Fodor's 2008

LONDON

Where to Stay and Eat
for All Budgets

Must-See Sights
and Local Secrets

Ratings You Can Trust

Fodor's Travel Publications   New York, Toronto, London, Sydney, Auckland
www.fodors.com

FODOR'S LONDON 2008
Editor: Amy B Wang

Editorial Production: Bethany Cassin Beckerlegge
Editorial Contributors: Robert Andrews, Nuha Ansari, Puja Chugani, Christi Daugherty, Erica Duecy, Stephen Heyman, Julius Honnor, James Knight, Helen Lewis, Katrina Manson, Christina Valhouli, Alex Wijeratna
Maps & Illustrations: David Lindroth, cartographer; William Wu; additional cartography provided by Henry Columb, Mark Stroud, and Ali Baird, Moon Street Cartography: Bob Blake and Rebecca Baer, map editors
Design: Fabrizio La Rocca, creative director; Guido Caroti, art director; Ann McBride and Chie Ushio, designers
Photography: Melanie Marin, senior picture editor
Cover Photo (Covent Garden): David Noton/Masterfile
Production/Manufacturing: Angela McLean

ISBN 978–1–4000–1790–4

ISSN 0149–631X

SPECIAL SALES
This book is available at special discounts for bulk purchases for sales promotions or premiums. Special editions, including personalized covers, excerpts of existing books, and corporate imprints, can be created in large quantities for special needs. For more information, write to Special Markets/Premium Sales, 1745 Broadway, MD 6-2, New York, New York 10019, or e-mail specialmarkets@randomhouse.com.

AN IMPORTANT TIP & AN INVITATION
Although all prices, opening times, and other details in this book are based on information supplied to us at press time, changes occur all the time in the travel world, and Fodor's cannot accept responsibility for facts that become outdated or for inadvertent errors or omissions. **So always confirm information when it matters,** especially if you're making a detour to visit a specific place. Your experiences—positive and negative—matter to us. If we have missed or misstated something, **please write to us.** We follow up on all suggestions. Contact the London editor at editors@fodors.com or c/o Fodor's at 1745 Broadway, New York, NY 10019.

PRINTED IN THE UNITED STATES OF AMERICA
10 9 8 7 6 5 4 3 2 1

Be a Fodor's Correspondent

Your opinion matters. It matters to us. It matters to your fellow Fodor's travelers, too. And we'd like to hear it. In fact, we need to hear it.

When you share your experiences and opinions, you become an active member of the Fodor's community. That means we'll not only use your feedback to make our books better, but we'll publish your names and comments whenever possible. Throughout our guides, look for "Word of Mouth," excerpts of your unvarnished feedback.

Here's how you can help improve Fodor's for all of us.

Tell us when we're right. We rely on local writers to give you an insider's perspective. But our writers and staff editors—who are the best in the business—depend on you. Your positive feedback is a vote to renew our recommendations for the next edition.

Tell us when we're wrong. We're proud that we update most of our guides every year. But we're not perfect. Things change. Hotels cut services. Museums change hours. Charming cafés lose charm. If our writer didn't quite capture the essence of a place, tell us how you'd do it differently. If any of our descriptions are inaccurate or inadequate, we'll incorporate your changes in the next edition and will correct factual errors at fodors.com immediately.

Tell us what to include. You probably have had fantastic travel experiences that aren't yet in Fodor's. Why not share them with a community of like-minded travelers? Maybe you chanced upon a beach or bistro or B&B that you don't want to keep to yourself. Tell us why we should include it. And share your discoveries and experiences with everyone directly at fodors.com. Your input may lead us to add a new listing or highlight a place we cover with a "Highly Recommended" star or with our highest rating, "Fodor's Choice."

Give us your opinion instantly at our feedback center at www.fodors.com/feedback. You may also e-mail editors@fodors.com with the subject line "London Editor." Or send your nominations, comments, and complaints by mail to London Editor, Fodor's, 1745 Broadway, New York, NY 10019.

You and travelers like you are the heart of the Fodor's community. Make our community richer by sharing your experiences. Be a Fodor's correspondent.

Happy traveling!

Tim Jarrell, Publisher

CONTENTS

MAPS

LONDON IN FOCUS

ABOUT THIS BOOK

Our Ratings

Sometimes you find terrific travel experiences and sometimes they just find you. But usually the burden is on you to select the right combination of experiences. That's where our ratings come in.

As travelers we've all discovered a place so wonderful that its worthiness is obvious. And sometimes that place is so experiential that superlatives don't do it justice: you just have to be there to know. These sights, properties, and experiences get our highest rating, **Fodor's Choice**, indicated by orange stars throughout this book.

Black stars highlight sights and properties we deem **Highly Recommended,** places that our writers, editors, and readers praise again and again for consistency and excellence.

By default, there's another category: any place we include in this book is by definition worth your time, unless we say otherwise. And we will.

Disagree with any of our choices? Care to nominate a place or suggest that we rate one more highly? Visit our feedback center at fodors.com.

Budget Well

Hotel and restaurant price categories from ¢ to $$$$ are defined in the opening pages of chapters 15 and 16. For attractions, we always give standard adult admission fees; reductions are usually available for children, students, and senior citizens. Want to pay with plastic? **AE, D, DC, MC, V** following restaurant and hotel listings indicate if American Express, Discover, Diners Club, MasterCard, and Visa are accepted.

Restaurants

Unless we state otherwise, restaurants are open for lunch and dinner daily. We mention dress only when there's a specific requirement and reservations only when they're essential or not accepted—it's always best to book ahead.

Hotels

Hotels have private bath, phone, TV, and air-conditioning and operate on the European Plan (aka EP, meaning without meals), unless we specify that they use the Continental Plan (CP, with a Continental breakfast), Breakfast Plan (BP, with a full breakfast), or Modified American Plan (MAP, with breakfast and dinner) or are all-inclusive (AI, including all meals and most activities). We always list facilities but not whether you'll be charged an extra fee to use them, so when pricing accommodations, find out what's included.

Symbols

Many Listings

★	Fodor's Choice
★	Highly recommended
✉	Physical address
↔	Directions
⬱	Mailing address
☎	Telephone
🖷	Fax
⊕	On the Web
✍	E-mail
⬓	Admission fee
☉	Open/closed times
Ⓤ	Tube stations
▤	Credit cards

Hotels & Restaurants

🏨	Hotel
⬐	Number of rooms
☖	Facilities
¶⊙¶	Meal plans
✗	Restaurant
⬑	Reservations
↘	Smoking
⸙⸙	BYOB
✗🏨	Hotel with restaurant that warrants a visit

Other

☾	Family-friendly
⇨	See also
✉	Branch address
☞	Take note

Experience London

Pedestrians crossing the Hungerford Bridge over the River Thames

WORD OF MOUTH

"The key to London's extraordinary museums and art galleries is that they're mostly free. So popping into several not only costs no money, but there are no ticket queues. And they'll still be there in a hundred years' time. Don't treat them like shrines: treat them like a city center park, that you just slip into for a couple of minutes. Above all, in London, be spontaneous."

—flanneruk

LONDON TODAY

So the weather stinks, no one smiles, and it takes far too long to get around—just what is it that makes London such a great place to be?

No Single London

To be sure, London is not an easy city for the visitor: most Londoners have about as much time for tourists as they do for toxic waste. But this, bizarrely, can be the city's greatest charm. Without the attention of strangers, you can lose yourself in London like in no other city in the world. A million different Londons exist cheek by jowl: from beggars on Bond Street to penthouses in Peckham, the extremes—of rich and poor, tranquility and raucousness, style and squalor—can be found right on top of one another. Despite its enormous size, London is still the fastest-growing city in Europe, which means about the only certainty is that it will not stay still.

Food and Drink

Recently, licensing laws have changed so that pubs and bars can now serve alcohol later. It may not have completely curbed the uncouth binge-drinking that Brits are famed for, but it has certainly made the capital a more sophisticated place, where you can take in a show and not have to make a mad dash for a cocktail afterwards. There are signs that the city is getting healthier as well: following Scotland's (and New York's) lead, there is now a smoking ban in all pubs and bars. Cyclists are now so common on London streets, and occasionally pavements, that pedestrians are starting to consider them a menace. High streets are filling up with organic health food stores and wheatgrass sandwich bars among the "greasy spoon" cafés.

Transport remains the gripe of choice in the city, whether it's delays at Waterloo or stuck Tube trains, and it replaces the weather as clichéd ice-breaker. Mayor Ken Livingstone continues his love-hate relationship with Londoners, determined to push through an extension to the Congestion Charge, a daily tax on vehicles entering and leaving central portions of the city. Claiming to ease traffic and save the environment, it is maligned and applauded in equal measure.

Highs and Lows

No one, least of all Londoners, expected London to win its bid to host the 2012 Olympics, but this event will shape much

---

DID YOU KNOW?

■ With more than 7 million residents, London is the largest city in the European Union. It's among the most densely populated, too, following Copenhagen, Brussels, and Paris. The city's ethnic mosaic includes communities from 34 different countries.

■ Up to about £2,000 (nearly $4,000) of taxpayers' money can be used to purchase a wig for a London judge, who often still wears the antiquated accessory. Barristers and solicitors (lawyers) must pay for their own wigs and often buy them used.

■ More than 100 species of fish, including smelt (which locals say has an odor resembling their beloved cucumber sandwiches), live in the Thames. In 1957 naturalists reported no signs of life in the river. The Thames looks brown because of sediment but is

of the city's development over the next several years. The strength of the bid was built on the social development and infrastructure benefits, which will outlast the event itself, and transform London's eastern side, making an impact far beyond the sporting arena.

London 2012 is also inexorably linked to the biggest shadow that hangs over the city: the threat of terrorism. The July 7 bombings that left 52 dead occurred the day after the announcement of London's successful Olympic bid in 2005. Since then, Londoners have lived with news of fresh arrests, plots foiled, and cells broken. For the most part, the post-9/11 environment has increased the city's resolve, and Londoners take the strain with considerable good humor. The multi-cultural soup that makes up the city means that everyone has a point of view on the debate, and a healthy interest in U.S. foreign policy. This has led to a popular new sport in the capital, American-baiting, which will often include playful swipes at the current U.S. administration. While it can occasionally be galling to be stereotyped, don't mistake this for anti-Americanism.

Political and Cultural Intrigue

2007 saw arguably the most important political development of the decade as the Tony Blair era came to an end, when he stepped down as British Prime Minister to hand the reins of power to Chancellor Gordon Brown—all without a public ballot

The Blair–Brown show has fascinated the public almost as much as the capital's other favorite relationship, between supermodel Kate Moss and troubled musician Pete Doherty. Their marriage of catwalk and guitar brings together two of the most potent icons of contemporary London, with lashing of excess and élan.

Culturally, life remains as rich and diverse as ever. Once the dominion of the super-DJ, London nightlife is now all about live music and smaller, intimate clubs that feel more like impromptu parties than organized affairs. Local acts including Lily Allen, Razorlight, Mika, and Dirty Pretty Things are impossible to ignore. The hip-hop scene, led by the likes of Sway, Plan B, and Just Jack, is stronger than ever.

actually Europe's cleanest metropolitan estuary.

■ Despite being surrounded by more than 5,000 pubs and bars, Londoners drink less than the average British resident. Twenty-three percent of men in London drank 22 or more units of alcohol per week from 2001 through 2002, compared with 27% in Great Britain as a whole.

■ The Tube is the world's biggest subway system. With 253 mi of routes and 275 stations, it covers more ground than systems in New York, Paris, and Tokyo.

■ There are 481 foreign banks in the city, more than in any other world financial center. The London Stock Exchange deals with almost twice as

many foreign companies as the New York Stock Exchange.

■ City taxi drivers must pass a training test that requires between two and four years of preparation. Eight or nine of every ten applicants drop out before completion.

LONDON PLANNER

When to Go

The heaviest tourist season runs mid-April through mid-October, with another peak around Christmas—though the tide never really ebbs. Spring is the time to see the countryside and the royal London parks and gardens at their freshest; fall to enjoy near-ideal exploring conditions. In late summer, be warned: air-conditioning is rarely found in places other than department stores, modern restaurants, hotels, and cinemas in London. Winter can be rather dismal, but all the theaters, concerts, and exhibitions go full speed.

When Not to Go

One good time to avoid is the October "half-term" when schools in the capital take a break for a week and nearly all attractions are flooded by children. Arriving at the start of August can be a very busy time, and the weather makes Tube travel a nightmare. And trying to shop in central London the week before Christmas is an insane idea best left only to desperate Londoners who have forgotten to buy presents.

Addresses

Central London and its surrounding districts are divided into 32 boroughs—33, counting the City of London. More useful for finding your way around, however, are the subdivisions of London into postal districts. Throughout the guide we've given the full postal code for most listings. The first one or two letters give the location: N means north, NW means northwest, and so on. Don't expect the numbering to be logical, however. (You won't, for example, find W2 next to W3.) The general rule is that the lower numbers, such as W1 or SW1, are closest to the city center.

Getting Around

London is, above all, a walker's city, and will repay every moment you spend exploring on foot. Of course, that may be of diminished appeal when you've got 30 minutes to scramble to the other side of town. Here are other options:

■ By far the easiest and most practical way to get around is on the Underground, or "Tube." Trains runs daily from early morning to night and provide a comprehensive service throughout the center with lines out to the suburbs. If you'll be traveling a lot around town, buy a Travelcard pass (from £4.60 per day), which offers unlimited use of the Tube, buses, and the commuter rail.

■ The commuter rail system is an overground network that connects outlying districts and suburbs to the center. Prices are comparable to those of the Underground, and you can easily transfer between the Underground and other connecting rail lines at many Tube stations.

■ Buses crisscross all over town, and are a great way to see the city. Their routes are more complicated than the Tube, but by reading the route posted on the main bus stop and watching the route on the front of the bus, you won't go far wrong. Services are frequent.

■ Note: The Tube is undergoing a major overhaul over the next several years. Keep an eye out for signs that will be posted in all stations when work is underway, with information on line closures and alternative routes.

London Hours

■ Most businesses are closed on Sunday and national (bank) holidays. Banks are open weekdays 9:30–4:30; offices are generally open 9:30–5:30.

■ The major national museums and galleries are open daily, with shorter hours on weekends than weekdays. Often there is one late-night opening a week.

■ The usual shop hours are Monday–Saturday 9–5:30. Around Oxford Street, Kensington High Street, and Knightsbridge, hours are 9:30–6, with late-night opening hours (until 7:30 or 8 PM) on Wednesdays or Thursdays.

Deal or No Deal?

There's no getting around it—today's exchange rates really maul the pockets of American tourists. But it's much better to accept this fact in advance and factor it into your holiday planning, tailoring outings and trips that will reflect your interests.

Often, booking in advance, harnessing low season deals, and taking advantage of Internet specials for flights and hotel rooms can cut down on costs. London is also great at offering things for free, and the quality of the culture, entertainment, relaxation, and fun to be had in the city means that if you target your spending wisely, you'll go home penny-pinched but satisfied.

	What it costs in London	What it costs in New York
Pair of theater tickets	£20–£70	$50–$200
Museum admission	Usually free; sometimes £5–£10	Usually $5–$20; sometimes free
Fast-food value meal	£4	$4
Tall latte	£2.15	$3.19
Pint of beer in	£3 and up	$6 and up
1-mi taxi ride before tips	£5	$5
Subway ride within city center	£3	$2

How's the Weather?

It's virtually impossible to forecast London weather, but you can be fairly certain that it will *not* be what you expect. It's generally mild—with some savage exceptions, especially in summer. In short, be prepared for anything: layers and an umbrella are your friends. The following are the average daily maximum and minimum temperatures for London.

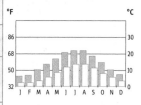

WHAT'S WHERE
CENTRAL LONDON

If London contained only its landmarks, it would still rank as one of the world's top destinations. But England's capital is more: a heady mix of old and new, reflecting fast-moving changes in fashion, lifestyle, and architecture, with an unconquered heritage of more than 2,000 years. *The following numbers refer to chapters.*

2 Westminster & Royal London. This is the place to embrace the "tourist" label. Snap pictures of the mounted horse guards, play with the pigeons in Trafalgar Square, and visit stacks of art in the national galleries. It's well worth braving the crowds to wander ancient Westminster Abbey and its historic bounty.

3 St. James's & Mayfair. You might not have the wallet for London's most prestigious district, but the window-shopping in Mayfair is free. St. James's is the ultimate enclave of old money and gentleman's London. Here you'll find the noted private members' clubs of Pall Mall, and the starched shirts and cigars of Jermyn Street, where you can shop like the Duke of Windsor.

4 Soho & Covent Garden. More sophisticated than seedy these days, the heart of London puts Theatreland, strip joints, Chinatown, and the trendiest of film studios side by side. Nearby Charing Cross Road is

a bibliophile's dream, but steer clear of the hectic hordes in Leicester Square, London's answer to Times Square.

5 Bloomsbury & Legal London. The literary and left-wing set that made Bloomsbury world famous has left little trace, but the area nevertheless remains the heart of brainy London. The University of London and the Law Courts are worth a passing glance; stop for a good while in the incomparable British Museum.

6 The City. London's Wall Street might be the oldest part of the capital, but thanks to futuristic skyscrapers and a sleek Millennium Bridge, it looks like the newest. Fans of ages gone by won't be disappointed, however: head for the dome of St. Paul's Cathedral, the storybook Tower Bridge, and grisly tales from the Tower of London.

7 The East End. Once famed for the 19th-century slums immortalized by Charles Dickens, today the area has become the oh-so-fashionable epicenter of London's contemporary art scene. For the spit-and-sawdust experience of market London on the weekend, dive into the wares at Spitalfields, Petticoat Lane, Brick Lane (popular for curry houses and bagel bakeries), and Columbia Road's much-loved flower market.

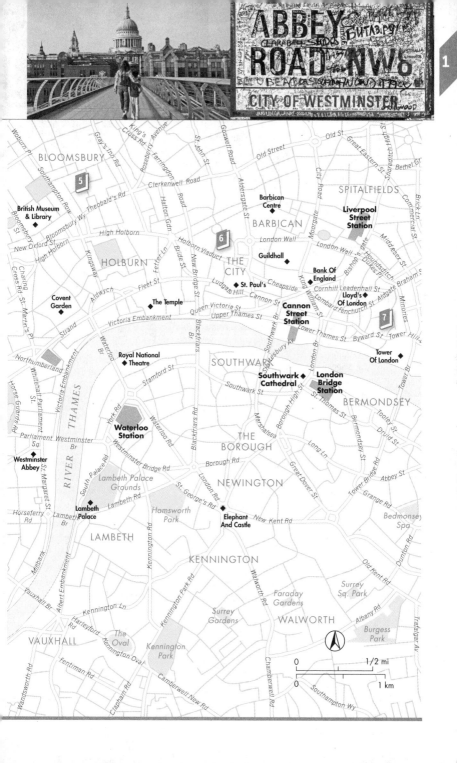

WHAT'S WHERE

8 The South Bank. Diehard culture vultures could spend a lifetime here. The South Bank Arts Complex—including the Royal National Theatre and Royal Festival Hall, Shakespeare's Globe, the Design Museum, and the Tate Modern—pretty much seals the artistic deal. Or take it all in from high on the British Airways London Eye.

9 Kensington & Chelsea. While the boutiques of King's Road have lost much of their heady '60s swagger, the museums are as awe-inspiring as ever. The playful Science Museum and the gargantuan Natural History Museum are the most fun for children. For a slightly more affordable alternative to King's Road, get shopping on High Street Kensington.

10 Knightsbridge & Belgravia. On your mark, get set, shop. While rich locals take cover in Knightsbridge's elegant houses and sleepy squares, flash your cash at the capital's snazziest department stores, Harrods and Harvey Nichols. Also check out the "mews" (posh alleyways) of Belgravia, London's most splendidly aristocratic enclave.

11 Notting Hill & Bayswater. To develop an effortlessly hip London demeanor, hang out in its most coveted residential area. Notting Hill, around Portobello Road, is a trendsetting square mile of multiethnicity, galleries, small shops, and see-and-be-seen-in restaurants. Bayswater mixes gaudy Arab fashions and fresh food shops; some think it has an appealing edginess, others a nouveau riche élan.

12 Regent's Park & Hampstead. For poetic inspiration, visit Keats House, where the poet penned his immortal "Ode to a Nightingale." Village-like Hampstead is a must: sweet streets, pavement cafés, delis, and outdoor swimming on the heath in "the Lido."

13 Greenwich. Quaint Thameside streets make for excellent rummaging ground for trendy antiques. Throw in some brilliant sights, Christopher Wren architecture, and the Greenwich Meridian Line, and you have one of the best excursions beyond the cut and thrust of London.

14 The Thames Upstream. As an idyllic retreat from the city, stroll around London's stately gardens and enjoy a beer close by once-powerful palaces at Chiswick, Kew Palace and Gardens, Richmond, and Putney. Better yet, take a river cruise along Old Father Thames for views of rolling greenery, and land up at the famous maze at Hampton Court Palace, England's version of Versailles.

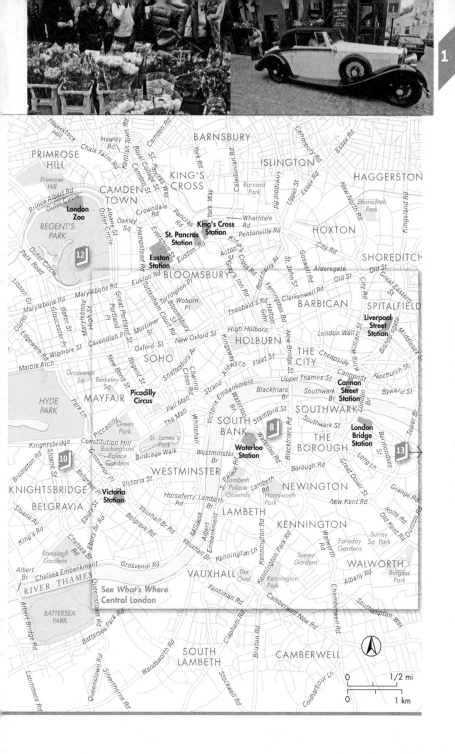

1

TOP LONDON ATTRACTIONS

Westminster Abbey

(A) The most exciting church in the land is the final resting place for the men and women who built Britain. Its great Gothic hall continues to play a part in the formation of the kingdom, having hosted nearly every coronation since 1308.

Buckingham Palace

(B) Not the prettiest royal palace, but a must-see for the glimpse it affords of modern royal life. The opulence of the state rooms open to the public provides plenty to gasp at, and don't forget the collection of china and carriages at the Queen's Gallery and Royal Mews next door.

St. Paul's Cathedral

(C) No matter how many times you have been before, the scale and elegance of Sir Christopher Wren's masterpiece never fail to take the breath away. Climb the enormous dome, third largest in the world, to experience the freaky acoustics of the Whispering Gallery, and higher still for fantastic views across London.

Tower of London

(D) The Tower is London at its majestic, idiosyncratic best. This is the heart of the kingdom—with foundations dating back nine centuries, every brick tells a story, and the axe-blows and fortunes that have risen and fallen within this turreted mini-city provide an inexhaustible supply of intrigue.

British Museum

(E) If you want to journey through time and space without leaving the confines of Bloomsbury, a visit to the British Museum has hours of eye-catching artifacts from the world's greatest civilizations, including the Elgin Marbles, the Rosetta Stone, and the Sutton Hoo treasure.

Shakespeare's Globe Theatre

(F) You can catch a Shakespeare play almost every night of the year in London. But standing on a floor of leaves and sawdust, in a painstakingly re-created version of the galleried Tudor theater for which he wrote is a special thrill.

Hampton Court Palace

(G) This collection of buildings and gardens won over Henry VIII to become his favorite royal residence. Its Tudor charm, augmented by Wren's touch, and a picturesque upstream Thames location make it a great day out—not even dour Oliver Cromwell, who moved here in 1653, could resist its charms.

Tate Modern

(H) More of an event than the average museum visit, Tate Modern, housed inside a striking 1930s power station, is a hip, immensely successful addition to the London gallery landscape. Passing judgment on the latest controversial temporary exhibit inside the giant turbine hall has become almost a civic pastime among art-loving Londoners.

National Gallery

(I) Whatever the collective noun is for a set of Old Masters—A palette? A canvas?—there are enough here to have the most casual art enthusiast purring with admiration. When you've finished, enjoy pedestrianized Trafalgar Square on the doorstep.

GREAT ITINERARIES

No Time to Spare?

If you're caught on the hop, your best bet is to head for a bus that is heading over the river. You can't beat that combination of classic red, murky water, and the skyline.

Crowning Glories

This regal runaround packs more into a day than most cities can offer in a week. Hit Westminster Abbey early to avoid the crowds, then cut through St. James's Park to catch the Changing of the Guard at 11:20 AM at Buckingham Palace. (If the Palace doors are open, enjoy a peek at royal life.) Take a quick detour to the Tudor delights of St. James's Palace, old haunt of Charles I, before a promenade down the Mall past the Regency glory of Carlton House Terrace and through Admiralty Arch to Trafalgar Square.

■TIP➡Get an early start and a hearty breakfast, as this selection of treasures will likely keep you on your feet all day.

After lunch, choose from the treasures of the National Gallery, the Who's Who of the National Portrait Gallery, or a brass rubbing in the crypt of St. Martin-in-the-Fields if the children's interest is flagging. This should leave time for a stately stroll down Whitehall—past Downing Street, Horse Guards Parade, and Banqueting House—to the Houses of Parliament, where you have the option of prebooking a tour, or trying to get in to see a debate.

■TIP➡Her Majesty's mounted guardsmen make a great photo op—you may even see Prince Harry, who joined the Regiment of the Blues and Royals, responsible for his grandmother's personal protection, after completing officer training at Sandhurst.

If you have any time or energy left, stroll through Green and Hyde Parks to Kensington Palace, childhood home of Queen Victoria, and (for little aspiring princesses everywhere) the Royal Dress Collection.

Museum Magic

London has one of the finest collections of museums in the world, and certainly no other comparable city offers so much for free. Many resemble state-of-the-art, hands-on playgrounds; others take a more classical approach. One of the latter is the British Museum in Bloomsbury, an Aladdin's cave of artifacts from across the world. This is ideal for either a half- or full-day browse. If you want to combine your day with other visits, pop into the nearby museum of architect Sir John Soane, the Theatre Museum, or the newly refurbished London Transport Museum.

■TIP➡The excellent restaurant in the British Museum's Great Court looks down on its library, where Karl Marx would shift uncomfortably, greatly afflicted by boils, as he researched *Das Kapital*.

Alternatively, South Kensington's "Museum Mile" on Cromwell Road houses a triple-whammy, any one of which would make for a substantial half-day's worth of diversion: the Victoria & Albert Museum, the Natural History Museum, and the Science Museum.

Retail Therapy

It's not hard to shop 'til you drop in London's West End. Start with the upscale on New Bond Street in order to save your afternoon frazzled look for nearby Oxford Street. Home to (take a deep breath here) Cerruti, Chanel, Cartier, De Beers, Dolce & Gabbana, Armani, Jimmy Choo, Versace, Swarovski, Bulgari, Tiffany, Prada, and Gucci, it's an awesome sweep of expense and elegance.

TIP➡ Men should not pass up a chance to browse the shirts on show at nearby Savile Row, famed for its high-quality tailoring, and accessories on Jermyn Street.

Oxford Street encompasses four Tube stations and is unbeatable for mass-market shopping. Run the gauntlet of high-street designers, cheap odds and ends, department stores, and ferocious pedestrians: it's seriously busy, but you're pretty much guaranteed a buy.

A more sedate but utterly fashionable experience can be found in Knightsbridge, wandering between Harvey Nichols and Harrods department stores. Take a south down Sloane Street to Sloane Square and head out along King's Road, home to boutiques galore and once capital of London's swinging sixties.

TIP➡ To catch a glimpse of how to design your home to match your new couture clothes, visit the Conran Shop at 81 Fulham Road, parallel to the Kings' Road.

To dip into the ever-expanding world of urban chic, try an afternoon in the Portobello street market in Notting Hill, where you can pick up remnants of various bygone ages: glassware, furniture, art and clothes, from boiler suits to Thai silk dresses. Portobello has wised up to tourist prices in recent years, so a trip out to Spitalfields (covered) market on a Sunday is worth considering, especially for a sample of the East End. Finally, for the younger crowd, Camden market has grunge and clubbing wear in spades.

Village People
The easiest village to reach is Hampstead, 20 minutes from the city center by Tube,

but a world away in character. It's home to a thriving arts scene, a history of left-wing poets and writers (including John Keats), some of the most gorgeous Georgian houses in London (hence the occasional jibe of "Champagne Socialism"), and a great range of smart shops, bistros, and French delicatessens.

TIP➡ If you're in Hampstead, don't miss the chance to get out onto the Heath, moodier and wilder than many of London's other open spaces.

To the west, leave the slightly suburban center of Richmond behind to get down to the riverside, or head for the vast expanse of the park next door, which breaks all remaining links with city life.

The fantastic views bestowed on Greenwich, to the south of the Thames, ensure you never forget how close the city is—and yet this village's nautical past creates an almost seaside feel. The National Maritime Museum and its collection of fine buildings, as well as two very good markets, make it a worthwhile day trip.

To the east, Bethnal Green is a village in the midst of an urban renaissance. Visit the flower market of Columbia Road, the Children's Museum, and the paths along the canal.

TIP➡ To appreciate fully how tribal London's villagers can be, try asking which part of the city they come from or live in. The responses you'll get—"Haggerston," "Tufnell Park," "Turnham Green," "Camberwell," "Battersea"—indicate a dizzying array of identities, often consisting of a few neighboring streets.

FREE (AND ALMOST FREE)

The exchange rate may sting, but there's one conversion that'll never change: £0 = $0. Here are our picks for the top free things to do in London.

ART

Many of London's biggest and best cultural attractions are free to enter, and the number of museums offering free entry is staggering. Donations are often more than welcome, and special exhibits usually cost extra.

Major Museums

British Museum
Imperial War Museum
Museum of London
National Gallery
National Maritime Museum, Queen's House, and Royal Observatory
National Portrait Gallery
Natural History Museum
Science Museum
Tate Britain
Tate Modern
Victoria & Albert Museum

Smaller Museums & Galleries

Burgh House and the Hampstead Museum
Clown's Gallery and Museum
Courtauld Permanent Exhibition (Free on Monday only)
Hogarth House
Houses of Parliament
ICA Gallery (£2.50)
Museum of Childhood
Serpentine Gallery
Sir John Soane's Museum
Theatre Museum
Wallace Collection
Whitechapel Art Gallery

CONCERTS

■ St. Paul's Cathedral, St. Martin-in-the-Fields, St. George Bloomsbury, and St. James's Church have regular lunchtime concerts, as does St. George Bloomsbury on Monday, Hyde Park Chapel on Thursday, and St. Giles in the Fields on Friday. There are regular organ recitals at Westminster Abbey.

■ Of the music colleges, the Royal Academy of Music, the Royal College of Music, the Guildhall, the Trinity College of Music, and the Royal Opera House have regular recitals; the Trinity College of Music holds recitals at lunchtime on Tuesday.

■ For contemporary ears, the area outside the National Theatre on the South Bank (known as the Djanogly Concert Pitch) reverberates to live world music weekdays at 6 o-, and on Saturday at 1 o- and 6 o-.

■ You can catch decent open-mike nights for unsigned acts and singer-songwriters at the River Bar (just south of Tower Bridge) every Wednesday, and Roadhouse (in Covent Garden) every Monday. Blues lovers should not miss the legendary Billy Chong Blues Revue band jam every Monday at the Globe pub in Hackney. The Palm Tree, in Mile End, is another great East End pub that hosts accomplished local jazz players on weekends.

FILM, THEATER & OPERA

■ If all seats have been sold, the English National Opera sells standing tickets for the back of the Dress and Upper Circles at £10 each. Check at the box office.

Standing tickets with obstructed views for the ballet or the opera at the Royal Opera House start at £7.

Sloane Square's Royal Court Theatre, one of the U.K.'s best venues for new playwriting, has restricted-view, standing-room-only tickets at the downstairs Jerwood Theatre for 10 pence (yes, £0.10), available one hour before the performance.

The Battersea Arts Club (BAC) has pay-what-you-can night on Tuesdays.

The Prince Charles Cinema in the West End shows weekday movie matinees for £3.50.

OFFBEAT EXPERIENCES

Go to the Public Record Office in Kew or Islington if you have a few hours to kill and want to track down some ancient branch of the family tree. Even if you don't have any leads, browsing through sheaves of ancient ledgers is great fun.

London has some of the finest parks in the world, and enjoying them won't cost you a pretty pence. Keen ornithologists can join free bird-watching walks in Hyde Park, while dedicated strollers touched by royal nostalgia can take the 7-mi Diana, Princess of Wales Memorial Walk through Hyde, Green, and St. James's Parks.

There are free spectacles throughout the year, but one of the most warmly enjoyed is Guy Fawkes' Night (November 5), when parks throughout the country hold spectacular fireworks displays.

On New Year's Eve thousands of revelers descend on Trafalgar Square and the South Bank to watch more free fireworks.

The Underground usually runs all night, and is free into the new year.

Finally, set aside some time for random wandering. London is a great walking city because so many of its real treasures are untouted: tiny alleyways barely visible on the map, garden squares, churchyards, shop windows, sudden vistas of skyline or park. With comfortable, weatherproof shoes and an umbrella, walking might well become your favorite free activity here.

SIGHTSEEING ON THE CHEAP

Join real Londoners on the top deck of a double-decker bus. You can use your Zones 1 and 2 Travelcard or buy tickets from machines at the bus stops for the following routes:

Bus 11: King's Road, Sloane Square, Victoria Station, Westminster Abbey, Houses of Parliament and Big Ben, Whitehall, Trafalgar Square, the Strand, Fleet Street, and St. Paul's Cathedral.

Bus 12: Bayswater, Marble Arch, Oxford Street, Piccadilly Circus, Trafalgar Square, Horse Guards, Whitehall, Houses of Parliament and Big Ben, Westminster Bridge.

Bus 19: Sloane Square, Knightsbridge, Hyde Park Corner, Green Park, Piccadilly Circus, Shaftsbury Avenue, Oxford Street, Bloomsbury, Islington.

Bus 88: Oxford Circus, Piccadilly Circus, Trafalgar Square, Whitehall, Houses of Parliament and Big Ben, Westminster Abbey, Tate Britain.

LONDON LIKE A LOCAL

Those unforgettable London moments aren't found in picture postcard places like Trafalgar Square, but in far more prosaic settings: at the bar of a friendly pub, amid the clutter of an antique shop, on a park bench in a smart residential garden, or in a centuries-old church beneath the glass and steel towers of the City.

Wander About a Market

London's markets are perfect for an aimless Sunday morning potter, along with locals who aren't quite sure what they're doing there either. The most fun is Portobello, full of great clothes and jewelry from local designers, and plenty of cafés and pubs to drop into along the way.

Discover Pub Culture

While fashionable coffee shops now dot every street, it's still the pub that Londoners are drawn to the minute the working day finishes. Don't get sucked into the big chains, such as Pitcher and Piano or All Bar One—head instead for the ones with kooky names straight out of a Monty Python sketch. Scuffed carpets, dartboards, and old chaps propping up the bar are all essential.

Go to Any Football Match

London doesn't get much more authentic than a 30,000-strong stadium on match day. In these emotional pressure-cookers, thousands of fans come to drink, swear, sing, and live every moment of their team's fortunes. Lower-division games (Brentford, Crystal Palace, Millwall, Leyton Orient, or Queens Park Rangers) will be less heavily subscribed and cheaper to watch.

Eat at a Greasy Spoon

The fatty delights of a classic London caff are best sampled after a night's excessive partying. A classic "Full English" breakfast will consist of fried bacon, sausage, egg, tomatoes, and mushrooms—and, for the adventurous, black pudding, washed down with a mug of strong tea. Take a selection of red-top tabloid newspapers to peruse for the full effect.

Take a Night Bus Home

Like the street sweepers they overtake, these buses pick up the living leftovers of a thousand different nights out in the capital. Sometimes there are so many stops that it seems it will be dawn before you get to where you want to go, but the endless procession of passengers (and the speed and humor of their banter) is what makes the trip interesting.

Visit a Park

When Londoners need to escape the city, they head for its green spaces. Sometimes it's to read the papers; other times to feed the ducks or play football. The parks boast an incredible range of free events, from music festivals to bird-watching. Favorites include Hyde Park in the west, Regent's Park in the north, St. James's Park in the city center, and Victoria Park in the east.

Party in Hoxton

This neighborhood is no longer the ultra-hip brother-in-charms to Manhattan's Lower East Side that it once was, but maybe it's all for the better. Nowadays, the mullet-headed fashionistas and art school drop-outs accommodate angular City slickers in the most predictable destination for a guaranteed good night out. Round off your night, or get it going, with a hearty curry on nearby Brick Lane, home to London's Bangladeshi community.

LONDON WITH KIDS

Education Without Yawns

Natural History Museum. It doesn't get much more awe-inspiring than blood-sucking bats, fake earthquakes, and a life-size blue whale. Just make sure you know your diplodocus from your dodo.

Regent's Park Zoo. City? What city? Disappear into the animal kingdom among the enclosures, complete with sessions for kids afraid of spiders (even bird-eating ones!).

Tower of London. Perfect for playing princess in front of the crown jewels. Not so perfect for imagining what becomes of the fairytale—watch your royal necks.

Science Museum. Special effects, virtual voyages, and interactive galleries: delving into the scientific abyss has never been more hands-on or fun.

V&A Museum. Decorative arts might sound a bit too sophisticated, but weekends at the museum are all set up for children under 12, with activities like metal detecting and interactive murder mysteries.

London Dungeons. Gore galore plunges you into murky depths of history, with gruesome rides and special effects scary enough to frighten the coolest of cats.

Performances

Applaud street performers. You can't beat the cacophony of jugglers, fire eaters, unicyclists, and the human statues tantalizing crowds in Covent Garden.

Enjoy Regent's Park Open Air Theatre. Welcome to the land of fairy dust and magic. Don't miss an evening performance under the stars of Midsummer Night's Dream in summer.

Watch films in 3D. So they just want to watch television? Blow their minds with the IMAX cinema, Britain's largest screen, which plays fantastical 3D films to audiences bespectacled in green-and-red glasses.

Sing along to musicals. Move over, Broadway: you can't beat a song and dance number from London's West End.

Activities

Ride the London Eye. Ferris wheel–loving kids will think they've hit the mother lode when they see Europe's biggest observation wheel.

Climb Monument. Those 311 steps up London's tribute to the Great Fire of 1666 are perfect for tiring out hyperactive kids, and the panorama from the top is well worth the climb.

Clamber on the lions. Challenge your child to pick a perch in Trafalgar Square, the capital's tourist hotspot, and climb one of the four tall stone lions at the foot of Nelson's column.

Cruise the Thames. See the sights in one fell swoop from the heart of London's waterways.

Paddle on the Serpentine. Pack a picnic and take a row boat out into the middle of Hyde Park's famed lake, settle back, and tuck in to lunch.

Lose your kids at Hampton Court. It might be more than 300 years old, but the quest to reach the middle of the world-famous hedge maze remains as challenging as ever.

OFF THE BEATEN PATH

So you've "done" London umpteen times before and think you've seen all there is to see? Think again. You just need to get outside the box. Not even the locals will have thought of some of these attractions, which makes them ideal bragging material to take home with you.

Bermondsey Antiques Market

If you want a brush with the cheeky types straight out of British gangster flicks, pop down to this former paradise for stolen goods. An old royal license (now canceled) ensured that stuff bought here did not have to be returned. Small stalls start setting up at 4 AM each Friday, so arrive early with a flashlight to scout for the best bargains. An ominous redevelopment of the market beckons, so enjoy its raffish charm while you can.

Reclaim the Beach

When the tides are right, usually best in spring and autumn, a small section of the Thames on the South Bank retreats enough to reveal a tiny stretch of sand beach. Cue a Baywatch-style celebration, complete with BBQs, music, dancing, and conversation with strangers. Don't forget to bring your own beer.

Smithfields Meat Market

If you're suffering from a little transatlantic jet lag, a visit to London's last remaining meat market, running until dawn on the edge of the City, provides a welcome late-night diversion. It's one of the few places you can see old-fashioned tradesmen at work, buying, selling, and packing all kinds of meat and offal. Nearby pubs have early-morning licenses and, naturally, serve some great cuts of meat.

Vauxhall City Farm

You have probably heard of London Zoo: this inner-city farm, hidden right away just south of the river behind Britain's spy headquarters, is a much more hands-on day out for children, with donkey rides, lessons in pony grooming, and milking demonstrations all available.

Highgate Cemetery

The timeless gaze of the stone angels that stand watch over this resting place of London souls is impossible to shrug off. Everlasting home to Communist theorist Karl Marx and novelist George Eliot, the 1839 Victorian cemetery of neo-Gothic statues and sarcophagi, fought over by the ivy, evokes sadness and beauty.

Brixton Life

Much-maligned and much-avoided, the focal point of London's African-Caribbean community is well worth exploring. Brixton's Victorian streets offer hair extension and nail salons, jerk chicken joints, and market stalls selling yams and plantains. Ignore the sniffy remarks from types north of the river; Brixton's bars and clubs make it one of the best bets for a night out in London.

Watch a Trial

If you came to London for spectacle, take a trip to a trial at the Old Bailey, the highest court in the land. Stories more twisted and compelling than anything on screen, strange costumes and wigs, command performances—it's true drama, without the West End ticket prices.

"I have seen the Mississippi. That is muddy
water. I have seen the St. Lawrence. That is
crystal water. But the Thames is liquid history."
—John Burns

A TOUR OF THE THAMES

The twists and turns of the Thames River through the heart of the
capital make it London's best thoroughfare and most compelling viewing point. Once famous for sludge, silt, and sewage, the Thames
is now the cleanest city river in the world. Every palace, church,
theater, wharf, museum, and pub along the bank has a tale to tell,
and traveling on or alongside the river is one of the best ways to
soak up views of the city.

A BRIEF HISTORY

The Thames has come a long way—and not just from its 344-km (214-mi) journey from a remote Gloucestershire meadow to the sea. In the mid-19th century, the river was dying, poisoned by sewers that flushed into the river. The "Big Stink" was so awful that cholera and typhoid killed more than 10,000 in 1853, and Parliament abandoned sitting in 1858. "The odour is hardly that of frankincense," said one contemporary of the 1884 drought that forced down water levels, leaving elegant Victorian nostrils exposed to slimy ooze on the banks.

Joseph Bazalgette, star civil engineer of his time, was commissioned to design a new sewage system, and by the 1900s nearly all was forgiven. (His efforts did not go unappreciated: Bazalgette was later knighted.) Today 7.2 million people get their drinking water from the Thames.

A marvelous array of boating options can put you port to starboard with ancient mariners, regatta rowers, houseboat gents, gin-palace queens, and even the odd naval officer. Lack sea legs? You can still enjoy the river: not much beats a wander beside London's waterway, strolling beneath strings of dangling lights at night, sipping the view from riverside cafés, or stepping out over splendid and inventive bridges to see skyline and water shimmer and sparkle.

ROWERS' ROW

Every spring Britain's oldest universities, Oxford and Cambridge, compete not with their brains but with their brawn, in the **Boat Race,** which began in 1829. The race is 4¼ miles upstream from Putney Bridge to Chiswick Bridge: expect clashing oars, clenched teeth, and the occasional sinking (there have been six). The best views are from Hammersmith at the Surrey bend, which is also where most of the pubs are clustered. ⊕ www.theboatrace.org

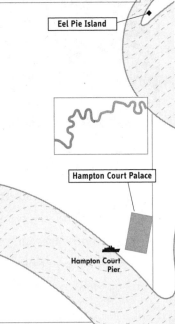

Eel Pie Island

Hampton Court Palace

Hampton Court Pier

HAMPTON COURT PALACE TO PUTNEY

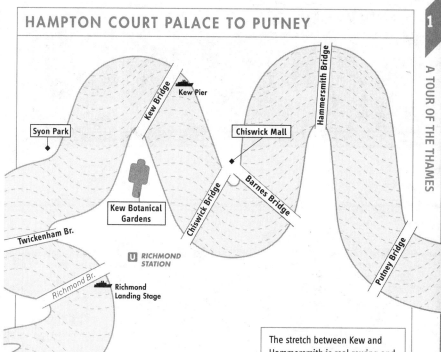

Kew Bridge

Kew Pier

Hammersmith Bridge

Syon Park

Chiswick Mall

Chiswick Bridge

Barnes Bridge

Kew Botanical Gardens

Twickenham Br.

Putney Bridge

U RICHMOND STATION

Richmond Br.

Richmond Landing Stage

Teddington

Kingston Bridge

The stretch between Kew and Hammersmith is real rowing and riverside-pub territory, with a picturesque parade past Strand-on-the-Green by Kew Bridge.

Hampton Court Palace is a suitably lavish start or end to any trip on the Thames. The river skirts the grounds, giving magnificent views over the Tudor palace that Henry VIII and his daughter Elizabeth I made home, and continues north to **Kingston Bridge**, starting point for the epic river voyage of Jerome K. Jerome's *Three Men in a Boat* and home to hectic summer regattas. At **Teddington**, where the poet Alexander Pope and writer Horace Walpole entertained their female admirers in the 18th century, the river turns tidal but remains quiet and unspoiled all the way to **Kew**, passing herons and fine stately homes standing proud on the banks. From **Twickenham Bridge** you round the old deer park (to the south) and **Syon Park** (north), which has belonged to the Duke of Northumberland's family for centuries. Beyond that is an even greater treat—the UNESCO World Heritage Site of **Kew Botanical Gardens**. All manner of rowboats set up for one, two, four, or eight people pull hard under **Chiswick Bridge** and **Barnes (railway) Bridge,** past the expensive riverside frontage of **Chiswick Mall** and under **Hammersmith Bridge**, to **Putney** and **Fulham**—smart urban villages facing each other across the banks.

WANDSWORTH TO BLACKFRIARS

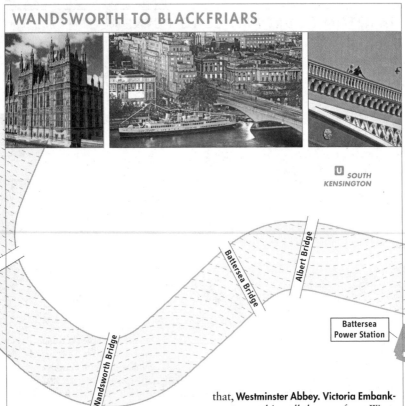

U SOUTH KENSINGTON

Albert Bridge

Battersea Bridge

Wandsworth Bridge

Battersea Power Station

Beyond **Wandsworth Bridge**, the early part of this stretch by **Battersea Bridge**, rebuilt in 1890, was London's real industrial heartland, the southern side chock full of cottage housing for laborers, artisans at work, and factories.

After **Albert Bridge**—glorious at night, with lights like luminescent pearls sweeping down on strings—the Thames is a metropolitan glory of a river, charging through fashionable **Chelsea** and past **Battersea Power Station**, under Chelsea, Vauxhall and Lambeth Bridges, with **Lambeth Palace** to the south.

The real treat of this stretch is the view of the **Houses of Parliament** and, beyond

that, **Westminster Abbey. Victoria Embankment**, stretching all the way from Westminster to Blackfriars, was once all grim mudflats. In 1878 it became the country's first electrically illuminated street, and today it is all fine architecture, trees, and gardens—perfect strolling territory.

You can't miss the **British Airways London Eye,** whose parts were brought down the Thames one by one before being assembled on-location. Look out too for the London Aquarium and the Dalí show, housed in the baroque-style County Hall.

The **Golden Jubilee Bridges** by **Embankment,** two beautifully lit steel-cabled pedestrian walkways, are perfect for reaching the **South Bank**.

Look out for the golden eagle, a monument to World War I RAF fighters, and

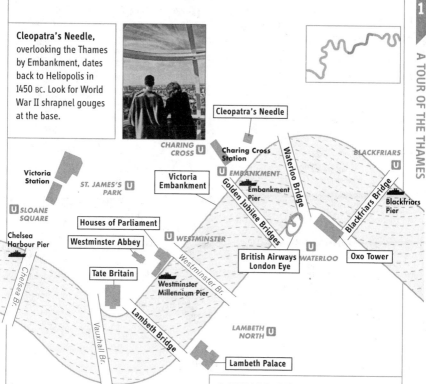

Cleopatra's Needle, overlooking the Thames by Embankment, dates back to Heliopolis in 1450 BC. Look for World War II shrapnel gouges at the base.

Cleopatra's Needle

CHARING CROSS U · Charing Cross Station · Cleopatra's Needle

Victoria Station · ST. JAMES'S PARK U · Victoria Embankment · U EMBANKMENT · Waterloo Bridge · BLACKFRIARS U

U SLOANE SQUARE · Golden Jubilee Bridges · Embankment Pier · Blackfriars Bridge · Blackfriars Pier

Chelsea Harbour Pier · Houses of Parliament · U WESTMINSTER · Chelsea Br. · Westminster Abbey · British Airways London Eye · WATERLOO U · Oxo Tower

Tate Britain · Westminster Br. · Westminster Millennium Pier · U

Vauxhall Br. · Lambeth Bridge · LAMBETH NORTH U

Lambeth Palace

Cleopatra's Needle. For the ultimate double-decker bus-viewing moment, look at **Waterloo Bridge**, once known as Ladies Bridge because it was built by female labor during World War II. The bridge has great views of the South Bank.

Further on is the **Oxo Tower**, whose red-glass letters were designed in 1928 to spell out the brand name while circumventing tight laws on exterior advertising.

By **Blackfriars Bridge**, named after the monks who wore black robes and lived on the north bank during the Middle Ages, the river used to run red by the riverside tanneries and slaughterhouses.

A WHALE OF A TALE

In January 2006, newspapers across the country were full of photos of a northern bottlenose whale swimming past the House of Commons. The "little" lost mite (18 feet long and weighing 7 tons) had wandered up the estuary. Thousands came to watch the rescue mission, which failed when she died on a barge taking her to the open sea. But her memory lives on: her bones are now part of the research collection at the Natural History Museum.

MILLENNIUM BRIDGE TO THAMES FLOOD BARRIER

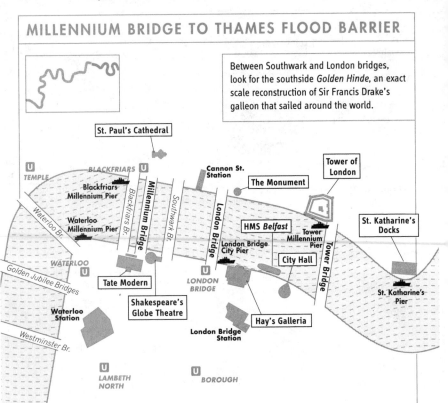

Between Southwark and London bridges, look for the southside *Golden Hinde*, an exact scale reconstruction of Sir Francis Drake's galleon that sailed around the world.

The **Millennium Bridge** is the newest span across the river: **St. Paul's Cathedral** and **Tate Modern** eye each other magnificently from either side of the once worryingly wobbly strip of a bridge. Farther on, the reconstructed **Shakespeare's Globe Theatre** is resplendent in whitewash and brown timber on the South Bank. **London Bridge** is admittedly not the river's finest, but it is the birthplace of the city. Some say the river ceases to be picturesque after St. Paul's, but we disagree: look for the flaming crown of the **Monument,** Sir Christopher Wren's tribute to those who died in the 1666 Great Fire of London.

Moored outside the Victorian shopping mall **Hay's Galleria** is **HMS *Belfast*,** Europe's last existing armored warship that saw action in World War II, now a floating naval museum on nine decks.

The splendid **Tower of London** sits proudly opposite the shining egg of **City Hall** (also

LONDON BRIDGE

Viking invaders destroyed London Bridge in 1014, hence the nursery rhyme "London Bridge is falling down." By 1962, London Bridge really *was* falling down again, its 1831 incarnation unable to take the strain of traffic. It was saved by American tycoon Robert McCulloch, who—possibly confusing the bridge with its much more splendid neighbor, Tower Bridge—bought it in 1968 for $2.46 million and had it shipped, stone by stone, to Lake Havasu in Arizona.

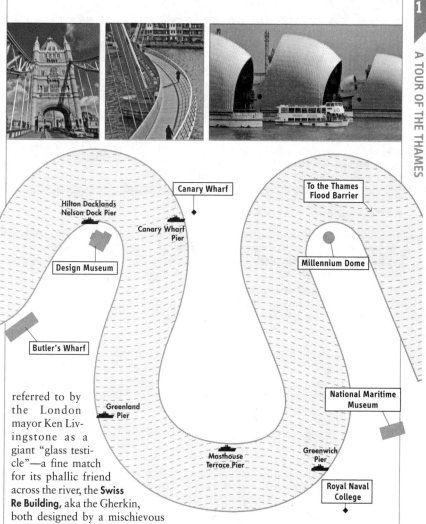

referred to by the London mayor Ken Livingstone as a giant "glass testicle"—a fine match for its phallic friend across the river, the **Swiss Re Building**, aka the Gherkin, both designed by a mischievous Norman Foster). They frame the 1894 **Tower Bridge**, a magnificent feat of engineering and style, which leads past the elegant confines of **St. Katharine's Docks**, the trendy restaurants of **Butler's Wharf**, and the **Design Museum**.

For the pièce de résistance of London's redevelopment, stay on the river until you reach the bright lights and tall reflective sides of **Canary Wharf**, the city's new business district, robotic in its modernity.

Step back in time at **Greenwich**, with the glorious **Royal Naval College** and the **National Maritime Museum**. Round the bend and you're back to the future, with the alien spaceship **Millennium Dome** and the **Thames Flood Barrier** looming.

PLANNING

"On the smallest pretext of holiday or fine weather the mighty population takes to the boats," wrote Henry James in 1877. You can follow in the footsteps of James, who took a boat trip from Westminster to Greenwich, or make up your own itinerary.

■ Frequent daily tourist-boat services are at their height between April and October.

■ In most cases you can turn up at a pier, and the next departure won't be far away. However, it never hurts to book ahead if you can.

■ Westminster and Tower piers are the busiest starting points, usually with boats heading east.

■ **TIP→** For a rundown of all the options, along with prices and timetables, contact **London River Services** (☎ 020/7222-1234 ⊕ www.tfl.gov.uk/river), which gives details of all the operators sailing various sections of the river.

■ The trip between Westminster Pier and the Tower of London takes about 30 minutes, as does the trip between the Tower and Greenwich.

■ A full round-trip can take several hours. Ask about flexible fares and hop on/off options at the various piers.

THE BEST WAYS TO EXPERIENCE THE THAMES WHILE . . .

Going off the beaten path (literally)	020/7928–3132　　　www.londonducktours.co.uk　　£17.50	
	London Ducktours offers sightseeing with a twist—amphibious patrol vehicles used in World War II have been painted like rubber duckies and traverse land and sea.	Departs from the London Eye (on land): Weekdays 10:30, noon, and 1:30; weekends 10–3:30 every 30 mins.
Saving time and money	020/7887–8888　　　www.tate.org.uk/tatetotate　　£4.30	
	The playfully polka-dotted *Tate Boat* ferries passengers across the river from the Tate Britain to the Tate Modern, with a stop at the London Eye in between.	Departs from the pier at either museum: Daily every 40 mins. Approximately 18 mins. one-way.
Impressing a date or client	020/7695–1800　　　www.bateauxlondon.com　　£19.50–£29.50 (lunch), £65–£99 (dinner)	
	For ultimate glamour (and expense), look into lunch and dinner cruises with **Bateaux London,** often formal affairs with surprisingly good two- to five-course meals. Variations include jazz brunch cruises on Sundays.	Departs from Embankment Pier: Daily 8 PM (boarding begins 45 mins. prior to departure). Approximately 3 hours.
Enjoying on-board entertainment	020/7740–0400　　　www.citycruises.com　　£66	
	The *London Showboat* lives up to its name, with four-course meals, snazzy cabaret acts from West End musicals, and after-dinner dancing.	Departs from Westminster Pier: Apr.–Oct., Wed.–Sun. 7 PM; Nov.–Mar., Thurs.–Sat. 7 PM (boarding begins 15 mins. prior to departure). Approximately 3½ hours.

(top) Big Ben and the Houses of Parliament at night. (bottom) The boys of Westminster Abbey Choir perform at Evensong.

(top) Horseback riding in Hyde Park. (bottom) Students study the Parthenon sculptures in the British Museum.

(top) Crossing the Millennium Bridge to St. Paul's Cathedral. (bottom) Raising a pint (or two) in a London pub.

(top) The ice-skating rink in the courtyard of Somerset House in winter. (bottom left) A compelling display of confectionery at Yauatcha in Soho. (bottom right) The Swiss Re Tower, one of the City's more recognizable buildings, at dusk.

(top) Design Museum, South Bank. (bottom) Museum-goers ponder an installation at the Tate Modern.

(top) The view mid-"flight" from a pod on the London Eye. (bottom) A cricket match in progress at Lord's.

(top) Changing of the Guard at Buckingham Palace. (bottom) The Great Court of the British Museum.

The London Eye and South Bank at night.

Westminster &
Royal London

Lord Chancellor's Procession from Westminster Abbey to the House of Lords

WORD OF MOUTH

"One evening we attended Evensong at Westminster Abbey. It never ceases to amaze me how similar religious services are. Had I only been half awake, I might not have known I was in an Anglican church."

—geribrum

"The National Portrait Gallery is great because you feel immediately connected to the paintings as you recognize the subjects.

—sarahkay

GETTING ORIENTED

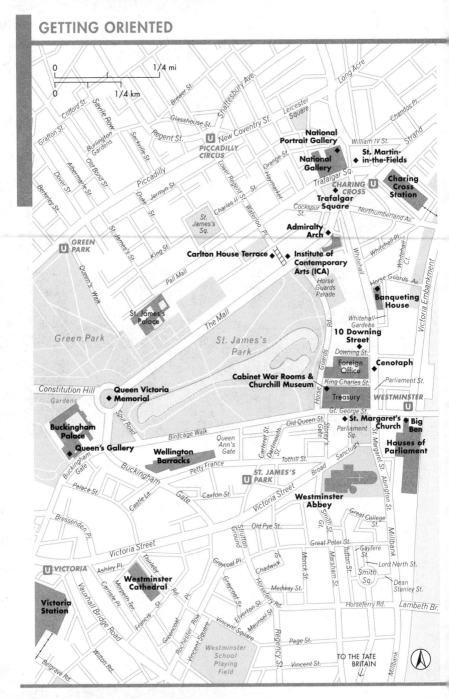

0   1/4 mi

0   1/4 km

2

TOP 5 REASONS TO GO

■ **Trafalgar Square:** Clamber onto one of the grand lions at the foot of Nelson's Column and gaze down ceremonial Whitehall.

■ **Cabinet War Rooms & Churchill Museum:** Listen to Churchill's wartime radio entreaties to the British people from this cavernous underground wartime hideout.

■ **Changing of the Guard:** Keep pace with the marching soldiers, resplendent in red and black, as they mark the daily routine.

■ **National Portrait Gallery:** Visit Bonnie Prince Charlie and Henry VIII before getting lunch upstairs with the best views of the monuments.

■ **Thames tours:** Ride the boat from Tate Britain to Tate Modern, and soak up the best views of Westminster and the London Eye en route.

FEELING PECKISH?

To the left of the visitor entrance to Westminster Abbey, you can get a coffee and a rich chocolate brownie (or three) from the vendor cart—nothing special, but cheap and useful on a chilly day.

Gordon's Wine Bar (⌗ *47 Villiers St., WC2N* ☎ *020/7930-1408* ⊕ *www.gordonswinebar.com*), the oldest in London, is hidden belowground among vaulted brick arches and bathed in candlelight. A range of bottles will suit any budget, and buffet food includes excellent beef. Take your glass outside if the weather's good.

There's great food and drink at **Inn the Park** (⌗ *St. James's Park, SW1* ☎ *020/7451-9999* ⊕ *www.innthepark.com*) and the outdoor pinewood deck makes for fantastic people-watching in the summer.

GETTING THERE

Trafalgar Square—easy to access and smack dab in the center of the action—is a good place to start. Take the Tube to Embankment (District and Circle lines) and walk north until you cross the Strand, or alight at Charing Cross (Bakerloo, Jubilee, and Northern lines), where the Northumberland Avenue exit deposits you on the southeast corner of the Square.

MAKING THE MOST OF YOUR TIME

You could spend a lifetime absorbing the rich history of this part of London. More practically, try to leave at least two days if you want to dip into the full gamut of attractions without feeling horribly rushed.

If Royal London is what you want, make a day of Buckingham Palace or Westminster Abbey, the Queen's Gallery, and the Guards Museum at Wellington Barracks. If you've a more constitutional bent, visit the Houses of Parliament and the Cabinet War Rooms.

NEAREST PUBLIC RESTROOMS

If you get caught short in Westminster Abbey, there are paid loos (50 p) across the street at the bottom of Victoria Street. Banqueting House and Queen's Gallery have some of the quietest, most dashing restrooms in London.

Sightseeing
★★★★★

Nightlife
☆☆☆★★

Dining
☆☆★★★

Lodging
☆☆☆☆★

Shopping
☆☆☆★★

This is postcard London at its best. Crammed with red buses, statues of statesmen, dazzling monuments, and ancient nooks and crannies, the area unites politics, high art, and religion. (Oh, and the Queen lives here, too.) Whether roaming aboveground or deep beneath the surface, there are constant marvels. Such grand dames as Buckingham Palace, Big Ben, Westminster Abbey, and the National Gallery sit alongside lesser-known but nevertheless gallant knights of the realm: tiny, lovingly curated museums and buildings heavy with the lives and legacies of those who have shaped London's seat of power. If you have time to visit only one part of London, this is it.

WHAT'S HERE

Royal London is so packed with sights it's difficult to know where to even *look* at times, let alone where to go, but the basic layout is simple if you think of three distinct areas—Buckingham Palace, Westminster and Whitehall, and Trafalgar Square—grouped at the corners of triangular St. James's Park.

Trafalgar Square is the official center of London, with **Nelson's Column** rising from the center. To its north, the **National Gallery** and **National Portrait Gallery** offer prime viewing of the greats of European art. Nearby **St. Martin-in-the-Fields** is one of London's best-loved churches and a popular venue for concerts; it has also provided lunch for the homeless for decades.

From Trafalgar Square two roads lead to the homes of very different ideas of governance: **Whitehall** leads to the **Houses of Parliament,** while **the Mall,** a wide, pink boulevard beyond the stone curtain of **Admiralty Arch,**

2

leads past **Carlton House Terrace** and the **Institute of Contemporary Arts** to the Queen's residence at **Buckingham Palace.** Heading down Whitehall, home to thousands of scurrying civil servants, the Queen's Lifeguards sit motionlessly on horses in front of Horse Guards Parade, while opposite is a historic warning to overweening royals, at the glorious Banqueting House. Its gorgeous painted ceiling, commemorating James I, would have been one of the final sights of his son, Charles I, before he was executed here before a crowd of thousands in 1649.

Downing Street, diagonally opposite, is home to the prime minister, traditionally resident at the famed **No. 10,** along with his Chancellor and several other higher-ups. For an example of the famous British stiff upper lip in the face of adversity, the pristinely preserved **Cabinet War Rooms & Churchill Museum,** set underground near the Foreign Office, offer a rare insight into how military officials and civil servants went about their quest to win World War II. Whitehall also houses monuments to those lost in war, or to those who made the fight possible: look out for the **Cenotaph,** designed by Edwin Lutyens in 1920 in commemoration of the 1918 armistice. Parliament Square faces the neo-Gothic **Houses of Parliament,** set beside the Thames, where members of the Houses of Commons and Lords decide the laws of the day.

Westminster Abbey, a colossus of a parish church that once housed monks and even served as parliament for a few years, stands proudly opposite. It's also possibly the most celebrity-filled burial ground in the world— the final resting place of monarchs, poets, and politicians. In its shadow is the no less interesting **St. Margaret's Church,** home to intrigue throughout the ages and many a parliamentary wedding. For the headquarters of the Catholic church in the United Kingdom, visit the neo-Byzantine **Westminster Cathedral,** farther south alongside Victoria Street. A short trot along **Birdcage Walk,** on the south side of St. James's Park, takes you past **Wellington Barracks,** home to and museum of the Queen's Guard (visit the shop: a toy soldier lover's dream), until you reach the golden glint of the **Queen Victoria Memorial** in the middle of the roundabout facing Buckingham Palace. The building opens its doors to the public only in summer, but the next-door Queen's Gallery, open all year, is worth a visit for the impressive collection of paintings, furniture, and sparkling jewels acquired by successive royals, while **Royal Mews** houses the royal cars, carriages, and coaches. Finally, farther south toward Pimlico, **Tate Britain** focuses on British artists of yesterday and today.

PLACES TO EXPLORE

Admiralty Arch. Gateway to the Mall—no, not an indoor shopping center but one of the very grand avenues of London—this is one of London's stateliest urban set pieces. On the southwest corner of Trafalgar Square, the arch, which was named after the adjacent Royal Navy headquarters, was designed in 1908–11 by Sir Aston Webb as a two-part memorial to Queen Victoria, along the ceremonial route to Buckingham Palace; the second part is the Victoria Memorial just outside the palace. As you pass under the enormous triple archway—though not through the central arch, opened only for state occasions—the environment changes along with the color of the road, for you're exiting frenetic Trafalgar

A BRIEF HISTORY

The Romans may have gunned for the City, but England's royals went for Westminster. London's home of democracy started out as Edward the Confessor's palace, when he moved his cramped court west in the 11th century. He founded Westminster Abbey in 1050, where every British monarch has been crowned since. Under the Normans, the palace of Westminster was an elaborate and French-speaking affair. The politicos finally got their hands on it in 1529 (when Henry VII and his court shifted up to the roomier Whitehall Palace), but nearly lost it forever with the Gunpowder Plot of 1605, when Catholic militants attempted to blow the prototypical Parliament to smithereens.

Inigo Jones's magnificent Banqueting House is the only surviving building of Whitehall Palace, and was the setting for the 1649 beheading of Charles I. The Westminster we see today took shape during the Georgian and Victorian periods, as Britain reached the zenith of its imperial power. Grand architecture sprang up, and Buckingham Palace became the principal royal residence in 1837, when Victoria acceded to the throne. Trafalgar Square and Nelson's Column were built in 1843, to mark Britain's most famous naval victory, and the Houses of Parliament were rebuilt in 1858 in the trendy neo-Gothic style of the time.

Square and entering the Mall (rhymes with shall)—the elegant avenue that leads directly to the palace. ⊠ *The Mall, Cockspur St., Trafalgar Sq., Westminster, SW1* Ⓤ *Charing Cross.*

Banqueting House. This is all that remains today of the Tudor Palace of Whitehall, which was (according to one foreign visitor) "ill-built, and nothing but a heap of houses." James I commissioned Inigo Jones (1573–1652), one of England's great architects, to do a grand remodeling. Influenced during a sojourn in Italy by Andrea Palladio's work, Jones brought Palladian sophistication and purity back to London with him. The resulting graceful and disciplined classical style of Banqueting House must have stunned its early occupants. In the quiet vaults beneath, James would escape the stresses of being a sovereign with a glass or two. His son, Charles I, enhanced the interior by employing the Flemish painter Peter Paul Rubens to glorify his father and the Stuart dynasty in vibrant painted ceiling panels. As it turned out, these allegorical paintings, depicting a wise monarch being received into heaven, were the last thing Charles saw before he was beheaded by Cromwell's Parliamentarians in 1649. But his son, Charles II, was able to celebrate the restoration of the monarchy in this same place 20 years later. The old palace is also the setting for lunchtime concerts, held 1–2 PM. Call or check the Web site for details. ⊠ *Whitehall, Westminster, SW1A* ☎ *020/7930–4179, 0870/751–5178 recorded information, 0870/751–5187 concert tickets* ⊕ *www.hrp.org.uk* ☎ *£4.50, includes free audio guide* ☉ *Mon.–Sat. 10–5, last admission 4:30. Closed Christmas wk* Ⓤ *Charing Cross, Embankment, Westminster.*

Fodor'sChoice   **Buckingham Palace.** Buckingham Palace tops many a must-see list and
★   has become perhaps *the* symbol of the royal family—although the

QUEEN VICTORIA MEMORIAL

You can't overlook this monument if you're near Buckingham Palace, which it faces from the traffic island at the west end of the Mall. The monument to Queen Victoria was conceived by Sir Aston Webb as the nucleus of the larger memorial which includes Admiralty Arch at one end, and the ceremonial route down the Mall to the Palace; it was executed by the sculptor Thomas Brock, who was knighted on the spot when the memorial was revealed to the world in 1911. Many wonder why he was given that honor, since the thing is Victoriana incarnate: the frumpy queen glares down the Mall, with golden-winged Victory overhead and her siblings Truth, Justice, and Charity, plus Manufacture, Progress-and-Peace, War-and-Shipbuilding, and so on—in Osbert Sitwell's words, "tons of allegorical females ... with whole litters of their cretinous children"—surrounding her. The Mall and Spur Rd., St. James's, SW1 ⓤVictoria, St. James's Park.

building itself is no masterpiece and has housed the monarch only since Victoria (1819–1901) moved here from Kensington Palace on her accession in 1837. Compared to other great houses and palaces in London, it's a more modern affair. Originally Buckingham House and the home of George III, it was remodeled by John Nash on the accession of George IV in 1820. Nash overspent his budget by about half a million pounds and was dismissed by Parliament after George's death. Although Queen Victoria added the east front (by Edward Blore, facing the Mall) to accommodate her prodigious state entertaining, Nash's gorgeous designs can still be enjoyed at the core of the palace. The Portland stone facade dates only from 1913 (the same stone used for the Victoria Memorial outside the Palace and Admiralty Arch at the foot of the Mall), and the interior was renovated and redecorated only after it sustained World War II bomb damage.

The palace contains 19 state rooms, 52 royal and guest bedrooms, 188 staff bedrooms, 92 offices, and 78 bathrooms—a prerequisite for the 450 people who work there, and the mere 50,000 who are entertained during the year. The private royal apartments are in the north wing; when the Queen is in residence, the royal standard is raised. The state rooms are where much of the business of royalty is played out—investitures, state banquets, and receptions for the great and good—and these are open to the public while the royal family is away during the summer. A visit makes for a fascinating glimpse into another world: the fabulously gilt interiors are not merely museum pieces but pomp and pageantry at work. Highlights of the tour include the **Quadrangle,** bordered by the many offices and apartments for employees in this extraordinary miniature village. Beyond the gates you may see the changing of the guard, which adds to the experience. The **Grand Hall,** followed by the **Grand Staircase** and **Guard Room,** gives a taste of what's to follow: lines of cool marble pillars, gold leaf galore on ceilings and walls, and light, bright rooms with massive, twinkling chandeliers. Nash's ornate designs unfold through the numerous drawing rooms—beginning with the **Green Drawing Room**—each equally spectacular, filled with treasures brought from the Prince Regent's original palatial home, Carlton House. (Some of the most exquisite pieces in the world, such as the cabinet with gemstone-decorated panels and the precious Sèvres porcelain, found their way to the palace after the French Revolution.) The **Throne Room**, in opulent theatrical baroque style, has the original 1953 coronation throne, among others. The **Picture Gallery** is a feast of renowned art. The collection was begun by Charles I, and includes masterpieces by Rubens, Vermeer, Van Dyck, Cuyp, and Canaletto. (More from the Royal Collection can be seen in the **Queen's Gallery**, near the south side of the palace.) The **Ballroom** has videos of royal events, and you can also see the dubbing sword used in the investitures held here, where the Queen touches those to become "Sirs" and "Dames." The **State Dining Room,** with its elaborate ceiling and walls of kingly portraits, has views over the palace gardens. The **Blue Drawing Room** is splendor in overkill and the set for prebanquet drinks. The bow-shaped **Music Room** features lapis lazuli columns between arched floor-to-ceiling windows, while the **White Drawing Room** is a sensation of white-and-gold plasterwork: a crescendo on which to end the tour.

Unless you have an invitation to one of the Queen's summer garden parties, the most you'll see of the 45-acre grounds is a walk along the south side. This addition to the tour gives views of the garden (west) front of the palace and the 19th-century lake. The walled oasis has plenty of wildlife—it contains more than 350 types of wildflowers.

Fodor'sChoice
★ Behind the front palace gates, the **Changing of the Guard**, with all the ceremony monarchists and children adore, remains one of London's best free shows and culminates in front of the palace. Marching to live music, the guards proceed up the Mall from St. James's Palace to Buckingham Palace. Shortly afterward, the replacement guard approaches from Wellington Barracks via Birdcage Walk. Then within the forecourt, the old guard symbolically hands over the keys to the palace to the replacement guard.

> **PHOTO OP**
>
> The best place for a photo opportunity alongside one of the guardsmen is at St. James's Palace, or try to keep up alongside them during the daily morning Changing the Guard. They leave St. James's at about 10:30 AM, for Buckingham Palace. Failing that, shuffle up to the mounted horse guards on the Whitehall side, there all day long.

The ceremony, more properly known as **Guard Mounting,** lasts about 45 minutes and usually takes place on schedule, but the guards sometimes cancel because of bad weather; check the signs in the forecourt or phone. Get there by 10:30 AM to grab a spot in the best viewing section at the gate facing the palace, since most of the hoopla takes place behind the railings in the forecourt. Be sure to prebook tour reservations of the palace with a credit card by phone. ⊠*Buckingham Palace Rd., St. James's, SW1* ☎*020/7766–7300* ⊕*www.royal.gov.uk* ☎*£15, includes audio tour, credit-card reservations subject to booking charge*☉*Late*

July–late Sept., daily 9:45–6, last admission 3:45; confirm dates, which are subject to Queen's mandate. Changing of the Guard Apr.–July, daily 11:30 AM*; Aug.–Mar., alternating days only 11:30* AM ▤ AE, MC, V* U *Victoria, St. James's Park.*

★ **Cabinet War Rooms & Churchill Museum.** It was from this small warren
☾ of underground rooms—beneath the vast government buildings of the Foreign Office—that Winston Churchill and his team directed Britain's troops in World War II. Designed to be bomb-proof, the complex is less museum, more fossilized time warp, as the whole has been preserved almost exactly as it was when the last light was turned off at the end of the war. Every clock shows almost 5 PM, and the furniture, fittings, and paraphernalia of a busy, round-the-clock war office are in situ, down to the colored map pins.

During air raids, the leading government ministers met here and the Cabinet Room is still arranged as if a meeting were about to convene. In the Map Room, the Allied campaign is charted on wall-to-wall maps with a rash of pin holes showing the movements of convoys. In the hub of the room, a bank of different-colored phones known as the "Beauty Chorus" linked the War Rooms to control rooms around the nation. The Prime Minister's Room holds the desk from which Churchill made his morale-boosting broadcasts; the Telephone Room (a converted broom cupboard) has his hotline to FDR. You can also see the restored suite of rooms that the PM used for dining, cooking, and sleeping. Telephonists and clerks who worked 16-hour shifts slept in lesser quarters in unenviable conditions; it would not have been unusual for a secretary in pajamas to scurry past a field marshal en route to a meeting.

An exciting addition to the Cabinet War Rooms is the **Churchill Museum,** which opened in 2005 on the 40th anniversary of his death. Different zones explore his life and achievements—and failures, too— through objects and documents, many of which, such as his personal papers, had never previously been made public. Central to the exhibition is an interactive timeline, with layers of facts, figures, and tales. If you visit in August, there are late-night openings and 1940s-style musical events; phone for details. ⊠ *Clive Steps, King Charles St., Westminster, SW1A* ☏ *020/7930–6961* ⊕ *www.iwm.org.uk* ▤ *£11, includes audio tour* ☉ *Daily 9:30–6; last admission 5* U *Westminster.*

Carlton House Terrace. This is a glorious example of Regency architect John Nash's genius. Between 1812 and 1830, under the patronage of George IV (Prince Regent until George III's death in 1820), Nash was the architect of the grand scheme for Regent Street, which started here and ended with the sweep of neoclassical houses encircling Regent's Park. The Prince Regent, who lived at Carlton House, had plans to build a country villa at Primrose Hill (to the north of the park), connected by a grand road—hence Regent Street. Even though it was considered a most extravagant building for its time, Carlton House was demolished after the prince's accession to the throne. Nash's Carlton House Terrace, no less imposing, with white-stucco facades and massive Corinthian columns, was built in its place. It was a smart address and one that prime ministers Gladstone (1856) and Palmerston (1857–75) enjoyed. Today Carlton House Terrace houses the Royal College of Pathologists (No. 2), the Royal Society (No. 6, whose members included Isaac Newton and Charles Darwin), the Turf Club (No. 5), and, at No. 12, the **Institute of Contemporary Arts,** better known as the ICA. ✉ *The Mall, St. James's, W1* Ⓤ *Charing Cross.*

Downing Street. Looking like an unassuming alley but for the iron gates at both its Whitehall and Horse Guards Road approaches, this is the location of the famous **No. 10,** London's modest version of the White House. The Georgian entrance is deceptive, though, since the old house now leads to a large mansion behind it, overlooking the Horse Guards Parade. Only three houses remain of the terrace built circa 1680 by Sir George Downing, who spent enough of his youth in America to graduate from Harvard—the second man ever to do so. **No. 11** is traditionally the residence of the chancellor of the exchequer (secretary of the treasury), and **No. 12** is the party whips' office. No. 10 has officially housed the prime minister since 1732. Just south of Downing Street, in the middle of Whitehall, you'll see the **Cenotaph,** a stark white monolith designed in 1920 by Edwin Lutyens to commemorate the 1918 armistice. On Remembrance Day (the Sunday nearest November 11, Armistice Day) it's strewn with red poppies to honor the dead of both world wars and all British and Commonwealth soldiers killed in action since; the first wreath is laid by the Queen and there's a march past by war veterans. ✉ *Whitehall, Westminster, SW1* Ⓤ *Westminster.*

Ⓒ **Horse Guards Parade.** Once the tiltyard of Whitehall Palace, where jousting tournaments were held, the Horse Guards Parade is now notable mainly for the annual Trooping the Colour ceremony, in which the Queen takes the Royal Salute, her official birthday gift, on the second Saturday in June. (Like Paddington Bear, the Queen has two birthdays; her real one is on April 21.) There is pageantry galore, with marching bands—the occasional guardsman fainting clean away from the heat building up under his weighty bearskin—and throngs of onlookers. Covering the vast expanse of the square that faces Horse Guards Road, opposite St. James's Park at one end and Whitehall at the other, the ceremony is televised. At the Whitehall facade of Horse Guards, the changing of two mounted sentries known as the **mounted guard** provides what may be London's most popular photo opportunity. ✉ *Whitehall,*

BEARSKIN, NOT BUSBY

While on duty, Guards soldiers are required to remain utterly aloof—they may not speak (some people attempt to make them laugh), may not swat errant flies from their noses, and in theory may not keel over under the weight of their enormous, saunalike hats. Called bearskins (not busbies, as is sometimes incorrectly assumed) after the material from which they are made, the headwear was taken as a trophy from the French after the victory of the Battle of Waterloo.

London's Great Architects

Great architectural achievements in London have often been motivated by disasters and misfortunes. Like a phoenix, London rose from the ashes in a frenzy of rebuilding after the Great Fire of 1666 had destroyed four-fifths of the city. Three centuries later, more fire, caused by the German air raids in the Second World War, flattened huge chunks of London. Gray civic buildings and tower blocks rose from the rubble. As a result of these intense civic reconstructions, a few individuals had the opportunity to leave significant marks on the city.

Inigo Jones (1573–1652), one of England's first great architects, was almost single-handedly responsible for the resurgence of classical styles of architecture in the early 17th century. Often directly modeling his work after that of Italian architect Andrea Palladio, Jones was highly influential during his time, as the Palladian style quickly spread throughout England. His most famous works include St. Paul's Church at Covent Garden and the magnificent Banqueting House on Whitehall.

Sir Christopher Wren (1632–1723) was given the Herculean task of overseeing the rebuilding of London following the Great Fire. His ambitious plans for a complete redesign of the formerly medieval city, drawn up within a week after the fire, were shot down by landowners, businesspeople, and private citizens intent on a quicker reconstruction. It remains a mystery what effect Wren's membership in the secretive Masonic Lodge had on his efforts. Nevertheless, Wren was responsible for 51 new churches (all in the City) and the amazing St. Paul's Cathedral. Only 23 of the City churches still survive, the finest of which are St. Bride's (Fleet Street), St. Mary Abchurch (Abchurch Yard), and St. Stephen's Walbrook (Walbrook Street). A wander through the deserted streets of the City past the churches is a rewarding way to spend a weekend afternoon.

John Nash (1752–1835) completely redesigned a large section of the city stretching from the Mall northward to Regent's Park and also remodeled Buckingham Palace. He is largely responsible for the look of much of central London; it was his idea to clear Trafalgar Square of its royal stables to make room for the public space as it exists today. For an insight into Nash's vision for London, walk from Buckingham Palace along the Mall, past his white stucco Carlton House Terrace to your left. Walk across Trafalgar Square to Haymarket, where Nash built the Haymarket Theater. Then walk the length of Regent Street, passing on the way All Souls Church, Langham Place, and Park Crescent, which leads into Regent's Park from its southern end.

Westminster, SW1 ⊗ Queen's mounted guard ceremony Mon.–Sat. 11 AM, Sun. 10 AM Ⓤ *Westminster.*

NEED A BREAK?

The Wesley Café (⊠ *Storey's Gate, Westminster, SW1* ☎ *020/7222–8010*) is a popular budget haunt for office workers around Westminster, and a good stopping point if you don't want to go farther along Victoria Street in search of food. It's almost opposite Westminster Abbey, in the crypt of Central Hall, a former Methodist church.

★ **Houses of Parliament.** Overlooking the Thames, the Houses of Parliament are, arguably, the city's most famous and photogenic sight, with the Clock Tower—which everyone calls Big Ben—keeping watch on the corner and Westminster Abbey ahead of you across Parliament Square.

> **TRIP TIP**
>
> The easiest time to get into the Commons is during an evening session—Parliament is still sitting if the top of the Clock Tower is illuminated.

The Palace of Westminster, as the complex is still properly called, was established by Edward the Confessor in the 11th century. It has served as the seat of English administrative power ever since. Henry VIII was the last king to hold court here, as after 1529 he moved a few steps away to the finer and more expansive Whitehall Palace. At the Reformation, the Royal Chapel here was secularized and became the first meeting place of the Commons, with the two groups sitting across from each other in the choir. The Lords settled in the White Chamber. These, along with everything but the **Jewel Tower** and **Westminster Hall,** were destroyed in 1834 when "the sticks"—the arcane elmwood "tally" sticks notched for loans paid out and paid back, kept beneath the Lords' Chamber, on which the court had kept its accounts until 1826—were incinerated, and the fire got out of hand. Westminster Hall, with its remarkable hammer-beam roof, was the work of William the Conqueror's son, William Rufus. It's one of the largest remaining Norman halls in Europe, and its dramatic interior was the scene of the trial of Charles I.

After the fire, Charles Barry and Augustus Pugin married their Renaissance and Gothic styles into the building you see today: Barry's classical proportions offset by Pugin's ornamental flourishes—although the latter were toned down by Gilbert Scott when he rebuilt the bomb-damaged House of Commons after World War II. The two towers were Pugin's work. The **Clock Tower** was completed in 1858 after long delays due to bickering over the clock's design. (Barry designed the faces in the

> **WHO WAS BIG BEN?**
>
> Some say Ben was "Big Ben" Caunt, heavyweight boxing champ; others, Sir Benjamin Hall, the sizeable Westminster building works commissioner.

end.) It contains the 13-ton bell known as Big Ben, which chimes the hour (and the quarters). At the southwest end of the main Parliament building is the 336-foot-high **Victoria Tower.**

The building itself, which covers 8 acres, is a series of chambers, lobbies, and offices joined by more than 2 mi of passages. There are two Houses, Lords and Commons. The former includes hereditary peers—earls, lords, viscounts, and other aristocrats—and life peers, whose titles are not inherited. The House of Commons is made up of 659 elected Members of Parliament (MPs). The political party with the most MPs forms the government, its leader becoming prime minister;

2

other parties form the Opposition. Since 1642, when Charles I tried to have five MPs arrested, no monarch has been allowed into the House of Commons. The state opening of Parliament in November consequently takes place in the House of Lords. Visitors aren't allowed many places in the Houses of Parliament, though the Visitors' Galleries of the House of Commons do afford a view of democracy in process where the banks of green leather benches seat the opposing MPs.

When they speak, it's not directly to each other but through the Speaker, who also decides who will get the floor each day. Elaborate procedures notwithstanding, debate is often drowned out by raucous jeers and insults. When MPs vote, they exit by the "Aye" or the "No" corridor, thus being counted by the party whips. In 2004 security in the chamber was spectacularly breached on two separate occasions, when fervent "father" protestors threw a purple flour–bomb from the Visitors' Gallery, after which a glass screen was installed. A later incident saw the traditionally dressed tail-coated security men wrestle "hunt" protestors to the floor of the chamber.

Other public areas of the 1,100-room labyrinth are punctuated with stirring frescoes commissioned by Prince Albert. You pass these on your way to the Visitors' Galleries—if, that is, you're patient enough to wait in line for hours (the Lords line is shorter) or have applied in advance for the special "line of route" tour for overseas visitors in Summer Opening (late July–August and mid-September–early October). Tickets can be prebooked by phone or on the Web site; alternatively, you can take a chance and buy same-day tickets from the ticket office opposite the Houses of Parliament. The tour takes you through the Queen's Robing Room, Royal Gallery, House of Lords, Central Hall (where MPs meet their constituents—the lucky ones get to accompany their MP to a prestigious tea on the terrace), House of Commons, and out into the spectacular Westminster Hall. Watch for the "VR" (Victoria Regina) monograms in the carpets and carving belying the "medieval" detailing as 19th-century work. The time to catch the action is Question Time—when the prime minister defends himself against the attacks of his "right honorable friends" on Wednesday between noon and 2:30 PM (it's also live on BBC2). Overseas visitors should check tour dates and details on the Parliament's Web site. The next best time to visit is either chamber's regular Question Time, held on Monday, Tuesday, and Thursday from noon to 2:30 PM.

For a special exhibition devoted to the "History of Parliament: Past and Present," head to the **Jewel Tower,** across the street from Victoria Tower, on Abingdon Street (also called Old Palace Yard), south of Parliament Square. Not to be confused with the other famed jewel tower at the Tower of London, this was the stronghold for Edward III's treasure in 1366. It's also one of the original parts of the old Palace of Westminster and still retains some original beams; part of the moat and medieval quay still remain. (The tower is run by English Heritage, with a small charge for entry.) Be sure to have your name placed in advance on the waiting list for the twice-weekly tours of the **Lord Chancellor's Residence**, a popular attraction since its spectacular renovation. ⊠*St. Stephen's Entrance, St. Margaret St., Westminster, SW1* ☎*020/7219–4272 Commons information, 020/7219–3107 Lords information, 020/7222–2219 Jewel Tower, 020/7219–2184 Lord Chancellor's Residence, 0870/906–3773 summer tours* ⊕*www.parliament.uk* ☞*Free, £7 summer tours* ⊙*Commons Mon. 2:30–10:30, Tues. and Wed. 11:30–7:30, Thurs. 11:30–6:30, Fri. 9:30–3 although not every Fri.; Lords Mon.–Thurs. 2:30–10; Lord Chancellor's Residence Tues. and Thurs. 10:30–12:30. Closed Easter wk, late July–early Sept., 3 wks for party conference recess mid-Sept.–early Oct., and 3 wks at Christmas* Ⓤ*Westminster.*

Institute of Contemporary Arts (ICA). Behind its incongruous white-stucco facade, at No. 12 Carlton House Terrace, the ICA has provided a stage for the avant-garde in performance, theater, dance, visual art, and music since it was established in 1947. There are two cinemas; a library of video artists' works; great bookshop; a café; a hip bar; and a team of adventurous curators. ⊠*The Mall, St. James's, SW1* ☎*020/7930–3647* ⊕*www.ica.org.uk* ☞*1-day, weekday membership £1.50; weekends, £2.50; additional charge for cinema screenings* ⊙*Daily noon–9:30* Ⓤ*Charing Cross, Piccadilly Circus.*

NEED A BREAK?

The ICAfé is windowless but brightly lighted, with hot dishes, salads, quiches, and desserts—it's very popular at lunchtime so come early. The upstairs bar has lighter food and windows overlooking the Mall. Both are open daily from noon and subject to the £1.50 one-day membership fee.

The Mall. This stately, 115-foot-wide processional route (pronounced like "shall") sweeping from Admiralty Arch to the Queen Victoria Memorial at Buckingham Palace is an updated 1904 version of the traditional rambling promenade that was used centuries before. The street was originally laid out around 1660 for the game of *paille-maille* (a type of croquet crossed with golf), which also gave the parallel road Pall Mall its name, and it quickly became the place to be seen. Samuel Pepys, Jonathan Swift, and Alexander Pope all wrote about it, and it continued as the beau monde's social playground into the early 19th century, long after the game had gone out of vogue. ■TIP➜Be sure to stroll along the Mall on Sunday when the road is closed to traffic. ⊠*The Mall, St. James's, SW1* Ⓤ*Charing Cross, Green Park.*

Fodor'sChoice
★
☾

National Gallery. You could spend a day perusing one of the largest and best collections of western European paintings, and still not reach full immersion—all for free. Hard to believe that the nation's collection began with a nucleus of 38 paintings on show in a wealthy banker's house in Pall Mall (there's a painting of the paintings at the house of John Julius Angerstein in the Victoria & Albert Museum). Even though the collection included works by Raphael, Rembrandt, Titian, and Rubens, it was hardly likely to rival the Louvre, so Parliament agreed in 1824 to a building in Trafalgar Square, the capital's central point. The gallery fills the north side of the square, with Nelson's column in the cen-

ter, and after a welcome redesign, which stopped traffic roaring past the gallery door, pedestrians can now walk between the two and appreciate William Wilkins's impressive colonnaded neoclassic facade. By the end of the 19th century, enthusiastic directors and generous patrons had turned the National Gallery into one of the world's foremost collections, with works from painters of the Italian Renaissance and earlier, from the Flemish and Dutch masters, the Spanish school, and of course the English tradition, including Hogarth, Gainsborough, Stubbs, and Constable.

Completed in 1991, the large Sainsbury Wing was designed by American architect Robert Venturi and houses the Early Renaissance collection. It's a popular part of the museum, with many excellent exhibitions as well as the National Dining Rooms, the restaurant overlooking Trafalgar Square on Level 1. On the opposite side of the museum from the Sainsbury Wing, the Getty entrance opened in 2004 and provides access at street level to the updated East Wing. Gone is the previous dark, dingy Victorian atmosphere; now you progress into the gallery through a daylighted, bright stone staircase with sleek black marble into a modern double-level atrium. It makes a fabulous entrance to the Central Hall and the Titian collection. Accompanying the redesign are superior visitor facilities, a better store for the must-have postcards and books, and a café.

Worthy of a look are the exhibitions in the Sunley Room and Room 1, where works are organized along a theme ("Bosch and Bruegel," for instance) or focus on an artist, such as El Greco. Alternatively, begin at an "Art Start" terminal in the Sainsbury Wing or East Wing Espresso Bar. The interactive screens give you access to information on all of the museum's holdings; you can choose your favorites, and print out a free personal tour map.

The following is a list of 10 of the most familiar works, to jog your memory, whet your appetite, and offer a starting point for your own exploration. The first five are in the Sainsbury Wing. In chronological order: (1) **Van Eyck** (circa 1395–1441), *The Arnolfini Portrait*. A solemn couple holds hands, the fish-eye mirror behind them mysteriously illuminating what can't be seen from the front view. (2) **Uccello** (1397–1475), *The Battle of San Romano*. In a work commissioned by the Medici family, the Florentine commander on a rearing white warhorse leads armored knights into battle against the Sienese. (3) **Bellini** (circa 1430–1516), *The Doge Leonardo Loredan.* The artist captured the Venetian doge's beatific expression (and snail-shell "buttons") at the beginning of his 20 years in office. (4) **Botticelli** (1445–1510), *Venus and Mars.* Mars sleeps, exhausted by the love goddess, oblivious to the lance wielded by mischievous putti and the buzzing of wasps. (5) **Leonardo da Vinci** (1452–1519), *The Virgin and Child.* This haunting black chalk cartoon is partly famous for having been attacked at gunpoint, and it now gets extra protection behind glass and screens. (6) **Caravaggio** (1573–1610), *The Supper at Emmaus.* A cinematically lighted, freshly resurrected Christ blesses bread in an astonishingly domestic vision from the master of chiaroscuro. (7) **Velázquez** (1599–1660), *The Toilet of Venus.* "The Rokeby Venus," named for its previous home in Yorkshire, has the most famously beautiful back in any gallery. She's the only surviving female nude by Velázquez. (8) **Constable** (1776–1837), *The Hay Wain.* Rendered overfamiliar by too many greeting cards, this is the definitive image of golden-age rural England. (9) **Turner** (1775–1851), *The Fighting Téméraire.* Most of the collection's other Turners were moved to the Tate Britain; the final voyage of the great French battleship into a livid, hazy sunset stayed here. (10) **Seurat** (1859–91), *Bathers at Asnières.* This static summer day's idyll is one of the pointillist extraordinaire's best-known works.

Glaring omissions from the above include some of the most popular pictures in the gallery, by Piero della Francesca, Titian, Holbein, Bosch, Bruegel, Rembrandt, Vermeer, Canaletto, Claude, Tiepolo, Gainsborough, Ingres, Monet, Renoir, and van Gogh. You can't miss the two most spectacular works on view—due to their mammoth size—Sebastiano del Piombo's *Sermon on the Mount* and Stubbs's stunning *Whistlejacket.* These great paintings aren't the only thing glowing in the rooms of the National Gallery—thanks to government patronage and lottery monies, salons here now gleam with stunning brocades and opulent silks. Rubens's *Samson and Delilah* has never looked better.

The collection of Dutch 17th-century paintings is one of the greatest in the world, and pieces by Hals, Hooch, Ruisdel, Hobbema, and Cuyp are shown in wonderful natural light and gracious surroundings. ✉ *Trafalgar Sq., Westminster, WC2* ☎ *020/7747–2885* ⊕ *www.nationalgallery.org.uk* 🎟 *Free, charge for special exhibitions* ☉ *Daily 10–6, Wed. until 9; 1-hr free guided tour starts at Sainsbury Wing daily at 11:30 and 2:30, and additionally 6 and 6:30 Wed, 12:30 and 3:30 Sat.* Ⓤ *Charing Cross, Leicester Sq.*

ART FOR KIDS

If you visit the National Gallery during the school vacations, there are special programs and trails for children that are not to be missed. Neither are the free weekday lunchtime lectures and Ten Minute Talks, which illuminate the story behind a key work of art. Check the information desk, or Web site, for details.

2

The National Dining Rooms (☎ *020/7747-2869*) in the Sainsbury Wing of the National Gallery is open daily 10 AM–5:30 PM and serves a fashionable British lunch, including oysters, roasts, and a great selection of cheeses. The All Day Bakery keeps longer hours and has a lighter menu. There is a superb view from huge windows overlooking Trafalgar Square. The National Café (☎ *020/7747-5945*) on Level 0 in the East Wing makes a fun stop, even if you're not visiting the gallery. Close to the Getty entrance, it has a good range of snacks, lunches, and drinks, including traditional tea with scones. A children's menu is available, and it's open 8 AM–11 PM on weekdays.

Fodor'sChoice
★
☺

National Portrait Gallery. An idiosyncratic collection that presents a potted history of Britain through its people, past and present, this museum is an essential stop for all history and literature buffs, where you can choose to take in a little, or a lot. The spacious, bright galleries are accessible via a state-of-the-art escalator, which lets you view the paintings as you ascend to a skylighted space displaying the oldest works in the Tudor Gallery. At the summit, a sleek restaurant, open beyond gallery hours, will satiate skyline droolers. Here you'll see one of the best landscapes for real: a panoramic view of Nelson's Column and the backdrop along Whitehall to the Houses of Parliament. Back in the basement are a lecture theater, computer gallery, bookshop, and café.

Walking through the Photography Gallery is like looking at an upmarket celebrity or society magazine. In the Tudor Gallery—a modern update on a Tudor long hall—is a Holbein cartoon of Henry VIII; Stubbs's self-portrait hangs in the refurbished 17th-century rooms; and don't miss the Hockney portraits in the modern Balcony Gallery, hanging alongside photographs, busts, caricatures, and paintings. Some of the faces are obscure and will be just as unknown to you if you're English, because the portraits outlasted their sitters' fame—not so surprising when the portraitists are such greats as Reynolds, Gainsborough, Lawrence, and Romney. But the annotation is comprehensive, the layout is easy to negotiate—chronological, with the oldest at the top—and there's a separate research center for those who get hooked on particular personages. Don't miss the absorbing mini-exhibitions in the Studio and Balcony Galleries; and there are temporary exhibitions in the Wolfson Gallery, on subjects as diverse as "Between Worlds: Voyagers to Britain 1700–1850" to contemporary fashion photography from Terry O'Neill to Mario Testino. ⌂ *St. Martin's Pl., Covent Garden, WC2* ☎ *020/7312-2463 recorded information* ⊕ *www.npg.org.uk* ☞ *Free, charge for special exhibitions* ☼ *Mon.–Wed., weekends 10–6, Thurs. and Fri. 10–9* Ⓤ *Charing Cross, Leicester Sq.*

★ **The Queen's Gallery.** The former chapel at the south side of Buckingham Palace is now a temple of art and rare and exquisite objects, acquired by kings and queens over the centuries. Although Her Majesty herself is not the personal owner, she has the privilege of holding these works for the nation. Step through the splendid portico (designed by John Simpson) into elegantly restrained, spacious galleries whose walls are

Modern Architecture

The renaissance of modern architecture in the capital has two major cues: the City boom and the brouhaha of the millennium. During the mid-'80s, the financial City deregulated and broke its boundaries socially, geographically—spreading east to Docklands—and architecturally, too. New buildings surged upward between the traditional classic pillars of Wren and Soane. Richard Rogers was responsible for the strident and beautiful Lloyds building in the City early on in 1986, although the sexiness stakes have been upped by Sir Norman Foster, whose recent portfolio includes the groundbreaking "Gherkin," the cucumber-shaped tower for the Swiss Re headquarters (30 St. Mary Axe) in 2003, and, on the vegetable theme again, the mushroom-shaped City Hall for the London Assembly headquarters by Tower Bridge in 2002. Other architects have complemented rather than outshone their neighbors, such as Stirling, who designed No. 1 Poultry to work with the surrounding Wren, Hawksmoor, and Lutyens designs.

The millennium celebrations also inspired many updates for old institutions, such as Norman Foster's awesome glass roofing and design of the Great Court at the British Museum. Glass is featured again in Rick Mather's revamp of the Maritime Museum and the Wallace Collection, and likewise in Dixon-Jones's internal facelift at the National Portrait Gallery and overhaul of the Royal Opera House. Richard Rogers broke the mold with the inspiring and controversial Millennium Dome, and not to be forgotten are other stars of the millennium: the bridges and the wheel. Foster's sculpted "blade of light" pedestrian footbridge had a wobbly beginning, but is now a firm attraction (at the doorstep of the tremendous Tate Modern powerstation makeover by Herzog & de Meuron). The Hungerford Bridge by Lifschutz Davidson from Charing Cross to the South Bank Arts Centre crept into the postmillennium, but is no less dazzling. The British Airways London Eye observation wheel by David Marks and Julia Barfield was almost eclipsed by the publicity surrounding the Dome downriver, yet it opened on time to spectacular success—and remains a tourist magnet and landmark on the constantly regenerating London horizon.

hung with some truly great works. An audio guide takes you through the treasures.

A rough timeline of the major monarch collectors starts principally with King Charles I. An avid appreciator of painters, Charles established the basis of the Royal Collection, purchasing works by Mantegna, Raphael, Titian, and Dürer (it was under royal patronage that Rubens painted the Banqueting House ceiling). During the Civil War many masterpieces were sold abroad and subsequently repatriated by Charles II. George III, who bought Buckingham House, scooped up a notable collection of Venetian (including Canaletto), Renaissance (Bellini and Raphael), and Dutch art (Vermeer), and patronized English contemporary artists such as Gainsborough, Hoppner, and Beechey. He also took a liking to American artist Benjamin West. The Prince Regent, George IV, transformed his father's house into a palace, filling it with fine art across the board from paintings to porcelain. In particular, he had a good eye for Rembrandt, contemporary equestrian works by Stubbs, and lavish portraits by Lawrence. Queen Victoria had a penchant for Landseer animals and landscapes, Frith's contemporary scenes, and portraits by Winterhalter. Finally,

> **DID YOU KNOW?**
>
> The miniature of Jane Austen by her sister Cassandra is the only likeness that exists of the great novelist.

Edward VIII indulged Queen Alexandra's love of Fabergé, while many royal tours around the empire produced gifts of gorgeous caliber, such as the Cullinan diamond from southern Africa and the emerald-studded belt from India.

The Queen's Gallery displays merely a selection from the Royal Collection in themed exhibitions, while more than 3,000 objects reside in museums and galleries in the United Kingdom and abroad: check out the National Gallery, the Victoria & Albert Museum, the Museum of London, and the British Museum. ■TIP→The E-gallery provides an interactive electronic version of the collection, allowing the user to open lockets, remove a sword from its scabbard, or take apart the tulip vases. It's probably the closest you could get to eyeing practically every diamond in the sovereign's glittering diadem. ⊠*Buckingham Palace, Buckingham Palace Rd., St. James's,*

> **KEEP IN MIND**
>
> At the Queen's Gallery, look out for the latest portrait of the Queen herself, often on show. She has the most reproduced image in history, with more than 180 billion incarnations on postage stamps alone.

SW1 ☎*020/7766–7301* ⊕*www.royal.gov.uk* ☑*£7.50, joint ticket with Royal Mews £13.50* ☉*Daily 10–5:30; last admission 4:30* Ⓤ *Victoria, St. James's Park.*

○ **Royal Mews.** Fairy-tale gold-and-glass coaches and sleek Rolls-Royce state cars emanate from the Royal Mews, next door to the Queen's Gallery. The John Nash–designed Mews serves as the headquarters for Her Majesty's travel department (so beware of closures for state visits), complete with the Queen's own special breed of horses, ridden by wigged postilions decked in red-and-gold regalia. Between the stables and riding school arena are exhibits of polished saddlery and riding tack. The highlight of the Mews is the splendid golden Coronation Coach, not unlike an art gallery on wheels, with its sculpted tritons and sea gods. Mews were originally falcons' quarters (the name comes from their "mewing," or feather shedding), but the horses gradually eclipsed the birds. Royal Household staff guide your tour. ⊠*Buckingham Palace Rd., St. James's, SW1* ☎*020/7766–7302* ⊕*www.royal.gov.uk* ☑*£7, joint ticket with Queen's Gallery £13.50* ☉*Apr.–July and Oct., Sat.–Thurs. 11–4; Aug. and Sept., daily 10–5, no guided tours; last admission 45 min before closing* Ⓤ *Victoria, St. James's Park.*

Fodor's Choice **St. James's Park.** With three palaces at its borders (the Palace of West-
★ minster, the Tudor **St. James's Palace,** and Buckingham Palace) St.
☺ James's Park is acclaimed as the most royal of the royal parks. It's also
London's smallest, most ornamental park, as well as the oldest; it was
acquired by Henry VIII in 1532 for a deer park. The land was marshy
and took its name from the lepers' hospital dedicated to St. James.
Henry VIII built the palace next to the park, which was used for hunting only—dueling and sword fights were forbidden. James I improved
the land and installed an aviary and zoo (complete with crocodiles).
Charles II (after his exile in France and because of his admiration for
Louis XIV's formal Versailles Palace landscapes) had formal gardens
laid out, with avenues, fruit orchards, and a canal. Lawns were grazed
by goats, sheep, and deer.

About 17 species of birds—including pelicans, geese, ducks, and swans
(which belong to the Queen)—now breed on and around Duck Island
at the east end of the lake, attracting ornithologists at dawn. Later on
summer days the deck chairs (which you must pay to use) are crammed
with office workers lunching while being serenaded by music from
the bandstands. One of the best times to stroll the leafy walkways
is after dark, with Westminster Abbey and the Houses of Parliament
rising above the floodlighted lake. The hugely popular Inn the Park
restaurant is a wood and glass pavilion with a turf roof that blends
in beautifully with the surrounding landcape; it's a restful place for a
meal or a snack on a nice day. ⊠ *The Mall or Horse Guards approach,
or Birdcage Walk, St. James's, SW1* ⊕ *www.royalparks.gov.uk* Ⓤ *St.
James's Park, Westminster.*

St. Margaret's Church. Dwarfed by
its neighbor, Westminster Abbey,
St. Margaret's was founded in the
12th century and rebuilt between
1486 and 1523. As the parish
church of the Houses of Parliament it's much sought after for
weddings: Samuel Pepys married
here in 1655, Winston Churchill
in 1908. The east Crucifix-
ion window celebrates another
union, the marriage of Prince
Arthur and Catherine of Aragon.

> **QUIRKY LONDON**
>
> Sir Walter Raleigh is among the
> notables buried at St. Margaret's,
> only without his head, which had
> been removed at Old Palace Yard,
> Westminster, and kept by his wife,
> who was said to be fond of ask-
> ing visitors, "Have you met Sir
> Walter?" as she produced it from
> a velvet bag.

Unfortunately, it arrived so late that Arthur was dead and Catherine
had married his brother, Henry VIII. ⊠ *Parliament Sq., Westminster,
SW1* Ⓤ *Westminster.*

☺ **St. Martin-in-the-Fields.** The small medieval chapel that once stood here,
probably used by the monks of Westminster Abbey, was indeed surrounded by fields. These gave way to a grand rebuilding, completed
in 1726, and St. Martin's grew to become one of Britain's best-loved
churches. James Gibbs's classical temple-with-spire design also became
a familiar pattern for churches in early Colonial America. Though it has
to compete for attention with Trafalgar Square's many prominent struc-

tures, its spire is actually slightly taller than Nelson's Column. It's a welcome sight for the homeless, who have sought soup and shelter here since 1914. The church is also a haven for music lovers; the internationally known Academy of St. Martin-in-the-Fields was founded here, and a popular program of concerts continues today. (However, although the interior is a wonderful setting, the wooden benches can make it hard to give your undivided attention to the music.) St. Martin's is often called the royal parish church, partly because Charles II was christened here. The crypt is a hive of lively activity, with a café and bookshop; plus the **London Brass-Rubbing Centre,** where you can make your own lifesize souvenir knight, lady, or monarch from replica tomb brasses, with metallic waxes, paper, and instructions provided from about £5; and the **Gallery in the Crypt,** showing contemporary work. ⊠ *Trafalgar Sq., Covent Garden, WC2* ☏ *020/7766–1100, 020/7839–8362 evening-concert credit-card bookings* ⊕ *www.stmartin-in-the-fields.org* ⊙ *Church daily 8–8; crypt Mon.–Sat. 10–8 (brass-rubbing center until 6), Sun. noon–6; box office Mon.–Sat. 10–5* Ⓤ *Charing Cross, Leicester Sq.*

> **FREE CONCERTS**
>
> Free lunchtime concerts take place Monday, Tuesday, and Friday, 1–2 PM. Tickets are available from the box office in the crypt.

NEED A BREAK?

St. Martin's Café in the Crypt, with its high-arched brick vault, serves full meals, sandwiches, snacks, traditional tea, and wine. The choice here, which includes vegetarian dishes, is one of the best available for such a central location.

Fodor'sChoice
★
☺

Tate Britain. The gallery, which first opened in 1897, funded by the sugar magnate Sir Henry Tate, is the older sister of Tate Modern, on the south bank of the Thames. Although the building is not quite as awe-inspiring as T.M., it has lovely, bright galleries and is a very user-friendly place to wander and explore great British art over 500 years from 1500 to the present. It also hosts the annual Turner Prize exhibition with its accompanying furor about the state of contemporary art, from about October to January each year. The Linbury Galleries on the lower floors stage temporary exhibitions, while the upper floors show the permanent collection. Each room has a theme and includes key works by major British artists: Van Dyck, Hogarth, and Reynolds rub shoulders with Rossetti, Sickert, Hockney, and Bacon, for example. Not to be missed is the generous selection of Constable landscapes.

The Turner Bequest consists of J. M. W. Turner's personal collection; he left it to the nation on condition that the works be displayed together. The James Stirling–designed Clore Gallery (to

> **CRAVING MORE ART?**
>
> Step down to the river and take the Tate to Tate shuttle boat (dotted with playful Damien Hirst spots) across to the Tate Modern; it runs between the two museums via the London Eye every 40 minutes.

the right of the main gallery) opened in 1987 to fulfill his wish, and it should not be missed. You can rent an audio guide with commentaries by curators, experts, and some of the artists themselves. ✉ *Millbank, Westminster, SW1* ☎ *020/7887–800, 020/7887–8008 recorded information* ⊕ *www.tate.org.uk* ✆ *Free, exhibitions £3–£10* ☉ *Daily 10–5:50* Ⓤ *Pimlico (signposted 5-min walk).*

NEED A BREAK?
Rather than search for a suitable place in Pimlico or Victoria, you can eat well right at the Tate. The Tate Britain Café has drinks, sandwiches, and cakes, and is open daily from 10 AM to 5:30 PM. The Rex Whistler Restaurant is almost a destination in itself, with its celebrated Rex Whistler murals and a daily fixed-price three-course lunch menu (around £15) and à la carte choices. Ingredients celebrate British produce, such as Cornish crab, Welsh lamb, organic smoked salmon, and Stilton cheese. Children's portions are available. It's open for lunch Monday through Saturday noon to 3 and Sunday noon to 4; breakfast and afternoon tea are also served on weekends.

Trafalgar Square. This is the center of London, by dint of a plaque on the corner of the Strand and Charing Cross Road from which distances on U.K. signposts are measured. It's the home of the **National Gallery** on its north side, and **Nelson's Column** at the heart of the square, flanked by two generals who distinguished themselves in the service of empire in India: **Charles Napier,** conqueror of Sind, and **Henry Havelock,** who recaptured Cawnpore (Kanpur) for the British during the Indian rebellion of 1857. Great events, such as the Christmas Tree lighting ceremony, New Year's Eve, royal weddings, political protests, and sporting triumphs always see the crowds gathering in the city's most famous square.

The commanding open space is built on the grand scale demanded by its central position in the metropolis of a great imperial power. From the 13th century the site housed the Royal Mews for the royal hawks and falcons. As falconry became less popular, the space was used for horse stables and barracks until 1830, when John Nash had the buildings torn down as part of his Charing Cross Improvement Scheme. Nash exploited the square's natural incline—it slopes down from north to south—making it a succession of high points from which to look down the imposing carriageways that run dramatically away from it toward the Thames, the Houses of Parliament, and Buckingham Palace. Upon Nash's death, the design baton was passed to Sir Charles Barry and then to Sir Edwin Lutyens.

On the southern point of the square, en route to Whitehall, is the **equestrian statue of Charles I.** After the Civil War and the king's execution, Oliver Cromwell, then the leader of the "Commonwealth," commissioned a scrap dealer, brazier John Rivett, to melt the statue. The story goes that Rivett buried it in his garden and made a fortune peddling knickknacks wrought, he claimed, from its metal, only to produce the statue miraculously unscathed after the restoration of the monarchy—and to make more cash reselling it to the authorities. In 1767 Charles II had it placed where it stands today, near the spot where his father

Continued on p. 60

WESTMINSTER ABBEY

A monument to the rich—and often bloody and scandalous— history of Great Britain, Westminster Abbey rises on the Thames skyline as one of the most iconic sites in London.

The mysterious gloom of the lofty medieval interior is home to more than 600 statues, tombs, and commemorative tablets. About 3,300 people, from kings to composers to wordsmiths, are buried in the abbey. It has been the scene of 14 royal weddings and no less than 38 coronations—the first in 1066, when William the Conqueror was made king here.

TOURING THE ABBEY

There's only one way around the abbey, and as there will almost certainly be a long stream of shuffling tourists at your heels, you'll need to be alert to catch the highlights. Enter by the north door.

When you enter the church, look up to your right to see the ❶ **painted-glass rose window,** the largest of its kind.

The ❷ **Coronation Chair,** at the foot of the Henry VII Chapel, has been briefly graced by nearly every regal posterior since Edward I ordered it in 1301. Look for the graffiti on the back of the Coronation chair. It's the work of 18th- and 19th-century visitors and Westminster schoolboys who carved their names there.

In front of the ❸ **High Altar,** which was used for the funerals of Princess Diana and the Queen Mother, is a black-and-white marble pavement laid in 1268. The intricate Italian Cosmati work contains three Latin inscriptions, one of which states that the world will last for 19,683 years.

The ❹ **Chapel of Henry VII** contains the tombs of Henry VII and his queen, Elizabeth of York. Close by are monuments to the young daughters of James I, and an urn purported to hold the remains of the so-called Princes in the Tower—Edward V and Richard. Interestingly, arch enemies Elizabeth I and her half-sister Mary Tudor share a tomb here. An inscription reads: "Partners

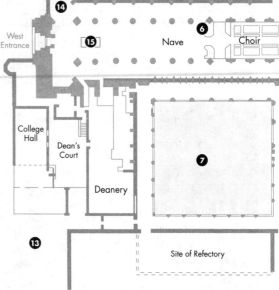

both in throne and grave, here rest two sisters, Elizabeth and Mary, in the hope of the Resurrection."

The ❺ **Chapel of St. Edward the Confessor** contains the shrine to the pre-Norman king. Because of its great age, it is closed off to the public; you must join a tour with the verger to be admitted to the chapel. (Details are available at the admission desk; there is a small extra charge.)

In the choir screen, north of the entrance to the choir, is a marble ❻ **monument to Sir Isaac Newton.**

A door from the south transept and south choir aisle leads to the calm of the ❼ **Great Cloisters.**

Geoffrey Chaucer was the first poet to be buried in ❽ **Poets' Corner** in 1400. Other memorials include: William Shakespeare, William Blake,

Map

North Entrance

1 North Transept

North Ambulatory

Sanctuary **5**   **2**   **4**   **3**

South Ambulatory

South Transept

8

9

10

11

12

The **10** **Abbey Museum** includes a collection of deliciously macabre effigies made from the death masks and actual clothing of Charles II and Admiral Lord Nelson (complete with eye patch).

The **11** **Little Cloister** is a quiet haven, and just beyond, the **12** **College Garden** is a delightful diversion. Filled with medicinal herbs, it has been tended by monks for more than 900 years.

John Milton, Jane Austen, Samuel Taylor Coleridge, William Wordsworth, and Charles Dickens.

The medieval **9** **Chapter House** is adorned with 14th-century frescoes. The King's Council met here between 1257 and 1547. Be sure to look at the floor, one of the finest surviving tiled floors in the country.

The **13** **Dean's Yard** is the best spot for a fine view of the massive flying buttresses above.

14 **A plaque to Franklin D. Roosevelt** is one of the Abbey's very few tributes to a foreigner.

The **15** **Grave of the Unknown Warrior,** in memory of the soldiers who lost their lives in both world wars, is near the exit of the abbey.

QUIRKY LONDON

Near the Henry VII chapel, keep an eye open for St. Wilgefort, who was so concerned to protect her chastity that she prayed to God for help and woke up one morning with a full growth of beard.

A BRIEF HISTORY

960 AD Benedictine monastery founded on the site by King Edward and King Dunstan.

1045–65 King Edward the Confessor enlarges the original monastery, erecting a stone church in honor of St. Paul the Apostle. Named "west minster" to distinguish from "east minster" (St. Paul's Cathedral).

1065 The church is consecrated on December 28. Edward doesn't live to see the ceremony.

1161 Following Edward's canonization, his body is moved by Henry III to a more elaborate resting place behind the High Altar. Other medieval kings are later buried around his tomb.

1245–54 Henry III pulls down the abbey and starts again with a new Gothic style influenced by his travels in France. Master mason Henry de Reyns ("of Rheims") constructs the transepts, north front, and rose windows, as well as part of the cloisters and Chapter House.

1269 The new abbey is consecrated and the choir is completed.

1350s Richard II resumes Henry III's plan to rebuild the monastery. Henry V and Henry VII continue as benefactors.

1503 The Lady Chapel is demolished and the foundation stone of Henry VII's Chapel is laid on the site.

1540 The abbey ceases to be used as a monastery.

1560 Elizabeth I refounds the abbey as a Collegiate Church. From this point on it is a "Royal Peculiar," exempt from the jurisdiction of bishops.

1745 The western towers, left unfinished from medieval times, are finally completed, based on a design by Sir Christopher Wren.

1995 Following a 25-year restoration program, saints and allegorical figures are added to the niches on the western towers and around the Great West Door.

PLANNING YOUR DAY

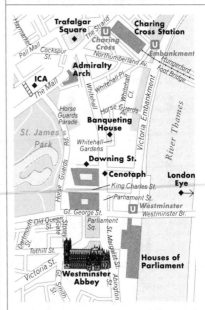

GETTING HERE: The closest Tube stop is Westminster. When you exit the station, walk west along Great George Street, away from the river. Turn left on St. Margaret Street.

CONTACT INFO: ✉ Broad Sanctuary, Westminster SW1 ☎ 020/7222–5152 ⊕ www.westminster-abbey.org.

ADMISSION: Adults: Abbey and museum £10. **Family ticket** (2 adults and 2 children): £24. **Children under 11:** free.

HOURS: The abbey is a house of worship. Services may cause changes to the visiting hours on any given day, so be sure to call ahead.
Abbey: Weekdays 9:30–3:45, Wed. until 6, Sat. 9:30–1:45; closes 1 hr after last admission.
Museum: Daily 10:30–4.
Cloisters: Daily 8–6.
College Garden: Apr.–Sept., Tues.–Thurs., 10–6; Oct.–Mar., Tues.–Thurs. 10–4.
Chapter House: Daily 10:30–4.

WESTMINSTER ABBEY

WHAT'S NEARBY: To make the most of your day, arrive at the abbey early (doors open at 9:30), then make an afternoon visit to the Parliament buildings and finish with a sunset ride on the **London Eye.** Post-flight, take a walk along the fairy-lit South Bank and have dinner (or a drink in the bar) with a view, at the **Oxo Tower Restaurant** (☎ 020/7803–3888). There's live jazz every evening starting at 7:30 PM.

Please note that overseas visitors can no longer visit the **Houses of Parliament** during session. However, tours of the buildings are available in August and September. For more information and booking call ☎ 0870/90–3773. Also, it's advisable to prebook tickets for the London Eye. Do this online at www.londoneye.com, or call 0870/990–8883.

IN A HURRY?

If you're pressed for time, concentrate on the following four highlights: the Coronation Chair; Tombs of Queen Elizabeth I and Mary Queen of Scots in the Chapel of Henry VII; Poets' Corner; and Grave of the Unknown Warrior.

THINGS TO KNOW

■ Photography and filming are not permitted anywhere in the abbey.

■ In winter the interior of the abbey can get quite cold; dress accordingly.

■ For an animated history of the museum, join one of the tours that depart from the information desk at 10, 11, 2, and 2:30 daily.

■ Touring the abbey can take half a day, especially in summer, when lines are long.

■ To avoid the crowds, make sure you arrive early. If you're first in line you can enjoy parts of the abbey in relative calm before the mad rush descends.

■ If you want to study up before you go, visit www.westminster-abbey.org, which includes an in-depth history and self-guided tour of the abbey. Otherwise pick up a free leaflet from the information desk.

■ On Sundays the abbey is not open to visitors. Join a service instead. Check the Web site for service times, as well as details of concerts, organ recitals, and special events.

was executed in 1649. Each year, on January 30, the day of the king's death, the Royal Stuart Society lays a wreath at the foot of the statue. ⊠ *Trafalgar Sq., Westminster, SW1* Ⓤ *Charing Cross.*

⟳ **Wellington Barracks.** These are the headquarters of the Guards Division, the Queen's five regiments of elite foot guards (Grenadier, Coldstream, Scots, Irish, and Welsh) who protect the sovereign and patrol her palace dressed in tunics of gold-purled scarlet and tall fur "bearskin" helmets of Canadian brown bearskin. If you want to learn more about the guards, or view every kind of toy model soldier, visit the **Guards Museum;** the entrance is next to the Guards Chapel. ⊠ *Wellington Barracks, Birdcage Walk, Westminster, SW1* ☎ *020/7414–3428* ⊕ *www.theguardsmuseum.com* ⊠ *£2* ☉ *Daily 10–4; last admission 3:30* Ⓤ *St. James's Park.*

Westminster Cathedral. Amid the concrete jungle of Victoria Street lies this remarkable neo-Byzantine find, seat of the Cardinal of Westminster, head of the Roman Catholic Church in Britain, and consequently London's principal Roman Catholic church. Faced with the daunting proximity of Westminster Abbey, the architect, John Francis Bentley, flew in the face of fashion by rejecting neo-Gothic in favor of the Byzantine idiom, which still provides maximum contrast today. The asymmetrical redbrick Byzantine hulk, dating only from 1903, is banded with stripes of Portland stone and abutted by a 273-foot-high campanile at the northwest corner, which you can scale by elevator. The interior is still incomplete, but worth seeing for its brooding mystery and its rich and colorful marble-work. Look out for the stations of the cross (stopping points for prayer or contemplation) by Eric Gill, the beautiful mosaic work on the roof of Holy Souls Chapel, and the striking baldachino—the enormous stone canopy standing over the altar and giant cross in front of it. The nave is the widest in the country and is constructed in green marble, which has a Byzantine connection—it was cut from the same place as the 6th-century St. Sophia's in Istanbul, and was almost confiscated by warring Turks as it traveled across the country. Just inside the main entrance is the tomb of Cardinal Basil Hume, who held the seat for more than 25 years. The Bell tower, containing Big Edward, can be climbed. There's a café in the crypt. ⊠ *Ashley Pl., Westminster, SW1* ☎ *020/7798–9055* ⊕ *www.westminstercathedral.org.uk* ⊠ *Tower £2* ☉ *Cathedral daily 7–7. Tower Apr.–Sept., daily 9–5; Oct.–Mar., Thurs.–Sun. 9–5* Ⓤ *Victoria.*

St. James's & Mayfair

Piccadilly Circus

WORD OF MOUTH

"Even if it means a few steps out of your way, strolling through St. James's Park can be a way to get from A to B."

—nessundorma

"The Sir John Soane museum is always good for an offbeat place to visit, and the Wallace Collection is also a fantastic place to spend a couple of hours—with lunch or tea and window shopping somewhere on Marylebone Street after."

—trvlgrl

GETTING ORIENTED

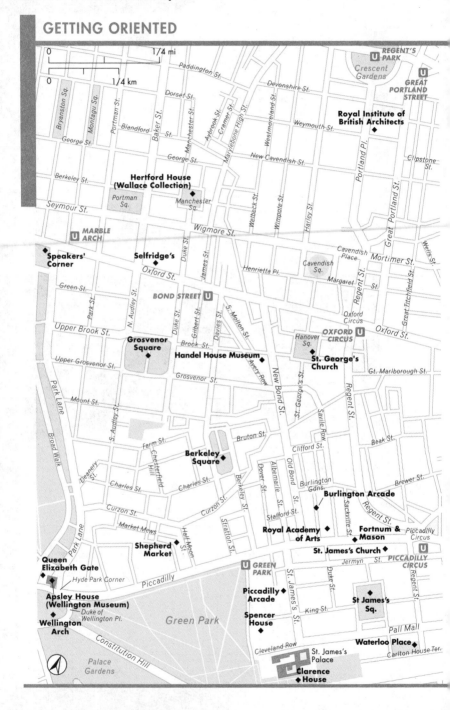

0   1/4 mi

0   1/4 km

REGENT'S PARK

Crescent Gardens

GREAT PORTLAND STREET

Paddington St.

Dorset St.

Devonshire St.

Weymouth St.

Royal Institute of British Architects

Blandford St.

George St.

New Cavendish St.

Clipstone St.

George St.

Hertford House (Wallace Collection)

Berkeley St.

Portman Sq.

Manchester Sq.

Seymour St.

Wigmore St.

MARBLE ARCH

Cavendish Place

Mortimer St.

Speakers' Corner

Selfridge's

Oxford St.

Cavendish Sq.

Margaret St.

Green St.

Henrietta Pl.

Upper Brook St.

BOND STREET

Oxford Circus

Oxford St.

OXFORD CIRCUS

Grosvenor Square

Brook St.

Hanover Sq.

St. George's Church

Upper Grosvenor St.

Handel House Museum

Gt. Marlborough St.

Grosvenor St.

Mount St.

Farm St.

Bruton St.

Clifford St.

Beak St.

Berkeley Square

Savile Row

Charles St.

Charles St.

Burlington Gdns.

Brewer St.

Curzon St.

Burlington Arcade

Market Mews

Stafford St.

Royal Academy of Arts

Fortnum & Mason

Piccadilly Circus

Shepherd Market

Half Moon St.

St. James's Church

PICCADILLY CIRCUS

Queen Elizabeth Gate

Hyde Park Corner

GREEN PARK

Jermyn St.

Piccadilly

Apsley House (Wellington Museum)

Duke of Wellington Pl.

Piccadilly Arcade

St James's Sq.

Wellington Arch

Spencer House

King St.

Pall Mall

Green Park

Cleveland Row

Waterloo Place

Constitution Hill

St. James's Palace

Carlton House Ter.

Palace Gardens

Clarence House

TOP 5 REASONS TO GO

■ **Claridge's Bar:** Unwind with afternoon tea at this art deco gem after a shopping spree in Mayfair.

■ **Fortnum & Mason:** Stock up on fine teas and quintessentially British foods, before living it up in the 1707 wine bar with some chablis and smoked salmon.

■ **Marylebone High Street:** Although it's just north of frenetic Oxford Street, you'll feel a whole world away as you wander by the chic restaurants and boutiques.

■ **Royal Academy of Arts:** Visit the Summer Exhibition, a breathtaking affair showcasing some of the best sculpture and painting in the art world.

■ **Green Park:** Grab a sandwich at Marks & Spencer across Piccadilly and settle down for a picnic on the grass, a lovely escape from the congestion of central London.

FEELING PECKISH?

Edgware Road, running north from Marble Arch, is full of Middle Eastern cafés, restaurants, pastry shops, and kebab houses. The Maroush and Ranoush chains are the best known, great for a post-shopping shawarma or falafal sandwich.

Pret A Manger on busy Piccadilly, opposite the Royal Academy, has windows to watch the world go by. It's one of a high-standard chain of cafés that specializes in a selection of sandwiches and pastries for breakfast and lunch. Eat in or take your sandwich across to Green Park.

GETTING HERE

There are four Tube stops on the Central Line that will leave you smack in the center of these neighborhoods: Marble Arch, Bond Street (also Jubilee Line), Oxford Circus (also Victoria and Bakerloo lines), and Tottenham Court Road (also Northern Line). You can also take the Piccadilly or Bakerloo Line to the Piccadilly Circus Tube stop, the Piccadilly to the Hyde Park Corner stop, or the Piccadilly, Victoria, or Jubilee line to the Green Park stop.

The best bus is the 8, which circles around via New Bond Street to Oxford Street, and skirts the eastern edge of Green Park to Grosvenor Place.

MAKING THE MOST OF YOUR TIME

Reserve at least a day to see the sites in St. James's and Mayfair, but choose carefully, as this is one of London's most densely packed, dynamic districts. The only areas to avoid are the Tube stations at rush hour, and Oxford Street if you're claustrophobic. At all costs, stay away from Oxford Circus around 5 PM, when rushing commuters can, at times, resemble an East African wildebeest migration.

Sightseeing
☆★★★★

Nightlife
☆☆★★★

Dining
☆★★★★

Lodging
☆★★★★

Shopping
☆★★★★

Smart, stylish, and so very British, St. James's and Mayfair comprise the heart and soul of London's West End. South of frenetic Oxford Street, you can feel the history and privilege of old London converging with the chic tempo and affluence of new London. Along these streets you will also find the greatest concentration of fine hotels, posh department stores, opulent restaurants and nightclubs, swanky galleries, top auction houses, big hedge funds, and international corporations—the sense of being somewhere important is all-encompassing in the sparkling streets of St. James's and Mayfair.

WHAT'S HERE

Architecture buffs and fine-art connoisseurs will want to see the Christopher Wren–designed **St. James's Church** as well as **St. James's Square,** home of the London Library. The well-known quarters for gentlemen's clubs, **Pall Mall** is an excellent example of 18th- and 19th-century patrician architecture and home to **Waterloo Place,** where a number of famous statues have been erected, among them a stunning portrait of Florence Nightingale. An equally regal statue of Franklin D. Roosevelt, a British memorial to the 32nd U.S. President, stands under London's oldest plane trees in the center of the distinguished **Grosvenor Square** across from the U.S. Embassy.

The **Royal Academy of Arts** is one of London's historic gems, a cultured place to seek solace from nearby swarming Piccadilly Circus. At the opposite end of Piccadilly is another aesthete's lair, the grand home of the Duke of Wellington, **Apsley House** (or Wellington Museum); before it stands **Wellington Arch** and next to it, one of London's newest monuments, the New Zealand Memorial, opened in 2006; it commemorates the "strong and enduring relation-ship" between the two countries. Fine-art enthusiasts should save an hour or two for **Hertford House** at **Manchester Square,** north of Oxford Street, which contains the delightful (and not often crowded) **Wallace Collection,** an exhibition of fine art and artifacts collected by four generations of Marquesses of

> ## ROYALTY IN AISLE 9
>
> Built in 1788, Fortnum & Mason sent hams to the Duke of Welling-ton's army and baskets of treats to Florence Nightingale in the Crimea. (It also happens to be the Queen's grocery store.)

Hertford. Afterwards, stroll up **Marylebone High Street** for some shopping or a drink in one of London's most stylish neighborhoods, one with a distinctly younger feel than Mayfair.

Those for whom shopping is paramount will relish a mosey along **Old Bond Street, South Molton Street, Mount Street, Savile Row,** and **Jermyn Street,** where you will find the most exclusive shops in London. The some-what overwhelmingly commercialized **Regent Street** is also fun for a few blocks if you fancy popping into Liberty, or the sleek Apple Store. Those keen on architecture should continue north along Regent's Street to the **Royal Institute of British Architects** (RIBA) at **Portland Place.** It's a 1934 Art Deco structure standing as a beautiful, stark counterpoint to the remaining 18th-century Adam houses on this elegant street. Shoppers and historians alike will enjoy **Fortnum & Mason** at 181 Piccadilly. This old-fashioned fine-foods store feels lifted from another century with ornate murals decorating the walls, glass cabinets and brass fixtures casting a dazzling glow all around, and smiling salespeople tending to your every need (a rarity in London). Its restaurants are beloved of old ladies who've come up from the country for the day. Another historic shop (or group of shops) in this district is **Burlington Arcade.** Built in 1818 by the Earl of Burlington, this covered royal walkway is one of the most elegant places to purchase fine wares in London. South of Piccadilly, the **Piccadilly Arcade** is no less historic, although rather more eccentric.

Finally, St. James's &.Mayfair has a fascinating musical and oratorical heritage that spans several centuries. If you visit 25 Brook Street you'll be a guest in the former home of famed baroque composer Friedrich Handel. A painstakingly restored Georgian, the house is now a live-music venue with weekly recitals, as well as a museum of Handel's life, called **Handel House Museum.** At **Hanover Square** you'll come upon the splendid **St. George's Church,** where often during the holidays choral concerts are held. All Souls Church at **Langham Place** is home to innu-merable classical concerts broadcast regularly by the BBC. Another notable musical site is No. 3 Savile Row, former headquarters of the Beatles' Apple Records label. If seeing this makes you want to "twist and shout," you might see fit to stop at **Speakers' Corner** in Hyde Park and join the ranks of figures such as Karl Marx, George Orwell, and Marcus Garvey, among others throughout history, who have exercised their right to let off steam in public.

A BRIEF HISTORY

The name Mayfair derives from the 15-day May fair that was once held in the web of small streets known as Shepherd Market, but was brought to an end by the upper classes who lived there and felt it was drawing undesirables to their polished part of town. The beautiful St. James's Park, meanwhile, stands as an idyllic emblem of this elite past: it's the oldest royal park in London and all that remains of the royal hunting grounds that once traversed the city to Islington, Marylebone, and Hampstead. Henry VIII acquired the park in 1532 for a deer park; he also built the neighboring, Tudor brick St. James's Palace. Another historic site, Lancaster House, was built for the Duke of York in the 1820s, but is most famous as the locale of the 1978 conference that ended white rule in the African nation that is now Zimbabwe.

The equally illustrious Clarence House, built in 1825 for the Duke of Clarence (later William IV), is now the home of Prince Charles and Camilla Parker Bowles, Duchess of Cornwall. And Spencer House, one of the most stunning 18th-century mansions in London, is home to the ancestors of the late Princess Diana of Wales. On a more somber note, if you follow the signs through Hyde Park you can find Marble Arch, once the city's gallows and now just a massive yet graceful arch that marks the merge of Bayswater Road and Oxford Street.

PLACES TO EXPLORE

Fodor'sChoice ★ ☾ **Apsley House (Wellington Museum).** For Hyde Park Corner read "hero's corner"; even in the subway, beneath the turmoil of traffic, the Duke of Wellington's heroic exploits are retold in murals. The years of war against the French, and the subsequent final defeat of Napoléon at the Battle of Waterloo in 1815 made Wellington—Arthur Wellesley—the greatest soldier and statesman in the land. The house is flanked by imposing statues: opposite is the 1828 Decimus Burton **Wellington Arch** with the four-horse chariot of peace as its pinnacle (open to the public as an exhibition area and viewing platform). Just behind Wellington Arch, and cast from captured French guns, the legendary **Achilles** statue points the way with thrusting shield to the ducal mansion from the tip of Hyde Park. Next to Apsley House is the elaborate gateway to the park, designed and built by Burton at the same time as the Wellington Arch.

Once known as No. 1, London, because it was the first and grandest house at the old tollgate from Knightsbridge village, this was long celebrated as the best address in town. Built by Robert Adam and later refaced and extended, this housed the Duke of Wellington from 1817 until his death in 1852. As the Wellington Museum, it has been faithfully restored, complete with Wellesley's uniforms, weapons, a fine collection of paintings, and his porcelain and plate collections acquired as a result of his military successes. His extensive art collection includes Dutch Old Masters, Velázquez, Goya, Rubens, and Correggio. There are portraits of his adversary Napoléon Bonaparte, and a huge, towering statue of a naked Napoléon by Canova in the stairwell. The free audio guide highlights the most noted works and the superb decor. The most stunning is the Waterloo Gallery, where the annual banquet for officers who fought beside Wellington was held. With its heavily sculpted and gilded ceiling, its feast of Old Master paintings on red damask walls, and commanding gray candelabra, it's a veritable orgy of opulence. There are commemorative weekends on either side of Waterloo Day, and the day itself when entry to the house is free, with special events and costumed guides. Telephone or check the Web site for details. ⊠ *Hyde Park Corner* ☎ *020/7499–5676* ⊕ *www.english-heritage.org. uk* ⊗ *Apr.–Nov., Tues.–Sun. 10–5; Dec.–Mar., Tues.–Sun. 10–4. Also open bank holiday Mon.* ☺ *£5.10, joint ticket with Wellington Arch £6.30* Ⓤ *Hyde Park Corner.*

Bond Street. This world-class shopping haunt is divided into northern "New" (1710) and southern "Old" (1690) halves. On New Bond Street you'll find **Sotheby's,** the world-famous auction house, at No. 35. But there are other ways to flirt with financial ruin on Old Bond Street: the mirror-lined Chanel store, the vainglorious marble acres of Gianni Versace, and the boutique of the more sophisticated Gucci, an array of fine jewelers including Tiffany's, and art dealers Colnaghi, Léger, Thos. Agnew, and Marlborough Fine Arts. **Cork Street,** which parallels the top half of Old Bond Street, is where London's top dealers in contemporary art have their galleries—where you're welcome to browse. Ⓤ *Bond St., Green Park.*

Burlington Arcade. Perhaps the finest of Mayfair's enchanting covered shopping alleys is the second oldest in London, built in 1819 for Lord Cavendish, to stop the hoi polloi from throwing rubbish into his garden at Burlington House, which is behind the arcade. It's still patrolled by top-hatted officials, who preserve decorum by preventing you from singing, running, or carrying open umbrellas. The arcade is also the main link between the Royal Academy of Arts and its extended galleries at 6 Burlington Gardens. ⊠ *Piccadilly, Mayfair, W1* Ⓤ *Green Park, Piccadilly Circus.*

Clarence House. The London home of Queen Elizabeth the Queen Mother for nearly 50 years, Clarence House is now the Prince of Wales

---

NAPOLEON DYNAMITE

Unmissable, in every sense (and considered rather too athletic for the time), is the gigantic Canova statue of a nude (but fig-leafed) Napoléon, which presides over the grand staircase that leads to the many elegant reception rooms.

BERKELEY SQUARE

As anyone who's heard the old song knows, the name rhymes with "starkly." Not many of its original mid-18th-century houses are left, but look at Nos. 42–46 (especially No. 44, which the architectural historian Sir Nikolaus Pevsner thought London's finest terraced house) and Nos. 49–52 to get some idea of why it was once London's top address—not that it's in the least humble now. Private members' nightclub Annabel's is one current resident. Berkeley Sq., Mayfair, W1 Ⓤ Green Park.

3

Royal Attractions

The Queen and the Royal Family attend approximately 400 functions a year, and if you want to know what they are doing on any given date, turn to the *Court Circular*, printed in the major London dailies, or check out the royal family Web site, ⊕ *www. royal.gov.uk*, for the latest pictures and events. Trooping the Colour is usually held on the second Saturday in June, to celebrate the Queen's official birthday. This spectacular parade begins when she leaves Buckingham Palace in her carriage and rides down the Mall to arrive at Horse Guards Parade at 11 exactly. To watch, just line up along the Mall with your binoculars!

Another time you can catch the Queen in all her regalia is when she and the Duke of Edinburgh ride in state to Westminster to open the Houses of Parliament. The famous gilded coach, such an icon of fairytale glamour, parades from Buckingham Palace, escorted by the brilliantly uniformed Household Cavalry—on a clear day, it's to be hoped, for this ceremony takes place in late October or early November, depending on the exigencies of Parliament.

But perhaps the most relaxed, least formal time to see the Queen is during Royal Ascot, held at the racetrack near Windsor Castle—a short train ride out of London—usually during the third week of June (Tuesday–Friday). After several races, the Queen invariably walks down to the paddock on a special path, greeting race goers as she proceeds. Americans wishing to reserve a seat in the Royal Enclosure should apply to the **American Embassy** (✉ *24 Grosvenor Sq., Mayfair, London W1*) before the end of March. But remember: you must be sponsored by two guests who have attended Ascot at least seven times before.

and the Duchess of Cornwall's residence. The Regency mansion was built by John Nash for the Duke of Clarence, who found living in St. James's Palace quite unsuitable. Since then it has remained a royal home for princesses, dukes, and duchesses, including the present monarch, Queen Elizabeth, after her marriage. The rooms have been sensitively preserved as the Queen Mother chose, with the addition of many works of art from the Royal Collection. You'll find it less palace, and more home (for the Prince and his sons William and Harry) with informal family pictures and comfortable sofas. The tour (by timed ticket entry only) is of the ground-floor rooms and includes the Lancaster Room, so called because of the marble chimneypiece presented by Lancaster county to the newly married Princess Elizabeth and the Duke of Edinburgh. Like Buckingham Palace, Clarence House is open only in summer, and tickets must be booked in advance. ✉ *The Mall, St. James's, SW1* ☏ *020/7766–7303* ⊕ *www.royal.gov.uk* ✉ *£7.50* ☉ *Aug.–mid-Oct.* Ⓤ *Green Park.*

Grosvenor Square. This square (pronounced "*Grove*-na") was laid out in 1725–31 and is as desirable an address today as it was then. Americans certainly thought so—from John Adams, the second president, who as ambassador lived at No. 38, to Dwight D. Eisenhower, whose wartime headquarters was at No. 20. Now the ugly '50s block of the U.S. Embassy occupies the entire west side, and a British memorial to Franklin D. Roosevelt stands in the center. There is also a memorial to those who died in New York on September 11, 2001. The little brick chapel used by Eisenhower's men during World War II, the 1730 Grosvenor Chapel, stands a couple of blocks south of the square on South Audley Street, with the entrance to pretty **St. George's Gardens** to its left. Across the gardens is the headquarters of the English Jesuits as well as the society-wedding favorite, the mid-19th-century Church of the Immaculate Conception, known as Farm Street because of its location. ⊠*Mayfair, W1* Ⓤ *Bond St.*

🕑 **Handel House Museum.** The former home of the composer, where he lived for more than 30 years until his death in 1759, is a celebration of his genius. It's the first museum in London solely dedicated to one composer, and that is made much of with room settings

> **HERE'S WHERE**
>
> Interestingly, the Handel House Museum also has a petite exhibition of photos of Jimi Hendrix, who lived in the adjoining house 1968–69.

in the contemporary fine Georgian style. You can linger over original manuscripts (there are more to be seen in the British Library) and gaze at portraits—accompanied by live music if the adjoining music rooms are being used by musicians in rehearsal. Some of the composer's most famous pieces were created here, including *Messiah* and *Music for the Royal Fireworks*. To hear a live concert here—there's a busy evening program of jazz and chamber music—is to imagine the atmosphere of rehearsals and "salon" music in its day. Handel House makes a perfect cultural pit-stop after shopping on nearby Bond and Oxford streets, and if you come on Saturday, there are free art and music activities for kids. The museum occupies both No. 25 and the adjoining house, where life in Georgian London is displayed in exhibit space (another musical star, Jimi Hendrix, lived here for a brief time in the 1960s, indicated by a blue plaque outside the house and a small exhibition of photos of the star). Occasional tours of the flat, currently administrative offices and not usually open to the public, can be arranged. Phone or check the Web site for details. ⊠*25 Brook St., Mayfair, W1* ☎*020/7495–1685* ⊕*www.handelhouse.org* 🔊*£5* 🕙 *Tues.–Sat. 10–6, Thurs. 10–8, Sun. noon–6* Ⓤ *Bond St.*

Marble Arch. John Nash's 1827 arch, moved to its present location in 1851, stands amid the traffic whirlpool where Bayswater Road segues into Oxford Street, and where Park Lane links up to the Wellington Arch at Hyde Park Corner. Search the sidewalk on the traffic island opposite the cinema to find the stone plaque that marks (roughly) the place where the Tyburn Tree stood for four centuries, until 1783. This was London's central gallows, a huge wooden structure with hanging accommodations for 21. Cross over (or under—there are signs to help in the labyrinth) to the northeastern corner of Hyde Park to Speakers' Corner. ⊠*Park La., Mayfair, W1* Ⓤ *Marble Arch.*

★ **Marylebone High Street.** A favorite of style sections everywhere, this street forms the heart of Marylebone Village, a vibrant, upscale residential neighborhood that encompasses the squares around the High Street and nearby Marylebone Lane. It's hard to believe that you're just a few blocks north of Oxford Street as you wander in and out of Marylebone's shops and boutiques. Some noteworthy stops along the way are La Fromagerie (2–4 Moxon St.), an excellent cheese shop; Daunt Books (Nos. 83–84), a travel bookshop; and on Sundays, a large farmers' market in a car park just behind the High Street. It becomes less intimate when you get to busy Marylebone Road, but Marylebone Town Hall is worth a look if you're heading that way—perhaps for a stroll in the park or to take the kids to Madame Tussauds. ⊠ *Marylebone, W1* Ⓤ *Bond Street.*

> **BIBLIOPHILE ALERT**
>
> From the giant Waterstone's megastore and genteel Hatchard's on Piccadilly, to G. Heywood Hill on Curzon Street and Maggs Bros. in Berkeley Square, Mayfair is a heavenly hunting ground for booklovers. Ⓤ Green Park.

Piccadilly Circus. Although it may *seem* like a "circus" with its traffic and the camera-clickers clustered around the steps of **Eros,** the name refers to the five major roads that radiate from it. The origins of "Piccadilly" are from the humble tailor on the Strand named Robert Baker who sold picadils—a collar ruff all the rage in courtly circles—and built a house with the proceeds. Snobs dubbed his new-money mansion Piccadilly Hall, and the name stuck.

Eros, London's favorite statue and symbol of the *Evening Standard* newspaper, is not in fact the Greek god of erotic love at all, but the angel of Christian charity, commissioned in 1893 from the young sculptor Alfred Gilbert as a memorial to the philanthropic Earl of Shaftesbury (the angel's bow and arrow are a sweet allusion to the earl's name). It cost Gilbert £7,000 to cast the statue he called his "missile of kindness" in the novel medium of aluminum, and because he was paid only £3,000, he promptly went bankrupt and fled the country. (Not to worry—he was knighted in the end.) Beneath the modern bank of neon advertisements are some of the most elegant Edwardian-era buildings in town. ⊠ *St. James's, W1* Ⓤ *Piccadilly Circus.*

Fodor's Choice ★ **Royal Academy of Arts.** Burlington House was built in the Palladian style for the Earl of Burlington around 1720, and it's one of the few surviving mansions from that period. The chief occupant today is the Royal Academy of Arts (RA), and a statue of one of its famed members, Sir Joshua Reynolds, with artist's palette in hand, is prominent in the piazza of light stone and fountains by Michael Hopkins. It's a tranquil, elegant space for sculpture exhibits, and has a café with outdoor tables in summer. Further exhibition space has been afforded with the opening of 6 Burlington Gardens, the old Museum of Mankind, reached through the elegant walkway of Burlington Arcade. The collection of works by Academicians past and present as well as its most prized piece, the *Taddeo Tondo* (a sculpted disk) by Michelangelo of the Madonna and Child, on display in the Sackler Wing. The RA has an active program of temporary exhibitions; hugely successful exhibitions here have included Monet in the 20th Century (1999), Van Dyck (1999), and a Rodin retrospective (2006). Every June, the RA puts on the **Summer Exhibition,** a huge and always surprising collection of sculpture and painting by Royal Academicians and a plethora of other artists working today. ⊠ *Burlington House, Piccadilly, Mayfair, W1* ☎ *020/7300–8000, 020/7300–5760 recorded information* ⊕ *www.royalacademy.org. uk* ✑ *Admission varies according to exhibition* ☉ *Sat.–Thurs. 10–6, Fri. 10–10* Ⓤ *Piccadilly Circus, Green Park.*

NEED A BREAK?

The Royal Academy Restaurant has hot dishes at lunchtime, very good vegetarian options, and an extensive salad selection that is inexpensive for such a posh location. The walls are covered in Stanley Spencer murals. It's open weekdays 10–5:30, with a dinner menu on Friday from 6:15 to 10:30.

Royal Institute of British Architects (RIBA). An Art Deco gem in elegant Portland Place, RIBA was built by Grey Wornum in 1934. Its distinctive Portland Stone facade stands out amid the surrounding 18th-century mansions, and large bronze doors lead to a spacious foyer with a wide marble staircase. There's a wonderful architecture bookstore inside, and you can enjoy your reading in impeccable Art Deco surroundings over lunch or coffee in the upstairs café. ⊠ *Park La., 66 Portland Pl., Marylebone, W1* Ⓤ *Regent's Park or Great Portland Street.*

St. James's Church. Set back from the street behind a courtyard, the church is filled most days with an antiques and crafts market. Completed in 1684, this was the last of Sir Christopher Wren's London churches and his own favorite. It contains one of Grinling Gibbons's finest works, an ornate limewood reredos (the screen behind the altar). The organ is a survivor of Whitehall Palace and was brought here in 1691. A 1940 bomb scored a direct hit here, but the church was subsequently completely restored, albeit with a fiberglass spire. The interior is again showing signs of wear and water damage, and a new restoration project is in the planning stages. It's a lively place, offering all manner of lectures and concerts. The courtyard hosts different markets: on Tuesday antiques and small collectibles; Wednesday to Saturday arts and crafts. ⊠ *Piccadilly, St. James's, W1* ☎ *020/7734–4511, 020/7381–0441 for concert program and tickets* ⊕ *www.st-james-piccadilly.org* Ⓤ *Piccadilly Circus, Green Park.*

St. James's Palace. With its solitary sentry posted at the gate, this surprisingly small palace of Tudor brick was once a home for many British sovereigns, including the first Elizabeth and Charles I, who spent his last night here before his execution. Today it's the working office of another Charles—the Prince of Wales. The front door actually debouches right onto the street, but he always uses a back entrance. Royals who live within the palace are Princess Alexandra and her husband, Sir Angus Ogilvy. Matters to ponder as you look (you can't go in): the palace was named after a hospital for women lepers, which stood here during the 11th century; Henry VIII had it built; foreign ambassadors to Britain are still accredited to the Court of St. James's even though it has rarely been a primary royal residence; and the present Queen made her first speech here. Friary Court out front is a splendid setting for Trooping the Colour, part of the Queen's official birthday celebrations. Everyone loves to take a snap of the scarlet-coated guardsman standing sentinel outside the imposing Tudor gateway. Note that the changing of the guard at St. James's Palace only occurs on days when the guard at Buckingham Palace is changed. See entry for Buckingham Palace for details. ⊠*Friary Court, St. James's, SW1* ⊕*www.royal.gov.uk* Ⓤ*Green Park*.

St. James's Square. One of London's oldest and leafiest squares was also the most snobbish address of all when it was laid out around 1670, with 14 resident dukes and earls installed by 1720. Since 1841, No. 14—one of the several 18th-century residences spared by World War II bombs—has housed the **London Library**, founded by Thomas Carlyle, and which, with its million or so volumes, is considered the best private humanities library in the land. You can go in and read the famous authors' complaints in the comments book—but not the famous authors' books, unless you become a member. Other notable institutions around the square include the **East India Club** at No. 16, and the **Naval and Military Club** (known as the "In and Out" after the signage on its gateposts) at No. 4. ⊠*St. James's, SW1* ⊕*www.londonlibrary. co.uk* Ⓤ*Piccadilly Circus*.

★ **Selfridges.** With its row of massive Ionic columns, this huge store was opened three years after Harry Gordon Selfridge came to London from Chicago in 1906. Now British-run, Selfridges rivals Harrods in size and stock, and it's finally rivaling its glamour, too, since investing in major face-lift operations. *(For more on Selfridges, see Chapter 19, Shopping.)* ⊠*400 Oxford St., Mayfair, W1* ☎*020/7629–1234* ⊕*www. selfridges.com* ⊙ *Weekdays 10–8, Sat. 9:30–8, Sun. 11:30–6* Ⓤ*Marble Arch, Bond St.*

★ **Spencer House.** Ancestral abode of the Spencers—Diana, Princess of Wales's family—this great mansion is perhaps the finest example of 18th-century elegance, on a domestic scale, extant in London. Superlatively restored by Lord Rothschild, the house was built in 1766 by Palladian architect John Vardy for the first Earl Spencer, heir to the first Duchess of Marlborough. Henry Holland, who was employed by the Prince Regent, added modifications. The gorgeous Doric facade, its pediment adorned with classical statues, makes immediately clear Earl Spencer's passion for the Grand Tour and the classical antiquities of the past. Inside, James "Athenian" Stuart decorated the gilded State Rooms, including the Painted Room, the first completely neoclassical room in Europe. The most ostentatious part of the house (and the Spencers did not shrink from ostentation—witness the £40,000 diamond shoe buckles the first countess proudly wore) is the florid bow window of the Palm Room: covered with stucco palm trees, it conjures up both ancient Palmyra and modern Miami Beach. The garden, of Henry Holland design, has been restored with planting of the time. Both the house and garden can be seen by guided tour only in limited numbers, so book in advance. ⊠*27 St. James's Pl., St. James's, SW1*

☎*020/7499–8620* ⊕*www.spencerhouse.co.uk* ✉*£9* ☉*Sept.–Dec. and Feb.–July, Sun. 10:45–4:45; guided tour leaves approx. every 25 min; tickets on sale Sun. at 10:30. Garden: late May–July, separate charge for tour* Ⓤ*Green Park.*

★ **Wallace Collection.** Assembled by four generations of Marquesses of
☾ Hertford and given to the nation by the widow of Sir Richard Wallace, illegitimate son of the fourth, this collection of art and artifacts is important, exciting, undervisited—and free. As at the Frick Collection in New York, Hertford House itself is part of the show: the fine late-18th-century mansion, built for the Duke of Manchester, contains a basement floor with educational activities, several galleries, and a courtyard, covered by a glass roof, with the upscale Wallace Restaurant.

The first marquess was a patron of Sir Joshua Reynolds, the second bought Hertford House, the third—a flamboyant socialite—favored Sèvres porcelain and 17th-century Dutch painting; but it was the eccentric fourth marquess who, from his self-imposed exile in Paris, really built the collection, snapping up Bouchers, Fragonards, Watteaus, and Lancrets for a song (the French Revolution having rendered them dangerously unfashionable), augmenting these with furniture and sculpture and sending his son Richard out to do the deals. With 30 years of practice behind him, Richard Wallace continued acquiring treasures after his father's death, scouring Italy for majolica and Renaissance gold, then moving most of it to London. Look for Rembrandt's portrait of his son, the Rubens landscape, Gainsborough and Romney portraits, the Van Dycks and Canalettos, the French rooms, and of course the porcelain. The highlight is Fragonard's *The Swing*, which conjures up the 18th-century's let-them-eat-cake frivolity better than any other painting around. Don't forget to smile back at Frans Hals's *Laughing Cavalier* in the Big Gallery or pay your respects to Thomas Sully's enchanting *Queen Victoria*, which resides in a rouge-pink salon (just to the right of the main entrance). There is a fine collection of armor (which you can try on for size) and weaponry in the basement as a break from all the upstairs gentility. ✉*Hertford House, Manchester Sq., Mayfair, W1* ☎*020/7563–9500* ⊕*www.wallacecollection.org* ✉*Free, charge for special exhibitions* ☉*Daily 10–5* Ⓤ*Bond St.*

NEED A BREAK?
The Wallace Restaurant brings the outside in, in the elegant setting of the glass-roofed courtyard of the Wallace Collection. It's open for breakfast, lunch, and afternoon tea, and for dinner on weekends. The brasserie menu highlights French food from pâtés and cheeses to oysters and succulent steaks. If you don't want to indulge your budget too much, you can just linger over coffee or afternoon tea in the gorgeous surroundings. It's open Sunday–Thursday 10–4:30, Friday–Saturday 10 AM–11 PM.

Wellington Arch. Opposite the Duke of Wellington's mansion, Apsley House, this majestic stone arch surveys the busy traffic rushing around Hyde Park Corner. Designed by Decimus Burton and built in 1828, it was created as a grand entrance to the west side of London and echoes the design of that other landmark gate, Marble Arch. Both were tri-

St. James's & Mayfair Dining

MODERATE DINING

Bentley's, Seafood, 11–15 Swallow St.

Bellamy's, Brasserie, 18–18A Bruton Pl.

Cecconi's, Italian, 5A Burlington Gardens

Le Caprice, Modern British, Arlington House, Arlington St.

Momo, Moroccan, 25 Heddon St.

The Wolseley, Austrian, 160 Piccadilly

EXPENSIVE DINING

Gaucho Grill, Steakhouse, 25 Swallow St.

Gordon Ramsay at Claridge's, French, Claridge's, 55 Brook St.

Greenhouse, French, 27A Hay's Mews

Le Gavroche, French, 43 Upper Brook St.

Locanda Locatelli, Italian, 8 Seymour St.

L'Oranger, French, 5 St. James's St.

Nobu, Japanese, Metropolitan Hotel, 19 Old Park La.

The Ritz, French, 150 Piccadilly

Sketch: Gallery, Modern British, 9 Conduit St.

The Square, French, 6–10 Bruton St.

AFTERNOON TEA

Brown's, 33 Albermarle St.

Café at Sotheby's, Sotheby's, 34 New Bond St.

Claridge's, Brook St.

The Dorchester, 53 Park La.

Fortnum & Mason, St. James's Restaurant, 4th fl., 181 Piccadilly

Patisserie Valerie at Sagne, 105 Marylebone High St.

The Ritz, 150 Piccadilly

umphal arches commemorating Britain's victory against France in the Napoleonic Wars, and both were moved after their construction to ease the Victorian traffic situation. The Wellington Arch was constructed at the same time as the Apsley Gate (also Burton's design); you'll see the same highly ornamental green gates within the Wellington Arch. Atop the building, the Angel of Peace descends on the quadriga, or four-horse chariot of war. This replaced the Duke of Wellington on his horse, which was considered too large and hence moved to army barracks in Aldershot. A step inside the arch reveals the stories behind the building and statue, and explores other great arches across the world. Without doubt, the highlight is to walk around the top of the arch and enjoy the brilliant panoramas over the park, including glimpses into the private gardens of Buckingham Palace. In summer, Wellington Arch is the starting point for English Heritage themed walks. ⊠*Hyde Park Corner, Mayfair, SW1* ☎*020/7930–2726* ⊕*www.english-heritage. org.uk* ⊡*£3* ☉*Apr.–Oct., Wed.–Sun. 10–5; Nov.–Mar., Wed.–Sun. 10– 4* Ⓤ*Hyde Park Corner.*

Soho & Covent Garden

Eclectic shops fill these two neighborhoods.

WORD OF MOUTH

"The main business for buskers [in Covent Garden] is in the day-time, when the shops and stalls are open. The area is full of interesting-looking shops…. West from the piazza, King Street takes you towards Leicester Square via New Row to St. Martin's Lane, but before you cross over towards Charing Cross Road, turn left and look for Goodman's Court for echoes of Victorian back alleys."

—PatrickLondon

GETTING ORIENTED

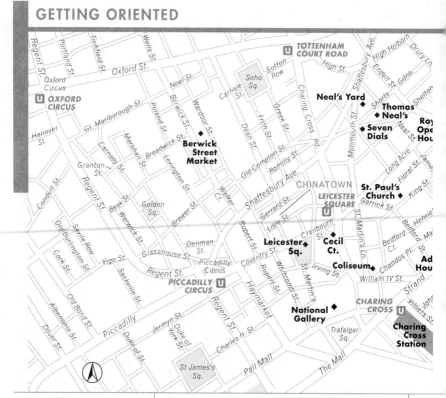

GETTING THERE	TOP 5 REASONS TO GO

Take any train to the Piccadilly Circus station (on the Piccadilly and Bakerloo lines or Leicester Square and Northern lines for Soho). Get off at Covent Garden on the Piccadilly Line for Covent Garden and Embankment (Bakerloo, Northern, District, and Circle lines) or Charing Cross (Northern, Bakerloo, and main railway lines) for the area south of the Strand.

■ **Hearing Big Ben:** Let its surprisingly familiar chimes waft down as you stroll down the Embankment.

■ **Royal Opera House:** Applaud as a ballerina collects roses at the end of her performance, but make sure you visit even if you're not going to the opera.

■ **Courtauld Gallery:** Admire your favorite impressionist painting up close in the Courtauld Gallery, then discover Cranach the Elder's mischievous *Adam and Eve*.

■ **Somerset House:** Watch the skaters and ice-wall climbers on a December evening.

■ **Chinatown:** Eat the best Cantonese, Singaporean, Thai, and Malaysian food outside of Asia.

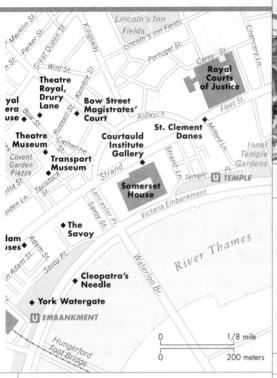

4

MAKING THE MOST OF YOUR TIME

You can comfortably tour all the sights in Covent Garden in a day. Visit the small but perfect Courtauld Gallery on Monday before 2 [pm] when it's free. That leaves plenty of time to visit the market-place, watch the street entertainment, and do a bit of shopping, with energy left over for a night on the town (or "on the tiles," as the British say) in Soho.

GAY LONDON

The bars and clubs along Old Compton Street in Soho are popular with affluent, stylish gay men. There are some very smart nightclubs in the area.

Madame Jo Jo's (⊠ *8–10 Brewer St.* ⊕ *www.madamejojos.com*) has been around for nearly 50 years, with a range of different, popular club nights. The club's Kitsch Cabaret, which can be booked online, is so popular (with straights as well as gays) that it's booked up weeks in advance.

FEELING PECKISH?

Although they may set out a few tables, the coffee shops and snack bars along the Covent Garden market buildings can be overpriced and of iffy quality. It's usually best to head for Soho when the munchies strike.

The enormous **Chuen Cheng Ku** (⊠ *17 Wardour St., Soho, W1* ☎ *020/7437–1398*) in Chinatown serves dim sim from steaming carts all day, in an atmosphere like something out of an old movie.

Maison Bertaux (⊠ *28 Greek St., Soho, W1* ☎ *020/7437–6007*) has been around since the end of the 19th century. Decor is spartan but fab French cakes, tarts, and savory quiches more than make up for that. Nobody's mother ever baked this well.

Neal's Yard Bakery & Tearoom (⊠ *6 Neals Yard, Covent Garden, WC2* ☎ *020/7836–5199*) sells vegetarian food, delicious cakes, and salad-filled sandwiches in a relaxed, kid-friendly atmosphere.

Sightseeing
☆☆★★★

Nightlife
☆★★★★

Dining
☆★★★★

Lodging
☆☆☆★★

Shopping
☆☆★★★

Once a red-light district, the Soho of today delivers more "grown-up" than "adult" entertainment, although there are flashbacks of its seedier days. Theaters, restaurants, pubs, and clubs merge with the first-run cinemas of Leicester Square and the venerable venues (Royal and English National Operas) of Covent Garden to create the mega-entertainment district known as the West End. Throughout the day, Covent Garden's historic piazza is packed with shoppers, backpackers, and sightseers, while Soho reverts to the business side of its lively, late-night scene—ad and media execs, film distributors, actors, and agents all looking for each other.

WHAT'S HERE

This is one of London's oldest districts. The streets turn and wind, or end abruptly in blank walls, and it's easy to lose your sense of direction and get lost. Even Londoners carry local maps (their trusty *Pocket A to Zs*) that they consult now and then. But having what locals would call "a good mooch around" is half the fun.

Unless you're involved in the media and movie business or looking to buy some fruit and vegetables at the **Berwick Street Market** (⇨ *Shopping, Chapter 19*), Soho is more of a nighttime entertainment district than a place for strolling and sightseeing. If you do find yourself in this part of town, you can take refuge in **Soho Square** and its 19th-century garden, a calm spot for a sandwich lunch amongst the frenzy. If you like theater, head for the half-price ticket kiosk in **Leicester Square** early; browse a bit in the antiquarian booksellers along tiny **Cecil Court,** between Charing Cross Road and St. Martin's Lane; then aim for **Cleopatra's Needle** (a

60-foot obelisk predating its arbitrary namesake, and London itself, by centuries) on Victoria Embankment near Embankment Station. From there you can ferret your way to the Strand through the small 18th- and early-19th-century lanes, passing the **Adam Houses** along the way.

The Savoy, just off the strand in its own little court is a good place to have a posh (and expensive) cream tea or a cocktail in the American Bar. **Somerset House** is just beyond, after the intersection with a half-circular road, the Aldwych. The **Courtauld Institute Gallery** and its shop are just under the archway leading to Somerset House. Once you've gone through the entry, a huge 18th-century piazza opens out. The former government buildings around it, built for George III, have been opened to the public since the Millennium and now house several good museums. It's lovely to stop here for a snack or a tea in warm weather and watch London children playing in the fountains. In winter an outdoor skating rink is set up.

Covent Garden starts north of the Strand. Drury Lane intersects the middle of Aldwych, passing one of London's oldest playhouses, **Theatre Royal, Drury Lane.** If you take a right onto Russell Street you come to the corner of Bow Street, one of the area's best intersections for things to do. Standing on the corner, you'll be within about 50 paces of **Bow Street Magistrates' Court,** the **Royal Opera House,** the **Theatre Museum,** and **London's Transport Museum.** You'll also be in sight of the Covent Garden Piazza, bustling with tourists and shoppers and loads of ways to spend your money.

It's likely that entertainers will be regaling the crowds in front of **St. Paul's Church,** known as the actor's church, on the west end of the market. They may look like ordinary buskers, but this is hallowed ground--the first Punch and Judy show was performed here--and they've had to pass strict auditions to be licensed. If they make you smile, don't forget to leave a coin.

North of Long Acre, catercorner to the Tube station, and closed to traffic halfway down, is **Neal Street,** one of Covent Garden's liveliest and most youthful pedestrian shopping areas. Here you can buy everything you never knew you needed--from vintage aviators' jackets to shoes with heels lower than toes to collapsible top hats.

Off Neal Street, on Earlham Street, is **Thomas Neal's**--an upscale, designer clothing and housewares mall named after the founder (in 1693) of the star-shaped cobbled junction of tiny streets nearby, called **Seven Dials**--a surprisingly residential enclave, with lots going on behind the tenement-style warehouse facades. If you walk down St. Martin's Lane from the Seven Dials, you'll see the **London Coliseum,** home of the English National Opera, on your left.

On Shorts Gardens, off Neal Street, is **Neal's Yard** (note the comical, water-operated wooden clock), originally just a whole-foods wholesaler and now an entire holistic village, with therapy rooms, an organic bakery, the superb Neal's Yard Dairy, a great vegetarian café, and Neal's Yard Remedies. There's also the Donmar Warehouse, one of London's

A BRIEF HISTORY

In the 18th century, Casanova lived and loved here before returning to Venice. Almost as soon as development covered what had been a royal park and hunting ground, Soho earned a reputation for entertainment, bohemianism, and cosmopolitan tolerance. When the minions of public decency decided to end Soho's sex trade in 1991, with tough licensing laws and zero-tolerance of soliciting, they cracked down on an old Soho tradition that still resurfaces from time to time.

For centuries Soho was also an immigrant slum. French Hugenots in the 1680s, followed by Germans, Russians, Poles, Greeks, Italians, and Chinese, settled and brought their ethnic cuisines with them. So when dining out became fashionable after World War I, Soho was the natural place for restaurants to flourish.

For 300 years, Covent Garden was a convent garden. In 1630, Inigo Jones turned it into Britain's first planned public square. But wealthy Londoners preferred their own gated gardens, and within 50 years the piazza became a fruit-and-vegetable market. Despite the development of the Royal Opera in the 19th century, the area became run-down and was scheduled to be demolished in the 1970s. A local campaign saved it and the restored market opened in 1980, with upscale boutiques and stalls selling hand crafted goods.

best and most innovative theaters, where film director Sam Mendes (*American Beauty, Road to Perdition, Jarhead*) made his name.

PLACES TO EXPLORE

The Adam Houses. All that remains of what was once a regal riverfront row of houses on a three-acre site, connected by arches and streets below grade, are a few of the structures, but such is their quality that they are worth a detour off the Strand to see. The work of 18th-century Scottish architects and interior designers (John, Robert, James, and William Adam, known collectively as the Adam brothers), the original development was damaged in the 19th century during the building of the embankment, and demolished in 1936 to be replaced by an art deco tower. The original houses still standing are protected, and give a glimpse of their former grandeur. Nos. 1–4 Robert Street and Nos. 7 and 10 Adam Street are the best. At the **Royal Society of Arts** (⊠ 8 *John Adam St.* ☎ *020/7930–5115* ⊕ *www.rsa.org.uk* ☞ *Free* ♡ *1st Sun. of month, 10--1*), you can see a suite of Adam rooms; no reservations are required. ⊠ *The Strand, Covent Garden, WC2* Ⓤ *Charing Cross, Embankment.*

Courtauld Institute Gallery. One of London's most beloved art collections, the Courtauld is to your left as you pass through the archway into the grounds of the beautifully restored, grand 18th-century classical **Somerset House.** Founded in 1931 by the textile magnate Samuel Courtauld to house his remarkable private collection, this is one of the world's finest impressionist and Postimpressionist galleries, ranging from Bonnard to van Gogh. A déjà vu moment with Cézanne, Degas, Seurat, or Monet awaits on every wall (Manet's *Bar at the Folies-Bergère* is the star), with bonus post-Renaissance works thrown in. Botticelli, Brueghel, Tiepolo, and Rubens are also represented, thanks to the exquisite bequest of Count Antoine Seilern's Princes Gate collection. German Renaissance paintings, bequeathed in 1947 include the colorful and delightfully wicked *Adam and Eve* by Lucas Cranach the Elder. There are also some bold and bright Fauvist paintings. Don't miss the little café downstairs. The Courtauld Institute of Art (on the other side of the entrance archway) is part of London University and trains art historians and conservators. ⊠ *The Strand, Covent Garden, WC2* ☎ *020/78482526* ⊕ *www. courtauld.ac.uk* ✉ *£5, free Mon. 102, except bank holidays* ☉ *Daily 106; last admission 5:15* Ⓤ *Covent Garden, Holborn, Temple.*

★ **Covent Garden Piazza.** The 1840 market building around which Covent Garden pivots is known as the Piazza. Inside, the shops are mostly higher-class clothing chains, plus a couple of cafés and some knick-knack stores that are good for gifts. There's the superior **Apple Market** for crafts on most days, too. If you turn right, you'll reach the indoor **Jubilee Market,** which, with its stalls of clothing, army surplus gear, and more crafts and knickknacks, is disappointingly ordinary. In summer it may seem that everyone you see around the Piazza (and the crowds are legion) is a fellow tourist, but there's still plenty of office life in the area. Londoners who shop in the area tend to head for Neal Street and the area to the left of the subway entrance rather than the touristy market itself. By the church in the square, street performers—from global musicians to jugglers and mimes—play to the crowds, as they have done since the first English Punch and Judy Show, staged here in the 17th century. ⊠ *Covent Garden, WC2* Ⓤ *Covent Garden.*

Leicester Square. This square (pronounced "Lester") is showing no sign of its great age. Looking at the neon of the major movie houses, the fast-food outlets (plus a useful Häagen-Dazs café), and the disco entrances, you'd never guess it was laid out around 1630. By the 19th century it was already bustling and disreputable, and now it's usually one of the few places crowded after midnight—with suburban teenagers, backpackers, and London's swelling ranks of the homeless. That said, it's not a threatening place, and the liveliness can be quite cheering. But be on your guard—any place so full of tourists and people a little the worse for wear is bound to attract pickpockets, and Leicester Square certainly does. In the middle is a statue of a sulking Shakespeare, clearly wishing he were somewhere else and perhaps remembering the days when the cinemas were live theaters—burlesque houses, but live all the same. Here, too, are figures of Hogarth, Reynolds, and Charlie Chaplin,

> **CHEAP TICKETS**
>
> One landmark certainly worth visiting is the **Society of** London Theatre ticket kiosk (TKTS), on the southwest corner of Leicester Square, which sells half-price tickets for many of that evening's performances. It's open Monday-Saturday from 10 AM to 7 PM, and Sunday from noon to 3 PM. One window sells matinee tickets and other tickets for evening performances, so make sure you join the correct line. Watch out for illegal ticket touts, who target tourists around the square.

and underneath, but not visible, is a £22 million electrical substation. On the northeast corner, in Leicester Place, stands the church of **Notre Dame de France,** with a wonderful mural by Jean Cocteau in one of its side chapels. ⊠*Covent Garden, WC2* Ⓤ *Leicester Sq.*

☼ **London's Transport Museum.** Normally housed in the old Flower Market at the southeast corner of the Covent Garden Piazza, the museum was closed for redevelopment at this writing and scheduled to reopen by late 2007. Visit the museum Web site for access information and to see if a public opening coincides with your London visit. ☎*020/ 75657299* ⊕*www.ltmuseum.co.uk.*

Royal Opera House. London's premier opera and ballet venue was designed in 1858 by E.M. Barry, son of Sir Charles, the House of Commons architect, and is the third theater on the site. The first theater opened in 1732 and burned down in 1808; the second opened a year later, only to succumb to fire in 1856.

The entire building, which was given a spectacular overhaul, retains the magic of the grand Victorian theater but has been made more accessible. The glass-and-steel Floral Hall (so badly damaged by fire in the 1950s it was used only for storing scenery) is the most wonderful feature; you can wander around and drink in (literally, in the foyer café) the interior during the day. The same is true of the Amphitheatre Bar and Piazza concourse, where you can have lunch while looking out at a splendid panorama across the city. There are free lunchtime chamber concerts and lectures as part of the policy to dispel the Opera House's elitist tag. *For more on the Royal Opera House, see Arts & Entertainment, Chapter 18.* ⊠*Bow St., Covent Garden* ☎*020/73044000* ⊕*www.royaloperahouse.org* Ⓤ*Covent Garden.*

St. Paul's Church. If you want to commune with the spirits of Vivien Leigh, Noël Coward, Edith Evans, and Charlie Chaplin, this might be just the place. Memorials to them and many other theater greats are found in this 1633 work of the renowned Inigo Jones, who, as the King's Surveyor of Works, designed the whole of Covent Garden Piazza. St. Paul's has been known as "the actors' church" since the Restoration, thanks to the neighboring theater district and St. Paul's prominent parishioners (well-known actors often read the lessons at services). Fittingly, its portico was where the opening scene for *Pygmalion* was staged. St. Paul's Church (Wren's St. Paul's cathedral is eastward in the City) is across the Covent Garden Piazza, often punctuated with street entertainers. They are continuing in a very old tradition. ■ TIP→**London diarist Samuel Pepys, writing in the 17th century, reports watching the first Punch and Judy show in English on the Tuscan portico of this church.** ⊠*Bedford St., Covent Garden, WC2* Ⓤ*Covent Garden.*

Fodor'sChoice **Somerset House.** An old royal palace once stood on the site, but the
★ 18th-century building that finally replaced it was the work of Sir William Chambers (172696) during the reign of George III. It was built to
☼ house government offices, principally those of the Navy; for the first time in more than 100 years these gracious rooms are on view for free, including the Seamen's Waiting Hall and the Nelson Stair. In addition,

the Navy Commissioners' Barge has returned to dry dock at the Water Gate. The rooms are on the south side of the building, by the river. The **Courtauld Institute Gallery** occupies most of the north building, facing the busy Strand. Between is the cobbled Italianate courtyard where Admiral Nelson used to walk, the scene of an ice rink in the winter holiday season as well as summer concerts and other cultural events. Cafés and a restored river terrace adjoin the property, and a stone-and-glass footbridge leads up to Waterloo Bridge, which you can walk across to get to the South Bank.

> ### ICE-SKATING
>
> It's hard to beat the skating experience at Somerset House, where during December and January a rink is set up in the spectacularly grand courtyard of this central London palace. Adults £9.50£12, children £6. Popularity is enormous, and if you can't get a ticket, other venues such as Hampton Court and the Natural History Museum are following Somerset House's lead in having temporary winter rinks. ☎020/78454670 ⊕ www.somerset-house.org. uk/icerink.

4

In the vaults of the house is **The Gilbert Collection,** a museum of intricate works of silver, gold snuff boxes, and Italian mosaics. The micro-mosaics on tables, portrait miniatures, and jewelry are made in such fine detail that you might think they're painted, so be glad if you're offered a magnifying glass—it's the best way to fully appreciate the fine detail. The **Hermitage Rooms** are the showcase for a selection of rotating exhibitions from the collections of the State Museum in St. Petersburg, and other Hermitage-related activities. The opening show consisted of a selection of jewels, antiquities, portraits, and miniatures amassed by Catherine the Great, one of the greatest collectors of all time. Subsequent exhibitions have included masterpieces of the Walpole Collection: Britain's first Prime Minister gathered works by such artists as Rembrandt, Rubens, Van Dyck, and Poussin, which were then sold to Catherine the Great. It's ironic that these pieces have returned to the country for the first time in more than 200 years. ⊠ *The Strand, Covent Garden, WC2* ☎*020/78454600 information, 020/78454630 Hermitage information* ⊕*www.somerset-house. org.uk* ⊠*Somerset House free, visit 1 collection £5, 2 collections £8, or get 3-day pass for unlimited visits over 3-day period to all collections £12* ⊗ *Daily 106; last admission 5:15* Ⓤ *Charing Cross.*

Ⓢ **Theatre Museum.** This mostly belowground museum aims to re-create the excitement of theater itself. There are usually programs in progress allowing children to get in a mess with makeup or have a giant dressing-up session. Permanent exhibits paint a history of the English stage from the 16th century to Mick Jagger's jumpsuit, with tens of thousands of theater playbills and sections on such topics as Hamlet through the ages and pantomime—the peculiar British theatrical tradition when men dress as ugly women, known as Panto Dames, and girls wear tights and play princes. There's a little theater in the bowels of the museum and a ticket desk for "real" theaters around town, plus an archive holding video recordings and audiotapes of significant British theatri-

Soho & Covent Garden Dining

BUDGET DINING

Bar Italia, Café, 22 Frith St.

Food for Thought, Vegetarian, 31 Neal St.

Maison Bertaux, Café, 28 Greek St.

New Piccadilly, Café, 8 Denman St.

MODERATE DINING

Andrew Edmunds, Mediterranean, 46 Lexington St.

Arbutus, Modern British, 6364 Frith St.

Bertorelli's, Italian, 44A Floral St.

Browns, Brasserie, 8284 St. Martin's La.

Fung Shing, Chinese, 15 Lisle St.

J Sheekey, Seafood, 2832 St. Martin's Ct.

Joe Allen, American, 13 Exeter St.

L'Escargot, French, 48 Greek St.

Orso, Italian, 27 Wellington St.

Ping Pong, Asian, 45 Great Marlborough St.

EXPENSIVE DINING

Asia de Cuba, Asian, 45 St. Martins La.

The Ivy, British, 1 West St.

L'Atelier de Joël Robuchon, French, 1315 West St.

Lindsay House, Irish, 21 Romilly St.

Rules, British, 35 Maiden La.

Yauatcha, Chinese, 15 Broadwick St.

AFTERNOON TEA

The Savoy, Strand

cal productions. Like the London theater it represents, the museum is "dark" (closed) on Monday. ⊠ *7 Russell St., Covent Garden, WC2* ☏ *020/79434700* ⊕ *www.theatremuseum.org* ⊠ *Free* ⊗ *Tues.Sun. 106; last admission 5:30* Ⓤ *Covent Garden.*

Theatre Royal, Drury Lane. This is London's best-known auditorium and almost its largest. Since World War II, its forte has been musicals (past ones have included *The King and I, My Fair Lady, South Pacific, Hello, Dolly!,* and *A Chorus Line*)—though David Garrick, who managed it from 1747 to 1776, made its name by reviving the works of the by-then-obscure William Shakespeare. It enjoys all the romantic accessories of a London theater—a history of fires (it burned down three times, once in a Wren-built incarnation), riots (in 1737, when a posse of footmen demanded free admission), attempted regicides (George II in 1716 and his grandson George III in 1800), and even sightings of the most famous phantom of theaterland, the Man in Grey (in the Circle, matinees). The entrance is on Catherine Street. ⊠ *Catherine St., Covent Garden, WC2* ⊕ *www.theatre-royal.com* Ⓤ *Covent Garden.*

Bloomsbury & Legal London

Gordon Square, Bloomsbury

WORD OF MOUTH

"To me the British Museum is a destination that everyone should visit once in their life.... You could easily spend the entire day in the museum. So plan accordingly! The first time my wife and I visited we had a couple hours until closing and we thought 'eh, that's plenty of time.' We got the boot and we had barely left the first room. The next time we spent 4 hours in the Egyptian room. And this time we're taking another couple to share the experience."

–Kevin_C

GETTING ORIENTED

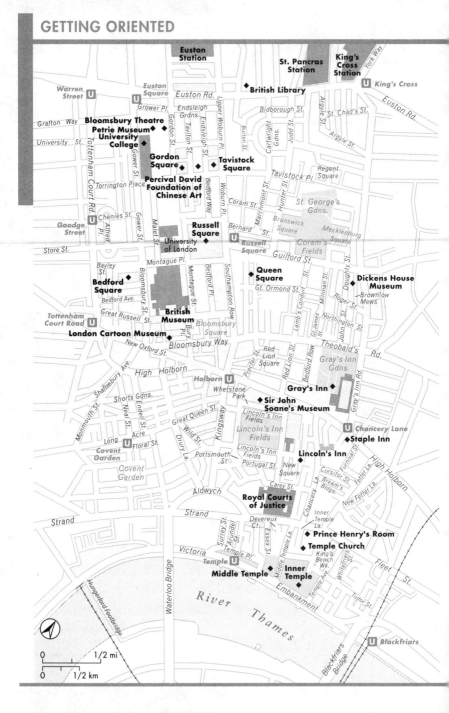

Euston Station

St. Pancras Station

King's Cross Station

Warren Street U

Euston Sq.

Euston Rd.

British Library

King's Cross U

King's Cross

Euston Rd.

Grower Pl.

Grafton Way

University St.

Endsleigh Gdns.

Bidborough St.

St. Chad's St.

Argyle St.

Argyle St.

Bloomsbury Theatre

Petrie Museum

University College

Gordon St.

Tavistock St.

Endsleigh St.

Upper Woburn Pl.

Burton St.

Cartwright Gdns.

Judd St.

Gordon Square

Tavistock Square

Tavistock Pl.

Regent Square

Percival David Foundation of Chinese Art

Torrington Place

Bedford Way

Woburn Pl.

Coram St.

Marchmont St.

Hunter St.

St. George's Gdns.

Goodge Street U

Chenies St.

Alfred Pl.

Gower St.

Malet St.

Bernard St.

Brunswick Square

Mecklenburg Square

Store St.

Russell Square

University of London

Montague Pl.

Russell Square U

Coram's Fields

Guilford St.

Doughty St.

Dickens House Museum

Bayley St.

Bedford Square

Bedford Ave.

Montague St.

Bedford Pl.

Southampton Row

Queen Square

Gt. Ormond St.

Lamb's Conduit

Gt. James St.

Millman St.

Roger St.

Northington St.

Brownlow Mews

Tottenham Court Road U

Great Russell St.

British Museum

Bloomsbury Square

Bloomsbury Way

Theobald's Rd.

London Cartoon Museum

New Oxford St.

Bury St.

Gray's Inn Rd.

Gray's Inn Gdns.

Shaftesbury Ave.

High Holborn

Procter St.

Red Lion Square

Red Lion St.

Bedford Row

Shorts Gdns.

Endell St.

Holborn U

Whetstone Park

Gray's Inn

Monmouth St.

Neal St.

Great Queen St.

Kingsway

Sir John Soane's Museum

Chancery Lane U

Long Acre

Floral St.

Wild St.

Drury La.

Lincoln's Inn Fields

Staple Inn

Covent Garden U

Covent Garden

Portsmouth St.

Lincoln's Inn Fields

Portugal St.

New Square

Lincoln's Inn

Cursitor St.

Furnival St.

Bream's Bldgs.

Fetter La.

High Holborn

Carey St.

Royal Courts of Justice

Chancery La.

Aldwych

Strand

Strand

Devereux Ct.

Inner Temple La.

New Fetter La.

Victoria Embankment

Surrey St.

Arundel St.

Temple Pl.

Essex St.

Middle Temple La.

Prince Henry's Room

Temple Church

Temple U

Middle Temple

Inner Temple

King's Bench Wk.

Temple Ave.

Whitefriars St.

Fleet St.

Tudor St.

Blackfriars U

Waterloo Bridge

Hungerford Footbridge

River Thames

Blackfriars Bridge

0   1/2 mi

0   1/2 km

TOP 5 REASONS TO GO

■ **British Museum:** It's never too late to start appreciating the treasures here that would take lifetimes to see.

■ **British Library:** Lay eyes on the original Magna Carta, an actual Gutenberg Bible, copies of Jane Austen's writings, and Shakespeare's First Folio.

■ **Museum Street:** Stroll along a street lined with independent galleries, antiquarian map shops, and delightful cafés.

■ **Percival David Foundation:** Visit the most comprehensive collection of Chinese ceramics outside of China.

■ **University of London:** Hang out at the Union with the day's paper while picking up the latest student fashion trends and eavesdropping on political discussions.

FEELING PECKISH?

At **Alfred** (⊠ *245 Shaftesbury Ave.*) sticky toffee pudding is the thing to order, and it should be slowly consumed.

The Hare and Tortoise Dumpling & Noodle Bar (opposite the Renoir Cinema on Brunswick Square) serves scrumptious Asian fast food until 10:30 PM, seven days a week. This bright café is a favorite with students and it's easy to see why: ingredients are all-natural, the portions huge, the service fast, and the bill always reasonable.

Truckles of Pied Bull Yard (across Kingsway, towards the British Museum on Bury Place) is a popular chain wine bar and café. Its main attraction is the courtyard where you can eat and drink away from the crowds and noise. The superb London Review Bookshop is here, too.

SAFETY

Come evening, avoid the region around King's Cross because it's known to be one of London's more unsavory neighborhoods, especially for nonnatives who don't know their way about town.

GETTING THERE

You can easily get to where you need to be on foot in Bloomsbury, and the Russell Square Tube stop on the Piccadilly Line leaves you right at the corner of Russell Square. The best Tube stops for the Inns of Court are Holborn on the Central and Piccadilly lines or Chancery Lane on the Central Line. Tottenham Court Road on the Northern and Central lines or Russell Square (Piccadilly Line) are best for the British Museum.

MAKING THE MOST OF YOUR TIME

Bloomsbury can be seen in a day, or in half a day, depending on your interests and your time constraints. If you plan to visit the Inns of Court as well as the British Museum, and you'd also like to get a feel for the neighborhood, then you may wish to devote an entire day to this literary and legal enclave, or come back on another day to visit the British Museum, which can be quite exhausting.

Unless you don't mind a lot of moving trucks, honking, and students carrying heavy loads through the streets, avoid Bloomsbury in mid-September, when the streets around Russell Square are filled with students moving into housing for the upcoming school session. At other times, it's a pleasure to wander through the quiet, leafy squares, examining Blue Plaques or relaxing at a streetside café. You can also pick up a "Museum Mile" map, which marks all the museums in this area, and use it to plan your path.

5

The hub of intellectual London, Bloomsbury is anchored by the British Museum and the University of London, which houses—among other institutions—the London School of Economics (LSE) and the School of Oriental and African Studies (SOAS). As a result, the streets and cafés around Bloomsbury's Russell Square are often crawling with students and professors engaged in heated conversation, while literary agents and academics surf the shelves of the antiquarian bookstores nearby.

WHAT'S HERE

Perhaps the best-known square in Bloomsbury is the large, centrally located **Russell Square,** with gardens laid out by Humphry Repton, a prominent English landscape designer often considered the successor to Capability Brown. Then there's the charming **Bedford Square** and **Queen Square,** dominated by a handful of hospitals. Scattered about the **University College** campus are **Woburn Square, Torrington Square, Tavistock Square,** and **Gordon Square.** Gordon Square, at one point home to Virginia Woolf, the Bells, John Maynard Keynes (all at No. 46), and Lytton Strachey (at No. 51), is now the location of the **Percival David Foundation of Chinese Art.** The redbrick **British Library** is a few blocks north, across busy Euston Road.

The area from Somerset House on the Strand, all the way up Kingsway to the Euston Road, is known as London's **Museum Mile** for the myriad historic houses and museums that dot the area. Though more often linked with its literary past—**Dickens House Museum,** where the author wrote *Oliver Twist,* is one of the most-visited sites in the area—Bloomsbury also happens to be where London's legal profession was born. In fact, the buildings associated with legal London were some of the few structures spared during the Great Fire of 1666, and so the serpentine alleys, cobbled courts, and historic halls frequented by the city's still-

A BRIEF HISTORY

Fundamental to the region's spirit of open expression and scholarly debate is the legacy of an elite corps of artists and writers who lived here during the first three decades of the 20th century. The "Bloomsbury Group" included the likes of Virginia Woolf, Charles Dickens, and E.M. Forster, authors who—much like the Beat poets of San Francisco or the jazz artists of the Harlem Renaissance—defined their neighborhood as well as an entire era.

The neighborhood's very British-sounding name, however, stems from that of Norman landowner William de Blemund who, in 1201, acquired what was then just a rural patch of land. In the early 1660s the Earl of Southampton built what became Bloomsbury Square and later, in the 18th century, a cluster of wealthy landowners acquired additional land, which led to the development of the neighborhood's center. Bloomsbury Market opened in 1730, and today the district is home to some of London's most picturesque parks, squares, and buildings, as well as London's four Inns of Court.

5

bewigged barristers ooze centuries of history. The massive, Gothic-style **Royal Courts of Justice** ramble for blocks all the way to the Strand, while the **Inns of Court—Gray's Inn, Lincoln's Inn, Middle Temple,** and **Inner Temple**—are where most British trial lawyers have offices to this day. In the 14th century the inns were lodging houses where the barristers lived so that people would know how to easily find them (hence, the label "inn"). **Temple Church,** the 500-year-old **Prince Henry's Room,** and the **Staple Inn,** one of London's oldest surviving half-timber buildings, are also here.

Artists' studios and design shops share space with tenants near the **British Museum,** bright and modern with its sweeping glass-roof Great Court. Not far off on Little Russell Street, the **London Cartoon Museum** sells original published editorials and strip cartoons, while farther north on Gordon Street the **Bloomsbury Theatre** presents foreign films, modern dance, and stand-up comedians. Guaranteed to raise a smile from the most blasé and footsore tourist is **Sir John Soane's Museum,** which hardly deserves the burden of its dry name.

PLACES TO EXPLORE

★ **British Library.** Since 1759, the British Library had been housed in the
☾ British Museum on Gordon Square. But space ran out long ago. The collection of around 18 million volumes now has a home in state-of-the-art surroundings, and if you're a researcher, it's a wonderful place to work (special passes are required). The library's treasures are on view to the general public: the Magna Carta, a Gutenberg Bible, Jane Austen's writings, Shakespeare's First Folio, and musical manuscripts by Handel and Sir Paul McCartney are on show in the John Ritblat Gallery. Also in the gallery are headphones—you can listen to some of the most interesting snippets in a small showcase of the **National Sound Archive** stored here (it's the world's largest collection, but is not on view), such as the voice of Florence Nightingale, and an extract from the Beatles' last tour interview. On weekends and during school vacations there are

Continued on p. 97

THE BRITISH MUSEUM

Anybody writing about the British Museum had better have a large stack of superlatives close at hand: most, biggest, earliest, finest. This is the golden hoard of nearly three centuries of the Empire, the booty brought from Britain's far-flung colonies.

The first major pieces, among them the Rosetta Stone and Elgin Marbles, were "acquired" from the French, who "found" them in Egypt and Greece. The museum has since collected countless goodies of worldwide historical significance: the Black Obelisk, some of the Dead Sea Scrolls, the Lindow Man. And that only begins the list.

The British Museum is a vast space split into 94 galleries, generally divided by continent or period of history, with some areas spanning more than one level. There are marvels wherever you go, and—while we don't like to be pessimistic—it is, yes, impossible to fully appreciate everything in a day. So make the most of the tours, activity trails, and visitors guides that are available ($\Rightarrow$ *Tours, page 114*).

The following is a highly edited overview of the museum's greatest hits, organized by area. Pick one or two that whet your appetite, then branch out from there, or spend two straight hours indulging in the company of a single favorite sculpture. There's no wrong way to experience the British Museum.

✉ Great Russell St., Bloomsbury WC1

☎ 020/7323–8920

⊕ www.thebritishmuseum.ac.uk

🎫 Free; donations encouraged. Tickets for special exhibits vary in price.

🕐 Galleries, including special exhibits, Sat.–Wed. 10–5:30, Thurs. and Fri. 10–8:30. Great Court Sun.–Wed. 9–6, Thurs.–Sat. 9 AM–11 PM. Reading Room library and information area daily 10–5:30, Reading Room viewing area Thurs. and Fri. 10–8:30.

Ⓤ Russell Square

(left) The Great Court
(top) *Cradle to Grave* by Pharmacopoeia

MUSEUM HIGHLIGHTS

Ancient Civilizations

The Rosetta Stone. Found in 1799 and carved in 196 BC by decree of Ptolemy V in Egyptian hieroglyphics, demotic, and Greek, it was this multilingual inscription that provided French Egyptologist Jean-François Champollion with the key to deciphering hieroglyphics. *Room 4.*

Colossal statue of Ramesses II. A member of the 19th dynasty (ca. 1270 BC), Ramesses II commissioned innumerable statues of himself—more than any other preceding or succeeding king. This one, a 7-ton likeness of his perfectly posed upper half, comes from his mortuary temple, the Ramesseum, in western Thebes. *Room 4.*

(top) Portland vase
(bottom) Colossal statue of Ramesses II

The Elgin Marbles. Perhaps these marvelous treasures of Greece shouldn't be here—but while the debate rages on, you can steal your own moment with them in the Parthenon Galleries. Carved in about 440 BC, these graceful decorations are displayed along with an in-depth, high-tech exhibit of the Acropolis; the **handless, footless Dionysus** who used to recline along its east pediment is especially well known. *Room 18.*

Mausoleum of Halikarnassos. All that remains of this, one of the Seven Wonders of the Ancient World, is a fragmented form of the original "mausoleum," the 4th-century tomb of Maussollos, King of Karia. The highlight of this gallery is the marble forepart of the **colossal chariot horse from the** *quadriga. Room 21.*

The Egyptian mummies. Another short flight of stairs takes you to the museum's most popular galleries, especially beloved by children: the Roxie Walker Galleries of Egyptian Funerary Archaeology have a fascinating collection of relics from the Egyptian realm of the dead. In addition to real corpses, wrapped mummies, and mummy cases, there's a menagerie of animal companions and curious items that were buried alongside them. *Rooms 62–63.*

Portland Vase. Made in Italy from cameo glass at the turn of the first century, it is named after the Dukes of Portland, who owned it from 1785 to 1945. It is considered a technical masterpiece—opaque white mythological figures cut by a gem-cutter are set on cobalt-blue background. *Room 70.*

The **Enlightenment Gallery** should be visited purely for the fact that its antiquarian cases hold the contents of the British Museum's first collections—Sir Hans Sloane's natural-history loot, as well as that of Sir Joseph Banks, who acquired specimens of everything from giant shells to fossils to rare plants to exotic beasts during his voyage to the Pacific aboard Captain Cook's *Endeavour. Room 1.*

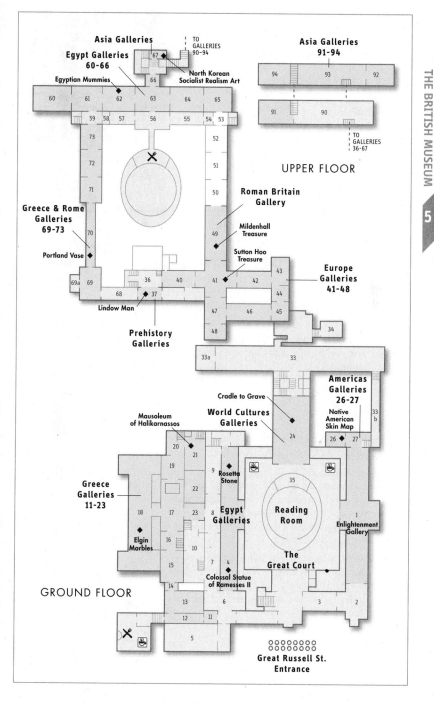

Asia Galleries

Egypt Galleries 60-66

Egyptian Mummies

TO GALLERIES 90-94

67

66

North Korean Socialist Realism Art

60 61 62 63 64 65

59 58 57 56 55 54 53

Asia Galleries 91-94

94 93 92

91 90

TO GALLERIES 36-67

73

72

71

52

51

50

UPPER FLOOR

Greece & Rome Galleries 69-73

Portland Vase

70

Roman Britain Gallery

49

Mildenhall Treasure

Sutton Hoo Treasure

43

Europe Galleries 41-48

69a 69 36 40 41 42 44

68 37 47 46 45

Lindow Man

48

34

Prehistory Galleries

33a 33

Americas Galleries 26-27

Native American Skin Map

33 b

Cradle to Grave

World Cultures Galleries

24

26 27

Mausoleum of Halikarnassos

20 21

19

9

Rosetta Stone

35

Greece Galleries 11-23

18

22

23

8

Egypt Galleries

Reading Room

1

Enlightenment Gallery

Elgin Marbles

17

16

10

The Great Court

15

7 4

14

Colossal Statue of Ramesses II

3 2

GROUND FLOOR

13

6

12 11

5

Great Russell St. Entrance

Asia

The Korea Foundation Gallery. Delve into striking examples of **North Korean Socialist Realism art** from the 1950s to the present and a reconstruction of a **sarangbang**, a traditional scholar's study, complete with hanji paper walls and tea-making equipment. *Room 67.*

World Cultures

Cradle to Grave. An installation by Pharmacopoeia, a collective of artists and a doctor, pays homage to the British nation's wellbeing—or ill-being, as it were. More than 14,000 drugs (the number estimated to be prescribed to every person in the U.K. in his lifetime) are encased in two lengths of nylon fabric resulting in a colorful tapestry of pills and tablets. *Room 24.*

The JP Morgan Chase North American Gallery. This is one of the largest collections of native culture outside North America, going back to the earliest hunters 10,000 years ago. Here a 1775 **native American skin map** serves as an example of the importance of such documents in the exploration and cartography of North America. Look for the beautifully displayed **native American costumes.** *Room 26.*

The Mexican Gallery. The most alluring pieces sit in this collection side by side: a 15th-century **turquoise mask of Xiuhtecuhtli**, the Mexican Fire God and Turquoise Lord, and a **double-headed serpent** from the same period. *Room 27.*

Britain and Europe

The Mildenhall Treasure. This glittering haul of 4th-century Roman silver tableware was found beneath the sod of a Suffolk field in 1942. *Room 49.*

The Sutton Hoo Treasure. Next door to the loot from Mildenhall—and equally splendid, including brooches, swords, and jewel-encrusted helmets)—the treasure was buried at sea with (it is thought) Redwald, one of the first English kings, in the 7th century, and excavated from a Suffolk field in 1938–39. *Room 41.*

Lindow Man. "Pete Marsh"—so named by the archaeologists who unearthed the body from a Cheshire peat marsh—was ritually slain, probably as a human sacrifice, in the 1st century and lay perfectly pickled in his bog until 1984. *Room 50.*

Colossal chariot horse from the *quadriga* of the Mausoleum at Halikarnassos

LOWER GALLERY

The three rooms that comprise the **Sainsbury African Galleries** are of the main interest here: together they present a staggering 200,000 objects, featuring intricate pieces of old ivory, gold, and wooden masks and carvings—highlighting such ancient kingdoms as the Benin and Asante. The displays include a collection of **55 throwing knives**; ceremonial garments including a dazzling pink and green **woman's coif** (*qufiya*) from Tunisia made of silk, metal, and cotton; and the *Oxford Man*, *a* 1992 woodcarving by Owen Ndou, depicting a man of ambiguous race clutching his Book of Knowledge.

THE NATION'S ATTIC: A HISTORY OF THE MUSEUM

The collection began when Sir Hans Sloane, physician to Queen Anne and George II, bequeathed his personal collection of curiosities and antiquities to the nation. The collection quickly grew, thanks to enthusiastic kleptomaniacs after the Napoleonic Wars—most notoriously the seventh Earl of Elgin, who obtained the marbles from the Parthenon and Erechtheion on the Acropolis in Athens during his term as British ambassador in Constantinople.

Soon thereafter, it seemed everyone had something to donate—George II gave the Royal Library, Sir William Hamilton gave antique vases, Charles Townley gave sculptures, the Bank of England gave coins. When the first exhibition galleries opened to visitors in 1759, the trustees agreed to admit only small groups guided by curators. The British Museum quickly became one of the most fashionable places to be seen in the capital, and tickets, which had to be booked in advance, were treated like gold dust.

The museum's holdings quickly outgrew their original space in Montague House. After the addition of such major pieces as the Rosetta Stone and other Egyptian antiquities (spoils of the Napoleonic War) and the Parthenon sculptures, Robert Smirke was commissioned to build an appropriately large and monumental building on the same site. It's still a hot ticket: the British Museum now receives more than 5 million visitors every year.

THE GREAT COURT & THE READING ROOM

The museum's classical Greek-style facade features figures representing the progress of civilization, and the focal point is the awesome Great Court, a massive glass-roofed space. Here is the museum's best-kept secret—an inner courtyard (now the largest covered square in Europe) that, for more than 150 years, had been used for storage.

The 19th-century Reading Room, an impressive 106-foot-high blue-and-gold-domed library, forms the centerpiece of the Great Court. The best way to marvel at it is to slip in, gaze at the 104,000 ancient tomes lining the shelves, and for a few moments join the weighty company of those who have used it as a literary and academic sanctuary over the past 150 years or so: H.G. Wells, Thomas Hardy, Lord Tennyson, Oscar Wilde, George Orwell, T.S. Eliot, and Beatrix Potter, to name a few.

(above) Reading Room

PLANNING YOUR VISIT

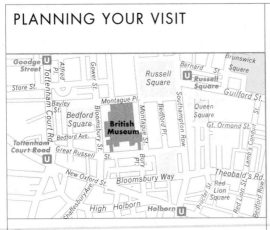

Tours

The **50-minute Eyeopener tour (free)** by museum guides does just what it says; ask for details at the information desk. The **90-minute Highlights tour (£8)** runs three times a day. After either of these tours, you can then dip back into the collections that most captured your imagination at your leisure.

An **audio version of the Highlights tour (£3.50)** is a less-animated but perhaps more relaxed way to navigate the galleries. Other audio tours focus on the Enlightenment and the Parthenon sculptures; another is designed for families.

Alternatively, the **Visitor's Guide (£5)** gives a brief but informative overview of the museum's history and is divided into self-guided themed tours.

Before you go, consider printing a **COMPASS tour (free)** from the museum's online navigation tool (www.thebritishmuseum.ac.uk/compass), which allows users to browse past and present exhibits as well as search for specific objects. A children's version can also be found here. Computer stations in the Reading Room offer onsite access to COMPASS.

> ■ TIP➜ The closest underground station to the British Museum is Russell Square on the Piccadilly line. However, since you will be entering via the back entrance on Montague Place, you will not experience the full impact of the museum's grand facade. To do so, alight at Holborn on the Central and Piccadilly lines or Tottenham Court Road on the Central and Northern lines. The walk from these stations is about 10 minutes.

WITH KIDS

■ Pick up the "Visiting with Children" leaflet, which has a guide to the top eight objects that attract the most attention from younger visitors.

■ The Reading Room has trails and activity backpacks for kids ages 2 to 6. There are also activity sheets for teens available.

■ Art materials are available for free from information points, where you can also find out about workshops, performances, storytelling sessions, and other free events.

■ Around the museum, there are Hands On desks open daily 11–4, which let visitors handle objects from the various collections.

WHERE TO REFUEL

The British Museum's self-service **Gallery Café** gets very crowded but serves a reasonably tasty menu beneath a plaster cast of a part of the Parthenon frieze that Lord Elgin didn't remove. It's open daily.

The **café in the Great Court** keeps longer hours and is a great place to people-watch and admire the spectacular glass roof while you eat your salad and sandwich.

If the weather is nice, exit the museum via the back entrance on Montague Place and amble over to **Russell Square,** which has grassy lawns, water fountains, and a glass-fronted café for post-sandwich coffee and ice cream.

hands-on demonstrations of how a book comes together. Feast your eyes also on the six-story glass tower that holds the 65,000-volume collection of George III, plus a permanent exhibition of rare stamps. If all this wordiness is just too much, you can relax in the library's piazza or restaurant, or take in one of the occasional free concerts in the amphitheater. ⊠ *96 Euston Rd., Bloomsbury, NW1* ☎ *020/7412-7332* ⊕ *www. bl.uk* ⊠ *Free, charge for special exhibitions* ⊙ *Mon. and Wed.–Fri. 9:30–6, Tues. 9:30–8, Sat. 9:30–5, Sun. 11–5 and bank holiday Mon.* Ⓤ *Euston, King's Cross.*

⊙ **Dickens House Museum.** This is the only one of the many London houses Charles Dickens (1812–70) inhabited that's still standing,

> ### KING'S CROSS STATION
>
> Known for its 120-foot-tall clock tower, this yellow brick, Italianate building with large, arched windows was constructed in 1851–52 as the London terminus for the Great Northern Railway. Harry Potter and fellow aspiring wizards took the Hogwarts Express to school from the imaginary platform 9¾ (platforms 4 and 5 were the actual shooting site) in the movies based on J.K. Rowling's popular novels. The station has put up a sign for platform 9¾ if you want to take a picture there—but please don't try to run through the wall. Euston Rd. and York Way, Euston, NW1 ☎0845/748–4950

and it would have had a real claim to his fame in any case because he wrote *Oliver Twist* and *Nicholas Nickleby* and finished *Pickwick Papers* here between 1837 and 1839. The house looks exactly as it would have in Dickens's day, complete with first editions, letters, and a tall clerk's desk (where the master wrote standing up, often while chatting with visiting friends and relatives). Down in the basement is a replica of the Dingley Dell kitchen from *Pickwick Papers*. A program of changing special exhibitions gives insight into the Dickens family and the author's works, with sessions where, for instance, you can try your own hand with a quill pen. Christmas is a memorable time to visit, as the rooms are decorated in traditional style: better than any televised costume drama, this is the real thing. ⊠ *48 Doughty St., Bloomsbury, WC1* ☎ *020/7405–2127* ⊕ *www.dickensmuseum.com* ⊠ *£5* ⊙ *Mon.–Sat. 10–5, Sun. 11–5; last admission 4:30* Ⓤ *Chancery La., Russell Sq.*

Gray's Inn. Although the least architecturally interesting of the four Inns of Court and the one most damaged by German bombs in the 1940s, this still has its romantic associations. In 1594 Shakespeare's *Comedy of Errors* was performed for the first time in its hall—which was restored after World War II and has a fine Elizabethan screen of carved oak. You must make advance arrangements to view the hall, but the secluded and spacious gardens, first planted by Francis Bacon in 1606, are open to the public. ⊠ *Gray's Inn Rd., Holborn, Bloomsbury, WC1* ☎ *020/7458–7800* ⊙ *Weekdays noon–2:30* Ⓤ *Holborn, Temple.*

★ **Lincoln's Inn.** There's plenty to see at one of the oldest, best-preserved, and most comely of the Inns of Court—from the Chancery Lane Tudor brick gatehouse to the wide-open, tree-lined, atmospheric Lincoln's Inn Fields and the 15th-century chapel remodeled by Inigo Jones in 1620.

5

✉ *Chancery La., Bloomsbury, WC2* ☎ *020/7405–1393* ⊘ *Gardens week-days 7–7, chapel weekdays noon–2:30; public may also attend Sun. service in chapel at 11:30 during legal terms* Ⓤ *Chancery La.*

Percival David Foundation of Chinese Art. This collection, belonging to the University of London, is dominated by ceramics from the Sung to Qing dynasties (10th to 19th centuries). ✉ *53 Gordon Sq., Bloomsbury, WC1* ☎ *020/7387–3909* ⊕ *www.pdfmuseum.org.uk* 🎟 *Free* ⊘ *Weekdays 10–12:30 and 1:30–5* Ⓤ *Russell Sq.*

Royal Courts of Justice. Here is the vast Victorian Gothic pile containing the nation's principal law courts, with 1,000-odd rooms running off 3½ mi of corridor. And here are heard the most important civil law cases—that's everything from divorce to fraud, with libel in between—and you can sit in the viewing gallery to watch any trial you like, for a live version of *Court TV*. The more dramatic criminal cases are heard at the Old Bailey. Other sights are the 238-foot-long main hall and the compact exhibition of judges' robes. Check out the gift shop also, where useful items (such as umbrellas) are emblazoned with the royal courts' crest. ✉ *The Strand, Bloomsbury, WC2* ☎ *020/7947–6000* ⊕ *www.hmcourts-service.gov.uk* 🎟 *Free* ⊘ *Weekdays 9:30–4:30; during Aug. there are no sittings and public areas close at 2:30* Ⓤ *Temple.*

★ **Sir John Soane's Museum.** Sir John (1753–1837), architect of the Bank of England, bequeathed his house to the nation on condition that nothing be changed. He obviously had enormous fun with his home: in the Picture Room, for instance, two of Hogarth's *Rake's Progress* series are among the paintings on panels that swing away to reveal secret gallery pockets with more paintings. Everywhere mirrors and colors play tricks with light and space, and split-level floors worthy of a fairground fun house disorient you. In a basement chamber sits the vast 1300 BC sarcophagus of Seti I, lighted by a domed skylight two stories above. (When Sir John acquired this priceless object for £2,000, he celebrated with a three-day party.) The elegant, tranquil courtyard gardens with statuary and plants are open to the public, and there's a below street-level passage, which joins two of the courtyards to the museum. ✉ *13 Lincoln's Inn Fields, Bloomsbury, WC2* ☎ *020/7405–2107* ⊕ *www.soane.org* 🎟 *Free, Sat. tour £3* ⊘ *Tues.–Sat. 10–5; also 6–9 on 1st Tues. every month; tours each Sat. at 2:30* PM Ⓤ *Holborn.*

Temple Church. Featuring "the Round"—a rare circular nave—this church was built by the Knights Templar in the 12th century. The Red Knights (so called after the red crosses they wore—you can see them in effigy around the nave) held their secret initiation rites in the crypt here. Having started poor, holy, and dedicated to the protection of pilgrims, they grew rich from showers of royal gifts, until in the 14th century they were charged with heresy, blasphemy, and sodomy, thrown into the Tower, and stripped of their wealth. You might suppose the church to be thickly atmospheric, but Victorian and postwar restorers have tamed its air of antique mystery. Still, it's a very fine Gothic-Romanesque church, whose 1240 chancel ("the Oblong") has been accused of perfection. ✉ *The Temple, Bloomsbury, EC4* ☎ *020/7353–3470* ⊕ *www.*

Bloomsbury & Legal London Dining

BUDGET DINING

Acorn House, Eclectic, 69 Swinton St.

Busabe Eathai, Thai, 22 Store St.

Lemonia, Greek, 89 Regent's Park Rd.

North Sea Fish Restaurant, Seafood, 7–8 Leigh St.

Villandry, French, 170 Great Portland St.

Yoisho, Japanese, 33 Goodge St.

MODERATE DINING

Elena's L'Étoile, Bistro, 30 Charlotte St.

Fino, Spanish, 33 Charlotte St.

Galvin Bistrot de Luxe, Bistro, 66 Baker St.

The Providores & Tapa Room, Asian, 109 Marylebone High St.

EXPENSIVE DINING

Crazy Bear, Thai, 26–28 Whitfield St.

Hakkasan, Chinese, 8 Hanway Pl.

Pied à Terre, French, 34 Charlotte St.

5

templechurch.com☉ *Wed.–Sat. 11–4, Sun. 1–4, and closures for special services* Ⓤ*Temple.*

University College. The college was founded in 1826 and set in a satisfyingly classical edifice designed by the architect of the National Gallery, William Wilkins. In 1907 it became part of the University of London, providing higher education without religious exclusion. The college has within its portals the **Slade School of Fine Art,** which did for many of Britain's artists what the nearby Royal Academy of Dramatic Art (on Gower Street) did for its actors. On view inside is a fine collection of sculpture by an alumnus, John Flaxman.

You can also see more Egyptian artifacts, if you didn't get enough at the neighboring British Museum, in the **Petrie Museum** (☎*020/7679– 2884* ⊕*www.petrie.ucl.ac.uk*), accessed from Malet Place, on the first floor of the DMS Watson building. It houses an outstanding, huge collection of fascinating objects of Egyptian archaeology—jewelry, toys, papyri, and some of the world's oldest garments. It has proved so popular with schoolchildren that it's now open Saturday 10–1 in addition to Tuesday–Friday 1–5. The South Cloisters contain one of London's weirder treasures: the clothed skeleton of one of the university's founders, Jeremy Bentham, who bequeathed himself to the college. ⊠*Gower St., Bloomsbury, WC1* Ⓤ*Euston Sq., Goodge St.*

The City

The Lloyd's of London Building

WORD OF MOUTH

"We arrived at the Tower of London just before 9:30 AM and went directly to the Crown Jewels, which were spectacular and completely uncrowded. I tried, unsuccessfully, to convince my dear husband that just ONE of those mere baubles would keep me happy forever … oh well, a girl can dream."

—fun4all4

GETTING ORIENTED

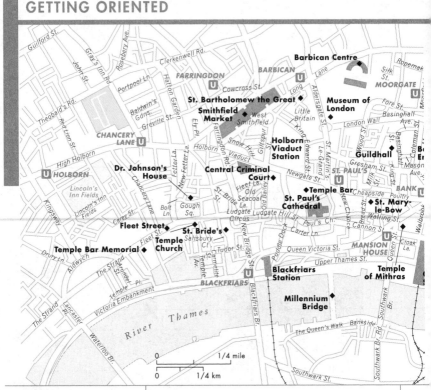

GETTING THERE	TOP 5 REASONS TO GO
The City is well served by a concentrated selection of underground stops in London. St. Paul's and Bank, on the Central Line, and Mansion House, Cannon Street, and Monument, on the District and Circle lines, deliver visitors to the heart of the City. Liverpool Street and Aldgate border the City's eastern edge, while Chancery Lane and Farringdon lie to the west. Barbican and Moorgate provide easy access to the theaters and galleries of the Barbican, while Blackfriars, to the south, leads to Ludgate Circus and Fleet Street.	■ **Monument:** Climb the 311 spiral steps to the top for dizzying views of the London skyline. ■ **St. Paul's Cathedral:** Talk into a wall of the Whispering Gallery and be heard on the opposite side. ■ **Tower of London:** Gaze in awe at the stunning Crown Jewels. ■ **Museum of London:** Relive the sights and sounds of Roman Londinium. ■ **Shops and the City:** Explore City outfitters and the upscale boutiques of Bow Lane and the Royal Exchange.

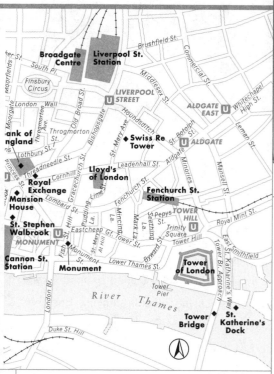

MAKING THE MOST OF YOUR TIME

The "Square Mile" is as compact as the nickname suggests, with very little distance between points of interest, making it easy to dip into the City for an afternoon stroll. For full immersion in the Tower of London, however, set aside half a day, especially if seeing the Crown Jewels is a priority. Allow an hour minimum each for the Museum of London, St. Paul's Cathedral, and the Tower Bridge. On weekends, without the scurrying suits, the City is nearly deserted, making it hard to find lunch—and yet this is when the major attractions are at their busiest. Come on a weekday if you can.

A GOOD WALK

Crossing the Millennium Bridge from the Tate Modern to St. Paul's is one of the finest walks in London for views of the river and the cathedral that towers over it. Dubbed the "blade of light," this shiny aluminum-and-steel construction was the result of a collaboration between architect Norman Foster and sculptor Anthony Caro.

FEELING PECKISH?

The friendly **Riverside Café Bar** (⊠ *St. Katherine's Way, E1* ☎ *020/7481–1464*) is one of the few places you're sure to find a good cup of hot chocolate and hot and cold meals, with waterside views of the luxurious yachts and gin palaces moored at the docks.

Sweetings (⊠ *39 Queen Victoria St., EC4* ☎ *020/7248–3062*) is not cheap, and closed in the evenings, but it serves one of the best fish lunches in London. Refuel here on Dover sole and Black Velvet, the local brew, and observe the pinstripes at play in their natural habitat.

When you're done exploring Fleet Street, repair to the famed **Ye Olde Cheshire Cheese** (⊠ *145 Fleet St., EC4* ☎ *020/7353–6170*) for a pint of old-fashioned ale and a snack. Parts of the building date from 1667, and it's one of London's best-loved pubs, rightly admired for its roaring log fires and dingy interior, where you can imagine Johnson and Boswell getting together for a literary confab.

Sightseeing
★★★★★
Nightlife
☆☆☆☆★
Dining
☆☆★★★
Lodging
☆☆☆☆★
Shopping
☆☆★★★

The City, as opposed to the city, is the capital's fast-beating financial heart. Behind a host of imposing neoclassical facades lie the banks and exchanges whose frantic trade determines the fortunes that underpin London. But the "Square Mile" is much more than London's Wall Street—the capital's economic engine room also has currency as a religious and political center. St. Paul's Cathedral has looked after Londoners' souls since the seventh century, and the Tower of London—that moat-surrounded royal fortress, prison, and jewel house—has taken care of beheading them. The City's maze of backstreets is also home to London's historic churches, marketplaces, and cozy pubs.

WHAT'S HERE

There are many starting points to explore the City, but **Temple Bar Memorial,** at the top of the Strand, is the site of the only surviving entry point—the gate itself was removed in 1878 to widen the road. From here, **Fleet Street,** the site of England's first printing press, was the undisputed seat of British journalism until the 1980s. The nearby church of **St. Bride's,** recognizable by its tiered wedding-cake steeple, is another Wren mini-masterpiece and still the church for journalists.

Nestled behind Fleet Street is **Dr. Johnson's House,** former home of the man who claimed that to be bored of London was to be bored of life. Eastward, **Ludgate Hill** provides the best approach to what's arguably London's most distinctive building, **St. Paul's Cathedral,** designed by Sir Christopher Wren and the fourth church to occupy the site. Opposite the Cathedral is **Temple Bar,** the original entrance to the City, painstakingly moved here brick-by-brick. To the south are clear views of the newly constructed **Millennium Bridge,** the pedestrian-only steel suspension bridge that links the City to the South Bank of the Thames. The **Central Criminal Court** (nicknamed **Old Bailey**), the highest court in the land, lies to the north, on the way to the famous 800-year-old **Smithfield Market,** whose Victorian halls are the site of a daily early-morning meat market.

Standing opposite is the ancient church of **St. Bartholomew the Great** and **St. Bartholomew Hospital,** both begun in 1123 by Henry I's favorite courtier Rahere, who caught malaria and, surviving, vowed to dedicate his life to serving the saint that had visited him in his fevered dreams.

FLEET STREET

The newspapers have abandoned Fleet Street (also known as "The Street of Shame") for more modern offices on the fringes of the City, but for a taste of print pomp, savor the art deco chrome-and-black majesty of the old Daily Express building, home to the best selling British newspaper of all time in the postwar era, regularly shifting 4 million copies a day.

The street named Little Britain leads to Aldersgate and the **Museum of London,** where archaeological displays include a portion of the original **Roman Wall** that ringed the City. This is a gateway to the modern **Barbican Centre,** a complex of arts venues and apartments that is all navigable above street level. To the southeast lies the **Guildhall,** headquarters of the Corporation of London that administers the City and the site of the only Roman amphitheater in London.

Nearby, the church of **St. Mary-le-Bow** and the narrow maze of streets just to its south, around **Bow Lane,** are great shopping haunts.

Cheapside leads to the epicenter of the City, the meeting point of a powerful architectural triumvirate: the **Bank of England,** the **Royal Exchange,** and **Mansion House,** where the Lord Mayor of the City of London (not to be confused with the Mayor of London, who works from City Hall on the South Bank) lives and entertains in traditionally lavish style. The Mansion House is next to another diverting and historic church, **St. Stephen Walbrook,** and the remains of the **Temple of Mithras,** at one time devoted to Bacchus, Roman god of wine and intoxication. Down King William Street lies **Monument,** built to commemorate the Great Fire of London of 1666. Northeast of its 202-foot-high tower are excellent views of two unmissable members of the City skyline: the **Lloyd's of London Building,** opened in 1986 and designed by Richard Rogers, and the **Swiss Re Tower,** popularly known as "the Gherkin," completed in 2004 by Foster and Partners. From here, following the river east past Trinity Gardens, is one of London's most absorbing and bloody attractions, the **Tower of London. Tower Bridge** is a suitably giddying finale; wind down among the wharves of **St. Katherine's Dock.**

A BRIEF HISTORY

Rising from the mud of the Thames as the Roman settlement of Londinium, in AD 47, this area marks the beginnings of the capital. It gained immediate momentum as a trading center for materials and goods shipped in from all corners of the fledgling colony. Centuries later, William the Conqueror began building the palace that was to become the Tower of London. It went from being Henry III's defensive shelter in the 13th century to, by Tudor times, the world's most forbidding and grisly prison, where two of Henry VIII's six wives were executed. During the Middle Ages, powerful guilds that nurtured commerce took root, followed by the foundation of great trading companies, such as the Honourable East India Company, which

started up in 1600.

The City's history has been punctuated by periods of chaos that have threatened to destroy it. The Great Fire of 1666 was the most serious, sparing but few of the cramped, labyrinthine streets, where the Great Plague of the previous year had already wiped out a huge portion of the population. Yet the gutted wastelands enabled a new start, driving out the plague-carrying rodents that had menaced London since the Middle Ages and forcing an architectural renaissance, led by Sir Christopher Wren. Further punishment came during the Blitz of World War II, when German bombers destroyed many buildings. Today's eclectic skyline reflects every period of its history, some sublime, some hideous.

PLACES TO EXPLORE

☾ **Bank of England.** Known for the past couple of centuries as "the Old Lady of Threadneedle Street," after someone's parliamentary quip, the Bank of England, which has been central to the British economy since 1694, manages the national debt and the foreign exchange reserves, issues banknotes, sets interest rates, looks after England's gold, and regulates the country's banking system. Sir John Soane designed the neoclassic hulk in 1788, wrapping it in windowless walls, which are all that survives of his building. It's ironic that an executive of so sober an institution should have been Kenneth Grahame, author of *The Wind in the Willows*. This and other facets of the bank's history are traced in the Bank of England Museum (entrance is around the corner on Bartholomew Lane). The characterful furniture and paraphernalia in wood and brass contrast starkly with the interactive computer games where you can try your hand as a money-market dealer. There are gold bars on which to gaze, too, and fun facts on fraudsters of yesteryear. ☒ *Threadneedle St., The City, EC4* ☎ *020/7601–5545* ⊕ *www. bankofengland.co.uk* ⬚ *Free* ☾ *Weekdays and Lord Mayor's Show day, 2nd Sat. in Nov., 10–5* Ⓤ *Bank, Monument.*

★ **Barbican Centre.** With two theaters; the London Symphony Orchestra and its auditorium; the Guildhall School of Music and Drama; a major art gallery for touring and its own special exhibitions; two cinemas; a convention center; an upscale restaurant, cafés, terraces with fountains, and literary bookshops; and living space in some of the most desirable tower blocks in town, the Barbican is an enormous 1980s concrete maze

A Da Vinci Code Tour

Although the real meaning behind Leonardo Da Vinci's art is ultimately unknowable, the real-life places in which Dan Brown set his best-selling suspense novel, *The Da Vinci Code*, are known throughout the world, and the book has inspired travelers to visit them. All the London sights in the book are in a compact area east and south of Trafalgar Square and are accessible by bus or the Tube. In the order the sights appear in *The Da Vinci Code*—with one exception, King's College—you can easily walk this 2-mi route.

Langdon, Neveu, and Teabing's whirlwind of events begins in Paris, but midway through—realizing that the clue to the cryptex might not be in France but in England—the three board Teabing's private plane for London. Once on the ground, the threesome, hastily interpreting their latest cryptex clue, make a mad dash down Fleet Street to a Knights of the Templar fortress. To launch your own tour, take the Tube to St. Paul's station and head west on Ludgate Hill to **Fleet Street,** continuing until you get to Temple, where you'll see the Temple Bar Memorial, a young bronze griffin.Opposite the statue is an elaborate stone arch through which you pass into Middle Temple Lane, which runs south all the way to the Thames. **Temple Church** (⊠ *Inner Temple La. off Fleet St., Bloomsbury* Ⓤ *Temple*) will be on your left as you head toward the river. After you've explored the church, reverse course to the statue and continue west.

Along the Strand you'll pass by **King's College London** (⊠ *The Strand, St. James's* Ⓤ *Temple*) where, in the book, a portion of the second cryptex's message, "In London lies a knight a Pope interred," finds new meaning for Langdon with the aid of a helpful King's College librarian's computer.

After exploring the campus, continue west on the Strand to Trafalgar Square. Just south of the square on Whitehall is the Horse Guards Parade, which edges **St. James's Park** (⊠ *Middle Temple La., St. James's* Ⓤ *St. James's Park, Westminster*). A character besotted with the Holy Grail has followed the trio to London, planning to usurp control of the secrets Langdon and Neveu continue to discover. Before he makes his move, though, he slips into St. James's Park to deal with an accomplice who has misbehaved.

Continue south to **Westminster Abbey** (⊠ *South side of Parliament Sq., Westminster* Ⓤ *Westminster*), the final scene of the trio's escapades in London. As Langdon and Neveu scour the tomb of Sir Isaac Newton for a final clue that will crack open the second cryptex, they receive a message from a rival character to meet in Westminster's Chapter House. In the ensuing struggle, they vanquish their nemesis. Sir Isaac Newton's grave and tomb are near the choir screen, at the north entrance to the choir.

An alternative to walking is to take Bus 11, which travels along Ludgate and Fleet Street to Trafalgar Square and Westminster. Note that Opus Dei's London office, which is mentioned in the book but is not open to the public, is more than 3 mi west of Westminster Abbey, just north (on Orme Court off Bayswater Road) of the northwest corner of Kensington Gardens. For full tours in the book's other key locales—Paris, Rome, and Scotland—pick up a copy of *Fodor's Guide to the Da Vinci Code*.

6

that Londoners either love or hate. Navigation around the complex is via the yellow lines running, Oz-like, along the floors, with signs on the walls, although it's still easy to get lost. Actors rate the theater acoustics especially high, and the steep rake of the seating makes for a good stage view. The dance, music, and theater programs have been transformed into a yearlong fest named BITE, which stands for Barbican International Theatre Events, and encompasses dance, puppetry, and music. The emphasis is on presenting tomorrow's names today, although there are performances by established companies and artists, such as Merce Cunningham. ⌧ *Silk St., The City, EC2* ☎ *020/7638–8891 box office* ⊕ *www.barbican.org.uk* ⌧ *Barbican Centre free, art gallery £6– £8, films £5–£7, concerts £5–£27, theater £3–£27* ⊗ *Barbican Centre Mon.–Sat. 9 AM–11 PM, Sun. noon–11 PM; gallery Wed. and Fri.–Mon. 11–8, Tues. and Thurs. 11–6; conservatory weekends noon–5:30 when not in use for private function; call first* Ⓤ *Moorgate, Barbican.*

★ **Dr. Johnson's House.** This is where Samuel Johnson lived between 1746 and 1759, compiling his famous dictionary in the attic as his health deteriorated. Built in 1700, it's the only one of Johnson's residences remaining today, its elegant Georgian lines make it exactly the kind of place you would expect the Great Bear, as Johnson was nicknamed, to live. It's a shrine to a most literary man who was passionate about London, and it includes a first edition of his *Dictionary of the English Language* among the mementos of Johnson and his friend and diarist James Boswell. ⌧ *17 Gough Sq., The City, EC4* ☎ *020/7353–3745* ⊕ *www.drjohnsonshouse. org* ⌧ *£4.50* ⊗ *May–Sept., Mon.–Sat. 11–5:30; Oct.–Apr., Mon.–Sat. 11–5; closed bank holidays* Ⓤ *Blackfriars, Chancery La.*

Guildhall. The Corporation of London, which oversees the City, has ceremonially elected and installed its Lord Mayor here for the last 800 years. The Guildhall was built in 1411, and though it failed to avoid either the 1666 or 1940 flames, its core survived. The Great Hall is a psychedelic patchwork of coats of arms and banners of the City Livery Companies, which inherited the mantle of the medieval trade guilds. Tradesmen couldn't even run a shop without kowtowing to these prototypical unions, and their grand banqueting halls, the plushest private dining venues in the City, are testimony to the wealth they amassed. Inside the hall, Gog and Magog, the pair of mythical giants who founded ancient Albion and the city of New Troy, upon which London was said to be built, glower down from their west-gallery grandstand in 9-foot-high painted lime-wood. The hall was also the site of famous trials, including that of Lady Jane Grey in 1553, before her execution at the Tower of London.

To the right of Guildhall Yard is the **Guildhall Art Gallery,** which includes portraits of the great and the good, cityscapes, famous battles, and a slightly cloying pre-Raphaelite section. The construction of the gallery led to the exciting discovery of London's only **Roman amphitheater,** which had lain underneath Guildhall Yard undisturbed for more than 1,800 years. It was excavated and now visitors can walk among the remains, although most of the relics can be seen at the Museum of London, through which guided tours can be booked.

The 1970s west wing houses the **Guildhall Library**; it has mainly City-related books and documents, plus a collection belonging to one of the city livery companies, the Worshipful Company of Clockmakers, in the **Clockmakers' Company Museum,** with more than 600 timepieces on show, including a skull-faced watch that belonged to Mary, Queen of Scots. It's one of the most important horological collections in the country. ⊠ *Gresham St., The City, EC2* ☎ *020/7606–3030, 020/7332–3700 gallery* ⊕ *www.cityoflondon.gov.uk* ✉ *Free; gallery and amphitheater £2.50* ⊙ *Mon.–Sat. 9:30–5; clockmaker museum weekdays 9:30–4:45; gallery Mon.–Sat. 10–5, Sun. noon–4, last admission 4:30 or 3:30* Ⓤ *St. Paul's, Moorgate, Bank, Mansion House.*

☉ ★ **Monument.** Commemorating the "dreadful visitation" of the Great Fire of 1666, this is the world's tallest isolated stone column. It is the work of Wren, who was asked to erect it "on or as neere unto the place where the said Fire soe unhappily began as conveniently may be." And so here it is—at 202 feet, exactly as tall as the distance it stands from Farriner's baking house in Pudding Lane, where the fire started. ⊠ *Monument St., The City, EC3* ☎ *020/7626–2717* ⊕ *www.cityoflondon.gov. uk* ✉ *£2; £6.50 joint ticket with Tower Bridge* ⊙ *Daily 9:30–5:30; hrs subject to change, call before visiting* Ⓤ *Monument.*

> **A VIEW TO REMEMBER**
>
> At the top of the Monument's 311-step spiral staircase (a better workout than any StairMaster) is a gallery providing fantastic views from the heart of the City that is helpfully caged to prevent suicidal jumps, which were a trend for a while in the 19th century.

☉ ★ **Museum of London.** If there's one place to get the history of London sorted out, right from 450,000 BC to the present day, it's here—although there's a great deal to sort out: Oliver Cromwell's death mask, Queen Victoria's crinolined gowns, Selfridges' art deco elevators, and the Lord Mayor's coach are just some of the goodies. The museum appropriately shelters a section of the 2nd- to 4th-century London wall, which you can view from a window inside. The displays—like one of the Great Fire, a 1940s air-raid shelter, a Georgian prison cell, a Roman living room, and a Victorian street complete with fully stocked shops—are complemented by rich soundscapes that atmospherically re-create London life through the ages. The archaeologists and curators at the museum regularly leap from AD to BC, as fresh building work in the city uncovers more treasures. None, though, have been as exciting as the ongoing project of preserving and displaying the Roman amphitheater at the Guildhall, and you can see the rewards of that excavation with the artifacts here. ⊠ *London Wall, The City, EC2* ☎ *020/7600–0807* ⊕ *www.museumoflondon.org.uk* ✉ *Free* ⊙ *Mon.–Sat. 10–5:50, Sun. noon–5:50; last admission 5:30* Ⓤ *Barbican.*

Old Bailey. This, the present-day **Central Criminal Court,** is where Newgate Prison stood from the 12th century right until the beginning of the 20th century. Called by the novelist Henry Fielding the "prototype of hell," few survived for long in the version pulled down in 1770. Those

6

who didn't starve were hanged, or pressed to death in the Press Yard, or they succumbed to the virulent gaol (the archaic British spelling of "jail") fever. The next model lasted only a couple of years before being torn down by raving mobs during the anti-Catholic Gordon Riots of 1780, to be replaced by the Newgate that Dickens described in several

> ### RISE AND SHINE
>
> If, for whatever reason, you're thirsting for a drink at 6 AM, head to the pubs around here, which are specially licensed to serve early-morning pints to market traders at the end of a hard day's night.

novels, including *Oliver Twist*. The Central Criminal Court replaced Newgate in 1907 and the most famous feature of the solid Edwardian building is the 12-foot gilded statue of Justice perched on top; she was intended to mirror the dome of St. Paul's. More intriguing are the ghoulish proceedings that unfold inside, which are open to the public—Crippen and Christie, two of England's most notorious wife-murderers, were both tried here. The day's hearings are posted on the sign outside, but there are security restrictions, and children under 14 are not allowed in; call the information line first. ⊠ *Newgate St., The City, EC4* ☎ *020/7248–3277 information* ⊕ *www.cityoflondon.gov.uk* ☉ *Public Gallery weekdays 10:30–1 and 2–5 (approx); line forms at Newgate St. entrance; closed bank holidays and day after* Ⓤ *St. Paul's.*

St. Bartholomew the Great. Reached via a perfect half-timber gatehouse atop a 13th-century stone archway, this is one of London's oldest churches. With the Dissolution of the Monasteries, Henry VIII had most of it torn down; the Romanesque choir loft is all that survives from the 12th century.

> ### HERE'S WHERE
>
> The ancient church St. Bartholomew the Great makes a guest appearance in the film *Four Weddings and a Funeral.*

On the other side of the road, the church's namesake St. Bartholomew's Hospital is home to a small museum. Facing both is Smithfield's meat market. ⊠ *Cloth Fair, West Smithfield, The City, EC1* ☎ *020/7606–5171* ⊕ *www.greatstbarts.com* ✉ *Church free; museum £4* ☉ *Church Tues.–Fri. 8:30–5 (Mar.–Oct. 8:30–4), Sat. 10–1:30, Sun. 8:30–1 and 2:30–8; museum Tues.–Fri. 10–4* Ⓤ *Barbican, Farringdon.*

St. Bride's. Appropriately named for anyone contemplating impending nuptials, the distinctively tiered steeple of this Christopher Wren–designed church gave rise to the shape of the traditional wedding cake. One early couple inspired to marry here were the parents of Virginia Dare, the first European child born in colonial America in 1587. As St. Paul's (in Covent Garden) is the actors' church, so St. Bride's belongs to journalists, many of whom have been buried or memorialized here. The poet John Milton lived in the churchyard for a while, and by 1664 the crypts were so crowded that diarist Samuel Pepys, who was baptized here, had to bribe the grave digger to "justle together" some bodies to make room for his deceased brother. Now the crypts house

Continued on p. 116

ST. PAUL'S CATHEDRAL

Sir Christopher Wren's maxim "I build for eternity" proves no empty boast.

Sublime, awesome, majestic, and inspirational are just some of the words to describe Wren's masterpiece, St. Paul's Cathedral—even more so now that it has been spruced up for its 300th anniversary in 2008.

This is the spiritual heart of the nation, where people and events are celebrated, mourned, and honored. As you approach the cathedral your eyes are inevitably drawn skyward to the great dome, one of the largest in the world and an amazing piece of engineering. Visit in the late afternoon for evensong, and let the choir's voices transport you to a world of absolute peace in a place of perfect beauty, as pristine as the day it was completed.

TOURING ST. PAUL'S

Enter the cathedral via the main west entrance, and walk straight down the length of the nave to the central Dome Altar. Nobody can resist making a beeline for the dome, so start your tour beneath it, standing dead center on the beautiful sunburst floor, Wren's focal mirror of the magnificent design above. The dome crowns the center of the cathedral and rises to 364 feet. You will need to crick your neck upward for a remarkable spectacle—but save your strength for the "great climb" to get some fantastic views.

THE CATHEDRAL FLOOR

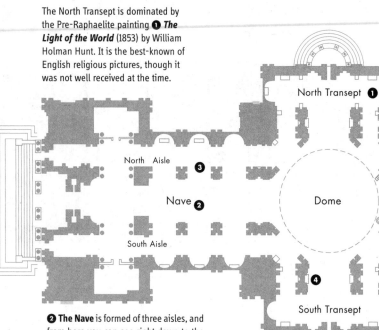

The North Transept is dominated by the Pre-Raphaelite painting ❶ *The Light of the World* (1853) by William Holman Hunt. It is the best-known of English religious pictures, though it was not well received at the time.

North Transept ❶

North   Aisle   ❸

Nave ❷

Dome

South Aisle

❹

South Transept

❷ **The Nave** is formed of three aisles, and from here you can see right down to the High Altar at the far end of the Choir, more than 100 yards away. Take time to admire the mastery of space and light.

In the north aisle of the Nave is Flaxman's grandiose ❸ **monument to the Duke of Wellington,** who sits astride his faithful charger, Copenhagen, the horse who carried him through the Battle of Waterloo.

The South Transept displays a ❹ **monument to Admiral Lord Nelson,** Britain's favorite naval hero, leaning on an anchor. Other memorials commemorate the explorer Captain Robert Scott and the British landscape painter J.M.W. Turner.

CELEBRITY STATUS

St. Paul's has witnessed many momentous processions along its checkered nave. The somber state funerals of heroes Admiral Lord Nelson and the Duke of Wellington, and of Sir Winston Churchill, drew huge crowds. It was here, also, that the fairy-tale wedding of Prince Charles and Lady Diana Spencer took place, and the jubilees of Queen Victoria, George V, and the present Queen were celebrated.

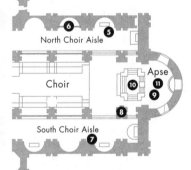

North Choir Aisle

Choir

Apse

South Choir Aisle

The North Choir Aisle features the beautiful ❺ **gilded gates** by Jean Tijou, perhaps the most accomplished artist in wrought iron of all time, as well as Henry Moore's sculpture ❻ *Mother and Child,* its simple lines complementing the ornate surroundings.

The South Choir Aisle contains a ❼ **marble effigy of John Donne,** who was Dean of old St. Paul's for his final 10 years (he died in 1631). This is the only statue to have survived the Great Fire of London intact.

The Choir contains the ❽ **Bishop's Throne** or cathedra, hence the name cathedral. Look aloft to the fabulous mosaics. Don't miss the exquisite, delicate carvings by Grinling Gibbons, in particular on the case of the ❾ **great organ,** one of the Cathedral's greatest artifacts. It was designed by Wren and played by such illustrious figures as Handel and Mendelssohn.

❿ **The High Altar,** with its glorious canopy, is a profusion of marble and carved and gilded oak.

The Apse is home to the ⓫ **American Memorial Chapel,** which honors the more than 28,000 U.S. soldiers who died while stationed in the U.K. during World War II. The lime-wood paneling incorporates a rocket as a tribute to the United States' achievements in space.

MUSICAL FRICTION

The organ, with its cherubs and angels, was not installed without controversy. The mighty instrument proved a tight fit, and the maker, known as Father Schmidt, and Wren nearly came to blows. Wren was reputed to have said he would not adapt his cathedral for a mere "box of whistles."

6

ST. PAUL'S CATHEDRAL

THE DOME

The dome is the crowning glory of the cathedral, a must for visitors.

At 99 feet, the ❶ **Whispering Gallery** is reached by 259 spiral steps. This is the part of the cathedral with which you bribe children—they will be fascinated by the acoustic phenomenon: whisper something to the wall on one side, and a second later it transmits clearly to the other side, 107 feet away. The only problem is identifying your whisper from the cacophony of everyone else's. Look down onto the nave from here and up to the monochrome frescoes of St. Paul by Sir James Thornhill.

More stamina is required to reach the ❷ **Stone Gallery**, at 175 feet and 378 steps from ground level. It is on the exterior of the cathedral and offers a vista of the city and the River Thames.

For the best views of all—at 280 feet and 530 steps from ground level—make the trek to the small ❸ **Golden Gallery**, the highest point of the outer dome. A hole in the floor gives a vertiginous view down. You can see the lantern above through a circular opening called the oculus. If you have a head for heights you can walk outside for a spectacular panorama of London.

The top of the dome is crowned with a ❹ **ball and cross**. At 23 feet high and weighing approximately 7 tons, it is the pinnacle of St. Paul's.

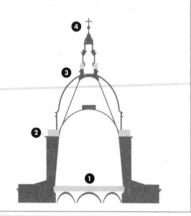

A BRIEF HISTORY

The cathedral is the masterpiece of Sir Christopher Wren (1632–1723), completed in 1710 after 35 years of building and much argument with the Royal Commission. Wren had originally been commissioned to restore Old St. Paul's, the Norman cathedral that had replaced, in its turn, three earlier versions, but the Great Fire left so little of it standing that a new cathedral was deemed necessary.

Wren's first plan, known as the New Model, did not make it past the drawing board; the second, known as the Great Model, got as far as the 20-foot oak rendering you can see here today before it, too, was rejected, whereupon Wren is said to have burst into tears. The third, however, known as the Warrant Design (because it received the royal warrant), was accepted, with the fortunate coda that the architect be allowed to make changes as he saw fit. Without that, there would be no dome, because the approved design had featured a steeple. Parliament felt that building was proceeding too slowly (in fact, 35 years is lightning speed, as cathedrals go) and withheld half of Wren's pay for the last 13 years of work. He was pushing 80 when Queen Anne finally coughed up the arrears.

■ TIP→ To see Wren's Great Model, you must join a Triforium Tour (Mon. and Tues. at 11:30 and 2, Fri. at 2). These one-hour tours include a visit to the library and a glimpse of the famous geometrical staircase. The visit ends in the Trophy Room, where Wren's Great Model is on display. The tour costs £14 per person and includes entry to the cathedral and access to the crypt and galleries. It's best to book in advance by calling 020/7246-8357 or sending an e-mail to visits@stpaulscathedral.org.uk.

THE CRYPT

A visit to the vast crypt is a time for reflection and contemplation, with some 200 memorials to see. If it all becomes too somber, take solace in the café or shop near the crypt entrance.

The ❶ **tomb of the Duke of Wellington** comprises a simple casket made from Cornish granite. He is remembered as a hero of battle, but his name lives on in the form of boots, cigars, beef Wellington, and the capital of New Zealand.

Here lies ❷ **Admiral Nelson,** killed at the Battle of Trafalgar in 1805. His body was preserved in alcohol for the journey home, and his pickled remains were buried here beneath Cardinal Wolsey's unused 16th-century sarcophagus.

Surrounded by his family and close to a plethora of iconic artists, musicians, and scientists, the ❸ **tomb of Sir Christopher Wren** is a modest affair. A simple slab marks the resting place with an inscription that concludes "Lector, si monumentum requiris, circumspice" (Reader, if you seek his monument, look around).

The beautiful ❹ **O.B.E. Chapel** (dedicated 1960) is a symbol of the Order of the British Empire, an order of chivalry established in 1917 by George V. The theme of sovereign and Commonwealth is represented in the glass panels.

The vast ❺ **treasury** houses the cathedral's plate, although a good deal has been lost or stolen over the centuries—in particular in a daring robbery of 1810—and much of the display comes from other London churches.

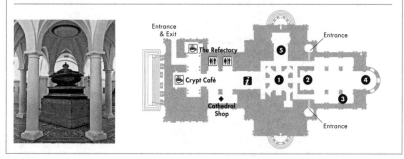

PLANNING YOUR DAY

WHAT'S NEARBY: After an early start and a morning spent at the cathedral, stroll over the Millennium Bridge (don't forget to look back for a great view of St. Paul's) and have lunch at Tate Modern. The restaurant at the top of the gallery has spectacular views of London.

CONTACT INFO: ⊠ *St. Paul's Churchyard, Ludgate Hill EC4* Ⓜ *St. Paul's* ☎ *020/7236-4128* ⊕ *www. stpauls.co.uk*

ADMISSION: Adults: cathedral, crypt, ambulatory, and gallery £9.50. **Family ticket** (2 adults, 2 children): £22.50. **Children 7–16:** £3.50.

Tours: A guided tour of the cathedral and crypt lasts 1½–2 hours and costs £3. Tours start at 11, 11:30, 1:30, and 2. Rental audio tours cost £3.50 and last 45 min.

HOURS: The cathedral is a house of worship. Services may cause changes to the visiting hours on any given day, so be sure to call ahead.

Cathedral: Mon.–Sat. 8:30–4:30 (last admission at 4).
Shop: Mon.–Sat. 9–5, Sun. 10:30–5.
Crypt café: Mon.–Sat. 9–5, Sun. 10–5.

a museum of the church's rich history, and a bit of Roman sidewalk. ✉ *Fleet St., The City, EC4* ☎ *020/7427–0133* ⊕ *www.stbrides.com* ✉ *Free* ☾ *Weekdays 8–6, Sat. 11–3, Sun. for services only 10–1, 5–7:30; crypt closed Sun.* Ⓤ *Chancery La.*

St. Mary-le-Bow. This church is another classic City survivor; various versions have stood on the site since the 11th century. In 1284 a local goldsmith took refuge here after committing a murder, only to be killed inside the church by enraged relatives of his victim. The church was abandoned for a time afterward, but started up again, and was rebuilt in its current form after the Great Fire. Wren's 1673 incarnation has a tall steeple for a City church (only St. Bride's is taller) and one of the most famous sets of bells around—a Londoner must be born within the sound of the "Bow Bells" to be a true cockney. The origin of that idea was probably the curfew rung on the bells during the 14th century, even though "cockney" only came to mean Londoner three centuries later, and then it was an insult. The Bow takes its name from the bow-shaped arches in the Norman crypt. The garden contains a statue of local boy Captain John Smith, who founded Virginia in 1606 and was later captured by Native Americans. ✉ *Cheapside, The City, EC2* ☎ *020/7248–5139* ⊕ *www.stmarylebow.co.uk* ☾ *Mon.–Thurs. 6:30 AM–5:45 PM, Fri. 6:30 AM–4 PM* Ⓤ *Mansion House.*

> **DID YOU KNOW?**
>
> The traditional definition of "Cockneys"—East End London residents with their own accent and dialect—is that they were born within hearing distance of the bells of St Mary-le-Bow church. The Cockney dialect includes rhyming slang ("apples," as in "apples and pears," to mean "stairs") and adapting Yiddish words such as schtum and kosher. In recent years, the term "mockney" has become a lighthearted term of abuse for posh types who try to sound Cockney.

NEED A BREAK?

The Place Below (☎ 020/7329–0789), in St. Mary-le-Bow's crypt, is packed with City workers weekdays at lunchtime—the self-service vegetarian menu includes soup and quiche, which are particularly good. Lunches are served from 10:30 until 2:30, weekdays only. It's also open for breakfast from 7:30 AM.

St. Stephen Walbrook. This is the parish church many think is Wren's best, by virtue of its practice dome, which predates the one at St. Paul's by some 30 years. Yet there's far more to the history of the Church than as a dry run for its next-door big brother. There has been a church here since the 7th century, built on the site of an older Roman shrine. Inside the church, called "the most perfectly proportioned interior in the world" by one admirer, two sights warrant investigation: Henry Moore's 1987 central marble altar, which sits beneath the dome ("like a lump of Camembert," say critics), and, well, a telephone—an eloquent tribute to that savior of souls, Rector Chad Varah, who founded the Samaritans, givers of phone aid to the suicidal, here in 1953. ✉ *Walbrook St., The City, EC4* ☎ *020/7626–8242* ⊕ *www.ststephenwalbrook.net* ☾ *Weekdays 10–4* Ⓤ *Bank, Cannon St.*

Continued on p. 124

6

THE TOWER OF LONDON

The Tower is a microcosm of the city itself—a sprawling, organic hodgepodge of buildings that inspires reverence and terror in equal measure. See the block on which Anne Boleyn was beheaded, marvel at the Crown Jewels, and pay homage to the ravens who keep the monarchy safe.

An architectural patchwork of time, the oldest building of the complex is the fairytale White Tower, conceived by William the Conqueror in 1078 as both a royal residence and a show of power to the troublesome Anglo-Saxons he had subdued at the Battle of Hastings. Today's Tower has seen everything, as a palace, barracks, a mint for producing coins, an archive, an armoury, and the Royal menagerie (home of the country's first elephant). Equally enticing is the stunning opulence of the Crown Jewels, kept on-site in the heavily fortified Jewel House. Most of all, though, the Tower is known for death: it's been a place of imprisonment, torture, and execution for the realm's most rabid traitors. These days, unless you count the killer admission fees, there are far less morbid activities taking place in the Tower, but it still breathes London's history and pageantry from its every brick and offers hours of exploration.

TOURING THE TOWER

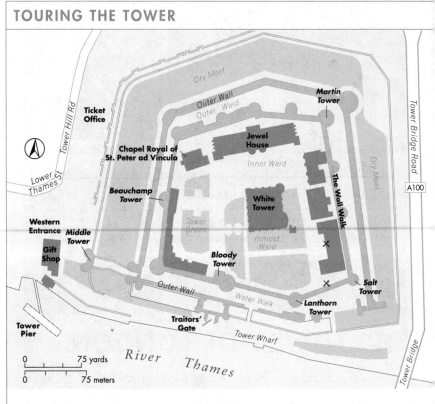

Ticket Office

Tower Hill Rd

Lower Thames St

Dry Moat

Outer Wall
Outer Ward

Martin Tower

Tower Bridge Road

A100

Jewel House

Chapel Royal of St. Peter ad Vincula

Inner Ward

Dry Moat

The Wall Walk

Beauchamp Tower

White Tower

Western Entrance
Middle Tower

Tower Green

Inmost Ward

Gift Shop

Bloody Tower

Salt Tower

Outer Wall

Water Walk

Lanthorn Tower

Tower Pier

Traitors' Gate

Tower Wharf

Tower Bridge

0 — 75 yards
0 — 75 meters

River Thames

Entry to the Tower is via the **Western Entrance** and the **Middle Tower,** which feed into the outermost ring of the Tower's defenses.

Water Lane leads past the dread-inducing **Traitors' Gate,**

GOLD DIGGER?

Keep your eyes peeled as you tour the Tower: according to one story, Sir John Barkstead, goldsmith and Lieutenant of the Tower under Cromwell, hid £20,000 in gold coins here before his arrest and execution at the Restoration of Charles II.

the final point of entry for many Tower prisoners.

Toward the end of Water Lane, the **Lanthorn Tower** houses by night the ravens who keep the kingdom safe, and by day a timely high-tech reconstruction of the Catholic Guy Fawkes's plot to blow up the Houses of Parliament in 1605.

The **Bloody Tower** earned its name as the apocryphal site of the murder of two young princes, Edward and Richard, who disappeared from the Tower after being put there in 1483 by their uncle, Richard III. Two little skeletons (now in

Westminster Abbey) were found buried close to the White Tower in 1674 and are thought to be theirs.

The **Beauchamp Tower** housed upper-class miscreants: Latin graffiti about Lady Jane Grey can be glimpsed today on its walls.

Like a prize gem set at the head of a royal crown, the **White Tower** is the centerpiece of the complex. Its four towers dominate the Inner Ward, a fitting and forbidding reminder of Norman strength at the time of the conquest of England.

Jewel House, Waterloo Barracks

ROYAL BLING

The Crown of Queen Elizabeth, the Queen Mother, from 1937, contains the exotic 105-carat Koh-i-Noor (mountain of light) diamond.

Once inside the White Tower, head upstairs for the **Armouries,** where the biggest attraction, quite literally, is the well-endowed suit of armor worn by Henry VIII. There is a matching outfit for his horse.

Other fascinating exhibits include the set of Samurai armor presented to James I in 1613 by the emperor of Japan, and the tiny set of armor worn by Henry VIII's young son Edward.

The **Jewel House** in **Waterloo Barracks** is the Tower's biggest draw, perfect for playing pick-your-favorite-crown from the wrong side of bulletproof glass. Not only are these crowns, staffs, and orbs encrusted with heavy-duty gems, they are invested with the authority of centuries of monarchical power in England, since the 1300s.

Outside, pause at **Tower Green,** permanent departure point for the few prisoners whose executions were consid-ered too sensitive for the vagaries of nearby Tower Hill. The Tower's most famous female victims—Anne Boleyn, Margaret Countess of Salisbury, Catherine Howard, and Lady Jane Grey—all went this decorous way.

Behind a well-kept square of grass stands the **Chapel Royal of St. Peter ad Vincula,** a delightful Tudor church and final resting place of six beheaded Tudor bodies. ■ TIP→ **Visitors are welcome for services and can also enter after 4:30 PM daily.**

The **Salt Tower,** reputedly the most haunted corner of the complex, marks the start of the **Wall Walk,** a bracing promenade along the stone spiral steps and battlements of the Tower that looks down on the trucks, taxis, and shimmering high-rises of modern London.

The Wall Walk ends at the **Martin Tower,** an old home of the Crown Jewels and now host to an exhibit that explains the art of fashioning royal headwear and includes 12,314 cut and uncut diamonds and the frames of five royal crowns.

On leaving the Tower, browse the **gift shop,** and wander the wharf that overlooks the Thames, leading to a picture-postcard view of Tower Bridge.

TIME KILLERS

Some prisoners managed to keep themselves plenty amused: Sir Walter Raleigh grew tobacco on Tower Green, and in 1561 suspected sorcerer Hugh Draper carved an intricate astronomical clock on the walls of his Salt Tower cell.

WHO ARE THE BEEFEATERS?

First of all, they're not technically known as Beefeaters, but as Yeoman Warders, first appointed as special bodyguards to King Henry VII following the Battle of Bosworth Field in 1485. No one quite knows where the term "Beefeater" originated: it may be from the French *buffetiers* (palace guards) or from "befeathered," in relation to their hats, although the most likely origin is that these guards could eat from the King's table.

Originally, the Yeoman Warders also served as jailers of the Tower, doubling as torturers when necessary. (So it would have been a Beefeater tightening the thumb screws, or ratchetting the rack another notch on some unfortunate prisoner. Smile nicely.) Today 36 Yeoman Warders, along with the Chief Yeoman Warder and the Yeoman Gaoler, live within the walls of the Tower with their families, in accommodations in the Outer Ward. They stand guard over the Tower, conduct tours, and lock up at 9:53 PM every night with the Ceremony of the Keys.

■ TIP→ Tickets to the Ceremony of the Keys are available by writing several months in advance; check the Tower Web site for details.

HARK THE RAVENS!

Legend has it that should the hulking black ravens ever leave, the White Tower will crumble and the kingdom fall. Charles II, no doubt jumpy after his father's execution and the monarchy's short-term fall from grace, made a royal decree in 1662 that there should be at least six of the carrion-eating nasties present at all times. There have been some close calls. During World War II, numbers dropped to one, echoing the precarious fate of the war-wracked country. In 2005, two (of eight) died over Christmas when Thor—the most intelligent but also the largest bully of the bunch—killed new recruit Gundolf, named after the Tower's 1070 designer. Pneumonia put an end to Bran, leaving lifelong partner Branwen without her mate.

■ DID YOU KNOW? In 1981 a raven named Grog, perhaps seduced by his alcoholic moniker, escaped to an East End pub after 21 years at the Tower. Others have been banished for "conduct unbecoming."

The six that remain, each one identified by a colored band around a claw, are much loved by the Yeoman Warder Raven Master for their fidelity (they mate for life) and their cheek (capable of 440 noises, they are witty and scolding mimics). It's not only the diet of

blood-soaked biscuits, rabbit, and scraps from the mess kitchen that keeps them coming back. Their lifting feathers on one wing are trimmed, meaning they can manage the equivalent of a lop-sided air-bound hobble but not much more. For the first half of 2006 the ravens were moved indoors full-time as a preventive measure against avian flu but have since been allowed out and about again. In situ they are a territorial lot, sticking to Tower Green and the White Tower, and lodging nightly by Wakefield Tower. They've had free front-row seats at all the most grisly moments in Tower history—Anne Boleyn's execution included.

■ TIP→ Don't get too close to the ravens: they are prone to pecking and not particularly fond of humans, unless you are the Tower's Raven Master.

And *WHAT* are they wearing?

A pike (or halberd), also known as a partisan, is the Yeoman Warder's weapon of choice. The Chief Warder carries a staff topped with a miniature silver model of the White Tower.

Anyone who refers to this as a costume will be lucky to leave the Tower with head still attached to body: this is the ceremonial uniform of the Yeoman Warders, and it comes at a cool £13,000 a throw.

The black Tudor bonnet is made of velvet; the blue undress consists of a felt top hat, with a single Tudor rose in the middle.

This Tudor-style ruff helps date the ceremonial uniform, which was first worn in 1552.

Insignia on a Yeoman Warder's upper right arm denote the rank he carried in the military.

The medals on a Yeoman Warder's chest are more than mere show: all of the men come from distinguished careers as senior non-commissioned officers (think screaming company sergeant major) in the army, navy, and air force.

This version of the royal livery bears the insignia of the current Queen ("E" for Elizabeth) but originally dates from Tudor times. The first letter changes according to the reigning monarch's Christian name; the second letter is always an "R" for *rex* (king) or *regina* (queen).

Slits in the tunic date from the times when Beefeaters were expected to ride a horse.

Red socks and black patent shoes are worn on special occasions. Visitors are more likely to see the regular blue undress, introduced in 1858 as the regular working dress of the Yeoman Warders.

The red lines down the trousers are a sign of the blood from the swords of the Yeoman Warders in their defense of the realm.

(IN)FAMOUS PRISONERS OF THE TOWER

Anne Boleyn   Lady Jane Grey   Sir Walter Raleigh

Sir Thomas More. A Catholic, Sir Thomas steadfastly refused to attend the coronation of Anne Boleyn (Henry VIII's second wife) or to recognize the multi-marrying king as head of the Church of England. Sent to the Tower for treason, in 1535 More lost his head.

Anne Boleyn. The first of Henry VIII's wives to be beheaded, Anne, who failed to provide the king with a son, was accused of sleeping with five men, including her own brother. All six got the chop in 1536. Her severed head was held up to the crowd, and her eyes were said to be moving and her lips mouthing prayer.

Margaret, Countess of Salisbury. Not the best-known prisoner in her lifetime, she has a reputation today for haunting the Tower. And no wonder: the elderly 70-year-old was condemned by Henry VIII in 1541 for a potentially treacherous bloodline (she was the last Plantagenet princess) and hacked to death by the executioner after she refused to put her head on the block like a common traitor and attempted to run away.

Queen Catherine Howard. Henry VIII's fifth wife was locked up for high treason and infidelity and beheaded in 1542 at age 20. Ever eager to please, she spent her final night practicing how to lay her head on the block.

Lady Jane Grey. The nine-days-queen lost her head in 1554 at age 16. Her death was the result of sibling rivalry gone seriously wrong, when Protestant Edward VI slighted his Catholic sister Mary in favor of Lady Jane as heir, and Mary decided to have none of it.

Guy Fawkes. The man who tried to bring down the Houses of Parliament and kill the king in the deadly Catholic Gunpowder Plot of 1605 was first incarcerated in the chambers of the Tower, where King James I requested he be tortured in ever-worsening ways. Perhaps unsurprisingly, he confessed. He met his seriously grisly end in the Old Palace Yard at Westminster, where he was hung, drawn, and quartered in 1607.

Sir Walter Raleigh. Once a favorite of Elizabeth I, he offended her by secretly marrying her Maid of Honor and was chucked in the Tower. As a conspirator against James I, he paid with his life. A frequent visitor to the Tower (he spent 13 years there in three stints), he managed to get the Bloody Tower enlarged on account of his wife and growing family. He was finally executed in 1618 in Old Palace Yard, Westminster.

Josef Jakobs. The last man to be executed in the Tower was caught as a spy when parachuting in from Germany and executed by firing squad in 1941. The chair he sat in when he was shot is preserved in the Royal Armouries' artifacts store.

FOR FURTHER EVIDENCE...

A trio of buildings in the Inner Ward, the **Bloody Tower, Beauchamp Tower,** and **Queen's House,** all with excellent views of the execution scaffold in Tower Green, are the heart of the Tower's prison accommodations and home to a permanent exhibition about notable inmates.

TACKLING THE TOWER (without losing your head)

☎ 0870/756-6060 ⊕ www.hrp.org.uk 💷 £16, children 16 and under £9.50, children under 5 free. Family tickets (2 adults, 3 children) £45 🕓 Mar.-Oct., Tues.-Sat. 9-6, Sun. and Mon. 10-6; last admission at 5. Nov.-Feb., Tues.-Sat. 9-5, Sun. and Mon. 10-5; last admission at 4 Ⓤ Tower Hill

■ TIP→ You can buy tickets from automatic kiosks on arrival, or up to seven days in advance at any Tube station. Avoid lines completely by booking by telephone (☎ 0870/756-7070, weekdays 9-9, weekends 10-5) or online.

WITH KIDS: The Tower's centuries-old cobble-stones are not exactly stroller-friendly, but strollers are permitted inside most of the buildings. If you do bring one, be prepared to leave it temporarily unsupervised (the stroller, that is—not your child) outside the White Tower, which has no access. There are baby-changing facilities in the Brick Tower restrooms behind the Jewel House.

■ TIP→ Tell your child to find one of the Yeoman Warders if he or she should get lost; they will in turn lead him or her to the By-ward Tower, which is where you should meet.

MAKING THE MOST OF YOUR TIME: Without doubt, the Tower is worth two to three hours. A full hour of that would be seriously well spent

by joining one of the Yeoman Warders' tours. It's hard to better their insight, vitality, and humor—they are knights of the realm living their very own fairytale castle existence.

The Crown Jewels are worth the wait, the White Tower is essential, and the Medieval Palace and Bloody Tower should at least be breezed through.

■ TIP→ It's best to visit on weekdays, when the crowds are smaller.

IN A HURRY? If you have less than an hour, head down Wall Walk, through a succession of towers, which eventually spit you out at the Martin Tower. The view over modern London is quite a contrast.

TOURS: Tours given by a Yeoman Warder leave from the main entrance near Middle Tower every half-hour from 10 AM to 4 PM, and last about an hour. Beefeaters give occasional 30-minute talks in the Lanthorn Tower about their daily lives. Both tours are free.

GOOD SOUVENIRS: You can live like a king yourself with a few choice purchases in the Tower gift shop: an elegant bottle of walnut or bramble liqueur goes for £8.50, and sparkling tiaras start at £37.99. Regal on a budget? Pick up a Mario Testino postcard of Princess Diana for £0.75.

The City Dining

BUDGET DINING

Canteen, British, 2 Crispin Pl.

Coach & Horses, British, 26–28 Ray St.

E Pellicci, Café, 332 Bethnal Green Rd.

Original Lahore Kebab House, Pakistani, 2 Umberston St.

The Real Greek, Greek, 15 Hoxton Market

Sông Qué Café, Vietnamese, 134 Kingsland Rd.

MODERATE DINING

Moro, Mediterranean, 34–36 Exmouth Market

St. John, British, 26 St. John St.

St. John Bread & Wine, British, 94–96 Commercial St.

Simpson's Tavern, British, 38½ Cornhill, at Ball Ct.

Sweetings, Seafood, 39 Queen Victoria St.

EXPENSIVE DINING

Club Gascon, French, 57 West Smithfield

Plateau, French, Canada Place, Canada Square

☾ **Tower Bridge.** Despite its venerable, nay, medieval, appearance, this is
FodorsChoice a Victorian youngster. Constructed of steel, then clothed in Portland
★ stone, it was deliberately styled in the Gothic persuasion to complement
the Tower next door, and it's famous for its enormous bascules—the
"arms," which open to allow large ships through. Although this still
happens occasionally, when river traffic was dense the bascules were
raised about five times a day.

The exhibition **Tower Bridge Experience** is a fun tour inside the building
to discover how one of the world's most famous bridges actually
works, and to see the fantastic views on the outside. First, take in the
romance of the panoramas from the east and west walkways between
those grand turrets. On the east, the modern super-structures and ships
of Docklands, and west, the best look at the steel and glass "futuristic
mushroom" that is Greater London Assembly's City Hall, the Tower of
London, St. Paul's, and the Monument. Then back down to the nitty-
gritty of the inner workings, which you learn about through hands-
on displays and films. ☎ *020/7403–3761* ⊕ *www.towerbridge.org.
uk* ✉ *£5.50; joint ticket available for Monument* ☾ *Daily 9:30–5:30;
last entry at 5* Ⓤ *Tower Hill.*

The East End

WORD OF MOUTH

"I've posted about Spitalfields before. I think it's a great way to spend a Sunday morning. Depending on your stamina there are four East End markets going on, in order from earliest to latest opening: Brick Lane, Columbia Road Flower Market, Petticoat Lane, and Spitalfields (my favorite of the four)."

-obxgirl

GETTING ORIENTED

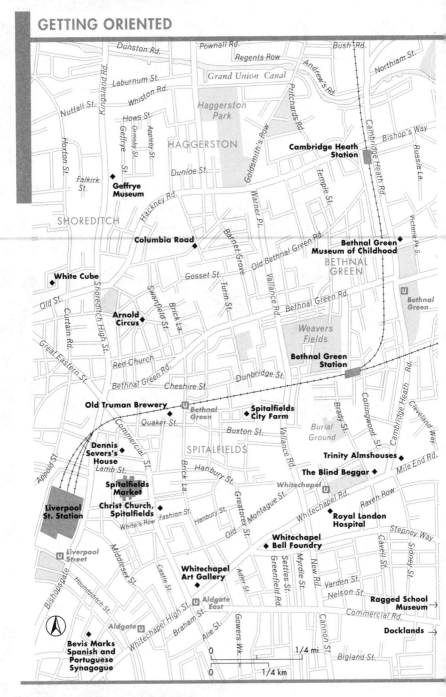

TOP 5 REASONS TO GO

■ **Geffrye Museum:** Stroll around the walled herb garden, then have afternoon tea at the glass-fronted museum café.

■ **Columbia Road flower market:** Take advantage of jet lag and arrive early on a Sunday morning.

■ **Brick Lane shopping:** Poke about the thrift stores and vintage clothes shops on (and around) Brick Lane.

■ **Spitalfields Market:** Hunt for original accessories while eating organic chocolate cake on weekends.

■ **East End nightlife:** Have a hedonistic night out bar- and club-crawling in Hoxton and Shoreditch.

FEELING PECKISH?

Inside Spitalfields Market is **Canteen** (☎ 0845/656–1122), an open-plan eatery with long communal tables that serves predominantly British dishes made with additive-free ingredients. Hot chocolate with rum or freshly squeezed juices provide perfect liquid accompaniment.

At **Coffee@Brick Lane** (✉ 154 Brick La. ☎ 020/7247–6735), organic, shade-grown coffee is served in shabby-chic surroundings with worn Chesterfield sofas for lounging. Sandwiches and soups are basic but tasty.

The **Market Coffee House** (✉ 50–52 Brushfield St. ☎ 020/7247–4110) offers sandwiches such as Scotch beef with horseradish and watercress on a roll or bagel, along with fresh soup, ploughman's lunches, and English muffins.

SAFETY

Around the central hubs of Hoxton, Shoreditch, Spitalfields, and Brick Lane, you're unlikely to experience any trouble during daylight hours; even after dark it's relatively safe. However, if you're venturing into Whitechapel or out toward Bethnal Green and Mile End, be vigilant. Muggings are common and visitors should be on their guard at all times.

GETTING THERE

The best Tube stops to start from are Whitechapel or Aldgate East on the District–Hammersmith and City lines, or Aldgate on the Metropolitan and Circle lines.

MAKING THE MOST OF YOUR TIME

The East End isn't picturesque, but it's vibrant, colorful, and exciting. It offers adventure, and if you want to spend a lot of time here you'll enjoy exploring its hidden corners. Spitalfields Market bustles all weekend, while Brick Lane is at its best on a Sunday morning—also the time to visit Columbia Road for its glorious flower market.

If you're planning to explore the East End art scene, pick up an East End Art Map at the Whitechapel Art Gallery to help you navigate around the many small galleries and art spaces here.

As far as the nightlife goes, there's no time limit here. Start as soon as you like after your shopping—Hoxton's bars are your best bet—and finish as far into the following morning as your stamina will allow.

A GOOD WALK

There are some thrilling walks that illustrate the progress of Jack and other murderers around the East End: recommended is the **Blood and Tears Walk: London's Horrible Past** (☎ 020/7625–5155), which departs daily from Barbican Tube station.

7

Sightseeing
☆☆★★★

Nightlife
★★★★★

Dining
☆★★★★

Lodging
☆☆☆☆☆

Shopping
☆★★★★

Made famous by Dickens and infamous by Jack the Ripper, the East End is one of London's most hauntingly evocative neighborhoods. It may have fewer conventional tourist attractions but is rich in folk history, architectural gems, and feisty burgeoning culture. Once home to French Huguenots, then Ashkenazi Jews, the area now has a large Bangladeshi community, whose influence is everywhere from innumerable curry houses to glittering sari shops to colorful street festivals. Since the early 1990s the area has attracted students and creative types, lured by the low rents and old industrial spaces; these days it is becoming increasingly affluent, as people rush to buy up and renovate the relatively affordable Georgian terrace houses. To experience the East End at its most lively, make sure you visit on the weekend—here it's possible to shop, eat, drink, and party your way through a whole 72 hours.

WHAT'S HERE

Near the Aldgate East Tube stop, behind Houndsditch, is the **Bevis Marks Spanish and Portuguese Synagogue,** London's oldest synagogue, named after the street on which it stands.

The George Yard Buildings once stood behind No. 90 Whitechapel High Street; nowadays you'll come across the famous **Whitechapel Art Gallery** instead. A few steps east is the **Whitechapel Bell Foundry**; and, nearby, Osborn Street, which soon becomes **Brick Lane,** the heart of the Bangladeshi East End and home to the **Old Truman Brewery.** ■ TIP→The

Sunday morning junk market on Brick Lane adds further complements to the rewarding vintage-clothes shopping in this area.

On the west end of Fournier Street, sits Nicholas Hawksmoor's soaring masterpiece, **Christ Church, Spitalfields,** along with some fine early Georgian houses. On Lamb Street are the two northern entrances to **Spitalfields Market.** ■ TIP→ Look out for work by young designers, whose one-off accessories make original gifts, and join the office workers for some pie and mash. If you have kids, they might have fun going to **Spitalfields City Farm,** a few blocks away on Weaver Street. On Folgate Street, just off Commercial Street, is **Dennis Severs's House.**

Arnold Circus is a perfect circle of Arts and Crafts–style houses around a central raised bandstand; this is the core of the Boundary Estate— "model" housing built by Victorian philanthropists for the slum-dwelling locals and completed as the 20th century began. Two streets north is **Columbia Road,** which on Sunday (8–2) gets buried under forests of shrubs and blooms of all shapes and sizes during London's main plant and **flower market.** Prices are ultralow, and lots of the Victorian shop windows around the stalls are filled with horticultural wares, accessories, and antiques. ■ TIP→ Arrive early to see the market in full sway and at its best. You can pick up coffee and a bagel for breakfast here from food stalls on the street.

On Kingsland Road, the **Geffrye Museum** occupies a row of early-18th-century almshouses. That bastion of contemporary art, the **White Cube** gallery, lies to the west in the very hip Hoxton Square. To the east, meanwhile, is the quirky **V&A Museum of Childhood.**

Farther east still, toward Mile End, are the former **Trinity Almshouses,** with the statue of William Booth on the very spot where the first Salvation Army meetings were held. On the northwest corner of Cambridge Heath Road, is the **Blind Beggar** pub, with the **Royal London Hospital** a few yards to the left and its **Archives** behind.

PLACES TO EXPLORE

Bevis Marks Spanish and Portuguese Synagogue. Named after the street on which it stands, this is London's oldest and most splendid synagogue. Embellished with rich woodwork for the benches and galleries, marble columns, and many plunging brass chandeliers, it's beautiful simplicity. The wooden ark resembles a Wren-style screen, and contains the sacred scrolls of the five books of Moses. When Cromwell allowed the Jews to return to England in 1655 (they had been expelled in 1290), there was no Jewish community, and certainly no place to worship openly. The site chosen to build a new synagogue in 1701 already had religious connections, as the house that stood here before, Burics Marks, was owned by the Abbot of Bury St. Edmunds; over the years the name reevolved. ✉ *Bevis Marks, East End, EC1* ☎ *020/7626–1274* ⊙ *Mon.–Wed., Fri., and Sat. 11:30–1, Sun. 10:30–12:30* Ⓤ *Aldgate East, Liverpool St.*

The Blind Beggar. This is the Victorian den of iniquity where Salvation Army founder William Booth preached his first sermon. Also, on the south side of the street stands a stone inscribed HERE WILLIAM BOOTH COM-

A BRIEF HISTORY

The argument goes that the East End is the "real" London—since East Enders are born "within the sound of Bow Bells," they are deemed to be Cockney through and through. The district began as separate villages—Whitechapel and Spitalfields, Shoreditch, Mile End, and Bethnal Green—melding together during the 19th century. Nowadays it's home to London's Bangladeshi community and more recent immigrants from other parts of the world, including China and Africa, making this the most culturally diverse area of London. Since the East End was heavily bombed in World War II, and subsequently rebuilt with public housing estates, it's not the best-looking part of the capital, although pockets of historic housing do remain. With a steady flow of affluent Londoners attracted by the East End's proximity to the City and single-family homes, the area today is a far cry from the gang culture of such notorious East Enders as the Kray twins of the '60s.

Two centuries earlier, neighboring Spitalfields provided sanctuary for the French Huguenots. They had fled here to escape persecution in Catholic France around 1685, and found work in the nascent silk industry, many of them becoming prosperous master weavers. Today Spitalfields and Shoreditch are London's most exciting bohemian neighborhoods, together with Hoxton, just north of here. There are stylish boutiques (especially on Cheshire Street) and cafés, artists' studios, and galleries, thanks to the plentiful old, derelict, industrial spaces that were bought up cheaply and have been imaginatively remodeled.

MENCED THE WORK OF THE SALVATION ARMY, JULY 1865, marking the position of the first Sally Army platform; back by the pub a statue of William Booth stands where the first meetings were held. Booth didn't supply the pub's main claim to fame, though. The Blind Beggar's real notoriety dates only from March 1966, when Ronnie Kray—one of the Kray twins, the former gangster kings of London's East End underworld—shot dead rival "godfather" George Cornell in the saloon bar. The original Albion Brewery, celebrated home to the first bottled brown ale, was next door. ⊠ *337 Whitechapel Rd., East End, E1* Ⓤ *Whitechapel.*

Christ Church, Spitalfields. This is the 1729 masterpiece of Wren's associate, Nicholas Hawksmoor. Hawksmoor built only six London churches; this one was commissioned as part of Parliament's 1711 "Fifty New Churches Act." The idea was to score points for the Church of England against such nonconformists as the Protestant Huguenots. (It must have worked; in the churchyard, you can still see some of their gravestones, with epitaphs in French.) As the local silk industry declined, the church fell into disrepair, and by 1958 the structure was crumbling, with the looming prospect of demolition. But after 25 years—longer than it took to build—and a huge local effort to gather funds, the structure has now been completely restored and is a joy to behold, from the colonnaded portico and tall spire to its bold, strident baroque-style interior. As a concert venue, particularly during the annual Spitalfields Festival, it truly comes into its own. ■ TIP→ **If you're lucky enough to be in town**

Jack the Ripper

Within the shadow of the City walls is London's oldest synagogue, the Bevis Marks, while Whitechapel is where the Salvation Army was founded and the original Liberty Bell was forged. However, what everyone remembers most about this area is the Victorian slum streets that were stalked by the most infamous serial killer of all, Jack the Ripper.

At No. 90 Whitechapel High Street once stood George Yard Buildings, where Jack the Ripper's first victim, Martha Turner, was discovered in August 1888. A second murder occurred some weeks later, and on Hanbury Street, behind a seedy lodging house

at No. 29, is where Jack the Ripper left his third mutilated victim, "Dark" Annie Chapman. A double murder followed, and then, after a month's lull, came the death on this street of Marie Kelly, the Ripper's last victim and his most revolting murder of all. He had been able to work indoors this time, and Kelly, a young widow, was found strewn all over the room, charred remains of her clothing in the fire grate. Jack the Ripper's identity never has been discovered, although theories abound, which, among others, include a cover-up of a prominent member of the British aristocracy, the artist Walter Sickert, and Francis Twomblety, an American quack doctor.

during the Spitalfields Festival held every summer and winter, then don't miss the chance to attend a classical concert in this atmospheric ecclesiastical venue. ⊠ *Commercial St., East End, E1* ☎ *020/7247–7202* ⊙ *Tues. 11–4, Sun. 1–4* Ⓤ *Aldgate East.*

★ **Dennis Severs's House.** Enter this extraordinary time machine of a house with your imagination primed to take part in the plot. The Georgian terraced house belonged to the eponymous performer-designer-scholar from Escondido, California, who dedicated his life not only to restoring his house but also to raising the ghosts of a fictitious Jervis family that might have inhabited it over the course of two centuries. Dennis Severs created a replica of Georgian life, without electricity but with a butler in full 18th-century livery to light the candles and lay the fires—for the Jervises. The rooms are shadowy set pieces of rose-laden Victorian wallpapers, Jacobean paneling, Georgian wing chairs, baroque carved ornaments, "Protestant" colors (upstairs), and "Catholic" shades (downstairs). ■TIP→ **The "Silent Night" candlelight tours, each Monday, are the most theatrical and memorable way to "feel" the house, a magical experience relished by both Londoners and out-of-towners.** ⊠ *18 Folgate St., East End, E1* ☎ *020/7247–4013* ⊕ *www. dennissevershouse.co.uk* ⊠ *£8 for Sun., £5 for Mon. open house; £12 for candlelight Mon. evenings* ⊙ *1st and 3rd Sun. of month 2–5, 1st and 3rd Mon. noon–2. Call for hrs for "Silent Night" Mon., reservations essential* Ⓤ *Liverpool St.*

★ **Geffrye Museum.** An antidote to the grand, high-society town-house interiors of the rich royal boroughs in the center of town, here's where you can discover what life was like for the general masses. It's a small museum where you can walk through a series of room sets that re-cre-

Street Smarts

Brick Lane and the narrow streets running off it offer a paradigm of the East End's development. Its population has moved in waves: communities seeking refuge, others moving out in an upwardly-mobile direction.

Brick Lane has seen the manufacture of bricks (during the 16th century), beer, and bagels, but nowadays it's becoming the hub of artistic bohemia, especially at the Old Truman Brewery with its calendar of diverse cultural activities. It's also the heart of Banglatown—Bangladeshis make up one-third of the population in this London borough, and you'll see the surrounding streets have their names written in Bengali—and where you find some of the best kebabs and curries in town, along with ethnic video shops, colorful saris, and stacks of sticky sweets. On Sunday morning the entire street is packed with stalls in a companion market to the nearby **Petticoat Lane**.

Flower and Dean streets, past the ugly 1970s housing project on **Thrawl Street** and once the most disreputable street in London, was where Abe Sapperstein, founder of the Harlem Globetrotters, was born in 1908.

Fournier Street contains fine examples of the neighborhood's characteristic Georgian terraced houses, many of them built by the richest of the early-18th-century Huguenot silk weavers (see the enlarged windows on the upper floors). Most of those along the north side of Fournier Street have now been restored by conservationists; others still contain textile sweatshops—only now the workers are Bengali.

Wilkes Street, with more 1720s Huguenot houses, is north of the Christ Church, Spitalfields, while neighboring **Princelet Street** was once important to the East End's Jewish community. Where No. 6 stands now, the first of several thriving Yiddish theaters opened in 1886, playing to packed houses until the following year, when a false fire alarm, rung during a January performance, ended with 17 people being crushed to death and so demoralized the theater's actor-founder, Jacob Adler, that he moved his troupe to New York. Adler played a major role in founding that city's great Yiddish theater tradition—which, in turn, had a significant effect on Hollywood.

Elder Street, just off Folgate, is another gem of original 18th-century houses. On the south and east side of Spitalfields Market are yet more timewarp streets that are worth a wander, such as **Gun Street,** where artist Mark Gertler (1891–1939) lived at No. 32.

ate everyday domestic interiors from the Elizabethan period through postwar 1950s utility. Originally, the museum was a row of almshouses for the poor, built in 1716 by Sir Robert Geffrye, former Lord Mayor of London, which provided shelter for 50 pensioners over the course of 200 years. The houses were rescued from closure by keen petitioners (the inhabitants were relocated to a healthier part of town) and were transformed into the Geffrye Museum in 1914. The former almshouses were restored to their original condition, with most of the internal woodwork intact, including the staircase, upper floors, closets, and paneling. There are also displays on the almshouses' history and on the kinds of people who lived there. To discover more, you can attend

The East End Art Scene

It was only inevitable that the once arty Islington area (the N1 postal district, which rubs streets with the less elegant end of the Regent's Canal toward the City, EC1) would become too expensive and gentrified for the artists themselves. Hoxton, on a corner of Islington just off the City Road, with its cheap industrial units and more artisan Georgian–Victorian terraced streets, was the logical next stop.

The seal of boho approval came when Damien Hirst's agent and the most important modern art dealer in town, Jay Jopling (married to artist-photographer Sam Taylor-Wood), set up the White Cube gallery at 48 Hoxton Square. Impoverished artists, however, are not newcomers to the area—in the 1960s, Bridget Riley set up an outfit here to find affordable studio space for British artists—but the latest wave this side of the millennium has changed the face of this formerly down-at-the-heels neighborhood. It's now undeniably hip to be in Hoxton.

From the Barbican in the City to Whitechapel in the East End, as many as 30 art galleries have opened, showing the latest works of the YBAs (Young British Artists). A spread of trendy real estate has taken a firm grip across the City Road into E1, principally Shoreditch, Spitalfields, and "Banglatown"—the nickname for the neighborhood around Brick Lane where Bengali shops and homes have created a slice of South Asia. Where less-than-glam buildings for the poor (such as the Jewish Soup Kitchen off Commercial Street, Spitalfields) once stood are now loft-style luxury apartments. Boutiques, bars, clubs, and restaurants have followed in their wake, and the Eastside—as it has been coined—is unapologetically brimming with energy.

a regular "bring a room to life" talk. The museum's extension wing opened in 1998 and houses the 20th-century galleries, a lovely café overlooking the garden, and a bookshop stuffed full of great gifts. ✉*Kingsland Rd., East End, E2* ☎*020/7739–9893* ⊕*www.geffrye-museum.org.uk* ☜*Free*☉*Tues.–Sat. 10–5, Sun. noon–5* Ⓤ*Old St., then Bus 243; Liverpool St., then Bus 149 or 242.*

Old Truman Brewery. This is the only one of the former East End breweries still standing. It's a handsome example of Georgian and 19th-century industrial architecture, and in 1873 was the largest brewery in the world. The buildings, which straddle Brick Lane, are a conglomeration of art, craft, and photo studios, and now established as capital cool. The Atlantis Gallery, host of the sell-out Body Worlds exhibition in 2002, is a major focus—visitors were crammed inside to watch a live autopsy as part of the exhibition. Less controversial events include fashion showcases for young, upcoming designers, and fringe events. The Vibe Bar is a hot spot to chill out behind a traditional Georgian facade—it also has a great outdoor space. ✉*91 Brick La., East End, E1* ⊕*www.trumanbrewery.com* Ⓤ*Aldgate East.*

Royal London Hospital. Founded in 1740, the Royal London was once as nasty as its then-neighborhood near the Tower of London. Waste was carried out in buckets and dumped in the street; bedbugs and alcoholic nurses were problems; but according to hospital records patients didn't die—they were "relieved." In 1757 the hospital moved to its present site, the building of which is the core of the one you see today. By then it had become one of the best hospitals in London, and it was enhanced further by the addition of a small medical school in 1785, and again, 70 years later, an entire state-of-the-art medical college. Thomas John Barnado, who went on to found the famous Dr. Barnado's Homes for Orphans, came to train here in 1866. Ten years later the hospital grew to become the largest in the United Kingdom, and now, though mostly rebuilt since World War II, it remains one of London's most capacious. To get an idea of the huge medical leaps forward, walk through the main entrance and garden to the crypt of St. Augustine with St. Philip's Church (alternatively, go direct two blocks south to the entrance on Newark Street), to the **Royal London Hospital Museum** (⊗ *Weekdays 10–4:30*), where displays of medical paraphernalia, objects, and documentation illustrate the 250-year history of this East London institution. The museum often closes on short notice, so call before you go. ⊠ *Whitechapel Rd., East End, E1* ☎*020/7377–7608* ⊕*www.bartsandthelondon.org.uk* ⊠*Free* ⊗ *Hospital and garden daily 9–6* Ⓤ*Whitechapel.*

↻ **Spitalfields City Farm.** This little farm, squashed into an urban landscape, raises a selection of farm animals, including some rare breeds, to help educate city kids in country matters. A tiny farm shop sells freshly laid eggs and organic seasonal produce. ⊠ *Weaver St., off Pedley St., East End, E1* ☎*020/7247–8762* ⊕*www.spitalfieldscityfarm. org* ⊠*Free* ⊗ *Tues.–Sun. 10–4* Ⓤ*Aldgate East, Liverpool St.*

Spitalfields Market. There's been a market here since the mid-17th century, but the current version is overflowing with crafts and design shops and stalls, restaurants and bars (with a pan-world palette, from tapas to Thai), and different-purpose markets every day of the week. The nearer the weekend, the busier it all gets, culminating in the arts-and-crafts and green market on Sunday—the best day to go. *For more on Spitalfields Market, see* ⇨ *Shopping, Chapter 19.* ⊠*65 Brushfield St., East End, E1* ☎*020/7247–8556* ⊕*www.spitalfields.co.uk* ⊠*Free* ⊗ *Daily 10–7; market stalls weekdays 10–3, Sun. 9:30–5* Ⓤ*Liverpool St.*

↻ **V&A Museum of Childhood.** This is the East End outpost of the Victoria & Albert Museum—in fact, this entire iron, glass, and brown-brick building was transported here from South Kensington in 1875. Since then, its contents have grown into the biggest toy collection in the world. The large Dolls' Houses collection is a bit like the Geffrye Museum zapped into miniature, with houses of every period. Each genre of plaything has its own enclosure, so if teddy bears are your weakness, you need waste no time with the train sets. The museum's title is justified in the fascinating—and possibly unique—galleries on the social history of childhood from baby dolls to Beanie Babies. There's also a soft-play area for little kids and a long list of "Drop-In" activities, including a dressing-up area with old-fashioned clothes, and floor-size board games such as Snakes and Ladders—guaranteed to send parents into a world of nostalgia, and children to a tranquil land before techno took its hold.

✉ *Cambridge Heath Rd., East End, E2* ☎ *020/8983–5200* ⊕ *www. museumofchildhood.org.uk* ⊑ *Free* ⊙ *Daily 10–5:45, last admission 5:30* Ⓤ*Bethnal Green.*

White Cube. The original White Cube had cramped quarters in genteel St. James's—this outpost was set up to take advantage of the massive open spaces of the East End's former industrial units. Damien Hirst, Tracey Emin, Gilbert and George, Sam Taylor-Wood, and other trailblazers have shown here, and gone on to become internationally renowned. The building looks, appropriately enough, like a white cube—it has a glassed-in upper level called "Inside the White Cube," where international guest curators are invited to show their projects. ✉ *48 Hoxton Sq., Hoxton, N1* ☎ *020/7930–5373* ⊕ *www.whitecube. com* ⊑ *Free* ⊙ *Tues.–Sat. 10–6* Ⓤ*Old St.*

Whitechapel Art Gallery. Housed in a spacious 1901 art nouveau building, this has an international reputation for its shows, which are often on the cutting edge of contemporary art. The American painter Jackson Pollock exhibited here in the 1950s, as did pop artist Robert Rauschenberg in the '60s, and David Hockney had his first solo show here in the '70s. Other exhibitions highlight the local community and culture, and there are programs of lectures, too. The Whitechapel Café serves remarkably inexpensive, home-cooked, whole-food hot meals, soups, and cakes. Pick up an East End Art Map for 50p to help you with the rest of your gallery hopping. ✉ *Whitechapel High St., East End, E1* ☎ *020/7522–7888* ⊕ *www.whitechapel.org* ⊑ *Free; charge for special exhibitions* ⊙ *Tues.–Fri. 11–5, Thurs. 11–9, weekends 11—6* Ⓤ *Aldgate East.*

7

The South Bank

A pod, mid-flight, on the British Airways London Eye

8

WORD OF MOUTH

"The view from the London Eye is fantastic—and worth every penny. You can see for miles, and get good views of St. Paul's, Trafalgar Square, Buckingham Palace, and of course Parliament and Westminster Abbey."

—jules4je7

GETTING ORIENTED

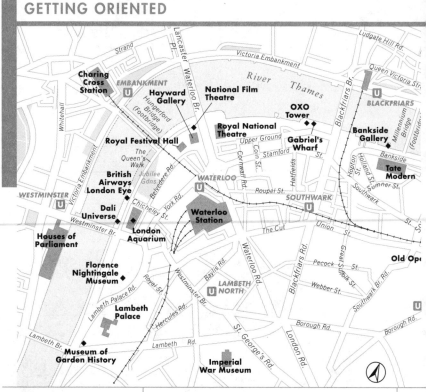

GETTING THERE	TOP 5 REASONS TO GO

GETTING THERE

For the South Bank use Westminster station on the Jubilee or Northern line, from where you can walk across Westminster Bridge; Embankment on District, Circle, Northern, and Bakerloo lines, where you can walk across Hungerford Bridge; or Waterloo on the Jubilee, Northern, and Bakerloo lines, where it's a five-minute walk to the Royal Festival Hall.

In the east, alternatively, use Tower Gateway on the Docklands Light Railway (DLR). London Bridge on the Northern and Jubilee lines is but a five-minute stroll from Borough Market and Southwark Cathedral.

TOP 5 REASONS TO GO

■ **Golden Jubilee Bridge:** Walk across the footbridge at dusk, then east along a fairy-light embankment towards the Oxo Tower.

■ **Shakespeare's Globe Theatre:** Catch a performance on a summer's eve.

■ **Royal Festival Hall:** Celebrate the new look of the "people's palace" with a concert or a drink in the foyer.

■ **Tate Modern:** Observe one of the changing installations—always impressive and humbling—in the turbine hall.

■ **Borough Market:** Spend a Saturday morning gauging your way through stalls of organic produce.

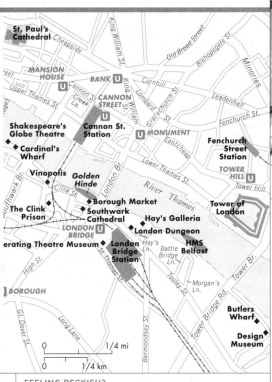

MAKING THE MOST OF YOUR TIME

Don't attempt the South Bank all in one go. Not only will you exhaust yourself, but you will miss out on the multifarious delights that it has to offer.

The Imperial War Museum demands a couple of hours, with the nearby Museum of Garden History providing an hour of further distraction.

To take in the South Bank galleries, such as Bankside and the Hayward, you'll need at least a day; the Tate Modern alone deserves a whole morning or afternoon, especially if you want to do justice to both the temporary exhibitions and the permanent collection.

The Globe Theatre requires about two hours for the exhibition theater tour and two to three hours for a performance. Finish with drinks or dinner at the Oxo Tower or a stroll west along the riverbank and then across Hungerford Bridge.

FEELING PECKISH?

At Gabriel's Wharf have a sit-down meal at the **Gourmet Pizza Co.** (☎ 020/7928–3188) or grab a sandwich or coffee at one of the smaller establishments open during the day here.

For exquisite hand-made pastries, along with daily specials such as chicken paella or vegetarian moussaka, stop at the bijou premises of **Konditor & Cook** (✉ 10 Stoney St. ☎ 020/7407–5100), the star of the handful of eateries to be found at Borough Market.

SAFETY

At night, it's best to stick to where the action is at the Butler's Wharf restaurants, the Oxo Tower, the National Theatre, the National Film Theatre, and the Royal Festival Hall. Stray farther south of the embankment and it quickly begins to feel deserted.

Sightseeing
★★★★★

Nightlife
☆☆★★★

Dining
☆☆★★★

Lodging
☆☆☆☆★

Shopping
☆☆☆★★

Culture, history, sights: the South Bank has it all. Stretching from the Imperial War Museum in the southwest as far as the Design Museum in the east, high-caliber art, music, film, and theater venues concertina up alongside the likes of an aquarium, a wine museum, historic warships, and a foodie-favorite market. Three structures dominate the skyline: the looming stack of Tate Modern, housed in an old power station; the distinctive Oxo Tower; and the one ring to rule them all, the British Airways London Eye. Meanwhile, pedestrians cross between the north and south banks using the futuristic Hungerford footbridges and the curvaceous Millennium Bridge, purposely dragging their feet as they take in the busy life of the Thames.

WHAT'S HERE

Lambeth Palace, by Lambeth Bridge, was for about 800 years the London base of the Archbishop of Canterbury, head of the Church of England. Much of the palace is hidden behind great walls, and even the Tudor gatehouse, visible from the street, is closed to the public, but you can stand here and absorb the historical vibrations echoing from momentous events. The delightful **Museum of Garden History** in St. Mary's church next door. A little farther east along Lambeth Road is the impressive **Imperial War Museum**; the best view of the Houses of Parliament can be had on the embankment between Lambeth and Westminster bridges.

A few steps from Westminster Bridge sits the **Florence Nightingale Museum** in St. Thomas's Hospital. Back on the embankment is County Hall, former home of the Greater London Council, the capital's old governmental body; it now houses the **London Aquarium** and the surrealist museum **Dalí Universe.**

Prominently above this company of sights is the **British Airways London Eye,** with crowds of people milling around waiting for their turn, spilling onto **Jubilee Gardens** next to County Hall. Continuing

TRIP TIP

Make sure you're hungry when you arrive at Borough Market as there's plenty of opportunity to taste the traders' delicious produce.

along the curve of the river, you come to Hungerford Bridge and the Charing Cross railway bridge; the **Golden Jubilee Bridges** are anchored to the railway bridge and run on either side of it. These deposit pedestrians at the **South Bank Centre,** home to the newly renovated **Royal Festival Hall,** the **Hayward Gallery,** the **National Film Theatre,** and the **National Theatre.** This area is alive with activity, especially in summer, with skateboarders, urban runners, secondhand-book stalls, street entertainers, and a series of plaques pointing out landmarks on the opposite side of the river.

The famous **Oxo Tower** sits on Upper Ground in the Coin Street Community neighborhood. Here also is **Gabriel's Wharf,** a small marketplace of shops and restaurants. Past Blackfriars Bridge is the monolithic former power station turned museum, **Tate Modern,** and the minuscule **Bankside Gallery.** Stretching from the Tate back across the river to the St. Paul's Cathedral steps in the City is the now-wobble-free sweep of the **Millennium Bridge.**

After the Tate, it's the reconstructed Jacobean **Shakespeare's Globe Theatre** that steals the show. On the right of the theater is the 17th-century **Cardinal's Wharf,** where Wren lived while St. Paul's Cathedral was being built.

The well-signposted Thames Path leads downriver to **Vinopolis,** the world's first museum, shop, and restaurant complex celebrating wine— now with tributes to whiskey and gin as well. This stands at the entrance to a dark, cobbled alley, an appropriate route to the dismal **Clink Prison.** On Clink Street you can discern the west wall, with a rose-window outline, of the ruins of Winchester House, which was the palace of the Bishops of Winchester until 1626.

The red, yellow, and black *Golden Hinde* nestles in the dry St. Mary Overie Dock, while the legendary **Borough Market,** held every Friday afternoon and Saturday, is the rowdier neighbor of **Southwark Cathedral.** *(For more on Borough Market, see F Chapter 19, Shopping.)* Joiner Street runs beneath the arches of London's first (1836) railway. On St. Thomas Street, the **Old Operating Theatre Museum** nestles under the shadow of London Bridge station.

Halfway down Tooley Street is the grisly **London Dungeon;** a little farther toward the river is **Hay's Galleria,** a small parade of bars and restaurants, offices, and shops, beneath an arched glass atrium roof supported by tall iron columns. At the bottom of Morgan's Lane is **HMS Belfast.** Just before Tower Bridge is the massive, glass, Darth Vader–helmet build-

A BRIEF HISTORY

Southwark, the oldest borough in England, was once infamous for being London's outlaw neighborhood. Although situated just across London Bridge, it was conveniently outside the city walls and laws and was therefore the ideal location for the theaters, taverns, and cockfighting arenas—not to mention brothels—that served as after-hours entertainment in the Middle Ages. However, it was only the brave that chose to stay out once the sun had set on this side of the river. Following a matinee performance of *Henry V* or *Romeo and Juliet,* the hordes of plebeians that flocked to Shakespeare's popular Globe Theatre were more eager to scuttle back to the safety of their hearths than take their chances with whatever lurked in the shadows of a twilight South Bank.

For centuries the North London jibe about needing a passport to cross the mighty Thames may have held true. But, in the mid-20th century people began to hold their tongues as the South Bank emerged as one of the capital's most creative hubs. The development began in the 1950s with the construction of the Royal Festival Hall, part of the postwar, morale-boosting Festival of Britain in 1951, and was followed by the additions of the Hayward Gallery in the '60s and the Royal National Theatre in the '70s. In the '80s the Design Museum and wharfside developments at Gabriel's Wharf and Butlers Wharf attracted a fresh influx of residents and further development downriver; with the '90s came the refurbishment of the Oxo Tower and the breathtaking reconstruction of Shakespeare's Globe Theatre. The architectural celebrations continued apace with showcase projects for the new millennium, such as Tate Modern and the British Airways London Eye—still a favorite with both Londoners and out-of-towners alike.

Even the previously lesser-frequented parts of the South Bank are now a magnet for visitors. The city's oldest market, Borough Market—or "London's Larder"—has become an essential foodie destination, where celebrity chefs go in search of farm-fresh produce. Just a short walk east, Bermondsey (or "Beormund's Eye" as it was known in Saxon times), with its artist studios and pretty streets, is being bought up by fashion-conscious homemakers in search of the new Hoxton.

ing of **City Hall,** designed by the prolific Sir Norman Foster and home to the London Assembly.

Past the bridge a path leads to **Butlers Wharf,** an '80s warehouse conversion of deluxe loft apartments, restaurants, and galleries—but once the dingy, dangerous shadowlands where Dickens killed off Bill Sikes in *Oliver Twist.* Here are munch-monster center, the Gastrodrome, and the **Design Museum,** where you can take another long-lasting view of the Thames and Tower Bridge.

PLACES TO EXPLORE

Bankside Gallery. Two artistic societies—the Royal Society of Painter-Printmakers and the Royal Watercolour Society—have their headquarters here. Together they mount exhibitions of current members' work, usually for sale, alongside artists' materials and books—a great place for finding that exclusive, not too expensive gift. There are also regular themed exhibitions. Note that the gallery usually closes for a few days between exhibitions, so check ahead for details before you go. ⊠ 48 Hopton St., South Bank, SE1 ☎ 020/7928–7521 ⊕ www.banksidegallery.com ⊠ Free ⊙ Daily 11–6 Ⓤ Blackfriars, Southwark, St. Paul's.

☺ ★ **British Airways London Eye.** To mark the start of the new millennium, architects David Marks and Julia Barfield conceived an entirely new vision: a beautiful and celebratory structure, which would allow people to see this great city from a completely new perspective—on a giant wheel. As well as representing the turning of the century, a wheel was seen as a symbol of regeneration and the passing of time. The London Eye is the larg-

YOUR EYE QUEUE
Buy your ticket online, over the phone, or at the ticket office in advance to avoid the long lines.

est observation wheel ever built, and in the top 10 tallest structures in London. From design to construction it took seven years to complete. The 25-minute slow-motion ride inside one of the enclosed passenger capsules is so smooth you'd hardly know you were suspended over the Thames, moving slowly round. On a clear day you can take in a range of up to 25 mi, viewing London's most famous landmarks from a fascinating angle. If you're looking for a special place to celebrate, champagne and canapés can be arranged ahead; check the Web site for details. ⊠ Jubilee Gardens, South Bank, SE1 ☎ 0870/990–8883 ⊕ www.ba-londoneye.com ⊠ £13.50 ⊙ June–Sept., daily 9:30 AM–10 PM; Oct.–May, daily 9:30–8 Ⓤ Waterloo.

☺ **The Clink Prison.** Giving rise to the term "clink," or jail, this institution was originally the prison attached to Winchester House, palace of the Bishops of Winchester until 1626. One of five Southwark establishments, it was the first to detain women, most of whom were called "Winchester geese"—a euphemism for prostitutes—which were endemic in Southwark, especially around the bishops' area of jurisdiction, which was known as "the Liberty of the Clink" so called because their graces' solution was to license prostitution rather than ban it. You'll discover, in graphic detail, how a grisly Tudor prison would operate on a code of cruelty, deprivation, and corruption. ⊠ 1 Clink St., South Bank, SE1 ☎ 020/7403–0900 ⊕ www.clink.co.uk ⊠ £5 ⊙ Weekdays 10–6, weekends 10–9; last admission 1 hr before closing Ⓤ London Bridge.

Dalí Universe. Here is Europe's most comprehensively arranged collection by master surrealist Salvador Dalí. The many exhibits—from art to sculpture, to furniture, to jewelry—are organized in themes (Sensuality and Femininity, Religion and Mythology, and Dreams and Fantasy), and thus the museum tries to give visitors a reflection of how Dalí thought out his work. There are more than 500 pieces on show, but highlights undoubtedly include the *Mae West Lips Sofa,* the *Lobster Telephone,* and *Spellbound* for the Hitchcock movie. Although there's much to take in, this museum has a much more commercial flavor and lacks the intimacy of other Dalí museums. ⊠ County

Hall, Riverside Bldg., Westminster Bridge Rd., South Bank, SE1
☎*0870/744–7485* ⊕*www.daliuniverse.com* 🖵*£12* ⊙*Daily 10–6:30;
last entry at 5:30* Ⓤ*Waterloo, Westminster.*

🕲 **Design Museum.** This was the first museum in the world to elevate everyday design and design classics to the status of art by placing them
in their social and cultural context. Fashion, creative technology, and
architecture are explored with thematic displays from the museum's permanent collection of design classics, and temporary exhibitions provide
an in-depth focus on such subjects as the work of great designers such
as Charles Eames and Isamu Noguchi, or thematic shows on the Bau-
haus or book design. The museum looks forward, too, by showcasing
innovative contemporary designs and technologies, an area that kids
find absorbing (there are free activity packs to spark their interest further). All of this is supplemented by a busy program of lectures, events,
and talks, including a workshop for kids. If you're in need of suste-
nance, there's the trendsetting Blueprint Café (designed by who else but
Terence Conran), with its river terrace and superb views. For quicker
snacks at a lower price, the museum's own café is on the ground floor
beside the Thames footpath. The museum store sells good-quality, high-
design products. Entry to both cafés and the store is free. ✉*28 Shad
Thames, South Bank, SE1* ☎*0870/833–9955* ⊕*www.designmuseum.
org* 🖵*£7* ⊙*Daily 10–5:45, last admission at 5:15* Ⓤ*London Bridge;
DLR: Tower Gateway.*

▌OFF THE
BEATEN
PATH

Dulwich Picture Gallery. A highly distinguished small gallery, the Dulwich has impressive works by Rembrandt, Van Dyck, Rubens, Poussin, and Gainsborough, among others, with three critically acclaimed
international loan exhibitions each year. Anyone who fell in love with
Sir John Soane's house may wish to make the overground train journey (12 minutes from London Bridge or Victoria) here, since this gallery was also designed by the visionary architect. You'll also enjoy the
Picture Gallery Café, which opens onto landscaped gardens, before or
after a wander around Dulwich Village, with its handsome 18th-cen-
tury houses strung out along its main street. Most of the land around
here belongs to the famous local school, the Dulwich College Estate,
founded in the early 17th century by the actor Edward Alleyn, and
this keeps strict control of modern development. Opposite the gallery,
Dulwich Park is a well-kept municipal park with a particularly fine
display of rhododendrons in late May. ✉*College Rd., Dulwich Village, Southwark, SE21* ☎*020/8693–5254* ⊕*www.dulwichpicturegal-
lery.org.uk* 🖵*£4, free on Fri.* ⊙*Tues.–Fri. 10–5, weekends and bank
holiday Mon. 11–5* Ⓤ*National Rail: West Dulwich from Victoria or
North Dulwich from London Bridge.*

Florence Nightingale Museum. Here you can learn all about the founder
of the first school of nursing, that most famous of health-care reformers, "the Lady with the Lamp." See the reconstruction of the barracks
ward at Scutari, Turkey, where she tended soldiers during the Crimean
War (1854–56) and earned her nickname. Here you also find a Victorian East End slum cottage showing what she did to improve living
conditions among the poor—and the famous lamp. The museum is in

St. Thomas's Hospital, which was built in 1868 to the specifications of Florence Nightingale. Most of it was bombed to bits in the Blitz, then rebuilt to become one of London's teaching hospitals. ⊠ *2 Lambeth Palace Rd., entrance parallel to embankment on Lambeth Palace Rd., South Bank, SE1* ☎ *020/7620–0374* ⊕ *www.florence-nightingale. co.uk* ⊠ *£5.80* ☯ *Weekdays 10–5, last admission 4, weekends 10–4:30, last admission 3:30* Ⓤ *Waterloo or Westminster, then walk over bridge.*

NEED A BREAK?

Gabriel's Wharf. This cluster of specialist shops, cafés, and restaurants is part of the Coin Street Community neighborhood and bustles with activity during the daytime. You can hire bicycles here from the London Bicycle Tour Company (☎ 020/7928–6838). ⊠ 52 Upper Ground, South Bank, SE1 ☎ 020/7401–2255 ⊕ www.gabrielswharf.co.uk ⊠ Free ☯ Shops and studios Tues.–Sun. 11–6 Ⓤ Blackfriars, Waterloo.

☯ **Golden Hinde.** Sir Francis Drake circumnavigated the globe in this little galleon, or one just like it. This exact replica made a 23-year round-the-world voyage—much of it spent along U.S. coasts, both Pacific and Atlantic—and has settled here to continue its educational purpose. If you want information along with your visit, book a tour in advance. ⊠ *St. Mary Overie Dock, Cathedral St., South Bank, SE1* ☎ *08700/11– 8700* ⊕ *www.goldenhinde.org* ⊠ *£5.50, £5 for prebooked guided tour* ☯ *Times vary, call ahead* Ⓤ *London Bridge, Mansion House.*

Hayward Gallery. The gray, windowless bunker tucked behind the South Bank Centre concert halls has had to bear the brunt of architectural criticism over the years, but that's changed with a foyer extension that gives more daylight, more space for exhibits, a café, and better access. The highlight of the project is an elliptical mirrored glass pavilion by New York–based artist Dan Graham. Exhibitions here encompass a range of art media, crossing history and cultures, bridging the experimental and established. It's consistently on the cutting edge of new developments in art and critical theory, finding new ways to present the well known, from Picasso to Lichtenstein, and as a prominent platform for up-and-coming artists. ⊠ *South Bank Centre, South Bank, SE1* ☎ *020/7921–0813* ⊕ *www.hayward.org.uk* ⊠ *Mon. £2.50, Tues.–Sun. £5* ☯ *Sat.–Mon., Thurs. 10–6, Tues. and Wed. 10–8, Fri. 10–9* Ⓤ *Waterloo.*

☯ **HMS Belfast.** At 613 feet, this is one of the largest and most powerful cruisers the Royal Navy has ever had. It played an important role in the D-Day landings off Normandy, left for the Far East after the war, and has been becalmed here since 1971. On board there's a riveting outpost of the **Imperial War Museum,** which tells the Royal Navy's story from 1914 to the present and shows you about life on a World War II battleship (with interactive push button games and quizzes), from mess decks and bakery to punishment cells and from operations room to engine room and armaments. ⊠ *Morgan's La., Tooley St., South Bank, SE1* ☎ *020/7940–6300* ⊕ *www.iwm.org.uk* ⊠ *£8.50* ☯ *Mar.–Oct., daily 10–6; Nov.–Feb., daily 10–5; last admission 45 min before closing* Ⓤ *London Bridge.*

☾ **Imperial War Museum.** Despite its title, this museum of 20th-century
★ warfare does not glorify bloodshed but emphasizes understanding
through evoking what life was like for citizens and soldiers alike
through the two world wars. There's an impressive amount of hardware at the main entrance with accompanying interactive material,
including a Battle of Britain Spitfire, a German V2 rocket, tanks, guns,
and submarines—and from here you can peel off to the various sections of the museum. Sights, sounds, and smells are used to re-create
the very uncomfortable Trench Experience in the World War I gallery,
which is equally as effective as The Blitz Experience in the World War
II gallery: a 10-minute taste of an air raid in a street of acrid smoke
with sirens blaring and searchlights glaring. There are two galleries
of war art on the second floor (by Henry Moore, John Singer Sargent,
Stanley Spencer, and William Orpen, to name a few), poetry, photography, and documentary film footage. There's also a permanent
Holocaust exhibition, and a Crimes Against Humanity exhibition,
which is not suitable for younger children. More recent wars attended
by British forces are commemorated, too, in the Victoria and George
Cross Gallery. Don't miss the intriguing Secret War Gallery, which
charts the history of agents' intrepid work in the wars and the incep-
tion of MI5 and MI6, the government's secret services.

The museum is housed in an elegant domed and colonnaded building, erected in the early 19th century to house the Bethlehem Hospital
for the Insane, better known as the infamous Bedlam. By 1816, when
the patients were moved here, they were no longer kept in cages to be
taunted by tourists (see the final scene of Hogarth's *Rake's Progress*
at Sir John Soane's Museum for some sense of how horrific it was),
since reformers—and George III's madness—had effected more humane
standards of confinement. Bedlam moved to Surrey in 1930. There's a
lovely, bright café where you can rest after your trek south of the river.
⊠*Lambeth Rd., South Bank, SE1* ☎*020/7416–5320* ⊕*www.iwm.org.
uk* ≊*Free* ♥ *Daily 10–6* Ⓤ*Lambeth North.*

☾ **London Aquarium.** The curved, colonnaded, neoclassic hulk of County
Hall once housed London's local government administration (now
located at the Norman Foster–designed City Hall building farther
downriver by Tower Bridge). Now it's where you can catch a dark and
thrilling glimpse of the waters of the world, focused around a superb
three-level aquarium full of sharks and stingrays, among other common
and rarer breeds. There are also educational exhibits, hands-on displays,
feeding displays, and piscine sights previously unseen on these shores.
It's not the biggest aquarium you've ever seen—especially if you've been
to SeaWorld—but the exhibit is well arranged on several subterranean
levels, with areas for different oceans, water environments, and climate
zones, including a stunning coral reef, and the highlight: the rain forest,
which is almost like the real thing. There are regular feeding times and
free talks throughout the day, while the aquarium also runs a conservation breeding scheme—so look out for new additions to the tanks.
⊠*County Hall, Riverside Bldg., Westminster Bridge Rd., South Bank,*

SE1 ☎ *020/7967–8000* ⊕ *www.londonaquarium.co.uk* ✆ *£9.75* ☼ *Daily 10–6; last admission at 5* Ⓤ *Westminster, Waterloo.*

☾ **London Dungeon.** Here's the goriest, grisliest, most gruesome attraction in town, where realistic waxwork people are subjected in graphic detail to all the historical horrors the Tower of London merely tells you about. Tableaux depict famous bloody moments—like Anne Boleyn's decapitation and the martyrdom of St. George—alongside the tor-

> **DUNGEON TIPS**
>
> Naturally, children absolutely adore this place, but be warned—nervous kiddies may find it too frightening. Expect long lines on weekends and during school holidays.

ture, murder, and ritual slaughter of lesser-known victims, all to a sound track of screaming, wailing, and agonized moaning. There are displays on the Great Plague, the Great Fire of London, and Jack the Ripper; to add to the fear and fun, costumed characters leap out of the gloom to bring the exhibits to life. ✉ *28–34 Tooley St., South Bank, SE1* ☎ *020/7403–7221* ⊕ *www.thedungeons.com* ✆ *£14.95* ☼ *Mid-Apr.–mid-July, daily 10–5:30; mid-July–mid-Sept., daily 10–7.30; mid-Sept.–mid-Nov., daily 10–5.30; mid-Nov.–mid-Apr. daily 10:30–5; phone to confirm dates* Ⓤ *London Bridge.*

Museum of Garden History. The first of its kind in the world, the museum is set in St. Mary's Church, next to Lambeth Palace. Founded in 1977, the museum has built up one of the largest collections of historic garden tools, artifacts, and curiosities, as well as an expanding library. Alongside the museum is a replica 17th-century knot garden, a peaceful haven of plants that can be traced back to that period. The garden also contains the tombs of the John Tradescants (the elder and younger), enthusiastic collectors of curiosities and adventurous plant hunters—who introduced many familiar blooms, such as lilac, to these shores—and memorials to William Bligh, captain of the *Bounty*, and the Sealy family of Coade stone fame. The shop has gifts in the plant vein, and there's a café. ✉ *Lambeth Palace Rd., South Bank, SE1* ☎ *020/7401–8865* ⊕ *www.museumgardenhistory.org* ✆ *Suggested donation £3* ☼ *Daily 10:30–5* Ⓤ *Vauxhall.*

☾ **Old Operating Theatre Museum.** All that remains of one of England's oldest hospitals, which stood here from the 12th century until the railway forced it to move in 1862, is the room where women went under the knife. The theater was bricked up and forgotten for a century but has now been restored into an exhibition of early-19th-century medical practices: the operating table onto which the gagged and blindfolded patients were roped; the box of sawdust underneath for catching their blood; the knives, pliers, and handsaws the surgeons wielded; and—this was a theater in the round—the spectators' seats. So authentic are the surroundings that they were used in the film *The Madness of King George.* Next door is a sweeter show: the **Herb Garret,** with displays of medicinal herbs used during the same period. ✉ *9A St. Thomas St., South Bank, SE1* ☎ *020/7188–2679* ⊕ *www.*

thegarret.org.uk ⌧*£4.25* ⊘ *Daily 10:30–5. Closed Dec. 15–Jan. 5* Ⓤ*London Bridge.*

Oxo Tower. Long a London landmark to the cognoscenti, the art deco–era Oxo building has graduated from its former incarnations as a power-generating station and warehouse into a vibrant community of artists' and designers' workshops, a pair of restaurants, as well as five floors of community homes. There's an observation deck for a super river vista (St. Paul's to the east, and Somerset House to the west), and a performance area on the first floor, which comes alive all summer long—as does the entire surrounding neighborhood. All the designers and artisans rely on you to disturb them whenever they're open, whether buying, commissioning, or just browsing. The biggest draw remains the Oxo Tower Restaurant extravaganza for a meal or a martini. ⌧*Barge House St., South Bank, SE1* ☎*020/7401–3610* ⊕*www.oxotower.co.uk* ⌧*Free* ⊘ *Studios and shops Tues.–Sun. 11–6* Ⓤ*Blackfriars, Waterloo.*

Southwark Cathedral. Pronounced "Suth-uck," this is the second-oldest Gothic church in London, after Westminster Abbey, with parts dating back to the 12th century. Although it houses some remarkable memorials, not to mention a program of lunchtime concerts, it's seldom visited. It was promoted to cathedral status only in 1905; before that it was the priory church of St. Mary Overie (as in "over the water"—on the South Bank). Look for the gaudily renovated 1408 tomb of the poet John Gower, friend of Chaucer, and for the Harvard Chapel. Another notable buried here is Edmund Shakespeare, brother of William. ■**TIP➔The Refectory serves light lunches and tea daily 10–5.** ⌧*Montague Close, South Bank, SE1* ☎*020/7367–6700* ⊕*www.southwark.anglican.org* ⌧*Free, suggested donation £4* ⊘ *Daily 8–6* Ⓤ*London Bridge.*

Ⓒ
Fodor'sChoice
★
Tate Modern. This structure was built as a power station in the 1930s, and after a dazzling renovation by Herzog & de Meuron, it currently provides a magnificent space for the Tate's collection of modern art. The vast Turbine Hall is a dramatic entrance point to the museum. On permanent display in the galleries are classic works from 1900 to the present day, by Matisse, Picasso, Dalí, Moore, Bacon, Warhol, and the most-talked-about British upstarts. The works are not grouped by artist but are arranged thematically—Landscape, Still Life, and the Nude—on different levels, reached by a moving staircase, which is a feature in its own right. You could spend a rainy day here exploring the building, visiting the superb bookshop, and at the restaurant with gorgeous views across the river; alternatively, come for the latest barnstorming exhibition (there are usually pricey, timed tickets for major special exhibitions), which is more often than not a talking point at smart dinner parties across London. ⌧*Bankside, South Bank, SE1* ☎*020/7887–8888* ⊕*www.tate.org.uk* ⌧*Free* ⊘ *Sun.–Thurs. 10–6, Fri. and Sat. 10–10* Ⓤ*Blackfriars, Southwark.*

Continued on p. 154

"*Within this wooden O...*"
—*William Shakespeare, Henry V*

SHAKESPEARE & THE GLOBE THEATRE

At Shakespeare's Globe Theatre, they say the Bard does not belong to the British; he belongs to the world. Not a day has gone by since the Restoration when one of his plays isn't being performed or reinterpreted somewhere. But here, at the site of the original Globe, in a painstaking reconstruction of Shakespeare's own open-air theater, is where seeing one of his plays can take on an ethereal quality.

If you are exceedingly well read and a lover of the Bard, then chances are a pilgrimage to his Globe Theatre is already on your list. But if Shakespeare's works leave you wondering why exactly the play is the thing, then a trip to the Globe—to learn more about his life or to see his words come alive—is a must.

The Globe Theatre in Shakespeare's Day

In the 16th and 17th centuries, a handful of theaters—the Rose, the Swan, the Globe, and others whose names are lost—rose above the higgledy-piggledy jumble of rooftops in London's rowdy Southwark neighborhood. They were round or octagonal open-air playhouses, with galleries for the "quality" members of society, and large, open pits for the raucous mobs. People from all social classes, from royalty down to the hoi polloi, shared the communal experience of drama in these places. Shakespeare's Globe was one.

A fire in 1613 destroyed the first Globe, which was quickly rebuilt; however, Oliver Cromwell and waves of other reformers put an end to all the Southwark playhouses in the 1640s. By the time American actor and director Sam Wanamaker visited in 1949, the only indication that the world's greatest dramatist created popular entertainment here was a plaque on a brewery wall. Wanamaker was shocked to find that all evidence of the playwright's legendary playhouse had vanished into air.

And thereby hangs a tale.

Wanamaker's Dream

Over the next several decades, Wanamaker devoted himself to the Bard. He was director of the New Shakespeare Theatre in Liverpool and, in 1959, joined the Shakespeare Memorial Theatre Company (now the Royal Shakespeare Company) at Stratford-upon-Avon.

SHAKESPEARE'S ALL-TIME TOP 10

1. *Romeo and Juliet*. Young love, teenage rebellion, and tragedy are the ingredients of the greatest tearjerker of all time.

2. *Hamlet* (*right*). The very model of a modern antihero and origin of the most quoted line of any play: "To be or not to be..."

3. *A Midsummer Night's Dream*. Spells and potions abound as the gods use humans for playthings; lovers' tiffs are followed by happy endings for all.

4. *Othello*. Jealousy poisons love and destroys a proud man.

5. *The Taming of the Shrew*. The eternal battle of the sexes.

6. *Macbeth*. Ambition, murder, and revenge. Evil gets its just reward.

7. *The Merry Wives of Windsor*. A two-timing rascal gets his comeuppance from a pack of hysterically funny gossips.

8. *Richard III*. One of literature's juiciest villains. The whole audience wants to hiss.

9. *The Tempest*. On a desert island, the concerns of men amaze and amuse the innocent Miranda: "Oh brave new world, that has such people in't."

10. *King Lear*. A tragedy of old age, filial love, and grasping, ungrateful children.

Finally, in the 1970s he began the project that would dominate the rest of his life: reconstructing Shakespeare's theater, as close to the original site as possible.

Today's Globe was re-created using authentic Elizabethan materials and craft techniques—green oak timbers joined only with wooden pegs and mortise-and-tenon joints; plaster made of lime, sand, and goat's hair; and the first thatched roof in London since the Great Fire. The complex,

200 yards from the site of the original Globe, includes an exhibition center, cafés, and restaurants. (The shell of a 17th-century-style theater, built adjacent to the Globe to a design by Inigo Jones, awaits further funds for completion.)

FUN FACT: Plays are presented in the open air (and sometimes the rain) to an audience of 1,000 on wooden benches in the bays, and 500 "groundlings," who stand on a carpet of filbert shells and clinker, just as they did nearly four centuries ago.

The eventual realization of Wanamaker's dream, a full-scale, accurate replica of the Globe, was the keystone that supported the revitalization of the entire district. The new Globe celebrates Shakespeare, his work, and his times, and as an educational trust it is dedicated to making the Bard continually fresh and accessible for new audiences. Sadly, Wanamaker died before construction was completed, in 1997. In Southwark Cathedral, a few hundred yards west of the Globe, a memorial to him stands beside the statue memorializing Shakespeare himself.

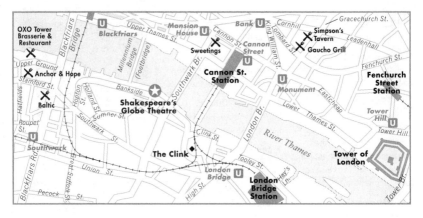

Visiting the Globe

✉ 21 New Globe Walk, Bankside, South Bank

☎ 020/7401-9919 box office, 020/7902-1400 New Shakespeare's Globe Exhibition

🌐 www.shakespeares-globe.org

💷 Exhibition admission £9, family ticket (2 adults, 3 children) £25; ticket prices for plays vary (£5-£32).

🕓 Exhibition May–early Oct., daily 10–5; mid-Oct.–Apr., daily 9–noon and 12:30–5; plays May–early Oct., call for performance schedule.

Ⓤ Southwark, then walk to Blackfriars Bridge and descend the steps; Mansion House, then cross Southwark Bridge; Blackfriars, then walk across Blackfriars Bridge; St. Paul's, then cross Millennium Bridge.

The season of plays is limited to the warmer months, from May to the first week in October, with the schedule announced in late January on the theater's Web site. Tickets go on sale in mid-February. The box office takes phone and mail orders as well as in-person sales, but the most convenient way to buy tickets is online. Book as early as possible.

FUN FACT: "Groundlings"–those with £5 standing-only tickets–are not allowed to sit during the performance. Reserve an actual seat, though, on any one of the theater's three levels, and you can join the "Elizabethan" crowd.

If you do have a seat, you can rent cushions for £1 (or bring your own) to soften the backless wooden benches. A limited number of backrests are also available for rent for £3. The show must go on, rain or shine, warm or chilly—so come prepared for whatever the weather throws at you. Umbrellas are banned, but you can bring a raincoat or buy a cheap Globe rain poncho, which doubles as a great souvenir.

MAKING THE MOST OF YOUR TIME
Give yourself plenty of time: there are several cafés and restaurants, as well as fascinating interactive exhibitions, and theater tours with occasional live demonstrations. Performances can last up to three hours.

WITH CHILDREN
Childsplay, a program for 8- to 11-year-olds, is held once a month during matinées. While Mom and Dad enjoy the play, children—helped by actors, musicans, and teachers—learn the background and story and become accustomed to Shakespearean language. By the time they are admitted to the theater for the last 15 minutes of the play, the children have become Shakespeare enthusiasts for life.

A regular workshop for kids, run with the Metropolitan Police, the National Archives, and the National Forensic Service, uses modern forensic techniques to solve real Elizabethan crimes and mysteries.

Year-Round at Shakespeare's Globe

Shakespeare's Globe Exhibition is a comprehensive display built under the theater (the entry is adjacent) that provides background material about the Elizabethan theater and about the surrounding neighborhood, Southwark. The exhibition describes the process of building the modern Globe and the serious research that went into it.

FUN FACT: In Shakespeare's day, this was a rough part of town. The Bear Gardens, around the corner from the Globe, was where bear baiting, a cruel animal sport, took place. Farther along, the Clink (now a museum) was the local *gaol* (jail).

Daily live demonstrations include Elizabethan dressing, stage fighting, and swordplay, performed by drama students and stage-fighting instructors from the Royal Academy of Dramatic Art (RADA) and the London Academy of Music and Dramatic Art (LAMDA).

FUN FACT: Many performances are done in Elizabethan dress. Costumes are handmade from period materials—wool, silk, cotton, animal skins, and natural dyes.

Admission also includes a tour of the theater. On matinee days, the tour visits the archaeological site of the nearby (and older) Rose Theatre.

SPECIAL EVENTS

The Frost Fair, held annually the weekend before Christmas, commemorates several extraordinary winters in the 17th century when the Thames froze over and fairs took place on the ice. It includes street theater, Morris Dancing, sword fighting, and food and crafts stalls. Admission is £1, and there is special reduced admission to the Theatre and Exhibition during the fair.

Shakespeare's Birthday, April 23, is celebrated every year with free all-day admission to the theater and exhibitions, free performances, and public access to the Globe stage, giving all comers a chance to entertain the groundlings. The line of would-be thesps wraps around the block.

FUN FACT: Shakespeare's casts were all male, with young men and boys playing the female roles. A live demonstration in the costume exhibit shows how this was done—and how convincing it can be.

Vinopolis. Spread over 2 acres between the Globe Theatre and London Bridge, you can take a virtual tour of the world's wine cultures, and have an opportunity to put your skills to the taste. The four restaurants claim to offer more wines by the glass than anywhere else in the city, and you can, of course, buy. Keep in mind that the last entry is two hours before the scheduled closing time, and you should allow at least two hours for a tour. ⊠ *1 Bank End St., South Bank, SE1* ☎ *0870/444–4777* ⊕ *www. vinopolis.co.uk* 🖃 *£16* ⊗ *Mon., Fri., and Sat. noon–9, Tues.–Thurs. and Sun. noon–6* Ⓤ *London Bridge.*

> **WHEN TO GO**
>
> Avoid going to the Tate Modern on weekends, when visitor numbers are at their greatest. Visit during the week or join the cool crowd on Friday evenings when it's open until 10 PM.

The South Bank Dining

AT A GLANCE

BUDGET DINING
Baltic, Eastern European, 74 Blackfriars Rd.

The Table, Café, 83 Southwark St.

MODERATE DINING
Anchor & Hope, Modern British, 36 The Cut

Chez Gérard, Steak, 9 Belvedere Rd.

Oxo Tower Restaurant & Brasserie, Modern British, Oxo Tower Wharf

EXPENSIVE DINING
Chez Bruce, French, 2 Bellevue Rd.

Kensington & Chelsea

The great entrance hall of the Natural History Museum

9

WORD OF MOUTH

"I don't know how to properly describe the Chelsea Flower Show. For five days a year, it takes over the sizeable compound of the Royal Hospital Chelsea; enormous temporary buildings sprout from the parade grounds and entire landscapes are created that will endure just a week. The best thing I can say is this: if you are ever in London at the end of May, go. And don't settle, as we did, for a half-day ticket. Spring for the (gulp) full-day pass. You won't regret it."

—Neal_Sanders

GETTING ORIENTED

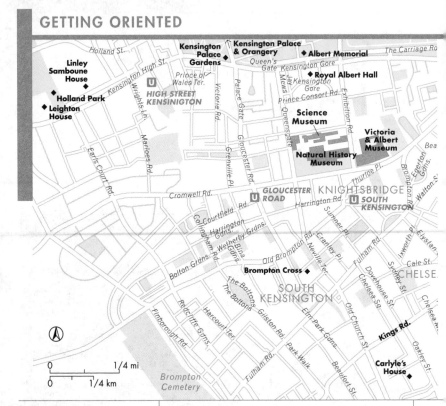

GETTING HERE

Depending on where you're headed, there are several useful Tube stations for Kensington & Chelsea: Sloane Square and High Street Kensington on the District and Circle lines; Earls Court on the Piccadilly Line; and South Kensington and Gloucester Road on the District, Circle, and Piccadilly lines.

TOP 5 REASONS TO GO

■ **The V&A Museum:** Sketch in the sculpture court, where even stools are provided—then have a glass of wine under the Chihuly chandelier.

■ **Natural History Museum:** Watch a child catch on that the museum's new animatronic T. rex has noticed *him*—and is licking its dinosaur chops.

■ **Science Museum:** Kids of all ages (this includes you) can enjoy this "painlessly educational" museum.

■ **The Proms:** Sing along at the end of a Proms concert in Royal Albert Hall. (Even better: watch the English concertgoers drop their inhibitions and join in, too.)

■ **King's Road pubs:** Chat with a Chelsea Pensioner, in full red-uniformed regalia, over a pint.

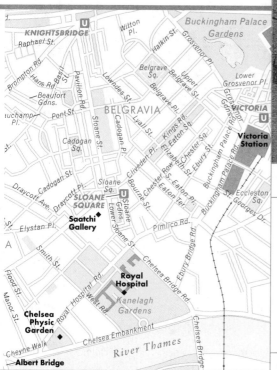

MAKING THE MOST OF YOUR TIME

You could fill three or four days in this borough: a shopping stroll along the length of King's Road is easily half a day. Add lunch and some time weaving back and forth between King's Road and the river and you can fill a day. Give yourself a half-day, at least, for the Victoria & Albert Museum and a half-day for either the Science or Natural History Museum.

A GOOD RUN

The short circuit around the Thames between Chelsea Bridge and Albert Bridge is a pleasant 1½-mi run. From Chelsea Bridge run west along Chelsea Embankment. The wooded park on the other side is Battersea Park with its Peace Pagoda in the middle. Turn left across the river on the Albert Bridge. Then turn left into Battersea Park and run along the cinder path beside the river. Now the view is of Chelsea. There are good public bathrooms and drinking fountains in the park. Emerge from the park and turn left across Chelsea Bridge back to the starting point.

FEELING PECKISH?

The Café at the V&A (⊠ *Victoria & Albert Museum, Cromwell Rd., SW7* ☎ *020/7581–2159*) serves breakfast, light snacks, tea, and full meals throughout the day, all in a very grand room at modest prices. You can eat in the courtyard if the weather's good, or have a buffet supper on late nights. Stop by just to see the original Arts & Crafts decor, one of William Morris's earliest commissions, with stained-glass panels by Edward Burne Jones.

NEAREST PUBLIC RESTROOMS

Peter Jones, the big department store in Sloane Square, has several large, clean restrooms that are free to use. Don't be shy about entering any pub and asking for the "loo." Even if you aren't a customer, nobody will mind. Usually, in this part of town, the restrooms are clean and well maintained.

Sightseeing
☆★★★★

Nightlife
☆☆☆☆★

Dining
☆★★★★

Lodging
☆★★★★

Shopping
☆★★★★

The Royal Borough of Kensington & Chelsea has always been home to world-famous movers and shakers. There are more blue plaques (historic markers) here than in any other part of London, three superb shopping districts, a royal palace, and one of the best concentrations of museums in the world. Kensington is more established, with some breathtaking private residences, while equally well-heeled Chelsea basks in its literary and artistic connections: the youth culture of the '60s was virtually invented here. Today, though more conservative than cutting-edge, it still attracts its fair share of hipsters to its villagelike neighborhoods.

WHAT'S HERE

As you head north from the Thames, the Royal Borough changes, layer by layer. The lawns and parkland of Wren's impressive **Royal Hospital** stretch down to the river near Chelsea Bridge, in the southeast corner. It's about a mile west along the Embankment to **Cheyne Walk,** a lovely street dating back to the 18th century, **Chelsea Physic Garden,** and **Carlyle's House,** with all their arty and historic associations. The blue plaques commemorating important residents along here are amazing. On the way, notice the **Albert Bridge,** a candy-color Victorian confection of a suspension bridge.

To the right of the Royal Hospital runs the Royal Hospital Road, along which is the National Army Museum. If you're a shopaholic, zig-zag north, through pleasant residential streets to **King's Road** *(Shopping, Chapter 19),* for retail therapy and for a bit of culture at the newly relocated **Saatchi Gallery,** which is doing its best to restore the cutting edge to the neighborhood. Once you hit King's Road, ramble up and down the tiny Georgian lanes of pastel-color houses, especially **Jubilee Place** and **Burn-sall Street,** that run off it to the north, leading to the hidden "village square" of **Chelsea Green.**

Alternatively, if you'd rather just continue shopping, you can literally charge your way down King's Road, from Sloane Square to World's End. The shopping area recently christened as **Brompton Cross** doesn't appear on most maps, but if you aim west, as the crow flies, from Sloane Square to the intersection of the Fulham Road and Brompton Road, you'll find a small but choice collection of fashion and homeware shops.

> ### LONDON AT NIGHT
>
> The Albert Bridge, alight with thousands of lights, its reflection sparkling on the river, is one of London's great romantic views.

Near South Kensington tube station is the heart of a small French community, centered around the French school, known as the **Lycée,** and a good place to look for a light snack or a coffee before attempting the South Kensington museums: the **Victoria & Albert Museum,** the **Science Museum,** and the **Natural History Museum** are all around the corner.

The **Royal Albert Hall,** with its bas reliefs that make it look like a redbrick Wedgwood pot, is the next layer, about ¼ mi north, past the museums and Imperial College on Exhibition Road. Facing the Albert Hall, across Kensington Gore in Kensington Gardens, is the **Albert Memorial,** a monument to Prince Albert and the British Empire. **Kensington Palace** and its **Orangery** are diagonally across the park, with the gated **Kensington Palace Gardens** running behind it. If you walk it, you can see why it earned the nickname "Billionaires' Row"—it's lined with palatial white-stucco houses designed by a selection of the best architects of the mid-19th century.

Kensington High Street, together with **Kensington Church Street,** is yet another great shopping and snacking area. Turn into Derry Street or Young Street, on either side of Barkers Arcade, and enter **Kensington Square,** one of the most complete 17th-century residential squares in London. Holland Park is about ¾ mi farther west, with the entrance on Park Close, off Ilchester Road. Both **Leighton House** and the **Linley Sambourne House** are nearby as well.

PLACES TO EXPLORE

✩ **Holland Park.** The former grounds of the Jacobean Holland House opened to the public only in 1952. It was originally owned by Sir Walter Cope, the wealthy Chancellor of James I, and many treats are to be found within its 60 acres. Holland House itself was nearly flattened by World War II bombs, but the east wing remains, now incorporated into a youth hostel and providing a fantastical stage for the April–September **Open Air Theatre** (☎ 0845/230–9769 *box office* ⊕ *www.opera-hollandpark.com*). The glass-wall Orangery also survived to host art exhibitions and wedding receptions. Next door the former Garden Ballroom has become the upmarket Belvedere restaurant; nearby is a lovely café. From the Belvedere's terrace you see the formal Dutch Garden, planted by Lady Holland in the 1790s with the first English

A BRIEF HISTORY

Kensington and Chelsea were separate villages, each with royal connections, until united in 1965. Chelsea, south of King's Road (Charles II's private way from St. James to Fulham), was settled before the Domesday Book and already fashionable when two of Henry VIII's wives lived there. Artists and writers flocked to the area in the 19th century, establishing a creative colony in Cheyne Walk; at one time Turner, Whistler, John Singer Sargent, Dante Gabriel Rossetti, and Oscar Wilde were residents. In the '60s it was the turn of the Rolling Stones and the Beatles; in the '70s Bob Marley wrote "I Shot the Sheriff" in a flat off Cheyne Walk. It's now one of London's most expensive streets, completely unaffordable for latter-day Bob Marleys.

Kensington laid its first royal stake when King William III, fed up with the vapors of the Thames, bought a country place there in 1689 and converted it into Kensington Palace. Courtiers followed, but the village kept its rural quality well into the Victoria's reign when, in the building boom of the 1850s, large landowners developed their farms into vast tracts of smart town houses. Queen Victoria's consort, Prince Albert, added the jewel in the borough's crown when he turned the profits of the Great Exhibition of 1851 into South Kensington's metropolis of museums.

dahlias. North of that are woodland walks; lawns populated by peacocks, guinea fowl, and the odd, awkward emu; a fragrant rose garden; great banks of rhododendrons and azaleas, which bloom profusely in May; a well-supervised children's Adventure Playground; and even a Japanese water garden, legacy of the London Festival of Japan. If that's not enough, you can watch cricket on the Cricket Lawn on the south side or tennis on the several courts. ☺ *Daily dawn–dusk* Ⓤ *Holland Park, High St. Kensington.*

★ **Kensington Palace.** For more than 300 years, royals have lived here in grand style. The original building, Nottingham House, needed 12 years of renovation by Wren and Hawksmoor, who had been commissioned by King William III and Queen Mary to turn it into a proper palace. During the subsequent three reigns, it underwent much further refurbishment—accompanied by numerous royal deaths: William III died here in 1702, Queen Anne in 1714, George I in 1727, and George II in 1760, after which it ceased to be a royal residence. It was also here that the 18-year-old Princess Victoria was called from her bed in June 1837 by the Archbishop of Canterbury and the Lord Chamberlain, to be told of the death of her uncle, William IV, and her accession to the throne. The State Apartments, including the late Princess Margaret's rooms are on show on the first floor. The Duke and Duchess of Gloucester and Prince and Princess Michael of Kent have private apartments here.

On the Garden Floor is the palace's visitor entrance, which takes you into the Red Saloon and Teck Saloon, where the **Royal Ceremonial Dress Collection** displays garments dating to the 18th century. State and occasional dresses, hats, shoes, and gloves from the present Queen's wardrobe are showcased, as are some incredible evening gowns worn by that most fashionable of royal icons, the late Princess Diana. Other displays interpret the symbolism of ceremonial court dress and also show the labor that went into producing this attire. Some dazzlers of note are the coronation robes of Queen Mary and George V and a regal mantua—a 6-foot-wide court dress that recalls the truth that part of the aristocratic game was to impress your fellow courtiers with your clothes.

Similarly, the State Apartments, especially the King's Apartments, reminded visitors none too subtly

PRINCESS DIANA

The late Diana, Princess of Wales lived at Kensington Palace until her death in 1997 and is possibly most notable by the absence of references to her, save for the display of her dresses in the Royal Ceremonial Dress Collection. Her apartments were in the northwest wing of the palace. People still leave flowers at the palace gates for her, particularly on the anniversary of her death.

of regal power. The King's Grand Staircase is the impressive starting point of the tour, with superb trompe-l'oeil paintings by William Kent showing courtiers looking down. The Presence Chamber (used for formal receptions), painted with mythical gods in the Italian "grotesque" style, is a red-and-gold assault on the eyes, packed with paintings. Look out for the cherubic overmantel carvings by Grinling Gibbons. Next follows the more intimate Privy Chamber, reflected by its comparatively tranquil decor. The Mortlake tapestries commissioned by Charles I represent the seasons, and the lavish painted ceiling alludes to the godlike status of monarchs. Roman columns and gilded decor in the Cupola Room, where Princess Victoria was christened, reminded the royal visitor that being admitted beyond the Presence Room was a mark of status (note that although the ceiling appears to be domed it's actually as flat as a pancake). These rooms lack chairs because only the monarch would have been seated.

Next come the rooms where Victoria had her ultrastrict upbringing, restored with items that belonged to her and Prince Albert. Originally part of the King's Apartments, these bedrooms and dressing rooms seem pleasantly domestic compared with the grandeur of the state rooms. The King's Gallery, which precedes the private apartments of Queen Anne, and later of Queen Mary, returns to the gilded theme—by Thornhill (of St. Paul's Cathedral fame)—with rich red damask walls. The copies of Van Dyck's Charles I portraits (the originals are at the Queen's Gallery, Buckingham Palace) dominate the scene, along with two pieces by Tintoretto. The tour ends with the Queen's Staircase, which leads into the garden: undoubtedly the true natural gem of the palace, and which provided the original attraction for the green-thumbed William and Mary. If you visit in spring, the tulips, which were a favorite of Mary's, reign supreme in a riot of color. The Orangery, built for Queen Anne, was the scene of many a royal family party; you can take a cup of tea here, before admiring the Sunken Garden with its fountains and Tudor design which echoes Hampton Court.

The palace was also home to the late Princess Margaret, and a photographic exhibition, "Number 1A Kensington Palace: from Courtiers' Lodgings to Royal Home," in her former apartments shows what life was like for the residents of this part of the palace from 1700. The Princess and Lord Snowdon transformed the place in the 1960s, mixing modern with 18th-century, a blend evidenced in the entrance hall, Snowdon's study, the guest bedroom, and garden room. ✉ *The Broad Walk, Kensington Gardens, Kensington, W8* ☎ *0870/751–5180 advance booking and information* ⊕ *www.hrp.org.uk* 🕮 *£11.50; discounted joint tickets for one other palace, specified at time of purchase, are available* ⊙ *Mar.–Oct., daily 10–6; Nov.–Feb., daily 10–5; last admission 1 hr before closing* Ⓤ *Queensway.*

Linley Sambourne House. Filled with delightful Victorian and Edwardian antiques, fabrics, and paintings, the home of *Punch* cartoonist Edward Linley Sambourne in the 1870s is one of the most charming 19th-century London houses extant—small wonder that it was used in Merchant and Ivory's *A Room with a View*. An Italianate house, it was the scene for society parties when Anne Messel was in residence in the 1940s. Being Kensington, there's a royal connection, too: her son, Antony Armstrong-Jones, married the late Princess Margaret, and their son has preserved the connection by taking the name Viscount Linley. Admission is by guided tours, given by costumed actors. There are set tour times on weekends, and you can call in advance for a tour appointment on other days. ✉ *18 Stafford Terr., Kensington, W8* ☎ *020/7602–3316* ⊕ *www.rbkc.gov.uk* 🕮 *£6* ⊙ *Guided tours weekends 10, 11:15, 1, 2:15, 3:30* Ⓤ *High St. Kensington.*

☾ **Natural History Museum.** Architect Alfred Waterhouse had relief pan-

Fodor'sChoice   els scattered across the outrageously ornate French Romanesque–style

★   terra-cotta facade of this museum, depicting extant creatures to the left of the entrance, extinct ones to the right. The museum is full of cutting-edge exhibits, with all the wow-power and interactives necessary to secure interest from younger visitors.

Upon entering the museum's central hall you'll come face-to-face with the most potent symbol of extinction—the dinosaurs—as a giant diplodocus skeleton dominates the many archways to the Life Galleries. From here you can follow the Waterhouse Way to further dinosaur exploration in Gallery 21, where velociraptors and oviraptors slug it out, *Jurassic Park*–style, in a vivid animatronic reconstruction. Don't be surprised when the dinos notice you—the fierce, animatronic Tyrannosaurus Rex senses when human prey is near and "responds" in character. Nearby, you can visit the first T. rex jaw ever discovered—its teeth are nearly 7 inches long. It's easy to spend all day here, but there are later developments of beastly evolution to discover: en route to the first of these, in the Human Biology Gallery (22), you pass through a birth-simulation chamber. In the Mammal Galleries (23 and 24), a massive 82-foot blue whale suspended on two levels is the centerpiece of the displays showing man's relationship with creatures large and small, from fossils to ferocious beasts. From here you can delve further into this field of biodiversity by continuing on to the new Darwin Centre, which show-

Historic Plaque Hunt

As you wander around London, you'll see lots of small, blue, circular plaques on the sides and facades of buildings, describing which famous, semifamous, or obscure but brilliant person once lived there. The first was placed outside Lord Byron's birthplace (now no more) by the Royal Society of Arts. There are around 700 blue plaques, erected by different bodies—you may even find some green ones which originated from Westminster City Council—but English Heritage now maintains the responsibility, and if you want to find out the latest, check the Web site ⊕www.english-heritage.org.uk. Below are some of the highlights:

James Barrie (100 Bayswater Rd., Hyde Park, W2); **Hector Berlioz** (58 Queen Anne St., Marylebone, W1); **Elizabeth Barrett Browning** (50 Wimpole St., Marylebone, W1); **Robert Browning** (17 Warwick Crescent, Hyde Park, W2); **Frederic Chopin** (4 St. James's Place, St. James's, W1); **Sir Winston Churchill** (28 Hyde Park Gate, Kensington, SW7); **Captain James Cook** (88 Mile End Rd., Mile End, E1); **T. S. Eliot** (3 Kensington Court Gardens, Kensington, W8); **Mahatma Gandhi** (20 Baron's Court Rd., West Kensington, W14); **George Frederic Handel** (25 Brook St., Mayfair, W1); **Karl Marx** (28 Dean St., Soho, W1); **Wolfgang Amadeus Mozart** (180 Ebury St., Belgravia, SW1); **Sir Isaac Newton** (87 Jermyn St., St. James's, SW1); **Florence Nightingale** (10 South St., Mayfair, W1); **George Bernard Shaw** (29 Fitzroy Sq., Bloomsbury, W1); **Percy Bysshe Shelley** (15 Poland St., Soho, W1); **Mark Twain** (23 Tedworth Sq., Chelsea, SW3); **Oscar Wilde** (34 Tite St., Chelsea, SW3); **William Butler Yeats** (23 Fitzroy Rd., Camden, NW1).

cases the museum's entire collection—all 22 million creatures—from a tiny Seychellian frog to the Komodo dragon lizard. In the Creepy Crawlies Gallery (33), there's a super-enlarged scorpion so nightmarish that it makes tarantulas seem cute. If this is your field of fun, then you might want to zip down to the basement for hands-on activities in the Investigate section, where you can handle actual objects, from old bones to bugs.

The Earth Galleries are also unmissable, if you have the time and stamina, and could make an alternative museum tour beginning, as there's a secondary museum entrance at the Exhibition Road end. No less stunning in effect, a giant escalator takes you into a globe, around which are representations of our solar system. There is a choice of levels—and Earth surfaces—to explore, such as "The Power Within" (Gallery 61), where you can feel an earthquake simulation and get the inside facts on volcanoes. The museum has an outdoor ice-skating rink from November to January, and a very popular Christmas fair. ✉ *Cromwell Rd., South Kensington, SW7* ☎ *020/7942–5000* ⊕ *www.nhm.ac.uk* ✆ *Free* ⊙ *Daily 10–5:50, last admission 5:30; daily tours from main information desk* Ⓤ *South Kensington.*

Royal Albert Hall. This domed, circular 8,000-seat auditorium (as well as the Albert Memorial, opposite) was made possible by the Victorian public, who donated funds for it. More money was raised by selling 1,300 future seats at £100 apiece—not for the first night but for every night for 999 years. (Some descendants of purchasers still use the seats.) The Albert Hall is best known for its annual July–September BBC Promenade Concerts (the "Proms"), with bargain-price standing (or promenading, or sitting-on-the-floor) tickets sold on the night of concert. *For more on Royal Albert Hall, see Arts & Entertainment, Chapter 18.* ⊠*Kensington Gore, Kensington, SW7* ☎*020/7589–8212* ⊕*www. royalalberthall.co.uk* ⊡*Prices vary with event* Ⓤ*South Kensington.*

Royal Hospital. The hospice for elderly and infirm soldiers was founded by Charles II in 1682 as his troops had hitherto enjoyed not so much as a meager pension and were growing restive after the civil wars of 1642–46 and 1648. Charles wisely appointed the great architect Sir Christopher Wren to design this small village of brick and Portland stone set in manicured gardens (which you can visit) surrounding the Figure Court—named after the 1692 bronze figure of Charles II dressed up as a Roman soldier—and the Great Hall (dining room) and chapel. The latter is enhanced by the choir stalls of Grinling Gibbons (who did the bronze of Charles, too), the former by a vast oil of Charles on horseback by Antonio Verrio, and both are open to the public.

The "Chelsea Pensioners" are recognizable by their traditional scarlet frock coats with gold buttons, medals, and tricorne hats. The pensioners celebrate Charles II's birthday—May 29, Oak Apple Day—by draping oak leaves on his statue and parading around it in memory of a hollow oak tree that expedited the king's miraculous escape from the 1651 Battle of Worcester. Also in May, and usually the third week, the Chelsea Flower Show, the year's highlight for thousands of garden-obsessed Brits, is held here. Run by the Royal Horticultural Society, the mammoth event takes up vast acreage here, and the surrounding streets throng with visitors. ⊠*Royal Hospital Rd., Chelsea, SW3* ☎*020/7730–0161* ⊕*www.chelsea-pensioners.org.uk* ⊡*Free* ⊗*Mon.–Sat. 10–noon and 2–4* Ⓤ*Sloane Sq.*

Saatchi Gallery. Charles Saatchi, who made his fortune building an advertising empire that successfully "rebranded" Margaret Thatcher's Conservative Party, is an astute art collector who has made acquisitions that regularly create headlines. Saatchi's personal collection, exhibited in his large private gallery, reflects the leading edge of the British avant-garde. Paula Rego, Damien Hirst, Rachel Whiteread, Janine Antoni, and Tracey Emin have all been shown. At this writing, the new location in Chelsea, complete with stark white galleries, a bookshop and café, was scheduled to open by fall 2007; check the Web site for updates. ⊠*Duke of Yorks HQ Building, Kings Rd., Chelsea, SW3* ☎*020/7823–2363* ⊕*www.saatchi-gallery.co.uk* Ⓤ*Sloane Sq.*

Ⓒ   **Science Museum.** This, the third of the great South Kensington museums, Fodor's Choice   stands behind the Natural History Museum in a far plainer building. It ★   has loads of hands-on exhibits, with entire schools of children apparently decanted inside to interact with them; but it is, after all, painlessly educational. Highlights include the Launch Pad gallery, which demonstrates basic scientific principles (try the plasma ball, where your hands attract "lightning"—if you can get them on it); *Puffing Billy,* the oldest steam locomotive in the world; and the actual *Apollo 10* capsule. But don't be mistaken in thinking this is kids-only territory—there's plenty here for all ages. The Wellcome Wing, a space-age addition devoted to contemporary science, medicine, and technology, includes a 450-seat IMAX cinema. ⊠*Exhibition Rd., South Kensington, SW7* ☎*0870/870–4868* ⊕*www. sciencemuseum.org.uk* ✉*Free, charge for the cinema shows and special exhibitions* ☉*Daily 10–6* Ⓤ*South Kensington.*

♻ **Victoria & Albert Museum.** Recognizable by the copy of Victoria's impe-
Fodor'sChoice rial crown on the lantern above the central cupola, this institution is
★ always referred to as the V&A. It's a huge museum, showcasing the applied arts of all disciplines, all periods, all nationalities, and all tastes, and it's a wonderful, generous place to get lost in, full of innovation and completely devoid of pretension. Prince Albert, Victoria's adored consort, was responsible for the genesis of this permanent version of the 1851 Great Exhibition, and his queen laid its foundation stone in her final public London appearance, in 1899. From the start, the V&A had an important role as a research institution, and that role continues today.

There are many beautiful diversions: one minute you're gazing on the Jacobean oak four-poster Great Bed of Ware (one of the V&A's most prized possessions, given that Shakespeare immortalized it in *Twelfth Night*) and the next you're in the celebrated Dress Collection, coveting a Jean Muir frock. ▪TIP➡ **As a whirlwind introduction, you could take a free, one-hour daily tour, or a 30-minute version on Wednesday evening. Otherwise, follow your own whims around the enormous space, but updated areas of the museum are worthy destinations.**

The British Galleries are an ambitious addition that heralds British art and design from 1500 to 1900. Here you'll see such major pieces as George Gilbert Scott's model of the Albert Memorial, and the first-ever English fork made in 1632, but you'll also discover fascinating facts behind the designs, such as the construction of a 16th-century bed and the best way for women in cumbersome hooped skirts to negotiate getting in and out of carriages. Throughout the galleries are interactive corners for all ages, where you can discover, design, and build—from your own family emblem to period chairs. The Whiteley Silver Galleries, opened in October 2002, bring more than 500 shining examples of silver together. From ancient medieval reliquaries to the Napoleonic period, to contemporary pieces, it's a stunning collection, and the largest in the United Kingdom.

The Jameel Gallery of Islamic Art opened in 2005 with a fresh display of the museum's collection of Islamic decorative arts: on show are ceramics and fine textiles, portraits from Iran's Qajar period, and the exquisite Erbil carpet, lit up once every 20 minutes for better viewing. The fourth floor Architecture Gallery brings together riches from the RIBA (Royal Institute of British Architects) archives and the V&A's architectural col-

AT A GLANCE

Kensington & Chelsea Dining

MODERATE DINING

Aubaine, French, 260–262 Brompton Rd.

The Pig's Ear, Modern British, 35 Old Church St.

PJ's Bar & Grill, American, 52 Fulham Rd.

Racine, Brasserie, 239 Brompton Rd.

EXPENSIVE DINING

Bibendum, Modern British, Michelin House, 81 Fulham Rd.

Gordon Ramsay at Royal Hospital Road, French, 68–69 Royal Hospital Rd.

Tom Aikens, French, 43 Elystan St.

AFTERNOON TEA

Kandy Tea House, 4 Holland St.

The Orangery at Kensington Palace, Kensington Gardens

lection. It's a fascinating, interactive space, with architectural models, plans, and manuscripts.

Unchanged, but still spectacular, is the Glass Gallery, where a collection spanning four millennia is reflected between room-size mirrors under designer Danny Lane's breathtaking glass balustrade. The V&A's outstanding glass collection includes a massive Dale Chihuly chandelier in the entrance dome—the only Chihuly piece on public display in the U.K. Don't miss the pure art, too: the Raphael Galleries house seven massive cartoons the painter completed in 1516 for his Sistine Chapel tapestries (now in the Pinoteca of the Vatican Museums in Rome). ■ TIP→**The V&A has many interesting lectures, tours, and special events, especially on the late-opening days and weekends—peruse the Web site before you leave for London.** The huge, walk-through shop is the museum in microcosm, and quite the best place to buy art nouveau or arts-and-crafts gifts. ✉ *Cromwell Rd., South Kensington, SW7* ☎ *020/7942–2000* 🌐 *www.vam.ac.uk* 🎫 *Free* ⏲ *Thurs.–Tues. 10–5:45, Wed. and last Fri. of month 10–10; tours daily at 10:30, 11:30, 1:30, and 3:30, and Wed. at 7:30* PM Ⓤ *South Kensington.*

Knightsbridge & Belgravia

Arriving at Harrods

WORD OF MOUTH

"We walked through small streets of Knightsbridge, just beautiful on a sunny crisp Sunday morning, and came along the side of the [Brompton] Oratory.… We had a few minutes to explore the Oratory (neo-renaissance style) before the 11:00 Mass, which was sung in Latin. It was quite the ethereal experience as we drifted into dozing with what sounded like the heavenly chorus for our lullabye. The homily was quite good (I was awake for that part), and the church was full."

—noe847

GETTING ORIENTED

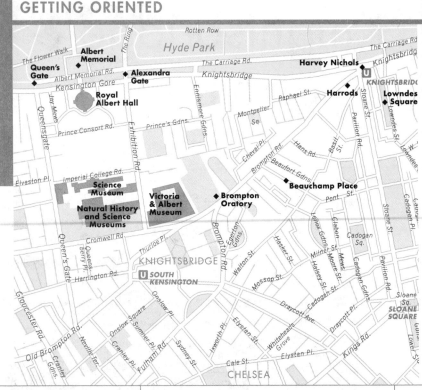

GETTING HERE

For Knightsbridge, take the Piccadilly Line to Knightsbridge Station, then either the Harrods exit on Brompton Road (or, for Harvey Nichols, the Sloane Street exit). Hyde Park Corner on the Piccadilly Line is near the northeast corner of Belgrave Square, while Victoria Station (District, Circle, and Victoria lines) and Sloane Square (District and Circle lines) are equidistant from the shops along Elizabeth Street.

TOP 5 REASONS TO GO

■ **Harrods food halls:** Notice the glistening mosaic of fresh fish under the actual mosaic ceilings of these esteemed underground culinary corridors.

■ **Harvey Nichols:** Find a designer dress in your size, for 80% off, in the Harvey Nicks January sales.

■ **Brompton Oratory:** Listen to the Schola Cantorum, with its brilliant boys' choir, sing a Mozart Mass.

■ **Beauchamp Place:** Spot celebs at the latest hot restaurant while taking a break from your shopping marathon.

■ **Patisserie Valerie:** Sink your teeth into a Paris Brest pastry at the venerable, art nouveau patisserie on Brompton Road.

NEAREST PUBLIC RESTROOMS

If you need a restroom, choose Harvey Nicks over Harrods. Harrods charges £1 to use its highly luxurious facilities.

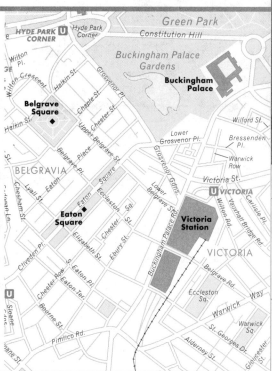

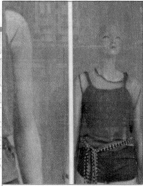

MAKING THE MOST OF YOUR TIME

Spending time here is mostly about stamina. Take a break between Harvey Nichols and Harrods to shop in smaller stores, stroll Beauchamp Place, or have a snack. To do justice to this area, don't plan on visiting far-away shopping neighborhoods on the same day. St. James's and Mayfair, including Fortnum's and the Bond Street arcades, are close enough for determined shoppers.

There's not much to do in Belgravia besides stroll leisurely and soak up the atmosphere. If you rush up and down its streets, you'll have missed the point.

10

A GOOD WALK

Just across Knightsbridge, at the end of Sloane Street, brave the complicated pedestrian crossing and go under the arch of the building that straddles the street. You'll be in Hyde Park, near the Hyde Park Barracks of one of the Queen's Household Regiments. If you're lucky, you may catch them exercising the horses on Rotten Row.

FEELING PECKISH?

With five branches, **Pâtisserie Valerie** (⊠ *215 Brompton Rd., SW3* ☎ *020/7832–9971*) is a London institution. The one down the road from Harrods, across from the Brompton Oratory, serves light meals and dazzling pastries in a bustling atmosphere.

Yo! Sushi is one of the quick, casual restaurants on Harvey Nichol's fifth floor.

The **Café** in Harvey Nicks is great for shopping breaks, light meals, and people-watching as well.

SAFETY

Knightsbridge is a safe area, but beware of pickpockets in crowded Tube stations and department stores. Quiet Belgravia is so heavily watched by a mélange of doormen, chauffeurs, embassy security staff, and security cameras that it feels like the safest place on earth. Still, remain alert, and don't flash expensive watches and jewelry.

Sightseeing
☆☆☆☆★

Nightlife
☆☆☆☆★

Dining
☆☆☆★★

Lodging
☆☆★★★

Shopping
★★★★★

Britain's reputation as a nation of shopkeepers is well kept in Knightsbridge, home of Harrods, Harvey Nichols, and the latest international designers, as well as a clutch of jewelers where you can drop some serious cash on very serious baubles. In short: Knightsbridge is *must*-go territory for shopaholics. In Belgravia, to the east, the frenetic pace is replaced with all the peace and quiet money can buy. Grand, white terraces of aristocratic town houses, part of the Grosvenor estate, are owned by the Dukes of Westminster. Many are leased to embassies but a remarkable number remain homes of the discreet, private wealthy.

WHAT'S HERE

There's no getting away from it. This is shop-'til-you-drop territory of the highest order. With two world-famous department stores, **Harrods** and **Harvey Nichols,** a few hundred yards apart, and every bit of space between and around taken up with designer boutiques, chain stores, and jewelers, it's hard to imagine why anyone who doesn't like shopping would even think of coming here.

If the department stores seem overwhelming, **Beauchamp Place** (pronounced "Beecham"), a left off Brompton Road and four streets west of Harrods, is a good tonic. It's lined with equally chic and expensive boutiques, but they tend to be smaller, more personal, and less hectic.

Another place to find peace and quiet (of a less expensive kind) is **Brompton Oratory,** the area's ornate and historic Catholic Church. If you're lucky, you may catch a rehearsal of the church's famous boys' choir. Remember this is an active place of worship.

Once you've maxed out your credit cards, a peaceful stroll in Belgravia may be just the thing. Walk east along the Brompton Road until it ends at Knightsbridge (the name of a street as well as the district) across Sloane Street. Pass Harvey Nichols and turn right into **Lowndes Square.** At the bottom of the square, continue on Lowndes Street to **West Halkin Street,** which leads into **Belgrave Square.** These are some of the grandest houses in London and, although many of them are embassies, several are still private homes.

Leave the square along Belgrave Place, admiring the lovely, Westminster-white houses. **Eaton Square,** lined with substantial terraces, most divided into large flats

A BRIEF HISTORY

Like the Westbourne River, bridged in the ancient past to give this area its name, the history of Knightsbridge is buried under modern London. In the mid-16th century it was the site of a leper colony and considered a dangerous, malodorous place—a far cry from today, when the biggest dangers are to your bank balance. Belgravia is part of a nearly 300-acre central-London estate formed by a marriage of noble families in 1677. It was used as waste ground for grazing sheep until developed by Thomas Cubitt in the 19th century.

or town houses, is the next major intersection. Often, the only people on the streets are professional dog walkers and chauffeurs. Turn right on Eaton Square, and right again after one block, onto **Elizabeth Street.** Some people call this area Belgravia, others Pimlico–Victoria. Either way, now that you've had a break, it's time to shop again, and this street is the place to be.

PLACES TO EXPLORE

Belgrave Square. The square, as well as the streets leading off it, are genuine elite territory and have been since they were built in the mid-1800s. The grand, porticoed mansions were created as town residences for courtiers, conveniently close to the monarch—Buckingham Palace is virtually around the corner. Walk down Belgrave Place toward Eaton Place and you pass two of Belgravia's most beautiful mews: Eaton Mews North and Eccleston Mews, both fronted by grand Westminster-white rusticated entrances right out of a 19th-century engraving. ■ TIP➡Traffic really whips around Belgrave Square so be careful.

Brompton Oratory. This is a late product of the mid-19th-century English Roman Catholic revival led by John Henry Cardinal Newman (1801–90), who established the oratory in 1884 and whose statue you see outside. Architect Herbert Gribble, a previously unknown 29-year-old, won the competition to design the place, an honor that you may conclude went to his head when you see the vast, incredibly ornate interior. It's punctuated by treasures far older than the church itself, like the giant *Twelve Apostles* in the nave, carved from Carrara marble by Giuseppe Mazzuoli in the 1680s and brought here from Siena's cathedral. ✉ *Brompton Rd., Kensington, SW7* ☎ *020/7808–0900* ⊕ *www.bromptonoratory.com* ✉ *Free* ⊗ *6:30 AM–8 PM. Services weekdays 7 AM, 10, 12:30, and 6 PM, Sat. 7 AM, 8:30 Latin, 10, and 6 PM; Sun. 7 AM, 8,*

10

Knightsbridge & Belgravia Dining

MODERATE DINING	EXPENSIVE DINING	AFTERNOON TEA
Amaya, Indian, 15–19 Halkin Arcade, Motcomb St.	**The Capital,** French, 22–24 Basil St.	**Harrods,** 87–135 Brompton Rd.
The Enterprise, Modern British, 35 Walton St.	**Le Cercle,** Modern French, 1 Wilbraham Pl.	**The Lanesborough,** Hyde Park Corner
La Poule au Pot, French, 231 Ebury St.	**Rasoi Vineet Bhatia,** Indian, 10 Lincoln St.	
	Zafferano, Italian, 15 Lowndes St.	
	Zuma, Japanese, 5 Raphael St.	

9 *Tridentine Latin, 10, 11 Sung Latin), 12:30, 4:30* PM, *and 7* Ⓤ *South Kensington.*

Harrods. Just in case you don't notice it, this well-known shopping destination frames its domed terra-cotta Edwardian outline in thousands of white lights each night. The 15-acre Egyptian-owned store's sales weeks are world-class, and inside it's as frenetic as a stock-market floor. Its motto, *Omnia, omnibus, ubique* (Everything, for everyone, everywhere) is not too far from the truth. Don't miss the extravagant Food Hall, with its stunning art nouveau tiling in the neighborhood of meat and poultry and continuing on in the fishmongers' territory, where its glory is rivaled by displays of the sea produce itself. *For more on Harrods, see* ⇨ *Shopping, Chapter 19.* ✉ *87–135 Brompton Rd., Knightsbridge, SW1* ☎ *020/7730–1234* ⊕ *www.harrods.com* ☉ *Mon.–Sat. 10–7, Sun. noon–6* Ⓤ *Knightsbridge.*

Harvey Nichols. This is fashionista central and a must for anyone who has been watching *Absolutely Fabulous,* dahling—in which case you'll already know to call it Harvey Nicks. The housewares on the fourth floor are as deliciously of the moment as the clothing and accessories for men and women. *For more on Harvey Nichols, see* ⇨ *Shopping, Chapter 19.* ✉ *109–125 Knightsbridge, Knightsbridge, SW1* ☎ *020/7235–5000* ⊕ *www.harveynichols.com* ☉ *Mon.–Sat. 10–8, Sun. noon–6* Ⓤ *Knightsbridge.*

Notting Hill & Bayswater

Bayswater Road

WORD OF MOUTH

"Half a mile east of Notting Hill is Bayswater, where the Tube station is surrounded by small cafés, restaurants, and shops, often with an Arabic flavor ..."

—ben_haines_london

GETTING ORIENTED

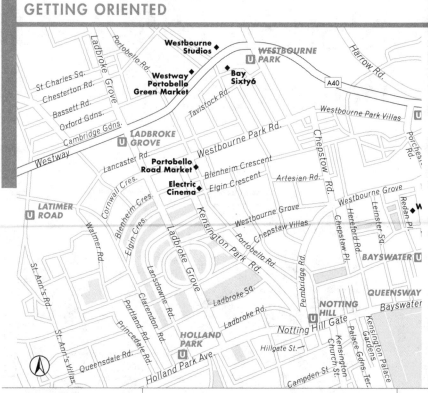

GETTING THERE

For Portobello Market and environs, the best Tube stops are Ladbroke Grove and Westbourne Park (Hammersmith and City lines); ask for directions when you emerge. The Notting Hill stop on the District, Circle, and Central lines enables you to walk the length of Portobello Road on a downhill gradient.

A GOOD WALK

To gape at Notting Hill's grandest houses, stroll over to Lansdowne Road, Lansdowne Crescent, and Lansdowne Square—two blocks west of Kensington Park Row.

TOP 5 REASONS TO GO

■ **Westbourne Grove:** People-watch at a sidewalk café in this swank section of the neighborhood.

■ **Portobello Road Market:** Seek and ye shall find; go early-morning antiques hunting at London's most famous market.

■ **Notting Hill shopping:** Browse for vintage designer pieces at Notting Hill's numerous secondhand and retro clothing stores.

■ **Notting Hill Carnival:** Experience the explosion of color, culture, and music that is the Notting Hill Carnival, held over two days every August bank holiday.

■ **Electric Cinema:** Catch a movie reclined on a two-seater leather sofa, beer and bar snacks at hand.

MAKING THE MOST OF YOUR TIME

Saturday is Notting Hill and Portobello Road's most fun and frenetic day. You could easily spend a whole day shopping, eating, and drinking here. You may prefer to start at the end of Portobello Road and work backward, using the parks for relaxation after your shopping exertions. Do the same on Friday if you're a flea-market fan. Sunday, the Hyde Park and Kensington Gardens railings all along Bayswater Road are hung with dubious art, which may slow your progress; this is also prime perambulation day for locals. The perimeter of the two parks alone covers a good 4 mi, and it's about half as far again around the remainder of the route. You could cut out a lot of park without missing out on essential sights and walk the whole thing in a brisk three hours.

SAFETY

At night, be wary of straying too far off the main streets as it gets "edgier" toward Ladbroke Grove's high-rise estates and surrounding areas.

FEELING PECKISH?

For healthy fast food, it's hard to beat the canteen at **Fresh & Wild** (⊠ *208–212 Westbourne Grove* ☎ *020/7229–1063*). In addition to the stellar salad bar, there are daily hot specials. Once you've had your fill, stock up on tasty snacks from the store for later, too.

Tea houses are back in vogue in the capital, with celebrity clientele airing their graces at **Tea Palace** (⊠ *175 Westbourne Grove* ☎ *020/7727–2600*). Choose from 150 different infusions.

Sightseeing
☆☆★★★

Nightlife
☆☆★★★

Dining
☆☆★★★

Lodging
☆☆★★★

Shopping
☆★★★★

North of the Royal Parks and once the estate of the Bishop of London's trustees, Bayswater is now a bustling hub of tourist restaurants, mid-price hotels, and high street shopping. To the west is the more enticing Notting Hill, a trend-setting square mile of ethnicity, music, and markets, with lots of restaurants to see and be seen in, as well as younger, more egalitarian modern-art galleries. The style-watching media here dubbed the local residents Notting Hillbillies. The whole area has mushroomed around one of the world's great antiques markets, Portobello Road. A Saturday morning spent here is almost obligatory, and people travel from all boroughs of the capital to soak up its chic, multicultural vibe, where the cool urban crowd meets and melds with the posh people of West London.

WHAT'S HERE

In Bayswater, the main thoroughfare of **Queensway** is a rather peculiar, cosmopolitan street of ethnic confusion, late-night cafés and restaurants, a skating rink, and the **Whiteleys** shopping-and-movie mall. Turn left at the end into **Westbourne Grove,** however, and you've entered the Notting Hill of the film sets, replete with chic boutiques and charity shops laden with the cast-offs from wealthy residents. You'll reach the famous **Portobello Road** after a few blocks, with the beautifully restored early-20th-century **Electric Cinema** at No. 191. Turn left for the Saturday antiques market and shops, right to reach the Westway overpass and the grocery and flea market. The stalls at **Westway Portobello Green Market** are occupied by junk, bric-a-brac, secondhand threads, and clothes and accessories by young, up-and-coming designers. Nearby on Acklam Road are the **Westbourne**

Continued on p. 182

HYDE PARK & KENSINGTON GARDENS

Every year millions of visitors descend on the royal parks of Hyde Park and Kensington Gardens, which sit side by side and roll out over 625 acres of grassy expanses that provide much-craved-for respite from London's frenetic pace. The two parks incorporate formal gardens, fountains, sports fields, great picnic spots, shady clusters of ancient trees, and even an outdoor swimming pool.

(counterclockwise from top right)
Morning fog on Rotten Row, Hyde Park

Albert Memorial

Diana Princess of Wales Memorial Playground

Inline-skating, Hyde Park

Although it's probably been centuries since any major royal had a casual stroll here— you're more likely to bump into Madonna and Guy Ritchie than Her Royal Highness these days—the parks remain the property of the Crown, which saved them from being devoured by the city's late-18th-century growth spurt.

Today the luxury of such wide open spaces continues to be appreciated by the Londoners who steal into the parks before work for a session of tai chi, say, or on weekends when the sun is shining. Simply sitting back in a hired deck chair or strolling through the varied terrain is one of the most enjoyable ways to spend time here.

KENSINGTON GARDENS

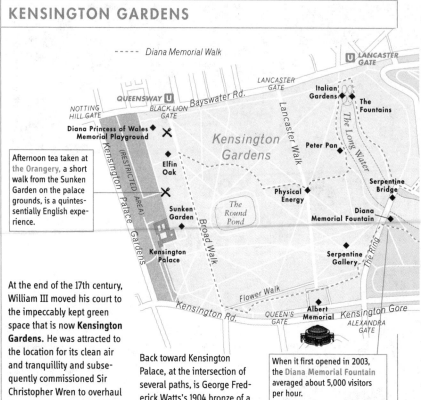

Afternoon tea taken at the Orangery, a short walk from the Sunken Garden on the palace grounds, is a quintessentially English experience.

At the end of the 17th century, William III moved his court to the impeccably kept green space that is now **Kensington Gardens.** He was attracted to the location for its clean air and tranquillity and subsequently commissioned Sir Christopher Wren to overhaul the original redbrick building, resulting in the splendid **Kensington Palace.**

To the north of the palace complex is the early-20th-century **Sunken Garden,** complete with a living tunnel of lime trees (i.e., linden trees) and golden laburnum.

On western side of the **Long Water** is George Frampton's 1912 *Peter Pan,* a bronze of the boy who lived on an island in the Serpentine and never grew up and whose creator, J.M. Barrie, lived at 100 Bayswater Road, not 500 yards from here.

Back toward Kensington Palace, at the intersection of several paths, is George Frederick Watts's 1904 bronze of a muscle-bound horse and rider, entitled **Physical Energy.** The **Round Pond** is a magnet for model-boat enthusiasts and duck feeders.

Near the Broad Walk, toward Black Lion Gate, is the **Diana Princess of Wales Memorial Playground,** an enclosed space with specially designed structures and areas on the theme of Barrie's Neverland. Hook's ship, crocodiles, "jungles" of foliage, and islands of sand provide a fantasy land for kids—more than 70,000 visit every year. Just outside its bounds is Ivor Innes's *Elfin*

When it first opened in 2003, the Diana Memorial Fountain averaged about 5,000 visitors per hour.

Oak, the remains of a tree carved with scores of tiny woodland creatures.

One of the park's most striking monuments is the **Albert Memorial.** This Victorian high-Gothic celebration of Prince Albert is adorned with marble statues representing his interests and amusements.

Diminutive as it may be, the **Serpentine Gallery** has not been afraid of courting controversy with its temporary exhibitions of challenging contemporary works.

11

HYDE PARK & KENSINGTON GARDENS

HYDE PARK

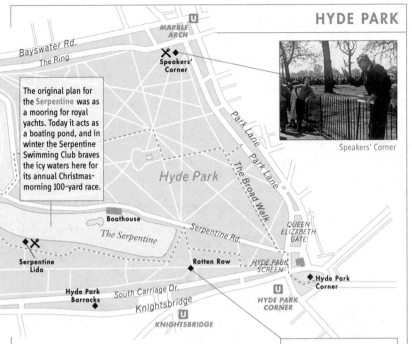

MARBLE ARCH

Bayswater Rd.

The Ring

Speakers' Corner

The original plan for the Serpentine was as a mooring for royal yachts. Today it acts as a boating pond, and in winter the Serpentine Swimming Club braves the icy waters here for its annual Christmas-morning 100-yard race.

Park Lane

Park Lane

The Broad Walk

Hyde Park

Boathouse

The Serpentine

Serpentine Rd.

QUEEN ELIZABETH GATE

Serpentine Lido

Rotten Row

HYDE PARK SCREEN

Hyde Park Corner

Hyde Park Barracks

South Carriage Dr.

Knightsbridge

HYDE PARK CORNER

KNIGHTSBRIDGE

Speakers' Corner

Hyde Park was once the hunting ground of King Henry VIII. This stout, bawdy royal more or less stole Hyde Park, along with the smaller St. James's and Green parks, from the monks of Westminster in 1536. The public wasn't to be granted access to Hyde Park's delights until James I came to the throne and opened up limited parts to "respectably dressed" plebeians.

It was Charles I, in the 1700s, however, who was to shape the Hyde Park that visitors see today. Once he had created **the Ring** (North Carriage Drive), which forms a curve north of the **Serpentine** and boathouses, Charles allowed the general public to roam free. During the Great Plague of

1665, East Enders and City dwellers fled to the park, seeking refuge from the black bilious disease.

The stone **Serpentine Bridge**, built in 1826 by George Rennie, marks the boundary between Hyde Park and Kensington Gardens. **Rotten Row,** a corruption of the French *route de roi* (king's road), runs along the southeastern edge of Hyde Park and is still used by the Household Cavalry, who live at the **Hyde Park Barracks**—a high-rise and a long, low, ugly red block—to the left. This is where the brigade that mounts the guard at Buckingham Palace resides; you can see them at about 10:30 AM, as they leave to perform their duty in full regalia, plumed

Rotten Row was the first artificially lit highway in Britain. In the late 17th century, William III was concerned that his walk to from Kensington Palace to St. James's Park was too dangerous, so he ordered 300 lamps to be placed along the route.

helmets and all, or await the return of the guard about noon.

On the south side of the 1930s **Serpentine Lido** (open to swimmers from June to September) is the £3.6 million oval **Diana Memorial Fountain**.

Ever since the 1827 legislation of public assembly, **Speakers' Corner** near Marble Arch has provided an outlet for political debate: on Sundays, it's an unmissable spectacle of vehement, sometimes comical, and always entertaining orators.

ENJOYING THE PARKS

Ride. **Hyde Park Riding Stables** keeps horses for hacking the sand tracks. Group lessons (usually just a few people) are £49 per person per hour, £53 on weekends. Private lessons are £65 Tuesday–Friday, £85 on weekends. ⊠ 63 Bathurst Mews, Bayswater W2 ☎ 020/7723-2813 ⊕ www.hydeparkstables.com Ⓤ Lancaster Gate.

Row. **The Serpentine** has paddleboats and rowboats for £6 per person per hour, kids £2.50, March through October from 10 AM to 5 PM, later in good weather in summer. ☎ 020/7262-1330).

Run. You can run a **4-mi route** around the perimeter of Hyde Park and Kensington Gardens or a **2½-mi route** in Hyde Park alone if you start at Hyde Park Corner or Marble Arch and encircle the Serpentine.

Skate. On Friday, skaters of intermediate ability and upward meet at 8 PM at the Duke of Wellington Arch, Hyde Park Corner, for the **Friday Night Skate,** an enthusiastic two-hour mass skating session, complete with music and whistles. If you're a bit unsure on your wheels, arrive at 7:30 PM for the free lesson on how to stop. The **Sunday Rollerstroll,** a more laid-back version of the same thing, runs on Sunday afternoons; meet at 2 PM ⊕ www.thefns.com Ⓤ Hyde Park Corner.

Swim. **Serpentine Lido** is technically a beach on a lake, but a hot day in Hyde Park is surreally reminiscent of the seaside. There are changing facilities, and the swimming section is chlorinated. There is also a paddling pool, sandpit, and kids' entertainer in the afternoons. It's open daily from June through September, 10–5:30; admission £3.50, children £0.80 (£0.60 after 4 PM). ☎ 020/7706-3422 ⊕ www.serpentinelido.com Ⓤ Knightsbridge.

WHERE TO REFUEL

✕ The **Lido Café,** near the Diana Memorial Fountain, has plenty of seating with views across the Serpentine Lake.

✕ The **Honest Sausage** at Speakers' Corner is the place to grab a free-range sausage sandwich or organic bacon roll before enjoying the circus of debate.

✕ The **Broadwalk Café & Playcafe** next to the Diana Memorial Playground has a children's menu.

✕ The **Orangery** beside Kensington Palace is a distinctly more grown-up affair for tea and cakes.

SPEAKERS' CORNER

Once the site of public executions and the Tyburn hanging trees, the corner of Hyde Park at Cumberland Gate and Park Lane now harbors one of London's most public spectacles: Speakers' Corner. This has been a place of assembly and vitriolic outpourings and debates since the mid-19th century. The pageant of free speech takes place every Sunday afternoon.

Anyone is welcome to mount a soapbox and declaim upon any topic, which makes for an irresistible showcase of eccentricity—one such being the (now-deceased) Protein Man. Wearing his publicity board, the Protein Man proclaimed that the eating of meat, cheese, and peanuts led to uncontrollable acts of passion that would destroy Western civilization. The pamphlets he sold for four decades along the length and breadth of Oxford Street are now collector's items. Other more strait-laced campaigns have been launched here by the Chartists, the Reform League, the May Day demonstrators, and the Suffragettes.

PRACTICAL INFO

ADMISSION: Free for both parks

HOURS: Kensington Gardens 6 AM–dusk; Hyde Park 5 AM–midnight

CONTACT INFO: ☎ 020/7298–2100, ⊕ www.royalparks.gov.uk

GETTING HERE: Ⓤ **Kensington Gardens:** Kensington High Street, Queensway, Lancaster Gate, South Kensington. **Hyde Park:** Hyde Park Corner, Knightsbridge, Lancaster Gate, Marble Arch

EVENTS: Major events, such as rock concerts and festivals, road races, and talks, are regular features of the parks' calendar; check online for what's on during your visit.

Each summer, a different modern architect designs an outdoor pavilion for the Serpentine Gallery, the venue for outdoor film screenings, readings, and other such cultural soirees.

From June to August, Hyde Park hosts the Royal Parks Summer Festival, with live jazz evenings, opera, and plays all over the park grounds.

(left) Horseback riding, Hyde Park

(top) The Fountains, Kensington Gardens

(bottom) The Serpentine, Hyde Park

TOURS: There are **themed guided walks** about once a month, usually on Thursday or Friday afternoons. They are free but must be booked in advance. Check online or call the park offices for dates and details.

A 45-minute tour (£4.50) of the **Albert Memorial** is available. It's held at 2 and 3 PM on the first Sunday of the month. There's no need to book in advance unless you are part of a big group, in which case call 020/7495–0916.

Kensington Palace is open for tours daily 10–6 (last admission at 5). For tickets (£11.50) and information call 0870/751–5180 or visit www.hrp.org.uk.

Studios, an office complex with a gallery, restaurant, and bar open to the public, and the capital's best skateboarding park, **Bay Sixty6.**

PLACES TO EXPLORE

★ **Portobello Road.** Tempted by tassels, looking for a 19th-century snuff spoon, an ancient print of North Africa, or a dashingly deco frock (just don't believe the dealer when he says the Vionnet label just fell off), or hunting for a gracefully Georgian silhouette of the Earl of Chesterfield? Head to Portobello Road, world famous for its Saturday antiques market (arrive before 9 AM to find the real treasures-in-the-trash; after 10, the crowds pack in wall to wall). Actually, the Portobello Market is three markets: antiques, "fruit and veg," and a flea market. The street begins at Notting Hill Gate, though the antiques stalls start a couple of blocks north, around Chepstow Villas. Lining the sloping street are also dozens of antiques shops and indoor markets, open most days—in fact, serious collectors will want to do Portobello on a weekday, when they can explore the 90-some antiques and art stores in relative peace. Where the road levels off, around Elgin Crescent, youth culture and a vibrant neighborhood life kick in, with all manner of interesting small stores and restaurants interspersed with the fruit and vegetable market. This continues to the Westway overpass ("flyover" in British), where London's best flea market (high-class, vintage, antique, and secondhand clothing; jewelry; and junk) happens Friday and Saturday, then on up to Golborne Road. There's a strong West Indian flavor to Notting Hill, with a Trinidad-style Carnival centered along Portobello Road on the August bank-holiday weekend. *(For more on Portobello Road, see ⇨ Shopping, Chapter 19.)* Ⓤ *Notting Hill Gate, Ladbroke Grove.*

QUEEN'S ICE BOWL

London's most central year-round ice-skating rink is the **Queens Ice Bowl,** where the per-session cost, including skate rental, is £6.50 for both adults and children. ✉ *17 Queensway, Bayswater, W2* ☏ *020/7229–0172* Ⓤ *Queensway.*

Regent's Park & Hampstead

Lord's Cricket Ground

WORD OF MOUTH

"I lived [in Hampstead] many years ago, and loved walking around the neighborhood—past John Keats house, the cafe where Orwell used to play chess, pubs, and of course the Heath."

—Carlux

GETTING ORIENTED

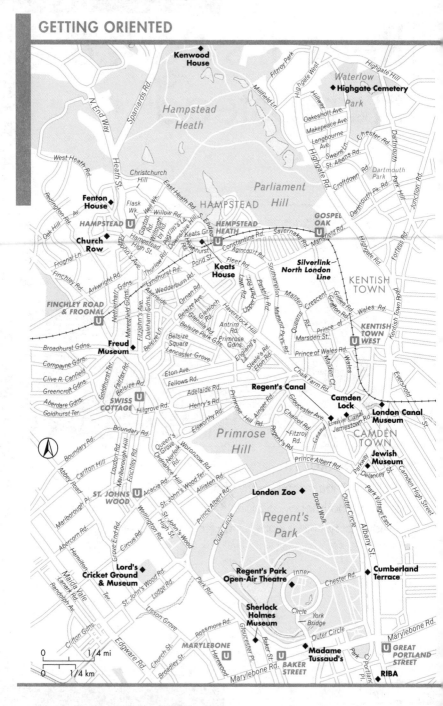

12

TOP 5 REASONS TO GO

■ **Primrose Hill:** Tackle the hill on a beautiful day with a friend, a stocked picnic basket, and a blanket, then enjoy the view from the top for a few long hours.

■ **Queen's Pub:** Nurse a pint at this Regent's Park Road pub where celebrities have been known to pop in.

■ **London Zoo:** Traipse through the walk-through forest and come face-to-face with a group of black-capped squirrel monkeys.

■ **Keats House:** Pick a plum from the tree planted outside on the original site that inspired "Ode to a Nightingale."

■ **Everyman Cinema:** Indulge in tapas and drinks at the cinema's sophisticated bar and lounge.

FEELING PECKISH?

For a substantial but still speedy meal on the hoof, stop at the **Hampstead Creperie** (⊠ *77 Hampstead High St., Hampstead, NW3* ☎ *020/7372–0081*), which serves authentic sweet and savory French crepes from a little cart on the street.

The excellent, thin-crust pizzas at **The Lansdowne** (⊠ *90 Gloucester Ave., Primrose Hill, NW1* ☎ *020/7483–0409* Ⓜ *Chalk Farm*) are just as good as any Italian's. Atypical here are the pizza toppings (fennel, chorizo, and aubergine, to name a few) and the pub's low-key, family-friendly atmosphere.

Bar Gansa (⊠ *2 Inverness St., Camden Town, NW1* ☎ *020/7267–8909*) offers tapas—small dishes for sharing—among other larger Spanish favorites, such as paella.

Marine Ices (⊠ *8 Haverstock Hill, Camden Town, NW3* ☎ *020/7482–9003*) has a window dispensing ice cream to strollers, and pasta, pizza, and sundaes inside the market at Camden Lock.

GETTING HERE

Reaching Hampstead by Tube is as easy as it looks: simply take the Edgewater branch of the Northern Line to the Hampstead stop. To get to Regent's Park, take the Bakerloo Line to Regent's Park Tube station or, for Primrose Hill, Swiss Cottage, St. John's Wood, and Belsize Park, the Swiss Cottage and St. John's Wood stops on the Jubilee Line or the Chalk Farm stop on the Northern Line.

MAKING THE MOST OF YOUR TIME

Depending on your pace and inclination, both Regent's Park and Hampstead can realistically be covered in a day. It might be best to spend the morning in Hampstead, then head south toward Regent's Park in the afternoon so that you're closer to central London come nightfall, if that is where your hotel is. It's advisable to stay out of Hampstead Heath and Regent's Park proper after nightfall unless there's an event (such as a play or concert) taking place on the greens.

A GOOD WALK

There really are no bad walks to be had in Hampstead. Once there, the village is best explored on foot, and Hampstead Heath will lead you by way of marked footpaths on a healthy jaunt through its sprawling green. The neighborhoods around Regent's Park—as well as the park itself—are also best explored on foot.

Sightseeing
☆★★★★

Nightlife
☆☆☆★★

Dining
☆☆☆★★

Lodging
☆☆☆☆★★

Shopping
☆☆★★★

If you feel the urge to escape the flurry of central London, hop the Tube or a bus going north for an afternoon spent in the snug shelter of Regent's Park and Hampstead. A leisurely stroll along these peaceful streets, with gorgeous Georgian architecture and lush greenery, will provide a taste of how laid-back (albeit moneyed) Londoners live. A longtime rendezvous of literati, these city districts contain two leafy parks, a handful of important historical sites, and some of the most stunning town-house architecture in the world (think any Merchant Ivory film). Excellent bookshops, contemporary boutiques, and cozy cafés line tree-shaded blocks abuzz with locals: you won't find souvenir stands here.

WHAT'S HERE

Despite the proliferation of residential neighborhoods in Regent's Park, the region does include its share of tourist sites. The **Sherlock Holmes Museum** at the northern end of Baker Street is at the exact address of Holmes's fictional abode and contains wax figures in the exhibition area and an antiques shop on the ground floor. **Madame Tussauds** is around the corner, and just inside the 112-acre **Regent's Park** along the Outer Circle is the **Regent's Park Open-Air Theatre** where, in summer, you can take in a Shakespeare play and a cocktail at the adjoining outdoor bar (that is, if you don't already have tickets for a match at the **Lord's Cricket Ground & Museum**). Design and art buffs will want to visit renowned 19th-century architect John Nash's **Cumberland Terrace** in the park, and continue south along the park to Portland Place to the Art Deco **Royal Institute of British Architects (RIBA)**.

12

If you're feeling energetic or if you have children to entertain, try wandering north within Regent's Park—past the daydreamers, dog-walkers, and soccer players—to the **London Zoo**, one of the oldest zoos in the world and still one of the best. Continue your "urban safari" along **Regent's Canal** (the more common name for the Grand Union Canal) past bankside willows and the zoo animals to **Camden Lock**, where you'll come upon the stalls and merchants of colorful **Camden Market.** Or make the trek up **Primrose Hill,** the name of both the nearby neighborhood and a 206-foot incline inside the park crisscrossed by walking paths.

PRIMROSE HILL

Primrose Hill offers some of the best views of the city and also happens to be the site of a series of well-known photographs of the Rolling Stones. Although the Stones also made music in this neighborhood, they did not use nearby Abbey Road studios where the Beatles famously recorded their entire output.

A couple of noteworthy museums are also within walking distance from Regent's Park: the **Jewish Museum,** which traces the history of the Jewish community in Britain from the Norman Conquest to the present day, and the **London Canal Museum,** where you can take a guided trip through London's slender waterways aboard a specially designed narrowboat. The **Freud Museum** is in the building where Sigmund Freud lived and worked just after he fled Austria following the German annexation of World War II, while Hampstead's oldest surviving house, **Fenton House,** is nearby on Hampstead Grove. George Eliot and Karl Marx are buried at **Highgate Cemetery,** adjacent to the immense **Hampstead Heath.** With its steep slopes toward Spaniard's Road, the heath offers views of the city comparable to those one would experience from the top of Primrose Hill. If you're walking around Hampstead Heath in the summer, you may also wish to stop for a concert at **Kenwood House,** a 17th-century mansion containing a collection of priceless art, including Vermeer's *Guitar Player.*

PLACES TO EXPLORE

🕲 **Camden Lock.** What was once just a pair of locks on the Grand Union Canal has now developed into London's third-most-visited tourist attraction. It's a vast honeycomb of markets that sell just about everything, but mostly crafts, clothing (vintage, ethnic, and young designer), and antiques. Here, especially on weekends, the crowds are dense, young, and relentless. *(For more on Camden Lock, see ⇨ Shopping, Chapter 19.)* ✉ *Camden High St., Camden Town, NW1* ⊕ *www.camdenlock. net* ☉ *Daily 10–6* Ⓤ *Camden Town, Chalk Farm.*

NEED A BREAK?

You will not go hungry in Camden Town. Among the countless cafés, bars, pubs, and restaurants, the following stand out for good value and good food. Within the market at Camden Lock there are various stalls selling the usual hot dogs, but you can also find good Chinese takeout, and other ethnic food if you don't mind standing as you eat outdoors, or finding a canalside bench.

A BRIEF HISTORY

Much like New York City's Greenwich Village, the cliché about Regent's Park and its bordering enclaves (Primrose Hill, Swiss Cottage, and St. John's Wood) is that the majority of folks here claim to be artists—and yet the cost of a coffee at a café along Regent's Park Road will run you as much as, if not more than, one in Central London. In the last decade, real estate prices in these neighborhoods have skyrocketed and the elephants of the London Zoo now call some of the best-dressed folks in town neighbors.

In the early 18th century the commercial development of the mineral springs in Hampstead led to its success as a spa; people traveled from miles around to drink the pure waters from Hampstead Wells, and small cottages were hastily built to accommodate the influx. Though the spa phenomenon was short-lived, Hampstead remained a favorite place for many artistic figures whose legacies still permeate the landscape.

In December 2005 Hampstead was the site of the biggest fire in Europe since World War II. It erupted in one of its oil refineries: remarkably, no one was injured and the village suffered little damage.

Fenton House. This is Hampstead's oldest surviving house. Now a National Trust property, it has an interesting collection of antiques and period interiors, along with some 17th-century-style gardens. Baroque enthusiasts can join a tour of the large collection of keyboard instruments, given by the curator, and there's a summer series of concerts on these very same instruments on Thursday evenings. Call ahead for details. ⊠ *Hampstead Grove, Hampstead, NW3* ☎ *020/7435-3471* ⊕ *www.nationaltrust.org.uk* ✉ *£4.90, joint ticket with 2 Willow Road £6.70* ☉ *Mar., weekends 2–5; Apr.–Oct., Wed.–Fri. 2–5, weekends 11–5* Ⓤ *Hampstead.*

Freud Museum. The father of psychoanalysis lived here for a year, between his escape from Nazi persecution in his native Vienna in 1938 and his death in 1939. Many of his possessions emigrated with him and were set up by his daughter, Anna (herself a pioneer of child psychoanalysis), as a shrine to her father's life and work. Four years after Anna's death in 1982 the house was opened as a museum. It replicates Freud's famous consulting rooms, particularly through the presence of *the* couch. You'll find Freud-related books, lectures, and study groups here, too. ⊠ *20 Maresfield Gardens, Hampstead, NW3* ☎ *020/7435-2002* ⊕ *www.freud.org.uk* ✉ *£5* ☉ *Wed.–Sun. noon–5* Ⓤ *Swiss Cottage, Finchley Rd.*

Ⓒ
Fodor'sChoice
★
Hampstead Heath. For an escape from the ordered prettiness of Hampstead, head to the heath—a wild park where wolves once roamed and washerwomen laundered clothes for aristocrats—which spreads for miles to the north. From its top, at Spaniards Road, there are stunning views for miles to the city. There are signposted paths, but these can be confusing. Maps are available from Hampstead newsagents and bookshops, or the information center at the Gospel Oak entrance, Gordon House Road, where you can also get details about the history of the

HAMPSTEAD PONDS

Hampstead Ponds, three Elysian little lakes, are surrounded by grassy lounging areas. Originally the lakes were pits, where clay was dug out for making bricks up until the 19th century. The women's lake is particularly secluded (though crowded in summer) and open all year, as is the men's; opening times vary with sunrise and sunset. The Mixed Pond is open May through September, 7 AM to 7 PM. All have murky-looking but clean, fresh water, and all are free.

Less murky is **Hampstead Lido,** open May through September. A swim here is £4 for the day (7 AM–6:30 PM). In winter the pool is open mornings only (7–12:30, £2). The 1930s Grade II–listed swimming pool underwent a £2.9 million refurbishment in 2005. ⊠ *E. Heath Rd., Hampstead, NW3* ☎ *020/7485–4491* Ⓤ *Tube or National Rail: Hampstead Heath.*

12

Heath and the flora and fauna growing there. ⊠ *Hampstead, NW3* ☎ *020/7482–7073 Heath Information Centre* ⊕ *www.cityoflondon.gov. uk* Ⓤ *Gospel Oak or Hampstead Heath Silverlink Line from Highbury & Islington underground for south of Heath; Hampstead underground, then walk through Flask Walk, Well Walk for east of Heath; Golders Green underground, then Bus 210, 268 to Whitestone Pond for north and west of Heath.*

Ⓒ ★ **Highgate Cemetery.** Highgate is not the oldest cemetery in London, but certainly it's the most celebrated. Such was its popularity that the acreage increased across the other side of the road, and this additional east side contains probably the most visited grave, of Karl Marx, where you also find George Eliot, among other famous names. The older west side was once part of a mansion owned by Sir William Ashurst, Lord Mayor of London in 1693. When the cemetery was consecrated in 1839, Victorians came from miles around to enjoy the architecture and the view. Both are impressive, from the moment you enter the grand wrought-iron gateway into a sweeping courtyard for horses and carriages. The highlight of the 20-acre site is the colonnaded Egyptian Avenue leading to the Circle of Lebanon, built around an ancient cypress tree—a legacy of Ashurst's garden—with catacombs skirting the edges. By the 1970s it was unkempt and neglected until a group of volunteers, the Friends of Highgate Cemetery, undertook the huge upkeep. Tours are arranged by the Friends, and among the numerous beautiful stone angels and beloved animals—memorials once hidden by wild brambles—they will show you the most notable graves, which include Michael Faraday and Christina Rossetti. ■ TIP→ Children under eight are not admitted; nor are dogs, cell phones, and video cameras. ⊠ *Swains La., Highgate, N6* ☎ *020/8340–1834* ⊕ *www.highgate-cemetery.org* 🎫 *£2, £3 for tours; £1 camera usage charge* ☉ *Call for opening times and visitor information; hrs vary according to whether a funeral service is scheduled* Ⓤ *Archway, then Bus 210 to Highgate Village.*

Hampstead's Historic Eateries

Hampstead is full of restaurants, including a few that have been here forever. Try the **Coffee Cup** (⊠ 74 *Hampstead High St., Hampstead, NW3* ☎ 020/7435–7565), which has been serving English breakfasts all day to locals since the 1950s, from 8 until late (and you can get steak sandwiches and pasta, too).

The **Hampstead Tea Rooms** (⊠ 9 *South End Rd., Hampstead, NW3* ☎ 020/7435–9563) has been run by the same owners for more than 30 years, selling sandwiches, pies, pastries, and cream cakes, on drool view in the window.

The quaintest pub in Hampstead, complete with fireplace and timber frame, is the **Hollybush** (⊠ 22 *Holly Mount,*

Hampstead, NW3 ☎ 020/7435–2892), which dates back to 1807. Tucked away on a side street, with cozy wooden booths inside, it's open until 11 each night and serves traditional English lunches and dinners, often to the accompaniment of live Irish music.

Close by Hampstead Heath, walking east along Gordon House Road, a historic pub stands at the northwest edge, at the tollhouse between Spaniards Road and Hampstead Lane. The **Spaniards Inn** (⊠ *Spaniards Rd., Hampstead, NW3* ☎ 020/8731–6571) is little changed since the early 18th century, when (they say) the notorious highwayman Dick Turpin hung out here. Keats also drank here, as did Shelley and Byron.

Jewish Museum. This museum tells a comprehensive history of the Jews in London from Norman times, though the bulk of the exhibits date from the end of the 17th century (when Cromwell repealed the laws against Jewish settlement) and later. The Ceremonial Art Gallery holds a collection of rare pieces, and the Audio Visual Gallery follows London Jewish life from cradle to grave. The museum's branch at the Sternberg Centre in Finchley covers social history, with exhibits and tape archives on the Holocaust, in the words of survivors. ⊠ *Raymond Burton House, 129 Albert St., Camden Town, NW1* ☎ 020/7284–1997 ⊕ *www.jewishmuseum.org.uk* ⊠ *£3.50* ☾ *Sun. 10–5, Mon.–Thurs. 10–4* Ⓤ *Camden Town* ⊠ *Sternberg Centre, 80 East End Rd., Finchley, N3* ☎ 020/8349–1143 ⊠ *£2* ☾ *Sun. 10:30–4:30, Mon.–Thurs. 10:30–5* Ⓤ *Finchley Central.*

Keats House. Here you can see the plum tree under which the young Romantic poet composed "Ode to a Nightingale," many of his original manuscripts, his library, and other possessions he managed to acquire in his short life. It was in February 1820 that Keats coughed blood up into his handkerchief and exclaimed, "I know the color of that blood; it is arterial blood. I cannot be deceived in that color. That drop of blood is my death warrant. I must die." He left this house in September, moved to Rome, and died of consumption there, in early 1821, at age 25. There are frequent guided tours and special events on Wednesday evenings (such as poetry readings); call or check the Web site for details. ⊠ *Keats House, Wentworth Pl., Keats Grove, Hampstead, NW3* ☎ 020/7435–2062 ⊕ *www.keatshouse.org.uk* ⊠ *£3.50, valid for 1* *yr* ☉ *Tues.–Sun. 1–5* Ⓤ *Hampstead or overground Silverlink Hampstead Heath from Highbury & Islington.*

☚ **Kenwood House.** Perfectly and properly Palladian, this mansion was first
★ built in 1616 and remodeled by Robert Adam in 1764. Adam refaced
most of the exterior and added the splendid library, which, with its
curved painted ceiling, rather garish coloring, and gilded detailing, is the
sole highlight of the house for decorative arts and interior buffs. What is
unmissable here is the **Iveagh Bequest,** a collection of paintings that the
Earl of Iveagh gave the nation in 1927, starring a wonderful Rembrandt
self-portrait and works by Reynolds, Van Dyck, Hals, Gainsborough,
and Turner. Top billing goes to Vermeer's *Guitar Player,* one of the most
beautiful paintings in the world. In front of the house, a graceful lawn
slopes down to a little lake crossed by a trompe-l'oeil bridge—all in perfect 18th-century upper-class taste. The rest of the grounds are skirted
by Hampstead Heath. Nowadays the lake is dominated by its concert
bowl, which stages a summer series of orchestral concerts, including
an annual performance of Handel's *Music for the Royal Fireworks,*
complete with fireworks. A popular café, the Brew House, is part of the
old coach house, and has outdoor tables in the courtyard and terraced
garden. Call in advance, as some parts may be closed to the public as
restoration of the house's Deal staircase is underway. ✉*Hampstead
La., Hampstead, NW3* ☎*020/8348–1286* ⊕*www.english-heritage.org.
uk* ✇*Free* ☉*House Apr.–Oct., daily 11–5; Nov.–Mar., daily 11–4. Gardens daily dawn–dusk* Ⓤ*Golders Green, then Bus 210.*

☚ **London Canal Museum.** Here, in a former ice-storage house, you can
learn about the rise and fall of London's once extensive canal network. Outside, on the Battlebridge Basin, float the gaily-painted narrow
boats of modern canal dwellers—a few steps and a world away from
King's Cross, which remains one of London's least salubrious neighborhoods. The quirky little museum is accessible from Camden Lock
if you take the towpath. ✉*12–13 New Wharf Rd., Camden Town,
N1* ☎*020/7713–0836* ⊕*www.canalmuseum.org.uk* ✇*£3* ☉*Tues.–Sun.
10–4:30; last admission 3:45* Ⓤ*King's Cross.*

☚ **London Zoo.** The zoo opened in 1828 and peaked in popularity during
★ the 1950s, when more than 3 million people passed through its turnstiles
every year. A modernization program focusing on conservation and education is underway. A great example of this is a huge glass pavilion—the
Web of Life—which puts these aims into action. Other zoo highlights
include the Casson Pavilion (which closely resembles the South Bank
Arts Complex); the graceful Snowdon Aviary, spacious enough to allow
its tenants free flight; and Berthold Lubetkin's 1936 Penguin Pool, now
home to porcupines. Don't miss the penguins' new home, though, where
feeding time tends to send small children into raptures. Recent additions
include a desert swarming with locusts, meerkats perching on termite
mounds, bats and hummingbirds, and an otter exhibit with underwater viewing. There's also a new walk-through forest where visitors
can come face-to-face with a group of black-capped squirrel monkeys.
London zoo is owned by the Zoological Society of London (a charity), and much work is done here in wildlife conservation, education,

and the breeding of endangered species. Male lion Lucifer was brought to the zoo in November 2004 in the hopes that he would breed with the young lioness Abi. For animal encounter sessions with keepers, and feeding times, check the information board at admission. ⊠*Regent's Park, NW1* ☎*020/7722–3333* ⊕*www.*

> **HERE'S WHERE**
>
> The London Zoo's reptile house is a special draw for Harry Potter fans—it's where Harry first talks to snakes, to alarming effect on his horrible cousin, Dudley.

londonzoo.co.uk ✆*£12* ☼*Late Oct.–Mar., daily 10–4, mid-Feb.–mid-Oct., daily 10–5:30; last admission 1 hr before closing* Ⓤ*Camden Town, then Bus 274.*

Lord's Cricket Ground & Museum. If you can't manage to lay your hands on tickets for a cricket match, the next best thing is to take a tour of the spiritual home of this most English of games. Founded by Thomas Lord, the headquarters of the MCC (Marylebone Cricket Club) opens its "behind the scenes" areas to visitors. You can see the Long Room with cricketing art on display; the players' dressing rooms; and the world's oldest sporting museum, where the progress from gentlemanly village-green game to world-class sport over 400 years is charted. Don't miss the prize exhibit: the urn containing the Ashes (the remains of a cricket ball burned by Australia fans mourning their defeat at the hands of the MCC in 1883), and even smaller, the poor sparrow that met its death by a bowled ball. More up-to-date is the eye-catching Media Centre building, which achieved high scores in the architectural league. The tour is not available during matches, but the museum remains open to match ticket holders. ⊠*St. John's Wood Rd., St. John's Wood, NW8* ☎*020/7616–8656* ⊕*www.lords.org* ✆*£10* ☼*Apr.–Sept., daily 10–2, not during major matches. Oct.–Mar., daily noon–2* Ⓤ*St. John's Wood.*

🕐 **Madame Tussauds.** One of London's busiest sights, this is nothing more and nothing less than the world's premier exhibition of lifelike waxwork models of celebrities. Madame T. learned her craft while making death masks of French Revolution victims, and in 1835 set up her first show of the famous ones near this spot. Top billing still goes to the murderers in the Chamber of Horrors, who stare glassy-eyed at visitors—one from an electric chair, one sitting next to the tin bath where he dissolved several wives in quicklime. What, aside from ghoulish prurience, makes people stand in line to invest in London's most expensive museum ticket? It's the thrill of rubbing shoulders with Shakespeare, Martin Luther King Jr., the Queen, and the Beatles—most of them dressed in their very own outfits—in a single day.

■**TIP→** Beat the crowds by calling in advance for timed entry tickets, or booking online. ⊠*Marylebone Rd., Regent's Park, NW1* ☎*0870/400–3000 for timed entry tickets* ⊕*www.madame-tussauds.com* ✆*From £15; prices vary according to day and season, call for details, or check Web site* ☼*Weekdays 9:30–5:30, weekends 9–6* Ⓤ*Baker St.*

CLOSE UP

A Trip to Abbey Road

For countless Beatlemaniacs and baby boomers, No. 3 Abbey Road is one of the most beloved spots in London. Here, outside the legendary Abbey Road Studios, is the most famous zebra crossing in the world, immortalized on the Beatles' 1969 *Abbey Road* album. This footpath became a mod monument when, on August 8 of that year, John, Paul, George, and Ringo posed—walking symbolically *away* from the recording facility—for photographer Iain Macmillan for the famous cover shot. In fact, the recording facility's Studio 2 is where the Beatles recorded their entire output, from "Love Me Do" onward, including *Sgt. Pepper's Lonely Hearts Club Band* (early 1967).

The studios are closed to the public, but tourists like to Beatle-ize themselves by taking the same sort of photo. ■ TIP➔ It's tempting to try to re-create "the" photo, but be careful: rushing cars make Abbey Road a dangerous intersection. One of the best—and safer—ways Beatle-lovers can enjoy the history of the group is to take one of the smashing walking tours offered by the **Original London Walks** (☏ *020/7624–3978* ⊕ *www.walks. com*), including "The Beatles In-My-Life Walk" (11:20 AM at the Baker Street Underground on Saturday and Tuesday) and "The Beatles Magical Mystery Tour" (10:55 AM at Underground Exit 3, Tottenham Court Road, on Sunday and Thursday), which cover nostalgic landmark Beatles spots in the city.

Abbey Road is in the elegant neighborhood of St. John's Wood, a 10-minute ride on the Tube from central London. Take the Jubilee Line to the St. John's Wood Tube stop, head southwest three blocks down Grove End Road, and be prepared for a heart-stopping vista right out of Memory Lane.

⟳ ★ **Regent's Park.** The youngest of London's great parks, Regent's Park, was laid out in 1812 by John Nash, working for his patron, the Prince Regent (hence the name), who was crowned George IV in 1820. The idea was to re-create the feel of a grand country residence close to the center of town, with all those magnificent white-stucco terraces facing in on the park. As you walk the Outer Circle, you'll see how successfully Nash's plans were carried out, although the focus of it all—a palace for the prince—was never actually built (George was too busy fiddling with the one he already had, Buckingham Palace). The most famous and impressive of Nash's terraces would have been in the prince's line of vision from the planned palace. **Cumberland Terrace** has a central block of Ionic columns surmounted by a triangular Wedgwood-blue pediment that's like a giant cameo. Snow-white statuary personifying Britannia and her empire (the work of the on-site architect, James Thomson) single it out from the pack. The noted architectural historian Sir John Summerson described it thus: "the backcloth as it were to Act III, and easily the most breathtaking architectural panorama in London."

As in all London parks, planting here is planned with the aim of having something in bloom in all seasons, but if you hit the park in May, June, or July, head first to the Inner Circle. Your nostrils should lead you to **Queen Mary's Gardens,** a fragrant 17-acre circle that riots with roses in summer and heather, azaleas, and evergreens in other seasons. The **Broad Walk** is a good vantage point from which to glimpse the minaret and golden dome of the **London Central Mosque** on the far west side of the park. If it's a summer evening or a Sunday afternoon, witness a remarkable phenomenon. Wherever you look, the sport being enthusiastically played is not cricket but softball, now Britain's fastest-growing participant sport (bring your mitt).

BOATING

You can spend a vigorous afternoon rowing about **Regent's Park Boating Lake** (☎ *020/7724–4069*), where rowboats hold up to five adults and cost £6 per hour per person, £4.50 for kids, approximately March through October. Hours vary with daylight, weather, and park opening times.

You're likely to see cricket, too, plus a lot of dog walkers—not for nothing did Dodie Smith set her novel *A Hundred and One Dalmatians* in an Outer Circle house. ☎ *020/7486-7905* ⊕ *www.royalparks.gov. uk* ⊗ *5* AM–*dusk* Ⓤ *Baker St., Regent's Park.*

Regent's Park Open-Air Theatre. The company has mounted Shakespeare productions here every summer since 1932; everyone from Vivien Leigh to Jeremy Irons has performed here. *A Midsummer Night's Dream* is the one to catch—never is that enchanted Greek wood more lifelike than it is here, augmented by genuine bird squawks and a rising moon. The park can get chilly, so bring a blanket; rain stops the play only when heavy. ⊠ *Open-Air Theatre, Regent's Park, NW1* ☎ *0870/060- 1811* ⊕ *www.openairtheatre.org* ⊗ *June–Aug., evening performances 7:30, matinees 2:30* Ⓤ *Baker St., Regent's Park.*

Sherlock Holmes Museum. Outside Baker Street station, by the Marylebone Road exit, is a 9-foot-high bronze statue of the celebrated detective. Keep your eyes peeled, for close by his image, "Holmes" himself, in his familiar deerstalker hat, will escort you to his abode at 221B Baker Street, the address of Arthur Conan Doyle's fictional detective. Inside, "Holmes's housekeeper" conducts you into a series of Victorian rooms full of Sherlock-abilia. It's all so realistic, you may actually begin to believe in Holmes's existence. ⊠ *221B Baker St., Regent's Park, NW1* ☎ *020/7935-8866* ⊕ *www.sherlock-holmes.co.uk* ⊴ *£6* ⊗ *Daily 9:30–6* Ⓤ *Baker St.*

Greenwich

The Painted Hall, Old Royal Naval College

WORD OF MOUTH

"It was raining when I visited Greenwich, but armed with a sturdy brolly and an enthusiastic travel companion I still enjoyed my visit very much. The surrounding park area is also very beautiful and the town itself charming, even when the weather isn't perfect. Check what the Observatory's and Maritime Museum's winter hours are ahead of time, however. Bundle up and enjoy!"

—Rebecka

GETTING ORIENTED

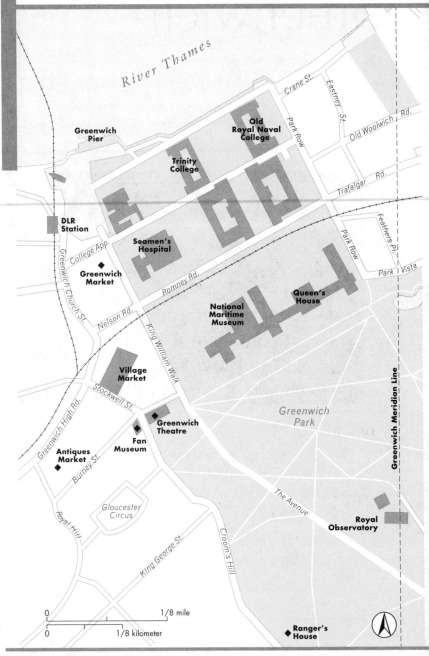

13

TOP 5 REASONS TO GO

■ **Greenwich Meridian Line:** Stand astride time.

■ **Old Royal Naval College Chapel:** Listen to a lunchtime concert amid neo-Grecian surroundings.

■ **Trafalgar Tavern:** Take a pint and whitebait dinner over the night-lighted Thames on the tavern's terrace.

■ **National Maritime Museum:** Relive the *Titanic's* last moments with rescued artifacts and underwater footage of the wreck.

■ **Greenwich Market:** Rifle through retro lighting and clothing stalls.

FEELING PECKISH?

The **Gipsy Moth Pub** (✉ *60 Greenwich Church St., SE10* ☎ *020/8858–0786*), behind the *Cutty Sark,* is the town's only memorial to another classic ship: the yacht that Sir Francis Chichester sailed single-handedly around the world in the 1960s. The galley here is expensive, but the beer garden makes up for it.

Up by the Royal Observatory is **The Honest Sausage** (⊕ *www.honestsausage.com*) beside the Wolfe monument, serving up delicious homemade organic sausages, and huge jacket potatoes drenched in onion gravy. The views are great, too.

For the best pub in Greenwich, head for the **Trafalgar Tavern** (✉ *Park Row, SE10* ☎ *020/8858–2909* ⊕ *www.trafalgartavern.co.uk*), with excellent views of the Thames. It's a grand place to have a pint and some upscale grub.

GETTING THERE

The Jubilee Line runs through Docklands from Canary Wharf to north Greenwich for the Millennium Dome. The zippy "driverless" Docklands Light Railway (DLR) runs to Cutty Sark station from Canary Wharf or Bank. Or take the DLR to Island Gardens and retrace the steps dockworkers used to take back and forth on the old Victorian Foot Tunnel under the river.

The best way to arrive, however—time and weather permitting—is like a sea admiral of old: by water. Note, though, that this journey takes over an hour from central London. *(For more on river ferries and cruising the Thames, see Chapter 1, Experience London.)*

MAKING THE MOST OF YOUR TIME

Set apart from the rest of London, Greenwich is worth a day to itself, to make the most of walks in the rolling parklands and to immerse yourself in its richness of maritime art and entertainment. The boat trip takes about an hour from Westminster Pier (next to Big Ben), or 25 minutes from the Tower of London, so factor in enough time for the round-trip. For the craft markets, a weekend trip is best.

NEAREST PUBLIC RESTROOMS

Duck into the tourist information center (near the Old Royal Naval College), whose loos are free.

Sightseeing
☆★★★★

Nightlife
☆☆☆☆★

Dining
☆☆☆★★

Lodging
☆☆☆☆★

Shopping
☆☆★★★

Visit Greenwich and you'll discover what makes Londoners tick. Situated on the Greenwich Meridian Line at 0° longitude, this smart Thames-side town literally marks the beginning of time. For an island nation whose reputation was built on sea-faring adventure, Britain's centuries-old maritime tradition lays anchor here. Fans of elegant architecture will be in heaven-on-sea, while landlubbers can wander acres of rolling parkland and immaculately kept gardens. And while the world-famous *Cutty Sark* may have been tragically destroyed by fire in 2007, trading traditions live on in Greenwich's maze of market stalls that sell a Davy Jones locker's worth of bric-a-brac, antiques, and retro gear.

WHAT'S HERE

A visit to Greenwich feels like a trip to a seaside town, but one with more than its fair share of historic sites and visitor attractions, all fairly close to one another. The **Old Royal Naval College** should be your first port of call. It's the village's most grandiose building, with an atmospheric history tour spanning the days when, as the Greenwich Hospital, wounded sea veterans were fed a daily diet of five pints of beer. Within the grounds are the immaculately preserved Chapel, designed by Sir Christopher Wren, and Painted Hall, with frescoes depicting scenes of naval grandeur (suitably pro-British for a dead Nelson to lay there in state in 1806).

Heading south, Inigo Jones's 1616 Palladian villa, the **Queen's House** (also known as the "House of Delight"), has a good collection of oil paintings, including a wide-eyed seven-year-old Elizabeth I, scenes of Britain's seafaring ascent, and the occasional oceanic punch-up. An elegant colonnade connects to the **National Maritime Museum,** which has oodles of interactive exhibits that bring the seas to life: rigs creaking in the wind, sailors shouting, grainy footage of the Titanic, and the lucky toy pig that saved one little girl's life.

> **HERE'S WHERE**
>
> Queen's House also formed the set for the Hollywood movie of Jane Austen's classic *Sense and Sensibility.*

13

Behind the Maritime Museum, a path through beautiful **Greenwich Park,** into which Henry VIII introduced deer to give himself a good hunt, rises steeply to the **Royal Observatory,** where it's hard to resist the urge—no matter how old you are—to bestride two hemispheres by standing over the **Greenwich Meridian Line.**

Beyond the Wolfe Monument is **Ranger's House,** which houses the private art collection of 19th-century diamond millionaire Julius Wernher. Look out for a lovingly tended rose garden next to it, housing such eclectic species as Ice Cream, Tequila Sunrise, Remember Me, and Grandpa Dickson.

Down Croom's Hill, past rows of Georgian houses and the Roman Catholic Church is the **Fan Museum,** an idiosyncratic labor of love dedicated to treasured examples throughout the ages, from ivory, tortoiseshell, and mother-of-pearl exhibits right up to the modern extractor fan. **Greenwich Theatre,** opposite the Fan Museum, leads onto the main drag, Greenwich Church Street, with the bohemian **Village Market** on the corner and, a little farther on, the lively weekend **Greenwich Market.**

Heading east on the River Path takes in the delightful **Trafalgar Tavern,** with magnificent views over the Thames and gracious buildings on the right. Less than a mile farther on, toward north Greenwich, rises Richard Rogers's **Millennium Dome.** Farther

> **FUN FACT**
>
> Charles Dickens was among many guests who would arrive by boat to take a light whitebait fish supper, on offer to visiting patrons to this day.

downstream, in the next-door neighborhood of Woolwich, lies the **Thames Flood Barrier** and its adjacent visitor center.

PLACES TO EXPLORE

Fan Museum. In two newly restored houses dating from the 1820s, opposite the Greenwich Theatre, is this highly unusual museum. The 2,000 fans here, which date from the 17th century onward, compose the world's only such collection, and the history and purpose of these objects, often exquisitely crafted from ivory, mother-of-pearl, and tortoiseshell, are explained in satisfying detail. It was the personal vision—and fan collection—of Helene Alexander that brought it into being, and the workshop and conservation and study center that she has also set up ensure that this anachronistic art has a future. ■ TIP➔**If your interest is really piqued, you can attend fan-making workshops. Ask at the desk for details.** ✉*12 Croom's Hill, Greenwich, SE10*

A BRIEF HISTORY

Although these days Greenwich is a thriving neighborhood with smart boutiques, organic groceries, pubs, and restaurants, this was not always the case. In the 17th century the diarist Samuel Pepys bemoaned the slew of invalids clogging up the streets. For almost 200 years, Greenwich Hospital was home to the war-wounded of the British Navy's numerous sea spats, who were housed at the Christopher Wren–designed building, one of the best-known in London. It closed in 1869, and was reincarnated as the Old Royal Naval College for training young officers and is the setting of many a blockbusting period film today.

Greenwich was originally home to one of England's finest Tudor palaces, and the birthplace of Henry VIII, Elizabeth I, and Mary I. Much of the palace fell into disrepair, but the site was reinvigorated with the construction of the Queen's House—built by the masterful Inigo Jones in 1616 and considered the first "classical" building in England.

More recently, Greenwich became synonymous with the hopelessly ambitious Millennium Dome, which currently lies empty like an abandoned spaceship. However, there are plans to bring it to life again as an entertainment and sports arena, and it's slated to host the gymnastics events of the 2012 Olympic Games in London.

In May of 2007, the Cutty Sark—what had been the world's last remaining tea clipper and one of Greenwich's most popular sights—burned down in a devastating (and suspicious) fire. At this writing, plans were underway to raise funds to restore the ship.

☎ 020/8305–1441 ⊕ www.fan-museum.org ✉ £4 ⊗ Tues.–Sat. 11–5, Sun. noon–5 Ⓤ DLR: Greenwich.

Greenwich Market. Established as a fruit-and-vegetable market in 1700, and granted a royal charter in 1849, the glass-roof market now offers arts and crafts Friday through Sunday, and antiques and collectibles on Thursday and Friday. Shopping for crafts is a pleasure, as in most cases you're buying directly from the artist. ✉ College Approach, Greenwich, SE10 ☎ 020/7515–7153 ⊕ www.greenwich-market.co.uk ⊗ Fri.–Sun. 9:30–5:30, Thurs. 7:30–5:30 Ⓤ DLR: Cutty Sark.

OFF THE
BEATEN
PATH

Village Market. If you're around Greenwich Market during the weekend, the nearby Village Market on Stockwell Street has bric-a-brac and books, and it's well known among the cognoscenti as a good source for vintage clothing.

Antiques Market. On the opposite block to the Village Market, the weekend Antiques Market on Greenwich High Road has more vintage shopping, and browsing among the "small collectibles" makes for a good half-hour diversion.

National Maritime Museum. Following a millennial facelift, one of Greenwich's star attractions has been completely updated to make it one of London's most fun museums. Its glass-covered courtyard of beautifully grand stone, dominated by a huge revolving propellor from a powerful

The Docklands Renaissance

13

But for the river, Roman Londinium, with its sea link to the rest of the world, would not have grown into a world power. Life was played out by the riverside, and palaces redolent of Venice—such as Lambeth, Greenwich, Somerset House, Westminster, and Whitehall—were built. Dock warehouses sprang up during the 18th century from the trade with the Indies for tea and coffee, spices, and silks (some now converted into museums and malls, such as Hay's and Butler's wharves).

Trade took a gradual downturn after World War II, leading to the docks' degeneration when larger vessels pushed trade farther downriver to Tilbury. It took a driverless railway and Britain's tallest building to start a renaissance. Now, what was once a desolate and dirty quarter is known as the Docklands, a peninsula of waterways with cutting-edge architecture, offices, water-based leisure and cultural activities, restaurants, and bars.

The best way to explore is on the **Docklands Light Railway (DLR),** whose elevated track appears to skim over the water past the swanky glass buildings where the railway is reflected in the windows. On foot, however, the Thames Path has helpful plaques along the way, with nuggets of historical information.

The **Museum in Docklands,** on a quaint cobbled quayside, beside the tower of Canary Wharf, is worth a visit for its warehouse building alone. With uneven wood floors, beams, and pillars, the museum used to be a storehouse for coffee, tea, sugar, or rum from the West Indies—hence the name West India Quay. The fascinating story of the old port and the river is told using films, together with interactive displays and reconstructions. Roaming visitor assistants are also on hand to help with further explanation and interesting anecdotes. ⊠ *No. 1 Warehouse, West India Quay, Hertsmere Rd., East End, E14* ☎ *0870/444-3857* ⊕ *www.molg.org. uk* ⊠ *£5; tickets valid for 1 yr* ☉ *Daily 10–6; last admission 5:30* Ⓤ *Canary Wharf; DLR: West India Quay.*

In its time, the **Ragged School Museum** was the largest school in London and a place where impoverished children could escape their deprived homes to get free education and a good meal. The museum re-creates the children's experiences with a time-capsule classroom, dating from the 1880s. It's an eye-opener for adults, and a fun experience for kids who get the chance to work just like Victorian children did more than 100 years ago in one of the many organized workshops. ⊠ *46–50 Copperfield Rd., East End, EC3* ☎ *020/8980–6405* ⊕ *www.raggedschoolmuseum.org.uk* ⊠ *Free* ☉ *Wed. and Thurs. 10–5, 1st Sun. of month 2–5* Ⓤ *Mile End; DLR: Limehouse.*

If you have time to travel farther downstream to the old Royal Dockyard at Woolwich, you'll find, adjacent to it, a brilliant exhibition of the Royal Artillery, *Firepower!* (☎ *020/8855–7755* ⊕ *www.firepower.org.uk* Ⓤ Woolwich Arsenal station). Complete with smoke and sound effects, it explores the role of the gunner in film, from the discovery of gunpowder to the Gulf War. Also on show are tanks and guns—some complete with battle scars, and most with individual investigative touch-screen storyboards. Housed in the old regal buildings of the Royal Arsenal leading down to the river shore, there's a powerful sense of the Thames and its lingering effect on the capital's history.

frigate, is reminiscent of the British Museum. The collection spans seascape paintings to scientific instruments, interspersed with the heroes of the waves. A permament Nelson gallery contains the uniform he wore, complete with bloodstain, when he met his end there in 1805. Allow at least two hours in this absorbing, adventurous place; if you're in need of refreshment the museum

> **A VIEW TO REMEMBER**
>
> Construction on the Queen's House was granted by Queen Anne only on the condition that the river vista from the house was preserved, and there are few more majestic views in London than the awe-inspiring symmetry that Wren achieved.

has a good café with views over Greenwich Park. The **Queen's House** is home to the largest collection of maritime art in the world, including works by William Hogarth, Canaletto, and Joshua Reynolds. Inside, the Tulip Stair, named for the fleur-de-lis–style pattern on the balustrade, is especially fine, spiraling up without a central support to the Great Hall. The Great Hall itself is a perfect cube, exactly 40 feet in all three dimensions, decorated with paintings of the Muses, the Virtues, and the Liberal Arts. ⊠ *Romney Rd., Greenwich, SE10* ☎ *020/8858–4422* ⊕ *www. nmm.ac.uk* ⊡ *Free* ⊙ *Apr.–Sept., daily 10–6; Oct.–Mar., daily 10–5; last admission 4:30* Ⓤ *DLR: Greenwich.*

★ **Old Royal Naval College.** Begun by Christopher Wren in 1694 as a rest home, or hospital for ancient mariners, this became instead a school for young ones in 1873. Today the University of Greenwich and Trinity College of Music have classes here. You'll notice how the structures part to reveal the Queen's House across the central lawns. Behind the college are two buildings you can visit. The **Painted Hall,** the college's dining hall, derives its name from the baroque murals of William and Mary (reigned 1689–95; William alone 1695–1702) and assorted allegorical figures. James Thornhill's frescoes, depicting scenes of naval grandeur with a suitably pro-British note of propaganda, were painstakingly done over installments in 1708–12 and 1718–26, and good enough to earn him a knighthood. It's still used for dining, making merry, schools, and weddings today. In the opposite building stands the **College Chapel,** which was rebuilt after a fire in 1779 and is altogether lighter, in a more restrained, neo-Grecian style. ■ TIP→ **Trinity College of Music holds free classical music concerts in the chapel every Tuesday lunchtime.** ⊠ *Old Royal Naval College, King William Walk, Greenwich, SE10* ☎ *020/8269–4747* ⊕ *www.oldroyalnavalcollege.org* ⊡ *Free, guided tours £4* ⊙ *Painted Hall and Chapel Mon.–Sat. 10–5, Sun. 12:30–5, last admission 4:15; grounds 8–6* Ⓤ *DLR: Greenwich.*

Ranger's House. This handsome, early-18th-century villa, which was the Greenwich Park Ranger's official residence during the 19th century, is hung with Stuart and Jacobean portraits. But the most interesting diversion is the Wernher Collection, more than 650 works of art with a north European flavor, amassed by diamond millionaire Julius Wernher at the turn of the 20th century. After making his money in diamond mining, he chose to buy eclectic objects, sometimes beautiful, often downright quirky, like the silver coconut cup. Sèvres porcelain and Limoges enamels, the largest jewelry collection in the country, and some particularly bizarre reliquaries form part of this fascinating collection. Wernher's American wife, Birdie, was a strong influence and personality during the belle epoque, which is easy to imagine from her striking portrait by Sargent. The house also makes a superb setting for concerts, which are regularly scheduled here. ☒ *Chesterfield Walk, Blackheath, Greenwich, SE10* ☎ *020/8853–0035* ⊕ *www.english-heritage.org.uk* ☒ *£5.50* ⊙ *Apr.–Sept., Sun.–Wed. 10–5; Oct.–Mar., by appointment only. Closed Jan. and Feb.* Ⓤ *DLR: Greenwich; no direct bus access, only to Vanbrugh Hill (from east) and Blackheath Hill (from west).*

> ### FUN FACT
>
> Prance around the lightning-cracked Elizabeth Oak in Greenwich Park and you'll be in good historic company—it's so called after Elizabeth I's own flights of fancy in youth.

13

⟳ **Royal Observatory.** Founded in 1675 by Charles II, this imposing institution was designed the same year by Christopher Wren for John Flamsteed, the first Royal Astronomer. The red ball you see on its roof has been there since 1833, and drops every day at 1 PM, although it started to malfunction in 2006. This Greenwich Timeball and the Gate Clock inside the observatory are the most visible manifestations of Greenwich Mean Time—since 1884, the ultimate standard for time around the world. Greenwich is on the **prime meridian** at 0° longitude. A brass line laid among the cobblestones here marks the meridian, one side being the eastern, one the western hemisphere. Right above the prime meridian line, a funky green laser shoots out across London, and at night it can be seen for several miles.

In 1948 the Old Royal Observatory lost its official status: London's glow had grown too intense, and the astronomers moved to Sussex, while the Astronomer Royal decamped to Cambridge, leaving various telescopes, chronometers, and clocks for you to view. An excellent exhibition on the solution to the problem of measuring longitude includes John Harrison's famous clocks, H1–H4, now in working order. There may be some closures to parts of the museum in preparation for the unveiling of Time and Space, a major development that adds a Planetarium and new galleries to the observatory. ☒ *Greenwich Park, Greenwich, SE10* ☎ *020/8858–4422* ⊕ *www.rog.nmm.ac.uk* ☒ *Free* ⊙ *Apr.–Sept., daily 10–6; Oct.–Mar., daily 10–5; last admission 4:30* Ⓤ *DLR: Greenwich.*

> ### A GOOD WALK
>
> Whether you go into the Royal Observatory or not, a walk up the steep path from the National Maritime Museum to the top of the hill gives you fantastic views across all of London, topped off with £1-a-slot telescopes to scour the skyline. Time it to catch the golden glow of late afternoon sun on Canary Wharf Tower and head back into town via the rose garden behind Ranger's House.

Thames Barrier Visitors' Centre. Learn what comes between London and its famous river—a futuristic-looking metal barrier that has been described as the eighth wonder of the world. Multimedia presentations, a film on the Thames' history, working models, and views of the barrier itself put the importance of the relationship between London and its river in perspective. ⊠ *Unity Way, Eastmoor St., Woolwich, SE18* ☎ *020/8305–4188* ⊕ *www.thamesbarrierpark.org.uk* ✉ *£1* ☉ *Apr.– Sept., daily 10:30–4:30; Oct.–Mar., daily 11–3:30* Ⓤ *National Rail: Charlton (from London Bridge), North Greenwich (Jubilee Line), then Bus 161 or 472.*

The Thames Upstream

Visitors tackling the garden maze at Hampton Court Palace

WORD OF MOUTH

"[Hampton Court Palace is] a must-see part of your trip to London. You get to experience the feel of life in the castle more than in other royal palaces. You can take the tour at your own pace and there are all sorts of activities to keep you busy.... While we were there, there were games on the lawn in the courtyard for children. It's much more interactive and memorable overall than Windsor."

–Kim from Tennessee

GETTING ORIENTED

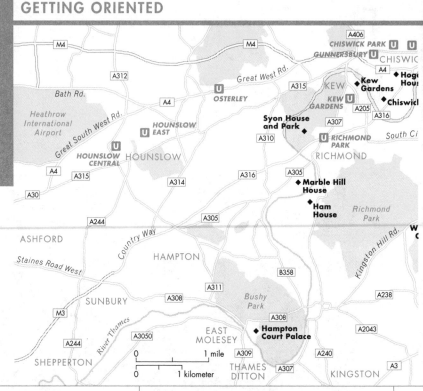

A GOOD WALK

From Chiswick House, follow Bur-lington Lane and take a left onto Hogarth Lane—which is anything but a lane—to reach Hogarth's House. Chiswick's Church Street (reached by an underpass from Hogarth's House) is the nearest thing to a sleepy country village street in all of London. Follow it down to the Thames and turn left at the bottom to reach the 18th-century riverfront houses of Chiswick Mall, referred to by locals as "Millionaire's Row." There are several pretty riverside pubs near Hammersmith Bridge.

MAKING THE MOST OF YOUR TIME

Hampton Court Palace requires at least half a day to experi-ence the most of its magic, although you could make do with an afternoon at Richmond Park, or a couple of hours for any of the other attractions. Because of the distances involved between the sights, too much traveling eats into your day. The best option is to concentrate on one of the sights, adding in a brisk park visit, one stately home, and a riverside promenade, before rounding off with an evening pint.

NEAREST PUBLIC RESTROOMS

Richmond Park, Kew Gardens, and all the stately homes have public toilets available.

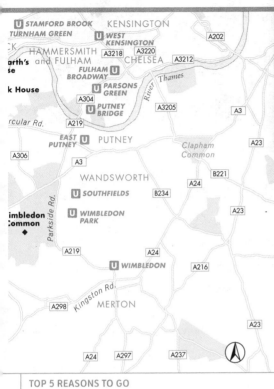

GETTING THERE

The District Line is the best of the Tube options, stopping at Turnham Green (in the heart of Chiswick but a fair walk from the houses), Gunnersbury (for Syon Park), Kew Gardens, and Richmond.

For Hampton Court, overland train is your only option: South West trains run from Waterloo, also stopping at Chiswick station (best for Chiswick House or Hogarth's House), Kew Bridge, Richmond (for Ham House), and St. Margaret's, best for Marble Hill House. Silverlink, another overland London service, also stops at Gunnersbury, Kew Gardens, and Richmond.

A pleasant, if slow, way to go is by river. Boats depart upriver from Westminster Pier, by Big Ben, for Kew (1½ hours), Richmond (2–3 hours), and Hampton Court (3–4 hours depending on tides) several times a day in summer, less frequently from October through March. The boat trip is worth taking only if you make it an integral part of your day out, and be aware that it can get very breezy on the water.

TOP 5 REASONS TO GO

■ **Hampton Court Palace:** Get lost in the leafy walls of the palace's maze as dusk falls.

■ **Richmond Park:** Take a misty early-morning stroll and catch sight of red deer.

■ **Richmond village:** Browse the antiques shops and go back in time.

■ **Kew Gardens:** Explore the giant stems of weird and wonderful plants at the Royal Botanic Gardens.

■ **Thames-side views:** Enjoy a pint from the creaking balcony of a centuries-old riverside pub as the boats row home.

The upper stretch of the Thames unites a string of lustrous riverside pearls—Chiswick, Kew, Richmond, Putney—taking in friendly streets, horticultural delights, regal magnificence, and Henry VIII's fiendish outdoor labyrinth at Hampton Court Palace. Achieving a noble hat-trick of homes, gardens, and parks, the neighborhoods dotted along the way are as proud of their village-y feel as of their stately history, with many a pleasing pub nestled at the water's edge. After the bustle of the West End, here the pace slackens delightfully, and it becomes easy to forget you're in a capital city.

CHISWICK & KEW

Chiswick is the nearest Thames-side destination to London. It's a low-key district, content with its good run of restaurants, stylish shops, and film-star residents, but it is also proud of the seething moral authority of its most famous son: William Hogarth, one of Britain's best-loved painters, lived here, and tore the fabric of the 18th-century nation to pieces in his slew of satirical engravings. Incongruously stranded among Chiswick's terraced homes are a number of fine 18th-century houses, and a charming little village survives, populated by London's affluent middle-class families.

A mile or so beyond Chiswick is Kew, and the village atmosphere here makes this one of the most desirable areas of outer London. The biggest draw for visitors, though, are the Royal Botanic Gardens.

PLACES TO EXPLORE

Chiswick House. Built circa 1725 by the Earl of Burlington (the Lord Burlington of Burlington House, Piccadilly, home of the Royal Academy, and, of course, the Burlington Arcade) as a country residence in which to entertain friends, and as a kind of temple to the arts, this is the very model of a Palladian villa, inspired by the Villa Capra near Vicenza in northeastern Italy. The house fans out from a central octagonal room in perfect symmetry, guarded by statues of Burlington's heroes, Palladio himself and his disciple Inigo Jones. Burlington's friends—Pope, Swift, Gay, and Handel among them—were well qualified to adorn a temple to the arts. Burlington was a great connoisseur and an important patron of the arts, but he was also an accomplished architect in his own right, fascinated by—obsessed with, even—the architecture and art of the Italian Renaissance and ancient Rome, with which he'd fallen in love during his Italian Grand Tour. Along with William Kent (1685–1748), who designed the interiors and the rambling gardens here, Burlington did a great deal toward the dissemination of Palladian ideals around Britain: Chiswick House sparked enormous interest, and you'll see these forms reflected in hundreds of later English stately homes both small and large. Sitting in acres of spectacular Italianate gardens filled with classical temples, statues, and obelisks, it's home to the sumptuous interiors of William Kent, including the Blue Velvet Room with its gilded decoration and intricate ceiling paintings. It also houses a fabulous collection of paintings and furniture. ⊠ *Burlington La., Chiswick, W4* ☎ *020/8995–0508* ⊕ *www.english-heritage. org.uk* ⊠ *£4* ⊙ *Apr.–Oct., Sun., Wed.–Fri., and bank holidays 10–5, Sat. 10–2; closed some Sat. afternoons; Nov.–Mar., by appointment only* Ⓤ *Turnham Green, Chiswick.*

Hogarth's House. Home to William Hogarth, the satirical painter and engraver, from 1749 until his death in 1764. Unprotected from the six-lane Great West Road, which remains a main route to the West Country, the poor house is besieged by surrounding traffic, but it's worth visiting for its little museum containing his amusing moralistic engravings, such as *Beer Street, Marriage a la Mode, The Harlot's Progress,* and the most famous of all, the *Rake's Progress* series of 1735.

> ### BOAT RACES
>
> A great place to buy Hogarth prints is at **Fosters** (⊠ *183 Chiswick High Rd., W4* ☎ *020/8995–2768*), the oldest shop in Chiswick. Run by a husband-and-wife team, the shop has its original Georgian frontage, creaking floorboards, and a glorious number of original Victorian novels and essays. It also offers handwritten gift vouchers from £10 to £50,000.

■ TIP→ Look out too for the 300-year-old mulberry tree in the garden, a vain attempt to get silkworms to breed in England. ⊠ *Hogarth La., Chiswick, W4* ☎ *020/8994–6757* ⊠ *Free* ⊙ *Apr.–Sept., Tues.–Fri. 1–5, weekends 1–6; Oct.–Mar., Tues.–Fri. 1–4, weekends 1–5* Ⓤ *Turnham Green.*

NEED A BREAK?

Pubs are the name of the game here at Chiswick's portion of the Thames. Many pubs sit on the bank of the river, offering watery vistas to accompany stout pints of brew. The Bell & Crown (⊠ *72 Strand-on-the-Green, Chiswick, W4* ☎ *020/8994–4164*) is the first pub on the riverside path from Kew Bridge, with a riverside conservatory to check those breezes. The Blue Anchor (⊠ *13 Lower Mall, Hammersmith, W6* ☎ *020/8748–5774*) is a cozy 18th-century watering hole, with rowing memorabilia lining the walls. The Dove (⊠ *19 Upper Mall, Hammersmith, W6* ☎ *020/8748–5405*) retains the charm of its 300-plus-year heritage. If you can find a spot on the tiny terrace, it's a tranquil place to watch the energetic oarsmen.

★ **Kew Gardens.** The Royal Botanic Gardens at Kew are a spectacular 300 acres of public gardens, containing more than 30,000 species of plants. In addition, this is the country's leading botanical institute, and has been named a World Heritage Site by UNESCO. There are also strong royal associations. Until 1840, when Kew Gardens was handed over to the nation, it had been the grounds of two royal residences: the White House (formerly Kew House) and Richmond Lodge. George II and Queen Caroline lived at Richmond Lodge in the 1720s, while their eldest son, Frederick, Prince of Wales, and his wife, Princess Augusta, came to the White House during the 1730s. The royal wives were keen gardeners. Queen Caroline got to work on her grounds, while next door Frederick's pleasure garden was developed as a botanical garden by his widow after his death. She introduced all kinds of "exotics," foreign plants brought back to England by botanists. Caroline was aided by a skilled head gardener and by the architect Sir William Chambers, who built a series of temples and follies, of which the crazy 50-story **Pagoda** (1762), visible for miles around, is the star turn. The celebrated botanist Sir Joseph Banks (1743–1820) then took charge of Kew, which developed rapidly in both its roles—as a landscaped garden and as a center of study and research.

The highlights of a visit to Kew are the two great 19th-century greenhouses filled with tropical plants, many of which have been there as long as their housing. Both the **Palm House** and the **Temperate House** were designed by Sir Decimus Burton, the first opening in 1848, the second in 1899. The Temperate House was the biggest greenhouse in the world, and today contains the largest greenhouse plant in the world, a Chilean wine palm rooted in 1846. You can climb the spiral staircase almost to the roof and look down on this and the dense tropical profusion from the walkway. The **Princess of Wales Conservatory,** the latest and the largest plant house at Kew, was opened in 1987 by Princess Diana. Under its bold glass roofs, designed to maximize energy conservation, there are no fewer than 10 climatic zones.

Plants may be beautiful to look at, and they have many medicinal uses, but how many plants are used in making fabrics, paper, and many more items? In **Museum No. 1,** near the Palm House, an interesting exhibition of the economic botany collections shows which plants "… help the merchant, physician, chemist, dyer, carpenter and artisans to find raw materials of their profession correctly named." It's free, but opening hours are seasonal, so check beforehand. The plant houses make Kew worth visiting even in the depths of winter, but in spring and summer the gardens come into their own. In late spring the woodland nature reserve of Queen Charlotte's Cottage Gardens is carpeted in bluebells; a little later, the Rhododendron Dell and the Azalea Garden become swathed in brilliant color. High summer brings glorious displays of roses and water lilies, and fall is the time to see the heather garden, near the pagoda. Whatever time of year you visit, something is in bloom, and your journey is never wasted. The main entrance is between Richmond Circus and the traffic circle at Mortlake Road. ⊠ *Kew Rd., Kew* ☏ *020/8332–5655* ⊕ *www.kew.org* 🎫 *£12.25* ⊙ *Gardens Apr.–Oct., weekdays 9:30–6:30, weekends 9:30–7:30; Nov.–Mar., daily 9:30– 4:30* Ⓤ *Kew Gardens.*

Kew Palace and Queen Charlotte's Cottage. To this day quietly domestic Kew Palace remains the smallest royal palace in the land. The house and gardens offer a glimpse into the 17th century. Originally known as the Dutch House, it was bought by King George II to provide more room in addition to the White House (another royal residence that used to exist on the grounds) for the extended royal family. In spring there's a romantic haze of bluebells. ⊠ *Kew Gardens, Kew* ⊕ *www.hrp.org. uk* 🎫 *£5, in addition to ticket for Kew Gardens.*

14

NEED A BREAK?

Maids of Honour (⊠ *288 Kew Rd., Kew* ☏ *020/8940–2752*), the most traditional of Old English tearooms, is named for the famous tarts invented here and still baked by hand on the premises. Tea is served in the afternoon, Tuesday–Saturday 2:30–5:30. If you can't wait for tea and want to take some of the lovely cakes and pastries to eat at Kew Gardens or on Kew Green, the shop is open Tuesday–Saturday 9:30–6 and on Monday until 1 PM.

RICHMOND

Named after the palace Henry VII built here in 1500, Richmond is still a welcoming and extremely pretty riverside "village," with many handsome (and expensive) houses, antiques shops, a Victorian theater, London's grandest stately home, and, best of all, the largest of London's royal parks.

PLACES TO EXPLORE

★ **Ham House.** To the west of Richmond Park, overlooking the Thames and nearly opposite the oddly named Eel Pie Island, the house was built in 1610 by Sir Thomas Vavasour, knight marshal to James I, then refurbished later the same century by the Duke and Duchess of Lauderdale, who, although not particularly nice (a contemporary called the duchess "the coldest friend and the most violent enemy that ever was known"), managed to produce one of the finest houses in Britain at the time. It's unique in Europe as the most complete example of a lavish Restoration period house, with a restored formal garden, which has become an influential source for other European palaces and grand villas. Produce from the garden can be enjoyed in the café in the Orangery. The library is filled with 17th- and 18th-century volumes; the original decorations in the Great Hall, Round Gallery, and Great Staircase have been replicated; and all the furniture and fittings are on permanent loan from the V&A. The gardens and outhouses (Ice House and Still House) are worth a visit in their own right, and are more conveniently open year-round. A tranquil and scenic way to reach the house is on foot, which takes about 30 minutes, along the eastern riverbank south from Richmond

Bridge. ✉ *Ham St., Richmond* ☎ *020/8940–1950* ⊕ *www.nationaltrust. org.uk* ⊡ *House, gardens, and outhouses £8* ☯ *House late Mar.–Oct., Sat.–Wed. 1–5. Gardens all year, Sat.–Wed., 11–6* Ⓤ *Richmond, then Bus 65 or 371.*

Marble Hill House. On the northern bank of the Thames, almost opposite Ham House, stands another mansion, this one a near-perfect example of a Palladian villa. Set in 66 acres of parkland, Marble Hill House was built in the 1720s by George II for his mistress, the "exceedingly respectable and respected" Henrietta Howard. Later the house was occupied by Mrs. Fitzherbert, who was secretly married to the Prince Regent (later George IV) in 1785. Marble Hill House was restored in 1901 and opened to the public two years later, looking very much like it did in Georgian times, with extravagant gilded rooms in which Ms. Howard entertained famous poets and wits of the age, including Pope, Gay, and Swift. A ferry service operates during the summer from Ham House across the river; access on foot is a half-hour walk south along the west bank from Richmond Bridge. Group tours can be arranged. ✉ *Richmond Rd., Twickenham, Richmond* ☎ *020/8892–5115* ⊕ *www. english-heritage.org.uk* ⊡ *£4* ☯ *Apr.–Oct., Sat. 10–2, Sun. and bank holidays 10–5; Nov.–Mar., prebooked tours only* Ⓤ *Richmond.*

☾ **Richmond Park.** Charles I enclosed this one in 1637 for hunting purposes, like practically all the other parks. Unlike the others, however, Richmond Park still has wild red and fallow deer roaming its 2,470 acres of grassland and heath and the oldest oaks you're likely to see—vestiges of the forests that encroached on London from all sides in medieval times. White Lodge, inside the park, was built for George II in 1729. Edward VIII was born here; now it houses the Royal Ballet School. You can walk from the park past the fine 18th-century houses in and around Richmond Hill to the river, admiring first the view from the top. ▪ TIP➔**There's a splendid, protected view of St. Paul's Cathedral from King Henry VIII's Mound. Established in 1710, it measures 10 mi and is the bane of over-enthusiastic town planners. Find it and you have a piece of magic in your sights.** ☎ *020/8948–3209* ⊕ *www. royalparks.gov.uk* ☯ *Mar.–Sept., daily 7* AM–*dusk; Oct.–Feb., daily 7:30* AM–*dusk* Ⓤ *Richmond.*

STAG LODGE STABLES

▪ Stag Lodge Stables has horses to ride in the big expanses of Richmond Park. Private lessons are £40 Tuesday to Friday, £50 on weekends. Riders with basic skills can rent a horse for a one-hour hack for £25, £35 on weekends. ✉ *Robin Hood Gate, Richmond Park, Richmond, TW10* ☎ *020/8974–6066* ⊕ *www.ridinginlondon.com* Ⓤ *Putney Bridge then Bus 85.*

▌ **NEED A BREAK?**

The Cricketers (✉ *Maids of Honour Row, Richmond Green, Richmond* ☎ *020/8940–4372*) serves a good pub lunch. The modern, partially glass-roofed Caffé Mamma (✉ *24 Hill St., Richmond* ☎ *020/8940–1625*) is a good spot for inexpensive Italian food.

🕙 **Syon House and Park.** The residence of Their Graces the Duke and Duch-
★ ess of Northumberland, this is one of England's most sumptuous stately
homes, and certainly the only one that's near a Tube station. Set in a
55-acre park landscaped by Capability Brown, the core of the house is
Tudor—two of Henry VIII's queens, Catherine Howard and Lady Jane
Grey, made pit stops here before they were sent to the Tower—but it
was redone in the Georgian style in 1761 by famed decorator Robert Adam. He had just returned from studying the sites of classical
antiquity in Italy and created two rooms here worthy of any Caesar:
the entryway is an amazing study in black and white, pairing neoclassical marbles with antique bronzes, and the Ante-Room contains 12
enormous verdantique columns surmounted by statues of gold—this,
no less, was meant to be a waiting room for the duke's servants and
retainers. The Red Drawing Room is covered with crimson Spitalfields
silk, and the Long Gallery is one of Adam's noblest creations (it was
used by Cary Grant and Robert Mitchum for a duel in the 1958 film
The Grass Is Greener). Elsewhere on the beautiful, rolling parkland is
a Victorian glass conservatory that's famous among connoisseurs for its
charm, not surprising as the designer, Fowler, was also responsible for
the grand Covent Garden Flower Market. ■TIP➔**On certain bank holidays and Sundays you can take a miniature steam train ride in the grounds.**
Also within the grounds, but not part of the Syon enterprise, are a
nature center and **The London Butterfly House** (☎*020/8560–7272* 🕙 *Daily
10–3:30*), with separate charges. ✉*Syon Park, Brentford* ☎*020/8560–
0882* ⊕*www.syonpark.co.uk* 🎫*£7.50 for house, gardens, conservatory, and rose garden; £3.75 gardens and conservatory* 🕙 *House late
Mar.–Oct., Wed., Thurs., Sun., and bank holidays 11–5; gardens daily
10:30–dusk* Ⓤ *Gunnersbury, then Bus 237 or 267 to Brentlea stop.*

HAMPTON COURT PALACE

Fodor'sChoice
★

Some 20 mi from central London,
on a loop of the Thames upstream
from Richmond, stands one of
London's oldest royal palaces. It
is actually two palaces in one: a
magnificent Tudor redbrick mansion, begun in 1514 by Cardinal
Wolsey, and a larger, late-17th-
century baroque structure, where
Christopher Wren designed the graceful south wing, one of the palace's
many highlights.

GOOD TO KNOW

There's a map available to guide
you around Hampton Court's
notorious maze if you're pressed
for time, but getting lost is much
more fun.

From the information center in the main courtyard, you can choose
which parts of the palace to explore—whether your taste is Tudor or
baroque—based on a number of self-guided walking routes. Throughout the palace, costumed interpreters and special programs, such as
cooking demonstrations in the cavernous Tudor kitchens, make history
fun. As you progress into the State Apartments through halls hung with
priceless paintings, you can easily imagine the ghost of Catherine Howard screaming her innocence of adultery to an unheeding Henry VIII.

14

Other highlights in the Tudor portion include Henry's Great Hall and the Chapel Royal (with its fan vaulting and azure ceiling). The routes continue with the later King's (William's) Apartments, the Queen's Apartments, and the Georgian Rooms. William and, especially, Mary loved Hampton Court and left their mark on the place—see their fine collections of Delftware and other porcelain. Be sure to look outside as you explore the baroque apartments. Famed throughout the world, the gardens were designed to please anyone gazing out the windows, as well as people strolling outside. ■ TIP➡ **Come Christmas season, there's ice-skating on a rink before the West Front of the palace—an unmissable mixture of pageantry and pleasure.**

The site beside the slow-moving Thames is idyllic, with 60 acres of fantastic ornamental gardens, lakes, and ponds, including William III's Privy Garden on the palace's south side. Its parterres, sculpted turf, and clipped yews and hollies—a hybrid of English and continental gardening styles—brilliantly set off Wren's addition. Other highlights are Henry VIII's Pond Garden, the enormous conical yews around the Fountain Garden, and the daffodil-lined paths of the Wilderness. On the east side of the house, 544 lime trees were replanted in 2004 along the Long Water, a canal built during the time of Charles II. The Great Vine, near the Banqueting House, was planted in 1768 and is still producing black Hamburg grapes. Perhaps best of all are the almost half mile of paths in the celebrated maze, which you enter to the north of the palace. It was planted in 1714 and is truly fiendish.

Royalty ceased living here with George III; poor George preferred the seclusion of Kew, where he was finally confined in his madness. The private apartments that range down one side of the palace are now occupied by pensioners of the Crown. Known as "grace and favor" apartments, they are among the most coveted homes in the country, with a surfeit of peace and history on their doorsteps. ⊠ *East Molesey on A308* ☎ *0870/752–7777* ⊕ *www.hrp.org.uk* ✉ *Palace, gardens, and maze £12.30, gardens only £4, maze only £3.50, park grounds free. Joint tickets available with Kensington Palace and Tower of London* ☉ *State apartments Apr.–Oct., daily 10–6, last admission at 5; Nov.–Mar., daily 10–4:30; grounds daily 7–dusk* Ⓤ *Richmond, then Bus R68; National Rail, South West: Hampton Court Station, 35 min from Waterloo.*

Where to Eat

London's dining scene never stays still.

WORD OF MOUTH

"There are several branches of Wagamama around central London now. Don't be put off by long queues snaking there way out of the doorways—you won't have to wait long and the food is worth it. Large bowls of Chinese noodle soups or Japanese soba or ramen noodles, stir fries etc. Not expensive. Long refectory shared tables."

–Kippy

Updated
by Alex
Wijeratna

THE SCENE

Swinging London rivals New York and Tokyo as one of the best places to eat in the world right now. The sheer diversity of restaurants here is unparalleled. Among the city's 6,700 restaurants are see-and-be-seen hotspots, casual ethnic eateries, innovative gastropubs, and temples to *haute* cuisine.

Now *the* premier global finance center, a wall of money has cascaded from the City's global finance markets to help spark the most fantastic restaurant boom that London has ever seen. To measure London's spectacular culinary rise, note that it was once a common dictum that the British ate to live while the French lived to eat.

Hell's Kitchen star Gordon Ramsay is setting the highest standard at his eponymous place at Royal Hospital Road in Chelsea, and the rest of the much-lauded high cuisine scene is dominated by world-class masters. French culinary legend Joël Robuchon recently launched an outpost of his L'Atelier concept, a high-concept French tapas joint; Michael Roux Jr. rules the roost at Le Gavroche; Eric Chavot sets a cracking pace at the Capital; and Tom Aikens commands his acclaimed, eponymous eatery in Chelsea.

For cheap eats, don't miss the city's unofficial dish, the ubiquitous Indian curry. The quality of other international cuisines also has grown in recent years, with London becoming known for its Malaysian, Spanish, Turkish, and North African restaurants. With all of the choices, traditional British food, when you track it down, appears as just one more exotic cuisine in the pantheon.

Whatever eating experience you seek, London can likely deliver. From dirt-cheap street food to posh multi-course meals, the city has become a destination for gustatory adventurers. In this chapter, we've uncovered the best of the best. Dig in, and enjoy!

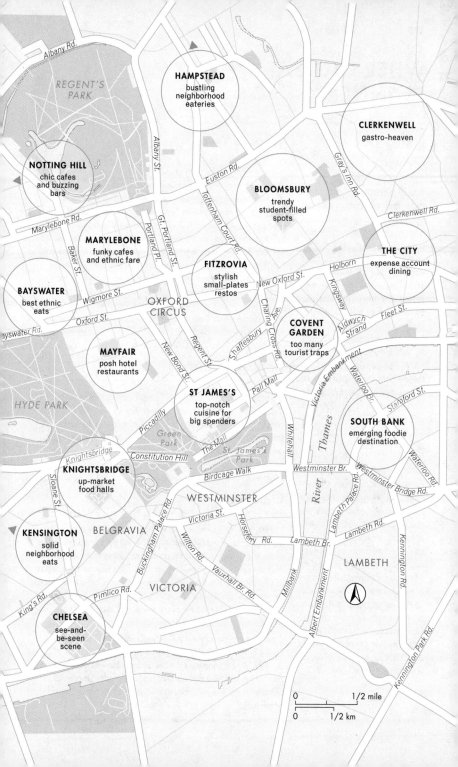

HAMPSTEAD
bustling
neighborhood
eateries

CLERKENWELL
gastro-heaven

REGENT'S
PARK

Albany Rd.

Albany St.

NOTTING HILL
chic cafes
and buzzing
bars

Euston Rd.

BLOOMSBURY
trendy
student-filled
spots

Gray's Inn Rd.

Clerkenwell Rd.

Marylebone Rd.

Gt. Portland St.

Portland Pl.

MARYLEBONE
funky cafes
and ethnic fare

Tottenham Court Rd.

FITZROVIA
stylish
small-plates
restos

New Oxford St.

Holborn

THE CITY
expense account
dining

Baker St.

Wigmore St.

OXFORD
CIRCUS

Charing Cross Rd.

Kingsway

Aldwych

Fleet St.

BAYSWATER
best ethnic
eats

Oxford St.

Bayswater Rd.

Shaftesbury Ave.

Strand

**COVENT
GARDEN**
too many
tourist traps

New Bond St.

Regent St.

MAYFAIR
posh hotel
restaurants

Victoria Embankment

Waterloo Br.

Stanford St.

HYDE PARK

ST JAMES'S
top-notch
cuisine for
big spenders

Pall Mall

Thames

SOUTH BANK
emerging foodie
destination

Waterloo Rd.

Piccadilly

Green
Park

The Mall

St. James's
Park

Whitehall

River

Westminster Bridge Rd.

Knightsbridge

Constitution Hill

Birdcage Walk

Westminster Br.

KNIGHTSBRIDGE
up-market
food halls

Sloane St.

WESTMINSTER

Lambeth Palace Rd.

Lambeth Rd.

Kennington Rd.

KENSINGTON
solid
neighborhood
eats

BELGRAVIA

Victoria St.

Horseferry Rd.

Lambeth Br.

LAMBETH

Buckingham Palace Rd.

Wilton Rd.

Vauxhall Br. Rd.

Millbank

Albert Embankment

King's Rd.

Pimlico Rd.

VICTORIA

CHELSEA
see-and-
be-seen
scene

Kennington Park Rd.

0 ⸻ 1/2 mile

0 ⸻ 1/2 km

WHERE TO EAT PLANNER

Eating Out Strategy

Where should we eat? With thousands of London eateries competing for your attention, it may seem like a daunting question. But fret not—our expert writers and editors have done most of the legwork. The 100-plus selections here represent the best this city has to offer—from hot pudding to *haute* cuisine. Search "Best Bets" for top recommendations by price, cuisine, and experience. Sample local flavor in the neighborhood features. Or find a review quickly in the alphabetical listings. Delve in, and enjoy!

Reservations

Plan ahead if you're determined to snag a sought-after reservation. Some renowned restaurants are booked weeks or months in advance. In the reviews, we mention reservations only when they're essential or not accepted, though it's always a good idea to book as far ahead as you can, and reconfirm when you arrive in London. Note that some top restaurants also now take credit card details and charge a penalty fee if you're a no-show.

What to Wear

When in England's style capital, do as the natives do: dress up to eat out. Whatever your style, dial it up a notch. Have some fun while you're at it. Pull out the clothes you've been saving for a "special" occasion and get a little glamorous. As unfair as it seems, the way you look can influence how you're treated—and where you're seated. Generally speaking, jeans and a button-down shirt will suffice at most table-service restaurants in the £ to ££ range. Moving up from there, many pricier restaurants require jackets, and some insist on ties. Shorts, sweatpants, and sports jerseys are rarely appropriate. Note in reviews that we mention dress only when men are required to wear a jacket or a jacket and tie.

Tipping and Taxes

Do not tip bar staff in pubs—though you can always offer to buy them a drink. In restaurants, tip 10% to 15% of the check for full meals if service is not already included; tip a small token if you're just having coffee or tea. If paying by credit card, double-check that a tip has not already been included.

Children

Unless your children behave impeccably, it's best to avoid the high-class establishments; you won't find a children's menu there, anyway. London's many Italian restaurants and pizzerias are popular with kids. Or take the little ones to Chinatown: it a fun cultural experience. China House serves kids' portions and offers Chinese arts-and-crafts activities from 1 PM to 4 PM every weekend. Activities vary but include magicians and origami experts.

Other family-friendly establishments include Pizza Express, Sticky Fingers, Tootsies Grill, and the brasserie chain Browns. At Smollensky's on the Strand, clowns and face painters provide entertainment on weekends. Finally, at Giraffe, there's a colorful interior, a children's menu, and a helpful staff.

Hours

In London you can find breakfast all day, but it's generally served between 7:30 AM and 10 AM. Workmen's cafés and sandwich bars for office workers are sometimes open from 7:30 AM, more upscale cafés from 9 AM to 10:30 AM. Lunch is between noon and 2 PM. Tea, often a meal in itself, is taken between 4 PM and 5:30 PM, while dinner or supper is typically eaten between 7:30 PM and 9:30 PM, though can be taken earlier. Many ethnic restaurants, especially Indian, serve food until midnight. Sunday is proper lunch day, and some restaurants are open for lunch only. Many restaurants are closed entirely on Sundays and on public holidays. Over the Christmas period, London virtually shuts down and it seems only hotels are prepared to feed travelers. Unless otherwise noted, the restaurants listed in this guide are open daily for lunch and dinner.

Prices

The democratization of restaurants in London has not translated into smaller checks, and London is an expensive city by most standards. A modest meal for two can easily cost £36 and the £100-a-head meal is not unknown. Damage-control strategies include making lunch your main meal—the top places have bargain lunch menus—or sharing an evening à la carte entrée and ordering a second appetizer instead. (Note that an appetizer, usually known as a "starter" or "first course," is sometimes called an "entrée," as it is in France, and that an entrée in England is dubbed the "main course" or simply "mains.") Seek out fixed-price menus, and watch for hidden extras on the check, i.e., bread or vegetables charged separately.

WHAT IT COSTS IN POUNDS STERLING

	£	££	£££	££££	£££££
AT DINNER	under £10	£10–£15	£16–£22	£23–£30	over £30

Price per person for an average main course or equivalent combination of smaller dishes at dinner. Note: If a restaurant offers only prix-fixe (set-price) meals, it has been given the price category that reflects the full prix-fixe price.

In this Chapter

15

Credit Cards

American Express, MasterCard, and Visa are accepted in most upscale restaurants, but pubs, small cafés, and indie eateries may take cash only.

BEST BETS FOR LONDON DINING

With thousands of restaurants to choose from, how will you decide where to eat? Fodor's writers and editors have selected their favorite restaurants by price, cuisine, and experience in the Best Bets lists below. In the first column, Fodor's Choice properties represent the "best of the best" in every price category. You can also search by neighborhood for excellent eats—just peruse the following pages. Or find specific details about a restaurant in the full reviews, listed alphabetically later in the chapter.

FODOR'S CHOICE ★

Anchor & Hope
Busabe Eathai
Canteen
The Capital
L'Atelier de Joël Robuchon
Le Gavroche
The Ledbury
Locanda Locatelli
Racine
Rasoi Vineet Bhatia
Royal China
Sông Quê Café
St. John
The Wolseley

By price

BEST £

Busabe Eathai
Food For Thought
Mandalay
Sông Quê Café

BEST ££

Acorn House
Anchor & Hope
Canteen
Original Lahore Kebab House
Pig's Ear

BEST £££

Galvin
Racine
Royal China
St. John
The Wolseley

BEST ££££

Le Cercle
Locanda Locatelli
Pied à Terre
Rasoi Vineet Bhatia
Yauatcha

BEST £££££

The Capital
L'Atelier de Joël Robuchon
Le Gavroche
Gordon Ramsay at Royal Hospital Road
The Ledbury

By cuisine

BRITISH

Canteen
St. John
St. John Bread and Wine
Rules
Sweetings

CHINESE

Fung Shing
Hakkasan
Ping Pong
Royal China
Yauatcha

FRENCH

Le Gavroche
Gordon Ramsay Royal Hospital Road
L'Atelier de Joël Robuchon
Pied à Terre
Tom Aikens

INDIAN

Amaya
Original Lahore Kebab House
Rasoi Vineet Bhatia

ITALIAN

Cecconi's
Locanda Locatelli
Orso
River Café
Zafferano

JAPANESE

Yoisho
Zuma

SPANISH

Fino
Moro

SEAFOOD

Bentley's
J Sheekey
North Sea Fish Restaurant
Sweetings

STEAKHOUSE

Chez Garard
Electric Brasserie
Gaucho Grill

VIETNAMESE

Busabe Eathai
E&O
Esarn Kheaw
Sông Qué Café

By experience

BUSINESS DINING

Gordon Ramsay at Claridges
Greenhouse
L'Oranger
Plateau
The Wolseley

BRUNCH

Cecconi's
Galvin Bistrot De Luxe
PJ's Grill
St. John Bread and Wine
The Wolseley

CELEB-SPOTTING

The Ivy
J Sheekey
Le Caprice
Nobu
The Wolseley

CHILD-FRIENDLY

Browns
High Road Brasserie
Joe Allen
The Ledbury

GASTROPUBS

Anchor & Hope
Coach & Horses
The Cow
The Enterprise
Pig's Ear

GOOD FOR GROUPS

Lemonia
Momo
Ping Pong
Royal China
Zuma

GREAT VIEW

Oxo Tower
Plateau
River Café
The Ritz
The Waterway

HOTEL DINING

Asia de Cuba
The Capital
Gordon Ramsay at Claridge's
Locanda Locatelli
The Ritz

LATE-NIGHT DINING

Hakkasan
J Sheekey
Joe Allen
Royal China

LUNCH PRIX-FIXE

The Capital
J Sheekey
Ping Pong
Racine
Tom Aikens

MOST POPULAR

Busabe Eathai
Canteen
Cecconi's
The Ivy
The Wolseley

QUIET MEAL

Almeida
Bellamy's
Bibendum
The Greenhouse
L'Oranger

SPECIAL OCCASION

Chez Bruce
Gordon Ramsay Royal Hospital Road
Le Caprice
Le Gavroche
The Ledbury

WINE LISTS

The Capital
Gordon Ramsay at Claridge's
The Greenhouse
Locanda Locatelli
The Square

PRE-THEATER

Arbutus
Bentley's
Browns
L'Escargot
Orso

HOT SPOTS

Acorn House
Canteen
Cecconi's
L'Atelier de Joël Robuchon
The Wolseley

ROMANTIC

J Sheekey
Julie's
L'Atelier de Joël Robuchon
La Poule au Pot
Rasoi Vineet Bhatia

BRASSERIES

Bellamy's
Electric Brasserie
High Road Brasserie
Racine
The Wolseley

15

ST. JAMES'S, MAYFAIR, & MARYLEBONE

Mayfair and St. James's—home to Buckingham Palace and Clarence House, where Prince Charles and Camilla live—have a decidedly old world, royal feel. Appropriately, most of the restaurants here are fit for a king.

This is where you'll find London's top restaurants including Gordon Ramsay at Claridge's, The Ivy, and Le Gavroche—dining experiences that are geared towards a well-heeled, deep-pocketed clientele. Mere mortals will have to make reservations months in advance to dine at any of these restaurants for dinner. But last-minute tables are sometimes available, and lunching here can be a great money-saving strategy.

If you're looking for something more low-key and wallet-friendly, head north to Marylebone where the scenery changes dramatically. Old World elegance is replaced by funky little cafes and restaurants with an indie spirit. Everything from Moroccan and Turkish to Thai is available here, as well as numerous local favorites. Just follow your nose. —Christina Valhouli

POSH NOSHING

Some of London's best restaurants can be found inside its hotels. David Tang's chic **China Tang** in the Dorchester serves dim sum and authentic Chinese cuisine (Park La., London W1, Mayfair, 020/7629–8888). **Angela Hartnett**, part of the Gordon Ramsay empire, serves up modern European cuisine with an Italian influence at the Connaught (16 Carlos Place, W1, Mayfair, 020/7592–1222). Celebrity chef **Brian Turner**'s self-named restaurant inside the Millennium Hotel Mayfair is where you'll find classic British dishes such as spit-roasted grouse, and Victoria Plum with clotted cream (Grosvenor Square, W1, Mayfair, 020/7596–3444)

LONDON'S HOTTEST TABLES

These restaurants are more than just see-and-be-seen hot-spots—excellent food adds to the buzz. If you're looking to save, visit at lunch when the set menu is usually a fraction of what it would cost to eat there at night.

×**Automat:** This trendy eatery, which resembles the interior of a carriage train, is one of the few places in London to serve an American-style brunch. Settle into a booth and tuck into comforting classics like mac-n-cheese and barbecue pork ribs *(33 Dover St., W1S, Mayfair, 020/7499–3033)*.

×**The Avenue:** This expansive, sleek restaurant serves modern British food that's surprisingly affordable. Try the crispy duck spring rolls or tender grilled scallops with celeriac puree *(7–9 St. James's St., SW1, St. James, 020/7321–2111)*.

×**Locanda Locatelli:** This sophisticated Italian restaurant, designed by David Collins, serves up traditional food with a twist. Try the homemade potato and mushroom gnocchi served with shavings of black truffles (8 Seymour St., W1, Marylebone, 020/7935–9088).

×**Wiltons:** If you've just been shopping among the traditional shirt-makers of Jermyn Street, pop in for lunch here. Opened in 1742, the atmosphere is dark and clubby, and the menu focuses on seafood (55 Jermyn St., SW1, St. James, 020/7629–9955).

DINING BY CUISINE

Austrian
The Wolseley, £££

Brasserie
Bellamy's, £££

French
Gordon Ramsay at Claridge's, £££££
Greenhouse, £££££
Le Gavroche, £££££
L'Oranger, ££££–£££££
The Ritz, £££££
The Square, £££££

Italian
Cecconi's, £££
Locanda Locatelli, ££££

Japanese
Nobu, ££££–£££££

Modern British
Le Caprice, £££
Sketch: Gallery, ££££

Moroccan
Momo, £££

Seafood
Bentley's, £££

Steakhouse
Gaucho Grill, ££££

A CULINARY MASTERPIECE

×Mourad Mazouz's restaurant **Sketch** (9 Conduit St., W1, 087/0777–4488) has developed a reputation for being one of the most innovative restaurants in London. The "gastro-complex" is housed in an 18th-century building, consisting of two restaurants, two bars, an art gallery, and a café. Its restaurant, headed by celebrity French chef Pierre Gagnaire, is pricey, but the set two-course lunch is a deal at £30. In the casual café, **Parlour**, outfitted with kooky mismatched furniture and Perspex deer heads, stop in for exquisite cakes, sandwiches, and tea service (Cream Tea with scones is a bargain at £8).

SOHO & COVENT GARDEN

Soho and Covent Garden is the city's playground, a late-night wonderland of glitz and greasepaint.

This area is London's cultural heart—home to media companies and strip clubs, late-night bars, and highbrow theater productions. In the last decade, high rents have forced out seedy businesses and ushered in topnotch restaurants, including **Yauatcha** (15–17 Broadwick St., W1D, Soho, 020/7494–8888) and **Lindsay House** (21 Romilly St., Soho, W1, 020/7439–0450), the latter so refined you have to ring a doorbell to be ushered in to its superb dining room.

Because of its popularity with tourists, Soho prices can be absurdly steep: £10 cocktails and £30 main courses are not out of the question. For a quick bite without breaking the bank, head to Chinatown's cobbled streets—the daytime dim sum trolley at **New World** (1 Gerrard St., W1, Soho, 020/7734–0396) is justly famous. Many clubs and bars stay open until 3 AM; a few even later. **Balans** (60 Old Compton St., W1D, Soho, 020/7439–2183) serves cocktails until 5 AM in the week, and 6 AM on Fridays and Saturdays. *–Helen Lewis*

BARS AND PUBS

Swedish import **Garlic and Shots** (14 Frith St., W1V, Soho, 020/7734–9505) delivers on that promise: Stock up on breath mints before trying the garlic beer. **K-Box** karaoke (7–9 Cranbourn St., WC2H, Soho, 020/7287–8868) lets you fulfill your pop-star dreams while cocktails loosen your vocal cords. Tucked behind Covent Garden plaza, the **Lowlander** (Drury La., WC2B, Covent Garden, 020/7379–7446) pub features 15 draught and 40 bottled beers. Private members' bar **Milk and Honey** (61 Poland St., W1F, Soho, 07000/655469) imports a New York vibe. Non-members can get in with a reservation before 11 PM.

MEAL DEALS AND STEALS

PRE- AND POST-THEATER DINING

For a prix-fixe deal on classic French food, head to **Café des Amis** (11–14 Hanover Place, WC2E, Covent Garden, 020/7379–3444), the ground floor of **L'Escargot** (48 Greek St., W1D, Soho, 020/7437–6828), or **Arbutus** (63 Frith St., W1D, Soho, 020/7734–4545), where two course before 7 PM will set you back less than £15. Philippe Starck–designed **Asia de Cuba** (45 St. Martin's La., WC2N, Covent Garden, 020/7636–4445) does three-course bento boxes for those in need of a quick bite, and **Bali Bali** (150 Shaftesbury Ave., WC2, Soho, 020/7836–2644) offers a pre-theater menu for £9 featuring six Malaysian and Indonesian dishes, served in a casual, family-run eatery that prides itself on authenticity.

BUDGET EATS AT ANY HOUR

Belgian: Cross the metal gantry in **Belgo Centraal** (50 Earlham St., WC2H, Covent Garden, 020/7813–2233), where a mound of mussels costs less than £10 and you can sample the largest selection of Belgian beers in the country. Continuing the Continental theme, the same road offers **Bunker Bierhall** (41 Earlham St., WC2H, Covent Garden, 020/7240–0606), where you can sit on the benches and quaff pilsner from a two-pint stein.

Italian: For those who prefer authentic Italian, there's **Amaretto** (116 Tottenham Court Rd., W1T, Soho, 020/7387–6234), a family-run restaurant featuring solid red-sauce cuisine, or **Spaghetti House** (30 St. Martin's La., WC2N, Trafalgar Square, 020/7836–1626), a local chain offering pizzas and pastas.

Pan-Asian: For dinner, drinks, and dancing in a hip, Asian-accented lounge, **The Langley** (5 Langley St., WC2H, Covent Garden, 020/7836–5005) offers great-value green curries, battered prawns, and other bar favorites in a futuristic space. Fusion pizza restaurant **Fire and Stone** (31–32 Maiden La., WC2E, Covent Garden, 020/7379–4793) serves traditional dough bases with toppings inspired by five continents, all below £9. The Koh Samui pizza features coconut curry sauce, roasted chicken, fried shallots, hot chiles, and mozzarella.

DINING BY CUISINE

American
Joe Allen, £££

Asian
Asia de Cuba, ££££
Ping Pong, ££

Brasserie
Browns, ££

British
Rules, £££–££££
The Ivy, £££–£££££

Café
Bar Italia, £
Maison Bertaux, £
New Piccadilly, £

Chinese
Fung Shing, £££
Yauatcha, ££££

French
L'Atelier de Joël Robuchon, £££££
L'Escargot, £££

Irish
Lindsay House, £££££

Italian
Bertorelli's, £££
Orso, ££

Mediterranean
Andrew Edmunds, ££

Modern British
Arbutus, £££

Seafood
J Sheekey, £££

Vegetarian
Food for Thought, £

BLOOMSBURY, FITZROVIA, & HAMPSTEAD

From the intellectual haunts of Bloomsbury and the chic dining scene of Fitzrovia to the leafy tranquillity of Hampstead, this area offers a diversity of dining experiences.

Bloomsbury is known as London's literary and academic center. It is home to the British Museum, the University of London, other universities, and numerous bookstores. Although Bloomsbury is known more as a residential area, there are many hotels in Russell Square, which is a convenient central location for visitors. Fitzrovia lies to the west of Bloomsbury, and here you will find a number of striking town houses as well as a wealth of stylish shops, hip bars, and trendy restaurants.

Hampstead lies in the north of London, and is best described as a leafy, quiet suburb. This neighborhood is a popular excursion destination for Londoners who want to escape the hustle and bustle of the city, with a stroll through peaceful Hampstead Heath to appreciate its meadows and woodland. The area is steeped in literary history, as many playwrights and writers had homes here. Hampstead has a number of cozy cafés, restaurants, and bustling pubs. —*Puja Chugani*

SUNDAY ROAST

Experience traditional English flavor at one of Hampstead's homey pubs: **The Wells** (30 Well Walk, NW3, 020/7794–3785) serves a traditional Sunday Roast with roast beef, Yorkshire pudding, and roasted vegetables: £20 for two courses, or £25 for three courses. For the "olde English" pub experience, complete with dim lighting, pot-bellied stove, and wood-paneled walls, soak up the ambiance at **Holly Bush** (22 Holly Mount, NW3, 020/7435–2892), housed in a 200-year-old building. The upscale pub fare emphasizes organic and local products, with a Sunday Roast featuring a choice of meats and vegetables. Price varies.

DINING TWO WAYS

	Save	Splurge
Chinese dim sum	Dim T (3 Heath St., NW3, Hampstead, 020/7435–0024) is a standby for traditional dumplings and noodles. The food is well-priced and it's kid-friendly.	Hakkasan (8 Hanway Pl., W1, Bloomsbury, 020/7927–7000) is where the stars go for dim sum. But the creative dishes and cocktails can be pricey.
Rustic Italian fare	Latium (21 Berners St., W1, Bloomsbury, 020/7323–9123) is a small venue with a big following. It's a bargain for simple pastas and great wines.	Passione (10 Charlotte St., W1, Bloomsbury, 020/7636–2833) offers delicious food in a stylish dining room. Check out the expert wine list.
Japanese charcoal-grilling	Jin Kichi (73 Heath St., NW3, Hampstead, 020/7794–6158) serves traditional char-grilled dishes. Meals are reasonably priced and there are set menus available.	Roka (37 Charlotte St., W1, Fitzrovia, 020/7580–6464) has a simple yet trendy design that showcases the restaurant's modern offerings, like glazed scallop skewers.

DINING BY CUISINE

Asian
The Providores & Tapa Room, £££

Bistro
Galvin Bistrot de Luxe, £££
Elena's L'Étoile, £££

Chinese
Hakkasan, ££££

Eclectic
Acorn House, ££

French
Pied à Terre, ££££–£££££
Villandry, ££

Greek
Lemonia, ££

Japanese
Yoisho, ££

Seafood
North Sea Fish Restaurant, ££

Spanish
Fino, £££

Thai
Busabe Eathai, £
Crazy Bear, ££££

GLOBAL TAPAS

The small-plates trend has caught on in London, especially in Bloomsbury and Fitzrovia. Here's where to go: **Fino** (33 Charlotte St., W1, Fitzrovia, 020/7813–8010) offers upscale Spanish tapas in the elegant basement dining room. Select a few dishes or try a set menu. **Salt Yard** (54 Goodge St., W1, Fitzrovia, 020/7637–0657) features tapas with a pan-European twist. **Siam Central** (14 Charlotte St., W1, Fitzrovia, 020/7436–7460) offers 30 "Thai tapas" for a new spin on the concept.

THE CITY, CLERKENWELL & SOUTHBANK

Clerkenwell has long been gastro-heaven, but now that the City stays busy weekends, and the Southbank is firmly on the foodie map, the area has emerged as a prominent dining destination.

This diverse area is one of the capital's most up-and-coming in terms of restaurants. The City's pubs and restaurants are busiest during the week, attracting bankers and lawyers in droves. Farther north, there's a more trendy, relaxed vibe, with good quality pubs in Farringdon such as **The Crown** (43 Clerkenwell Green, EC1, Clerkenwell, 020/7253–4973) and **The Peasant** (240 St. John St., EC1V, Islington, 020/7336–7726) attracting media types and well-heeled students.

The south bank of the Thames has transformed in the last decade into restaurant nirvana, with the Shad Thames area testament to the revival. A short walk from London Bridge tube, it's possible to eat on the riverbank at the Design Museum's acclaimed restaurant, The **Blueprint Café** (28 Shad Thames, SE1, Shad Thames, 020/7378–7031), or at one of the reasonably priced chains nearby.
—Helen Lewis

UNDER £10

Because these areas are traditional hangouts for high-earners, prices can be steep. But you can get grilled free-range chicken with aïoli and lemon cheesecake at "fresh fast food" restaurant **Leon** (12 Ludgate Circus, EC4M, Blackfriars, 020/7489–1580) for less than a tenner. For something a little more exotic, **Tas** (72 Borough High St., SE1, Borough, 020/7403–7200) serves accessible Turkish food such as grilled spicy sausages and lamb kebabs and has a set menu for just over £8. For traditional pub grub like bangers and mash, try the **Southwark Tavern** (22 Southwark St., SE1, Borough, 020/7403–0257).

OFF THE TOURIST TRACK

CHEF-CENTRIC CLERKENWELL

The area where the starchiness of the City fades into the relaxed artsiness of Islington is a fertile ground for restaurants. Within walking distance of Farringdon tube you can find Michelin-starred **Club Gascon** (57 W. Smithfield, EC1A, Clerkenwell, 020/7796–0600), serving mouthfuls of exquisite southwestern French cuisine, as well as **Bleeding Heart** bistro (off Greville St., EC1N, Clerkenwell, 020/7242–2056), regularly voted London's most romantic venue.

Just around the corner, marvel at some of the city's best-presented food at **The Clerkenwell Dining Rooms** (69–73 St. John St., EC1M, Clerkenwell, 020/7253–9000)—the two-course set lunch is only £15. Farther up, you could easily miss the minimalist white frontage of **St. John** (26 St. John St., EC1M, Smithfield, 020/7251–0848) but don't—this temple to carnivorousness is famed for its no-nonsense approach to offal. Try the signature bone marrow and parsley salad.

In the other direction, there's the "first gastropub," **The Eagle** (159 Farringdon Rd., EC1R, Clerkenwell, 020/7837–1353), where the marinated steak sandwich is highly recommended.

BUSTLING BOROUGH MARKET

Now 250 years old, Borough Market is a firm favorite with London's top chefs and passionate home cooks alike. On Saturdays, the unassuming location under the railway arches at London Bridge is packed with Londoners eager to pick up the finest and freshest food in the capital. There are more than 70 stalls, plus shops like **Neal's Yard Dairy** (6 Park St., SE1, Borough, 020/7645–3554), where cheeses are stacked floor to ceiling, and great restaurants. Foodies keen on sampling roast beef with all the trimmings should head to **Roast** (Floral Hall, SE1, Borough, 020/7940–1300). For Spanish ham and manzanilla sherry, try the offerings at **Tapas Brindisa** (18–20 Southwark St., SE1, Borough, 020/7357–8880). If French flavors are what you're craving, enjoy duck confit with a glass of red at cozy French brasserie **La Cave** (Basement Bank Chambers, Montague Place, SE1, Borough, 020/7378–0788).

DINING BY CUISINE

British

Canteen, ££

Coach & Horses, ££

Simpson's Tavern, ££–£££

St. John, £££

St. John Bread & Wine, £££

Cafés

E Pellicci, £

The Table, £

Eastern European

Baltic, ££

French

Chez Bruce, ££££

Club Gascon, £££££

Plateau, £££££

Greek

The Real Greek, ££

Mediterranean

Moro, £££

Modern British,

Anchor & Hope, ££–£££

Oxo Tower Restaurant & Brasserie, £££

Pakistani

Original Lahore Kebab House, ££

Seafood

Sweetings, £££

Steak

Chez Gérard, £££

Vietnamese

Sông Qué Café, ££

CHELSEA, KENSINGTON & KNIGHTSBRIDGE

If you're wealthy, fabulous, famous, or all three, chances are you'll be living—and dining—in one of these neighborhoods.

Chelsea, Kensington, and Knightsbridge are home to some of the city's best restaurants and shops (do Gordon Ramsay and Harvey Nichols ring a bell?). Chelsea, made famous in the swinging '60s as the birthplace of punk, is where you'll find yummy mummies bombing around in their Range Rovers, which locals have nicknamed "Chelsea tractors." Known for its shopping, Chelsea's restaurants range from glamorous boîtes to little places ideal for a bite on the go.

In upscale Knightsbridge, where you'll find Harrods and the high-end boutiques of Sloane Street, the restaurants are just as polished as the residents. Come here for an amazing dining experience, but don't expect any bargains. Nearby, Kensington is a residential neighborhood with a wider range of restaurants to choose from, from little French bistros to funky Vietnamese places. —*Christina Valhouli*

TEA TIME

The tradition of afternoon tea, which started in 1830, has never really gone out of style. Served between 3 PM and 5 PM, tea is popular among ladies who lunch as well as those seeking an elegant experience. Glamorous spots to imbibe include **The Berkeley** in Knightsbridge (Wilton Place, SW1, 020/7235–6000), **The Orangery** at Kensington Palace (Kensington Gardens, W8, 020/7376–0239), and **The Ritz** in Green Park (150 Piccadilly, 020/7493–8181). Expect to pay £30 per person. On a budget? Get your fill of pastries at the shabby-chic **Maison Bertaux** in Soho (28 Greek St., 020/7437–6007).

REFUELING STOPS FOR SHOPPERS

Whether you're looking for a quick bite or a more relaxing meal, there are plenty of options for every budget.

Londoners love **Wagamama** (Lower ground floor, Harvey Nichols, 109–125 Knightsbridge, SW1, 020/7201–8000) for its healthy, cheap, and cheerful noodles and rice dishes. This branch is located inside Harvey Nichols.

Celebs like Gwyneth Paltrow and Victoria Beckham are fans of **Zuma** (5 Raphael St., Knightsbridge, SW7, 020/7584–1010). Try the cocktails made with lychees and lemongrass, and splurge on the chef's tasting menu, featuring Wagyu beef, a selection of sushi, and miso cod.

The closest thing to a BBQ shack in central London, **The Big Easy** (332–334 Kings Rd., Chelsea, SW3, 020/7352–4071) serves up heaping portions of barbecue ribs and pulled-pork sandwiches, all washed down by tasty margaritas.

Tucked away in a little courtyard off the King's Road, **Phat Phuc Noodle Bar** (151 Sydney St., Chelsea, SW3, 078/7039–3863) is a casual eatery where you can grab a big bowl of steaming pho or a plate of summer rolls, then sit outside to gobble it down.

Located inside the Sloane Square hotel, the **Chelsea Brasserie** (Sloane Square, Chelsea, SW1, 020/7896–9988) is an informal but stylish place to have lunch.

DINING BY CUISINE

American
PJ's Bar & Grill, ££
Brasserie
Racine, £££
French
Aubaine, £££
Le Cercle, ££££
Gordon Ramsay at Royal Hospital Road, £££££
La Poule au Pot, £££–££££
The Capital, £££££
Tom Aikens, £££££
Indian
Amaya, £££
Italian
Zafferano, £££££
Japanese
Zuma, ££££
Modern British
The Pig's Ear, ££
Enterprise, ££–££££

RISING STAR: TOM AIKENS

Bad boy **Tom Aikens** was the youngest British chef to be awarded two Michelin stars but he's equally famous for his wild behavior. His eponymous restaurant (43 Elystan St., SW3, 020/7584–2003) is one of the finest in town, offering unexpected riffs on classic preparations, like curried frogs' legs with tomato salad and quail-egg beignets. The £29 lunch menu is a fantastic deal; at dinner, three-courses runs £65. A more casual option is **Tom's Kitchen** in Chelsea (27 Cale St., 020/7349–0202), where you can start with a cocktail in the "bar and games room" before enjoying a meal in the brasserie-style dining room. The deep-fried pigs ears with shallot-caper mayo gets raves, as does pan-friend veal loin over tomato-caper linguine.

NOTTING HILL & BAYSWATER

Notting Hill's trendy atmosphere, designer shops, and hip residents, and Bayswater's numerous ethnic eateries continue to entice Londoners and tourists to this area.

Notting Hill, located west of Bayswater and north of Kensington, has earned a reputation as one of London's more fashionable neighborhoods, with numerous boutiques, chic cafés and restaurants, buzzing bars, and the famous Portobello Road Market's collection of antiques shops, vintage clothes stands and delicious food stalls. The gentrification of Notting Hill has led to an increase in the number of young working professionals moving to the area and prices are rising accordingly. If you are in London at the end of August, be sure to check out the revelry and fanfare of the Notting Hill Carnival.

Bayswater is known for its diversity of communities and restaurants. This neighborhood's main street, Queensway, boasts some of the best inexpensive ethnic restaurants in London. It's here that you will find Greek, Indian, Chinese, and Persian restaurants all within walking distance of each other. Affordable accommodations and shops are plentiful here, making this a popular destination for tourists. —*Puja Chugani*

SNACKING SPOT

Portobello Road Market is one of London's most popular outdoor markets. Get there early on Saturday morning (the market is open from 8 AM–5 PM) to beat the crowds. Peruse the antiques and vintage clothes and when you've built up an appetite, head to the *other* side of the market for snacks. You'll find fresh fruit and vegetable stands, bakeries, olive and cheese purveyors, and numerous hot food stalls peddling sweet and savory crepes, sausages and hamburgers, fried prawns, and grilled kebabs.

How to get there: Take the tube to Ladbroke Grove or Notting Hill Gate station and follow the signs (and crowds).

A GASTROPUB TOUR

These upscale pubs specialize in the kind of high-quality, innovative fare you'd be more likely to find in a proper restaurant than a low-key bar setting. Dining here is an excellent way to experience local cuisine and a great pint of beer.

✕**The Cow Dining Room** (89 Westbourne Park Rd., W2, Notting Hill, 020/7221–0021) is one of the best-known gastropubs in London. Eat at the stylish bar or head upstairs to the slightly more formal dining room where you'll have more room to stretch out and enjoy your meal.

✕**The Westbourne** (101 Westbourne Park Villas, W2, Notting Hill, 020/7221–1332) offers hearty regional food and rustic dishes from the daily changing menu, with specials like Portuguese fish stew and grilled leg of Welsh lamb. It's an über-trendy spot popular with stylish locals.

✕**Prince Bonaparte** (80 Chepstow Rd., W2, Notting Hill, 020/7313–9491) is a cozy gastropub serving modern European cuisine. Stop in to try one of their more popular specialties: toad-in-the-hole, aka sausages in Yorkshire pudding.

✕**Ladbroke Arms** (54 Ladbroke Rd., W11, Notting Hill, 020/7727–6648) is the quintessential neighborhood gastropub. The menu changes frequently, but a trademark specialty is the chocolate fondant.

CHEAP EATS

If you're looking for a great meal that's not too pricey, head to Bayswater. These are our favorite bargain restaurants:

✕**Khan's** (13–15 Westbourne Grove, W2, Bayswater, 020/7727–5420) is renowned throughout London for its great Indian food at affordable prices.

✕**Alounak** (44 Westbourne Grove, W2, Bayswater, 020/7229–4158) is a local favorite featuring superb Iranian cuisine served in a comfortable dining room.

✕**Four Seasons Chinese** (84 Queensway, W2, Bayswater, 020/7229–4320) is always crowded, but that's a testament to the food quality at this affordable spot.

DINING BY CUISINE

Asian
E&O, £££

Asian
Mandalay, £

Brasserie
Notting Hill Brasserie, £££–££££

Electric Brasserie, ££–£££

British
Cow Dining Room, £££

Julie's, £££

The Salusbury, ££–£££

Chinese
Royal China, £££

Continental
Clarke's, £££££

French
The Ledbury, £££££

Middle Eastern
Alounak, ££

Modern British
The Waterway, ££

Thai
Churchill Thai Kitchen, £

RESTAURANTS (IN ALPHABETICAL ORDER)

££
ECLECTIC
Bloomsbury

Acorn House. London's top eco-friendly upmarket restaurant in resurgent King's Cross spearheads the trend for green dining. All ingredients are seasonal, sustainable, organic, fair-trade, or locally sourced. The water is purified on site, the staff uses biodeisel, the packaging is biodegradable, and all waste is recycled. London's ethical eaters love the concept, *and* they get to choose the size of portions to help reduce overconsumption. Wonderfully creative dishes range from yellow beetroot with potatoes to pheasant salad with dandelion. ⊠*69 Swinton St., WC1* ☎*020/7812–1842* ▭*AE, DC, MC, V* Ⓤ*King's Cross.*

£££
FRENCH
Covent Garden

Admiralty. This is a restaurant worthy of its imperial courtyard setting of Somerset House, just off the Strand. Admiralty does modern French cuisine with creative panache, like ham-hock ravioli with caramelized onions and pea-and-mint velouté, and roasted sea bass with baby bok choy and saffron sauce. There is outdoor seating in the summer on a terrace that overlooks the Thames. ⊠*Somerset House, Strand, , WC2* ☎*020/7845–4646* ▭*AE, DC, MC, V* ◷*No dinner Sun.* Ⓤ*Charing Cross.*

£££
BRASSERIE
Angel

Almeida. Angel's best bet for a decent classy meal, Almeida is a smart unshowy French brasserie which works well pre- and post-performance for the eponymous off–West End theater across the road. With lunch and theater deals at £17.50—before 6.30 PM or after 9.30 PM—you can't go wrong with classic dishes like tuna niçoise, Landes duck, or guinea fowl ratatouille. ⊠*30 Almeida St.,, N1* ☎*020/7354–4777* ▭*AE, DC, MC, V* Ⓤ*Angel.*

££
MIDDLE
EASTERN
Bayswater

Alounak. The Persian food at this raffish canteen may be tried and true but swarms of locals still come for the hot bread and kebabs that emerge from the clay oven by the door. Try chicken kebab or the *zereshk polo* (chicken with Iranian berries). Take Persian black tea and Persian sweets, but note that the sour yogurt drinks are not to everyone's taste. ⊠*44 Westbourne Grove, W2* ☎*020/7229–0416* ▭*DC, MC, V* Ⓤ*Queensway.*

£££
INDIAN
Knightsbridge

Amaya. The hard-to-fool freeholders of Knightsbridge rave about the posh curries at Amaya. The dark-wood paneling, terra-cotta statues, rosewood candles, and sparkly chandelier set a sensual upscale tone, but it's the *biryanis* and spicy grilled fish and meats from the open showkitchen that get customers' juices going. Watch the chefs produce the goods from the tandoor oven, *sigri* grill, and *tawa* skillet, but mind the prices—the bill adds up quickly. ⊠*15–19 Halkin Arcade, Motcomb St., SW1* ☎*020/7823–1166* ⌖*Reservations essential* ▭*AE, DC, MC, V* Ⓤ*Knightsbridge.*

££–£££
MODERN
BRITISH
South Bank

Anchor & Hope. Great things at reasonable prices come from the open kitchen at this permanently packed, no-reservations, exceptional gastropub on the Cut: Crab on toast, and cod with white beans are two standouts. It's informal, cramped, and highly original, and there are often dishes for groups (leg of lamb is a good 'un.) Expect to share a table, too. ✉*36 The Cut, SE1* ☎*020/7928–9898* ⚑*Reservations not accepted*☰*MC, V*☾*Closed Sun.* Ⓤ*Waterloo, Southwark.*

££ **Andrew Edmunds.** Rustic food at realistic prices defines this perpetually
MEDITERRANEAN jammed, softly lighted restaurant—though you'll wish it were larger
Soho and the seats more forgiving. Tucked away behind Oxford and Carnaby Streets, it's a favorite with the media crowd that comes for the daily-changing, fixed-price lunch menus. Starters and main courses draw on the taste of Ireland, the Mediterranean, and Middle East. Dressed crab, feta cheese and barley, or smoked duck with walnuts are all hale and hearty. ✉*46 Lexington St., W1* ☎*020/7437–5708*☰*MC, V*Ⓤ*Oxford Circus, Piccadilly Circus.*

£££££ **Angela Hartnett at the Connaught.** Pioneering female head chef Angela
MEDITERRANEAN Hartnett delights at the famous, quintessentially English mahogany-
Mayfair paneled dining rooms at the Connaught. She nods to Italy and the Mediterranean with braised duck and white beans, and squares off with apricot soufflé and amaretto ice cream. The clientele is business and mature, and Hartnett sometimes appears from the kitchens to chat with diners. ✉*The Connaught, Carlos Pl., W1* ☎*020/7592–1222* ⚑*Reservations essential*☰*AE, DC, MC, V*Ⓤ*Green Park.*

£££ **Arbutus.** Award-winning serious cooking at mid-range prices has turbo-
MODERN boosted Arbutus into the winners' enclosure of favorite Soho eateries.
BRITISH The £17.50 three-course pre-theater special is the steal of the year. Chef
Soho Anthony Demetre might surprise with Cornish sardines or pork belly carpaccio, and end with Valrhona chocolate soup. Eighty wines are offered in mid-size carafes—a fun way to match different wines with cracking grub. ✉*63–64 Frith St., W1* ☎*020/7734–4545*☰*AE, DC, MC, V*Ⓤ*Tottenham Court Rd.*

££££ **Asia de Cuba.** Like the trendy St. Martins Lane hotel it resides in, funky
ASIAN Asia de Cuba is designed by Philippe Starck. It's bold and loud—check
Covent Garden the dangly light bulbs, Latino music, satin-clad pillars, and mini-TVs. The food is Pan-Asian fusion, and customers are encouraged to share. The miso black cod is a crowd pleaser, likewise the calamari salad. It may not be cheap, but it sure is entertaining. ✉*45 St. Martins La., WC2* ☎*020/7300–5588*☰*AE, DC, MC, V*Ⓤ*Leicester Sq.*

£££ **Aubaine.** You'll be amazed how many pretty women hang out in sum-
FRENCH mer at Aubaine in Brompton Cross. They love the feminine ambience,
Chelsea the distressed gray wooden furniture, the flowers, in-house patisserie, terrace tables, and hot people watching. It's also the figure-friendly Gallic menu, featuring prawn salads, porcini risotto, grilled tuna, and smoked chicken tartines. Sit by Brompton Road and enjoy the best free catwalk in town. ✉*260–262 Brompton Rd., SW3* ☎*020/7052–0100*☰*AE, DC, MC, V*Ⓤ*South Kensington.*

££ **Baltic.** To dine (and drink) well in South Bank, perhaps after an art
EASTERN excursion to Tate Modern, stop into this airy, modernist oasis. Slick
EUROPEAN white walls, wooden beams, exposed walls, and an amber chande-
South Bank lier make the converted coach house a sophisticated spot for enjoying Eastern European fare. Under the same ownership as Chez Kristof in

15

Afternoon Tea

The quintessential English afternoon tea ritual has been quietly brewing among London polite society. Perhaps it's the new prim thing, but nevertheless, it is now ever so fashionable to take afternoon tea.

So, what is afternoon tea, exactly? Well, it means real tea (English breakfast, Earl Grey, Ceylon, Indian, or Chinese—and preferably loose leaf) brewed in a china pot, and usually served with china cups and saucers and silver spoons any time between 3 and 5:30 PM daily. In particularly grand places—like the bigger hotels—there should be elegant finger foods on a three-tiered silver tea stand: crustless cucumber, watercress, and egg sandwiches on the bottom; scones with Devonshire clotted cream and strawberry preserve in the middle; and rich fruitcake and fancies on top.

Dress is smart-casual in posh hotels, and conversation should by tradition avoid politics and religion. Babies and children are generally very welcome, with highchairs often available. Make reservations for all these below, unless otherwise noted.

Brown's Hotel. This revamped classic English Mayfair town-house hotel sets the standard at the Tea Room, where one of London's best-known afternoon teas is served. Brown's may rely on its reputation somewhat, but still, everyone swears by its divine armchairs. For £37.50, you get sandwiches, scones with cream and jam, tart, cakes, pastries, and shortbread. ⊠ 33 Albermarle St., W1 ☎ 020/7493–6020 ⊟ AE, DC, MC, V ⊙ Tea Mon.–Fri. 3–6, weekends 2–6 Ⓤ Green Park.

Café at Sotheby's. What could be better than perusing the finest art and antiques at this famous Mayfair auction house before afternoon tea? It's open from 9:30 AM and tends to book up days in advance. ⊠ Sotheby's, 34 New Bond St., W1 ☎ 020/7293–5077 ⊿ Reservations essential ⊟ AE, DC, MC, V ⊙ Tea weekdays 3–4:45 Ⓤ Green Park.

Claridge's. This is the real McCoy, with liveried footmen proffering sandwiches, scones, and superior pastries (£32.50 for traditional tea, £42.50 for champagne tea) in the palatial yet genteel foyer, to the sound of the resident "Hungarian orchestra." Also try the £40.50 Lawn Tennis tea, with strawberries and pink champagne. ⊠ Brook St., W1 ☎ 020/7629–8860 ⊟ AE, DC, MC, V ⊙ Tea served daily at 3, 5, 5:30 Ⓤ Bond St.

The Dorchester. Amid a maze of marble and gold leaf at this grand hotel on Park Lane, afternoon tea in the Promenade is best taken on comfy sofas and to the sound of the resident pianist. Teas are £29, £38, or £43, but book well ahead. ⊠ W1 ☎ 020/7629–8888 ⊟ AE, DC, MC, V ⊙ Mon.–Fri. 2:30–4:30 PM, weekends. 2:30–4:45 PM Ⓤ Kew Gardens.

Fortnum & Mason. Upstairs at the revamped 300-year-old Queen's grocers, three set teas are ceremoniously served: afternoon tea (sandwiches, scones, and cakes: £24), old-fashioned high tea (the traditional nursery meal, adding something more robust and savory: £26), and champagne tea (£34). ⊠ St. James's Restaurant, 4th fl., 181 Piccadilly, W1 ☎ 020/7734–8040 Ext. 2241 ⊟ AE, DC, MC, V ⊙ Tea Mon. 10–5:30, Tues.–Sat. 3–5:30 Ⓤ Green Park.

Harrods. For sweet-tooths, the fourth-floor Georgian Restaurant at this well-known department store has a high tea (£19.95 or £25.95) that will give you a sugar rush for a week. ✉ *87–135 Brompton Rd., SW3* ☎ *020/7730–1234* 🖃 *AE, DC, MC, V* ⊗ *Tea weekdays 3:45–5:30, Sat. 3.45–5:30* Ⓤ*Knightsbridge.*

Kandy Tea House. This tiny Sri Lankan tearoom off Kensington Church St. specializes in Ceylon tea. There's quaint cream tea (£7.50 per person) with homemade scones, clotted cream, and jam, or afternoon tea with cucumber sandwiches (£11 or £14). ✉ *4 Holland St., W8* ☎ *020/7937–3001* 🖃 *MC, V* ⊗ *Wed.–Fri. noon–5 PM, weekends noon–6 PM* Ⓤ*High St. Kensington.*

The Lanesborough. Tea in the Conservatory is as grand as it gets in the sumptuous former eighteenth century St. George's hospital on Hyde Park Corner. Tea (£28 or £37) is served delightfully to the sound of a resident pianist. ✉ *Hyde Park Corner, SW1* ☎ *020/7259–5599* 🖃 *AE, DC, MC, V* ⊗ *Mon.–Sat. 3:30–5:30 PM, Sun. 4–6:30 PM* Ⓤ*Hyde Park Corner.*

The Orangery at Kensington Palace. This Georgian, gorgeous, sunlight-flooded, yes, orangery is the perfect place for a light lunch or tea. You can get homemade soups and quiche, cakes, shortbread, pastries, and pots of Earl Grey. Go when it's balmy, or you'll freeze. ✉ *Kensington Gardens, , W8* ☎ *020/7376–0239* 🖃 *AE, MC, V* Ⓤ*High St. Kensington, Queensway.*

The Original Maids of Honour. A trip to Kew Royal Botanical Gardens is topped off with tea at Maids of Honour. The family-run business is famous for its cakes—puff pastry with sweet curd—made from a secret recipe. Prices are low, there's outdoor seating, and it's near Kew's main Victoria Gate entrance. ✉ *288 Kew Rd., TW9* ☎ *020/8940–2752* 🖃 *MC, V* ⊗ *Mon 9:30 AM–1 PM, Tues.–Sat. 9:30 AM–6 PM* Ⓤ*Kew Gardens.*

Patisserie Valerie at Sagne. Nibble on decadent patisseries with afternoon tea at this ever-reliable, reasonably priced, and stylish café. It's a perfect Marylebone High Street resting point, and you'll adore the towering cakes, chandelier, and murals on the walls. ✉ *105 Marylebone High St., W1* ☎ *020/7935–6240* 🖃 *AE, MC, V* ⊗ *Weekdays 7:30 AM–7 PM, Sat. 8 AM–7 PM, Sun. 9 AM–6 PM* Ⓤ*Marylebone.*

The Ritz. The Ritz's huge, stagy, sometimes cold and overly formal Palm Court orchestrates cake stands, silver pots, a harpist, and Louis XVI chaises, plus a great deal of rococo gilt and glitz, all for £35. Reserve four weeks ahead, more for weekends, but remember: no jeans or sneakers. ✉ *150 Piccadilly, W1* ☎ *020/7493–8181* 🖃 *AE, MC, V* ⊗ *Tea daily 11:30, 1:30, 3:30, 5:30, 7:30* Ⓤ*Green Park.*

15

Hammersmith, Baltic serves fine blinis (with caviar or smoked salmon) and tasty gravlax. Dill and rose petal are but two of the tasty infused vodkas on offer. ⊠74 Blackfriars Rd., SE1 ☎020/7928–1111 ☐AE, MC, V Ⓤ Southwark.

£ Bar Italia. This well-established caffeine stop and snack shop is a 24-hour haven for Soho-ites, theatergoers, and late-night clubbers. Expect panettone and pizza, rich chocolate cake, and real macchiato and cappuccino. The walls are full of nostalgic photos of Italian singers and sporting heroes, and it's the *primo* place in London to watch Italy play in soccer's World Cup. ⊠22 Frith St., W1 ☎020/7437–4520 ☐AE, DC, MC, V Ⓤ Leicester Sq.

CAFE
Soho

£££ Bellamy's. The posh Mayfair crowd loves this uppercrust French brasserie off Berkeley Square. The vibe is exclusive and discreet; the decor is classy and restrained; and the all-French wine list is reasonably priced. The menu weaves from scrambled eggs with Périgord truffles, through salt cod, coquilles St. Jacques, to entrecôte of beef, rillettes of duck, and *îles flottantes* ("floating islands"—custard topped with egg whites). Enter through the delicatessen next door to the restaurant. ⊠18–18A Bruton Pl., W1 ☎020/7491–2727 ☐AE, DC, MC, V Ⓤ Green Park.

BRASSERIE
Mayfair

£££–££££ Bentley's. Creamy fish pie or half a dozen oysters at the marble-top counter is the way to do it at Bentley's, Piccadilly's finest oyster bar. Richard Corrigan has led this classic old-school fish institution back to the premier league. Expect expert service, a clubby atmosphere, and high-quality fish dishes—the salmon, sole, herring, and sturgeon are all fresh and tasty. Tip: Keep Bentley's up your sleeve for pre- and post-theater for shows on nearby Shaftesbury Avenue, about five minutes away. ⊠11–15 Swallow St., W1 ☎020/7734–4756 ⌕Reservations essential ☐AE, MC, V Ⓤ Piccadilly Circus.

SEAFOOD
Mayfair

£££ Bertorelli. A stone's throw away from the Royal Opera House, Bertorelli is chic and reliable, and great for pre- or post-performance meals. The Italian food is tempting, and the menu is just inventive enough: dishes include grilled calves liver in balsamic reduction with pancetta wafers, and char-grilled beef with truffle oil. Assured, mature, and relaxed, Bertorelli's draws a host of faces from the world's of theater, opera, and ballet. There are a café-bar below and branches at Bloomsbury, Soho, and the City. ⊠44A Floral St., WC2 ☎020/7836–3969 ☐AE, DC, MC, V ⊙ Closed Sun. Ⓤ Covent Garden.

ITALIAN
Covent Garden

££££ Bibendum. This converted 1911 Michelin tire showroom, adorned with awesome stained glass and art deco prints, remains a smooth-running, London showpiece. Chef Matthew Harris cooks with Euro-Brit flair. Try calves' brains, any risotto, Pyrenean lamb with garlic and gravy, or tripe (just as it ought to be cooked). The £28.50 fixed-price lunch menu is money well spent, especially on Sunday. ⊠Michelin House, 81 Fulham Rd., SW3 ☎020/7581–5817 ⌕Reservations essential ☐AE, DC, MC, V Ⓤ South Kensington.

MODERN
BRITISH
South
Kensington

££   **Browns.** Crowd-pleasing, child-friendly English feeding is performed
BRASSERIE   well at this comfortable colonial-style brasserie chain. Salads, burg-
Soho   ers, and pastas dominate the menu, but don't overlook king prawns,
☙   lamb, roasted peppers, and especially the classic Browns steak-and-
Guinness pie. The Browns chain is seven-strong—from Kew to the
City. ✉*82–84 St. Martin's La., WC2* ☎*020/7497–5050* 🖃*AE, DC,
MC, V* Ⓤ*Leicester Sq.*

£   **Busaba Eathai.** Expect top value for money at this superior high-turnover
THAI   Thai canteen. It's fitted with bench seats and hardwood tables but is no
Bloomsbury   less seductive for the communal dining. The menu includes noodles, curries, and stir-fries. We recommend the chicken with butternut squash,
cuttlefish curry, or seafood vermicelli studded with prawn, squid, and
scallops. There's a crazy-busy site in Soho (106–110 Wardour St.), or
another near Selfridges department store (8–13 Bird St.). ✉*22 Store
St., WC1* ☎*020/7299–7900* ⌲*Reservations not accepted* 🖃*AE, MC,
V* Ⓤ*Tottenham Court Rd.*

££   **Canteen.** It's all posh pies and trendy British classics at this well-lit, ultra-
THAI   modern, diner-style canteen in Spitalfield's finance district. With booths
The City   and communal oak tables, a mainly City lunch crowd wolfs down
Coronation chicken and savory pies (chicken-and-tarragon and steak-
and-kidney are favorites), with mashed potatoes, greens, or mushy
peas. Finish with treacle tart or Eton Mess (strawberries, meringue, and
cream). Everything tastes good and is reasonably priced. ✉*2 Crispin
Place, E1* ☎*0845/686–1122* 🖃*AE, MC, V* Ⓤ*Liverpool St.*

£££££   **The Capital.** The French haute cuisine is sublime at this legendary club-
FRENCH   like hotel dining room that retains a grown-up atmosphere and formal
Knightsbridge   service. Chef Eric Chavot serves impeccable dishes in chic surroundings.
Go for exquisite smoked haddock carpaccio with quail eggs, roasted
scallops with black pudding, or halibut and Provençal tian. Desserts
like mint parfait with meringue are sensational, too. The set lunch
for £29.50 is an excellent value for this part of town. ✉*22–24 Basil
St., SW3* ☎*020/7589–5171* ⌲*Reservations essential* 🖃*AE, DC, MC,
V* Ⓤ*Knightsbridge.*

£££   **Cecconi's.** Enjoy all day buzz at this fashionable Italian brasserie oppo-
ITALIAN   site the Royal Academy on Burlington Gardens. Wedged between Sav-
St. James's   ile Row and New Bond St., the glam brigade pitch up for breakfast,
brunch, and Italian tapas (*cicchetti*) at the bar, and return for something
more formal later on. The green and brown Ilse Crawford interior is a
stylish setting for classics like veal Milanese, zucchini fritti, and Venetian calves liver. Note: It's a great refueling stop during a shopping
safari. ✉*5A Burlington Gardens, W1* ☎*020/7434–1500* ⌲*Reservations essential* 🖃*AE, DC, MC, V* Ⓤ*Green Park, Piccadilly Circus.*

££££   **Chez Bruce.** It's a coup to wrest the title of London's favorite restaurant
FRENCH   from the Ivy, and even more so for a casual neighborhood eatery south
South Bank   of the river on Wandsworth Common. Expect peerless yet relaxed service, and gustatory wonders from chef-proprietor Bruce Poole, ranging
from old fashioned braises and daubes to delicious offal preparations
and lighter, simply grilled fish dishes. The wines are great, the somme-

15

lier superb, and overall it's a warm, satisfying experience. ⊠*2 Bellevue Rd., SW17* ☎*020/8672–0114* ⌂*Reservations essential* ▤*AE, DC, MC, V* Ⓤ*Wandsworth Common rail.*

£££ **Chez Gérard.** Useful for a South Bank arts foray, it's one of a first-rate
STEAK chain of steak-*frites* restaurants—there are eight locations across Lon-
South Bank don. This one has widened the choice on the Gallic menu to include
more for those who don't eat red meat: for example, cod with mussels
and leeks. But for those with red-blooded cravings, beef steak with
shoestring fries and Béarnaise sauce remains the reason to visit. ⊠*9 Belvedere Rd., SE1* ☎*020/7202–8470* ▤*AE, DC, MC, V* Ⓤ*Waterloo.*

£££ **Chez Kristof.** This popular neighborhood eatery on salubrious Ham-
FRENCH mersmith Grove has a modern look with muted grays, whites, and
Hammersmith browns. The modern French brasserie food can be salty, but it's more
hit than miss—sea bream, ox cheek, pig's head, or veal trotters all sing
for their supper. Go for the party atmosphere and glamorous West
End vibe. Swarms of wealthy "Brackenbury village" locals gather here
all year round, but the place is especially packed in summer, when
sitting at a terrace table is the height of cool. ⊠*111 Hammersmith
Grove, W6* ☎*020/8741–1177* ⌂*Reservations essential* ▤*AE, DC,
MC, V* Ⓤ*Hammersmith.*

£ **Churchill Thai Kitchen.** There's a cult appeal to this super-value Thai
THAI kitchen attached to a traditional English pub swamped in horse tack,
Notting Hill bedpans, and Winston Churchill memorabilia. With big portions of all
dishes priced at £6, it's a bargain for this high-end W8 postal district,
and is filled with hungry customers most nights. The *pad thai* noodles
are a sure bet, as are the red or green curries. ⊠*Churchill Arms, 119
Kensington Church St., W8* ☎*020/7792–1246* ▤*MC, V* Ⓤ*Notting Hill
Gate, High Street Kensington.*

£££££ **Clarke's.** The great Sally Clarke's
CONTINENTAL daily changing, set-price din-
Notting Hill ners, £40 and up, at this white-
wash-and-flowers Kensington
townhouse contain ultrafresh
ingredients, plainly but perfectly
cooked, accompanied by Sally's
baked breads. There could be
Welsh lamb or Cornish plaice,
but everything's invariably delicious. The clientele is conservative and unbrash; many like to sit
in the basement dining room to
catch a view of the open kitchen.
⊠*124 Kensington Church St.,
W8* ☎*020/7221–9225* ⌂*Reservations essential* ▤*AE, MC,
V* ⊘*Closed Sun. No lunch Sat.*
Ⓤ*Notting Hill Gate.*

££££ **Club Gascon.** Elegant yet relaxed, Club Gascon is one of the sexist places
FRENCH to dine in all of London. Maybe it's the leather-wall interior, the cut
The City flowers, sublime service, or the way the new wave tapas-style southwestern French cuisine is served (on a rock rather than on a plate). The restaurant specializes in foie gras from start to finish: start with duck foie
gras "popcorn," and finish with it for dessert, served with grapes and
gingerbread. ⊠*57 West Smithfield, EC1* ☎*020/7796–0600* ⚑*Reservations essential* ⊟*AE, MC, V* ☻*Closed Sun. No lunch Sat.* Ⓤ*Barbican.*

££ **Coach & Horses.** Farringdon's leading gastropub gets it right across
BRITISH the board. The inside feels like a real English "boozer"—all etched
The City glass and original wooden screens. The ales are good, and the service
keen. You'll find Old Spot ham or Goosnargh chicken, and you can
eat outside during the summer. For that real English pub experience,
dine at the bar. ⊠*26–28 Ray St., EC1* ☎*020/7278–8990* ⊟*AE, MC,
V* Ⓤ*Farringdon.*

£££ **Cow Dining Room.** A chic gastropub, the Cow comprises a faux-Dublin
BRITISH 1950s backroom saloon bar that serves rock oysters, salmon cakes,
Notting Hill baked brill, and Cornish crab. Upstairs the chef whips up Brit special-
ties like roast chicken, ox tongue, Elwy lamb, and black pudding. Mil-
lionaire Notting Hill locals love the house special in the always-packed
bar area: draft Guinness with a pint of prawns. ⊠*89 Westbourne
Park Rd., W2* ☎*020/7221–0021* ⚑*Reservations essential* ⊟*MC, V*
Ⓤ*Westbourne Park.*

££££ **Crazy Bear.** Lavish art deco styling is the draw at this glamorous res-
THAI taurant in Fitzrovia, good for cocktails in the basement sunken lounge
Bloomsbury bar, and a light Thai meal upstairs. A glossy media crowd admire the
ostrich-hide chairs, Murano chandalier, and unmarked mirrored loos.
Start with crispy duck, tiger prawns, or steamed sea bass, and end with
cheesecake. ⊠*26–28 Whitfield St., W1* ☎*020/7631–0088* ⚑*Reserva-
tions essential* ⊟*AE, MC, V* ☻*Closed Sun.* Ⓤ*Goodge St., Tottenham
Court Rd.*

£ **E Pellicci.** It's Cockney bather and all-day English breakfasts at this land-
CAFE mark café near Brick Lane and Colombia Road markets. With stained
The City glass, deco marquetry, and pics autographed by *EastEnders* soap stars,
it's the hole-in-the-wall for the breakfast Londoners adore: eggs, bacon,
toast, baked beans, black pudding, and "bubble 'n' squeak" (cabbage
and mash potatoes). Your arteries may clog up, but at least the wallet survives: almost everything is under £5, including lasagna. ⊠*332
Bethnal Green Rd., E2* ☎*020/7739–4873* ⊟*No credit cards* ☻*Closed
Sun.* Ⓤ*Bethnal Green.*

£££ **E&O.** There's decent star-spotting at E&O, one of London's hip scene
ASIAN bars and restaurants off Portobello Road. E&O means Eastern and
Notting Hill Oriental, and the cute mix of Chinese, Japanese, Vietnamese, and Thai
dishes includes *beaucoup* vegetarian options. Don't skip the lychee
martinis, miso-marinated black cod, Thai-spiced rare beef, chili-spiked
tofu, or papaya salad. ⊠*14 Blenheim Crescent, W11* ☎*020/7229–
5454* ⚑*Reservations essential* ⊟*AE, DC, MC, V* Ⓤ*Ladbroke Grove.*

15

££–£££ **Electric Brasserie.** There's nowhere better for people-watching than the
BRASSERIE   Electric, on Portobello Road, a popular hangout from morning to night.
Notting Hill   Expect oysters, steaks, roasts, chunky sandwiches, and seafood plat-
ters. The bar is a great place to meet up with friends—or make new
ones. Check out the cocktail list, with a broad selection of Martinis
and Champagne cocktails. ✉*191 Portobello Rd., W11* ☎*020/7908–
9696* ⊟*AE, DC, MC, V* Ⓤ*Notting Hill.*

£££ **Elena's L'Étoile.** London's most renowned octogenarian maitre d' Elena
BISTRO   Salvoni presides over this atmospheric century-old Parisian-style politi-
Bloomsbury   cal salon—one of London's last unreconstructed French bistros. Trad
dishes of confit lamb, salmon cakes, crème brûlée, and apple tart join
newer treats, and most diners are guaranteed a smile from Elena even
if they're not her politician-actor-journalist regulars. ✉*30 Charlotte
St., W1* ☎*020/7636–7189* ⊟*AE, DC, MC, V* ⊘*Closed Sun. No lunch
Sat.* Ⓤ*Goodge St.*

££–££££ **The Enterprise.** An upper-class gastropub near Harrods and Brompton
MODERN   Cross, the Enterprise is filled with decorous types who complement
BRITISH   the eclectic decor—striped wallpaper, Edwardian side tables covered
Knightsbridge   with baskets, vintage books piled up in the windows, white linens,
and bunches of fresh flowers. The heartiness of the room makes for
a fun experience. Like the decor, the menu is eclectic—venison and
red wine, crab mayonnaise, and sea bass with roasted fennel are all
served with style. ✉*35 Walton St., SW3* ☎*020/7584–3148* ⊟*AE,
MC, V* Ⓤ*South Kensington.*

£ **Esarn Kheaw.** Get over the green dated decor, and focus on the excellent
THAI   food at this legendary hole-in-the-wall Thai on cosmopolitan Uxbridge
Hammersmith   Road in Shepherd's Bush in Hammersmith. Stray out of the comfort
zone with homemade chili sausages or catfish specials, or stick with
spicy classics like *pad thai* noodles. Either way, it's as authentic as it
comes. ✉*314 Uxbridge Rd., W12* ☎*020/8743–8930* ⊟*AE, DC, MC,
V* Ⓤ*Shepherd's Bush.*

£££ **Fino.** Trot through a spread of fine modern Spanish tapas and sip a glass
SPANISH   of Amontillado sherry, too; but watch the check—it all adds up. The set
Bloomsbury   menus for £17.95 or £28 are the best way to limit wallet strain. Set in
a buzzy basement, menu highlights include *pimentos de padron* (baby
green peppers), stuffed zucchini flowers, and tiger prawns. The meats
are divine, too, with selections like Iberico ham, chorizo, and wind-
dried beef. The entrance is on Rathbone Street. ✉*33 Charlotte St., W1*
☎*020/7813–8010* ⊟*AE, MC, V* ⊘*Closed Sun.* Ⓤ*Goodge St.*

£ **Food for Thought.** It may only be a '70s-style subterranean, unfussy veg-
VEGETARIAN   etarian café with no liquor license, but you'll often find a queue down
Covent Garden   the stairs here. It has communal tables and a zingy daily menu of soups,
quiches, stir-fries, bakes, and casseroles. Wheat-free, gluten-free, geneti-
cally modified-free, and vegan options are available, too. Note that it
closes at 8:30 PM. ✉*31 Neal St., WC2* ☎*020/7836–9072* ⊘*Reservations not accepted* ⊟*No credit cards* Ⓤ*Covent Garden.*

The Surrey Curry Scandal

In recent years, chicken tikka masala—a mild tomato-based curry filled with chunks of charcoal-cooked chicken—has virtually overtaken fish-and-chips as Britain's national dish. But buyer beware! If your order of the popular dish radiates an unnatural orange hue, it may contain illegal levels of artificial colorant.

Being a Brit these days generally involves loving curry. Whether or not the British are proud of their Empire's exploits, one happy consequence has been the growing popularity of delicious Indian cooking. Today there are more than 9,000 curry restaurants in the United Kingdom, employing more than 72,000 people, with sales of £3.2 billion a year. In contrast, just 30 years ago, there were fewer than 500 curry restaurants in the country.

But the delightfully colorful cuisine can have a hidden downside. In what has become known as the Surrey Curry Scandal, London tabloids in 2003 brought attention to a little-known problem facing Indian-food lovers throughout the nation. As the tabloid headlines screamed "Toxic Tikka," and "Curry to Dye For," the country learned that it was consuming "illegal and potentially dangerous" levels of artificial colorants in its favorite dish. Research from the UK's Food Standards Agency (FSA) had revealed that the majority of chicken tikka masala sold at restaurants in the county contained unacceptably high levels of chemical food colorants.

Before the scandal broke, most Brits had judged the superiority of their chicken tikka not by its taste, but by the brightness of its dyed-orange appearance. Even now, despite a nationwide educational campaign for restaurateurs and consumers, the problem still exists. Just be sure to ask about artificial coloring when you order. —Adam Gold

15

£££ **Fung Shing.** In terms of service and food, this cool-green restaurant is a
CHINESE   large cut above the other Lisle–Wardour Street Chinatown restaurants.
Soho   Especially exciting Cantonese dishes are the crispy baby squid, lobster
noodles, steamed scallops, and salt-baked chicken, served on or off the
bone with a bowl of broth. You'll find a steady flow of Chinese locals
and American tourists, many of whom like to sit in the airy backroom
conservatory. ⊠ *15 Lisle St., WC2* ☎ *020/7437–1539* ▤ *AE, DC, MC,
V* Ⓤ *Leicester Sq.*

£££ **Galvin Bistrot de Luxe.** The Galvin brothers successfully blaze a trail for
BISTRO   the bistro de luxe concept on Baker Street. Feted chefs Chris and Jeff
Bloomsbury forsake Michelin stars and cut loose under the brasserie banner. An
older crowd enjoys impeccable service in a handsome salon. There's no
finer crab lasagna around, and mains punch above their weight: rump
of lamb, pork with prunes, halibut with shrimp. ⊠ *66 Baker St., W1*
☎ *020/7935–4007* ▤ *AE, MC, V* Ⓤ *Baker St.*

££££ **Gaucho Grill.** You'll struggle to find a better steakhouse than this flag-
STEAKHOUSE ship Argentine steak emporium off Piccadilly, featuring rump, ribeye,
St. James's and everything in between. Order your steak *bleu,* rare, or *bien cuit,*
well done, and kick back amid the orgy of cowhide furnishings. At this

London's Best Curries

Brick Lane is known for its numerous curry houses and a local favorite is **Aladin's**. Legend has it that Prince Charles stopped by for a quick meal of chicken tikka masala during a visit of the East End. Though lacking in ambience, Aladin's makes up for it with low prices and its great chicken baltis. Note that it's BYOB. Average price of dinner for two: £15. ✉132 Brick La., E1, ☎020/7247-8210. Ⓤ Shoreditch and Aldgate East.

Tiffinbites is based on traditional Indian tiffin-packed lunches concept, each meal includes three dishes, such as chicken tikka masala, lamb rogan josh, and pilao rice. Other specialties include vegetable samosas and tandoori chicken. Tiffinbites attracts an office worker crowd during the day and takeaway is available at the Liverpool and Moorgate locations. Average price of dinner for two: £30. ✉ 22–23 Jubilee Place, E14, 020/7719–0333. Closest Tube: Canary Wharf. 22–23 Liverpool St., EC2M, ☎ 020/7626–5641. Closest tube: Liverpool St.; 24 Moorfield, EC2M, 020/7638–3951. ⊕www.tiffinbites.com. Ⓤ Moorgate.

Soho Spice offers Londoners one of the best-priced deals for Indian food. The restaurant is trendy and colorful, and the bar turns into a nightclub on Friday and Saturday night after 11

PM, which tends to attract a younger crowd. Other specialties include a range of kebabs and lamb curry. All main courses are served with rice, naan bread, dal (spiced lentils) and a vegetable. Average price of dinner for two: £35. ✉ 124–126 Wardour St., W1F, ☎ 020/7434-0808. ⊕www. sohospice.co.uk. Ⓤ Piccadilly. Oxford Circus and Tottenham Court Road.

Rooburoo is a modern and sophisticated newcomer to London's Islington neighborhood. The restaurant has quickly gained a reputation for modern spins on classic dishes and is especially popular with young professionals. Dishes include classic chicken tikka masala, as well as specialties such as Indian wraps and sea-bass fillets in banana leaves. Average price of dinner for two: £40. ✉ 21 Chapel Market, N1, ☎ 020/7278-8100. ⊕www.rooburoo.com. Ⓤ Angel.

Vama's upscale, stylish setting makes it a favorite among Chelsea's trendy crowd. The restaurant has won numerous awards and offers its own take on chicken tikka masala, as well as other popular dishes such as scallop masala and tandoori lamb chops. Average price of dinner for two: £60. ✉ 438 King's Rd., SW10, ☎ 020/7351-4118. ⊕www.vama.co.uk. Ⓤ Sloan Square or South Kensington.

four-floor ode to beef, there's little for vegetarians. ✉25 Swallow St., W1 ☎020/7734–4040 ▤AE, DC, MC, V Ⓤ Piccadilly Circus.

£££££   **Gordon Ramsay at Claridge's.** Celebrity chef and global franchise Gordon
FRENCH   Ramsay may not man the stoves but there's still a gracious atmosphere
Mayfair   at one of London's favorite celebration restaurants. Consider the three-
course lunches (£30), or the opulent set dinners (£60 and £75). Try pork
cheeks in honey or foie gras with Périgord truffle. Book months ahead—
a Sunday evening is more likely to yield success—and arrive early for
drinks at the hotel cocktail bar, which is one of the swankiest in town.
✉Claridge's, 55 Brook St., W1 ☎020/7499–0099 ⚉Reservations

essential. Jacket required ▭AE, DC, MC, V Ⓤ*Bond St.*

££££ **Gordon Ramsay at Royal Hospital**
FRENCH **Road.** The infamous Mr. Ramsay—
Chelsea of *Hell's Kitchen* fame—whips up a heavenly storm of white beans, lobster, foie gras, and shaved truffles at this fancy restaurant. He's one of Britain's finest chefs, and wins the highest accolades here, where tables are booked months in advance. For £90, splurge on seven courses; for £70, dance through a three-course dinner; or breeze through a £40 three-course lunch. ✉68–69 *Royal Hospital Rd., SW3* ☎020/7352–4441 ⚑*Reservations essential*▭*AE, DC, MC, V*☒*Closed weekends* Ⓤ*Sloane Sq.*

15

££££ **Greenhouse.** Tucked amid Mayfair mansions and approached via a spot-
FRENCH lighted decked garden, this elegant salon is for aficionados of top-class
Mayfair French cuisine at any price. Sit by the garden windows and feast on Anjou pigeon and pomegranate, wild sea bass with razor clams, or Limousin veal with salsify. The epic, 90-page wine book has 2,000 bottles, including Château d'Yquem (1887–1990). ✉*27A Hay's Mews, W1* ☎020/7499–3331 ⚑*Reservations essential*▭*AE, DC, MC, V*☒*Closed Sun. No lunch Sat.* Ⓤ*Green Park.*

£££ **Hakkasan.** It's *Crouching Tiger, Hidden Dragon* territory at this lauded
CHINESE Cantonese basement restaurant off Tottenham Court Road. Dimly lit
Bloomsbury and ultra stylish with black lattice screens, leather seats and an oak bar, Hakkasan is ideal for special-occasion dining. Go for exceptional dim sum (lunch only, noon to 3 PM), the nightclub vibe, the pretty people, the immaculate wait staff, and the hip evening cocktail scene. The restaurant is open until 1:30 AM Thursday through Sunday. ✉*8 Hanway Pl., W1* ☎020/7907–1888 ▭*AE, MC, V*Ⓤ*Tottenham Court Rd.*

£££ **High Road Brasserie.** Restaurateur to the stars Nick Jones (owner of
BRASSERIE Soho House) keeps turning out hits like this 80-seat all-day Euro
Chiswick brasserie in leafy Turnham Green. French windows, banquettes, and sidewalk dining provide the setting for comforting favorites at all hours, from egg white omelets and vichyssoise to sardines on toast and whole Dorset crab. The service is exemplary, and the buzz is constant. ✉*162–166 Chiswick High Rd., W4* ☎020/8742–7474▭*AE, MC, V*Ⓤ*Turnham Green.*

£££–£££££ **The Ivy.** The Ivy may have been pushed from its perch as London's
BRITISH favorite restaurant, yet it still is nearly impossible to get a reservation.
Covent Garden In a handsome wood-panel room with stained glass, an unexpected mix of celebrities and gawkers dines on Caesar salad, salmon cakes, and English classics like shepherd's pie and rhubarb fool. For paparazzi and

star-spotting ("Don't look now, dear, but that's Kate Moss!") this is the prime spot in London. The weekend lunch is a bargain at £21.50. If you can't score a reservation, try walking in for a table at the last minute. ⊠*1 West St., WC2* ☎*020/7836–4751* ⚲*Reservations essential* ▤*AE, DC, MC, V* Ⓤ*Covent Garden.*

£££
SEAFOOD
Covent Garden

J Sheekey. The A-list come here as an alternative to the Ivy, Nobu, or Cipriani. Linked with West End Theaterland, J Sheekey is one of Londoners' favorite haunts. It charms with warm wood paneling, alcove tables, and lava-rock bar tops. Opt for jellied eel, Dover sole, or the famous Sheekey fish pie. The £23.75 weekend lunch is a great deal. ⊠*28–32 St. Martin's Ct., WC2* ☎*020/7240–2565* ▤*AE, DC, MC, V* Ⓤ*Leicester Sq.*

£££
AMERICAN
Covent Garden

Joe Allen. West End thespians flock here after curtain fall, but more for the Broadway buzz than the decent American comfort food. Service can be flakey and the menu is undemanding: pastrami and fig is a typical starter, and mains include BBQ ribs with corn muffins. There are Yankee desserts, and secret burgers off menu, but it's the whiff of greasepaint that everyone adores. ⊠*13 Exeter St., WC2* ☎*020/7836–0651* ⚲*Reservations essential* ▤*AE, MC, V* Ⓤ*Covent Garden.*

£££
BRITISH
Notting Hill

Julie's. Does Julie's really have a draped-off dining room known as the "G-Spot"? The peek-a-boo alcoves at this cute '60s throwback ooze Victorian sensuality and have *allegedly* been the site all manner of naughtiness over the years. Movie stars and artists, royalty and rockers—from Mick Jagger to Capt. Mark Philips—have famously cavorted here. Now it's the next generation, like Kate Moss and Robbie Williams, who get carried away. The food is pricey and rather forgettable, but the racy memories abound. Poached pheasant with bread sauce, grilled sardines, or venison with mulled wine sauce are well-liked standards. ⊠*135–137 Portland Rd., W11* ☎*020/7229–8331* ▤*AE, MC, V* Ⓤ*Holland Park.*

£££££
FRENCH
Covent Garden

L'Atelier de Joël Robuchon. A-listers sit side-by-side at the counter and graze tapas-style at French legend Joël Robuchon's super seductive London outpost. Decked out in plush red and black, counter seating frames the ground-floor open kitchen, creating a spectacle that is pure culinary theater. Navigate exquisite French tapas—from frogs' legs to veal rib and quail with truffle mash. The £80 six-course tasting menu is a neat way to experience multiple flavors. There's also a smart cocktail bar, and a sit-down restaurant, La Cuisine, on the first floor. ⊠*13–15 West St., WC2* ☎*020/7010–8600* ▤*AE, DC, MC, V* Ⓤ*Leicester Square.*

£££
FRENCH
Soho

L'Escargot. Everything is classy at this old-time Soho institution on Greek Street that serves standout fare in a sassy art deco ground-floor salon and more ambitious dishes in the sophisticated first-floor Picasso Room, with Picasso artwork lining the walls. The fine wines go well with guinea fowl and Bayonne ham, roast pheasant with juniper, or any of the grilled fish dishes. Owned by restaurateur Marco Pierre White, L'Escargot is reliable, grown-up, and glamorous. ⊠*48 Greek St., W1* ☎*020/7437–2679* ▤*AE, DC, MC, V* ⊘*Closed Sun.* Ⓤ*Leicester Sq.*

££££–£££££ **L'Oranger.** The haute cuisine reaches great heights at this special place
FRENCH in aristocratic St. James's, whether leek-and-potato cappuccino, Dover
St. James's sole with langoustine, or the orange soufflé. The dining room is attrac-
tive and intimate—with polished silver, oak panels, flowers, and French
windows—and service is formal. Courtiers, business leaders, and the
Establishment great-and-the-good revel in the hushed surrounds. ⊠5
St. James's St., SW1 ☎*020/7839–3774* ⌖*Reservations essential* ⊟*AE,*
DC, MC, V ☉*Closed Sun. No lunch Sat.* Ⓤ*Green Park.*

£££–££££ **La Poule au Pot.** Americans love this delightful candlelight corner of
FRENCH France in Belgravia, where exposed walls, rustic furniture, and potted
Knightsbridge roses make for a romantic dining experience. Hardly spectacular, the
country cooking is pleasing and reliable. The goose with butterbeans
is strong and hearty, and there are some fine classics, like French onion
soup, steak with Béarnaise sauce, and cassoulet. Service comes with
bonhomie. ⊠*231 Ebury St., SW1* ☎*020/7730–7763* ⌖*Reservations*
essential ⊟*AE, DC, MC, V* Ⓤ*Sloane Sq.*

££££ **La Trompette.** Top-notch neighborhood dining doesn't get much bet-
FRENCH ter than La Trompette in outlying Chiswick. Linked to Chez Bruce
Chiswick in Wandsworth, La Trompette has a serious west London following
which goes ga-ga for the elegant food and chic surroundings. A £35
dinner might wow with steamed flounder and buttered mussels, followed by royal bream or daube of veal Provençal. The puddings stand
up to the mains and the sommelier is charm in a glass. ⊠*5–7 Devon-*
shire Rd., W4 ☎*020/8747–1836* ⌖*Reservations essential* ⊟*AE, MC,*
V Ⓤ*Turnham Green.*

£££ **Le Caprice.** Le Caprice commands the deepest loyalty of any restaurant
MODERN in London. Why? Because it gets everything right. It's the David Bailey
BRITISH prints, naff '80s Eva Jiricna interior, perfect service, and undemanding
St. James's menu that sits somewhere between Euro peasant and trendy fashion
plate. Sit at the counter and enjoy char-grilled squid with chorizo and
peppers, roasted duck with blood orange sauce, and rhubarb crumble
with custard—all enjoyed with an ample helping of celebrity spotting.
⊠*Arlington House, Arlington St., SW1* ☎*020/7629–2239* ⌖*Reserva-*
tions essential ⊟*AE, DC, MC, V* Ⓤ*Green Park.*

££££ **Le Cercle.** Prepare to be wowed by knockout new French cuisine at this
MODERN chic basement restaurant off Sloane Square. Dinky tapas-size portions
FRENCH of mushroom ravioli, gilt-head bream, or hare with Banyuls sauce arrive
Knightsbridge with style and demand to be shared. Four to six dishes will generally
do for a two-person party, and drinking wine by the glass adds to the
fun without breaking the bank. ⊠*1 Wilbraham Pl., SW1* ☎*020/7901–*
9999 ⌖*Reservations essential* ⊟*AE, MC, V* ☉*Closed Sun. and Mon.*
Ⓤ*Sloane Sq.*

£££££ **Le Gavroche.** Michel Roux Jr. outperforms at this clubby basement
FRENCH haven, which some critics rate the best formal dining in London. With
Mayfair silver domes and un-priced ladies' menus, Roux's mastery of classic
French cuisine will wow with signatures like his foie gras with cin-
namon-scented crispy duck pancake, Bresse chicken with truffles and
Madeira, or saddle of rabbit with Parmesan cheese. The set lunch is rela-

15

tively affordable at £46 (with water, a half-bottle of wine, and coffee). In fact, it may be the best way to eat here if you don't have an expense account, which most patrons clearly do. ⊠ *43 Upper Brook St., W1* ☎ *020/7408–0881* ⚑ *Reservations essential* ▤ *AE, DC, MC, V* ⊗ *Closed 10 days at Christmas. No lunch weekends* Ⓤ *Marble Arch.*

£££££
FRENCH
Notting Hill

The Ledbury. Notting Hill's hedge fund magnates have created a "strong buy" with this fantastic neighborhood fine dining restaurant housed in a handsome high-ceiling dining room. The £55 tasting menu is a tour de force that weaves from rabbit lasagna to sea bass with pumpkin gnocchi to foie gras with pear. Finish with the standout Sauternes custard with apricots and vanilla. Excellent service and a great sommelier round out this winning proposition. ⊠ *127 Ledbury Rd., W11* ☎ *0207/7792–9090* ▤ *AE, MC, V* Ⓤ *Westbourne Park.*

££
GREEK
Bloomsbury

Lemonia. Primrose Hill's favorite eternal Greek, vine-decked Lemonia is large and light, and always packed with hungry customers. Besides the usual *meze* starters, there are hearty mains like baked lamb in lemon and beef stewed in wine. Expect hoards of posh locals and the occasional mega film star. ⊠ *89 Regent's Park Rd., NW1* ☎ *020/7586–7454* ⚑ *Reservations essential* ▤ *MC, V* ⊗ *No lunch Sat. No dinner Sun.* Ⓤ *Chalk Farm.*

£££££
IRISH
Soho

Lindsay House. Irish chef Richard Corrigan fills up this creaky 1740s Georgian Soho town house with his personality and some of the finest food in town. He's known for his innovation—combining scallops with pork belly and veal sweetbreads with cauliflower, for example. But don't pass by excellent standards like Irish beef and mashed potatoes, and poached turbot with cockles and mussels. Petits fours with coffee will send you home oh-so-happy. ⊠ *21 Romilly St., W1* ☎ *020/7439–0450* ▤ *AE, DC, MC, V* ⊗ *Closed Sun.* Ⓤ *Leicester Sq.*

££££
ITALIAN
Mayfair

Locanda Locatelli. Celebrities like Madonna and Kate Moss are frequent patrons at Giorgio Locatelli's sexy Italian at the Churchill InterContinental. David Collins–designed with beige banquettes and cherrywood dividers, the food is mighty accomplished—silky risottos, handmade pastas, gorgeous grilled fish, beautiful desserts. Be bold, and try the calve's kidney or red mullet with olives, and lose yourself in the all-Italian wine list focused on Piedmont and Tuscany. ⊠ *8 Seymour St., W1* ☎ *020/7935–9088* ⚑ *Reservations essential* ▤ *AE, MC, V* Ⓤ *Marble Arch.*

£
CAFE
Soho

Maison Bertaux. Romantics cherish this tiny, two-story 1871 French patisserie because nothing has changed in decades. The pastries and gooey cakes are delightful; the éclairs are stuffed with light cream, and the rich Black Forest gâteau is studded with Morello cherries. Run by legendary owner Michelle Wade, there are commendable savories and a cute tea services. For the sake of other customers, try not to drool on the window display. ⊠ *28 Greek St., W1* ☎ *020/7437–6007* ▤ *No credit cards* Ⓤ *Leicester Sq.*

£ ASIAN Notting Hill **Mandalay.** Bargain lovers have caught on to this tiny stalwart Burmese café run by two brothers. All dishes are less than £7; bookings are recommended. Don't go for romance or atmosphere; instead, focus on the delicious papaya and cucumber salad, any of the fritters, and tilapia fish curry. Completely stuffed, you'll leave with change from £20. ✉ *444 Edgware Rd., W2* ☎ *020/7258–3696* ✍ *Reservations essential* ▭ *AE, DC, MC, V* Ⓤ *Edgware Rd.*

£££ MOROCCAN St. James's **Momo.** Mourad Mazouz—"Momo" to friends—rocks beau London with his Casbah-like North African restaurant off Regent Street. There are Moroccan rugs and fur-skin seats, plus a DJ and often live Maghreb music. Downstairs is the members-only Kemia Bar, and next door is Mô—a cozy Moroccan tearoom, open to all. The cuisine, although good, doesn't quite live up to the theatrical atmosphere, but that doesn't stop everyone from having a rockin' good time. ✉ *25 Heddon St., W1* ☎ *020/7434–4040* ✍ *Reservations essential* ▭ *AE, DC, MC, V* Ⓤ *Piccadilly Circus.*

15

£££ MEDITERRANEAN The City **Moro.** Up from the City, near Clerkenwell and Sadler's Wells dance theater, is Exmouth Market, a cluster of cute shops, an Italian church, and more fine restaurants like Moro. The menu includes a mélange of Spanish and North African flavors. Spiced meats, Serrano hams, salt cod, and wood-fired and char-grilled offerings are the secret to Moro's success. Sidle up to the zinc bar, or squeeze into a tiny table and lean in—it's noisy here. But then again, that's part of the buzz. ✉ *34–36 Exmouth Market, EC1* ☎ *020/7833–8336* ✍ *Reservations essential* ▭ *AE, DC, MC, V* ⏲ *Closed Sun.* Ⓤ *Farringdon.*

£ CAFE Soho **New Piccadilly.** Nothing has changed at this charming, family-run diner since its opening in 1951. The upturned lampshades, Formica tables, and bench seats remain; tea is served in Pyrex, and the food is cheap and cheery. Steak, chips, and spaghetti are £6.50; a banana split runs £1.75. Note that it closes at 8:30 PM daily. ✉ *8 Denman St., W1* ☎ *020/7437–8530* ▭ *No credit cards* Ⓤ *Piccadilly Circus.*

££££–£££££ JAPANESE Mayfair **Nobu.** Set in the Met, a so-hip-it-hurts hotel, soccer stars and models haunt London's top celebrity hangout and pay silly money for new-style sashimi with Peruvian flair, like yellowtail sashimi with jalapeño. For warm dishes, the miso-marinated black cod and rock-shrimp tempura are excellent. A spin off, Nobu Berkeley, thrives nearby, as does Ubon ("Nobu" backwards), in Canary Wharf. ✉ *Metropolitan Hotel, 19 Old Park La., W1* ☎ *020/7447–4747* ✍ *Reservations essential* ▭ *AE, DC, MC, V* Ⓤ *Hyde Park.*

££ SEAFOOD Bloomsbury **North Sea Fish Restaurant.** Come here and nowhere else for the British national dish of fish-and-chips—battered cod, thick fries with salt and vinegar, and a dollop of fresh tartar sauce. It's tricky to find: Head three blocks south of St. Pancras station and the British Library, then down Judd Street. They serve only freshly caught fish, which you can order grilled—but that would defeat the purpose. ✉ *7–8 Leigh St., WC1* ☎ *020/7387–5892* ▭ *AE, MC, V* ⏲ *Closed Sun.* Ⓤ *Russell Sq.*

£££–££££   **Notting Hill Brasserie.** There's something seductive about NHB, with
BRASSERIE   its side entrance, twinkle of live jazz in the bar, muted conversation,
Notting Hill   African artifacts, mini armchairs, and friendly service. The food is
imaginative, with strong and confident flavors. Feeling like fish? Try
monkfish with parsnip puree or sea bream with braised fennel. Meat
lovers should try the black pig cassoulet. ✉ *92 Kensington Park Rd.,
W11* ☎ *020/7229–4481* ▤ *AE, MC, V* Ⓤ *Notting Hill Gate.*

££   **Original Lahore Kebab House.** "Best budget curries in London" is the key
PAKISTANI   message for the Original Lahore Kebab House in insalubrious Aldgate.
The City   It may be BYOB and no-frills, but the Pakistani home-style cooking is
cheap and brilliant. Mutton *tikka*, grilled lamb chops, *tarka daal* lentils,
and karahi chicken are all super-spiced and fiery. A meal is nothing at
£15 a head, and knocks spots off anything on offer in nearby Brick
Lane's curry mile. ✉ *2 Umberston St., E1* ☎ *020/7481–9737* ▤ *MC,
V* Ⓤ *Aldgate.*

££   **Orso.** Showbiz folks flock to this mid-range Italian eatery in Covent
ITALIAN   Garden for its snappy attitude and thespian vibe, which it shares with
Covent Garden   sister restaurant Joe Allen, not far away. Menus change daily but always
include excellent pizza and pasta, plus entrées like roast sea bass. ✉ *27
Wellington St., WC2* ☎ *020/7240–5269* ⌂ *Reservations essential* ▤ *AE,
MC, V* Ⓤ *Covent Garden.*

£££   **Oxo Tower Restaurant & Brasserie.** More than two million customers have
MODERN   dined at this decade-old celebration venue on the eighth floor of the
BRITISH   Oxo Tower overlooking the Thames on the South Bank. Ceiling slats
South Bank   turn from white to blue, but who notices, with St. Paul's Cathedral,
the "Erotic Gherkin" office tower, and the majestic London skyline
across the water? The brasserie is cheaper than the pricey restaurant,
but both have great river views, especially in summer, with tables outside. Scottish lobster tempura, cod with Jerusalem artichokes, or plum-
and-sake sorbet are all bound to please. ✉ *Oxo Tower Wharf, , SE1*
☎ *020/7803–3888* ▤ *AE, DC, MC, V* Ⓤ *Waterloo.*

££££–£££££   **Pied à Terre.** Few restaurants can match the precision of Shane Osborn's
FRENCH   accomplished cuisine at this discreet townhouse on buzzing Charlotte
Bloomsbury   Street. The layout may be a touch intimate, but the food is sensational.
You'll marvel at scallop ceviche, and red mullet with baby squid. The
wine's heavy on French and the desserts will knock your socks off. ✉ *34
Charlotte St., W1* ☎ *020/7636–1178* ▤ *AE, MC, V* ☻ *Closed Sun. No
lunch Sat.* Ⓤ *Goodge St.*

££   **The Pig's Ear.** Heart-throb Prince William came with friends and split
MODERN   the check in the first-floor dining room at this classic gastropub off the
BRITISH   King's Road. Elbow in at the decorous ground-floor pub area, or choose
Chelsea   a more formal vibe in the wood-panel salon upstairs. You'll find creative
dishes on a short menu, like pig's ear, bone marrow, seared mackerel,
and Bavette steak, which are all typical, and executed … royally. ✉ *35
Old Church St., SW3* ☎ *020/7352–2908* ⌂ *Reservations essential* ▤ *AE,
DC, MC, V* Ⓤ *Sloane Sq.*

British Food Decoder

In London, local could mean any global flavor, but for pure Britishness, roast beef and Yorkshire pudding probably top the list. If you want the best-value traditional Sunday lunch, go to a pub. Gastropubs, where Sunday roasts are generally made with top-quality ingredients, are a good bet. The meat is usually served with crisp roast potatoes and carrots, and with the traditional Yorkshire pudding, a savory batter baked in the oven until crisp. A rich, dark meaty gravy is poured on top.

Other tummy liners include shepherd's pie, made with stewed minced lamb and a mashed-potato topping and baked until lightly browned on top; cottage pie is a similar dish, but made with minced beef instead of lamb. Steak-and-kidney pie is a delight when done properly: with chunks of lean beef and ox kidneys, braised with onions and mushrooms in a thick gravy, and topped with a light puff-pastry crust.

Fish-and-chips, usually cod or haddock, comes with thick "chips," or french fries, as we call them in the States. A ploughman's lunch in a pub is crusty bread, a strong-flavored English cheese with bite (cheddar, blue Stilton, crumbly white Cheshire, or smooth red Leicester), and tangy pickles with a side-salad garnish. For a hot, comforting dessert, seek out a sweet bread-and-butter pudding, made from layers of bread and dried currants baked in creamy custard until crisp. And one can't forgo English cream tea, which consists of scones served with jam and clotted cream, and sandwiches made with wafer-thin slices of cucumber—served as an accompaniment to properly brewed tea.

15

££ **Ping Pong.** High fives to Ping Pong for bringing dim sum to a younger, more fashionable crowd. So successful are the black lacquer decor, communal seating, fancy cocktails, and no-bookings formula that three clones have spawned across town, and queues at each one can snake out onto the street. Service is fast, making it a popular lunch spot. The £11.90 dim sum sets are a bargain from noon to 6 PM. ⊠ *45 Great Marlborough St., W1* ☎ *020/7851–6969* ⌲ *Reservations not accepted* ⊟ *AE, MC, V* Ⓤ *Oxford Circus.*

ASIAN
Soho

££ **PJ's Bar & Grill.** Enter PJ's and assume the Polo Joe lifestyle: wooden floors and stained glass, a slowly revolving propeller from a 1911 Vickers Vimy flying boat, and polo gear galore. The place is packed, relaxed, and efficient, and the menu, which includes all-American staples like steaks, salads, and brownies, will please all except vegetarians. PJ's opens late, and the bartenders are pros. Weekend brunch is *de rigueur* with the Chelsea set. ⊠ *52 Fulham Rd., SW3* ☎ *020/7581–0025* ⊟ *AE, MC, V* Ⓤ *South Kensington.*

AMERICAN
Chelsea

£££££ **Plateau.** Plateau's the top choice for an important Canary Wharf business meal or something more relaxed. In a slick all-white space, with tulip-shape chairs and majestic floor-to-ceiling glass windows overlooking Canada Square, Plateau has something for all business meetings; two bars, a terrace, a rotisserie room, a smoking room, and the main restaurant. Plates like cod with tamarind, venison with Savoy cabbage,

FRENCH
The City

or skate wing with capers are all dear, but pricey. ⊠*Canada Place, Canada Square, E14* ☏*020/7715–7100* ≜*Reservations essential* ▤*AE, DC, MC, V* Ⓤ*Canary Wharf.*

£££
ASIAN
Bloomsbury

The Providores & Tapa Room. New Zealander Peter Gordon scores high with his Pacific Rim fusion food in gastro-ville Marylebone. Have a sophisticated meal in the formal restaurant upstairs or try the more relaxed ground-floor Tapa Room. You'll find all sorts of exotica on the menu, from venison to kangaroo—and the whole well-heeled Marylebone village reading the papers on Sunday mornings. New Zealand venison with spiced quince, and Wagyu beef with tapioca and miso-mustard are typical delights. ⊠*109 Marylebone High St., W1* ☏*020/7935–6175* ▤*AE, MC, V* Ⓤ*Baker St.*

£££
BRASSERIE
Chelsea

Racine. It's all upscale buzz at this star of the Brompton Road dining scene, not far from Harrods or the V&A museum. Henry Harris's chic French brasserie de luxe excels because he does the simple things well—and doesn't overcharge. Classics like calves' brain, melted Raclette cheese fondue, and veal with foie gras hit the mark. Wines by the glass are fairly priced and the £18.50 dinner, available before 7:30 PM, is a good deal. ⊠*239 Brompton Rd., SW3* ☏*020/7584–4477* ▤*AE, MC, V* Ⓤ*South Kensington.*

££££
INDIAN
Knightsbridge

Rasoi Vineet Bhatia. Chef-proprietor Vineet Bhatia showcases the finest new Indian cuisine in London at this tony townhouse venue off the King's Road. Super seductive and decked with Indian prints and artifacts, Bhatia pushes the boundaries with signatures like wild mushroom rice with tomato ice cream or grilled lobster with cocoa and sour spices. Don't leave without sampling the chocolate samosas. ⊠*10 Lincoln St., SW3* ☏*020/225–1881* ▤*AE, DC, MC, V* Ⓤ*Sloane Sq.*

££
GREEK
The City

The Real Greek. London Greek cuisine shoots up several notches at this east-side Shoreditch favorite. Push costs down with a spread of *meze* starter dishes and *fagakia* mid-size plates. Lamb sweetbreads and grilled goat harken a real taste of the mainland and the all-Greek wine list gets stronger by the year. ⊠*15 Hoxton Market, N1* ☏*020/7739–8212* ≜*Reservations essential* ▤*MC, V* ☉*Closed Sun.* Ⓤ*Old St.*

£££££
FRENCH
St. James's

The Ritz. This palace of gilt, marble, mirror, and trompe l'oeil would moisten Marie Antoinette's eye. Add the view over Green Park and the Ritz's sunken garden, and it seems churlish to eat. But the cuisine stands up to the visuals, with super-rich morsels—foie gras, lobster, truffles, and caviar—all served with a flourish. Englishness is wrested from Louis XVI by a daily roast from the trolley. A set-lunch at £45 makes the check more bearable than the £80 you would pay for the Friday and Saturday cha-cha dinner-dance, which sadly is a dying tradition. ⊠*150 Piccadilly, W1* ☏*020/7493–8181* ≜*Reservations essential.* Jacket and tie ▤*AE, DC, MC, V* Ⓤ*Green Park.*

£££££
ITALIAN
Hammersmith

River Café. This canteen-style open-kitchen Italian restaurant sets the standard with its simple roasts, fresh salads, and char-grilled meats. Celebrated chefs Rose Gray and Ruth Rogers source ultra-fresh, impeccable seasonal ingredients, so expect crab with bruschetta, pumpkin and ricotta ravioli, and papardalle with wild duck ragù—plus one of London's highest checks. Remember: if you snag an evening table, this is in distant Hammersmith. You may be stranded if you haven't booked a cab. Note that tables clear out by 11 PM. ✉ *Thames Wharf, Rainville Rd., W6* ☎ *020/7386–4200* ⚑ *Reservations essential* ▤ *AE, DC, MC, V* Ⓤ *Hammersmith.*

£££ **Royal China.** The black and gold Biba-style louche decor is half the
CHINESE appeal at this flagship dim sum palace on Queensway. Expect queues
Bayswater and mirrored ceilings at this long-time favorite that churns out stacks of dim sum at a furious pace. Start with dumplings stuffed full of squid, pork, prawn, scallop, or crab, and follow up with spare ribs, Chinese greens, and pots of tea. There are other good branches at Baker Street, St. John's Wood, and Canary Wharf. ✉ *13 Queensway., W2* ☎ *020/7221–2535* ▤ *AE, DC, MC, V* Ⓤ *Queensway, Bayswater.*

£££–££££ **Rules.** Come, escape from the 21st century. Opened in 1798, London's
BRITISH oldest restaurant has seen everyone from Charles Dickens to Charlie
Covent Garden Chaplin and the current Prince of Wales pass through its doors. It's one of the most charming dining salons in London: plush red banquettes and lacquered yellow walls crammed with oil paintings, engravings, and Victorian cartoons. The menu includes historic British dishes—try roast beef and Yorkshire pudding or the steak-and-kidney pudding for a taste of the 18th century. In season, daily specials will include game from Rules' High Pennines estate. ✉ *35 Maiden La., WC2* ☎ *020/7836–5314* ▤ *AE, DC, MC, V* Ⓤ *Covent Garden.*

££–£££ **The Salusbury.** Trendy Queen's Park is dubbed "Notting Hill north"
BRITISH now thanks to winning venues like the Salusbury. Sitting at the heart
Notting Hill of the neighborhood action, it's a noisy residential boozer, with enough creative spunk in its dining room to keep the QP denizens coming back for more. The chops, braised meats, and slow roasts are mighty soothing during the cold winter months. ✉ *50–52 Salusbury Rd., NW6* ☎ *020/7328–3286* ▤ *MC, V* Ⓤ *Queen's Park.*

££–£££ **Simpson's Tavern.** This back-alley City chophouse was founded in 1757
BRITISH and is as racuous as ever. It draws ruddy-faced City folk, who love
The City old-school fare: steak-and-kidney pie, chump chops, potted shrimp, or the house specialty "stewed cheese" (cheese on toast with béchamel sauce). It is shared bench seating and service is idiosyncratic—one of its charms. ✉ *38½ Cornhill, at Ball Ct., , EC3* ☎ *020/7626–9985* ⚑ *Reservations not accepted* ▤ *AE, DC, MC, V* ☙ *Closed weekends. No dinner* Ⓤ *Bank.*

££££ **Sketch.** Fashionistas *get* the funky design thing at Mourad Mazouz's
MODERN madcap gastro-emporium off Regent Street. The lavish Gallery dining
BRITISH room, a true art gallery space by day, serves carbo-light contemporary
St. James's cuisine to a funky beat and video projections, and turns into a club Friday and Saturday nights, as soon as staff clears the floor. There are also cakes in the Parlour Room, lunch in the Glade area, and fine-dining "molecular gastronomy," aka science-based cuisine, in the first-floor Lecture Room, overseen by French star Pierre Gagnaire. ✉ *9 Conduit*

15

St., W1 ☎*0870/777–4488* ✎*Reservations essential* ▤*AE, DC, MC,
V* ☙*Closed Sun.* Ⓤ*Oxford Circus.*

££
VIETNAMESE
The City

Sông Qué Café. A trawl through trendy Hoxton is topped off at this
amazing-value Vietnamese canteen. Block out the scuzzy Kingsland
Road location and the gaudy decor and instead dive into green papaya
salad, tamarind prawns, Vietnamese pancakes, and oodles of *pho*
(beef broth with noodles and sliced steak). ✉*134 Kingsland Rd., E2*
☎*020/7613–3222* ▤*AE, MC, V* Ⓤ*Old St.*

£££££
FRENCH
Mayfair

The Square. Philip Howard's sophisticated set menus, from £25 to
£75, include haute French dishes such as crab lasagne and pigeon with
goose liver, followed perhaps by caramel mousse. Some grumble the
decor lacks character, but everything else purrs along. The clientele
is mainly corporate cats who appreciate impeccable service. There's a
long wine list and a knowledgeable sommelier. ✉*6–10 Bruton St., W1*
☎*020/7495–7100* ✎*Reservations essential* ▤*AE, DC, MC, V* ☙*No
lunch weekends* Ⓤ*Green Park.*

£££
BRITISH
The City

St. John. Fans come far and wide for Fergus Henderson's ultra-British
cooking at this stark-white converted smokehouse in trendy Clerkenwell. The architect-turned-chef's chutzpah is galling: one appetizer is
pigskin, and others, like gizzard or pig nose and tail, are marginally less
extreme. Entrées from bone marrow to woodcock can appear stark on
the plate but arrive with aplomb. Expect an all-French wine list, plus
malmsey and port. Try rice pudding with plums, or Eccles cakes. ✉*26
St. John St., EC1* ☎*020/7251–0848* ✎*Reservations essential* ▤*AE,
MC, V* ☙*Closed Sun. No lunch Sat.* Ⓤ*Farringdon.*

£££
BRITISH
The City

St. John Bread & Wine. The canteen cousin of St. John in Clerkenwell is
a winner no matter what meal of the day: have porridge and prunes
for breakfast, seed cake and Madeira for "elevenses," heart and picked
walnuts for lunch, and veal chops for dinner. Yummy bread is baked
on-site, and the wine is mainly French. This eatery is a good spot to
refuel after a visit to Brick Lane or Old Spitalfields markets. ✉*94–96
Commercial St., E1* ☎*020/7251–0848* ▤*AE, MC, V* Ⓤ*Aldgate East,
Liverpool St.*

£££
SEAFOOD
The City

Sweetings. Established in 1889, Sweetings is a remnant from the old
imperial City of London days. There are certain things Sweetings
doesn't do: reservations, dinner, coffee, and weekends. It does, however, do seafood. Not far from St. Paul's, it is patronized by City gents
who drink black velvet (i.e., Guinness and champagne) and eat potted
shrimp and roe on toast at raised counters. The oysters are fresh, and
puddings are grade-school favorites. ✉*39 Queen Victoria St., EC4*
☎*020/7248–3062* ✎*Reservations not accepted* ▤*AE, MC, V* ☙*Closed
weekends. No dinner* Ⓤ*Mansion House.*

£
CAFE
South Bank

The Table. Close to Borough food market, the Table is the smartest upscale self-service salad bar in town. Help yourself to a spread of Med-
inspired salads, pastas, bakes, and garnishes, laid out—you guessed
it—on a long table at this first floor modern canteen in an architects'
office, and pay by the weight. Dispel any reservations about DIY din-

ing—self-service never looked nor tasted so good. ⊠*83 Southwark St., SE1* ☎*020/7401–2760* ▭*AE, MC, V* Ⓤ*Southwark tube, London Bridge tube/rail.*

£££££ **Tom Aikens.** Flame-haired wonder chef Tom Aikens trained under French
FRENCH guru Joël Robuchon and excels at his slick modern eponymous res-
Chelsea taurant in deepest Chelsea. Prone to flights of fancy, his food on the
plate is highly elaborate: many swoon over his pig's head with pork
belly, poached oysters, and John Dory. There's a friendly sommelier to
help navigate the hefty wine list. ⊠*43 Elystan St., SW3* ☎*020/7584–
2003* ⏃*Reservations essential* ▭*AE, MC, V* Ⓤ*South Kensington.*

££ **Villandry.** Heaven for food lovers, this posh gourmet deli is crammed
FRENCH with fancy French pâtés, smelly cheese, fruit tarts, biscuits, organic veg,
Bloomsbury and obscure breads galore. There's a bar, charcuterie counter, and fash-
ionable dining room frequented by BBC staff and Labour politicos. A
popular breakfast is served weekdays from 8 AM. ⊠*170 Great Portland
St. W1* ☎*020/7631–3131* ▭*AE, MC, V* Ⓤ*Great Portland St.*

££ **The Waterway.** The quaint Little Venice, canal-side aspect is the big
MODERN appeal at this rated gastropub. The canal-facing outside decked ter-
BRITISH race is a sun trap in summer and heaves with local glitterati, who enjoy
Notting Hill Pimms, people-watching, and perfectly charred burgers. Inside is cozy
like a chalet, with a friendly open bar—all browns and burgundy—and
a small dining area. Expect competent cooking; roast cod and peas
is typical, and recommended. ⊠*54 Formosa St., W9* ☎*020/7266–
3557* ▭*AE, MC, V* Ⓤ*Warwick Ave.*

£££ **The Wolseley.** *Le tout* London enjoy grand elegance at this Viennese-style
AUSTRIAN grand café on Piccadilly, run by Chris Corbin and Jeremy King, some of
St. James's the city's top restaurateurs. Framed with black lacquerware, the classic
brasserie begins its long, decadent days with breakfast at 7 AM and is
open until midnight. Linger here morning, noon, and night for satisfying
fare like simple egg and bacon, wiener schnitzel, or Matjes herrings. For
dessert, go for the strudel and *kaiserschmarren*, a pancake with stewed
fruit. It's particularly good for afternoon tea and sinful pastries. ⊠*160
Piccadilly, W1* ☎*020/7499–6996* ▭*AE, DC, MC, V.*

££££ **Yauatcha.** It's all-day dim sum at this superbly lighted slinky Soho clas-
CHINESE sic. Expertly designed by Christian Liaigre—with an aquarium, candles,
Soho and a starry ceiling—the food is a match for the *Sex in the City* set-
ting. There is wicked dim sum (try anything with prawns or scallops)
and cocktails. Upstairs is a modern pastry shop. Note the quick table
turns, and ask to dine in the more romantic basement at night. ⊠*15
Broadwick St., W1* ☎*020/7494–8888* ⏃*Reservations essential* ▭*AE,
MC, V* Ⓤ*Oxford Circus.*

££ **Yoisho.** The Japanese keep this undiscovered bistro-style restaurant
JAPANESE mostly to themselves. It's tatty and poorly signed, but the food is
Bloomsbury famous, and a bargain for Fitzrovia. The grilled, skewered kushiyaki
dishes—like pork belly or chicken heart—are delectable, and there are
all sorts of dumplings, square omelets, rice balls, rice porridge, noodles,

15

and raw fish dishes. ⊠*33 Goodge St., W1* ☎*020/7323–0477* ▭*AE, MC, V* Ⓤ*Goodge St.*

£££££   **Zafferano.** Asprey-wearing Belgravians flock to Zafferano, one of Lon-
ITALIAN   don's best exponents of *cucina nuova.* The fireworks are in the kitchen,
Knightsbridge   and *what* fireworks they are: venison with polenta, and scallops with
pheasant ravioli are a dream. The desserts are *delizioso*, too, especially the chocolate tiramisu. ⊠*15 Lowndes St., SW1* ☎*020/7235–
5800* ✐*Reservations essential* ▭*AE, DC, MC, V* Ⓤ*Knightsbridge.*

££££   **Zuma.** Hurrah for this ever fashionable, Tokyo-style Japanese res-
JAPANESE   taurant. Superbly lighted and designed, with polished granite, blond
Knightsbridge   wood, and exposed pipes, it includes a bar, robata grill, and sushi
counter, which takes no reservations. Try maki rolls, taraba crab, eel
sushi, and black cod and hoba leaf, or *wagyu* beef. Grab the "sake
sommelier" to help navigate 30 varieties of rice wine. ⊠*5 Raphael
St., SW7* ☎*020/7584–1010* ✐*Reservations essential* ▭*AE, DC, MC,
V* Ⓤ*Knightsbridge.*

London
Dining & Lodging
Atlas

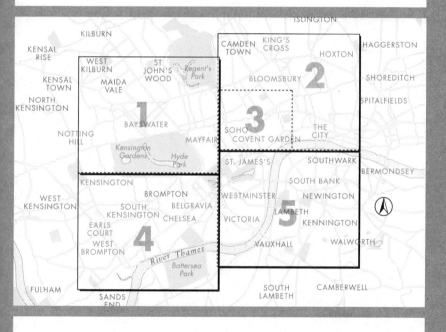

ISLINGTON

KILBURN

KENSAL RISE

WEST KILBURN

KENSAL TOWN

MAIDA VALE

ST JOHN'S WOOD

Regent's Park

NORTH KENSINGTON

1

BAYSWATER

NOTTING HILL

Kensington Gardens

Hyde Park

CAMDEN TOWN

KING'S CROSS

HAGGERSTON

HOXTON

BLOOMSBURY

2

SHOREDITCH

SPITALFIELDS

3

SOHO

COVENT GARDEN

THE CITY

MAYFAIR

KENSINGTON

ST. JAMES'S

SOUTHWARK

BERMONDSEY

BROMPTON

WEST KENSINGTON

SOUTH KENSINGTON

BELGRAVIA

CHELSEA

WESTMINSTER

SOUTH BANK

NEWINGTON

5

LAMBETH

KENNINGTON

EARLS COURT

WEST BROMPTON

4

VICTORIA

River Thames

Battersea Park

VAUXHALL

WALWORTH

FULHAM

SANDS END

SOUTH LAMBETH

CAMBERWELL

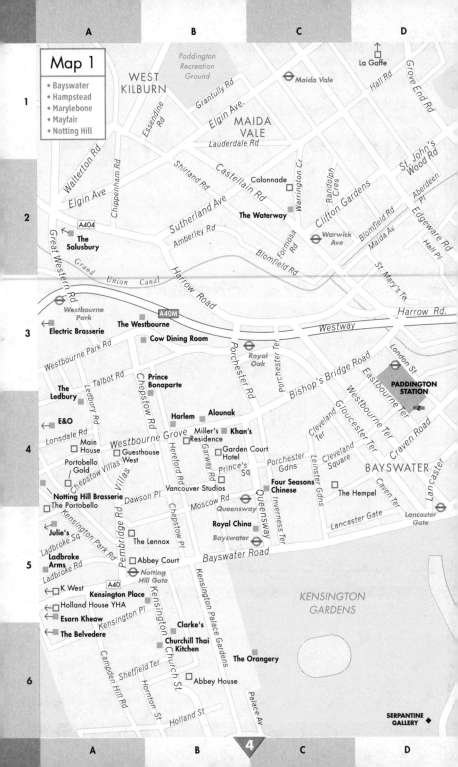

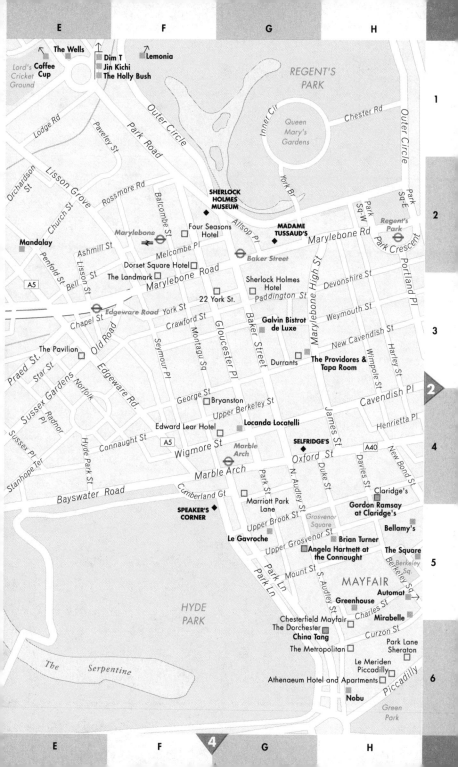

REGENT'S PARK

Chester Rd

Outer Circle

Inner Cir

Queen Mary's Gardens

1

Lord's Cricket Ground

The Wells

Coffee Cup

Dim T
Jin Kichi
The Holly Bush

Lemonia

Lodge Rd

Paveley St

Park Road

Outer Circle

Rossmore Rd

Balcombe St

York Br

Park Sq E

Park Sq-W

Regent's Park

2

Orchardson St

Church St

Lisson Grove

Ashmill St

Marylebone

Four Seasons Hotel

SHERLOCK HOLMES MUSEUM

Allsop Pl

MADAME TUSSAUD'S

Marylebone Rd

Park Crescent

Mandalay

Melcombe Pl

Dorset Square Hotel

The Landmark

Baker Street

Marylebone Road

Sherlock Holmes Hotel

Paddington St

Devonshire St

Weymouth St

Portland Pl

Penfold St

Lisson St

Bell St

A5

Chapel St

Edgware Road

York St

Crawford St

22 York St.

Galvin Bistrot de Luxe

New Cavendish St

Marylebone High St

Harley St

3

The Pavilion

Praed St

Star St

Old Road

Seymour Pl

Montagu Sq

Gloucester Pl

Baker Street

Durrants

The Providores & Tapa Room

Wimpole St

Sussex Gardens

Norfolk

Edgware Rd.

George St

Bryanston

Upper Berkeley St

Locanda Locatelli

James St

Cavendish Pl

Henrietta Pl

2

Radnor Pl

Connaught St

Edward Lear Hotel

A5

Wigmore St

Marble Arch

SELFRIDGE'S

A40

New Bond St

4

Sussex Pl

Stanhope Ter

Hyde Park St

Bayswater Road

Marble Arch

Oxford St

Duke St

Davies St

Claridge's

Cumberland Gt

Park St

N. Audley St

Gordon Ramsay at Claridge's

Bellamy's

SPEAKER'S CORNER

Marriott Park Lane

Grosvenor Square

Brian Turner

The Square

5

HYDE PARK

Park Ln

Park Ln

Le Gavroche

Upper Brook St

Upper Grosvenor St

Angela Hartnett at the Connaught

Mount St

S. Audley St

MAYFAIR

Berkeley Sq.

Automat

Greenhouse

Charles St

Mirabelle

Curzon St

Chesterfield Mayfair

The Dorchester

China Tang

The Metropolitan

Park Lane Sheraton

The Serpentine

Le Meriden Piccadilly

Athenaeum Hotel and Apartments

Piccadilly

6

Nobu

Green Park

E F G H

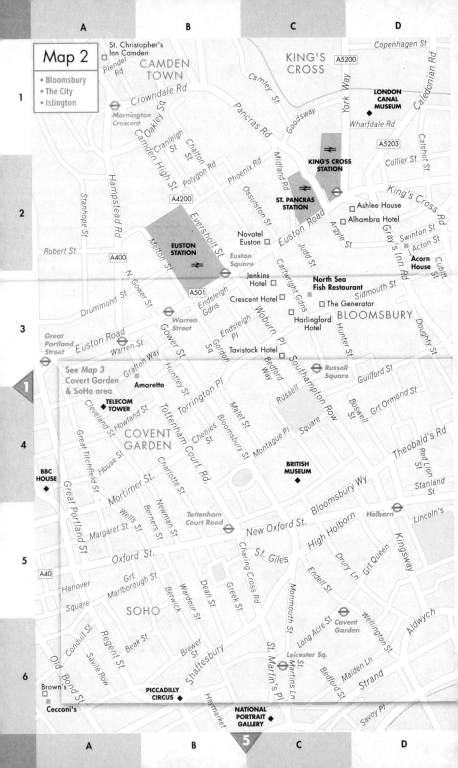

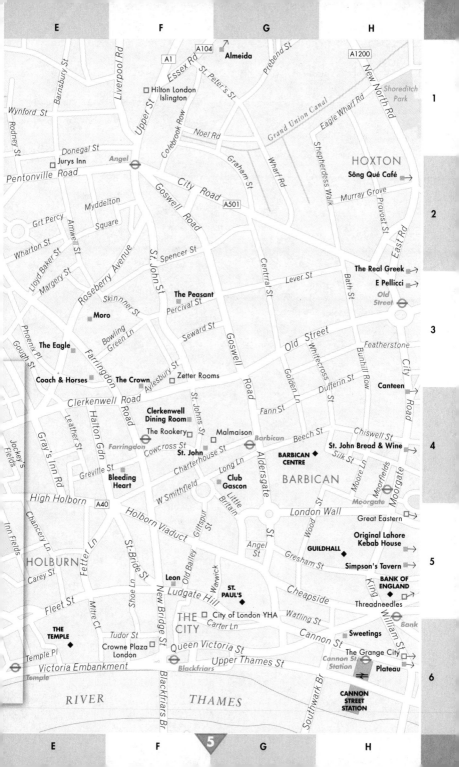

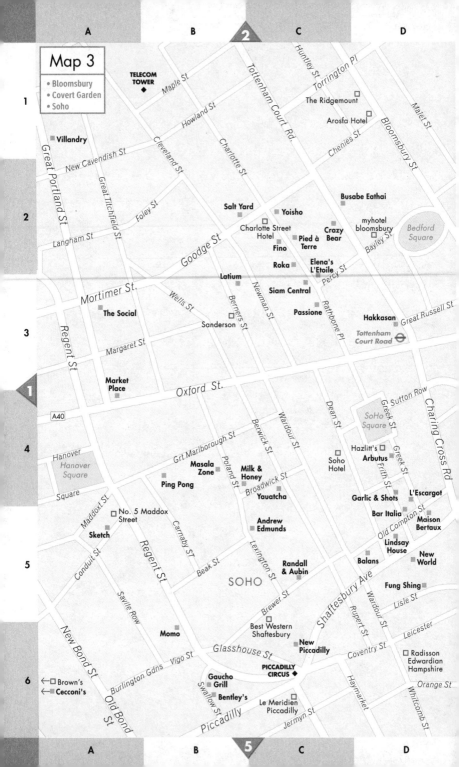

Map 3

- Bloomsbury
- Covert Garden
- Soho

1

2

3

1

A40

4

5

6

A **2** **B** **C** **D**

TELECOM TOWER ◆

Maple St

Howland St

Cleveland St

Charlotte St

Tottenham Court Rd.

Huntley St

Torrington Pl

The Ridgemount ☐

Arosfa Hotel ☐

Chenies St

Malet St

Bloomsbury St

■ Villandry

New Cavendish St

Great Titchfield St

Great Portland St

Foley St

Langham St

Goodge St

Salt Yard ■

Yoisho ■

Charlotte Street Hotel

Fino ■

Pied à Terre ■

Crazy Bear ■

Busabe Eathai ■

myhotel bloomsbury ☐

Bayley St

Bedford Square

Roka ■

Elena's L'Etoile ■

Percy St

Mortimer St.

Latium ■

Siam Central ■

Passione ■

Hakkasan ■

Great Russell St

The Social ■

Wells St

Berners St

Newman St

Rathbone Pl

Sanderson

Regent St

Margaret St

Tottenham Court Road ⊖

Market Place ■

Oxford St.

Dean St

Sutton Row

SoHo Square

Greek St

Charing Cross Rd

Hanover Hanover Square

Grt Marlborough St

Berwick St

Wardour St

Hazlitt's ☐

Arbutus ■

Frith St

Greek St

Square

Masala Zone ■

Poland St

Milk & Honey ■

Broadwick St

Soho Hotel ☐

Ping Pong ■

Yauatcha ■

Garlic & Shots ■

L'Escargot ■

Maddox St

No. 5 Maddox Street ☐

Carnaby St

Andrew Edmunds ■

Bar Italia ■

Old Compton St

Maison Bertaux ■

Sketch ■

Conduit St

Regent St

Beak St

Lexington St

Randall & Aubin ■

Lindsay House ■

Balans ■

New World ■

SOHO

Brewer St

Shaftesbury Ave

Rupert St

Wardour St

Fung Shing ■

Lisle St

Savile Row

Momo ■

Best Western Shaftesbury ☐

New Piccadilly ■

Coventry St

Leicester

Radisson Edwardian Hampshire ☐

New Bond St

Vigo St

Glasshouse St

PICCADILLY CIRCUS ◆

Haymarket

Orange St

Whitcomb St

← ☐ Brown's

← ■ Cecconi's

Burlington Gdns

Swallow St

Gaucho Grill ■

Bentley's ■

Le Meridien Piccadilly ☐

Old Bond St

Piccadilly

Jermyn St

A **B** **5** **C** **D**

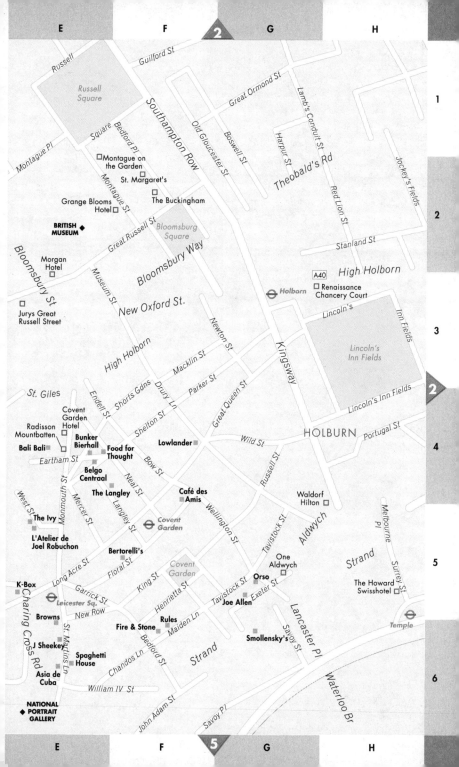

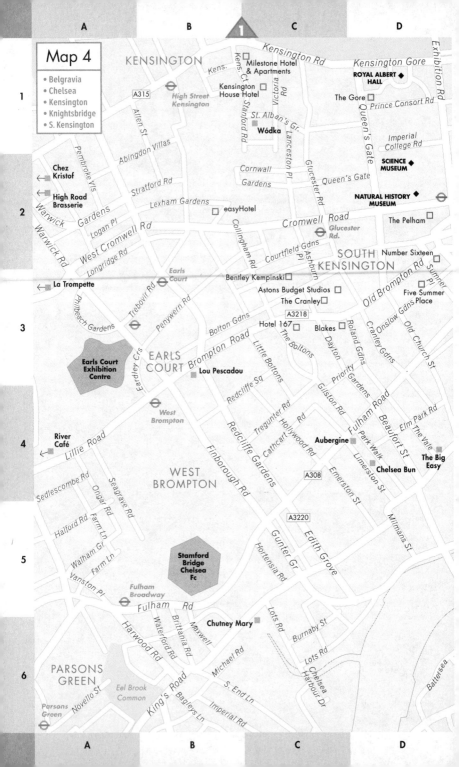

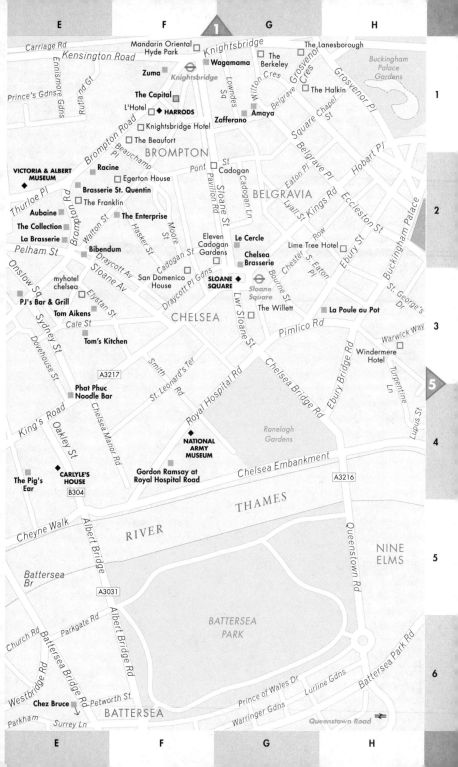

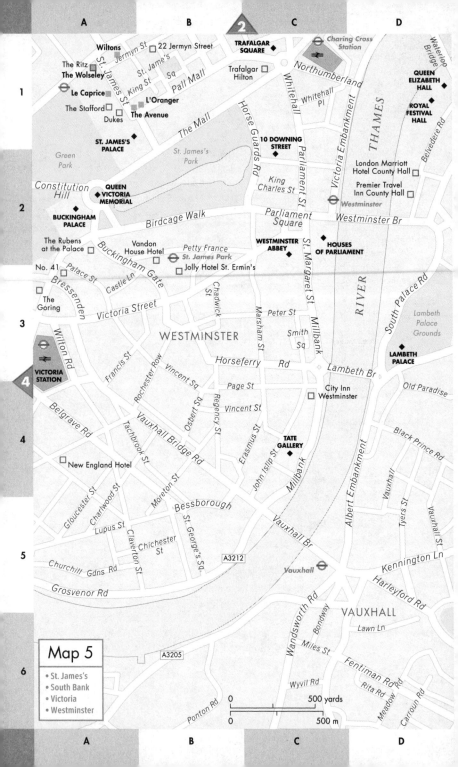

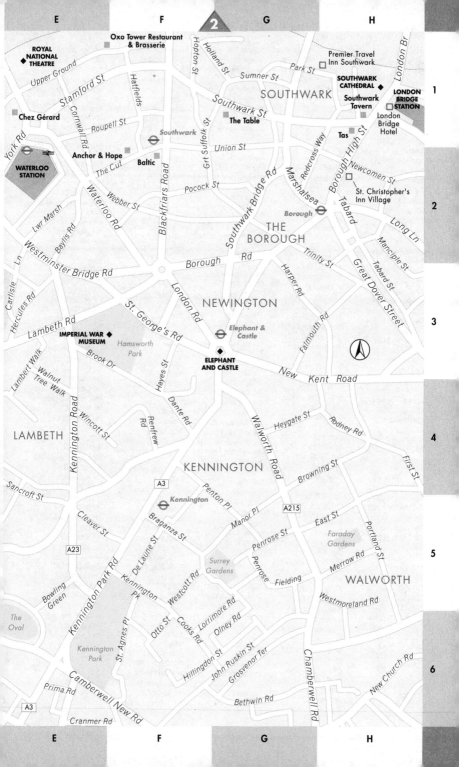

Where to Stay

The poshest hotels in London are known for their legendary service.

WORD OF MOUTH

"There is not one neighborhood in London that is 'close to everything.' London is a very large city. What is most important in my opinion is to have easy (close) access to a Tube station, and, even better, if possible, to a station that serves more than one Tube line."

—elaine

Updated
by Christi
Daugherty

THE SCENE

You'll find many things in London hotels: luxury, extraordinary service, and incredible views. But one thing you'll look long and hard for is a bargain. Accommodations have traditionally been expensive here, and—for Americans—the dollar-to-pound exchange rate has only made matters worse. If it's any consolation, London does luxury better than just about any city, so you'll get your money's worth.

For those on more moderate budgets, the situation is different. The city is just beginning to develop a base of moderately priced hotels that offer a high level of quality. Two places that have opened in recent years—Zetter Rooms and Guesthouse West—are great options in this category.

At the budget level, bed-and-breakfasts still dominate, and most are filled with chintz-covered armchairs, knickknacks, and resident pets. A sleek alternative are the new ultramodern, ultra-cheap "pod hotels"—loosely based on a popular concept in Tokyo. One, easyHotel, is a spinoff of the budget airline easyJet. A similar version called "Yotel" just opened in 2007. These are frill-free establishments with tiny rooms offering just the basics—bed, shower, toilet—but at very low prices (by London standards, anyway). They are not for the claustrophobic, as the rooms, or "pods," are tinier than a college dorm room.

Slightly more spacious are rooms in chain hotels that have opened in the center of town with cookie-cutter furnishings and basic, modern conveniences. The Best Western Shaftesbury and Premier Travel Inn County Hall are both good examples. And even at the very bottom of the price scale, accommodations can be unexpectedly trendy—just look at the slick simplicity of the Generator hostel.

WHERE SHOULD I STAY?

	Neighborhood Vibe	Pros	Cons
Bayswater & Notting Hill	Plenty of hotel options in an upscale, trendy area favored by locals and tourists.	Hotel deals abound in Bayswater; gorgeous greenery in Hyde Park; great shopping districts.	Few budget lodging options; residential areas may be too quiet at night for some.
Bloomsbury, Hampstead, Holborn & Islington	Diverse area that is part bustling business area, and part tranquil respite with tree-lined streets and meadows.	Easy access to Tube, and 15 minutes to city center; major sites, like British Museum are here; buzzing nightlife in Islington.	Busy streets filled with honking trucks and roving students; the area around King's Cross can be sketchy—avoid it at night.
The City & South Bank	London's financial district, where most of the city's banks and businesses are headquartered.	Central location with easy transportations access; great hotel deals in South Bank; many major sights nearby.	It can be as quiet as a tomb on after 8 pm; many nearby restaurants and shops close over the weekend.
Kensington	In a village-like setting, this is one of London's most upscale neighborhoods and a center of London's tourist universe.	Diverse hotel selection; great area for meandering walks; superb shopping district.	Depending on where you are, the nearest Tube might be a hike; residential area might be too quiet for some.
Knightsbridge, Chelsea & Belgravia	A glittering galaxy of posh department stores, boutiques, and fabulous hotels.	London's capital of high-end shopping with Harrod's; easy Tube access; gorgeous architecture.	Few budget hotel or restaurant options; beware of pickpockets in crowded Tube stations; not many sights here.
Mayfair, Marylebone & St. James's	Scenic area with many parks and leafy, tree-lined streets. Many tony eateries and shops nearby.	Chic hotels in one of the city's fanciest neighborhoods; low crime area; several Tube stops nearby.	Budget beds are few and far between; heavy traffic during commuting hours; pricey restaurants.
Soho & Covent Garden	A tourist hub with endless entertainment on the streets and in theaters and clubs—it's party central for young adults.	Buzzing area with plenty to see and do; late-night entertainment abounds; wonderful shopping district.	The area tends to be noisy at night; few budget hotels; keep your wits about you at night, and watch out for pickpockets.
Westminster & Victoria	This historic section, aka "Royal London" is home to major tourist attractions like Buckingham Palace.	Central area near tourist sites; easy Tube access; considered a safe area to stay.	Mostly expensive lodging options; few restaurants and entertainment venues nearby.

16

WHERE TO STAY PLANNER

Lodging Strategy

Where should we stay? With hundreds of London hotels, it may seem like a daunting question. But fret not—our expert writers and editors have done most of the legwork. The 120-plus selections here represent the best this city has to offer—from the best budget motels to the sleekest designer hotels. Scan "Best Bets" on the following pages for top recommendations by price and experience. Or find a review quickly in the listings. Search by neighborhood, then alphabetically. Happy hunting!

In This Chapter

Need a Reservation?

Yes. Hotel reservations are an absolute necessity when planning your trip to London, so book your room as far in advance as possible. Fierce competition means properties undergo frequent improvements. When booking inquire about any ongoing renovations lest you get a room within earshot of noisy construction. In this ever-changing city, travelers can find themselves temporarily, and most inconveniently, without commonplace amenities such as room service or spa access if their hotel is upgrading.

Facilities

The lodgings listed are the cream of the crop in each price category. All available facilities are mentioned, but some do cost extra. When pricing accommodations, always ask what's included. Modern hotels usually have air-conditioning, but B&Bs and hotels in older buildings often do not, and it is generally not the norm in London. You should specify if you wish to have a double bed. All hotels listed have private baths unless otherwise noted. Whatever the price, *don't* expect a room that's large by American standards. Like most of Europe, space is at a premium here.

Prices

If breakfast is included in the rate, we've noted it at the end of each review (CP for continental breakfast daily and BP for full breakfast daily). There may be significant discounts on weekends and in the off-season. ■ TIP→ **The Visit London Accommodation Booking Service (020/7932–2020, www. visitlondon.com) offers a best-price guarantee.**

WHAT IT COSTS In pounds

	£	££	£££	££££	£££££
HOTEL	under £70	£70–£120	£121–£180	£181–£250	over £250

Prices are for two people in a standard double room in high season, V.A.T. included.

BEST BETS FOR LONDON LODGING

Fodor's offers a selective listing of quality lodging experiences at every price range, from the city's best budget motel to its most sophisticated luxury hotel. Here, we've compiled our top recommendations by price and experience. The very best properties—in other words, those that provide a particularly remarkable experience in their price range—are designated in the listings with the Fodor's Choice logo.

FODOR'S CHOICE ★

Claridge's, p. 296
The Generator, p. 278
The Gore, p. 288
Grange City, p. 283
Guesthouse West, p. 274
The Connaught, p. 296
Mandarin Oriental, p. 293
Number Sixteen, p. 289
One Aldwych, p. 301
Renaissance Chancery Court, p. 281
The Rookery, p. 285
The Willett, p. 294
Zetter Rooms, p. 283

Best By Price

£

easyHotel, p. 287
The Generator, p. 278
Holland House YHA, p. 288

Morgan Hotel, p. 281
St. Christopher's Inn, p. 285

££

Guesthouse West, p. 274
Colonnade, p. 274
The Willett, p. 294

£££

Abbey Court, p. 274
L'Hotel, p. 292
Miller's Residence, p. 276
Number Sixteen, p. 289
Zetter Rooms, p. 283

££££

Charlotte Street Hotel, p. 278
The Gore, p. 288
Grange City, p. 283
Renaissance Chancery Court, p. 281
The Rookery, p. 285

£££££

Claridge's, p. 296
The Connaught, p. 296
The Stafford, p. 300
Mandarin Oriental, p. 293
One Aldwych, p. 301

Best By Experience

BEST SPAS

Bentley Kempinski, p. 287
Claridge's, p. 296
Great Eastern, p. 284
One Aldwych, p. 301
Renaissance Chancery Court, p. 281

HISTORIC HOTELS

The Cadogan, p. 291
Claridge's, p. 296
The Dorchester, p. 296
The Ritz, p. 299
The Rookery, p. 285

BEST BREAKFAST

The Dorchester, p. 296
K West, p. 275
The Milestone, p. 289
The Rookery, p. 285
Zetter Rooms, p. 283

BUSINESS TRAVELERS

Crowne Plaza, p. 283
Grange City, p. 283
Great Eastern, p. 284
Threadneedles, p. 286
Zetter Rooms, p. 283

BEST CONCIERGE

The Connaught, p. 296
The Dorchester, p. 296
The Lanesborough, p. 292
Mandarin Oriental, p. 293

MOST ROMANTIC

The Gore, p. 288
Number Sixteen, p. 289
The Pelham, p. 290
The Rookery, p. 285

MOST KID-FRIENDLY

22 Jermyn Street, p. 294
Best Western, p. 295
City Inn Westminster, p. 303
No. 5 Maddox Street, p. 299
Premier Travel Inn County Hall, p. 286

16

BAYSWATER & NOTTING HILL

£££–££££ **Abbey Court.** Sink deep into the Victorian era at this gracious, antique-laden white mansion on a quiet street off Notting Hill Gate. This place is hardly all eye-candy, though, as it strives to meet the needs of business travelers with amenities such as broadband Internet. A continental breakfast buffet is served in the conservatory. Bathrooms are tiny but modern with gray Italian marble; some have whirlpool baths. ⊠*20 Pembridge Gardens, Notting Hill, W2 4DU* ☎*020/7221–7518* 🖷*020/7792–0858* ⊕*www.abbeycourthotel.co.uk* 🛏*19 rooms, 3 suites* ☐*In-room: no a/c, safe, ethernet. In-hotel: restaurant, room service, concierge, laundry service, no-smoking rooms* 🖃*AE, DC, MC, V* �‖*CP* Ⓤ*Notting Hill Gate.*

££–£££ **Colonnade.** Near a canal filled with colorful narrow boats, this lovely town house rests in a quiet, residential area known as "Little Venice." From the Freud suite (Sigmund visited regularly in 1938) to the rooms with four-poster beds or balconies, you'll find rich brocades, velvets, and antiques. It's a former home, so each room is different; some are split-level. Extra touches in each include bathrobes and slippers, bowls of apples, and CD players. The 1920s elevator and the Wedgwood fireplace in the lobby add to the historic style of the place, but the new tapas bar is pleasantly modern. ⊠*2 Warrington Crescent, Bayswater, W9 1ER* ☎*020/7286–1052* 🖷*020/7286–1057* ⊕*www.theetoncollection.com* 🛏*15 rooms, 28 suites* ☐*In-room: safe, minibar, dial-up. In-hotel: restaurant, room service, bars, laundry service, parking (fee), no-smoking rooms, some pets allowed* 🖃*AE, DC, MC, V* Ⓤ*Warwick Ave.*

£–££ **Garden Court Hotel.** This attractive, small hotel is formed from two 19th-century town houses in a quiet garden square. Each room has a character of its own, some with original Victorian fittings. Note that some rooms are more recently refurbished than others, and not all have private bathrooms. Rooms with toilet and shower cost an extra £30, a hot breakfast also ups the bill, and family-size rooms are in the ££ category. The little, lush garden is a lovely hideaway when the sun shines. ⊠*30–31 Kensington Gardens Sq., Bayswater, W2 4BL* ☎*020/7229–2553* 🖷*020/7727–2749* ⊕*www.gardencourthotel.co.uk* 🛏*12 rooms, 10 with bath* ☐*In-room: no a/c. In-hotel: bar, no-smoking rooms, some pets allowed* 🖃*MC, V* �‖*BP* Ⓤ*Bayswater, Queensway.*

££–££££ **Guesthouse West.** The goal of this hip hotel is to offer high-class chic
Fodor's Choice at moderate prices. They almost get it right. The minimalist decor and
★ technology—cool black-and-white photos and flat-screen TVs—are very stylish. Rooms, however, are truly tiny, and there's no room service. The restaurant is child-friendly and packed with locals, and the bar is a beautiful homage to the 1930s. The hotel's relationship with a local spa and restaurant provides guests with discounts, and there are guaranteed seats for shows at the small Gate Theatre. If you fall deeply in love with the place you can "buy" a room for £235,000, which gives you "ownership" of it for 52 days of the year. ⊠*163–165 Westbourne Grove, Notting Hill, W11 2RS* ☎*020/7792–9800* 🖷*020/7792–9797* ⊕*www.guesthousewest.com* 🛏*20 rooms* ☐*In-room: DVD, dial-up, Wi-Fi.*

In-hotel: restaurant, bar, parking (fee), no-smoking rooms ☐*AE, MC, V* Ⓤ*Notting Hill Gate.*

££££ **The Hempel.** First, Anouska Hempel created the lush and lavish Blakes Hotel in South Kensington. Then she opened its opposite, the Hempel, an ultra-minimalist hotel famed for its lack of every color except white. It's an exquisite, pale wraith of a hotel, with an elegantly sculpted garden. There's nothing jarring or extraneous here, and no visible means of support beneath the furniture. A word of warning: The Hempel appeals mainly to style hounds, but its stark, minimalist sensibility is not for everyone. Those who love that sort of thing will be entranced. ✉*31–35 Craven Hill Gardens, Bayswater, W2 3EA* ☎*020/7298-9000* 🖷*020/7470-4666* ⊕*www.the-hempel.co.uk* ⤵*35 rooms, 12 suites* ⌂*In-room: safe, VCR, minibar, dial-up. In-hotel: restaurant, room service, bars, concierge, laundry service, Wi-Fi, parking (fee)* ☐*AE, DC, MC, V* Ⓤ*Lancaster Gate.*

££££ **K West.** The proudly edgy K West is hidden away inside a boring glass-and-steel building near the Shepherd's Bush tube stop, just outside Notting Hill. This is a grown-up place popular with business types, and *not* geared toward families with kids. Suites have two-person baths and drawers labeled "smut," where you'll find "adult entertainment" supplies. Dark wood, soft suede, and sleek beige walls combine to create a designer look in the bedrooms. And the minimalist style extends to the all-white hotel bar, dubbed the K Lounge. ✉*Richmond Way, Shepherd's Bush, W14 0AX* ☎*020/7674-1000* 🖷*020/7674-1050* ⊕*www.k-west. co.uk* ⤵*216 rooms, 6 suites* ⌂*In-room: safe, DVD, broadband, minibar. In-hotel: restaurant, room service, bar, gym, spa, laundry service, parking (fee), no-smoking rooms* ☐*AE, DC, MC, V* ⍥*CP* Ⓤ*Shepherd's Bush (Central).*

£££–££££ **The Lennox.** This sweet, white-stucco Victorian row house changed its name and underwent a full renovation in 2006, which brought in tasteful new carpets, furniture, and curtains but did not dent the hotel's friendly, low-key personality. Bedrooms have a traditional feel, but much of the swagged floral drapery is gone, replaced by crisp, clean fabrics that lend some elegance. Bathrooms are small but modern. Staff are so friendly they verge on jolly, and the location in Notting Hill, not far from the Portobello Road antiques market, couldn't be leafier—or lovelier. ✉*34 Pembridge Gardens, Notting Hill, W2 4DX* ☎*0870/850-3317* 🖷*020/7727-4982* ⊕*www.thelennox.com* ⤵*20 rooms* ⌂*In-room: no a/c (some), safe, VCR, dial-up Internet. In-hotel: room service, bar, laundry service, parking (fee), some pets allowed* ☐*AE, DC, MC, V* ⍥*BP* Ⓤ*Notting Hill Gate.*

££–£££ **Main House.** A brass lion door knocker marks Main House's Victorian front door, typical of Notting Hill. With just four rooms, this hotel offers nothing but a good night's sleep in an interesting Victorian home. Furnished with clean white linens, polished wood floors, modern furniture, and Asian art, it is uncluttered and delightfully spacious. The tiny urban terrace is a great place for stargazing or reading the morning paper. A day rate at the local health club is available, too. ✉*6 Colvile*

16

Rd., Notting Hill, W11 2BP 🕾*020/7221–9691* ⊕*www.themainhouse. com* ⇆*4 rooms* ⚒*In-room: VCR, Wi-Fi (some rooms). In-hotel: bicycles, laundry service, airport shuttle, parking (fee), no-smoking rooms, no elevator* ⊟*MC, V*⎮◎⎮*CP* Ⓤ*Notting Hill Gate.*

£££–££££   **Miller's Residence.** From the moment you ring the bell and are ushered up the winding staircase flanked by antiques and curios, you know you've entered a realm where history is paramount. The building is so packed with Jacobean, Victorian, Georgian, and Tudor antiques that if it weren't so elegant it might remind you of your grandmother's attic. Run by Martin Miller of *Miller's Antique Price Guides* fame, this town house serves as his home, gallery, and B&B. Rooms are named after Romantic poets. Sip a complimentary evening cocktail in the long, candlelit drawing room with fireplace, while mixing with other guests or the convivial staff. ⊠*111A Westbourne Grove, Notting Hill, W2 4UW* 🕾*020/7243–1024* 🖷*020/7243–1064* ⊕*www.millersuk.com* ⇆*6 rooms, 2 suites* ⚒*In-room: no a/c, dial-up. In-hotel: bar, concierge, laundry service* ⊟*AE, DC, MC, V*⎮◎⎮*CP* Ⓤ*Notting Hill Gate.*

££   **The Pavilion Hotel.** This eccentric Victorian town house calls itself the Pavilion *Fashion Rock 'n' Roll* Hotel, and that should give you an idea that this is a trendy address for fashionistas, actors, and musicians (that the owners are in their thirties is another hint). Often used for fashion shoots, the kitsch bedrooms veer wildly from Moroccan fantasy (the "Casablanca Nights" room) to acres of plaid ("Highland Fling") and satin ("Enter the Dragon"). You'll probably want to take some photos of your own here. Triples and family rooms are ideal for groups looking for space *and* style. ⊠*34–36 Sussex Gardens, Bayswater, W2 1UL* 🕾*020/7262–0905* 🖷*020/7262–1324* ⊕*www.pavilionhoteluk. com* ⇆*30 rooms* ⚒*In-room: no a/c, DVD (some), dial-up. In-hotel: room service, bar, laundry service, parking (fee), no-smoking rooms, no elevator* ⊟*AE, D, MC, V*⎮◎⎮*CP* Ⓤ*Paddington, Edgware Rd.*

£££–£££££   **The Portobello.** One of London's most famous hotels, the little Portobello (formed from two adjoining Victorian houses) is seriously hip and attracts scores of celebrities. It's a quirky place, decorated with utter abandon. In your room, you're likely to find an assortment of antiques, luxurious fabrics, statues, and bizarre bric-a-brac. Some rooms have balconies and claw-foot bathtubs. Room 16 has a round bed and an extraordinary Victorian "bathing machine" that actor Johnny Depp is said to have once filled with Champagne for Kate Moss, a former flame. ⊠*22 Stanley Gardens, Notting Hill, W11 2NG* 🕾*020/7727–2777* 🖷*020/7792–9641* ⊕*www.portobello-hotel. co.uk* ⇆*24 rooms* ⚒*In-room: no a/c (some), safe, VCR, Broadband, minibar. In-hotel: restaurant, room service, bar, concierge, laundry service, no-smoking rooms* ⎮◎⎮*CP* ⊟*AE, MC, V* ☺*Closed 10 days at Christmas* Ⓤ*Notting Hill Gate.*

££–£££   **Portobello Gold.** This no-frills B&B in the heart of the Portobello Road antiques area occupies the floor above the pub and restaurant of the same name. Flat-screen TVs are mounted on the wall, and the beds take up almost the entire tiny room in the doubles. The best of the bunch is the split-level apartment (£££) with roof terrace, small kitchen, and soothing aquarium. The casual restaurant serves international food at reasonable prices, and there's an Internet café that charges £1 per half hour. ✉ *95–97 Portobello Rd., Notting Hill, W11 2QB* ☎ *020/7460–4910* ⊕ *www.portobellogold.com* ⇨ *6 rooms, 1 apartment* ⚱ *In-hotel: restaurant, room service, bar, laundry service, Wi-Fi, no elevator* ▭ *MC, V* ❚◯❙ *CP* Ⓤ *Notting Hill Gate.*

££ **Vancouver Studios.** This little hotel in a listed Victorian town house is perfect for those wanting a home away from home. All rooms are like efficiency apartments, with minikitchens and microwaves, and you can even pre-order groceries, which are stocked in your mini-refrigerator upon arrival. Each studio has daily maid service as well as room service. Some rooms have working fireplaces, and one opens onto the leafy, paved garden. ✉ *30 Prince's Sq., Bayswater, W2 4NJ* ☎ *020/7243–1270* ⊟ *020/7221–8678* ⊕ *www.vancouverstudios.co.uk* ⇨ *45 studios* ⚱ *In-room: no a/c, kitchen, refrigerator, dial-up. In-hotel: room service, bar, laundry facilities, laundry service, parking (fee), no elevator* ▭ *AE, DC, MC, V* Ⓤ *Bayswater, Queensway.*

BLOOMSBURY, HAMPSTEAD, HOLBORN & ISLINGTON

£ **Alhambra Hotel.** One of the best bargains in Bloomsbury, this family-run hotel has singles as low as £32 and doubles as low as £45. Rooms tend to be small and look dated, but they're definitely good value. Some rooms have a private shower but no toilet (you share one down the hall); others have both. All rooms have a TV, all guests have access to free Wi-Fi, and tea/coffeemakers are available on request. It's not fancy, but it certainly is cheap. ✉ *17–19 Argyle St., Bloomsbury, WC1H 8EJ* ☎ *020/7837–9575* ⊟ *020/7916–2476* ⊕ *www.alhambrahotel.com* ⇨ *52 rooms* ⚱ *In-room: no a/c, no phone, Wi-Fi (some rooms). In-hotel: concierge, parking (fee), no-smoking rooms* ▭ *AE, MC, V* ❚◯❙ *BP* Ⓤ *King's Cross.*

£–££ **Arosfa Hotel.** The friendly owners, Mr. and Mrs. Dorta, and an interesting historical tidbit (the property once was the home of pre-Raphaelite painter Sir John Everett Millais) set this B&B apart from the Gower Street hotel pack. Rooms are simple and comfortable. Those at the back are far quieter and overlook the hotel's pleasant garden, although even at the front, the double glazing somewhat tames the din of the students on their way to and from class at nearby University College London. ✉ *83 Gower St., Bloomsbury, WC1E 6HJ* ☎ *020/7636–2115* ⊟ *020/7636–2115* ⇨ *15 rooms* ⚱ *In-room: no a/c, Wi-Fi (free). In-hotel: bar, no-smoking rooms, no elevator* ▭ *MC, V* ❚◯❙ *BP* Ⓤ *Goodge St.*

£ **Ashlee House.** This may be a hostel, but it attracts visitors of all ages, and is quite popular with older budget travelers, thanks to the lack of a curfew and a 24-hour reception desk. It has all the necessary hostel amenities including shared kitchen, free luggage storage, guided walking tours, and an Internet station. Staff are as cheerful as the decor, which is all sunny yellows and vivid pinks. Prices range from £9 per person for a dorm room to £26 per person for a double. ✉ *261 Gray's Inn Rd.,*

16

Holborn, WC1X 8QT ☎*020/7833–9400* 🖷*020/7833–9677* ⊕*www. ashleehouse.co.uk* ⟿*26 rooms, 175 beds* ⚲*In-room: no a/c, no phone, no TV. In-hotel: bar, laundry facilities, shared TV lounge, no-smoking rooms, Internet room (fee), kitchen, luggage storage, no elevator* ▤*MC, V* �◉*CP* Ⓤ*King's Cross.*

££–£££   **The Buckingham.** This Georgian town house near Russell Square is a great bargain for the money. Its spacious, attractively designed rooms are all studios and suites. Each has its own tiny kitchenette, giving you an alternative to eating in restaurants every night. All have marble-and-granite bathrooms and plenty of amenities. Staff are friendly, and the location is an easy walk from the British Museum and Covent Garden. ✉*11–13 Bayley St., Bedford Sq., Bloomsbury, WC1B 3HD* ☎*020/7636–2474* 🖷*020/7580–4527* ⊕*www.grangehotels.com* ⟿*17 rooms* ⚲*In-room: no a/c, dial-up Internet. In-hotel: bar, no-smoking rooms* ▤*MC, V* Ⓤ*Tottenham Court Rd.*

££££–£££££   **Charlotte Street Hotel.** On a busy street in the media hub around Soho, this hotel fuses the modern and traditional with real class. Bedrooms are beautifully decorated with unusual printed fabrics by designer and owner Kit Kemp, and bathrooms are lined with gleaming granite and oak, with walk-in showers and deep baths. Each bathroom has a flat-screen TV so you can catch up on the news while you soak with exclusive products by London perfumer Miller Harris. The restaurant, Oscar, is excellent, and the bar is a trendy local hangout. There's a public screening room with Ferrari leather chairs for watching a movie at the Sunday-night dinner-and-film club. Or you might just want to read a paper by the fire in the spacious drawing room. ✉*15 Charlotte St., Bloomsbury, W1P 1HB* ☎*020/7806–2000, 800/553–6674 in U.S.* 🖷*020/7806–2002* ⊕*www.charlottestreethotel.com* ⟿*44 rooms, 8 suites* ⚲*In-room: safe, VCR, minibar, broadband. In-hotel: restaurant, room service, bar, gym, concierge, laundry service* ▤*AE, DC, MC, V* Ⓤ*Goodge St.*

££   **Crescent Hotel.** Located on one of Bloomsbury's grand old squares, the Crescent is a friendly, old-fashioned B&B. Rooms are small and very simply decorated in cheery colors, and breakfast is big and hearty. Bathrooms are tiny and utilitarian—some have a bath and shower, others only a bath, a few have neither, so if you have a preference ask when you book. Guests can use the tennis courts and private gardens in the square—great for picnics on a sunny day. ✉*49–50 Cartright Gardens, Bloomsbury, WC1H 9EL* ☎*020/7383–2054* ⊕*www.crescenthoteloflondon.com* ⟿*27* ⚲*In-room: no a/c, dial-up. In hotel: tennis court, no elevator* ▤*MC, V* �◉*BP* Ⓤ*Russell Sq.*

£   **The Generator.** This is where the young, enthusiastic traveler comes to
Fodor's Choice   find fellow partiers. It's also the cleverest youth hostel in town. Set in a
★   former police barracks, its rooms are designed like prison cells, making the most of the bunk beds and dim lighting. The Internet café provides handy maps and leaflets. The Generator Bar has cheap drinks and a rowdy crowd, and the Fuel Stop cafeteria provides inexpensive meals. There are singles, twins, and dormitory rooms, each with a washba-

sin, locker, and free bed linen. Prices run from £10 per person for a bed in a 12-bed dorm room to £23 per person for a double room. ✉ *MacNaghten House, Compton Pl. off 37 Tavistock Pl., Bloomsbury, WC1H 9SE* ☎ *020/7388–7666* 🖷 *020/7388–7644* ⊕ *www.generatorhostels.com* ⇌ *215 beds* ⇗ *In-room: no a/c, no phone, no TV. In-hotel: restaurant, bars, concierge, airport shuttle, parking (fee), no-smoking rooms, Internet room (fee), kitchen, luggage storage* ▤ *MC, V* ⦿*CP* Ⓤ*Russell Sq.*

££–£££ **Grange Blooms Hotel.** Recently purchased by the reliable Grange hotels chain, this white Georgian town-house hotel offers a pleasant home away from home in a building just around the corner from the British Museum. Rooms are not too tiny by London standards, and those in the back of the hotel look out onto a leafy green garden. Decor in public areas is a bit stuffy, but not in an unpleasant way. You can get good deals by booking in advance through the Web site, and on the whole, it's good value for the money. ✉ *7 Montague St., Bloomsbury, WC1B 5BP* ☎ *020/7323–1717* 🖷 *020/7636–6498* ⊕ *www.grangehotels.com* ⇌ *26 rooms, 1 suite* ⇗ *In-room: no a/c, dial-up Internet. In-hotel: restaurant, room service, bar, some pets allowed, no elevator* ▤ *AE, DC, MC, V* Ⓤ*Russell Sq.*

££ **Harlingford Hotel.** The Harlingford is by far the sleekest and most contemporary of the Cartwright Gardens hotels. Bold color schemes and beautifully tiled bathrooms enliven the family-run place. Bedrooms aren't big, but they're attractive, quiet, and comfortable. Public rooms are similarly small but perfectly appointed. With space for four, the quad rooms are an excellent choice for traveling families. ✉ *61–63 Cartwright Gardens, Bloomsbury, WC1H 9EL* ☎ *020/7387–1551* 🖷 *020/7383–4616* ⊕ *www.harlingfordhotel.com* ⇌ *43 rooms* ⇗ *In-room: no a/c, dial-up. In-hotel: bar, tennis court, no elevator* ▤ *AE, DC, MC, V* ⦿*BP* Ⓤ*Russell Sq.*

££–£££ **Hilton London Islington.** Next door to the Islington Business Design Centre, this hotel is sleek and modern, standing out starkly in historic Islington. The hotel has standard, good-sized rooms with all the usual amenities meant to soothe the souls of the business travelers. For guests with time for aesthetics, the rooms higher up have panoramic views. There's a relaxing spa for those worn down by jetlag. ✉ *53 Upper St., Islington, N1 0UY* ☎ *020/7354–7700* 🖷 *020/7354–7711* ⊕ *www.hilton.com* ⇌ *183 rooms, 6 suites* ⇗ *In-room: safe, dial-up Internet. In-hotel: 3 restaurants, room service, bar, gym, spa, no-smoking rooms* ▤ *AE, DC, MC, V* ⦿*BP* Ⓤ*Angel.*

££ **Jenkins Hotel.** When this small hotel had a starring role in the British television series *Agatha Christie's Poirot,* it was filled with antiques. These days the Georgian exterior still looks the same, but inside it's been refurbished with simple but charming decor, small bathrooms, and everything you'll need for a good night's rest. Its excellent management and pleasant atmosphere led one London newspaper to recently include it among the city's top 10 hotel deals. ✉ *45 Cartwright Gardens, Bloomsbury, WC1H 9EH* ☎ *020/7387–2067* ⊕ *www.jenkinshotel.demon.co.uk* ⇌ *13* ⇗ *In-hotel: no elevator. In-room: safe,*

16

minibar, dial-up Internet, no a/c ☰ *MC,* V ⃝ BP Ⓤ *Russell Sq., King's Cross, Euston.*

££££ **Jurys Great Russell Street.** Originally designed by architect Sir Edwin Lutyens for the Young Women's Christian Association in the early 1930s, today this proud, neo-Georgian building is an upscale hotel aimed at corporate travelers during the week and leisure travelers on the weekend, when rates drop considerably. Throughout the reception area and lounge, much of the original design has been retained though it's furnished mostly with reproductions. Rooms are fairly spacious and have a classic look to them, but some could use a bit of a renovation nowadays. ✉ *16–22 Great Russell St., Bloomsbury, WC1B 3NN* ☎ *020/7347–1000* 🖷 *020/7347–1001* ⊕ *www.jurysdoyle.com* ⤴ *124 rooms, 6 suites* ⅙ *In-room: dial-up Internet, minibar. In-hotel: restaurant, room service, bars, concierge, laundry service, no-smoking rooms* ☰ *AE, DC, MC, V* Ⓤ *Tottenham Court Rd.*

££ **Jurys Inn.** Just a 10-minute walk from King's Cross station, this nondescript, utilitarian, U.K. chain hotel provides low-price accommodations. The rooms are basic but spacious, and can accommodate up to three adults or a family of four. Busy, trendy Upper Street, with its cafés, lively bars, and hip restaurants, is close by. ✉ *60 Pentonville Rd., Islington, N1 9LA* ☎ *020/7282–5500* 🖷 *020/7282–5511* ⊕ *www.jurysinn.com* ⤴ *229 rooms* ⅙ *In-room: Wi-Fi (some rooms). In-hotel: restaurant, bar, laundry service, parking (fee), no-smoking rooms* ☰ *AE, DC, MC, V* Ⓤ *Angel, King's Cross.*

££ **La Gaffe.** Italian Lorenzo Stella has welcomed people back to these early-18th-century shepherds' cottages, a short walk up one of Hampstead's magnificent hills, for more than 20 years. His restaurant has been going for nearly 40 years. Make no mistake: Rooms are tiny, with showers only, but many have canopy or four-poster beds, and all are sweetly designed. Between the two wings of the hotel is a raised summer patio. ✉ *107–111 Heath St., Hampstead, NW3 6SS* ☎ *020/7435–8965* 🖷 *020/7794–7592* ⊕ *www.lagaffe.co.uk* ⤴ *18 rooms, 3 suites* ⅙ *In-room: no a/c. In-hotel: restaurant, bar, concierge, laundry facilities, parking (no fee), no-smoking rooms, no elevator* ☰ *AE, MC, V* ⃝ CP Ⓤ *Hampstead.*

£££–£££££ **Montague on the Gardens.** What this hotel lacks in space it makes up for in charm with yards of fabric covering the walls and ceilings. Converted from a row of 1830s Georgian town houses, the Montague keeps the elegant, antique look alive with its period furnishings. Standard double rooms are small, but there are plenty of cozy public areas in which to unwind. The bar hosts jazz evenings, and the sitting room is filled with comfy furniture. The best views are from the small terrace and conservatories, where you can look out on a stretch of lawn running an entire city block. ✉ *15 Montague St., Bloomsbury, WC1B 5BJ* ☎ *020/7637–1001* 🖷 *020/7637–2516* ⊕ *www.redcarnationhotels.com* ⤴ *93 rooms, 11 suites* ⅙ *In-room: safe (some), minibar, dial-up. In-hotel: restaurant, room service, bar, gym, concierge, laundry service, no-smoking rooms* ☰ *AE, DC, MC, V* Ⓤ *Russell Sq.*

£–££ **Morgan Hotel.** This is a Georgian row-house hotel, family-run with charm and panache. Rooms are basic but attractive—the best are the little apartments (£££), which give you a bit more space to move around in. The tiny, paneled breakfast room is straight out of an 18th-century doll-house. Rooms have sunny decor; some have floor-to-ceiling windows, and the ones in the back overlook the British Museum. ⊠ *24 Bloomsbury St., Bloomsbury, WC1B 3QJ* ☎ *020/7636–3735* 🖷 *020/7636–3045* ⊕ *www.morganhotel.co.uk* ⇨ *15 rooms, 5 apartments* 🛇 *In-room: refrigerator (some), dial-up Internet. In hotel: no elevator* ⊟ *MC, V* ⏱ *BP* Ⓤ *Tottenham Court Rd. or Russell Sq.*

££££–£££££ **myhotel bloomsbury.** When myhotel opened in 1999 it was one of London's first minimalist boutique hotels, and the town raved about its plain white walls, feng shui philosophy, and a sense of style that turned a single perfect orchid in the foyer into art. But the buzz has moved elsewhere, and myhotel has struggled to catch up, repainting the cold white rooms with splashes of color, and equipping them with flat-screen TVs. The tiny "mybar" makes the place noisy and smoky on weekend evenings, and the fact that the in-house restaurant is a sushi bar may strike some as limiting when it comes to choosing lunch options. ⊠ *11–13 Bayley St., Bedford Sq., Bloomsbury, WC1B 3HD* ☎ *020/7667–6000* 🖷 *020/7667–6001* ⊕ *www.myhotels.com* ⇨ *78 rooms* 🛇 *In-room: safe (some), DVD (some), ethernet, Wi-Fi (some rooms), In-hotel: restaurant, room service, bar, gym, concierge, no-smoking rooms* ⊟ *AE, DC, MC, V* Ⓤ *Tottenham Court Rd.*

£–£££ **Novotel Euston.** Useful, but not all that stylish, this tower of a hotel is smack-dab in between King's Cross and Euston stations on busy, gritty Euston Road. It's popular with conference groups and business travelers, so all the guest rooms are generally pleasant, with good work spaces and comfortable beds. There are plenty of cappuccinos on hand in the busy lobby, and the restaurant is handy, but not about to win culinary awards. One exception to the bland, businesslike atmosphere here is the spectacular view—from the upper floors you can see for miles. ⊠ *100–110 Euston Rd., Bloomsbury, NW1 2AJ* ☎ *020/7666–9000* 🖷 *020/7666–9100* ⊕ *www.novotel.com* ⇨ *309 rooms, 3 suites* 🛇 *In-room: safe, Wi-Fi, mini-bar, satellite TV. In-hotel: restaurant, room service, bar, gym, concierge, laundry service, no-smoking rooms* ⊟ *AE, MC, V* Ⓤ *King's Cross, Euston.*

£££–££££ **Renaissance Chancery Court.** This landmark structure, built by the Pearl
Fodor'sChoice Assurance Company in 1914, houses this beautiful Marriott hotel. So
★ striking is the architecture that the building was featured in the film *Howard's End*. The spacious bedrooms are popular with business travelers and the decor has a masculine edge—lots of leather and dark red fabrics. The day spa in the basement is a peaceful cocoon. There's marble everywhere, from the floors in public spaces and the massive staircase to the in-room bathrooms. The restaurant, Pearl, is known for its modern European cuisine, and the bar, in an old banking hall, has elegant soaring ceilings. ⊠ *252 High Holborn, Holborn, WC1V 7EN* ☎ *020/7829–9888* 🖷 *0207/829–9889* ⊕ *www.renaissancehotels.com/loncc* ⇨ *343 rooms, 14 suites* 🛇 *In-room: safe, minibar, broadband.*

16

In-hotel: restaurant, room service, bar, gym, spa, concierge, laundry service, no-smoking rooms ⊟*AE, MC, V* ⓤ*Holborn.*

£ **The Ridgemount.** Mere blocks away from the British Museum and London's West End theaters, this guest house offers clean and neat rooms at a bargain. The public areas, especially the family-style breakfast room, are rather sweetly cluttered Victorian-style parlors. Some rooms overlook a leafy garden and some have their own bathroom (for about £15 extra per night). ⊠*65 Gower St., Bloomsbury, WC1E 6HJ* ☎*020/7636–1141* 🖷*020/7636–2558* ⊕*www.ridgemounthotel. co.uk* ⌨*32 rooms, 15 with bath* ☝*In-room: no a/c, no phone. In-hotel: no-smoking rooms, no elevator* ⊟*MC, V* ⓘⓞⓘ*BP* ⓤ*Goodge St.*

£££££ **Sanderson.** This surreal urban spa is housed in a converted 1950's textile factory with a lobby that looks like a design museum: Billowy fabrics serve as bathroom doors, and bedrooms have sleigh beds. The furniture is a mix of over-the-top Louis XV and postmodern pieces. Exercise addicts will find Agua (the "holistic bath house") and the indoor-outdoor fitness classes to be just what the doctor ordered. Foodies will surely want to try the hotel's popular, controversially expensive Spoon restaurant. The elegantly landscaped courtyard forms a romantic urban oasis, especially late at night, by candlelight. It doesn't get more "designer cool" than this place. ⊠*50 Berners St., Bloomsbury, W1T 3NG* ☎*020/7300–1400* 🖷*020/7300–1401* ⊕*www.sandersonlondon. com* ⌨*150 rooms* ☝*In-room: safe, VCR, Wi-Fi (fee). In-hotel: restaurant, room service, bars, gym, spa, concierge, laundry service, parking (fee), no-smoking rooms* ⊟*AE, DC, MC, V* ⓤ*Oxford Circus, Tottenham Court Rd.*

£–££ **St. Margaret's.** On a street full of budget hotels near the British Museum, St. Margaret's stands out with its attractively decorated rooms and Georgian-era exterior. The friendly family that runs the hotel is sure to welcome you by name if you stay long enough. Rooms are decorated with tasteful wallpaper and a light floral touch, as well as Georgian details such as fireplaces and beautiful cornice moldings. All stays of more than one night receive automatic discounts. Note: Not all rooms have private bathrooms, so ask when you book if this is important to you. ⊠*26 Bedford Pl., Bloomsbury, WC1B 5JL* ☎*020/7636– 4277* 🖷*020/7323–3066* ⊕*www.stmargaretshotel.co.uk* ⌨*64 rooms, 12 with bath* ☝*In-room: no a/c, dial-up Internet. In-hotel: bar, no-smoking rooms, Internet room; no elevator* ⊟*MC, V* ⓘⓞⓘ*BP* ⓤ*Russell Sq.*

£–££ **Tavistock Hotel.** This big, sprawling hotel off Russell Square makes for a convenient and affordable base to explore the British Museum and London's West End. The rooms are small and simply furnished, but clean and quiet with tea/coffeemakers. The hotel itself has plenty of amenities, including a relaxed bar and restaurant. It's a bit old-fashioned, and it won't win any style awards, but it's a solid option when money is an issue. ⊠*Tavistock Sq., Bloomsbury, WC1H 9EU* ☎*020/7278– 7871 reservations, 020/7636–8383 hotel* 🖷*020/7837–4653* ⊕*www. imperialhotels.co.uk* ⌨*343 rooms* ☝*In-hotel: restaurant, bar* ⊟*MC, V* ⓘⓞⓘ*CP* ⓤ*Russell Sq.*

£££–££££ **Zetter Rooms.** By day, nothing but business suits buzzes through the
Fodor'sChoice area between Holborn and Clerkenwell. By night, though, the ties are
★ loosened and it's all oh-so-trendy. One of London's latest "it" hotels,
Zetter reflects both personalities. The dizzying five-story atrium, art
deco staircase, and slick restaurant are your first indications of what
to expect at this converted warehouse: a breath of fresh air (and a little
space) in London's mostly Victorian hotel scene. Rooms are smoothly
done up in soft, dove gray and vanilla fabrics, and the views from the
higher floors are wonderful. It's all lovely to look at, and a bargain
by London standards. ⊠*86–88 Clerkenwell Rd., Holborn, EC1M
5RJ* ☎*020/7324–4444* 🖷*020/7324–4445* ⊕*www.thezetter.com* ⤏*59
rooms* ⌂*In-room: safe, CD, DVD, broadband (free), minibar, satellite
TV. In-hotel: restaurant, room service, bar, concierge, laundry service,
no-smoking rooms* ⊟*AE, MC, V* Ⓤ*Farringdon.*

THE CITY & SOUTH BANK

£ **City of London YHA.** On the doorstep of this hostel are St. Paul's Cathedral and the Millennium Bridge that leads to the Tate Modern. Once a
choir school, the hostel has an oak-panel chapel that's now used as a
meeting room. Most of the rooms have four to eight beds, but there are
a few singles, doubles, and triples. ⊠*36 Carter La., The City, EC4V
5AB* ☎*0870/770–5764* 🖷*020/7236–7681* ⊕*www.yha.org.uk* ⤏*193
beds* ⌂*In-room: no a/c, no phone, no TV. In-hotel: restaurant, bar,
laundry facilities, no-smoking rooms, Internet room (fee), no elevator*
⊟*AE, MC, V* ⏏*BP* Ⓤ*St. Paul's.*

£££££ **Crowne Plaza London—The City.** The shell of an old stationery warehouse,
on the former site of Henry VIII's Bridewell Palace, is now in its "nth"
reincarnation as a polished hotel. Don't let its all-business appearance
and financial-district location put you off. It's located just paces away
from the Tube, and soundproof windows block out City noise. At night,
of course, the soundproofing is wasted; so go elsewhere for a boisterous party scene. Minimalist rooms are smaller than at a typical Crowne
Plaza but reasonable by London standards. Head down to the hotel's
restaurant, Refettorio, for quality rustic Italian cuisine, including charcuterie, regional cheeses, and homemade pastas. ⊠*19 New Bridge St.,
The City, EC4* ☎*0870/400–9190* 🖷*020/7438–8080* ⊕*www.crowne-
plaza.com* ⤏*203 rooms, 14 suites* ⌂*In-room: safe, DVD (some), ethernet, minibar. In-hotel: restaurant, room service, bar, gym, concierge,
laundry service, Internet room (fee), parking (fee), no-smoking rooms*
Ⓤ*Blackfriars.*

££££ **Grange City.** With an eye on business, this sleek hotel in London's City
Fodor'sChoice has everything the workaholic needs to feel right at home—chic bed-
★ rooms subtly decorated in creams and chocolates, modern furnishings,
plenty of space (by London standards) in which to pace, broadband and
direct-dial phones, and more. The women-only wing has extra amenities
ranging from more powerful hair dryers to extra-secure doors with peep
holes and chain-locks. Ladies (and gentlemen) can exercise in the hotel's
magnificent columned swimming pool, and then linger over sushi at the

16

Koto Japanese Restaurant or sip cocktails in the Isis Lounge. ⊠ *8–14 Cooper's Row, The City, EC3N 2BQ* ☎ *020/7863–3700* 🖷 *030/7863–3701* ⊕ *www.grangehotels.com* ⤳ *307 rooms* ♿ *In-room: safe, ethernet, satellite TV, CD, mini-bar. In-hotel: 2 restaurants, room service, bar, pool, gym, spa, concierge, laundry service, no-smoking rooms* ⊟ *AE, MC, V* Ⓜ *Tower Hill, Aldgate, Monument.*

££££££ **Great Eastern.** This grand old Victorian railway hotel looks lavish and over-the-top on the outside, but inside it's all about modern, with polished wood, neutral colors, Frette linens, and contemporary art. You'll pine for nothing here—there are five restaurants (serving sushi, seafood, brasserie fare, pub food, and haute cuisine), a popular bar, a gorgeous spa, and a boutique selling the covetable Ren bath products with which all the hotel's bathrooms are stocked. Rooms on the fifth and sixth floors are modern lofts, with lots of light. Suites are beautifully designed. Note that the restaurants and bars are favored by locals, so this is not a total retreat from bustling London life. ⊠ *Liverpool St. at Bishopsgate, The City, E2M 7QN* ☎ *020/7618–5010* 🖷 *020/7618–5011* ⊕ *www.great-eastern-hotel.co.uk* ⤳ *246 rooms, 21 suites* ♿ *In-room: safe, DVD, CD, satellite television, broadband, minibar. In-hotel: 5 restaurants, room service (24-hours), bars, gym, spa, concierge, laundry service, no-smoking rooms* ⊟ *AE, DC, MC, V* Ⓤ *Liverpool St.*

££££ **London Bridge Hotel.** Just steps away from the London Bridge rail and Tube station, this thoroughly modern, stylish hotel is popular with business travelers, but leisure travelers will find it just as handy. Most of the South Bank's attractions are within easy walking distance, and it's a short stroll to London Bridge station to catch the tube. Each sleek room is understated and contemporary, with a calming, neutral decor. Three spacious two-bedroom apartments (*£££££*) come with kitchen, living room, and dining room. ⊠ *8–18 London Bridge St., South Bank, SE1 9SG* ☎ *020/7855–2200* 🖷 *020/7855–2233* ⊕ *www.london-bridge-hotel.co.uk* ⤳ *138 rooms, 3 apartments* ♿ *In-room: safe, kitchen (some), minibar, ethernet. In-hotel: restaurant, room service, bar, gym, concierge, laundry service, parking (fee), no-smoking rooms* ⊟ *AE, DC, MC, V* Ⓤ *London Bridge.*

£££££ **London Marriott Hotel County Hall.** This grand hotel has what many want—a view of the London Eye and the Houses of Parliament across the Thames. The building is a mammoth, spectacular, pedimented, and columned affair with bronze doors and marble lobby. Similarly, the decor in the guest rooms has a lot going on—floral bedcovers make strange bedfellows with chairs clad in pastel plaid. Still, the views are lovely, the fabrics luxurious, and it's got all the business-like bells and whistles you could ask for and a fantastic 24-hour health-and-fitness spa. ⊠ *County Hall, South Bank, SE1 7PB* ☎ *020/7928–5200* 🖷 *020/7928–5300* ⊕ *www.marriotthotels.com* ⤳ *200 rooms* ♿ *In-room: safe, ethernet, cable TV, minibar. In-hotel: 2 restaurants, room service, bars, pool, gym, spa, concierge, laundry service, parking (fee)* ⊟ *AE, DC, MC, V* Ⓤ *Westminster.*

££££ Malmaison. Part of a small chain of well-regarded UK boutique hotels, this Clerkenwell address is very trendy, with contemporary furnishings, clean lines, and all the extras. Stylish rooms are well decorated in neutral cream and beige, and have huge beds and CD systems with a library of music on demand, as well as satellite TVs and free broadband. The hotel prides itself on fast, quality room service, so breakfast in bed can be a pleasure. The whole package is a business traveler's dream. *⊠Charterhouse Sq., The City, EC1M 6AH*☎*020/7012–3700*🖷*020/7012–3702* ⊕*www.malmaison.com*📞*95 rooms, 2 suites* ⚒*In-room: safe, ethernet, minibar. In-hotel: restaurant, room service, bar, gym, concierge, laundry service, no-smoking rooms*🖃*AE, MC, V*⦿⧉*CP*Ⓤ*Barbican, Farringdon.*

££ Premier Travel Inn County Hall. It might be near the riverfront, but the Thames is obstructed by the nearby Marriott. Still, it's got an excellent location near the London Eye, and you get an incredible value here. Rooms are not very big, but they're nicely decorated, and the staff are helpful. Best of all for families on a budget are the foldout beds that let you accommodate two kids at no extra charge. *That's* a bargain. *⊠Belvedere Rd., South Bank, SE1 7PB*☎*0870/238–3300*🖷*020/7902–1619* ⊕*www.premiertravelinn.com*📞*313 rooms*⚒*In-room: no a/c, dial-up. In-hotel: 2 restaurants, bar, parking (fee), no-smoking rooms*🖃*AE, DC, MC, V*Ⓤ*Westminster.*

££ Premier Travel Inn Southwark. This excellent branch of the Premier Travel Inn chain is a bit out of the way on the Southbank, but it sits on a quiet cobbled lane, and is ideally located for visiting the Tate Modern museum or the Globe Theatre. Rooms are simple but attractively decorated, and all have the chain's signature 6-foot-wide beds (really two 3-foot-wide beds zipped together). Family rooms can accommodate four people. Ask for a room away from the elevators, which can be a little noisy. *⊠34 Park St., South Bank, SE1 9EF*☎*020/7089–2580 or 0870/990–6402*🖷*0870/990–6403* ⊕*www.premiertravelinn.com*📞*56 rooms*⚒*In-room: dial-up. In-hotel: parking (fee), no-smoking rooms*🖃*AE, DC, MC, V*Ⓤ*London Bridge.*

££££–£££££ **The Rookery.** This is an extraordinary hotel, where each beautiful double
Fodor'sChoice room is decorated with a lavish, theatrical flair and an eye for history.
★ Many have four-poster beds, each has a claw-foot bathtub, antique carved wooden headboard, and period furnishings, including exquisite salvaged pieces. In the Rook's Nest, the hotel's duplex suite, you can relax in an antique bath in the corner of the bedroom or enjoy a magnificent view of the City's historic buildings. The conservatory, with its small patio garden, is a relaxing place to unwind. Great deals are available here in the winter. *⊠12 Peter's La., at Cowcross St., The City, EC1M 6DS*☎*020/7336–0931*🖷*020/7336–0932* ⊕*www.rookeryhotel. com*📞*30 rooms, 3 suites*⚒*In-room: no a/c, safe, minibar, dial-up. In-hotel: room service, bar, concierge, laundry service, airport shuttle, parking (fee), no-smoking rooms*🖃*AE, DC, MC, V*Ⓤ*Farringdon.*

£ **St. Christopher's Inn Village.** Named for the patron saint of travelers, St. Christopher's Inn is the headquarters of a small, reliably good hostel

16

chain. It's actually made up of three hostels: the quiet Orient Espresso, the historic Inn, and party-hearty Village. You check into all of them at the St. Christopher's Inn Village. All the hostels are within walking distance, and all are cheap and cheerful, with swipe-card security and shared bathrooms. Along with the usual hostel offerings, it has the added benefit of a rooftop sauna and open-air hot tub. The sports bar in St. Christopher's is a good place to meet other travelers. ⊠*161–165 Borough High St., South Bank, SE1 1HR* ☎*020/7407–1856* 🖷*020/7403–7715* ⊕*www.st-christophers.co.uk* ⇆*166 beds at Village, 50 beds at Original, 36 beds at Orient Espresso; all without bath* ⏁*In-room: no a/c, no phone, no TV. In-hotel: restaurant, bar, laundry facilities, no-smoking rooms* ⊟*MC, V* Ⓤ*London Bridge, Borough* ⑩*CP.*

£££££ Threadneedles. Owned by the people who run the Colonnade in Bayswater, Threadneedles is a first-rate boutique hotel. The building is a former bank, and the hotel has beautifully adapted the vast old banking hall along with its luxurious marble and mahogany panels. Rooms are a good size for London, with big, comfortable beds and neutral coffee and cream colors, with dashes of deep burgundy. Bathrooms are modern and attractive, with plenty of marble. Given its location in the financial district, it's no surprise that this place looks as if it were custom-designed to please business travelers. Steep discounts are available by booking online in advance. ⊠*5 Threadneedle St., The City, EC2R 8AY* ☎*020/7657–8080* 🖷*020/7657–8100* ⊕*www.theetoncollection.com* ⇆*63 rooms, 6 suites* ⏁*In-room: safe, mini-bar, refrigerator, CD, DVD, satellite TV, in-room Wi-Fi. In-hotel: restaurant, room service, bar, concierge, laundry service, no-smoking rooms* ⊟*AE, DC, MC, V* Ⓤ*Bank.*

KENSINGTON

£–££ Abbey House. The main attractions of this Victorian town house are cheap prices and a convenient location near High Street Kensington's many shops. Inside, rooms look dated, and the decor is basic, but not unpleasant. Every room shares a bath with another. There are stairs and no elevator here, so it can be a burden for those with mobility problems. ⊠*11 Vicarage Gate, Kensington, W8 4AG* ☎*020/7727–2594* 🖷*020/7727–1873* ⊕*www.abbeyhousekensington.com* ⇆*16 rooms without bath* ⏁*In-room: no a/c, no phone. In-hotel: bar, no elevator* ⊟*No credit cards* ⑩*BP* Ⓤ*High Street Kensington.*

££–£££ Astons Budget Studios. Three redbrick Victorian town houses on a residential street hold Astons' comfortable studios and apartments. All are simple and well-designed, with tiny kitchenettes, and the apartments (*£££*) have marble bathrooms and other extra touches as well. The decor has a modern, blonde-wood look, and it all makes a nice alternative to normal hotel rooms. ⊠*31 Rosary Gardens, South Kensington, SW7 4NH* ☎*020/7590–6000, 800/525–2810 in U.S.* 🖷*020/7590–6060* ⊕*www.astons-apartments.com* ⇆*43 rooms, 12 suites* ⏁*In-room: no a/c, safe, kitchen, refrigerator, dial-up. In-hotel: concierge, airport* *shuttle, parking (fee), no-smoking rooms, some pets allowed, no elevator*☰*AE, MC, V*Ⓤ*Gloucester Rd.*

££££££ **Bentley Kempinski.** This opulent hotel is an elegant escape in Kensington. Housed in a creamy white Victorian building, its lobby is a gorgeous explosion of marble, with high ceilings and chandeliers. The bedrooms are almost palatial by London standards, with silk wallpaper, golden furnishings, and fine marble bathrooms with whirlpool baths—some have steam rooms. The two restaurants serve modern British cuisine with continental touches, while Malachite is a quiet bar for a brandy after dinner. Cigar lovers can drift to the Cigar Divan for Havana cigars and mature whiskies. The staff is obliging, and the marble Turkish steam room is a unique haven from the stresses of the day. ⊠*27– 33 Harrington Gardens, South Kensington, SW7 4JK*☎*020/7244– 5555*🖷*020/7244–5566*⊕*www.thebentley-hotel.com*⤶*52 rooms, 12 suites*⚲*In-room: safe, DVD, CD, broadband, minibar, butler service. In-hotel: 2 restaurants, bar, gym, spa, concierge, laundry service, airport shuttle, parking (fee), no-smoking rooms, some pets allowed*☰*AE, D, MC, V*Ⓤ*Gloucester Rd.*

££££££ **Blakes.** Designed by owner Anouska Hempel, Blakes is a fantasy packed with precious Biedermeier, Murano glass, and modern pieces collected from around the world. Each room is unique—some hark back to the days of the British empire, while others are minimalist spaces draped in diaphanous white fabric and stacked with white pillows. The foyer sets the tone with piles of cushions, black walls, rattan, and bamboo. The exotic Thai restaurant is a trendy delight. ⊠*33 Roland Gardens, South Kensington, SW7 3PF*☎*020/7370–6701*🖷*020/7373–0442*⊕*www. blakeshotels.com*⤶*38 rooms, 11 suites*⚲*In-room: no a/c (some), safe, mini-bar, DVD, CD, Wi-Fi. In-hotel: restaurant, room service, bar, gym, concierge, laundry service, parking (fee), Internet room (fee)*☰*AE, DC, MC, V*Ⓤ*South Kensington.*

££££ **The Cranley.** Old-fashioned British propriety is the overall feeling here at this small, Victorian town-house hotel. High ceilings, huge windows, and a pale, creamy color scheme make the bedrooms light and bright. Antique desks and four-poster or half-tester beds give the place historic authenticity. Even the bathrooms have traditional Victorian fittings—although the plumbing is completely modern. Afternoon tea and evening canapés are complimentary and tasty. Some rooms are big enough for families. ⊠*10–12 Bina Gardens, South Kensington, SW5 0LA*☎*020/7373–0123*🖷*020/7373–9497*⊕*www.thecranley.com*⤶*29 rooms, 5 suites, 4 apartments*⚲*In-room: safe, VCR, dial-up. In-hotel: room service, concierge, laundry service, parking (fee), no-smoking rooms*☰*AE, DC, MC, V*Ⓤ*Gloucester Rd.*

£ **easyHotel.** This budget hotel received loads of attention in when it opened in 2005 as London's first "pod hotel." Crammed into a big white town house are 34 tiny rooms, all with a double bed, private bathroom, and little else. Each is brightly decorated in the trademark orange-and-white of the Easy chain (which includes the Internet cafés easyEverything, the cruise line company easyCruise, and the budget air-

16

line easyJet). The idea behind the hotel is to provide quality basics (bed, sink, shower, and toilet) for little money. The tiny reception desk with one staff member can't offer much in terms of service, and if you want your room cleaned while you stay, it's an additional £10 a day. The concept is a huge hit—easyHotel is fully booked months in advance. ⊠*14 Lexham Gardens, Kensington, W8 5JE* ☎*020/7216–1717* ⊕*www.easyhotel.com* ⏎*34 rooms* ⚇ *In-room: no a/c, no phone. In-hotel: no-smoking rooms, no elevator* ⊟*MC, V* Ⓜ*Gloucester Rd.*

££££–£££££   **Eleven Cadogan Gardens.** This aristocratic, late-Victorian, gabled town house has a clubby feel—there's no sign, just a simple 11 above the door. Antiques, landscape paintings and portraits, coupled with some of that solid, no-nonsense furniture that *real* English country houses have in abundance make it seem like you're staying in a family home. The best rooms are at the back, overlooking a private garden. If you want to spare no expense and hire a chauffeur-driven car, there's one standing by. The complimentary freshly baked cake for afternoon tea, and sherry and canapés in the evening are excellent. ⊠*11 Cadogan Gardens, Sloane Sq., South Kensington, SW3 2RJ* ☎*020/7730–7000* 🖷*020/7730–5217* ⊕*www.number-eleven.co.uk* ⏎*62 rooms* ⚇ *In-room: safe, VCR, mini-bar, broadband. In-hotel: room service, bar, gym, concierge, currency exchange, laundry service, airport shuttle, babysitting service, Wi-Fi* ⊟*AE, DC, MC, V* Ⓤ*Sloane Square.*

£££   **Five Sumner Place.** Once you checked into this tall Victorian town house on a quiet residential street, you'll get your own key to the front door and instructions to make yourself at home. Guest rooms are elegantly decorated with designer fabrics, and a modern flair. If the weather is good, relax in the small garden. In the morning, take breakfast in the sunny (or rainy) conservatory. ⊠*5 Sumner Pl., South Kensington, SW7 3EE* ☎*020/7584–7586* 🖷*020/7823–9962* ⊕*www.sumnerplace.com* ⏎*17 rooms* ⚇ *In-room: minibar, Wi-Fi. In-hotel: room service, parking (fee), no-smoking rooms* ⊟*AE, MC, V* ⊦◎⊦*BP* Ⓤ*South Kensington.*

££££–£££££   **The Gore.** Just down the road from the Albert Hall, this gorgeous,
Fodor'sChoice   friendly hotel is run by the same people who run Hazlitt's and the
★   Rookery. The lobby looks like a set from a Luchino Visconti film, evoking a wealthy estate from centuries past. Upstairs are spectacular rooms—Room 101 is a Tudor fantasy with minstrel gallery, stained glass, and four-poster bed, and Room 211, done in over-the-top Hollywood style, has a tile mural of Greek goddesses in its bathroom. It's all lush and luxurious, but, as with anything eccentric, this place is not for everyone. ⊠*189 Queens Gate, Kensington, SW7 5EX* ☎*020/7584–6601* 🖷*020/7589–8127* ⊕*www.gorehotel.com* ⏎*54 rooms* ⚇ *In-room: no a/c, safe, VCR, minibar, dial-up. In-hotel: restaurant, room service, bar, concierge, laundry service, no-smoking rooms* ⊟*AE, DC, MC, V* Ⓤ*Gloucester Rd.*

£   **Holland House YHA.** Part Jacobean mansion and part 1970s addition, this is the most historic and pastoral of London's youth hostels. Dorm rooms overlook the wooded park, where black bunnies scamper and peacocks strut around the central Kyoto Gardens. High Street Kensington and civilization are just a few steps away. Inexpensive lunches and dinners are available. ✉*Holland Walk, Kensington, W8 7QU* ☎*0870/770–5866* 🖷*020/7376–0667* ⊕*www.hollhse.btinternet.co.uk* ↩*201 beds* ♿*In-room: no a/c, no phone, no TV. In-hotel: bar, tennis courts, laundry facilities, no-smoking rooms, Internet room (fee)* ⊟*AE, MC, V*⦿*BP* Ⓤ*High Street Kensington.*

££ **Hotel 167.** This white-stucco, Victorian corner house just a two-minute walk from the V&A is a funny old place. With its abstract art pieces and black-and-white tiled floor, the lobby is unique, but the bedrooms are an unimpressive mélange of new and old furniture and colorful fabrics. The breakfast room, on the other hand, is old-fashioned and charming, with wrought-iron furniture and sunny yellow walls. Its creative look and unpredictable approach has been the subject of a novel (*Hotel 167*, by Jane Solomon) and a song by the rock band Manic Street Preachers, but it's quite expensive for what you get. Note: Street traffic on busy Brompton Road makes rooms on that side of the hotel quite noisy, so this place is not for light sleepers. ✉*167 Old Brompton Rd., South Kensington, SW5 0AN* ☎*020/7373–3221* 🖷*020/7373–3360* ⊕*www. hotel167.com* ↩*18 rooms* ♿*In-hotel: no a/c, Wi-Fi, no elevator* ⊟*AE, DC, MC, V*⦿*CP* Ⓤ*Gloucester Rd.*

£££–££££ **Kensington House Hotel.** This refurbished 19th-century town house off High Street Kensington has attractive, streamlined rooms with large windows and contemporary furnishings. Rear rooms have views of trees and mews houses, and all rooms have extras such as tea/coffee-makers and bathrobes. ✉*15–16 Prince of Wales Terr., Kensington, W8 5PQ* ☎*020/7937–2345* 🖷*020/7368–6700* ⊕*www.kenhouse.com* ↩*41 rooms* ♿*In-room: no a/c, safe, dial-up. In-hotel: restaurant, room service, bar, laundry service, parking (fee), no-smoking rooms* ⊟*AE, DC, MC, V*⦿*CP* Ⓤ*High Street Kensington.*

£££££ **Milestone Hotel & Apartments.** This pair of intricately decorated Victorian town houses overlooking Kensington Palace and Gardens is an intimate, luxurious alternative to the city's more famous five-star hotels. Great thoughtfulness goes into the hospitality and everything is possible in this special place. You'll be offered a welcome drink upon arrival and, if you so desire, you can return to a post-theater midnight snack in your room or leave with a picnic basket for the park across the street. The staff is friendly and efficient, but never too familiar. Each sumptuous room is full of antiques; many have canopied beds. A favorite is the Ascot Room, which is filled with elegant hats of the kind worn at the famous races. ✉*1 Kensington Ct., Kensington, W8 5DL* ☎*020/7917–1000* 🖷*020/7917–1010* ⊕*www.milestonehotel.com* ↩*45 rooms, 12 suites, 6 apartments* ♿*In-room: safe, kitchen (some), DVD, CD, mini-bar, Wi-Fi. In-hotel: 2 restaurants, room service, bar, gym, concierge, laundry service, no-smoking rooms, some pets allowed* ⊟*AE, DC, MC, V*Ⓤ*High Street Kensington.*

£££–££££ **Number Sixteen.** In a white-portico row of Victorian houses, close to the
Fodor'sChoice South Kensington Tube and a short walk from the Victoria & Albert
★ Museum, Number Sixteen is a lovely luxury B&B. Rooms are spacious

16

and have marble- and oak-clad bathrooms. The style is not so much interior-designed as understated—new furniture and modern prints are juxtaposed with weighty oil paintings and antiques. The staff is friendly, so lingering in the drawing rooms is a pleasure, and drinks are served in the garden in summer. ⊠ *16 Sumner Pl., South Kensington, SW7 3EG* ☎ *020/7589–5232, 800/553–6674 in U.S.* 🖨 *020/7584–8615* ⊕ *www.firmdale.com* ⇆ *42 rooms* ♿ *In-room: no a/c (some), safe, VCR, minibar, dial-up. In-hotel: room service, bar, concierge, laundry service* ⊟ *AE, MC, V* ⦸ CP ⓤ *South Kensington.*

££££–£££££ **The Pelham.** Museum lovers flock to this sweet hotel across the street from the South Kensington tube station. The Natural History, Science, and Victoria & Albert museums are all a short stroll away, as is King's Road. At the end of a day's sightseeing, settle down in front of the fireplace in one of the two snug drawing rooms with their honor bars. The stylish, contemporary rooms by designer Kit Kemp have sash windows and marble bathrooms. Some top-floor rooms have sloping ceilings and casement windows. ⊠ *15 Cromwell Pl., South Kensington, SW7 2LA* ☎ *020/7589–8288, 800/553–6674 in U.S.* 🖨 *020/7584–8444* ⊕ *www.firmdale.com* ⇆ *47 rooms, 4 suites* ♿ *In-room: safe (some), VCR, minibar, dial-up. In-hotel: restaurant, room service, bar, concierge, parking (fee)* ⊟ *AE, MC, V* ⓤ *South Kensington.*

KNIGHTSBRIDGE, CHELSEA & BELGRAVIA

££££ **The Beaufort.** At this elegant, modern-styled boutique guesthouse, you get a lot for your money. Guests have a front-door key, access to the honor bar in the drawing room, and an in-room CD player and radio. The high-ceiling, contemporary rooms have muted, sophisticated colors. Rates include flowers, fruit, chocolates, cookies, and water in your room; free e-mail and movies via the TV; tea in the drawing room; and admission to a local health club. Junior suites include a free one-way airport transfer. Four of the rooms have pretty wrought-iron balconies. ⊠ *33 Beaufort Gardens, Knightsbridge, SW3 1PP* ☎ *020/7584–5252* 🖨 *020/7589–2834, 800/584–7764 in U.S.* ⊕ *www.thebeaufort.co.uk* ⇆ *20 rooms, 7 suites* ♿ *In-room: no a/c (some), safe, dial-up. In-hotel: room service, bar, concierge, laundry service, no-smoking rooms* ⊟ *AE, DC, MC, V* ⦸ CP ⓤ *Knightsbridge.*

£££££ **The Berkeley.** The elegant Berkeley successfully mixes the old and the new in a luxurious, modern building with a splendid penthouse swimming pool. The big bedrooms have either swags of William Morris prints or art deco touches. All have sitting areas, CD players, and big marble bathrooms. There are spectacular penthouse suites with their own conservatory terraces, and others with saunas or balconies. Dining venues include Marcus Wareing's high-class Pétrus restaurant, Gordon Ramsay's excellent and extremely popular Boxwood Café, the eclectic and sumptuous Blue Bar (which Madonna reportedly "adores"), and the whimsical Caramel Room where morning coffee and decadent doughnuts are served to slim ladies who look as if they've never eaten such a thing in their lives. ⊠ *Wilton Pl., Belgravia, SW1X 7RL*

☎ *020/7235–6000, 800/637–2869 in U.S.* 🖷 *020/7235–4330* ⊕ *www. the-berkeley.com* ⟿ *103 rooms, 55 suites* ♿ *In-room: safe, CD, DVD, broadband, minibar, voicemail, satellite TV. In-hotel: restaurant, room service, bar, pool, gym, spa, concierge, laundry service, airport shuttle, parking (fee), no-smoking rooms* ▤ *AE, DC, MC, V* Ⓤ *Knightsbridge.*

££££ **The Cadogan.** This is one of London's most historically naughty hotels. The Cadogan was once the home of Lillie Langtry, a scandalous actress and King Edward's mistress in the 1890s. Her home was turned into a hotel, where Oscar Wilde stayed in 1895 when he was arrested for "indecency" with a young man. A recent overhaul means much of the hotel's old stuffiness is gone—elegant golds and creams have replaced fussy florals. The drawing room has rich wood paneling and deep, comfortable armchairs, and is an excellent place for tea and people-watching. The small, sophisticated bar urges you to have a martini and a cigar. Breakfast offers healthy cereals and fruits alongside decadent pastries. ✉ *75 Sloane St., Chelsea, SW1X 9SG* ☎ *020/7235–7141* 🖷 *020/7245– 0994* ⊕ *www.cadogan.com* ⟿ *65* ♿ *In-room: VCR, minibar, Wi-Fi. In-hotel: restaurant, room service, bar, tea room, tennis courts, concierge, laundry service, no-smoking rooms* ▤ *AE, MC, V.*

££££ **The Capital.** Reserve well ahead if you want a room here—or if you want a table in the hotel's popular, top-quality French restaurant. This grand hotel in a formerly private house is the work of the Levin family, who also own nearby L'Hotel, and it exudes their impeccable taste: fine-grain woods, original prints, and soothing, country-chic furnishings. Ask for a front-facing room to get more space. If you're going for a deluxe double, ask for the L-shaped rooms in the atmospheric Edwardian wing, where each room has a desk. Nothing is ever too much here—mattresses are handmade, sheets are 450-thread count, bathrooms are marble. ✉ *22–24 Basil St., Knightsbridge, SW3 1AT* ☎ *020/759–1202, 800/926–3199 in U.S.* 🖷 *020/7225–0011* ⊕ *www. capitalhotel.co.uk* ⟿ *40 rooms, 8 suites* ♿ *In-room: safe, dial-up, minibar. In-hotel: restaurant, room service, bar, concierge, laundry service, parking (fee), no-smoking rooms, some pets allowed* ▤ *AE, DC, MC, V* Ⓤ *Knightsbridge.*

£££ **Egerton House.** This utterly peaceful, small hotel was the first in the group that includes the Franklin and Dukes hotels. Chintz, floral, or Regency-stripe bedrooms overlook the gorgeous gardens in back. The two drawing rooms, decorated in high-Victorian style, are good places to write letters or relax with a drink from the honor bar. ✉ *17–19 Egerton Terr., Knightsbridge, SW3 2BX* ☎ *020/7589–2412, 800/473– 9492 in U.S.* 🖷 *020/7584–6540* ⊕ *www.egertonhousehotel.co.uk* ⟿ *23 rooms, 6 suites* ♿ *In-room: VCR (some), minibar, dial-up. In-hotel: room service, bar, concierge, laundry service, parking (fee), no-smoking rooms* ▤ *AE, DC, MC, V* Ⓤ *Knightsbridge, South Kensington.*

£££ **The Franklin.** It's hard to imagine, while taking tea in this flowery hotel overlooking a quiet garden, that you're an amble away from busy Brompton and Cromwell roads and the splendors of the V&A Museum. A few of the rooms are small, but the marble bathrooms

16

are not, and the large garden rooms and suites are plush indeed. Some rooms have four-poster beds; all have antique furnishings. Tea is served daily in the lounge, and there's an honor bar. ✉ *28 Egerton Gardens, Knightsbridge, SW3 2DB* ☎ *020/7584–5533, 800/473–9487 in U.S.* 🖷 *020/7584–5449, 800/473–9489 in U.S.* ⊕ *www.franklinhotel.co.uk* ↩ *50 rooms* ᐃ *In-room: safe, VCR (some), dial-up. In-hotel: room service, bar, concierge, laundry service, parking (fee), no-smoking rooms* ⊟ *AE, DC, MC, V* Ⓤ *South Kensington.*

££££ **The Halkin.** This hotel's understated design is an escape from the clutter and flowery motifs of other hotels. Guests can chill out in the clean-cut, white marble lobby bar. In the earth-tone bedrooms, bedside control panels are used to adjust the lights and air-conditioning. It's akin to staying in the Design Museum, except that you have Knightsbridge and Hyde Park practically on your doorstep, and the exceptional Nahm Thai restaurant in the lobby. The Shambhala Health Club at the nearby Metropolitan Hotel is at your disposal as well. ✉ *5 Halkin St., Belgravia, SW1X 7DJ* ☎ *020/7333–1000* 🖷 *020/7333–1100* ⊕ *www.ihw. com* ↩ *41 rooms* ᐃ *In-room: safe, VCR, broadband. In-hotel: restaurant, bar, concierge, laundry service, parking (fee), no-smoking rooms* ⊟ *AE, DC, MC, V* Ⓤ *Hyde Park Corner.*

££££–£££££ **Knightsbridge Hotel.** Just off glamorous Knightsbridge near Harrods and Harvey Nichols in quiet Beaufort Gardens, this chic hotel is well placed for shoppers. The balconied suites and regular rooms are wrapped in bold fabrics, the beds piled high with warm duvets. All rooms have CD players, writing desks, and large granite-and-oak bathrooms. The fully loaded honor bar in the drawing room is an excellent place to unwind amid African sculptures and modern art. ✉ *10 Beaufort Gardens, Knightsbridge, SW3 1PT* ☎ *020/7584–6300, 800/553–6674 in U.S.* 🖷 *020/7584–6355* ⊕ *www.knightsbridgehotel.co.uk* ↩ *42 rooms, 2 suites* ᐃ *In-room: safe, VCR (some), dial-broadband, minibar* ⊟ *AE, MC, V* Ⓤ *Knightsbridge.*

£££–££££ **L'Hotel.** This is the kind of small hotel people fall in love with. Rooms are designed in classic Provençal style, with delicate wallcoverings, creamy bedcovers, and hand-made wrought-iron and wood furniture. The atmosphere is a bit like staying in a (particularly fabulous) home: You're given your own front-door key, and the staff leaves in the evening. Ask for a fireplace room, since they're the biggest. In the morning the French theme continues, and fresh croissants and baguettes are served in Le Métro cellar wine bar or in your room. You also have access to the restaurant and concierge services of the plush Capital Hotel, run by the same family, a few doors down the street. ✉ *28 Basil St., Knightsbridge, SW3 1AT* ☎ *020/7589–6286* 🖷 *020/7823–7826* ⊕ *www. lhotel.co.uk* ↩ *11 rooms, 1 suite* ᐃ *In-room: no a/c, VCR, dial-up. In-hotel: restaurant, bar, concierge, laundry service, parking (fee), no elevator* ⊟ *AE, V* ⊙ *CP* Ⓤ *Knightsbridge.*

£££££ **The Lanesborough.** Royally proportioned public rooms distinguish this multimillion-dollar, American-run hotel. Everything exudes richness—moiré silk, magnificent antiques and oil paintings, handwoven carpet—it's all so flowery and elaborate, it's like the lovechild of Liberace and Laura Ashley. To check in, sign the visitors' book, then retire to your room, where you are waited on by a personal butler. Guests at the Lanesborough have their own private butlers. Should you take the £5,000-per-night Royal Suite, the hotel will provide a chauffeur-driven Bentley and personal security guards. If you yearn for a bygone age and are willing to spend, this hotel is for you. ⊠*Hyde Park Corner, Belgravia, SW1X 7TA* ☎*020/7259–5599, 800/999–1828 in U.S.* 🖷*020/7259–5606, 800/937–8278 in U.S.* ⊕*www.lanesborough.com* 🖅*49 rooms, 46 suites* △*In-room: safe, minibar, ethernet. In-hotel: 2 restaurants, room service, bars, gym, concierge, laundry service, parking (fee), no-smoking rooms* ▤*AE, DC, MC, V* Ⓤ*Hyde Park Corner.*

££££££   Mandarin Oriental Hyde Park. Stay here, and the three greats of Knights-
Fodor'sChoice bridge—Hyde Park, Harrods, and Harvey Nichols—are on your door-
★   step. Built in 1880, the Mandarin Oriental is one of London's most elegant hotels. Bedrooms are traditional Victorian with hidden high-tech gadgets (Wi-Fi was recently added) and luxurious touches like Frette linen duvets, fresh orchids, and delicate chocolates. Miles of marble were used to fill the grand entrance. The Park restaurant, glittering Foliage, and quirky Mandarin Bar all attract Europe's jet setters. The service here is legendary and there's a butler on every floor, should you, for example, need a bit of help with the pillow menu. ⊠*66 Knightsbridge, Knightsbridge, SW1X 7LA* ☎*020/7235–2000* 🖷*020/7235–2001* ⊕*www.mandarinoriental.com* 🖅*177 rooms, 23 suites* △*In-room: safe, VCR, Wi-Fi, minibar. In-hotel: 2 restaurants, room service, bar, gym, spa, butler, concierge, laundry service, airport shuttle, parking (fee), no-smoking rooms* ▤*AE, DC, MC, V* Ⓤ*Knightsbridge.*

£££–£££££   myhotel chelsea. This small, chic hotel tucked away down a Chelsea side street is a charmer. Rooms are bijou small, but sophisticated, with mauve satin throws atop crisp white down comforters. Tiny bathrooms are made cheery with pale pink granite countertops. Flat-screen TVs, DVD players, and in-room Wi-Fi keep you digital. The beauty is in the details here—there's no restaurant, but the fire-warmed bar serves light meals and tea. There's no pool, but there's a spa. The guest library loans DVDs and books, and offers a quiet place to relax. Best of all, you can get a good deal if you book in advance via the Web site. ⊠*35 Ixworth Pl., Chelsea, SW3 3QX* ☎*020/7225–7500* 🖷*020/7225–7555* ⊕*www.myhotels.com* 🖅*45 rooms, 9 suites* △*In-room: safe, minibar, DVD, Wi-Fi. In-hotel: room service, bar, gym, spa, laundry service, no-smoking rooms, some pets allowed, minibar* ▤*AE, D, MC, V* Ⓤ*South Kensington.*

£££££   San Domenico House. Until 2006 this place was known as the Sloane, and the new owners have kept things much as they were in that popular hotel. The decor is still lavish, with gorgeous antiques, museum-quality paintings, luxurious fabrics draping the windows and beds, and marble baths. But gone are the days when you could buy the furniture—it was too hard to find pieces to replace the beautiful antiques that the guests took home. The roof terrace, which has upholstered garden furniture and a panoramic view of Chelsea, is the best place to relax, and the staff are endlessly helpful. ⊠*29 Draycott Pl., Chelsea, SW3*

16

2SH ☎*020/7581–5757, 800/324–9960 from the U.S.* 📠*020/7584–1348* ⊕*www.sandomenicohouse.com* ➪*14 rooms, 8 suites* ⚒*In-room: safe, VCR, digital Internet telephones. In-hotel: bar, concierge, laundry service, parking (fee)* 🟰*AE, DC, MC, V* Ⓤ*Sloane Square.*

££   **The Willett.** This lovely small hotel just off Sloane Square (handily
FodorśChoice located for shopping on the King's Road) is a bargain in this expensive
★   neighborhood. Its stained-glass windows and crystal chandeliers offer
easy proof that this was once an elegant home. The rooms are done
up in luxury fabrics and priced according to size—beware, the "small"
rooms are *tiny*, with beds squeezed creatively into closet-size spaces. But
the standard and deluxe rooms are spacious and elegantly decorated.
✉*32 Sloane Gardens, Chelsea SW1W 8DJ* ☎*020/7824–8415* ⊕*www.
eeh.co.uk* ➪*19* ⚒*In-hotel: restaurant, room service, bar, room service,
babysitting. In-room: cable TV, refrigerator (some), safe, no a/c (some
rooms)* 🟰*AE, MC, V* Ⓤ*Sloane Square* ⧖*BP.*

MAYFAIR, MARYLEBONE & ST. JAMES'S

££££   **22 Jermyn Street.** This historic guesthouse is on a fashionable shopping
☾   street near Fortnum & Mason. Flexible room configurations, including sitting rooms that convert to bedrooms, mean families have plenty
of space. In fact, the hotel rolls out the red carpet for children, providing anything from high chairs and coloring books to kiddie-sized
bathrobes to personal nannies. For grown-ups, there are access to a
nearby gym, complimentary newspapers, and a shoe shine. ✉*22 Jermyn St., St. James's, SW1Y 6HL* ☎*020/7734–2353, 800/682–7808
in U.S.* 📠*020/7734–0750* ⊕*www.22jermyn.com* ➪*5 rooms, 13 suites* ⚒*In-room: safe, VCR, Wi-Fi, minibar. In-hotel: room service, concierge, laundry service, airport shuttle, parking (fee)* 🟰*AE, DC, MC,
V* Ⓤ*Piccadilly Circus.*

££   **22 York Street.** This Georgian town house has a cozy, family feel with
pine floors and plenty of antiques. Pride of place goes to the central,
communal dining table where guests enjoy a varied continental breakfast of croissants, cheeses, yogurt, fruit, and cereal. A living room with
tea/coffeemaker is at guests' disposal as well. The homey bedrooms
are individually furnished with quilts and antiques. Triples and family rooms for four are available. ✉*22 York St., Mayfair, W1U 6PX*
☎*020/7224–2990* 📠*020/7224–1990* ⊕*www.22yorkstreet.co.uk* ➪*10
rooms* ⚒*In-room: no a/c. In-hotel: bar, no-smoking rooms, no elevator* 🟰*AE, MC, V* ⧖*CP* Ⓤ*Baker St.*

£££–££££   **Athenaeum Hotel and Apartments.** Fresh and gorgeous after a recent renovation, this smallish hotel overlooking Green Park offers plenty for
the money. Rooms are both comfortable and lavishly decorated, with
Hypnos beds, plasma screen televisions, and luxurious fabrics and bathrooms. If you need more space, you can choose one of its apartments
instead, with separate living and sleeping space, and tiny, fully equipped
kitchens. The spa downstairs is available only to guests, ensuring you
can always get an appointment. The restaurant offers butter-rich European cuisine, and a full afternoon tea here (£23) is an elegant experi-

ence. ✉*116 Piccadilly, Mayfair, W1J 7BJ*☎*020/7499–3464*⊕*www. athenaeumhotel.com*↩*123*⌂*In-hotel: restaurant, bar, spa, concierge, no-smoking rooms, gym. In-room: minibar, safes, broadband, satellite TV, CD, DVD, room service*☰*AE, MC, V*Ⓤ*Green Park*✦|*BP.*

£££ **Best Western Shaftesbury.** When the Best Western chain set up house in
♻ the midst of historic London, it did an admirable job of fitting in, certainly using as much chrome and frosted glass as anybody could ask for. Complimentary newspapers are scattered about, and bedrooms are ultramodern, with neutral rugs, white walls, dark curtains, and sleek furniture. The price reflects all this effort, so it's not the typical Best Western bargain, but it's pleasant and ideally situated in the heart of Theaterland. ✉*65–73 Shaftesbury Ave., Piccadilly, W1D 6EX* ☎*020/7871–6000*🖷*020/7745–1207*⊕*www.bestwestern.com*↩*69 rooms*⌂*In-room: DVD, ethernet. In-hotel: no-smoking rooms*☰*AE, MC, V*Ⓤ*Piccadilly Circus.*

£££££ **Brown's.** Founded in 1837 by James Brown, Lord Byron's "gentleman's gentleman," this hotel made up of 11 Georgian town houses holds a treasured place in London society. After renovations closed the venerable spot for more than a year, Margaret Thatcher hosted the reopening in 2005. The transformation is extraordinary. Public spaces once laden with chintz are now chic and contemporary. Everything is done up in cool neutral tones of coffee and cream; beds are new and firm; bathrooms are filled with marble and high-end bath products. All rooms have broadband and office space. The staff is still exceedingly professional and helpful. It's still Brown's, only better. ✉*34 Albemarle St., Mayfair, W1X 4BT*☎*020/7493–6020*🖷*020/7493–9381*⊕*www. brownshotel.com*↩*117 rooms, 19 suites*⌂*In-room: safe, VCR, broadband, minibar. In-hotel: 2 restaurants, room service, bar, gym*☰*AE, DC, MC, V*Ⓤ*Green Park.*

££ **Bryanston.** This family-run hotel, a few blocks north of Hyde Park and Park Lane, is an option for budget travelers who want to stay in this pricey area. The public rooms in its three converted Georgian houses are decorated in traditional English style: open fireplaces, leather armchairs, oil paintings. The bedrooms, on the other hand, are small and bland, with a faded pink color scheme, creaky floors, and tiny, old-fashioned bathrooms. In light of this, the prices could be cheaper. ✉*56–60 Great Cumberland Pl., Mayfair, W1H 8DD*☎*020/7262–3141*🖷*020/7262– 7248*⊕*www.bryanstonhotel.com*↩*81 rooms, 8 apartments*⌂*In-room: no a/c, kitchen (some) In-hotel: bar, concierge, laundry service, airport shuttle, parking (fee)*☰*MC, V*✦|*CP*Ⓤ*Marble Arch.*

£££–££££ **Chesterfield Mayfair.** Set deep in the heart of Mayfair, this four-star hotel is the former town house of the Earl of Chesterfield. The welcoming wood-and-leather public rooms match the dark-wood furnishings in the snug bedrooms, which are done in burgundy, browns, and forest green. Double rooms are the small side, but they are elegantly designed and the service is excellent. There are bargains to be had if you book online in advance. ✉*35 Charles St., Mayfair, W12 SEB*☎*020/7491– 2622*🖷*020/7491–4793*⊕*www.chesterfieldmayfair.com*↩*101 rooms,*

16

9 suites ⟡ In-room: safe (some), ethernet. In-hotel: 2 restaurants, room service, bar, gym, concierge, laundry service, no-smoking rooms, Wi-Fi in public rooms ▭ AE, DC, MC, V Ⓤ Green Park.

£££££–£££££
Fodor's Choice
★

Claridge's. Stay here, and you're staying at a hotel legend (founded in 1812), with one of the world's classiest guest lists. The friendly, liveried staff is not in the least condescending, and the rooms are never less than luxurious. Enjoy a cup of tea in the lounge, or retreat to the stylish bar for cocktails—or, better, to Gordon Ramsay's inimitable restaurant. The bathrooms are spacious (with enormous showerheads), as are the bedrooms (Victorian or art deco). The grand staircase and magnificent elevator complete with sofa and driver are equally glamorous. Perhaps Spencer Tracy said it best when he remarked that, when he died, he wanted to go not to heaven, but to Claridge's. ⊠ Brook St., St. James's, W1A 2JQ 🕾 020/7629–8860, 800/637–2869 in U.S. 🖷 020/7499–2210 ⊕ www.claridges.co.uk ⇆ 203 rooms ⟡ In-room: safe, VCR, dial-up, minibar. In-hotel: restaurant, bar, gym, spa, concierge, laundry service, airport shuttle, parking (fee), no-smoking rooms ▭ AE, DC, MC, V Ⓤ Bond St.

£££££
Fodor's Choice
★

The Connaught. Make reservations well in advance for this very exclusive hotel, the most understated of any of London's grand hostelries. Some guests learned from their grandparents to consider the petite Connaught their London home-away-from-home. Others—such as rock stars, politicians, and Hollywood celebrities—learned it all on their own. The bar and lounges have the air of an ambassador's residence, an impression reinforced by the imposing oak staircase, butler on each floor, and dignified staff. Each bedroom has a foyer, antique furniture (if you don't like the desk, they'll change it), and fresh flowers. One of Britain's most famous chefs, Angela Hartnett, oversees the two restaurants—Menu and Grill—which share an exceptional approach to modern European cuisine. ⊠ Carlos Pl., Mayfair, W1K 6AL 🕾 020/7499–7070 🖷 020/7495–3262 ⊕ www.theconnaughthotel-london.com ⇆ 75 rooms, 27 suites ⟡ In-room: safe, minibar, dial-up. In-hotel: 2 restaurants, room service, bars, gym, concierge, laundry service, airport shuttle, parking (fee), no-smoking rooms, Internet room ▭ AE, DC, MC, V Ⓤ Bond St.

£££££

The Dorchester. Few hotels this opulent manage to be as personable. The glamour level is off the scale: 1,500 square yards of gold leaf and 1,100 square yards of marble. Bedrooms (some not as spacious as you might expect) have Irish linen sheets on canopied beds, brocades, velvets, and Italian marble and etched-glass bathrooms with Floris toiletries. Furnishings throughout are English country-house style, with more than a hint of art deco, in keeping with the original 1930s building. The Dorchester is many things, but it's not subtle. The hotel has embraced modern technology, and employs "e-butlers" to help guests figure out the advanced Web TVs in the rooms. The recently renovated bar is receiving rave reviews, but its award-winning martinis don't come cheap (at £12.50). ⊠ Park Lane, Mayfair, W1A 2HJ 🕾 020/7629–8888 🖷 020/7409–0114 ⊕ www.dorchesterhotel.com ⇆ 195 rooms, 55 suites ⟡ In-room: safe, DVD, CD, raido, ether-

net, minibar. In-hotel: 3 restaurants, bar, gym, spa, concierge, laundry service, parking (fee), no-smoking rooms ⊟*AE, DC, MC, V* Ⓤ*Marble Arch, Hyde Park Corner.*

££££–£££££ **Dorset Square Hotel.** A fine pair of Regency town houses with design ideas *House & Garden* subscribers would love, this hotel is small but perfectly formed. Rooms are certainly not very big, but they're all beautifully decorated and each has its unique, luxurious style. Staff are subdued, but friendly. The beds could use an upgrade to more modern, firmer mattresses; those with back trouble may feel a pang or two in the morning. Still, this is a quirky, personable place, ideal for those looking for something elegant, but unique. The first-floor balconied Coronet rooms are the largest. ✉*40 Dorset Sq., Marylebone, NW1 6QN* ☎*020/7723–7874, 800/525–4800 in U.S.* 📠*020/7724–3328* ⊕*www. dorsetsquare.co.uk* ⤳*35 rooms, 3 suites* ⌂*In-room: no a/c (some), safe (some), VCR, minibar, dial-up. In-hotel: restaurant, room service, bar, concierge, laundry service, parking (fee), no-smoking rooms, some pets allowed* ⊟*AE, MC, V* Ⓤ*Baker St.*

£££££ **Dukes.** This small, exclusive, Edwardian-style hotel with a gas lantern–lighted courtyard entrance is in a discreet cul-de-sac. Overstuffed sofas, oil paintings of assorted dukes, and muted, rich colors create the perfect setting for sipping the finest dry martinis in town. Rooms are impeccably decorated in subdued colors and luxurious fabrics. The hotel's trump card is that, for such a central location, it's remarkably peaceful. ✉*35 St. James's Pl., St. James's, SW1A 1NY* ☎*020/7491–4840, 800/381–4702 in U.S.* 📠*020/7493–1264* ⊕*www.dukeshotel. co.uk* ⤳*80 rooms, 9 suites* ⌂*In-room: safe, DVD (some), satellite TV, minibar, Wi-Fi. In-hotel: restaurant, bar, gym, spa, concierge, laundry service, parking (fee)* ⊟*AE, DC, MC, V* Ⓤ*Green Park.*

£££ **Durrants.** A stone's throw from Oxford Street and the smaller, posher shops of Marylebone High Street, Durrants occupies a quiet corner almost near the Wallace Collection. It's a tasteful option, with old-English wood-paneling, leather armchairs, and dark-red patterned carpet. Note: Bedrooms at the back of the hotel are smaller than those at the front, but also quieter and air-conditioned. The building has served as a hotel since the late 18th century. ✉*26–32 George St., Mayfair, W1H 5BJ* ☎*020/7935–8131* 📠*020/7487–3510* ⊕*www.durrantshotel. co.uk* ⤳*87 rooms, 5 suites* ⌂*In-room: no a/c (some), dial-up. In-hotel: restaurant, room service, bar, concierge, laundry service* ⊟*AE, MC, V* Ⓤ*Bond St.*

£ **Edward Lear Hotel.** Named after a 19th-century poet famed for writing things nobody could really understand, this charming hotel occupies two historic town houses dating to the end of the 18th century. One was once the home of the eponymous writer, and his sweetly nonsensical words decorate the walls. Rooms are small and decorated in a simple but charming style, with flowery bedspreads and cream walls. Bathrooms are nothing fancy, but have all you need. Downstairs the sitting rooms are attractive and relaxing. Note that not all rooms have private bathrooms, so specify if that's important to you. Also, bed-

16

rooms facing the street can be a bit noisy—light sleepers should ask for rooms at the back. ⊠*28–30 Seymour St., Marylebone, W1H 7JB* ☎*020/7402–5401* ⊕*www.edlear.com* ⇨*31 rooms* ♿*In-room: dial-up, no a/c. In-hotel: lounge, no elevator* ☰*MC, V* Ⓤ*Marble Arch* ⍸Ⓞ⍸*BP.*

££ **Four Seasons Hotel.** Alas, this has nothing to do with *the* Four Seasons opposite Hyde Park; there are no stunning views over the Thames, no livery-clad footmen, no celebrities in the gilded bar. What this place has, however, are relatively affordable, basic bedrooms in soothing pastel colors close to Regent's Park. The conservatory is a light, airy space for breakfast. ⊠*173 Gloucester Pl., Regent's Park, NW1 6DX* ☎*020/7724–3461* 🖷*020/7402–5594* ⊕*www.4seasonshotel. co.uk* ⇨*28 rooms* ♿*In-room: no a/c, dial-up. In-hotel: room service, laundry service, no-smoking rooms, some pets allowed* ☰*AE, DC, MC, V* ⍸Ⓞ⍸*CP* Ⓤ*Baker St.*

£££££ **The Landmark.** This is one of London's grande dame hotels. Rich fabrics in neutral tones make the rooms welcoming and elegant, while high-speed Internet and doorbells that can be muted are welcome high-tech additions. The lovely, eight-story atrium Winter Garden is overlooked by odd-numbered rooms. Even standard rooms here are among the largest in London and have white marble bathrooms with plush robes. Despite all this luxury, it's worth mentioning that this is one of the few grand London hotels that doesn't force you to dress up. Still, it's a bit old-fashioned for some, and the busy neighborhood outside means this isn't a peaceful oasis. ⊠*222 Marylebone Rd., Marylebone, NW1 6JQ* ☎*020/7631–8000* 🖷*020/7631–8080* ⊕*www.landmarklondon. co.uk* ⇨*299 rooms, 47 suites* ♿*In-room: safe, satellite TV, ethernet, minibar. In-hotel: 2 restaurants, bars, pool, gym, spa, concierge, laundry service, no-smoking rooms* ☰*AE, DC, MC, V* Ⓤ*Marylebone.*

£££££ **Marriott Park Lane.** The ornate facade and beautiful interior of this swanky Marriott date to 1919. Today its useful location at the Oxford Street end of Park Lane gives access to great shopping on Bond Street and lovely strolls through Hyde Park. In spite of its size, the hotel has a boutique feel. The sizeable bedrooms are standard Marriott fare. The bar at the Marriott Park Lane has its own cocktail, the Crantini 140, a heady mix of white cranberries, vodka, and Cointreau. ⊠*140 Park La., Mayfair, W1K 7AA* ☎*020/7493–7000* 🖷*020/7493–8333* ⊕*www.marriott.com* ⇨*148 rooms, 9 suites* ♿*In-room: safe, cable TV, ethernet, minibar. In-hotel: restaurant, room service, pool, gym, spa, concierge, laundry service, no-smoking rooms, Wi-Fi in public areas* ☰*AE, DC, MC, V* Ⓤ*Marble Arch.*

£££££ **Le Meridien Piccadilly.** This massive 1908 building embodies fin-de-siècle elegance, carefully retaining its architectural features. Guest rooms vary between "traditional" (outdated, standard decor) and "executive" (stylish, minimalist decor), as well as in size. A few on the seventh floor have balconies overlooking Piccadilly. The hotel's Champneys, one of the most exclusive health clubs in London, is luxurious. ⊠*21 Piccadilly, Mayfair, W1J 0BH* ☎*020/7734–8000* 🖷*020/7437–3574* ⊕*www. lemeridien-piccadilly.com* ⇨*232 rooms, 35 suites* ♿*In-room: safe, eth-*

ernet, minibar. In-hotel: 2 restaurants, room service, bars, pool, gym, spa, concierge, laundry service, parking (fee), no-smoking rooms ⊟AE, DC, MC, V ⓤPiccadilly Circus.

££££££ **The Metropolitan.** Home to Nobu and the chic Met bar, this super-trendy hotel is a popular address for visiting fashion, music, and media folk. The lobby is sleek, white and modern, as are the bedrooms, which are designed by Keith Hobbs and have identical minimalist taupe-and-white furnishings. The best rooms overlook Hyde Park, but all rooms have a groovy minibar hiding the latest alcoholic and health-boosting beverages. ⊠*Old Park La., Mayfair, W1K 1LB* ☎*020/7447–1000, 800/337–4685 in U.S.* 🖷*020/7447–1100* ⊕*www.metropolitan. co.uk* ⟲*137 rooms, 18 suites* ⟳*In-room: safe, cableTV, VCR (some), ethernet, fax, minibar. In-hotel: restaurant, room service, bar, gym, concierge, laundry service, parking (fee), no-smoking rooms* ⊟*AE, DC, MC, V* ⓤ*Hyde Park Corner.*

££££££ **No. 5 Maddox Street.** With in-room kitchens, this hotel is a great option
Ⓒ for those who tire quickly of restaurants. Room service caters to every whim, delivering groceries and lending out CDs, videos and DVDs, or even a bicycle. Deluxe suites have balconies and working fireplaces. The suites are decorated with subtle, Asian-inspired touches like bamboo. The tiny kitchens are stocked with everything from sweets to herbal tea. Guests have access to a nearby health club. Note there's no elevator. ⊠*5 Maddox St., Mayfair, W1R 9LE* ☎*020/7647–0200* 🖷*020/7647–0300* ⊕*www.no5maddoxst.com* ⟲*12 suites* ⟳*In-room: safe, kitchen, refrigerator, VCR, Wi-Fi. In-hotel: restaurant, room service, concierge, laundry service, parking (fee), no elevator* ⊟*AE, DC, MC, V* ⓤ*Oxford Circus.*

££££££ **Park Lane Sheraton.** This is one of London's "old-school" classic hotels, with a long tradition of five-star style. While it's still a worthy option, it needs a makeover—especially in its 1980s-era bathrooms. But the Park Lane's public spaces still inspire fantasies. The ballroom, featured in the movies *Golden Eye* and *End of the Affair,* is exquisite. Afternoon tea in the Palm Court is a grand London tradition, although these days prices (which can exceed £30 per person) are a bit over the top. Many executive double rooms have sweeping views of Green Park, just across busy Piccadilly from the hotel. ⊠*Piccadilly, Mayfair, W1J BX* ☎*020/7499–6321* 🖷*020/7499–1965* ⊕*www.sheraton.com* ⟲*268 rooms, 39 suites* ⟳*In-room: safe, minibar, satellite TV, dial-up. In-hotel: 3 restaurants, room service, bar, gym, concierge, laundry service, parking (fee), no-smoking rooms* ⊟*AE, DC, MC, V* ⓤ*Hyde Park Corner.*

££££££ **The Ritz.** Memorialized in song by Irving Berlin, this hotel's very name conjures images of swagged curtains, handwoven carpets, and the smell of cigars, polish, and fresh lilies. The only thing that has been lost is a certain vein of moneyed naughtiness that someone like F. Scott Fitzgerald, at least, would have banked on. The bedrooms are bastions of pastel Louis XVI style, with gilded furniture and crystal chandeliers. The central lobby, with its chandelier and balconies circling above, is a photo opportunity waiting to happen. With a ratio of two staff mem-

16

bers to every bedroom, you're guaranteed personal service despite the hotel's massive size. However, you'll have to sit up straight: Formal dress is encouraged, jackets are required in the bar and restaurant, and jeans are not allowed in public areas. ☒ *150 Piccadilly, St. James's, W1J 9BR* ☎*020/7493–8181* 🖷*020/7493–2687* ⊕*www.theritzhotel. co.uk* ⤵*133 rooms* ♿*In-room: safe, VCR (some), dial-up. In-hotel: 2 restaurants, room service, bar, gym, concierge, laundry service, parking (fee), no-smoking rooms* ▭*AE, DC, MC, V* Ⓤ*Piccadilly Circus.*

£££–£££££ **Sherlock Holmes Hotel.** This was once a rather ordinary Hilton, until somebody noticed its location and had the brilliant idea of making it a boutique hotel. Add a beautiful bar for a bit of local buzz, and—presto!—the place took off like a rocket. You might say it was elementary. With wood floors and leather furniture, the bar is marvelously relaxing; rooms have a masculine edge with lots of earth tones, pin-stripe sheets, and hyper-modern bathrooms stocked with fluffy bathrobes. Beware that not all rooms are renovated to the same standard, and you could get stuck with a much less modern version. Still, overall, a handsome option near the good shopping of Marylebone High Street. Rooms are equipped with international electrical outlets, including those that work with American equipment. ☒ *108 Baker St., Marylebone, W1U 6LJ* ☎*020/7486–6161* 🖷*020/7958–5211* ⊕*www. sherlockholmeshotel.com* ⤵*119* ♿*In room: minibar, safes, Wi-Fi, satellite TV. In-hotel: restaurant, room service, bar, gym, spa, concierge, no-smoking rooms* ▭*AE, DC, MC, V* Ⓤ*Baker St.*

£ **St. Christopher's Inn Camden.** In bustling, hippie Camden Town just north of the center of London, this branch of the local hostel and backpacker hotel chain is perfectly situated for wandering around Camden Lock and Camden Market. The decor is in the usual cheap and cheery hostel style, and is kept in good condition. There's no curfew, and you get key-card security and 10% off food and drink in the raucous Belushi's bar on the ground floor. Rooms range from doubles to 10-bed dorms; linens are free. The lounge has cable TV. ☒ *48–50 Camden High St., Camden Town, NW1 0JH* ☎*020/7407–1856* 🖷*020/7403–7715* ⊕*www. st-christophers.co.uk* ⤵*52 beds, some without bath* ♿*In-room: no a/c, no phone, no TV. In-hotel: restaurant, bar, laundry facilities, no-smoking rooms, Internet room (fee)* ▭*MC, V* ⦿*CP* Ⓤ*Camden Town, Mornington Crescent.*

£££££ **The Stafford.** This is a rare find: a posh hotel that offers equal parts elegance and friendliness. It's hard to check in without meeting the gregarious manager, and his unshakable cheeriness must be infectious, for the staff are also upbeat and helpful. The location is one of the few peaceful spots in the area, down a small lane behind Piccadilly. Its 13 adorable carriage-house rooms, installed in the 18th-century stable block, are relative bargains; each individually decorated room has a cobbled mews entrance and gas-fueled fireplace, exposed beams, and CD player. The popular little American Bar has ties, baseball caps, and toy planes hanging from a ceiling modeled, presumably, on New York's 21 Club. A real find in the luxury category. ☒*St. James's Pl., St. James's, SW1A 1NJ* ☎*020/7493–0111* 🖷*020/7493–7121* ⊕*www.*

thestaffordhotel.co.uk ⌨*81 rooms* ⚒*In-room: dial-up. In-hotel: restaurant, bar* ▭*AE, DC, MC, V* Ⓤ*Green Park.*

SOHO & COVENT GARDEN

£££££ **Covent Garden Hotel.** In the midst of boisterous Covent Garden, this hotel is now the London home-away-from-home for a mélange of off-duty celebrities, actors, and style mavens. With painted silks, *style anglais* ottomans, and 19th-century Romantic oils, the public salons are perfect places to decompress over a glass of sherry from the honor bar. Guest rooms are *World of Interiors* stylish, each showcasing matching-but-mixed couture fabrics to stunning effect. For £30, the popular Saturday-night film club includes dinner in the brasserie and a film in the deluxe in-house cinema. ✉*10 Monmouth St., Covent Garden, WC2H 9HB* ☎*020/7806–1000, 800/553–6674 in U.S.* 🖨*020/7806–1100* ⊕*www.firmdale.com* ⌨*55 rooms, 3 suites* ⚒*In-room: safe, VCR, dial-up. In-hotel: restaurant, room service, gym, spa, concierge, laundry service* ▭*AE, MC, V* Ⓤ*Covent Garden.*

££££ **Hazlitt's.** Three connected early-18th-century houses, one of which was the last home of essayist William Hazlitt (1778–1830), make up this charming Soho hotel. It's a disarmingly friendly place, full of personality but devoid of elevators. Robust antiques are everywhere, most beds are four-posters, and every room has a Victorian claw-foot tub in its bathroom. There are tiny sitting rooms, wooden staircases, and more restaurants within strolling distance than you could patronize in a year. This is *the* London address for visiting antiques dealers and theater and literary types. ✉*6 Frith St., Soho, W1V 5TZ* ☎*020/7434–1771* 🖨*020/7439–1524* ⊕*www.hazlittshotel.com* ⌨*20 rooms, 3 suites* ⚒*In-room: no a/c (some), VCR, dial-up. In-hotel: room service, concierge, laundry service, parking (fee), no-smoking rooms, no elevators, some pets allowed* ▭*AE, DC, MC, V* Ⓤ*Tottenham Court Rd.*

££££–£££££ **The Howard Swissotel.** The rather spartan modern shell that encases the Howard Swissotel hides a contemporary, hip interior. It has a crisp brown color palette, with dark-wood furniture, light-wood floors, and lots of suede and leather. Some rooms have spectacular river views, and all have Lavazza coffee machines. Suites have the option of a riverside balcony. There's alfresco dining in the Asian fusion restaurant in good weather. ✉*Temple Pl., Covent Garden, WC2R 2PR* ☎*020/7836–3555* 🖨*020/7379–4547* ⊕*www.swissotel.com* ⌨*189 rooms* ⚒*In-room: safe, satellite TV, minibar, dial-up. In-hotel: restaurant, room service, bar, concierge, laundry service, parking (fee), no-smoking rooms* ▭*AE, D, MC, V* Ⓤ*Temple.*

£££££ **One Aldwych.** An understated blend of contemporary and classic results
Fodor'sChoice in pure, modern luxury here. Flawlessly designed inside an Edwardian
★ building, One Aldwych is coolly eclectic, with an artsy lobby, feather duvets, Italian linen sheets, and quirky touches (a TV in every bathroom, all-natural toiletries). It's the ultimate in 21st-century style, from the free, hotel-wide Wi-Fi, down to the gorgeous swimming pool in the awesome health club. Suites have amenities such as a private gym, a

16

kitchen, and a terrace. Breakfast is made with organic ingredients. The pool at One Aldwych has underwater speakers that play music you can hear only when you dive in. ✉*1 Aldwych, Covent Garden, WC2 4BZ* ☎*020/7300–1000* 🖷*020/7300–1001* ⊕*www.onealdwych.co.uk* ⇗*93 rooms, 12 suites* ♿*In-room: safe, kitchen (some), minibar, satellite TV, Wi-Fi. In-hotel: 2 restaurants, room service, bars, pool, gym, spa, concierge, laundry service, parking (fee), no-smoking rooms* ▭*AE, MC, V* Ⓤ*Charing Cross, Covent Garden.*

££££ **Radisson Edwardian Hampshire.** Right on Leicester Square and steps from the half-price ticket booth, this hotel is perfectly placed for theatergoers. Bedrooms are tiny and old-fashioned with plenty of rose prints, beige carpets, and shiny bedspreads, but the equally small bathrooms are modern. Public spaces exude plushness with thick carpets, gold chandeliers, and sparkling cut glass and mirrors. Rooms facing Leicester Square have lovely arched windows and great views, but can be a bit noisier, while those not facing the square tend to have views of nothing but blank brick walls. ✉*31–36 Leicester Sq., Covent Garden, WC2H 7LH* ☎*020/7839–9399* 🖷*020/7930–8122* ⊕*www.radissonedwardian. com* ⇗*119 rooms, 5 suites* ♿*In-room: safe, cable TV, minibar, Wi-Fi. In-hotel: restaurant, room service, bars, gym, concierge, laundry service, parking (fee), no-smoking rooms, some pets allowed* ▭*AE, DC, MC, V* Ⓤ*Leicester Square.*

££££ **Radisson Mountbatten.** Named after the late Lord Mountbatten, last viceroy of India and favorite uncle of Prince Charles, the hotel reflects Mountbatten's life with photos of the estate where he lived, plus some empire-themed furnishings and animal prints and figurines. Rooms are quite small and understated, cooly decorated in neutral tones and rich fabrics. Bathrooms are tiny, but stylish with lashings of Italian marble. Corner suites have the best views of the city, but they don't come cheap. ✉*20 Monmouth St., Covent Garden, WC2H 9HD* ☎*020/7836–4300* 🖷*020/7240–3540* ⊕*www.radissonedwardian.com* ⇗*143 rooms, 8 suites* ♿*In-room: safe, satellite TV, minibar, dial-up. In-hotel: restaurant, room service, bar, gym, concierge, laundry service, parking (fee), no-smoking rooms, some pets allowed* ▭*AE, DC, MC, V* Ⓤ*Covent Garden.*

££££–£££££ **Soho Hotel.** This redbrick, loft-like building opened its doors in 2004, making it the first upscale hotel in gritty Soho. The sleek boutique hotel's public rooms are boldly designed with bright fuchsia and acid green, but the large bedrooms are calmer, most with neutral, beige-and-cream tones, or subtle, sophisticated pinstripes, all offset by modern furniture. The bar and restaurant, Refuel, is one of the city's hotspots, and there are movie-screening rooms downstairs, in case the wide-screen TVs in the rooms aren't big enough. ✉*4 Richmond Mews, off Dean St., Soho, W1D 3DH* ☎*020/7559–3000* 🖷*020/7559–3003* ⊕*www. sohohotel.com* ⇗*85 rooms, 6 apartments* ♿*In-room: DVD, ethernet. In-hotel: room service, gym, concierge, no-smoking rooms* ▭*AE, MC, V* Ⓤ*Tottenham Court Rd.*

££££ Trafalgar Hilton. This fresh, contemporary hotel defies the Hilton norm. The rooms here, in either sky-blue or beige color schemes, keep many of the 19th-century office building's original features, and some have floor-to-ceiling windows with expansive views of Trafalgar Square. Twenty-one rooms are split-level, with upstairs space for chilling out with a CD or DVD and sleeping space below. Bathrooms take the cake with deep baths, full-size toiletries, eye masks, and mini-TVs. Go up to the roof garden for spectacular views of the Houses of Parliament, Westminster Abbey, and the British Airways London Eye. Better yet, ask for Room 303 to enjoy these exquisite views in privacy. ⊠ *2 Spring Gardens, Covent Garden, SW1A 2TS* ☎ *020/7870–2900* 🖷 *020/7870–2911* ⊕ *www.hilton.co.uk* ➯ *127 rooms, 2 suites* ⬩ *In-room: safe, satellite TV, DVD (some), minibar, games consoles (some), CD (some), ethernet. In-hotel: restaurant, room service, bar, concierge, laundry service, parking (fee), no-smoking rooms* ⊟ *AE, DC, MC, V* Ⓤ *Charing Cross.*

£££££ Waldorf Hilton. Following a massive overhaul, the Waldorf now has frosted glass, white marble, and understated modern bedrooms. The "Art + Tech" rooms cater to modern travelers' demands with plasma-screen TVs, complimentary fruit, herbal teas, and soft drinks, as well as innovative safes with laptop chargers. The "contemporary" rooms have retained period features while incorporating all the new gadgets. The Palm Court was inspired by the ballroom on that famous luxury ship the *Titanic*—and even doubled for it in the eponymous Hollywood movie. After a century, the weekend tea dances with big-band music are still going strong. ⊠ *Aldwych, Covent Garden, WC2B 4DD* ☎ *020/7836–2400* 🖷 *020/7836–7244* ⊕ *www.hilton.co.uk* ➯ *303 rooms* ⬩ *In-room: safe, satellite TV, minibar, ethernet. In-hotel: restaurant, room service, bar, pool, gym, spa, concierge, laundry service, parking (fee), no-smoking rooms* ⊟ *AE, DC, MC, V* Ⓤ *Charing Cross.*

16

WESTMINSTER & VICTORIA

££££ City Inn Westminster. In a rather stark steel-and-glass building steps from the Tate Britain, this member of a small UK chain has some rooms with spectacular views of Big Ben and the London Eye. Extras like floor-to-ceiling windows, CD players, and flat-screen TVs complement the contemporary, monochrome guest rooms. Cots, baby baths, Nickelodeon, special menus, and baby food are all on tap for kids. The restaurant and bar serve modern British cooking. ⊠ *30 John Islip St., Westminster, SW1P 4DD* ☎ *020/7630–1000* 🖷 *020/7233–7575* ⊕ *www.cityinn.com* ➯ *444 rooms, 16 suites* ⬩ *In-room: safe, DVD, broadband, CD, satellite TV. In-hotel: restaurant, room service, bar, gym, concierge, laundry service, parking (fee), no-smoking rooms* ⊟ *AE, MC, V* Ⓤ *Pimlico.*

££££–£££££ The Goring. Buckingham Palace is just around the corner, and visiting VIPs use the Goring as a convenient, suitably dignified base for royal occasions. The hotel, built in 1910 and now run by third-generation Gorings, retains an Edwardian style. It's a bit fussy—striped wallpaper and floral curtains are combined with patterned carpets and brass fittings—and would never be described as "modern." ✉*15 Beeston Pl., Grosvenor Gardens, Victoria, SW1W 0JW* ☎*020/7396–9000* 🖷*020/7834–4393* ⊕*www.goringhotel.co.uk* ⤵*68 rooms, 6 suites* ⚲ *In-room: safe, dial-up. In-hotel: restaurant, room service, bar, gym, concierge, laundry service, parking (fee), no-smoking rooms* ⊟*AE, DC, MC, V* Ⓤ*Victoria.*

££££–£££££   **Jolly Hotel St. Ermin's.** The hotel is just a short stroll from Westminster Abbey, Buckingham Palace, and the Houses of Parliament. An Edwardian anomaly in the shadow of modern skyscrapers, the hotel is set on a tiny cul-de-sac courtyard. The lobby is an extravaganza of Victorian stylings like cake-frosting stuccowork in shades of baby blue and creamy white. Guest rooms are tastefully decorated, but some are quite small. The hotel's Cloisters restaurant is an ornately carved 19th-century Jacobean-style salon, and one of the most magnificent rooms in which to dine in London. ✉*2 Caxton St., Westminster, SW1H 0QW* ☎*020/7222–7888* 🖷*020/7222–6914* ⊕*www.jollyhotels.it* ⤵*277 rooms, 8 suites* ⚲ *In-room: safe (some), dial-up, minibar. In-hotel: restaurant, room service, bar, laundry service, parking (fee), no-smoking rooms* ⊟*AE, DC, MC, V* Ⓤ*St. James's Park.*

££–£££   **Lime Tree Hotel.** On a street filled with budget hotels, the Lime Tree stands out for its gracious proprietors, the Davies family, who endeavor to provide a homey atmosphere as well as act as concierges. The flowery rooms include tea/coffeemakers. The triples and quads are suitable for families, but children under five are not allowed. The simple breakfast room covered with notes and gifts from former guests opens onto a garden. ✉*135–137 Ebury St., Victoria, SW1W 9RA* ☎*020/7730–8191* 🖷*020/7730–7865* ⊕*www.limetreehotel.co.uk* ⤵*25 rooms* ⚲ *In-room: no a/c, safe. In-hotel: no elevator, no kids under 5* ⦿|*BP* ⊟*MC, V* Ⓤ*Victoria.*

££   **New England Hotel.** This family-run B&B in a 19th-century town house is cheap(ish) and cheerful. The power showers, comfortable beds, and electronic key cards are pluses, but there's nothing fancy about the interior, and the bright color scheme is possibly too cheerful for some. Prices have gone up here in recent years without any substantial improvements to the hotel, making this less of a good deal than it once was. View this as a fall-back option if other, better budget places are booked up. ✉*20 Saint George's Dr., Victoria, SW1V 4BN* ☎*020/7834–8351* 🖷*020/7834–9000* ⊕*www.newenglandhotel.com* ⤵*25 rooms* ⚲ *In-room: no a/c, dial-up. In-hotel: parking (fee), no-smoking rooms, no elevator* ⊟*AE, DC, MC, V* ⦿|*BP* Ⓤ*Victoria.*

£££££   **No. 41.** This luxurious abode is not a formulaic, paint-by-numbers hotel. Its designer credentials are clear everywhere, from the unusual tiled floors to the extraordinary furnishings, which seem to have been drawn from every corner of the globe. Even the entrance is unique: You walk into a guests-only lift and are swept up to the fifthth-floor lobby. Sit for a second in the lobby and someone will offer you tea, cocktails, water—anything that crosses your mind can be yours in a second. Rooms, some of them split-level, are filled with high-tech gadgets to keep you in touch with the office back home, and a handy jar of jellybeans, should you feel the need for something sweet. When you're not working, you can relax on the butter-soft leather sofa in front of the fireplace, recline on the exquisite bed linens and feather duvets, or luxuriate in the marble bath. A "whatever, whenever" button on the telephone connects you with the helpful, amiable staff who provide exactly that. ☒ *41 Buckingham Palace Rd., Victoria, SW1W 0PS* ☎ *020/7300–0041* 🖷 *020/7300–0141* ⊕ *www.41hotel.com* ⤶ *14 rooms, 4 suites* ⟐ *In-room: safe, VCR, satellite TV, ethernet. In-hotel: room service, bar, concierge, laundry service, parking (fee), no-smoking rooms* ⊟ *AE, DC, MC, V* ⦿ *CP* Ⓤ *Victoria.*

£££££ The Rubens at the Palace. This hotel, which looks out over the Royal Mews of Buckingham Palace, provides the sort of deep comfort needed to soothe away a hard day's sightseeing, with cushy armchairs crying out for you to sink into them with a cup of Earl Grey. With decent-sized rooms—not quite furnished like the ones at the palace, it must be said—and a location that couldn't be more central, this hotel is a favorite with tour groups. Women traveling alone are offered special security, including an escort to and from your car. ☒ *39 Buckingham Palace Rd., Westminster, SW1W 0PS* ☎ *020/7834–6600* 🖷 *020/7233– 6037* ⊕ *www.rubenshotel.com* ⤶ *160 rooms, 13 suites* ⟐ *In-room: safe, VCR (some), minibar, dial-up. In-hotel: 2 restaurants, room service, bars, concierge, laundry service, parking (fee), no-smoking rooms* ⊟ *AE, DC, MC, V* Ⓤ *Victoria.*

£–££ Vandon House Hotel. Popular with students, backpackers, and families on a budget, this simply decorated hotel is close to Westminster Abbey and Buckingham Palace. Singles and some twin rooms share bathrooms, but the rest are suites with a shower only. Family rooms include a double bed and camp-style bunk bed, which could result in scuffles over who sleeps where. It's nothing fancy, but it's a friendly little place. ☒ *1 Vandon St., Westminster, SW1H 0AH* ☎ *020/7799– 6780* 🖷 *020/7799–1464* ⊕ *www.vandonhouse.com* ⤶ *32 rooms* ⟐ *In-room: no a/c. In-hotel: bar, laundry service, airport shuttle, no-smoking rooms, Wi-Fi* ⊟ *MC, V* ⦿ *CP* Ⓤ *St. James's Park.*

££ Windermere Hotel. This sweet little hotel will not let you forget that it stands on the site of London's first B&B, which opened here in 1881. It's draped in charmingly sunny floral fabrics, which look appropriate on the antique beds. Bathrooms are thoroughly modern, and the attached restaurant, small though it may be, is actually quite good. Unfortunately, prices have gone up substantially in recent years, making this less of a bargain than it once was. It's a decent option if you can't get a bargain at a plusher hotel for the same price. ☒ *142–144 Warwick Way, Victoria, SW1V 4JE* ☎ *020/7834–4163* 🖷 *020/7630–8831* ⤶ *22 rooms* ⊕ *www.windermere-hotel.co.uk* ⟐ *In-room: dial-up. In-hotel: room service, bar, no-smoking rooms, no elevator* ⊟ *MC, V* Ⓤ *Victoria.*

16

Lodging Alternatives

APARTMENT RENTALS

For a home base that's roomy enough for a family and that comes with cooking facilities, consider renting furnished "flats" (what apartments are called in Britain). These can save you money, especially if you're traveling with a group. If you're interested in home-exchange, but don't feel like sharing, some home exchange directories list rentals as well. If you want to deal directly with local agents, get a personal recommendation from someone who has used the company; there's no accredited rating system for apartment rental standards like the one for hotels. In addition to the options listed here, the London Tourist Board has accommodation lists; *see also the "Bed-and-Breakfasts & Apartment Agencies" section above.*

INTERNATIONAL AGENTS

At Home Abroad (⊠ *163 3rd Ave., No. 319, New York, NY 10003* ☎ *212/421–9165* ⊟ *212/533–0095* ⊕ *www.athomeabroadinc.com).* **Hideaways International** (⊠ *767 Islington St., Portsmouth, NH 03801* ☎ *603/430–4433 or 800/843–4433* ⊟ *603/430–4444* ⊕ *www. hideaways.com),* annual membership $145. **Hometours International** (⊠ *1108 Scottie La., Knoxville, TN 37919* ☎ *865/690–8484 or 866/367–4668* ⊕ *thor.he.net/~hometour/).* **Interhome** (⊠ *1990 N.E. 163rd St., Suite 110, North Miami Beach, FL 33162* ☎ *305/940–2299 or 800/882–6864* ⊟ *305/940–2911* ⊕ *www.inter-home.us).* **Vacation Home Rentals Worldwide** (⊠ *235 Kensington Ave., Norwood, NJ 07648* ☎ *201/767–9393 or 800/633–3284* ⊟ *201/767–5510* ⊕ *www.vhrww.com).* **Villanet** (⊠ *1251 N.W. 116th St., Seattle, WA 98177* ☎ *206/417–3444 or 800/964–1891* ⊟ *206/417–1832* ⊕ *www.renta-*

villa.com). **Villas and Apartments Abroad** (⊠ *183 Madison Ave., Suite 201, New York, NY 10016* ☎ *212/213–6435 or 800/433–3020* ⊟ *212/213–8252* ⊕ *www.vaanyc.com).*[/omit]**Villas International** (⊠ *4340 Redwood Hwy., Suite D309, San Rafael, CA 94903* ☎ *415/499–9490 or 800/221–2260* ⊟ *415/499–9491* ⊕ *www.villasintl.com).*

LOCAL AGENTS

Acorn Apartments (⊠ *103 Great Russell St., WC1B 3LA* ☎ *020/7813–3223* ⊟ *020/7813–3270* ⊕ *www. acorn-apartments.co.uk)* cost from £90. **The Apartment Service** (⊠ *5 Francis Grove, Wimbledon, SW19 4DT* ☎ *020/8944–1444* ⊟ *020/8944–6744* ⊕ *www.apartmentservice.com).* **Landmark Trust** (⊠ *01628/825–925* ⊕ *www.landmarktrust.org.uk),* for London apartments in unusual and historic buildings.

UNIVERSITY HALLS OF RESIDENCE

University student dorms can be ideal for single travelers as well as those on a tight budget who want to come to London in summer when deals on other lodgings are scarce. Walter Sickert Hall has year-round lodging in its "executive rooms" (six single and three twin), and breakfast is even delivered to your room. Beds are usually available for a week around Easter, and from mid-June to mid-September in all the university accommodations around town. As you might expect, showers and toilets are shared, and there are no bellhops to carry your bags or concierges to answer your questions.

UNIVERSITIES

City University Hall of Residence: Walter Sickert Hall (⊠ *Graham St., N1 8LA* ☎ *020/7040–*

8822 ⊜ 020/7040–8825 ⊕ www.city.
ac.uk/ems) costs £60 for a double
year-round and includes continental
breakfast. **London School of Economics Vacations** (☎ 020/7955–
7575 ⊜ 0207/955–7676 ⊕ www.
lsevacations.co.uk) costs £38 for a
double without a toilet to £62 for a
double with a toilet. You can choose
from a variety of rooms in their many
halls of residence around London. **University College London** (⊠ Residence
Manager, Campbell House, 5–10
Taviton St., WC1H 0BX ☎ 020/7679–
1479 ⊜ 020/7388–0060) costs £35–
£40 for a double and is open from
mid-June to mid-September.

HOME EXCHANGES
If you would like to exchange your
home for someone else's, join a
home-exchange organization, which
will send you its updated listings of
available exchanges for a year and
will include your own listing in at
least one of them. It's up to you to
make specific arrangements.

EXCHANGE CLUBS
HomeLink International (⊕ Box
47747, Tampa, FL 33647 ☎ 813/975–
9825 or 800/638–3841 ⊜ 813/910–
8144 ⊕ www.homelink.org); $110
yearly for a listing, online access, and
catalog; $70 without catalog. **Inter-
vac U.S.** (⊠ 30 Corte San Fernando,
Tiburon, CA 94920 ☎ 800/756–
4663 ⊜ 415/435–7440 ⊕ www.inter-
vacus.com); $125 yearly for a listing,
online access, and a catalog; $65
without catalog.

HOSTELS
No matter what your age, you can
save on lodging costs by staying at
hostels. In some 4,500 locations in
more than 70 countries around the
world, Hostelling International (HI), the
umbrella group for a number of na-

tional youth-hostel associations, offers
single-sex, dorm-style beds and, at
many hostels, rooms for couples and
family accommodations. Membership
in any HI national hostel association,
open to travelers of all ages, allows
you to stay in HI-affiliated hostels at
member rates; one-year membership
is about $28 for adults (C$35 for a
two-year minimum membership in
Canada, £14 in the United Kingdom,
A$52 in Australia, and NZ$40 in New
Zealand); hostels charge about $10–
$30 per night. Members have priority
if the hostel is full; they're also eli-
gible for discounts around the world,
even on rail and bus travel in some
countries. Members of the Boy Scouts
may want to consider London's useful Baden-Powell House, which offers
rooms for as little as $25 a night for
Scouts and their families. Non scouts
must pay a bit more.

ORGANIZATIONS
Baden-Powell House (⊠ 65–67
Queens Gate, London SW7 5JS
☎ 020/7584–7031 ⊜ 020/7590–
6902 ⊕ www.scoutbase.org.uk/hq/
bph/index.htm). **Hostelling International—USA** (⊠ 8401 Colesville
Rd., Suite 600, Silver Spring, MD
20910 ☎ 301/495–1240 ⊜ 301/495–
6697 ⊕ www.hiusa.org). **Hostelling
International—Canada** (⊠ 205
Catherine St., Suite 400, Ottawa,
Ontario K2P 1C3 ☎ 613/237–7884
or 800/663–5777 ⊜ 613/237–
7868 ⊕ www.hihostels.ca). **YHA England and Wales** (⊠ Trevelyan House,
Dimple Rd., Matlock, Derbyshire
DE4 3YH, UK ☎ 0870/870–8808,
0870/770–8868, or 0162/959–
2600 ⊜ 0870/770–6127 ⊕ www.yha.
org.uk).

16

BED-AND-BREAKFASTS & APARTMENT AGENCIES

If hotels are not your style, or if you're staying for a week or more and you're looking for a better deal, there are lots of options. You can stay with London families in small, homey B&Bs for an up-close-and-personal brush with city life, relax in a *pied-à-terre*, or rent an entire house—comfortable in the knowledge that you won't be startled awake by housekeeping the next morning. The benefits of using a B&B agency are substantial: The price is cheaper than a hotel room of comparable quality, and you have access to the kitchen so you don't have to eat every meal in a restaurant. The limitations are fairly minimal: Although you can arrange for daily maid service, there is no staff at your beck and call should you want something at odd hours, and most B&Bs and private homes are not located in the very center of the city (although many are in lovely and convenient neighborhoods like Notting Hill and Kensington). Prices for attractive rooms in privately owned homes start as low as £60 a night, and go up for more central neighborhoods and larger and more luxurious homes. It's an excellent option, both for seasoned travelers and for those trying to travel well without busting their budgets. Search the Web and call around to find the place that's right for you.

£–££ **At Home in London.** This service offers rooms in private homes in Knightsbridge, Kensington, Mayfair, Chelsea, and West London. Prices are very competitive and include breakfast, and rooms are all approved by the agency. Prices start at £28 a night per room, making this a great alternative to budget hotels. ⊠ *70 Black Lion La., Hammersmith, W6 9BE* ☎ *020/8748–1943* 🖷 *020/8748–2700* ⊕ *www.athomeinlondon. co.uk* ⊟ *MC, V* ⌖ *£7.50 per person booking fee.*

££ **Bulldog Club.** This reservation service offers delightful little London flats in sought-after neighborhoods. A three-year membership is about £25, with most properties available for about £105 per night. Full English breakfasts as well as other goodies are often provided. Most of the properties are in Knightsbridge, Kensington, and Chelsea. ⊠ *14 Dewhurst Rd., Kensington, W14 0ET* ☎ *020/7371–3202, 877/727–3004 in U.S.* 🖷 *020/7371–2015* ⊕ *www.bulldogclub.com* ⊟ *AE, MC, V.*

££–££££ **Coach House London Vacation Rentals.** Stay in the properties of Londoners who are temporarily away. Apartments and houses are primarily in Notting Hill, Kensington, and Chelsea. The extra touches—airport pickup, complimentary breakfast provisions, and a welcome drink with a representative—make this service personal. Homes also come with a phone number to call for help in planning your stay. ⊠ *2 Tunley Rd., Balham, SW17 7QJ* ☎ *020/8772–1939* 🖷 *0870/133–4957* ⊕ *www. chslondon.com* ⊟ *AE, MC, V* ⌖ *Payment by credit card only; 10% deposit required.*

£ **Host & Guest Service.** In business for 40 years, this service can find you a room based on a huge selection of B&Bs in London as well as the rest of the United Kingdom, even in rural areas. It's a great way to find excellent bargains in small hotels and guesthouses, knowing that all have been vetted by the agency. ⊠ *103 Dawes Rd., Fulham, SW6 7DU*

☎020/7385–9922 🖷020/7386–7575 ⊕*www.host-guest.co.uk* ▭*MC, V ᴥ Full payment in advance.*

££   **London B&B.** This long-established family-run agency has some truly spectacular—and some more modest—homes in central London. Check many of them out via its Web site before making a commitment. The staff here is most personable and helpful. ✉*437 J St., Suite 210, San Diego, CA 92101* ☎*800/872–2632* 🖷*619/531–1686* ⊕*www.londonbandb.com ᴥ 30% deposit required.*

££   **Primrose Hill B&B.** This is a small, friendly B&B agency genuinely "committed to the idea that traveling shouldn't be a rip-off." Expatriate American Gail O'Farrell has family homes (to which you get your own latchkey) in or near village-y Hampstead, all of which are comfortable. This used to be one of those word-of-mouth secrets, but now that everyone knows, book well ahead. ✉*14 Edis St., Regent's Park, NW1 8LG* ☎*020/7722–6869* ▭*No credit cards.*

££   **Uptown Reservations.** As the name implies, this B&B booking service accepts only the more upscale addresses and specializes in finding hosted homes or short-term apartments for Americans, often executives of small corporations. Nearly all the 85 homes on its register are in Knightsbridge, Belgravia, Kensington, and Chelsea. The private homes vary, of course, but all are good-looking. Self-catering rentals—ideal for families—start at £550 per week. 🖃*Box 50407, Chelsea, W8 5XZ* ☎*020/7937–2001* 🖷*020/7937–6660* ⊕*www.uptownres.co.uk* ▭*AE, MC, V ᴥ Facilities vary. Payment by bank transfer, U.S. check, or credit card; 20% deposit required.*

16

Pubs & Nightlife

The Prospect of Whitby, London's oldest riverside pub

WORD OF MOUTH

Many London pubs have a fascinating history and decor. Whether it is a beamed medieval, or has 'snobscreens' or a display of antiques, the choice is wide. The one often chosen is Ye Olde Cheshire Cheese where I have had a meal. It was like going into a rabbit's warren and we sat somewhere down in a basement. I found it slightly claustrophobic but not enough to spoil my meal."

—tod

PUBS & NIGHTLIFE PLANNER

Getting Around

If you're out past 12:30 AM, the best way to get home is by taxi (the tube stops running around 12:30 AM Monday–Saturday and midnight on Sunday. The best place to hail a taxi is at the front door of one of the major hotels; you can also have the staff at your last stop of the evening call one for you.

Liquor Laws

At the end of 2005, England and Wales relaxed their licensing laws and as many as 5,200 drinking establishments in London extended their opening hours. The new era marks the most notable change since 1915 of what many feel were draconian liquor laws that required most pubs to close at 11 PM. And although it's controversial, the new development only translates into a modest increase in overall licensing hours; only 14 bars and clubs are now open until dawn, while many still shut at 11, and others at midnight or a few short hours later.

Can I Take My Kids to the Pub?

As pubs increasingly emphasize what's coming out of the kitchen rather than what's flowing from the tap, whether or not to bring the kids has become a frequent question. The law dictates that patrons must be 18 years of age or older to drink alcohol in a pub unless they're having a meal in an area designated for eating. In such cases, 16-year-olds accompanied by an adult may drink beer or cider. Children 14 to 17 may enter a pub but are not permitted to purchase or drink alcohol, while children under 14 are not permitted in the bar area of a pub unless the pub has a "Children's Certificate" and they are accompanied by an adult. In general, however, pubs have a section set aside for families and welcome well-behaved children. If possible, it's probably best to call ahead—the bar staff will fill you in on their children's policy.

What to Wear

As a general rule, you can dress as you would for an evening in New York City; however, you will see fewer people in the upscale London nightspots wearing jeans and sneakers. British women are also prone to baring a bit more skin, so that sparkly, backless top you were saving for a Caribbean soirée might be just as suitable for a night out in London, weather permitting. In general, people are more likely to dress down than up for a trip to a gig or to the pub.

What's Happening Now

There are several Web sites, in addition to the print publications *The Evening Standard, Time Out London, Where London,* and *In London,* which will tell you who's playing where and when. Check out www.Londontown.com, www.AllinLondon.co.uk, www.Viewlondon.co.uk, or www.london.net/nightlife.

Updated by
Julius Honnor

London is a veritable utopia for excitement junkies, culture fiends, and those who—simply put—like to party. Virginia Woolf once wrote of London, "I step out upon a tawny-colored magic carpet ... and get carried into beauty without raising a finger. The nights are amazing, with all the white porticoes and broad silent avenues. And people pop in and out, lightly, divertingly, like rabbits...."

17

Most who visit London will, like Woolf, be mesmerized by the city's energy, which reveals itself in layers. Whether you prefer a romantic evening at the opera, rhythm and blues with fine French food, the gritty guitar riffs of East London, a pint and gourmet pizza at a local gastro-pub, or swanky cocktails and sushi at London's sexiest lair, the U.K. capital is sure to feed your fancy.

PUBS

Even today, competing with a thoroughly modern entertainment industry, the traditional pub is still a vital part of British life. It also should be a part of the visitor's experience, as there are few better places to meet Londoners in their local habitat. There are thousands of pubs in London—ever fewer of which still have original Victorian etched glass, Edwardian panels, and art nouveau carvings. The list below offers a few pubs selected for central location, historical interest, a pleasant garden, music, or good food, but you might just as happily adopt your own temporary "local."

Pubs in the capital are changing: 90-year-old licensing laws have finally been modernized, gastro-pub fever is sweeping London, and smoking in all pubs has been made illegal. At many places, char-grills are installed in the kitchen out back and nouveau pub grub, such as Moroccan chicken, is on the menu. Regardless of what you eat, however, you'll definitely want to order a pint.

■TIP→**Remember that what Americans call beer, the British call lager, often beers from continental Europe.** However, the real pub drink is "bitter," usually served at cellar temperature (that is, cooler than room temperature but not actually chilled). There's a movement to protect the traditional British cask-conditioned ale that is much less gassy. There are also plenty of other potations: Irish stouts like Guinness and Murphy's are thick, pitch-black brews you'll either love or hate; ciders, made from apples, are an alcoholic drink in Britain (Magner's cider, served over ice, is now ubiquitously fashionable); shandies are a mix of lager and lemonade (lemon soda). Discuss your choice of drink with the barman, turn to your neighbor, raise the glass, and utter that most pleasant of toasts, "Cheers."

Admiral Codrington. Named after a hero of the Napoleonic Wars, this rustic bar in a former market district was once the most popular meeting place for the upwardly mobile of Sloane Square (Lady Diana Spencer is said to have been a regular in her teaching days). The "Admiral Cod," as it's known, has recently been refurbished and now houses a modern courtyard with a removable glass roof, where excellent English fare is served at lunch and dinnertime; the adjoining original pub with its bare floorboards remains a popular spot with "Sloane Rangers." ☒ *17 Mossop St., Chelsea, SW3* ☎ *0871/332–4123* Ⓜ *South Kensington.*

The Albion. Hidden away from the hubbub of Upper Street in the laidback, leafy backstreets of Islington, the classy, ivy-clad Albion has a beer garden, straightforward pub food, and a good selection of beers. Sit out front and watch upscale North London go slowly by. ☒ *10 Thornhill Rd., Islington, N1* ☎ *020/7607–7450* Ⓜ *Angel.*

Fodor'sChoice ★ **Anchor and Hope.** One of London's most popular gastro-pubs, the Anchor and Hope doesn't take reservations, meaning queuing would-be diners snake around the red-walled, wooden-floored pub, kept happy by some good real ales and a fine wine list. The food is old-fashioned English (think salt cod, tripe, and chips) with a few modern twists. ☒ *36 The Cut, South Bank, SE1* ☎ *020/7928–9898* Ⓜ *Southwark.*

Black Friar. A step from Blackfriars Tube stop, this spectacular pub has an arts-and-crafts interior that is entertainingly, satirically ecclesiastical, with inlaid mother-of-pearl, wood carvings, stained glass, and marble pillars all over the place. In spite of the finely lettered temperance tracts on view just below the reliefs of monks, fairies, and friars, there is, needless to say, a nice group of beers on tap from independent brewers. ☒ *174 Queen Victoria St., The City, EC4* ☎ *020/7236–5474* Ⓜ *Blackfriars.*

Blue Anchor. This unaltered Georgian pub has been seen in the movie *Sliding Doors* and was the site where *The Planets* composer Gustav Holst wrote his *Hammersmith Suite.* Sit out by the river, or shelter inside with a good ale. ☒ *13 Lower Mall, Hammersmith, W6* ☎ *020/8748–5774* Ⓜ *Hammersmith.*

Cricketers. You'll find bowls of noodles and weekly quiz nights at this understated pub in one of London's wealthiest neighborhoods. It's also a fine place for a Pimm's (a British gin-based liquor). ■TIP→**On a summer's day, Cricketers makes a sublime vantage point for the cricket and the**

frolicking that take place on Richmond Green. ✉ *Maids of Honour Row, the Green, Richmond, TW9* ☎ *020/8940–4372* Ⓜ *Richmond.*

De Hems. London's only Dutch pub, straddling Chinatown and Shaftesbury Avenue, was founded in 1902. There are Oranjeboom and Fruli (strawberry beer) on tap among numerous other tasty and strong Dutch and Belgian beverages. Interestingly named Netherlands dishes, such as *bitterballen* (deep-fried meatballs) and *vlammetjes* (spicy spring rolls), are on the menu, and the place is almost always lively—sometimes bustling—up to the midnight closing time. ✉ *11 Macclesfield St., Chinatown, W1* ☎ *020/7437–2494* Ⓜ *Piccadilly Circus.*

Dove Inn. Read the list of famous ex-regulars, from Charles II and Nell Gwyn to Ernest Hemingway, as you wait for a beer at this smart, comely, and very popular 16th-century riverside pub by Hammersmith Bridge. If the Dove is too full, stroll upstream along the bank to the Old Ship or the Blue Anchor. ■ TIP➜**Please note, you must be 18 to be admitted to this pub.** ✉ *19 Upper Mall, Hammersmith, W6* ☎ *020/8748–9474* Ⓜ *Hammersmith.*

Engineer. A gastro-pub before anyone knew what the term meant, the Engineer has an upscale restaurant area (serving breakfast, lunch, and dinner), a stylish carved wooden bar with some good beers on tap, and a garden as well. Expect fresh cut flowers, a modern British menu on the chalkboard, and lots of young, beautiful people. ✉ *65 Gloucester Ave., Primrose Hill, NW1* ☎ *020/7483–0592* Ⓜ *Chalk Farm.*

French House. In the pub where the French Resistance convened during World War II, Soho hipsters and eccentrics rub shoulders now with theater people and the literati—more than shoulders, actually, because this tiny, tricolor-waving, photograph-lined pub is almost always packed. Note that in French style, only half-pints of beer are served here. ✉ *49 Dean St., Soho, W1* ☎ *020/7437–2799* Ⓜ *Tottenham Court Rd.*

Harp. This is the sort of friendly little local you might find on some out-of-the-way backstreet, except that it's right in the middle of town, between Trafalgar Square and Covent Garden. As a result, the Harp can get crowded, but the squeeze is worth it for a good range of real ales and a no-frills menu of British sausages, cooked behind the bar. ✉ *47 Chandos Pl., Covent Garden, WC2* ☎ *020/7836–0291* Ⓜ *Charing Cross.*

Fodor'sChoice **The Holly Bush.** A short walk up the hill from Hampstead Tube station, ★ the friendly Holly Bush was once a country pub before London spread this far north. It retains something of a rural feel. Separate rooms with stripped wooden floors and an open fire make it an intimate place to enjoy the great ales and organic pub food. ✉ *22 Holly Mount, Hampstead, NW3* ☎ *020/7435–2892* Ⓜ *Hampstead.*

★ **Island Queen.** This sociable Islington pub with ornate windows and warm, red decor has home-cooked food and a cozy upstairs lounge. Relax on the soft sofas with a Belgian beer or one of the guest ales. Playwright Joe Orton frequented the place; he lived—and died, murdered by his lover—next door. ✉ *87 Noel Rd., Islington, N1* ☎ *020/7704–7631* Ⓜ *Angel.*

17

Jerusalem Tavern. Owned by the excellent St. Peter's Brewery from Suffolk, the Jerusalem Tavern is one-of-a-kind. Small and endearingly eccentric, the beer, both bottled and on tap, is some of the best you'll find anywhere in London. Ancient Delft-style tiles meld with wood and concrete in a converted clockmakers shop dating back to the 18th century. It's often busy, especially after work. ⊠ *55 Britton St., Clerkenwell, EC1* ☎ *020/7490–4281* Ⓜ *Farringdon.*

★ **The Lamb.** Step back in time inside this intimate pub and feel the presence of Charles Dickens and his contemporaries who drank here. For private chats at the bar, you can close the delicate etched glass "snob-screen" to the bar staff, only opening it when you fancy another pint. ⊠ *94 Lamb's Conduit St., Bloomsbury, WC1* ☎ *020/7405–0713* Ⓜ *Russell Sq.*

Lamb & Flag. This refreshingly original 17th-century pub was once known as the Bucket of Blood because the upstairs room was used as a ring for bare-knuckle boxing. Now it's a friendly—and bloodless—pub, serving food (lunch only) and real ale. It's on the edge of Covent Garden, off Garrick Street. ⊠ *33 Rose St., Covent Garden, WC2* ☎ *020/7497–9504* Ⓜ *Covent Garden.*

The Lowlander. Calling itself a Belgian and Dutch beer café, Lowlander is a world away from English café culture. There are 14 beers on tap, with another 30 or so bottled options available to order from the long wooden tables. Exceptionally helpful staff are on hand to guide you, and Belgian fries with mayonnaise help absorb some of the alcohol. ⊠ *36 Drury La., Covent Garden, WC2B* ☎ *020/7379–7446* Ⓜ *Covent Garden or Holborn.*

Fodor's Choice ★ **Market Porter.** Opposite Borough Market, this atmospheric pub opens at 6 AM for the stall holders, stays open until late into the night, and always seems busy. Remarkably, it manages to remain a relaxed place, with helpful staff and happy customers spilling out onto the road right through the year. The selection of real ales is excellent and one of the widest in London. ⊠ *9 Stoney St., South Bank, SE1* ☎ *020/7407–2495* Ⓜ *London Bridge.*

Mayflower. An atmospheric 17th-century riverside inn with exposed beams and a terrace, this is practically the very place from which the Pilgrims set sail for Plymouth Rock. The inn is licensed to sell American postage stamps. ⊠ *117 Rotherhithe St., South Bank, SE16* ☎ *020/7237–4088* Ⓜ *Rotherhithe.*

★ **Museum Tavern.** Across the street from the British Museum, this friendly and classy Victorian pub makes an ideal resting place after the rigors of the culture trail. Karl Marx unwound here after a hard day in the Library. He could have spent his *Kapital* on any of six well-kept beers available on tap. ⊠ *49 Great Russell St., Bloomsbury, WC1* ☎ *020/7242–8987* Ⓜ *Tottenham Court Rd.*

The Nag's Head. It's best not to upset the landlord in this classic mews pub in Belgravia—he runs a tight ship and no cell phones are allowed. If that sounds like misery, the Victorian artifacts (including antique penny arcade games), high-quality beer, and old-fashioned pub grub should make up for it. ⊠ *53 Kinnerton St., Belgravia, SW1* ☎ *020/7235–1135* Ⓜ *Hyde Park Corner.*

Princess Louise. This fine, popular pub has an over-the-top Victorian interior—glazed terra-cotta, stained and frosted glass, and a glorious painted ceiling. It's not all show, either; the food is a cut above normal pub grub, and there's a good selection of excellent value Yorkshire real ales. ⊠ *208 High Holborn, Holborn, WC1* ☎ *020/7405–8816* Ⓜ *Holborn.*

★ **Prospect of Whitby.** Named after a ship, this is London's oldest riverside pub, dating from around 1520. Once upon a time it was called the Devil's Tavern because of the lowlife criminals—thieves and smugglers—who congregated here. Ornamented with pewter ware and nautical objects, this much-loved "boozer" is often pointed out from boat trips up the Thames. ⊠ *57 Wapping Wall, East End, E1* ☎ *020/7481–1095* Ⓜ *Wapping.*

The Running Horse. Sitting on the site of a building that dated back to 1720 and became a tavern in 1738, the newly refurbished Running Horse has good food and a degree of class that suits its location, a five-minute walk from the Bond Street Tube station. It's a perfect stopover for those needing a break from a jaunt through elegant Mayfair. ⊠ *50 Davies St., Mayfair, W1K* ☎ *020/7493–1275* Ⓜ *Bond St.*

Sherlock Holmes. This pub used to be known as the Northumberland Arms, and Arthur Conan Doyle popped in regularly for a pint, in the days before old black-and-white Basil Rathbone films played on loop on the pub's television. It figures in *The Hound of the Baskervilles*, and you can see the hound's supposed head and plaster casts of its huge paws among other Holmes "memorabilia" in the bar. Even if you're not a Conan Doyle fan, the beer is excellent. ⊠ *10 Northumberland St., Trafalgar Square, WC2* ☎ *020/7930–2644* Ⓜ *Charing Cross.*

★ **Spaniards Inn.** Ideal as a refueling point when you're on a Hampstead Heath hike, this historic, oak-beam pub has a gorgeous garden, scene of the tea party in Dickens's *Pickwick Papers*. Dick Turpin, the highwayman, frequented the inn; you can see his pistols on display. Before Dickens, Shelley, Keats, and Byron hung out here as well. It's extremely popular, especially on Sunday, when Londoners roll in for the tasty dishes, crackling fire, and amusing dog-washing machine in the parking lot. ⊠ *Spaniards Rd., Hampstead, NW3* ☎ *020/8731–6571* Ⓜ *Hampstead.*

★ **White Hart.** This elegant, family-owned pub on Drury Lane is one of the best places to mix with cast and crew of the stage. A female-friendly environment, a cheery skylight above the lounge area, a late license, and above-average pub fare make the White Hart a particularly sociable spot for a drink. ⊠ *191 Drury La., Covent Garden, WC2* ☎ *020/7242–2317* Ⓜ *Holborn.*

FodorśChoice
★ **White Horse.** This pub in well-to-do Parson's Green has a superb menu with a beer or wine chosen to match each dish. Open early for weekend brunch, the "Sloaney Pony" (named for its wealthy Sloane Square clientele) is enormously popular and a place to find many a Hugh Grant and Liz Hurley lookalike. The owner is an expert on cask-conditioned ale, with as many as 20 on tap, and there are more than 100 wines to choose from. ⊠ *1–3 Parson's Green, Parson's Green, SW6* ☎ *020/7736–2115* Ⓜ *Parsons Green.*

Windmill Tavern. Decorated floor to ceiling with photos of actors who have appeared across the road in the Old Vic Theatre, the Windmill Tavern has a friendly vibe and also does decent Thai food. ✉ *86 The Cut, Waterloo, SE1* ☎ *020/7207–3984* Ⓜ *Southwark.*

Windsor Castle. Rest here if you're on a Kensington jaunt, and save your appetite for the food, especially on Sunday, when they do a traditional roast. On other days you may find oysters, salads, fish cakes, and steak sandwiches. In winter a fire blazes; in summer an exquisite patio garden awaits. ✉ *114 Campden Hill Rd., Notting Hill, W8* ☎ *020/7243–9551* Ⓜ *Notting Hill Gate.*

Ye Grapes. This 1882 traditional (noisy and anti-chic, though far from cheap) pub has been popular since Victoria was on the throne. It's in the heart of Shepherd Market, the village-within-Mayfair, and is still home-away-from-home for a full deck of London characters. ✉ *16 Shepherd Market, Mayfair, W1* ☎ *020/7499–1563* Ⓜ *Green Park.*

Ye Olde Cheshire Cheese. Yes, it's a tourist trap, but it's also an extremely historic pub (it dates from 1667, the year after the Great Fire of London), and it deserves a visit for its sawdust-covered floors, low wood-beam ceilings, and the 14th-century crypt of Whitefriars' monastery under the cellar bar. But if you want to see the set of 17th-century pornographic tiles that once adorned the upstairs, you'll have to go to Blacks Museum. This was the most regular of Dr. Johnson's and Dickens's *many* locals. ✉ *145 Fleet St., The City, EC4* ☎ *020/7353–6170* Ⓜ *Blackfriars.*

NIGHTLIFE

As is true of nearly all cosmopolitan centers, the pace with which bars and clubs go in and out of fashion is mind-boggling. The phenomenon of absinthe has been replaced by bourbon's bite and the frenzy for the perfect cocktail recipe, while the dreaded velvet rope has been usurped by the doorbell-ringing mystique of members-only drinking clubs. The understated glamour of North London's Primrose Hill, which makes movie stars feel so at ease, might be considered dull by the über-trendy clubgoers of London's West End, while the price of a pint in Chelsea would be dubbed blasphemous by the musicians and poets of racially diverse Brixton. Meanwhile, some of the city's most talked-about nightlife spots are turning out to be those attached to some of its best restaurants and hotels—no wonder when you consider the increased popularity of London cuisine in international circles. Moreover, the gay scene in London continues to flourish.

Whatever your pleasure, however your whim turns come evening, chances are you'll find what you're looking for in London's ever-changing arena of activity and invention.

BARS

Today the London bar scene is known for its bizarre blends, its pioneering panache, and its highly stylish regulars. Time was, bars in London were just a stopover in an evening full of fun—perhaps the pub first, then a bar, and then it's off to boogie the night away at the nearest dance club. These days, however, bars have become less pit stops and more destinations in themselves. With the addition of dinner menus, DJs, dance floors, and the still-new later opening hours, people now stay into the wee small hours of the morning at many of London's most fashionable bars. From exotic spaces designed to look like African villages to classic art deco creations to cavernous structures housed in old railway stations, London's bar culture is as diverse as it is delicious.

All Star Lanes. One of London's newest chic bars is an unlikely combination—it's in a sleek, underground, retro bowling alley in the heart of literary Bloomsbury. Here, surrounded by 1950s Americana, you can sit on the red leather seats and choose from the largest selection of bourbons in London. ⊠ *Victoria House, Bloomsbury Pl., Bloomsbury, WC1* ☎ *020/7025–2676* ⊕ *www.allstarlanes.co.uk* ⊙ *Mon.–Wed. 5–11:30 PM, Thurs. 5–midnight, Fri. and Sat. noon–2 AM, Sun. noon–11 PM* Ⓜ *Holborn.*

★ **American Bar.** Festooned with a chin-dropping array of club ties, signed celebrity photographs, sporting mementos, and baseball caps, this sensational cocktail bar has superb martinis. ■ TIP➔ **Jacket required after 5** PM. ⊠ *Stafford Hotel, 16–18 St. James's Pl., St. James's, SW1A* ☎ *020/7493–0111* ⊙ *Weekdays 11:30 AM–11:30 PM, Sat. noon–3 PM and 5:30–11 PM, Sun. noon–2:30 PM and 6:30–10:30* Ⓜ *Green Park.*

Fodor'sChoice **Annex 3.** The same set behind the London-based Les Trois Garçons and
★ Loungelover (three antiques dealers) now have this richly decorated den of cocktail inventions to add to their roster. Infused with purple-and-red decor, dimly lighted crystal chandeliers, and walls that resemble the side of a giant Rubik's Cube, the très chic Annex 3 just off Regents Street serves a colorful mix of traditional and fruity drinks that will please most palates (as well as Japanese-influenced modern European fare for those who wish to nibble as they nurse). ⊠ *6 Little Portland St., Fitzrovia, W1W* ☎ *020/7631–0700* ⊙ *Weekdays 5 PM–midnight, Sat. 6 PM–midnight* Ⓜ *Oxford Circus.*

Babalou. Inside the crypt of a church, this intimate vaulted bar with North African overtones has restaurant and lounge areas. Brixton hipsters shake it up to top DJs spinning the decks, and knock back fancy cocktails at the bar. There's live music on Thursday nights. ⊠ *Brixton Hill, under St. Matthew's Church, Brixton, SW2* ☎ *020/7738–3366* ⊙ *Thurs. 7 PM–2 AM, Fri. and Sat. 7 PM–5 AM* Ⓜ *Brixton.*

Beach Blanket Babylon. In a Georgian house in Notting Hill, close to Portobello Market, this always-packed bar is distinguishable by its eclectic interior of indoor–outdoor spaces filled with Gaudí-esque curves and snuggly corners—like a fairy-tale grotto or a medieval dungeon. ⊠ *45 Ledbury Rd., Notting Hill, W11* ☎ *020/7229–2907* ⊙ *Mon.–Sat. noon–midnight, Sun. noon–11:30 PM* Ⓜ *Notting Hill Gate.*

17

Bedford and Strand. The wine bar is enjoying something of a renaissance in London, and this is one of the best of a new generation. It's sunk atmospherically down below the streets of Covent Garden, with dark wood and hanging shades; the wine list is short but excellently chosen, the service is faultless, and the bistro food is created with plenty of care. ⊠ *1A Bedford St., Charing Cross, WC2E* ☎ *020/7836–3033* ⊗ *Mon.– Sat. noon–midnight* Ⓜ *Charing Cross.*

The Blue Bar at the Berkeley Hotel. With Wedgwood-blue walls, Indian-style glass lanterns, and cozy seating arrangements in every corner, this baroque-style hotel bar is the ideal spot for a secretive tête-à-tête. Nurse a Blue Bar Martini (served dry with a blue cheese–stuffed olive) while taking in eclectic music ranging from Brazilian jazz to Tom Waits. ⊠ *Wilton Pl., Knightsbridge, SW1* ☎ *020/7235–6000* ⊗ *Mon.–Sat. 4* PM–*1* AM, *Sun. 3* PM–*midnight* Ⓜ *Knightsbridge.*

Cafe des Amis. This relaxed brasserie–wine bar near the Royal Opera House is the perfect pre- or post-theater spot—and a friendly enough place to go to on your own. More than 30 wines are served by the glass along with a good selection of cheeses. Opera buffs will enjoy the performance and production prints on the walls. ⊠ *11–14 Hanover Pl., Covent Garden, WC2* ☎ *020/7379–3444* ⊗ *Mon.–Sat. 11:30* AM–*1* AM Ⓜ *Covent Garden.*

Cinnamon Club. In the basement of what was once Old Westminster Library, the bar of this contemporary Indian restaurant has Bollywood scenes playing on a large screen, Asian-themed cocktails (mango mojito, Delhi mule), delicious bar snacks, and a clientele that includes fashionable young politicos. ⊠ *The Old Westminster Library, Great Smith St., Westminster, SW1* ☎ *020/7222-2555* ⊕ *www.cinnamonclub. com* ⊗ *Weekdays 11* AM–*midnight, Sat. 6* PM–*midnight* Ⓜ *Westminster.*

Fodor'sChoice ★ **Claridge's Bar.** This elegant Mayfair meeting place remains unpretentious even when it brims with beautiful people. The bar has an art deco heritage made hip by the sophisticated touch of designer David Collins. A library of rare champagnes and brandies as well as a delicious choice of traditional and exotic cocktails—try the Black Pearl—will occupy your taste buds. Request a glass of vintage Cristal (the only bar in London that serves it) or a smoke from the menu of fine cigars in the Macanudo Fumoir. ⊠ *55 Brook St., Mayfair, W1A* ☎ *020/7629–8860* ⊗ *Mon.–Sat. 11* PM—*1* AM, *Sun. 4* PM–*midnight* Ⓜ *Bond St.*

Fodor'sChoice ★ **Cocoon.** Pan-Asian restaurant Cocoon transforms itself into a sophisticated lounge bar (with DJ) Thursday through Saturday until 3 AM. Smack in the center of the West End on a landmark site, the Late Lounge with its soft peach decor and sanctuary-like setting serves caviar, oysters, a selection of appetizers, and desserts as well as champagne, sake, and cocktails with an oriental twist. If you're looking to make an impression, this sparkling spot holds sway. ⊠ *65 Regent St., St. James's, W1B* ☎ *087/1332–6347* ⊗ *Thurs.–Sat. 11* PM–*3* AM Ⓜ *Piccadilly.*

Fodor'sChoice ★ **Crazy Bear.** This sexy basement bar with cowhide stools and croc-skin tables feels like Casablanca in Fitzrovia. As you enter Crazy Bear, a spiral staircase leads to a mirrored parlor over which presides a 1947 Murano chandelier. But don't let the opulence fool you: waitresses here are warm and welcoming to an all-ages international crowd abuzz with chatter. A new chef means the menu now advertises drinks and dim sum. ✉ *26–28 Whitfield St., Fitzrovia, W1T* ☎ *020/7631–0088* ⊙ *Mon.–Sat. noon–11* Ⓜ *Goodge St.*

Cubana. Authentic Cuban style and ingredients make this a lively place for a cocktail or a bite to eat. Mojitos are exemplary, using organic raw cane sugar and piles of fresh mint. The place is decorated with everything from guns to chili fairy lights, and there's live salsa music every evening from Wednesday to Saturday. ✉ *48 Lower Marsh, South Bank, SE1* ☎ *020/7928–8778* ⊕ *www.cubana.co.uk* ⊙ *Mon. and Tues. noon–midnight, Wed. and Thurs. noon–1* AM, *Fri. noon–3* AM, *Sat. 5* PM–*3* AM Ⓜ *Waterloo.*

★ **Dogstar.** This popular South London hangout is frequented by local hipsters and counterculture types. The vibe is unpretentious and hip, and the modern Caribbean cuisine is a treat. The interior has been refurbished in "surrealist boudoir" style and top-name DJs play cutting-edge sounds (free Monday–Thursday). ✉ *389 Coldharbour La., Brixton, SW9* ☎ *020/7733–7515* 🖃 *Free–£5* ⊙ *Mon.–Thurs. 4* PM–*2* AM, *Fri. and Sat. noon–4* AM, *Sun. noon–2* AM Ⓜ *Brixton.*

Elbow Room. Designed in '60s pool-hall chic, Elbow Room has 11 tables, table tennis, leather-booth seating, and a neon-lighted bar. DJs and occasional bands put in late appearances. There are also branches in Shoreditch and Westbourne Grove. ✉ *89–91 Chapel Market, Islington, N1* ☎ *020/7278–3244* 🖃 *Free–£5* ⊙ *Mon. 5* PM–*2* AM, *Tues.–Thurs. noon–2* AM, *Fri. and Sat. noon–3* AM, *Sun. noon–midnight* Ⓜ *Angel.*

Hackney Central. A welcome addition to the East London nightlife scene, this bar and music club is the new incarnation of Hackney's old Victorian railway station. DJs and live bands perform in the bar upstairs, while food and drink flow in the restaurant and bar downstairs. ✉ *Amhurst Rd., Hackney, E8* ☎ *020/8986–5111* ⊕ *www.hackneycentral.com* 🖃 *Free–£15* ⊙ *Sun.–Thurs. 11* AM–*midnight, Fri. and Sat. 11* AM–*2* AM Ⓜ *National Rail: Hackney Central.*

Harlem. Backed by music producer Arthur Baker (the Elbow Room), Harlem re-creates New York in more ways than one, not the least of which is its size: the two rooms together equal the dimensions of an average Manhattan apartment. However, funky DJs, fresh tunes, and reasonably priced drinks—not to mention the excellent soul food served in the first floor restaurant—give Harlem a vibe all its own. ✉ *78 Westbourne Grove, Westbourne Grove, W2* ☎ *020/7985–0900* ⊙ *Mon.–Thurs. 11* AM–*2* AM, *Fri. 11* AM–*2:30* AM, *Sat. 10* AM–*2:30* AM, *Sun. 10* AM–*midnight* Ⓜ *Westbourne Park.*

Hoxton Square Bar & Kitchen. The rectangular concrete bar, reminiscent of a Swedish airport hangar, has long, comfortable sofas, plate-glass windows at the front and back, and outdoor tables overlooking leafy Hoxton Square. In the converted Lux cinema next door, there's a designated restaurant area serving venison and the like. The music policy here is anything but house, and creative types give the place good business. ✉ *2–4 Hoxton Sq., Hoxton, E1* ☎ *020/7613–0709* ⊙ *Sun.–Thurs. 11* AM–*1* AM, *Fri. and Sat. 11* AM–*2* AM Ⓜ *Old St.*

★ **Le Beaujolais.** Around 60 lovingly selected French wines are available here, where you can snack on delicious olives, charcuterie, and homemade *croque monsieur* sandwiches while snug and warm under the bottle-laden ceiling as a funky blues soundtrack plays. It's a romantic little spot and can get crowded just before theater performances, but has room again once the shows begin. ⊠ *25 Litchfield St., Leicester Square, WC2* ☎ *020/7836–2955* Ⓜ *Leicester Square.*

Long Bar at Sanderson Hotel. Dubbed by Vanity Fair as a "magical stage set for the world's high-profile travelers," the Philippe Starck-designed Sanderson Hotel envelops visitors in a fantasyland setting of billowy white decor and glass dividers. The dramatic, high-ceiling Long Bar (as the name suggests, the bar is 80-feet long) just off the lobby serves sushi and tapas as well as cocktails, providing a chic shopping break as well as an excellent perch for people-watching. ⊠ *50 Berners St., Fitzrovia, W1T* ☎ *020/7300–5587* ☉ *Mon. 11 AM–1 AM, Tue. and Wed. 11 AM–1:30 AM, Thurs.–Sat. 11 AM–3 AM, Sun. noon–10:30 PM* Ⓜ *Oxford Circus.*

Milk & Honey. An offshoot of the New York drinking club, this unmarked bar feels like a Prohibition-era speakeasy with its limited entrance for non-members, call-ahead policy, and doorbell entrance. Here cocktail maestro Dale DeGroff serves up more potent potions than the name suggests until 11 PM during the early half of the week. However, if you're unacquainted with the bar's rules of conduct, consider yourself fore-warned: "Gentlemen will not introduce themselves to ladies. Ladies … if a man you don't know speaks to you, please lift your chin slightly and ignore him." ⊠ *61 Poland St., Soho, W1F* ☎ *020/7000–655469* ⊕ *www.mlkhny.com* ☉ *Open to non-members weekdays 6 PM–11 PM, Sat. 7 PM–11 PM (in practice usually only early in the week)* ⚞ *Reservations essential* Ⓜ *Oxford Circus.*

★ **Nordic.** With Red Erik and Faxe draft beers, shooters called "Husky Poo" and "Danish Bacon Surprise," and crayfish tails and meatballs on the smorgasbord menu, Nordic takes its Scandinavian feel the whole way. This secluded, shabby-chic bar serves many couples cozied up among travel brochures promoting the Viking lands. The sassy, sweet Longberry is quite possibly the most delicious cocktail ever made. ⊠ *25 Newman St., Noho, W1* ☎ *020/7631–3174* ⊕ *www.nordicbar.com* ☉ *Weekdays noon–11 PM, Sat. 6 PM–11 PM* Ⓜ *Tottenham Court Rd.*

Oxo Bar. The views of London are inspiring from this eighth-floor bar near the Tate Modern on the south bank of the Thames. Most people come to eat at the excellent restaurant, but the bar is a wonderful place in its own right, expensive but still a striking spot for a predinner drink or a vertiginous nightcap. ⊠ *Bargehouse St., South Bank, SE1* ☎ *020/7803–3888* ☉ *Mon. and Tues. 11 AM–11 PM, Wed.–Sat. 11 AM–midnight, Sun. noon–10:30 PM* Ⓜ *Waterloo.*

Potemkin. Over 100 vodkas and some great cocktails are available at this modern Russian bar. Friendly staff will happily suggest where to start, and downstairs a restaurant serves up excellent Russian fare. ⊠ *144 Clerkenwell Rd., Clerkenwell, EC1* ☎ *020/7278–6661* ⊕ *www.potem-kin.co.uk* ☉ *Weekdays noon–11 PM, Sat. 6 PM–11 PM* Ⓜ *Farringdon or Chancery Lane.*

Smiths of Smithfield. This loft-style megabar with exposed wood beams, steel columns, and huge windows overlooks the Victorian Smithfield's market. Have a beer in the airy ground-floor pub, a cocktail in the intimate champagne-cocktail bar upstairs (open until 1 AM on weekends), or some fine British Modern cuisine in the restaurants. The 7 AM opening hour captures the fallout from nearby clubs. DJs spin records here in the evenings Wednesday through Saturday. ✉ *67–77 Charterhouse St., East End, EC1N* ☎ *020/7251–7950* ☉ *Mon.–Wed. 7 AM–11 PM, Thurs. 7 AM–12:30 AM, Fri. 7 AM–1 AM, Sat. 10 AM–1 AM, Sun. 9:30 AM–10:30 PM* Ⓜ *Farringdon.*

Ten West. At this sprawling South Beach–inspired bar under the Westway on Ladbroke Grove, retro-pattern wallpaper and cushy chairs are offset by lipstick-red latticework railings and chandeliers with marqueelike dividers throughout. Copper tables highlight the main event: simple canapés and cocktails with names like Collins Avenue and the Delano. Although the Miami theme borders on excessive, the tasty food and drinks somehow alleviate the overkill. ✉ *161–165 Ladbroke Grove, Ladbroke Grove, W10* ☎ *020/8960–1702* ⊕ *www.vertigo42.co.uk* ☉ *Sun.–Fri. 5 PM–midnight, Sat. noon–midnight* Ⓜ *Ladbroke Grove.*

COMEDY & CABARET

Amused Moose. This dark Soho basement is widely considered the best place to see breaking talent as well as household names doing "secret" shows. Ricky Gervais and Eddie Izzard are among those who have graced this stage and every summer a handful of the Edinburgh Fringe comedians preview here. The bar is open late and there are a DJ and dancing until 5 AM after the show. Tickets are usually discounted with a print-out from their Web site. ✉ *Moonlighting, 17 Greek St., Soho, W1* ☎ *020/7287–3727* ⊕ *www.amusedmoose.com* 🎟 *£9 and up* ☉ *Showtimes vary, call for details* Ⓜ *Tottenham Court Rd.*

Banana Cabaret. This pub is one of London's finest comedy venues. Well worth the trek, it's only 100 yards from Balham station, and there's a minicab office close by for those tempted to make a long night of it. ✉ *Bedford Pub, 77 Bedford Hill, Balham, SW12* ☎ *020/8673–8904* ⊕ *www.bananacabaret.co.uk* 🎟 *£12–£15* ☉ *Fri. 7:30 PM–2 AM, Sat. 6:30 PM–2 AM* Ⓜ *Balham.*

Canal Café Theatre. You'll find famous comics and cabaret performers every night of the week in this intimate, picturesque, canal-side venue. The long-running NewsRevue is a topical song and sketch show every night, Thursday–Sunday. ✉ *Bridge House, Delamere Terr., Little Venice, W2* ☎ *020/7289–6054* ⊕ *www.canalcafetheatre.com* 🎟 *£5–£9* ☉ *Mon.–Sat. 7:30 PM–11 PM, Sun. 7 PM–10:30 PM* Ⓜ *Warwick Ave.*

Comedy Café. In addition to lots of stand-up comedy, this popular dive in trendy Hoxton has Tex-Mex cuisine, a free open mike on Wednesday, and late-night disco on Saturday nights. ✉ *66 Rivington St., East End, EC2* ☎ *020/7739–5706* ⊕ *www.comedycafe.co.uk* 🎟 *Free–£15* ☉ *Wed. and Thurs. 7 PM–midnight, Fri. and Sat. 6 PM–1 AM* Ⓜ *Old St.*

★ **Comedy Store.** Known as the birthplace of alternative comedy, this is where the U.K.'s funniest stand-ups have cut their teeth before being

17

launched onto prime-time TV. Comedy Store Players entertain audiences on Wednesday and Sunday; the Cutting Edge team steps in every Tuesday; and weekends have up-and-coming comedians performing on the same stage as established talent. There's a bar with food also available. ■ TIP→ **Tickets can be booked through Ticketmaster or over the phone.** Note that children under 18 are not admitted to this venue. ⊠ *1A Oxendon St., Soho, SW1* ☎ *0870/060–2340* ⊕ *www.thecomedystore.co.uk* ⚏ *£10–£15* ⊙ *Shows Tues.–Thurs. and Sun. 8* PM–*10:15* PM, *Fri. and Sat. 8* PM–*10:15* PM *and midnight–2:30* AM Ⓜ *Piccadilly Circus, Leicester Sq.*

Fodor'sChoice **Soho Theatre.** This innovative theater programs excellent comedy shows
★ by established acts and award-winning new comedians. The bar downstairs, Café Lazeez, stays open until 1 AM. Check local listings or the Web site for what's on and book tickets in advance. ⊠ *21 Dean St., Soho, W1* ☎ *0870/429–6883* ⊕ *www.sohotheatre.com* ⚏ *£10–£17.50* Ⓜ *Tottenham Court Rd.*

DANCE CLUBS

The city that practically invented raves is always on the verge of creating something new and on any given night there's a club playing the latest in dance music. Because London is so ethnically diverse, the tunes that emanate from the DJ box are equally varied; an amalgamation of sounds infusing drum 'n' bass, hip-hop, deep house, Latin house, breakbeat, indie, and R&B.

The club scene here ranges from mammoth-size playgrounds like Fabric and Cargo to more intimate venues where you can actually hear your friends talk. Check the daily listings in *Time Out* for "club nights," which are themed nights that take place the same night every week, sometimes at the same clubs but often shifting locations. Another good way to learn about club nights is by picking up fliers in your favorite bar.

Bar Rumba. Though nothing special to look at, this smallish West End venue has a reputation for good fun. The staff is friendly and the club is almost always heaving with serious clubbers grooving to different styles of music each night. Stop by weekdays for cheap cocktails during a generously long happy hour. ⊠ *36 Shaftesbury Ave., Soho, W1* ☎ *020/7287–2715* ⚏ *£3–£12* ⊙ *Mon. 9* PM–*3* AM, *Tues. 6* PM–*3* AM, *Wed. 8* PM–*3* AM, *Thurs. 8* PM–*3:30* AM, *Fri. 7* PM–*4* AM, *Sat. 9* PM–*3:30* AM, *Sun. 8:30* PM–*2:30* AM Ⓜ *Piccadilly Circus.*

★ **The Cross.** Stone-floored and rustic, this theme-night, 650-capacity venue manages to be cool and comfortable at the same time. Under six abandoned railway arches, with wrought-iron railings and a Greek-style outdoor garden, the Cross lends itself to a mixed crowd. Theme nights vary from "polysexual" to gay to charity affairs to musically themed events. ☞ *Check Web site for details on theme nights and opening hrs.* ⊠ *Kings Cross Goods Yard, Arches 27–31, York Way, N1* ☎ *020/7837–0828* ⊕ *www.the-cross.co.uk* Ⓜ *Kings Cross.*

Fodor'sChoice **Cargo.** Housed under a series of old railway arches, this vast brick-wall
★ bar, restaurant, dance floor, and live-music venue pulls an international crowd with its hip vibe and diverse selection of music. Long tables

bring people together, as does the food, which draws on global influences and is served tapas-style. ✉ *83 Rivington St., Shoreditch, EC2* ☎ *0871/075–1741* ⊕ *www.cargo-london.com* ⊙ *Mon.–Thurs. noon–1* AM, *Fri. noon–3, Sat. 6* PM–3 AM, *Sun. 1* PM–midnight M *Old St.*

★ **The End.** This intimate club is owned and designed by clubbers for clubbers. Top-name DJs, a state-of-the-art sound system, and minimalist steel-and-glass decor—clubbing doesn't get much better than this. Next door, the AKA Bar is a stylish split-level Manhattan-esque cocktail bar with excellent food. ✉ *18 West Central St., Holborn, WC1* ☎ *020/7419–9199* ⊕ *www.endclub.com* ☐ *£5–£16* ⊙ *Mon. 10* PM–3 AM, *Wed. 10:30* PM–3 AM, *Thurs. 10* PM–4 AM, *Fri. 10* PM–5 AM, *and Sat. 10* PM–7 AM. *Also some Sun.* M *Tottenham Court Rd.*

Fabric. This sprawling subterranean club has been *the* place to be for the past few years. "Fabric Live" hosts drum 'n' bass and hip-hop crews and live acts on Friday; international big-name DJs play slow sexy bass lines and cutting-edge music on Saturday. Sunday is "Polysexual Night." The devastating sound system and bodysonic dance floor ensure that bass riffs vibrate through your entire body. ■ TIP → Get there early to avoid a lengthy queue, and don't wear a suit. ✉ *77A Charterhouse St., East End, EC1* ☎ *020/7336–8898* ⊕ *www.fabriclondon.com* ☐ *£12–£15* ⊙ *Fri. 9:30* PM–5 AM, *Sat. 10* PM–7 AM M *Farringdon.*

★ **KOKO.** KOKO is the latest name for this Victorian theater, formerly known as Camden Palace, that's seen acts from Charlie Chaplin to Madonna, and genres from punk to rave. Updated with lush reds not unlike a cockney Moulin Rouge, this is still one of London's most stunning venues. Sounds of live indie-rock, cabaret, funky house, and club classics keep the big dance floor moving, even when it's not heaving. ✉ *1A Camden High St., Camden Town, NW1* ☎ *0870/432–5527* ⊕ *www.koko.uk.com* ☐ *£3–£20* ⊙ *Fri. and Sat. 10* PM–4 AM, *also some Wed.* M *Mornington Crescent.*

Mass. In what was previously St. Matthew's Church, but is now an atmospheric club with Gothic overtones, winding stone steps lead to the main room where an extended balcony hangs over the dance floor. An unpretentious and friendly crowd dances, on rotating club nights, to reggae, drum 'n' bass, and R&B. ✉ *Brixton Hill, St. Matthew's Church, Brixton, SW2* ☎ *020/7738–7875* ⊕ *www.mass-club.com* ☐ *£5–£15* ⊙ *Wed. and Thurs., 10* PM–2 AM, *Fri. 10* PM–6 AM, *Sat. noon–7* PM *and 10* PM–6 AM M *Brixton.*

Ministry of Sound. It's more of an industry than a club, with its own record label, online radio station, and international DJs. The stripped down warehouse-style club has a super sound system and pulls in the world's most legendary names in dance. There are chill-out rooms, two bars, and three dance floors. ✉ *103 Gaunt St., South Bank, SE1* ☎ *020/7378–6528* ☐ *£10–£35* ⊙ *Fri. 10:30* PM–5 AM, *Sat. 11* PM–7 AM M *Elephant & Castle.*

★ **Notting Hill Arts Club.** Rock stars like Liam Gallagher and Courtney Love have been seen at this small basement club-bar. An alternative crowd swills beer to eclectic music that spans Asian underground, hip-hop, Latin-inspired funk, deep house, and jazzy grooves. What it lacks in looks it makes up for in mood. ✉ *21 Notting Hill Gate, Notting*

17

Hill, W11 ☎*020/7460–4459* ⊕*www.nottinghillartsclub.com* ✉*Free–*
£8 ⊘ *Weekdays 6* PM*–2* AM*, Sat. 4* PM*–2* AM*, Sun. 4* PM*–1* AM Ⓜ*Notting*
Hill Gate.

Pacha. London's version of the Ibizan superclub is in a restored 1920s
dancehall next to Victoria Coach Station. The classic surroundings—all
wood and chandeliers—don't stop the sounds from being eminently up-
to-date. The crowd is slightly older than average and stylish, but not
necessarily as monied as you might expect. ✉*Terminus Pl., Victoria,*
SW1 ☎*020/7833–3139* ✉*£15–£20* ⊘*Fri. 10* PM*–4* AM*, Sat. 10* PM*–6*
AM Ⓜ*Victoria.*

Tantra. This sexy dance club is decidedly not for wallflowers. With its
starry ceiling and leather furnishings, the sweeping space is chock-full
of fashionistas boogying the night away to the latest beats. Count on
expensive food and drink, but if you're up for a night of celeb-spotting
and stargazing amidst the London elite, Tantra crowns the list. ✉*62*
Kingly St., Soho, W1R ☎*0871/075–1754* ⊘*Mon.–Sat. 10:30* PM*–3*
AM Ⓜ*Piccadilly Circus.*

333. The last word in dance music for the trendy Shoreditch crowd.
Fashionable bright young things dance to drum 'n' bass, twisted disco,
and underground dance genres. There are three floors, each with its own
theme. You can chill on leather sofas at the relaxed Mother Bar upstairs,
open from 8 PM daily, which always has DJs. ✉*333 Old St., East End,*
EC1 ☎*020/7739–5949* ⊕*www.333mother.com* ✉*Free–£10* ⊘*Tues. hrs*
vary, Fri. and Sat. 10 PM*–5* AM*, Sun. 10:30* PM*–4* AM Ⓜ*Old St.*

ECLECTIC MUSIC

The Borderline. This important small venue has a solid reputation for
booking everything from metal to country and beyond. Oasis, Pearl Jam,
Blur, Sheryl Crow, PJ Harvey, Ben Harper, Jeff Buckley, and Counting
Crows have all played live here. ✉*Orange Yard off Manette St., Soho,*
W1 ☎*020/7434–9592* ⊕*www.meanfiddler.com* ✉*£5–£12* ⊘*Mon.–Sat.*
7 PM*–3* AM*, Sun. 7* PM*–11* PM Ⓜ*Tottenham Court Rd.*

Fodor'sChoice **Carling Academy Brixton.** This legendary Brixton venue has seen it all—
★ mods and rockers, hippies and punks. Despite a capacity of almost
5,000 people, this refurbished Victorian hall with original art deco
fixtures retains a clublike charm; it has plenty of bars and upstairs seating. ✉*211 Stockwell Rd., Brixton, SW9* ☎*0870/771–2000* ⊕*www.*
brixton-academy.co.uk ✉*£10–£30* ⊘*Opening hrs vary* Ⓜ*Brixton.*

Dingwalls. This midsize venue in the Camden Lock warehouses
caters to the full spectrum of musical tastes—country, jazz, blues,
folk, indie, and world beat. (▪TIP➔**Note that on Friday and Satur-**
day it becomes a comedy club, Jongleurs.) ✉*Middle Yard, Camden*
Lock off Camden High St., Camden Town, NW1 ☎*020/7267–*
1577 ⊕*www.dingwalls.com* ✉*£5–£20* ⊘*Tues.–Thurs. 7:30* PM*–*
midnight Ⓜ*Camden Town.*

93 Feet East. Knowing nods greet the bands in this cool but friendly
independent venue, with a courtyard out back for taking a breather,
or partaking in weekend barbecues. Up-and-coming guitar groups
and blues acts find their way here, while house DJs get you moving

and live hip-hop crews shake you off your seat with hefty bass lines. Short films are shown here on Sunday. ✉ *150 Brick La., East End, E1* ☎ *020/7247–3293* ⊕ *www.93feeteast.co.uk* 💷 *Free–£10* ☺ *Mon.–Thurs. 5 PM–11 PM, Fri. 5 PM–1 AM, Sat. noon–1 AM, Sun. noon–10:30 PM* Ⓜ *Aldgate East.*

100 Club. Since it opened in 1942, all the greats have played here, from Glenn Miller and Louis Armstrong on down to the best traditional jazz artists, British and American blues, R&B, and punk. This cool, inexpensive club now reverberates to rock, indie, and R&B—as well as traditional jazz, of course. You can still take jitterbug and jive lessons from the London Swing Dance Society. ✉ *100 Oxford St., Soho, W1* ☎ *020/7636–0933* ⊕ *www.the100club.co.uk* 💷 *£7–£15* ☺ *Mon. 7:30 PM–midnight, Tues.–Thurs. 7:30 PM–11 PM, Fri. 7:30 PM–12:30 AM, Sat. 7:30 PM–2 AM, Sun. 7:30 PM–11 PM* Ⓜ *Oxford Circus, Tottenham Court Rd.*

Shepherd's Bush Empire. Once a grand old theater and former BBC TV studio, this intimate venue with fine balcony views now hosts a great cross section of mid-league U.K. and U.S. bands. ✉ *Shepherd's Bush Green, Shepherd's Bush, W12* ☎ *0870/771–2000* ⊕ *www.shepherds-bush-empire.co.uk* 💷 *£10–£30* ☺ *Opening hrs vary* Ⓜ *Shepherd's Bush (H&C).*

★ **Spitz.** In buzzing Spitalfields Market, where the City interfaces with the East End, this two-level café-restaurant-gallery has eclectic music that includes world-beat, folk, jazz, Americana, and electronic sounds. The downstairs bar and bistro has DJs and live jazz free on Friday nights. ✉ *109 Commercial St., East End, E1* ☎ *020/7392–9032* ⊕ *www.spitz.co.uk* 💷 *Free–£15* ☺ *Mon.–Sat. 10 AM–midnight, Sun. 10 AM–10:30 PM* Ⓜ *Liverpool St.*

12 Bar Club. This rough-and-ready acoustic club hosts notable singer-songwriters. Four different acts of new folk, contemporary country, blues, and even ska and punk perform each night in this intimate venue. There's a good selection of bottled beer and gastro-pub food here. ✉ *22–23 Denmark Pl., West End, WC2* ☎ *020/7916–6989* ⊕ *www.12barclub.com* 💷 *£3–£10* ☺ *Mon.–Thurs. 7:30 PM–1 AM, Fri. and Sat. 7:30 PM–3 AM, Sun. 7 PM–12:30 AM. Café opens at 11 AM, Mon.–Sat.* Ⓜ *Tottenham Court Rd.*

★ **Union Chapel.** This beautiful old chapel has excellent acoustics and sublime architecture. The beauty of the space and its impressive multicultural programming have made it one of London's best musical venues, especially for acoustic shows. Performers have included Ravi Shankar, Björk, Beck, Beth Orton, and Bob Geldof, though nowadays you're more likely to hear lower-key alternative country, world music, and jazz. ✉ *Compton Terr., Islington, N1* ☎ *020/7226–1686 or 0870/120–1349* ⊕ *www.unionchapel.org.uk* 💷 *Free–£25* ☺ *Opening hrs vary* Ⓜ *Highbury & Islington.*

17

JAZZ & BLUES

Jazz in London is highly eclectic. You can expect anything from danceable, smooth tunes played at a supper club to groovy New Orleans–style blues to exotic world-beat rhythms, which can be heard at some of the less central venues throughout the capital. Musicians are a combination of Brits and visiting artists from the United States and elsewhere. London hosts the **London Jazz Festival** in November, which showcases top and emerging artists in experimental jazz. The **Ealing Jazz Festival,** at the end of July, claims to be the biggest free jazz event in Europe.

Ain't Nothin' but Blues. The name sums up this bar that whips up a sweaty and smoky environment. Local musicians, as well as some notable names, squeeze onto the tiny stage. There's good bar food of the chili-and-gumbo variety. Most weekday nights there's no cover. ✉ *20 Kingly St., Soho, W1* ☎ *020/7287–0514* 🖃 *Free–£5* ⊙ *Mon.–Wed. 6 PM–1 AM, Thurs. 6 PM–2 AM, Fri. and Sat. noon–3 AM, Sun. 7:30 PM–midnight* Ⓜ *Oxford Circus.*

★ **Bull's Head.** Its pleasant location (right on the Thames) and the big-name musicians who jam here regularly make the excursion to Bull's Head worthwhile. Jazz-and-blues shows start nightly at 8:30 PM (2 PM and 8 PM on Sunday). ■TIP→**They also offer 250 wines, 80 malt whiskies, and Thai food.** ✉ *373 Lonsdale Rd., Barnes Bridge, Barnes, SW13* ☎ *020/8876–5241* ⊕ *www.thebullshead.com* 🖃 *£7–£12* ⊙ *Mon.–Sat. noon–11 PM, Sun. noon–10:30 PM* Ⓜ *Hammersmith, then Bus 209 to Barnes Bridge.*

Dover Street Restaurant & Jazz Bar. Put on your blue-suede shoes and prepare to dance the night away—that is, after you've feasted from an excellent French Mediterranean menu. Fun for dates as well as groups, Dover Street Restaurant offers three bars, a DJ, and a stage with the latest live bands performing everything from jazz to soul to R&B, all this encircling linen-covered tables with a friendly staff catering to your every whim. ✉ *8–10 Dover St., Mayfair, W1S* ☎ *020/7491–7509* ⊕ *www.doverst.co.uk* 🖃 *Free–£15* ⊙ *Mon.–Thurs. noon–3 PM and 5:30 PM–3 AM, Fri. noon–3 PM and 7 PM–3 AM, Sat. 7 PM–3 AM* Ⓜ *Green Park.*

Fodor's Choice **Jazz Café.** A palace of high-tech cool in bohemian Camden—it remains
★ an essential hangout for fans of both the mainstream end of the repertoire and hip-hop, funk, rap, and Latin fusion. Book ahead if you want a prime table overlooking the stage, in the balcony restaurant. ✉ *5 Pkwy., Camden Town, NW1* ☎ *020/7916–6060 restaurant reservations, 0870/150–0044 standing tickets* ⊕ *www.jazzcafe.co.uk* 🖃 *£10–£25* ⊙ *Mon.–Thurs. 7 PM–1 AM, Fri. and Sat. 7 PM–2 AM, Sun. 7 PM–midnight* Ⓜ *Camden Town.*

Pizza Express Jazz Club Soho. One of the capital's most ubiquitous pizza chains also runs a great Soho jazz venue. The dimly lit restaurant hosts top-quality international jazz acts every night. The Italian-style thin-crust pizzas are good, too, though on the small side. The Hyde Park branch has a spacious jazz club in the basement that hosts mainstream acts. ✉ *10 Dean St., Soho, W1* ☎ *020/7439–8722* Ⓜ *Tottenham Court Rd.* ✉ *11 Knightsbridge, Hyde Park Corner, Knightsbridge, W1*

☎020/7235–5273 Ⓜ *Hyde Park Corner* ☜ *£10–£25* ☺ *Daily from 11:30* AM *for food; music 7:30* PM*–midnight.*

★ **Ronnie Scott's.** Since the '60s, this legendary jazz club has attracted big names. It's usually crowded and hot, the food isn't great, and service is slow—but the mood can't be beat, even since the sad departure of its eponymous founder and saxophonist. Reservations are recommended. ✉ *47 Frith St., Soho, W1* ☎ *020/7439–0747* ⊕ *www.ronniescotts.co.uk* ☜ *£15–£25 nonmembers, £5–£15 members, annual membership £165* ☺ *Mon.–Sat. 8:30* PM*–3* AM*, Sun. 7:30* PM*–11* PM Ⓜ *Leicester Sq.*

606 Club. Expect a civilized Chelsea club that showcases mainstream and contemporary jazz by well-known British-based musicians. ■ TIP➜**You must eat a meal in order to consume alcohol, so allow for an extra £10–£20.** Reservations are advisable. ✉ *90 Lots Rd., Chelsea, SW10* ☎ *020/7352–5953* ⊕ *www.606club.co.uk* ☜ *£8–£12 music charge added to bill* ☺ *Mon.–Wed. 7:30* PM*–1* AM*, Thurs. 8* PM*–1* AM*, Fri. and Sat. 8* PM*–1:30* AM*, Sun. 12:30* PM*–4* PM *and 8* PM*–midnight* Ⓜ *Earl's Court, Fulham Broadway.*

ROCK

Ever since the Beatles hit the world stage in the early 1960s, London has been at the epicenter of rock and roll. The city is a given stop on any burgeoning or established band's international tour. These days, since rock clubs have been granted later licenses, many shows now go past 11 PM. Fans here are both loyal and enthusiastic. It is, therefore, a good idea to buy show tickets ahead of time. The "Gigs and Tickets" section on ⊕ *www.nme.com* is a comprehensive search engine where you can easily book tickets online, and Time Out is another good source of upcoming shows.

The Astoria. This balconied theater hosts cutting-edge and big-name alternative bands (punk, metal, indie guitar). Shows start early, at 7 PM most nights; the building is often cleared, following gigs, for club events. ■ TIP➜**Note that it's closed on some Tuesdays and Wednesdays.** ✉ *157 Charing Cross Rd., West End, W1* ☎ *020/7434–9592* ⊕ *www.meanfiddler.com* ☜ *£8–£25* ☺ *Mon., Thurs., and Fri. 7* PM*–4* AM*, Tues., Wed., and Sun. 7* PM*–midnight, Sat. 6* PM*–4:30* AM Ⓜ *Tottenham Court Rd.*

★ **Barfly Club.** At one of the finest small clubs in the capital, punk, indie guitar bands, and new metal rock attract a nonmainstream crowd. Weekend club nights upstairs host DJs who rock the decks. ✉ *49 Chalk Farm Rd., Camden Town, NW1* ☎ *020/7691–4244* ⊕ *www.barflyclub.com* ☜ *£5–£8* ☺ *Mon.–Thurs. 7:30* PM*–midnight, Fri. and Sat. 8* PM*–3* AM*, Sun. 7:30* PM*–11* PM Ⓜ *Camden Town, Chalk Farm.*

Forum. The best medium-to-big-name rock performers consistently play at the 2,000-capacity club. It's a converted 1920 art deco cinema, with a balcony overlooking the dance floor. Consult the Web site for current listings. ✉ *9–17 Highgate Rd., Kentish Town, NW5* ☎ *020/7284–1001* ⊕ *www.meanfiddler.com* ☜ *£12–£25* ☺ *Opening hrs vary depending on concert schedule* Ⓜ *Kentish Town.*

17

The Garage. Popular with the younger set, this intimate, two-stage club has a solid reputation for programming excellent indie and rock outfits, including American bands. Club nights start after the gigs on weekends. ✉ *20–22 Highbury Corner, Islington, N1* 🕾 *020/7607–1818* ⊕ *www.meanfiddler.com* 🖃 *£5–£12* ♡ *Mon.–Wed. 8 PM–11:30 PM, Thurs. 8 PM–2 AM, Fri. and Sat. 8 PM–3 AM, Sun. 7 PM–midnight* Ⓜ *Highbury & Islington.*

Water Rats. This high-spirited pub hosted Bob Dylan on his 1963 tour, as well as the first Oasis gig. Alt-country, hip-hop, and indie guitar bands thrash it out most nights of the week. ✉ *328 Gray's Inn Rd., Euston, WC1* 🕾 *020/7336–7326* 🖃 *£5* ♡ *Mon.–Sat. 7:30 PM–11:30 PM* Ⓜ *King's Cross.*

THE GAY SCENE

The U.K. capital's gay and lesbian culture is as thriving as it is in New York or Los Angeles, with Soho serving as the hub of gay London. Clubs in London cater to almost every desire, whether that be the suited up Tommy Hilfiger–look-alike scene, cruisers taking on smoky dives, flamboyant drag shows, lesbian tea dances, or themed fetish nights. There's also a cornucopia of queer theatre and performance art that runs throughout the year. Whatever your tastes, you'll be able to satisfy them with a night on the town in London.

Choices are admittedly much better for males than females here; while many of the gay clubs are female-friendly, those catering strictly to lesbians are in the minority. The National Film Board puts on the Gay and Lesbian Film Festival in March. Pride London in June (an annual event encompassing a parade, sports, art, comedy, theater, music, cabaret, and dance) welcomes anyone and everyone, and had over half a million participants in 2006. This extravagant pageant spirals its way through London's streets, with major events taking place in Trafalgar Square and Leicester Square, then culminates in Victoria Embankment with ticketed parties continuing on afterwards. Visit ⊕ *www.pridelondon.org* for details.

For up-to-date listings, consult *Time Out, Boyz, Gay Times, Attitude,* or the lesbian monthly, *Diva.* Online directories include Gay to Z (⊕ *www.gaytoz.com*) and Rainbow Network (⊕ *www.rainbownetwork.com*).

BARS, CAFÉS & PUBS

Most bars in London are gay-friendly, though there are a number of cafés and pubs that are known as gay hangouts after-hours. Here's a listing of just a few that serve drinks until 11 PM (10:30 PM on Sunday).

Box. True to its name, this modern, industrial-chic café-bar is small and square. It's a staple on the preclub circuit and gets packed to the hilt with muscular boys. For peckish punters there's food before 5 PM daily. ✉ *32–34 Monmouth St., Soho, WC2* 🕾 *020/7240–5828* ♡ *Mon.–Sat. 11 AM–11 PM, Sun. noon–10:30 PM* Ⓜ *Leicester Sq.*

Candy Bar. The United Kingdom's first girls' bar is intimate, chilled, and cruisey, with DJs mixing the latest sounds. Pole-dancing and striptease are now also features on some nights. Men are welcome as guests. ✉ *4 Carlisle St., Soho, W1* ☎ *020/7494–4041* 🖹 *£5 after 9 PM, Fri. and Sat.* 🕙 *Mon.–Thurs. 5 PM–11:30 PM, Fri. and Sat. 5 PM–2 AM, Sun. 5 PM–10:30 PM* Ⓜ *Tottenham Court Rd.*

The Edge. *Poseurs* are welcome at this hip hangout. Straight groovers mingle with gay men over the four jam-packed floors. In summer, sidewalk tables provide an enviable view of Soho's daily street theater. ✉ *11 Soho Sq., Soho, W1* ☎ *020/7439–1313* 🕙 *Mon.–Sat. noon–1 AM, Sun. noon–11:30 PM* Ⓜ *Oxford Circus.*

Fodor'sChoice
★ **Friendly Society.** This haute moderne hotspot hops with activity almost any night of the week; the basement feels a bit like something out of Star Trek with its white-leather pod seats. Rumor has it that Madonna pops in from time to time, which makes sense as the place is known for being gay yet female-friendly. ✉ *79 Wardour St., Soho, W1D* ☎ *020/7434–3805* 🕙 *Weekdays 4–11, Sat. 2–11, Sun. 2–10:30* Ⓜ *Leicester Sq.*

Rupert Street. For smart boyz, this gay chic island among the sleaze has a lounge feel with brown-leather sofas and floor-to-ceiling windows. It's crowded and cruisey at night with preclubbers, civilized and café-like by day, with traditional British food served until 5 PM. ✉ *50 Rupert St., Soho, W1* ☎ *020/7292–7141* 🕙 *Mon.–Sat. noon–11 PM, Sun. noon–10:30 PM* Ⓜ *Leicester Sq., Piccadilly Circus.*

CLUBS

Many of London's best gay dance clubs are in mixed clubs like Fabric on themed nights designated for gays. Almost all dance clubs in London are gay-friendly, but if you want to cruise or mingle only with other gays, it's best to call ahead or check Web-site listings.

G.A.Y. London's largest gay party is at the Astoria on Monday, Thursday, Friday, and Saturday. Saturday night hosts big-name talent; regular guests include Kylie Minogue, Geri Halliwell, and a whole host of B-list TV celebrities. ■ TIP➔ **Buy advance tickets to avoid the long Saturday-night queue.** ✉ *157 and 165 Charing Cross Rd., Soho, WC2* ☎ *020/7434–9592* 🌐 *www.g-a-y.co.uk* 🖹 *£3–£15* 🕙 *Mon. and Thurs. 10:30 PM–4 AM, Fri. 11 PM–5 AM, Sat. 10:30 PM–5:30 AM* Ⓜ *Tottenham Court Rd.*

Fodor'sChoice
★ **Heaven.** With by far the best light show on any London dance floor, Heaven is unpretentious, loud, and huge, with a labyrinth of rooms, bars, and live-music parlors. Friday is more straight, while on Saturday there's also a gay comedy night (£10, 7 PM–11:30 PM). If you go to just one club, Heaven should be it. ✉ *The Arches, Villiers St., Covent Garden, WC2* ☎ *020/7930–2020* 🌐 *www.heaven-london.com* 🖹 *£4–£12* 🕙 *Mon. 10:15 PM–5:15 AM, Wed. 10:30 PM–3 AM, Fri. and Sat. 10:30 PM–6 AM* Ⓜ *Charing Cross, Embankment.*

Fodor'sChoice
★ **Sanctuary.** There's something for everyone at this Soho hotspot. If you're not in the mood to let loose to pumping house music on the dance floor downstairs, you can ascend to the candlelit upstairs and sip your cocktail on a shapely sofa. The pianist who regularly plays on the top floor has a loyal fan base, and there's a singer belting out show tunes on

17

Wednesday. ■TIP→Straight-friendly Sanctuary's happy hour (daily 5 PM–8 PM) is great value. ⊠*4–5 Greek St., Soho, W1* ☎*020/7434–3323* ⌨*£5 after 11 PM Fri. and Sat.*☺*Mon.–Sat. 5 PM–2 AM, Sun. 5 PM–12:30 AM* Ⓜ*Tottenham Court Rd.*

★ **The Shadow Lounge.** This fabulous little lounge and dance club glitters with faux jewels and twinkling fiber-optic lights over its sunken dance floor, which comes complete with pole for those inclined to do their thing around it. It has a serious A-list celebrity factor, with the glamorous London glitterati camping out in the VIP booth. Members are given entrance priority when the place gets full, especially on weekends, so show up early or prepare to queue. ⊠*5 Brewer St., Soho, W1* ☎*020/7287–7988* ⊕*www.theshadowlounge.co.uk* ⌨*£3–£10*☺*Mon.– Wed. 10 PM–3 AM, Thurs.–Sat. 9 PM–3 AM* Ⓜ*Leicester Sq.*

Sunday Sunday. A longtime fave with the girls, this is a very camp and fun Sunday ballroom, Latin, line-dance, time-warp disco. Tea and biscuits are served until 7 PM. ⊠*BJ's White Swan, 556 Commercial Rd., East End, E14* ☎*020/7780–9870* ⌨*£2*☺*Sun. 5:30 PM–midnight* Ⓜ*Aldgate East.*

Arts & Entertainment

A performance during the Proms at Royal Albert Hall

WORD OF MOUTH

"The Tate Modern is well worth a trip. It is huge with many exhibits. I am a bit of a philistine when it comes to art, and have to admit that I 'popped in' while passing, just to see what it was like. I was surprised to find I really enjoyed it, and spent a few hours there. I seem to remember that it is free (except any 'special' exhibitions). There are certainly areas where you can sit, and get an excellent view of the Thames."

—willit

ARTS & ENTERTAINMENT PLANNER

What's on Now

To find out what's showing now, the weekly magazine *Time Out* (£2.50, issued every Tuesday) is invaluable. The *Evening Standard* also carries listings, especially in the supplement "Metro Life," which comes with the Thursday edition, as do London's widely available free newspapers, many Sunday papers, and the Saturday *Independent, Guardian,* and *Times*. You can pick up the free fortnightly *London Theatre Guide* from hotels and tourist-information centers.

There are hundreds of small private galleries all over London with interesting work by famous and not-yet-famous artists. The bi-monthly free pamphlet "new exhibitions of contemporary art" ⊕ *www. newexhibitions.com*, available at most galleries, lists and maps nearly 200 art spaces in London. Expect to pay around £10 for entry into touring exhibitions, but most permanent displays and commercial galleries are free.

Top 5 for the Arts

■ **Stand with the 'plebs' in Shakespeare's Globe Theatre.** There are seats, but to really experience theater Shakespearean style you should stand in the yard, with the stage at eye-level.

■ **Visit the latest grand art installation in the Turbine Hall at the Tate Modern.** The enormity of the Tate's central space either intimidates or inspires artists challenged to fill it.

■ **Catch a world-class performance at the Proms.** There's a surprisingly down-to-earth atmosphere among the elated company at these great concerts.

■ **Enjoy a night at the National Film Theatre.** Mingle with the real aficionados at a showing of a black-and-white, little-remembered Hungarian classic.

■ **Watch a Hollywood star in a West End production.** Film stars often come to London to boost their artistic credibility in small-scale theaters.

Top 5 for Entertainment

■ **Ice-skate at Somerset House.** The courtyard of a grand old pile is a spectacular setting for a winter skate.

■ **Get late summer-evening returns at Wimbledon.** Play often continues well into warm sunny evenings on Wimbledon's show courts. Line up to get bargain returns from those who go home early.

■ **Watch a one-day international at Lords.** Cricket can go on and on, but a one-day international is short enough to guarantee some excitement and long enough to get some idea of the rules.

■ **Dress up for Ascot.** However much you spruce yourself up, you may still feel underdressed among the over-the-top fashions of the English upper classes.

■ **Watch a Premiership football game.** If you can manage to see a London derby, this is probably your best chance to understand the passionately tribal nature of the national game.

Updated by
Julius Honnor

Shakespearean theater and musical extravaganzas, the high passions of soccer and the genteel obscurities of cricket, enormous art installations and tiny Renaissance still lifes, magnificent operatics and cutting edge physical theater—if you're into going out, London will fill your fancy.

The arts in London have acquired some shiny new buildings and renovated homes, largely as a result of National Lottery money and the involvement on and off the city's stages by high-profile Hollywood figures, such as Kevin Spacey, who have given the theatrical scene extra pizzazz. The Donmar, Almeida, and Royal Court theaters have all been renovated to reveal their stripped-down, essential structures. The RSC has a new home and, saved from Bingo-hall oblivion, the legendary Hackney Empire theater is thriving again after a £15 million refurbishment. And there are new studios and a renovated theater for contemporary dance at the Place. But the biggest story is south of the river. Herzog and de Meuron's magnificent Tate Modern, in what was once the Bankside Power Station, is now cemented as one of the city's big attractions. The Tate has enlivened London's contemporary art scene and provides the main focus for a rejuvenated South Bank. Some of the more tourist-oriented shows and musicals suffer from a lack of visitors, but in many cases this economic pressure has made London's theatre more innovative and more accessible, creating a vibrant cultural scene in a better position than ever to play on the world stage.

Sport is taken increasingly seriously in Britain, nowhere more so than in the capital. Londoners may not be the fittest bunch—participation falls far short of enthusiasm of the armchair variety—but they can get excited by just about anything sporting. Winning the Olympics, to be staged in the city in 2012, only sharpened an existing enthusiasm for balls, wheels, and sports gear of all shapes and sizes, and the Olympics are already starting to bring increased investment into London's sporting facilities. Wimbledon, the FA Cup Final, the London Marathon, and international cricket are the big one-off events, though the weekly matches of Premiership football dominate for most of the year. Getting hold of a ticket for the most prominent occasions can be difficult, but

18

at all other levels (from lower-division football to greyhound racing) there's always a great selection of sporting entertainment on offer.

THE ARTS

Whether you fancy your art classical or modern, or as a contemporary twist on a time-honored classic, you'll find that London's arts scene pushes the boundaries. Watch a Hollywood star in a West End theater, or a troupe of Latin American acrobats. See a blockbuster contemporary art show at the Tate Modern, or a Holbein retrospective at the Tate Britain. There are international theater festivals, innovative music festivals, and obscure seasons of postmodern dance. Celebrity divas sing original-language librettos at the Royal Opera House; the Almeida Opera is more daring with its radical productions of new opera and music theater. Shakespeare's plays are brought to life at the reconstructed Globe Theatre, and challenging new writing is produced at the Royal Court. Whether you feel like the lighthearted extravagance of a West End musical or the next shark-in-formaldehyde sculpture at the White Cube, the choice is yours.

DANCE

Dance fans in London can enjoy the classicism of the world-renowned Royal Ballet, as well as innovative contemporary dance from several companies—including Rambert Dance Company, Matthew Bourne's New Adventures, Random Dance Company, The Michael Clark Company, Richard Alston Dance Company, Charles Linehan Company, DV8 Physical Theatre, Siobhan Davies, and Akram Khan—and scores of independent choreographers. The English National Ballet and visiting international companies perform at the Coliseum and at Sadler's Wells, which also hosts various other ballet companies and dance troupes. Encompassing the newly refurbished Royal Festival Hall, the South Bank Centre has a seriously good contemporary dance program that hosts top international companies and important U.K. choreographers, as well as multicultural offerings from Japanese Butoh and Indian Kathak to hip-hop. The Place and the Lilian Bayliss Theatre at Sadler's Wells are where you'll find the most daring, cutting-edge performances.

The biggest annual event is **Dance Umbrella** (☏ *020/8741–4040* ⊕ *www. danceumbrella.co.uk*), a seven-week season from September to November that hosts international and British-based artists at various venues across the city.

The following theaters are the key dance venues. Check weekly listings or ⊕ *www.londondance.com* for current performances and fringe venues.

The London Coliseum. The English National Ballet (⊕ www.ballet.org.uk) and other dance companies often perform in this restored Edwardian baroque theater (1904) with a magnificent auditorium and a rooftop glass dome with a bar and great views. ⊠*St. Martin's La., Covent Garden, WC2N* ☎*020/7632–8300* Ⓤ*Leicester Sq.*

Peacock Theatre. Sadler's Wells' West End annex, this modernist theater near the University of London offers commercial dance as well as ballet. ⊠*Portugal St., Holborn, WC2* ☎*0870/737–0337* ⊕*www.sadlerswells. com/peacock* Ⓤ*Holborn.*

The Place. The Robin Howard Dance Theatre is London's only theater dedicated to contemporary dance, and with tickets between £5 and £15 it's good value, too. *Resolution!* is the United Kingdom's biggest platform event for new choreographers. ⊠*17 Duke's Rd., Bloomsbury, WC1* ☎*020/7121–1000* ⊕*www.theplace.org.uk* Ⓤ*Euston.*

Riverside Studios. The two performance spaces are noted for postmodern movement styles and performance art. ⊠*Crisp Rd., Hammersmith, W6* ☎*020/8237–1111* ⊕*www.riversidestudios.co.uk* Ⓤ*Hammersmith.*

Fodor'sChoice ★ **Royal Opera House.** The renowned Royal Ballet performs classical and contemporary repertoire in this spectacular state-of-the-art Victorian theater. ⊠*Bow St., Covent Garden, WC2* ☎*020/7304–4000* ⊕*www. royaloperahouse.org* Ⓤ*Covent Garden.*

Fodor'sChoice ★ **Sadler's Wells.** Random Dance Company has its home in this lovely modern theater, which produces an excellent season of ballet and contemporary dance. The little Lilian Bayliss Theatre here has more left-field pieces. ⊠*Rosebery Ave., Islington, EC1* ☎*020/7863–8198* ⊕*www. sadlers-wells.com* Ⓤ*Angel.*

South Bank Centre. A diverse and exciting season of international and British-based contemporary dance companies is presented in the Queen Elizabeth Hall, Purcell Room, and Royal Festival Hall. ⊠*Belvedere Rd., South Bank, SE1* ☎*0870/380–0400* ⊕*www.rfh.org.uk* Ⓤ*Waterloo, Embankment.*

18

CLASSICAL MUSIC

Whether you want to go hear cellist Yo-Yo Ma at the Barbican or a Mozart requiem by candlelight, it's possible to hear first-rate musicians in world-class venues almost every day of the year. The London Symphony Orchestra is in residence at the Barbican Centre, although other top orchestras—including the Philharmonia and the Royal Philharmonic—also perform here. The Barbican also hosts chamber-music concerts with such celebrated orchestras as the City of London Sinfonia. Wigmore Hall, a lovely venue for chamber music, is renowned for its song recitals by up-and-coming young singers. The South Bank Centre has an impressive international music season, held in the Queen Elizabeth Hall and the small Purcell Room as well as in the Royal Festival Hall, now completely refurbished. Full houses are rare, so even at the biggest concert halls you should be able to get a ticket for £12. If you can't book in advance, arrive at the hall an hour before the performance for a chance at returns.

■TIP➡**Lunchtime concerts take place all over the city in smaller concert halls, the big arts-center foyers, and churches; they usually cost less than £5 or are free, and feature string quartets, singers, jazz ensembles, or gospel choirs.** St. John's, Smith Square, and St. Martin-in-the-Fields are

The Arts for Free

MUSEUMS & GALLERIES

Perhaps no other city in the world can match up to London's offerings of free art. Most of London's museums and galleries do not charge entrance fees. The monthly *Galleries* magazine, available from galleries themselves or online at ⊕ *www.artefact.co.uk*, has listings for all private galleries in the capital.

CONTEMPORARY MUSIC

Brixton's Dogstar pub has an excellent selection of DJs playing for free on weekday evenings. Ain't Nothing But the Blues in Soho has live blues most nights, often without a cover charge. Spitz, in Spitalfields Market, frequently has live music for free. The largest of the music superstores, such as Virgin Piccadilly and HMV Oxford Street, have occasional live performances of pop and rock bands, often to accompany album or single launches.

CLASSICAL MUSIC & JAZZ

The Barbican, the Royal National Theatre, and the Royal Opera House often have free music in their foyers or in dedicated spaces, usually of high standard. On the South Bank, free festivals and special performances often take place alongside the river.

Many of London's world-class music colleges give free concerts several times a week. The Royal Academy of Music and the Royal College of Music often have free concerts. St. Martin-in-the-Fields has free lunchtime concerts. Other churches, including Westminster Abbey and Christchurch Spitalfields, also have frequent free music. For the Proms, which run from July to September at the Royal Albert Hall, good seats are expensive, but hundreds of standing tickets are available at £4: not quite free, but a good value.

DRAMA & PERFORMANCE ARTS

Look out for occasional festivals where innovative performances take place on the South Bank. Check the newspapers and *Time Out* for upcoming performances.

PARK LIFE

London's parks come to life in summer with a wide-ranging program of music, dance, and visual arts. See ⊕ *www.royalparks.gov.uk* for details or phone ☎ 020/7298–2000 for a free printed program. Radio stations also organize free summer music concerts (generally aimed at the teenybopper set) in London parks, with lots of big-name pop stars, but entry is usually by ticket only and events are often oversubscribed. Other free festivals, such as the excellent Fruitstock, with a more eclectic mix of music, are easier to get into.

RADIO & TELEVISION

With so much broadcast material made in London, much of it recorded in front of live audiences, there are often opportunities to watch a free quiz show, current affairs debate, comedy, or even drama. Check the BBC Web site for forthcoming recordings or call **BBC Studio Audiences** (☎ 020/8576–1227 ⊕ *www.bbc.co.uk/tickets*). **Hat Trick Productions** (☎ 020/7434–2451 ⊕ *www.hattrick.co.uk*) makes a number of good comedy programs, including the excellent satirical current affairs program *Have I Got News for You.*

popular locations. Performances usually begin about 1 PM and last one hour.

Classical-music festivals range from the stimulating avant-garde Meltdown (curated each year by a prominent musician, recently Morissey and Patti Smith, ⊕*www.rfh.org.uk/meltdown*) at the South Bank Centre in June to the more conservative "Music On A Summer Evening" concerts at Kenwood House (⊕*www.picnicconcerts.com*) from July through August, at which you can listen to classical music outdoors. There are also church hall recitals in June and December during the Spitalfields Festival (⊕*www.spitalfieldsfestival.org.uk*), and in guildhalls, churches, and other venues in the square mile during the month-long City of London Festival (⊕*www.colf.org*) in June and July.

A great British tradition since 1895, the Henry Wood Promenade Concerts (more commonly known as the "Proms"; ⊕*www.bbc.co.uk/proms*) run eight weeks, from July to September, at the Royal Albert Hall. Despite an extraordinary quantity of high-quality concerts, it's renowned for its (atypical) last night: a madly jingoistic display of singing "Land of Hope and Glory," Union Jack–waving, and general madness. Demand for last-night tickets is so high you must enter a lottery. For regular Proms, tickets run £4–£80, with hundreds of standing tickets for £4 available at the hall on the night of the concert. ■TIP→**The last night is broadcast in Hyde Park on a jumbo screen, but even here a seat on the grass requires a paid ticket that can set you back around £20.**

Barbican Centre. Home to the London Symphony Orchestra (⊕www.lso.co.uk) and frequent host of the English Chamber Orchestra and the BBC Symphony Orchestra, the Barbican has an excellent season of big-name virtuosos. ⊠*Silk St., East End, EC2* ☎*020/7638–8891 box office* ⊕*www.barbican.org.uk* Ⓤ*Barbican or Moorgate.*

Cadogan Hall. Formerly a church, Cadogan Hall has now been turned into a spacious concert venue where the English Chamber Orchestra are regular performers. ⊠*5 Sloane Terrace, Kensington, SW1* ☎*020/7730–4500* ⊕*www.cadoganhall.com* Ⓤ*Sloane Square.*

Kenwood House. Outdoor concerts are held in the grassy amphitheater in front of Kenwood House on Saturday evenings from July to late August. ⊠*Hampstead Heath, Hampstead, NW3* ☎*0870/333–6206* ⊕*www.picnicconcerts.com* Ⓤ*Hampstead.*

★ **Royal Albert Hall.** Built in 1871, this splendid iron-and-glass–dome auditorium hosts a varied music program, including Europe's most democratic music festival, the Henry Wood Promenade Concerts—the Proms. The Hall is also open daily for daytime guided tours (£6). ⊠*Kensington Gore, Kensington, SW7* ☎*020/7589–8212* ⊕*www.royalalberthall.com* Ⓤ*South Kensington.*

St. James's Church. The organ was brought here in 1691 after fire destroyed its former home, the Palace of Whitehall. St. James's holds regular classical-music concerts, including free lunchtime recitals several times a week. ⊠*197 Piccadilly, St. James's, W1* ☎*020/7381–0441 concert program and tickets* ⊕*www.sjpconcerts.org* Ⓤ*Piccadilly Circus, Green Park.*

18

St. John's, Smith Square. This baroque church behind Westminster Abbey offers chamber music and organ recitals as well as orchestral concerts September through July. There are occasional lunchtime recitals for £7. ⊠ *Smith Sq., Westminster, W1* ☎ *020/7222–1061* ⊕ *www.sjss.org. uk* Ⓤ *Westminster.*

★ **St. Martin-in-the-Fields.** Popular lunchtime concerts (free but £3.50 donation suggested) are held in this lovely 1726 church, as are regular evening concerts. ■ TIP➔ **Stop for a snack at the Café in the Crypt.** ⊠ *Trafalgar Sq., Covent Garden, WC2* ☎ *020/7839–8362* ⊕ *www.smitf. org* Ⓤ *Charing Cross.*

South Bank Centre. After a £70 million refurbishment, the Royal Festival Hall reopened in 2007 with large-scale choral and orchestral works in newly improved acoustic surroundings. Both the Philharmonia and the London Philharmonic orchestras are based here. Another £20 million has been spent on the rest of the South Bank Centre, where other venues host smaller scale music performances; the Queen Elizabeth Hall has chamber orchestras and top-tier soloists, and in the intimate Purcell Room you can listen to chamber music and solo recitals. ⊠ *Belvedere Rd., South Bank, SE1* ☎ *0870/380–0400* ⊕ *www.sbc.org. uk* Ⓤ *Waterloo.*

Fodor's Choice **Wigmore Hall.** Hear chamber music and song recitals in this charming hall
★ with near-perfect acoustics. Don't miss the mid-morning Sunday concerts. ⊠ *36 Wigmore St., Marylebone, W1* ☎ *020/7935–2141* ⊕ *www. wigmore-hall.org.uk* Ⓤ *Bond St.*

FILM

There are many wonderful movie theaters in London and several that are committed to nonmainstream and repertory cinema, in particular, the National Film Theatre. Now almost 50 years old, the London Film Festival (⊕ *www.lff. org.uk*) brings hundreds of films made by masters of world cinema to London for 16 days each October into November, accompanied by often-sold-out events. The smaller, avant-garde Raindance Film Festival (⊕ *www.raindance.co.uk*) highlights independent filmmaking, also in October.

> ### WORD OF MOUTH
>
> "My daughter and I went to a movie in the Mayfair section of London. Not only were the seats reserved, but they were wonderfully upholstered and rocked back and forth. It was a struggle to watch the movie (as good as it was) versus taking a well-needed nap." –bronxgirl

West End movie theaters continue to do good business. Most of the major houses, such as the Odeon Leicester Square and the UCI Empire, are in the Leicester Square–Piccadilly Circus area, where tickets average £10. Monday and matinees are often cheaper, at around £5–£7, and there are also fewer crowds.

Check out *Time Out* or the *Guardian's* "Guide" section (free with the paper on Saturday) for listings.

☺ **Barbican.** In addition to Hollywood films, obscure classics and film festivals with Screen Talks are programmed in the three cinemas here. Saturday Family Film Club often has animation for the entire family. ✉*Silk St., East End, EC2* ☎*020/7382–7000 information, 020/7638–8891 box office* ⊕*www.barbican.org.uk/film* Ⓤ*Barbican.*

BFI London IMAX Cinema. The British Film Institute's glazed drum-shaped IMAX theater has the largest screen in the United Kingdom (approximately 75 feet wide and the height of five double-decker buses) playing state-of-the-art 2-D and 3-D films. ✉*1 Charlie Chaplin Walk, South Bank, SE1* ☎*0870/787–2525* ⊕*www.bfi.org.uk/imax* Ⓤ*Waterloo.*

★ **Curzon Soho.** This comfortable cinema runs an artsy program of mixed rep and mainstream films. There's also a Mayfair branch. Members (£25) get discounts. ✉*99 Shaftesbury Ave., Soho, W1* ☎*0870/756–4620* Ⓤ*Piccadilly Circus, Leicester Sq.* ✉*38 Curzon St., Mayfair, W1* ☎*0870/756–4621* ⊕*www.curzoncinemas.com* Ⓤ*Green Park.*

★ **The Electric Cinema.** This refurbished Portobello Road art house screens mainstream and international movies. The emphasis is on comfort, with leather sofas, armchairs, footstools, and mini coffee tables for your popcorn. ✉*191 Portobello Rd., Notting Hill, W11* ☎*020/7908–9696* ⊕*www.electriccinema.co.uk* Ⓤ*Ladbroke Grove, Notting Hill Gate.*

☺ **Everyman Cinema Club.** Kick off your shoes, curl up on the large comfy
★ sofas, and have tapas and champagne brought to you in front of an excellent selection of classic, foreign, cutting-edge, and almost-new Hollywood titles. This venue also screens major sports games and TV events, and is a popular place for Hampstead denizens to bring their kids. ✉*5 Hollybush Vale, Hampstead, NW3* ☎*020/7431–1777* ⊕*www.everymancinema.com* Ⓤ*Hampstead.*

ICA Cinema. Underground and vintage movies are shown in the avant-garde Institute of Contemporary Arts. ✉*The Mall, St. James's, SW1* ☎*020/7930–0493 information, 020/7930–3647 box office* ⊕*www.ica.org.uk* Ⓤ*Piccadilly Circus, Charing Cross.*

☺ **National Film Theatre (NFT).** With easily the best repertory programming in London, the NFT's three cinemas show more than 1,000 titles each year, favoring obscure, foreign, silent, forgotten, classic, noir, and short films over Hollywood blockbusters. ■ TIP→**The London Film Festival is based here at the NFT; throughout the year there are minifestivals, seminars, and guest speakers.** Members (£35) get priority bookings (useful for special events) and get £1 off each screening. ✉*Belvedere Rd., South Bank, SE1* ☎*020/7633–0274 information, 020/7928–3232 box office* ⊕*www.bfi.org.uk/incinemas/nft/* Ⓤ*Waterloo.*

Riverside Studios Cinemas. The selection at this converted movie studio changes almost daily. Admission fees are reasonable; £5.50 gets you entrance to a double bill. ✉*Crisp Rd., Hammersmith, W6* ☎*020/8237–1111* ⊕*www.riversidestudios.co.uk* Ⓤ*Hammersmith.*

☺ **Tricycle Theatre.** Expect the best of new British, European, and World Cinema, as well as films from the United States. There are occasional Irish, Black, and Asian Film Festivals, as well as a year-round program of film-related activities for children. ✉*269 Kilburn High Rd.,*

18

Kilburn, NW6 ☎ *020/7328–1900 information, 020/7328–1000 box office* ⊕ *www.tricycle.co.uk* Ⓤ*Kilburn.*

OPERA

The two key players in London's opera scene are the Royal Opera House (which ranks with the Metropolitan Opera House in New York) and the more innovative English National Opera (ENO), which presents English-language productions at the London Coliseum. Only the Theatre Royal, Drury Lane, has a longer theatrical history than the Royal Opera House, and the current theater—the third to be built on the site since 1858—completed a monumental 16-year renovation in 1999.

Despite occasional performances by the likes of Björk, the Royal Opera House struggles to shrug off its reputation for elitism. Ticket prices rise to £170. It is, however, more accessible than it used to be—the cheapest tickets are just £4. Conditions of purchase vary; call for information. Prices for the ENO are generally lower, ranging from around £15 to £75. You can get same-day balcony seats for as little as £5.

Almeida Opera and BAC Opera produce opera festivals that showcase new opera and cutting-edge music theater. In summer, Holland Park Opera presents the usual chestnuts in the open-air theater of leafy Holland Park. Bring a picnic and an umbrella. Serious opera fans should not miss the Glyndebourne Festival, where Pavarotti made his British debut. It's the jewel in the crown of the country-house opera circuit, and the greatest opera festival in the United Kingdom.

International touring companies often perform at Sadler's Wells, Barbican, South Bank Centre, and Wigmore Hall, so check the weekly listings for details.

★ **Almeida Theatre.** The Almeida Opera Festival in July has an adventurous program of new opera and music theater. ✉*Almeida St., Islington, N1* ☎*020/7359–4404* ⊕*www.almeida.co.uk* Ⓤ*Angel.*

English National Opera. ENO produces innovative opera for lower prices than the Royal Opera House. The company is based at the London Coliseum, which has emerged sparkling from an extensive refurbishment program with much improved facilities and reconfigured interior spaces. ✉*St. Martin's La., Covent Garden, WC2* ☎*0870/145–0200* ⊕*www. eno.org* Ⓤ*Leicester Sq.*

★ **Glyndebourne.** Fifty-four miles south of London, Glyndebourne is one of the most famous opera houses in the world. Six operas are presented from mid-May to late-August. The best route by car is the M23 to Brighton, then the A27 toward Lewes. There are regular trains from London (Victoria) to Lewes with coach connections to and from Glyndebourne. Call the information office for information about recommended trains for each performance. ✉*Lewes, BN8 5UU* ☎*01273/812321 information, 01273/813813 box office* ⊕*www.glyndebourne.com.*

Holland Park Opera. In summer new productions and well-loved operas are presented against the remains of Holland House, one of the first great houses built in Kensington. Ticket prices range from £30 to £40.

✉*Holland Park, Kensington High St., Kensington, W8* ☎*0845/230–9769* ⊕*www.operahollandpark.com* Ⓤ*Kensington High St.*

Fodor'sChoice **Royal Opera House.** Original-language productions are presented in this
★ extravagant theater, also home to the Royal Ballet. ■ TIP➜**Tickets range
in price from £5 to £185. It may be worth showing up on the morning of a
performance (the box office opens at 10** AM, **but queues for popular productions can start as early as 7** AM) **to purchase a same-day seat, of which 67 are
offered.** There are free lunchtime recitals most Mondays in the Linbury
Studio Theatre or the Crush Room (book tickets in advance), and three
summer concerts are broadcast live to a large screen in Covent Garden
Piazza. ✉*Bow St., Covent Garden, WC2* ☎*020/7304–4000* ⊕*www.
royalopera.org* Ⓤ*Covent Garden.*

THEATER

In London the play really *is* the thing, and chances are good you can see
a Sam Mendes Off–West End production, the umpteenth production of
Les Misérables, a Peter Brook deconstruction of Shakespeare, innovative physical theater from *Le Théatre de Complicité,* the latest offering
from *Cirque du Soleil* or Robert Lepage, or even a fringe production
above a pub. West End glitz and glamour continue to pull in the audiences, and so do the more innovative players. Only in London will a
Tuesday matinee of the Royal Shakespeare Company's *Henry IV* be sold
out in a 1,200-seat theater.

In London the words "radical"
and "quality," or "classical" and
"experimental," are not mutually
exclusive. The Royal Shakespeare
Company (⊕*www.rsc.org.uk*)
and the Royal National Theatre
Company often stage contemporary versions of the classics. The
Almeida, Battersea Arts Centre (BAC), Donmar Warehouse,
Royal Court Theatre, Soho The-
atre, and the Old Vic attract famous actors and have excellent reputations for new writing and innovative theatrical languages. These are the
places that shape the theater of the future, the venues where you'll see
an original production before it becomes a hit in the West End. (And
you'll see them at a fraction of the cost.)

18

Another great thing about the London theater scene is that it doesn't
shut down in summer—it's business as usual for the Royal Shakespeare
Company and Royal National Theatre. From mid-May through mid-
September you can see the Bard served up in his most spectacular
manifestation—at the open-air reconstruction of Shakespeare's Globe
Theatre. In addition, the Open Air Theatre presents a season of Shake-
speare-under-the-stars, from the last week in May to the third week
in September, in lovely Regent's Park. **London Mime Festival** (⊕*www.
mimefest.co.uk*) happens in January. Some theater festivals take place
throughout the year, so unlike other cities, there's always something

good to see in London. **Lift** (⊕ *www.liftfest.org.uk*), the London International Festival of Theatre, stages productions at venues throughout the city. **B.I.T.E.** *(Barbican International Theater Events)* presents top-notch, cutting-edge performances. Check *Time Out* for details. The Web sites ⊕ *www.londontheatre.co.uk,* ⊕ *www.whatsonstage. com,* and ⊕ *www.officiallondontheatre.co.uk* are both good sources of information about performances.

Theater-going isn't cheap. Tickets under £10 are a rarity; in the West End you should expect to pay from £15 for a seat in the upper balcony to at least £25 for a good one in the stalls (orchestra) or dress circle (mezzanine). However, as the vast majority of theaters have some tickets (returns and house seats) available on the night of performance, you may find some good deals. Tickets may be booked through ticket agents, at individual theater box offices, or over the phone by credit card. Be sure to inquire about any extra fees—prices can vary enormously but agents are legally obliged to reveal the face value of the ticket if you ask. All the larger hotels offer theater bookings, but they tack on a hefty service charge.

Ticketmaster (☎ 0870/060–0800 ⊕ *www.ticketmaster.co.uk*) sells tickets to a number of different theaters, although they charge a booking fee. You can book tickets in the United States through **Keith Prowse** (✉ *234 W. 44th St., Suite 1000, New York, NY 10036* ☎ *800/669–8687* ⊕ *www.keithprowse.com*). For discount tickets, **Society of London Theatre** (☎ 020/7557–6700) operates TKTS, a half-price ticket booth (☎ No phone) on the southwest corner of Leicester Square, and sells the best available seats to performances at about 25 theaters. It's open Monday–Saturday 10 AM–7 PM, Sunday noon–2 PM; there's a £2 service charge. Major credit cards are accepted. There's now also a TKTS booth at Canary Wharf station in Docklands, open Monday–Saturday 10 AM–3:30 PM.

★ **Almeida Theatre.** This Off–West End venue premieres excellent new plays and exciting twists on the classics. Hollywood stars often perform here. ✉ *Almeida St., Islington, N1* ☎ *020/7359–4404* ⊕ *www.almeida. co.uk* Ⓤ *Angel, Highbury & Islington.*

★ **BAC.** Battersea Arts Centre has an excellent reputation for producing innovative new work. Check out Scratch, a monthly, pay-what-you-can night of low-tech cabaret theater by emerging artists, and the BAC Octoberfest of innovative performance. Tuesday shows also have pay-what-you-can entry. ✉ *176 Lavender Hill, Battersea, SW11* ☎ *020/7223–2223* ⊕ *www. bac.org.uk* Ⓤ *British Rail: Clapham Junction.*

Barbican Centre. Built in 1982, the Barbican Centre puts on a number of performances by British and international theater companies as part of its year-round **B.I.T.E.** (Barbican International Theatre Events), which also features ground-breaking performance, dance, drama, and music theater. ✉ *Silk St., East End, EC2* ☎ *020/7638–8891* ⊕ *www.barbican. org.uk* Ⓤ *Barbican.*

Fodor's Choice ★ **Donmar Warehouse.** Hollywood stars often perform here in diverse and daring new works, bold interpretations of the classics, and small-scale musicals. It works both ways, too—former director Sam Mendes went straight from here to directing *American Beauty.* ⊠*41 Earlham St., Covent Garden, WC2* ☎*0870/060–6624* ⊕*www.donmar-warehouse. com* Ⓤ*Covent Garden.*

★ **Hackney Empire.** The history of this treasure of a theater is drama in its own right. Charlie Chaplin is said to have appeared here during its days as a thriving variety theater and music hall in the early 1900s. It reopenend in 2004 after a £15 million overhaul. ⊠*291 Mare St., Hackney, E8* ☎*020/8985–2424* ⊕*www.hackneyempire.co.uk* Ⓤ*National Rail: Hackney Central.*

★ **National Theatre.** When this theater opened in 1976 Londoners generally felt the same way about this low-slung, multilayered "Brutalist" block the color of heavy storm clouds and designed by Sir Denys Lasdun that they would feel a decade later about the Barbican Centre. But whatever its merits or demerits as a feature on the landscape, the Royal National Theatre has wonderful interior spaces that are definitely worth a tour. Interspersed with the three theaters, the 1,120-seat Olivier, the 890-seat Lyttelton, and the 300-seat Cottesloe, is a multilayered foyer with exhibitions, bars, and restaurants, and free entertainment. Musicals, classics, and new plays are in repertoire. ■TIP➔**An adventurous ticketing scheme means some National Theatre performances can be seen for as little as £10. Free performances outside in summer are also worth catching.** ⊠*South Bank Arts Centre, Belvedere Rd., South Bank, SE1* ☎*020/7452–3000* ◱*Tour £5* ◷*Foyer Mon.–Sat. 10 AM–11 PM; 1-hr tour of theater backstage Mon.–Sat. 10:15, 12:30, and 5:30* ⊕*www. nt-online.org* Ⓤ*Waterloo.*

The Old Vic. American actor Kevin Spacey is the artistic director of this grand 1818 Victorian theater, one of London's oldest. Legends of the stage have performed here, including John Gielgud, Vivian Leigh, Peter O'Toole, Richard Burton, Judi Dench, and Laurence Olivier, who called it his favorite theater. After decades of financial duress threatening to shut it down, the Old Vic is now safely under the ownership of a dedicated trust, though many of Spacey's productions have been widely criticized by afficionados. ⊠*The Cut, Southwark, SE1* ☎*0870/060–6628* ⊕*www.oldvictheatre.com* Ⓤ*Waterloo.*

Fodor'sChoice **Open Air Theatre.** On a warm summer evening, classical theater in the
★ pastoral, and royal Regent's Park is hard to beat for magical adventure. Enjoy a supper before the performance and during the intermission on the picnic lawn, and drinks in the spacious bar. ⊠*Inner Circle, Regent's Park, NW1* ☎*0870/060–1811* ⊕*www.openairtheatre.org* Ⓤ*Baker St., Regent's Park.*

★ **Royal Court Theatre.** Britain's undisputed epicenter of new writing, the RCT is now 50 years old and continues to produce gritty British and international drama. ■TIP➔**Don't miss the best deal in town—£10 tickets on Monday.** ⊠*Sloane Sq., Chelsea, SW1* ☎*020/7565–5000* ⊕*www. royalcourttheatre.com* Ⓤ*Sloane Sq.*

Novello Theatre. The Royal Shakespeare Company has taken up a five-year lease at this renovated theater, where they will take to the stage with innovative and consistently excellent productions of Shakespeare's plays. ⊠*Aldwych Covent Garden, WC2* ☎*0870/950–0940* ⊕*www.del-fontmackintosh.co.uk* Ⓤ*Covent Garden or Temple.*

18

FodorśChoice **Shakespeare's Globe Theatre.** This
★ faithful reconstruction of the
open-air playhouse, where Shakespeare worked and wrote many
of his greatest plays, re-creates
the 16th-century theater-going
experience. Standing room in the
"pit" right in front of the stage
costs £5. The season runs May
through September. *For more
on Shakespeare's Globe Theatre, see chapter 8.* ⊠ *New Globe
Walk, Bankside, South Bank, SE1*
☎ *020/7401–9919* ⊕ *www.shake-
speares-globe.org* ⓤ *Southwark,
Mansion House, walk across Southwark Bridge; Blackfriars, walk
across Blackfriars Bridge.*

> **CAUTION**
>
> Be very wary of ticket touts
> (scalpers) and unscrupulous ticket
> agents outside theaters and work-
> ing the line at TKTS (a half-price
> ticket booth)—they try to sell
> tickets at five times the price of
> the ticket at legitimate box offices.
> You might be charged £200 or
> more for a sought-after ticket (and
> you'll pay a stiff fine if caught
> buying a scalped ticket).

Soho Theatre. This sleek theater in the heart of Soho is devoted to foster-
ing new writing and is a prolific presenter of work by emerging writers. ⊠ *21 Dean St., Soho, W1* ☎ *0870/429–6883* ⊕ *www.sohotheatre.
com* ⓤ *Tottenham Court Rd.*

☉ **Tricycle Theatre.** The Tricycle is committed to the best in Irish, African-
Caribbean, Asian, and political drama, and the promotion of new plays.
⊠ *269 Kilburn High Rd., Kilburn, NW6 7JR* ☎ *020/7328–1000* ⊕ *www.
tricycle.co.uk* ⓤ *Kilburn.*

Young Vic. Ensconced in a new home near Waterloo, big names perform
here alongside young talent, often in daring, innovative productions of
classic plays. ⊠ *66 The Cut, Waterloo, South Bank, SE1* ☎ *020/7928–
6363* ⊕ *www.youngvic.org* ⓤ *Waterloo.*

CONTEMPORARY ART

In the 21st century, the focus of the city's art scene has shifted from
west to east, and from the past to the future. Helped by the prominence
of the Tate Modern, London's contemporary art scene has never been
so high-profile. In public-funded exhibition spaces like the Barbican
Gallery, Hayward Gallery, Institute of Contemporary Arts, Serpentine
Gallery, and Whitechapel Art Gallery, London now has a modern-art
environment on a par with Bilbao and New York. Young British Artists (YBAs, though no longer as young as they once were)—Damien
Hirst, Tracey Emin, Gary Hume, Rachel Whiteread, Jake and Dinos
Chapman, Sarah Lucas, Gavin Turk, Steve McQueen, and others—are
firmly planted in the public imagination. The celebrity status of British
artists is in part thanks to the annual Turner Prize, which always stirs
up controversy in the media during a monthlong display of the work
at Tate Britain.

British artists may complain about how the visual arts here are severely
underfunded, and about the rough ride they get in the media, but where
else would Damien Hirst's 6-meter-high bronze version of an anatomy
model fetch £1 million? Hirst and his Goldsmith's College contempo-

raries were catapulted to fame in the late 1980s, when they rented an unused Docklands warehouse to put on seminal shows like "Freeze." It coincided with a recession that saw West End galleries closing, and a property slump that enabled young artists to open trendy artist-run places in the East End.

West End dealers like Jay Jopling and, in particular, the enigmatic advertising tycoon and art collector Charles Saatchi, championed these Young British Artists. Depending on who you talk to, the Saatchi Gallery is considered to be either the savior of contemporary art or the wardrobe of the emperor's new clothes. Since 1992 Saatchi has shown several shows of YBA, including the period's most memorable sculptures—Damien Hirst's shark in formaldehyde, *The Impossibility of Death in the Mind of the Living* (sold to an American collector for $12 million), and Rachel Whiteread's plaster cast of a room, *Ghost*. The Saatchi Gallery will reopen in the Duke of York's Building in Chelsea in 2007, after its short-lived tenancy on the South Bank ended acrimoniously in 2005.

The South Bank, with the Tate Modern and the Hayward Gallery, may house the giants of modern art, but the East End is where the innovative action is. There are dozens of galleries in the fashionable spaces around Old Street, and the truly hip have already moved even farther east, to areas such as Bethnal Green. The Whitechapel Art Gallery continues to flourish, exhibiting exciting new British artists and, together with Jay Jopling's influential White Cube in Hoxton Square, is the new East End art establishment.

Barbican Centre. Innovative exhibitions of 20th-century and current art and design are shown in the Barbican Gallery and **The Curve** (⊠ *Free* ⊘ *Mon.–Sat. 11–8*). Recent highlights have included a retrospective of modernist architect Alvar Aalto and a look at photography and European 20th-century history. ⊠ *Silk St., East End, EC2* ☎ *020/7638–8891* ⊕ *www.barbican.org.uk* ⊠ *£6–£8, tickets cheaper if booked online in advance* ⊘ *Mon., Wed., Fri., and weekends 11–8, Tues. and Thurs. 11–6* Ⓤ *Barbican.*

The **Contemporary Art Society** (☎ *020/7612–0730* ⊕ *www.contempart. org.uk*) runs bus tours (£25 per person) for serious art enthusiasts the last Saturday of every month (except July, August, and December). ■ TIP➔**This is a great opportunity to get the inside scoop on off-the-beaten-track spaces. Book well ahead, as spaces fill up quickly.**

★ **Hayward Gallery.** This modern art gallery is a classic example of 1960s Brutalist architecture. It's part of the South Bank Centre and is one of London's major venues for important touring exhibitions. ⊠ *Belvedere Rd., South Bank Centre, South Bank, SE1* ☎ *0870/165–6000* ⊕ *www. hayward.org.uk* ⊠ *£5, Mon. half-price* ⊘ *Thurs. and Sat.–Mon. 10–6, Tues. and Wed. 10–8, Fri. 10–9* Ⓤ *Waterloo.*

Institute of Contemporary Arts. Housed in an elegant John Nash–designed Regency terrace, the ICA's three galleries have changing exhibitions of contemporary visual art. The ICA also programs contemporary drama, film, new media, literature, and photography. There's an arts bookstore, cafeteria, and bar. To visit you must be a member of the ICA; a day membership costs £2. ⊠*Nash House, The Mall, St. James's, SW1* ☎*020/7930–3647 or 020/7930–0493* ⊕*www.ica.org.uk* ✉ *Weekdays £2, weekends £3* ☉ *Daily noon–7:30* Ⓤ*Charing Cross.*

★ **Lisson.** Owner Nicholas Logsdail represents about 40 blue-chip artists, including minimalist Sol Lewitt and Dan Graham, at arguably the most respected gallery in London. The gallery is most associated with New Object sculptors like Anish Kapoor and Richard Deacon, many of whom have won the Turner Prize. A new branch, Lisson New Space, down the road at 29 Bell Street, features work by younger up-and-coming artists. ⊠*52–54 Bell St., Marylebone, NW1* ☎*020/7724–2739* ⊕*www. lissongallery.com* ✉*Free* ☉ *Weekdays 10–6, Sat. 11–5* Ⓤ*Edgware Rd. or Marylebone.* .

Photographer's Gallery. Britain's first photography gallery brought world-famous photographers like André Kertesz, Jacques-Henri Lartigue, and Irving Penn to the United Kingdom, and continues to program cutting-edge and provocative photography. The prestigious annual Deutsche Börse Photography Prize is exhibited and awarded here annually. There are a print sales room (closed Sunday and Monday), bookstore, and a café. ⊠*5 and 8 Great Newport St., Covent Garden, WC2* ☎*020/7831–1772* ⊕*www.photonet.org.uk* ✉*Free* ☉ *Mon.–Wed., Fri., and Sat. 11–6, Thurs. 11–8, Sun. noon–6* Ⓤ*Leicester Sq.*

Royal Academy. Housed in an aristocratic mansion and home to Britain's first art school (founded in 1768), the Academy is best known for its blockbuster special exhibitions—like the record-breaking Monet, and the controversial "Sensation" drawn from the Saatchi collection of contemporary British art. The annual Summer Exhibition has been a popular London tradition since 1769. ⊠*Burlington House, Soho, W1* ☎*020/7300–8000* ⊕*www.royalacademy.org.uk* ✉*From £8, prices vary with exhibition* ☉ *Sat.–Thurs. 10–6, Fri. 10 AM–10 PM* Ⓤ*Piccadilly Circus.*

Saatchi Gallery. Charles Saatchi's ultramodern gallery reopened in the Duke of York's HQ building in Chelsea in 2007 complete with a new bookshop and café-bar; its short-lived tenancy on the South Bank ended acrimoniously in 2005. ⊠*Duke of York's HQ, Sloane Sq., Chelsea, SW3 4RY* ☎*020/7823–2332* ⊕*www.saatchi-gallery.co.uk* Ⓤ*Sloane Sq.*

Serpentine Gallery. In a classical 1930 tea pavilion in Kensington Gardens, the Serpentine has an international reputation for exhibitions of modern and contemporary art. Man Ray, Henry Moore, Andy Warhol, Bridget Riley, Damien Hirst, and Rachel Whiteread are a few of the artists who have exhibited here. ⊠*Kensington Gardens, South Kensington, W2* ☎*020/7402–6075* ⊕*www.serpentinegallery.org* ✉*Donation* ☉ *Daily 10–6* Ⓤ*South Kensington or Knightsbridge.*

Fodor'sChoice **Tate Modern.** This converted power station is one of the largest
★ modern-art galleries in the world, so give yourself ample time to take it all in. The permanent collection, which includes work by all the major 20th-century artists, was rehung in 2006 and is now grouped by art movement rather than thematically. There are also blockbuster touring shows and solo exhibitions of international artists. ■TIP→**The café on the top floor has gorgeous views overlooking the Thames and St. Paul's Cathedral.** ⊠*Bankside, South Bank, SE1*

☎020/7887–8008 ⊕*www.tate.org.uk* ✉*Free–£8.50*⊙*Daily 10–6, Fri. and Sat. until 10* PM Ⓤ*Southwark.*

★ **Victoria Miro Gallery.** This important commercial gallery has exhibited some of the biggest names on the British contemporary art scene—Chris Ofili, the Chapman brothers, Peter Doig, to name a few. It also brings in exciting new talent from abroad. ✉*16 Wharf Rd., Islington, N1* ☎*020/7336–8109* ⊕*www.victoria-miro.com* ✉*Free*⊙*Tues.–Sat. 10–6* Ⓤ*Old St., Angel.*

Vilma Gold. This serious commercial gallery in Bethnal Green shows outré work by international and British artists. ✉*25B Vyner St., East End, E2* ☎*020/8981–3344* ⊕*www.vilmagold.com* ✉*Free*⊙*Thurs.–Sun. noon–6* Ⓤ*Bethnal Green.*

★ **White Cube.** Jay Joplin's influential gallery is housed in a 1920s light-industrial building on Hoxton Square. Many of its artists are Turner Prize stars—Hirst, Emin, Hume, et al., and many live in the East End, which supposedly has the highest concentration of artists in Europe. Farther west, White Cube opened a second gallery in a striking new building in Mason's Yard, St. James's in 2006. ✉*48 Hoxton Sq., East End, N1* ☎*020/7749–7450* ⊕*www.whitecube.com* ✉*Free*⊙*Tues.–Sat. 10–6* Ⓤ*Old St.*

★ **Whitechapel Art Gallery.** Established in 1897, this independent East End gallery is one of London's most innovative. Jeff Wall, Bill Viola, Gary Hume, and Janet Cardiff have exhibited here. ✉*80–82 Whitechapel High St., East End, E1* ☎*020/7522–7888* ⊕*www.whitechapel. org* ✉*Free–£8*⊙*Tues.–Sun. 11–6, Thurs. 11–9* Ⓤ*Aldgate East.*

SPORTS & THE OUTDOORS

18

In the wake of London's successful bid to host the Olympics in 2012, the city's sporting credentials and sporting facilities are receiving a massive boost. The salaries of some professional athletes in the United Kingdom put them among the highest paid people in the land, and sports stars are some of the country's most marketable personalities. The British are dead serious about sports. When things are going well for an English national team, especially in football, there's a definite "feel-good" factor that envelops the capital. And for spectators there's plenty to get excited about. Alongside the traditions of the Wimbledon Tennis Championships and boating on the Thames there's the slow tension of cricket, the multimillion pound industry that is modern football (soccer), the festive atmosphere of the Flora London Marathon, and possibilities to watch just about anything else sporting.

For participants, London is a great city for the weekend player of almost anything. It comes into its own in summer, when the parks sprout nets and goals and painted white lines, outdoor swimming pools open, and a season of spectator events gets under way. *For more on Hyde Park in particular, see chapter 11.* In winter there's the opportunity to ice-skate in some of Britain's most spectacular locations. If you feel like joining in, the London version of *Time Out* magazine, available in newsstands, is a great resource. On the Web, Sport England (⊕*www.activeplaces.com*) has a good database of information on local clubs, facilities, and organizations. Check ⊕*www.royalparks.gov.uk* for details on all of London's royal parks. The listings below concentrate on facilities available for various sports, and on the more accessible or well-known spectator events. Bring your gear, and branch out from that hotel gym.

BICYCLING

London is becoming more cycle-friendly, with special lanes marked for bicycles on some streets, especially in central London, and a network of cycle-only lanes, often along canal paths. ■ TIP→**If you plan to cycle much in the city, get the excellent London Cycling Guides, with useful information and detailed cycling routes through the city.** They're available free from bike shops, Tube stations, or by post via the Web site of **Transport for London** (☎*0845/305–1234* ⊕*www.tfl.gov.uk/cycles*). You can also use Transport for London's online journey planner to create recommended cycling routes and maps.

★ **London Bicycle Tour Company,** right beside the Oxo Tower on the South Bank, offers 3½-hour bike tours of the East End and West End, for £16.95. Reserve in advance by phone or on the Internet. You can also go it alone: bikes can be rented for £3 an hour or £16 for a day (£8 for each subsequent day). Or, if you prefer, there are in-line skates, tandems, and rickshaws for rent. ✉*1A Gabriel's Wharf, South Bank, SE1* ☎*020/7928–6838* ⊕*www.londonbicycle.com* Ⓤ*Waterloo.*

CRICKET

Fodor'sChoice **Lord's** has been hallowed turf for worshippers of England's summer
★ game since 1811. Tickets can be hard to procure for the five-day Test Matches (full internationals) and one-day internationals played here: obtain an application form and enter the ballot (lottery) to purchase tickets. Forms are sent out from early December or you can sign up online. Standard Test Match tickets cost between £40 and £65. County matches (Middlesex plays here) can usually be seen by lining up on match day. ✉*St. John's Wood Rd., St. John's Wood, NW8* ☎*020/7432–1000* ⊕*www.lords.org* Ⓤ*St. John's Wood.*

★ The **Oval,** home of Surrey County Cricket Club, is a slightly easier place than Lord's to witness the *thwack* of leather on willow, with tickets for internationals sold on a first-come first-served basis from late October. Though slightly less venerated than its illustrious cousin, the standard of cricket here is certainly no lower. Test match tickets range in price from £40 to £75. ✉*Kennington Oval, Kennington, SE11* ☎*020/7582–6660* ⊕*www.surreycricket.com* Ⓤ*Oval.*

EQUESTRIAN EVENTS

Racing   The main events of "the Season," as much social as sporting, occur just outside the city. Both Ascot and Epsom are best known for their big summer meets but racing happens at both throughout the year.

Making a Bet

Horses, greyhounds, football, and whether it will snow on the roof of the Meteorological Office on Christmas Day are all popular reasons for a "flutter" in all corners of the capital. Now that technology and the abolition of tax on betting have encouraged a massive surge in Internet wagers, you don't even need to leave home to put a pound on just about anything you want, or any combination of likely or unlikely events. If you do, however, you'll find London's ubiquitous bookmakers (Ladbroke and William Hill are the biggest) to be increasingly comfortable places with live satellite link-ups to sporting events around the world. At both equine and canine racecourses these chains are also represented, but here they struggle to compete for attention with the furious calling and signaling of the traditional bookies, whose tictac communications provide an alternative form of entertainment on the track.

★ Her Majesty attends **Royal Ascot** (⊠ *Grand Stand, Ascot, Berkshire* ☎ *01344/622211* ⊕ *www.royalascot.co.uk*) in mid-June, driving from Windsor in an open carriage for a procession before the plebes daily at 2. You'll need to book good seats far in advance for this event, although some tickets—far away from the Royal Enclosure and winning post—can usually be bought on the day of the race for £15. Grandstand tickets, which go on sale on the first working day of the year, cost £54. There are also Ascot Heath tickets available for a mere £3, but these only admit you to a picnic area in the middle of the race course. You'll be able to see the horses, of course, but that's not why people come to Ascot. The real spectacle is the crowd itself: enormous headgear is de rigueur on Ladies Day—the Thursday of the meet—and those who arrive dressed inappropriately (jeans, shorts, sneakers) will be turned away from their grandstand seats.

Fodor'sChoice **Derby Day** (⊠ *The Grandstand, Epsom Downs, Surrey* ☎ *01372/*
★ *470047* ⊕ *www.epsomderby.co.uk*), usually held on the first Saturday in June, is, after Ascot, the second biggest social event of the racing calendar; it's also one of the world's greatest races for three-year-olds. Lord Derby and Sir Charles Bunbury, the founders of the mile-and-a-half race, tossed a coin to decide who the race would be named after. It was first run in 1780. Tickets are between £10 and £35.

FOOTBALL

To refer to the national sport as "soccer" is to blaspheme. It is football, and its importance to the people and the culture of the country seems to grow inexorably. Massive injections of money from television, sponsorship, and foreign investors often fail to filter down through the game, leaving some lower-division clubs in financial difficulty, but public interest in millionaire stars in the domestic game is immense. The domestic season (August through May) culminates in the FA Cup Final, traditionally the biggest day in the sporting calendar, for which tickets are

18

about as easy to get as they are for the Super Bowl. Increasingly important, the European Champions League, a club competition, brings together many of the world's best players in a quest for continental glory and riches. The three or four top English clubs are involved. The FA Cup Final and international matches are once again being held at Wembley since the long-delayed rebuilding of the National Stadium.

For a real sample of this British obsession, nothing beats a match at the home ground of one of the London clubs competing in the Premier League, and a taste

of the electric atmosphere only a vast football crowd can generate. Try to book tickets (from about £25 upward) in advance. You might also check out London's lower division games: though the standard of football in League Two may not match that of the Premiership, tickets are cheaper and easier to get hold of, and the environment can be just as fervent. For more information on teams, games, and prices, look in *Time Out* magazine.

Premier League Teams

Arsenal is historically London's most successful club, and under the managerial reign of Arsene Wenger they have shed their boring image to become proponents of attractive, free-flowing football. They also have an impressive new stadium to match their ambitions. However, their pre-eminent position in the capital is threatened by London rival Chelsea. ⊠*Emirates Stadium, Ashburton Grove, Islington, N5* ☎*020/7704–4040* ⊕*www.arsenal.com* Ⓤ*Arsenal.*

Charlton Athletic has more passion than money and, despite a habit of outperforming expectations, their time in the top division may be limited. ⊠*The Valley, Floyd Rd., Greenwich, SE7* ☎*020/8333–4010* ⊕*www. cafc.co.uk* Ⓤ*National Rail: Charlton.*

Chelsea is owned by one of Russia's richest men, and the extra cash has brought in new players and an outspoken Portuguese manager. They won the Premiership in 2005 and 2006 and are now one of the best in Europe. ⊠*Stamford Bridge, Fulham Rd., Fulham, SW6* ☎*0870/300–2322* ⊕*www.chelseafc.co.uk* Ⓤ*Fulham Broadway.*

Fulham has now become a regular in the top division. Under the same owner as Harrods, they certainly possess the money and the self-confidence to stay with the big boys. ⊠*Craven Cottage, Stevenage Rd., Fulham, SW6* ☎*0870/442–1234* ⊕*www.fulhamfc.co.uk* Ⓤ*Putney Bridge.*

Tottenham Hotspur, or "Spurs," traditionally an exponent of attractive, positive football, has underperformed for many years, but in the last two or three seasons there have been some signs of a revival for the North London side. ⊠ *White Hart La., 748 High Rd., Tot-*

tenham, N17 ☎ 0870/420–5000 ⊕ www.spurs.co.uk Ⓤ National Rail: White Hart La.

West Ham is the team of London's East End. After years of failing to match the successes of their past they returned to top-flight football in 2005, and, now under Icelandic ownership, are looking to catch up with their London rivals. ⊠ Boleyn Ground, Green St., Upton Park, E13 ☎ 0870/112–2700 ⊕ www.whufc.com Ⓤ Upton Park.

RUGBY

An ancestor of American football that's played unpadded, Rugby Union raises the British blood pressure (especially on the Celtic fringes) enormously. To find out about top clubs playing rugby in and around the capital during the September to May season, peruse *Time Out* magazine. Rugby League, a slightly different game, is played almost exclusively in the north of England, but you can catch the one southern Super League team, Harlequins Rugby League, at the Twickenham Stoop.

★ **Twickenham** hosts the Rugby Union Six-Nations tournament, where relative newcomer Italy joins old-timers England, France, Scotland, Wales, and Ireland. During this competition, held January through March, rugby can rival even football for the nation's sporting attentions, and tickets for these matches are more precious than gold. The domestic Powergen Cup Final is fought out at Twickenham in early May. To get there, take National Rail to Twickenham station; the stadium is a 10-minute walk away. You can also take the Tube to Richmond and take a bus or walk 15 minutes to the ground. ⊠ Twickenham Rugby Football Ground, Whitton Rd., Twickenham, TW2 ☎ 0870/143–1111 ⊕ www.twickenhamstadium.com.

18

RUNNING

London is a delight for joggers. If you don't mind a crowd, popular spots include Green Park, which gets a stream of runners armed with maps from Piccadilly hotels, and—to a lesser extent—adjacent St. James's Park. Both can get perilous with deck chairs on summer days. You can run a 4-mi perimeter route around Hyde Park and Kensington Gardens or a 2½-mi route in Hyde Park alone if you start at Hyde Park Corner or Marble Arch and encircle the Serpentine. Most Park Lane hotels offer jogging maps for this, their local green space. Regent's Park has the most populated track because it's a sporting kind of place; the Outer Circle loop measures about 2½ mi.

Away from the center, there are longer, scenic runs over more varied terrain at Hampstead Heath: highlights are Kenwood, and Parliament Hill, London's highest point, where you'll get a fabulous panoramic sweep over the entire city. Richmond Park is the biggest green space of all, but watch for deer during rutting season (October and November). Back in town, there's a rather traffic-heavy 1½-mi riverside run along Victoria Embankment from Westminster Bridge to Blackfriars Bridge, or a beautiful mile among the rowing clubs and ducks along the Malls—Upper, Lower, and Chiswick—from Hammersmith Bridge.

If you don't want to run alone, call the **London Hash House Harriers** (☎020/8567–5712 ⊕ *www.londonhash.org*). They organize noncompetitive hour-long hare-and-hound group runs around interesting bits of town, with loops, shortcuts, and pubs built in. Runs start at Tube stations, usually at noon on Saturday or Sunday in winter, and at 7 PM on Monday in summer. The cost is £1.

SPAS

★ At **Agua** (in the Sanderson Hotel, but open to non-guests), the chic Philippe Starck minimalism is as much a part of the experience as the opulent treatments. Ancient eastern traditions combine with the clean lines of modernity and everything is unfailingly chic. Packages cost from £145 for a combination of three mud, massage, bath, or "bed of roses" treatments. ⊠*Sanderson Hotel, 50 Berners St., Fitzrovia, W1* ☎*020/7300–1414* ⊕*www.sandersonlondon.com* Ⓤ*Goodge St.*

There's a 36- by 14-meter indoor pool for serious lap swimmers at **Porchester Baths** (costing £3.95 a swim), plus a 1920s Turkish bath, sauna, and spa of refurbished grandeur at £20.35. It has separate sessions for men (Monday, Wednesday, Saturday) and women (Tuesday, Thursday, Friday). Sunday is mixed. ⊠*Queensway, Bayswater, W2* ☎*020/7792–2919* Ⓤ*Queensway.*

★ One of London's oldest spas, **The Sanctuary** still has the rope swing made famous by a naked Joan Collins in the 1970s movie *The Stud,* and although it lacks some of the modern design aesthetics of others in the city, it retains a dated sense of style. Day membership is £67–£77, or you can soothe away a hard day with an evening's pampering Wednesday to Friday 5 PM–10 PM for £43–£45. Women only. ⊠*12 Floral St., Covent Garden, WC2E* ☎*0870/770–3350* ⊕*www.thesanctuary.co.uk* Ⓤ*Covent Garden.*

SQUASH

There are four squash courts at **Finsbury Leisure Centre,** a popular sports center in the City frequented by execs who work nearby. You can book by phone without a membership, and you're most likely to get a court if you show up to play during Londoners' regular office hours, or possibly on weekends, when courts are less busy. A 40-minute court session costs £8.10 for nonmembers, £6 off-peak (before 5 PM or after 7 PM). ⊠*Norman St., Finsbury, EC1* ☎*020/7253–2346* Ⓤ*Old St.*

TENNIS

Many London parks have courts that are often cheap or even free:

★ **Holland Park** is one of the prettiest places to play, with six hard courts (two of which are floodlit) available all year. The cost here is £5.50 per hour, but only borough residents can book in advance. ✉*Holland Park, W8* ☎*020/7602–2226* Ⓤ*Holland Park*.

Islington Tennis Centre is about the only place where you don't need a membership to play indoors year-round, but you do need to reserve by phone. In addition to six indoor courts there are two outdoor courts; coaching is also available, as are "Pay and Play" sessions where you can turn up and be matched with a player of similar ability. Prices are £18 for the indoor courts and £8.50 for outdoors. Nonmembers can book up to five days ahead. ✉*Market Rd., Islington, N7* ☎*020/7700–1370* ⊕*www.aquaterra.org* Ⓤ*Caledonian Rd.*

☾ **Regent's Park Tennis Centre** has courts available to nonmembers for £9 an hour peak (weekdays 4 PM–9 PM, weekends all day) and £7 off-peak. There are also social tennis sessions every Sunday 1–4 PM, where you can arrive without a partner and get in on a game. Four courts are floodlighted for use in winter. Two junior courts are the centerpieces of the "Tennis Kid Zone," and there's also a café. ✉*York Bridge Rd., Inner Circle, Regent's Park, Marylebone, NW1* ☎*020/7486—4216* Ⓤ*Regent's Park*.

★ The **Wimbledon Lawn Tennis Championships** are famous among fans for the green, green grass of Centre Court; for strawberries and cream; and for rain, which always falls, despite the last-week-of-June–first-week-of-July high-summer timing. This event is the most prestigious of the four Grand Slam events of the tennis year. Whether you can get grandstand tickets is literally down to the luck of the draw, because there's a ballot system (lottery) for advance purchase. To apply, send a self-addressed stamped envelope (or an international reply coupon) between August 1 and December 15 in order to receive an application form; then return the completed form by December 31, and hope for the best.

There are other ways to see the tennis. About 500 Centre and Number 1 and 2 Court tickets are kept back to sell each day (except for the last four days), and fanatics line up all night for these, especially in the first week. Afternoon tickets collected from early-departing spectators are resold (profits go to charity). These can be excellent grandstand seats (with plenty to see—play continues until dusk). ▪ TIP→ **You can also buy entry to the grounds to roam matches on the outside courts, where even the top-seeded players compete early in the two-week period.** Get to South-fields or Wimbledon Tube station as early as possible and start queuing to be sure of getting one of these. ✉*Ticket Office, All England Lawn Tennis & Croquet Club, Box 98, Church Rd., Wimbledon, SW19 5AE* ☎*020/8946–2244* ⊕*www.wimbledon.org*.

18

If you don't fancy the crowds and snaking queues of Wimbledon, you can watch many of the top names in men's tennis play in the pre-Wimbledon **Stella Artois Tournament.** This, too, is usually oversubscribed, but you can join a mailing list and then apply online from January for a priority booking. ⊠*Queen's Club, Palliser Rd., West Kensington, W14* ☎*020/7385–3421* ⊕*www.stellaartoistennis.com* Ⓤ Barons Court.

YOGA

Life Centre, London's best yoga school specializes in the dynamic, energetic Ashtanga Vinyasa technique, though yoga classes also cater to 12 other different types. Beautiful premises enhance the experience. A huge variety of holistic health therapies is available upstairs. Classes cost from £10 to £13 and run all day every day. ⊠*15 Edge St., Kensington, W8* ☎*020/7221–4602* ⊕*www.thelifecentre.com* Ⓤ*Notting Hill Gate.*

Shopping

Portobello Road Market, Notting Hill

WORD OF MOUTH

"Portobello Road is best seen very early Saturday morning—and really no other tourist attractions are open then. So go to the market around 8 AM (earlier if you can manage, but on your first full day in London that might be difficult). By 10–10:30 AM it gets very crowded, so it is best to be leaving around then. Most tourist attractions open around 10, so the timing is perfect."

—janisj

SHOPPING PLANNER

Top 5

■ **Portobello Road Market.** This market is still the best for size, variety, and sheer street theater.

■ **Harrods Food Halls.** Noisy, colorful, and tempting, the food halls have long been a favorite. The mosaic of fresh fish assembled every day is a must-see.

■ **Liberty.** In a classic, half-timbered building, the store's historic connection with William Morris and the Arts and Crafts movement is maintained in a focus on design and truly beautiful things.

■ **Selfridges.** This is the best department store in London, with an astonishing selection of goods at prices that range from budget to astronomical.

■ **Hamleys.** With floor after floor of treasures for every child on your list, this is *the* London toyshop.

A Word About Service

Don't take it personally if sales-people seem abrupt—even rude. Service with a smile is a relatively new concept here, and it hasn't caught on everywhere.

Opening Hours

Most shops are open from about 9:30 or 10 AM to 6 or 6:30 PM. Some may open at 11 and stay open until 7. Because shop hours, particularly for the smaller shops, are varied, it's a good idea to phone ahead. Stores that have late shopping—and not all do—are usually open until 7 or 8 PM, on Wednesday or Thursday only. On Sunday, many shops open between 11 AM and noon and close at 5 or 6 PM.

Watch Your Language

The English have their own version of our mutual language. Here are a few confusing terms to watch for when out and about in the shops:

Pants means underwear. Every other type of long-legged bottoms (except jeans) are called **trousers.**

Knickers are ladies' undies. If you want pantyhose, ask for **tights.**

Jumper means sweater—unless it's a cardigan, in which case it's called a **cardie.** If you ask for a **sweater,** you may be offered a sweatshirt.

Men use **braces** to hold up their trousers; in England **suspenders** is another word for garters.

If you want some Adidas or Nike-type athletic shoes, ask for **trainers**—never sneakers.

Don't ask for a **pocketbook** or a **purse** if you mean a hand-bag—the former will be incomprehensible while the latter will produce a coin purse.

In the nightwear department, nightgowns are always **nighties** and bathrobes are always **dressing gowns.**

Updated by
Lisa Ritchie

Napoléon was being scornful when he called Britain a nation of shopkeepers, but with shopping one of today's most popular leisure activities, Londoners have had the last laugh. Not only does London have some of the finest stores in the world, it also has plenty of them—from grand department stores to exquisite specialty and designer shops. Like most other major cities, London has its share of national and global chain stores, but individuality still rules here and the real pleasure is in nosing out the unique.

You can shop like royalty and have your undies custom-made at Her Majesty's corsetiere Rigby & Peller in Knightsbridge, run down a leather-bound copy of *Wuthering Heights* at a Charing Cross bookseller, find antique toby jugs on Portobello Road, or drop in at Vivienne Westwood's landmark shop on the King's Road—Gwen Stefani and Kelly Osborne are fans. Whether you're out for fun or for fashion, London can be the most rewarding of hunting grounds.

19

Apart from bankrupting yourself, the only problem you may encounter is exhaustion. London is a town of many far-flung shopping areas. Real shophounds plan their excursions with military precision, taking in only one or two shopping districts in a day, with fortifying stops for lunch, tea, and a pint or glass of wine in the pub.

DEPARTMENT STORES

London's department stores range from Harrods—practically a national monument on the tourist trail—to many mid-range stores that cater to Londoners' everyday needs. A few rise above the pack for their fashion (Harvey Nichols), originality (Liberty), or sheer excitement (Selfridges). The best are scattered about the West End on Oxford Street, Regent Street, and Knightsbridge. Some, like Marks & Spencer, another British institution now known mostly for clothing and food, have branches

CAMDEN TOWN
cheap second-hand and club gear

CLERKENWELL
a historical hotspot for crafts and design

SHOREDITCH
edgy young designers

MARYLEBONE
small shops in village-like setting

NOTTING HILL
antiques, vintage clothing, and boho boutiques

OXFORD CIRCUS
global flagships, department stores, and street style on Carnaby

SOHO
books abound on Charing Cross Road

COVENT GARDEN
an urban-wear mecca around Seven Dials

MAYFAIR
catwalk names on Bond St., trad tailors on Savile Row

ST JAMES'S
old-fashioned specialists, from hatters to shirtmakers

KNIGHTSBRIDGE
luxe labels and, of course, Harrods

CHELSEA
the King's Rd. spans fashion to furniture

REGENT'S PARK

BLOOMSBURY

BAYSWATER

HYDE PARK

GREEN PARK

ST. JAMES'S PARK

WESTMINSTER

BELGRAVIA

VICTORIA

LAMBETH

1/2 mile

1/2 km

Albany Rd.

Park Rd.

Lisson Grove

Marylebone Rd.

Baker St.

Edgware Rd.

Wigmore St.

Oxford St.

Bayswater Rd.

Kensington Rd.

Brompton Rd.

Sloane St.

Pimlico Rd.

King's Rd.

Albany St.

Gt. Portland St.

Portland Pl.

New Bond St.

Regent St.

Euston Rd.

Tottenham Court Rd.

New Oxford St.

Charing Cross Rd.

Shaftesbury

Pall Mall

Piccadilly

Constitution Hill

Knightsbridge

Buckingham Palace Rd.

Wilton Rd.

Vauxhall Br. Rd.

Victoria St.

Birdcage Walk

The Mall

Holborn

Kingsway

Aldwych

Strand

Waterloo Br.

Victoria Embankment

Thames

River

Westminster Br.

Horseferry Rd.

Lambeth Br.

Lambeth Palace Rd.

Millbank

Albert Embankment

Gray's Inn Rd.

Whitehall

all over town. ■TIP→Unless you have Olympic levels of stamina, aim to anchor a shopping day with only one or two department stores, dipping in and out of the nearby boutiques in between.

Fenwick. Near the Oxford Street end of New Bond Street, Fenwick (pronounced *Fennick*) is a haven of realistically priced fashion in a shopping area where most things cost the earth. Five floors of chic clothes and accessories for men and women, lingerie, and home furnishings highlight lesser-known and emerging designers from all over Europe. Even the restaurants, Joe's on the second floor and Carluccio's in the basement, have style. Make sure to see the big selection of striking, semi-precious and costume jewelry on the ground floor. *(⇨Map A)* ⊠*63 New Bond St., Mayfair, W1* ☎*020/7629–9161* Ⓤ *Bond.*

Fodor'sChoice
★
Harrods. This Knightsbridge institution is an encyclopedia of luxury brands, with at least 500 departments and 20 restaurants packed onto seven floors across 4½ acres. In 2000, Harrods lost its Royal Warrants and some of its luster as a "top people's store." If you approach Harrods more as a tourist attraction than a fashion store you won't be disappointed: focus on the spectacular food halls, the huge ground-floor perfumery, the marble clad accessory rooms, and the outrageous *Egyptian* escalator—at the bottom there's a tacky shrine to Diana and Dodi. ■TIP→Be prepared to brave the crowds, and dress nicely, please—scruffy visitors are politely shown the door. *(⇨Map E)* ⊠*87–135 Brompton Rd., Knightsbridge, SW1* ☎*020/7730–1234* Ⓤ*Knightsbridge.*

★ **Harvey Nichols.** It's a block away from Harrods, but Harvey Nicks is not competing on the same turf, because its passion is fashion, all the way. There are nearly six floors of it, including departments for dressing homes and men, but the woman who invests in her wardrobe is the main target. Accessories here are out of this world—especially designer bags and shoes—and the store secures exclusives from many labels. The fourth floor has a chic home-design department, stocking such names as Armani Casa and Culti. A reservation at the Fifth Floor restaurant is coveted, but you can drop in at the chic, if noisy, Café for panoramic views of Knightsbridge and its fashionistas. *(⇨Map E)* ⊠*109–125 Knightsbridge, Knightsbridge, SW1* ☎*020/7235–5000* Ⓤ *Knightsbridge.*

John Lewis. This store's motto is "Never knowingly undersold," and for all kinds of goods at sensible prices, John Lewis is hard to beat. Chelsea locals think of Peter Jones, its brother store in Sloane Square, Chelsea, for classic fashions and home accessories. Both stores have big dress and furnishing fabrics, needlework, and knitting departments. Their bespoke, lined draperies set the gold standard, not only in London but in smart, traditional homes all over Britain. *(⇨Map B)* ⊠*278–306 Oxford St., Mayfair, W1* ☎*020/7629–7711* Ⓤ *Oxford Circus* ⌖ *Peter Jones:* ⊠*Sloane Sq., Chelsea, SW1* ☎*020/7730–3434* Ⓤ *Sloane Square.*

Fodor'sChoice
★
Liberty. With a wonderful black-and-white mock-Tudor facade, Liberty is a peacock among pigeons on humdrum Regent Street. In the 19th century, Liberty's designers, leaders in the art nouveau, Arts and Crafts, and aesthetic movements, created classic fabric and home-furnishing designs. Those Liberty prints are still world famous today. Inside, the

19

Know Your Shopping Personality

"What's the best place to shop in London?" is an unanswerable question, akin to "How long is a piece of string?" There are thousands of shops in London and dozens of neighborhoods worth shopping in. Identify your shopping personality to narrow your choices for a successful day or half-day outing.

Department Store Aficionado. Do you like the buzz of a big store, want to look at many different kinds of merchandise in one place, finish your shopping list fast? Head for the department stores. Selfridges, John Lewis, Fenwick, and Liberty are all clustered in the area around Oxford Circus and Bond Street Tube stations. Harvey Nichols and Harrods share Knightsbridge Tube.

Fashionista. When only the best designers will do, start at Harvey Nichols, in Knightsbridge, then take in the designer boutiques along Sloane Street before boarding the Tube for Green Park. From there, head up New and Old Bond streets, finishing at Fenwick. If you still have time and energy, aim for St. Christopher Place W1 or South Molton Street W1 for more fashion boutiques.

Eclectic. If you don't like to be pinned down and like beautiful workmanship and originality, start at Liberty on Regent Street then head for either the Holland Park/Notting Hill or Marylebone neighborhoods. Both provide enough idiosyncratic lifestyle shops for hours of browsing.

Funky & Avant-Garde. Aim for the Spitalfields/Brick Lane area on a Sunday. Take the Tube to Liverpool Street or Aldgate East, then follow the crowds of trendies. Brick Lane runs parallel to Commercial Street (where Spitalfields Market is located). The ladder of small streets between them is good for surprises.

Easygoing. If you like popping in and out of different shops, a bit of people-watching, and a few good spots for coffee or lunch, the mile and a half of the King's Road that starts in Sloane Square is ideal. You'll find small department stores like Peter Jones and Marks & Spencer, familiar chains, one-off boutiques, food and coffee shops, bookstores, electronics, music, children's goods, antiques, and high fashion all along the route.

store is a labyrinth of nooks and crannies stuffed with goodies. The carpet department is an exotic jumble of handmade Oriental and contemporary rugs, while furniture is an impressive archive spanning the mid-19th century to the present, worth a look even if you're not buying. The jewelry and accessories department contrasts the unusual and bohemian with deluxe international labels. Fashion, for men and women, focuses on quality and beautiful fabric. *(⇨ Map A) ✉ Regent St., Mayfair, W1 ☎ 020/7734–1234 Ⓤ Oxford Circus.*

Marks & Spencer. A major chain of stores that's an integral part of the British way of life, Marks & Spencer was once known for its moderately priced practical clothes and knitwear. Since about 1998 the store has been struggling to find its place in the new retail environment, so what particular fashion incarnation is in-store when you arrive is anybody's guess. Some classics—like beautiful, moderately priced sweaters ("jumpers" in British parlance)—seem to be holding their own and the lingerie remains outstanding. Look for M&S Simply Food shops popping up all over the place and trading on the store's reputation for prepared dishes you can pass off as your own. They're a good source of shortbread, tins of British biscuits and sweets, and jars of condiments you can take home. The Marble Arch branch is the flagship, and its fast stock turnover ensures that it carries the latest from the M&S designers' stable. *(⇨ Map B) ⊠ 458 Oxford St., Oxford Street, W1 ☎ 020/7935–7954 Ⓤ Marble Arch.*

Fodor'sChoice
★
Selfridges. This giant, bustling store is giving Harvey Nicks a run for its money as London's leading fashion department store. It's packed to the rafters with high-profile, popular designer clothes for everyone in the family. Revamped for the millennium, the store continues to break ground with its theatrical modern design—especially the men's and women's high-fashion Superbrands sections. The frenetic cosmetics department is, according to the store, the largest in Europe. There are so many zones with pulsating music that merge into one another—from fashion to sports gear to audio equipment—that you practically need a map. ■ TIP➡ **Don't miss the globe-spanning Food Hall on the ground floor; there's also a theater-ticket counter in the basement.** *(⇨ Map B) ⊠ 400 Oxford St., Oxford Street, W1 ☎ 0870/837–7377 Ⓤ Bond St.*

SPECIALTY STORES

ANTIQUES

Investment-quality items or lovable junk, London has lots. Try markets first—even for pedigree silver, the dealers at these places often have the best wares and the knowledge to match. The Silver Vaults in Chancery Lane and Bermondsey are the best. Some say that Portobello Road has become a bit of a tourist trap, but if you acknowledge that it's a circus and get into the spirit, it's a lot of fun. Just don't expect many bargains. Kensington Church Street is *the* antiques-shopping street, with both prices and quality high. Early English and European pottery as well as Oriental art porcelains are a specialty. Less stratospheric, an antiques enclave has sprung up around Alfie's Antique Market in Marylebone; the small shops lining Church Street sell everything from large-scale 19th-century English and European furniture to art deco ceramics and vintage shop fittings. Or, try your luck at auction against the dealers. Summer is usually a quiet period, but at any other time there are plenty of bargains to be had.

Listed here is a selection of the hundreds of stores to whet your appetite. ■ TIP➡ **Opening times vary: many places that are open on the weekend will close Monday or Tuesday.**

★ **Alfie's Antique Market.** A large and exciting labyrinth on several floors, it has dealers specializing in anything and everything, but particularly in vintage clothing and furniture. Highlights include the fabulous collection of cocktail dresses and kitsch bar accessories at The Girl Can't Help It, and Vincenzo Caffarrella's spectacular Italian lighting. In addition to the market, this end of Church Street is lined with excellent antiques shops. *(⇨ Map B) ⊠ 13–25 Church St., Regent's Park, NW8 ☎ 020/7723–6066 ۞ Closed Sun. and Mon. Ⓤ Edgware Rd.*

19

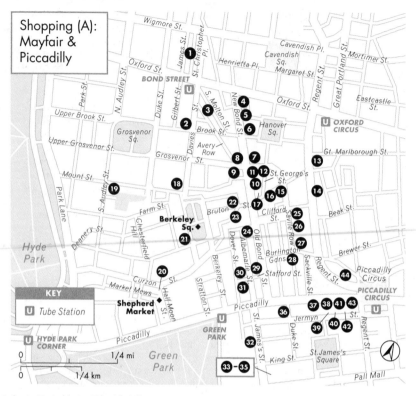

Shopping (A): Mayfair & Piccadilly

Antiquarius. About 10 minutes' walk from Sloane Square on the King's Road is an indoor antiques market with about 100 stalls selling collectibles, including items that won't bust your baggage allowance but may empty your bank account: art deco brooches, meerschaum pipes, silver salt cellars, and so on. (⇨ *Map F*) ⊠ *131–145 King's Rd., Chelsea, SW3* ☎ *020/7351–5353* ⊗ *Closed Sun.* Ⓤ *Sloane Square.*

Grays Antique Market. Dealers specializing in everything from Sheffield plate to Oriental antiquities assemble here under one roof, although the majority of stalls focus on jewelry. Bargains are not impossible, and proper pedigrees are guaranteed. Also try Grays in the Mews around the corner—it has less expensive merchandise, including the large Biblion bookshop and excellent vintage clothing at Vintage Modes. (⇨ *Map A*) ⊠ *58 Davies St., Mayfair, W1* ☎ *020/7629–7034* ⊗ *Closed Sun.; open Sat. in Dec. only* Ⓤ *Bond St.* ⊠ *1–7 Davies Mews, Mayfair, W1* ☎ *020/7629–7034* Ⓤ *Bond St.*

Hope and Glory. This is one of the many specialty stores in Kensington with commemorative china and glass from Victoria's reign to the present; there are also affordable lesser pieces. The entrance is on Peel Street. (⇨ *Map G*) ⊠ *131A Kensington Church St., Kensington, W8* ☎ *020/7727–8424* ⊗ *Closed Sun.* Ⓤ *Notting Hill Gate.*

★ **London Silver Vaults.** A basement conglomeration of around 40 dealers, it's a great place for the average Joe. Some pieces are spectacular, but you can also pick up a set of Victorian cake forks, jugs, cruet sets, candlesticks, and other smaller pieces for lower prices. ■TIP➔**As an especially cool feature, most of the silver merchants actually trade out of room-size, underground vaults.** (⇨ *Map C*) ⊠ *Chancery House, 53–64 Chancery La., Holborn, WC2* ☎ *020/7242–3844* ⊗ *Closed Sat. after 1, and Sun.* Ⓤ *Chancery La.*

Rupert Cavendish. This most elevated of dealers has the Biedermeier market cornered, with Empire and deco bringing up the rear. On a short stretch of the King's Road that's packed with high-quality antiques dealers, the shop is a museum experience. (⇨ *Map F*) ⊠ *610 King's Rd., Fulham, SW6* ☎ *020/7731–7041* ⊗ *Closed Sun.* Ⓤ *Fulham Broadway.*

AUCTION HOUSES

A few pointers on going to auction: you don't need bags of money; the catalog prices aren't written in stone; and if you're sure of what you want when you view the presale, then bid with confidence. It's easy to get carried away in the excitement of the moment, so keep your limit in mind or take along a friend to remind you. Listed below are the main houses, which all deal in fine art and furniture.

Bonhams. One of the more buyer-friendly places, this auction house has many interesting collections. Along with antiques, Bonhams specializes in 20th-century design. Its 2001 merger with the auction house Phillips increased the depth and scope of other specialty areas, such as Old Master paintings. Bonhams' flagship is now at the former Phillips site in New Bond Street, W1, and its Knightsbridge sales rooms are right across from Harrods. (⇨ *Map A and E*) ⊠ *101 New Bond St.,Mayfair, W1* ☎ *020/7447–7447* Ⓤ *Bond St.* ⊠ *Montpelier St., Knightsbridge, SW7* ☎ *020/7393–3900* Ⓤ *Knightsbridge.*

19

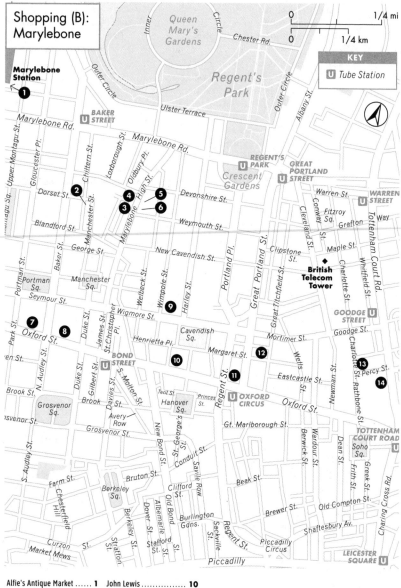

Shopping (B): Marylebone

KEY

U Tube Station

★ **Christie's.** Look here for great English country-house furniture in varying states of repair, paintings, prints, carpets, lighting, plus all manner of bona fide treasures. It's amazing what can be classed as infinitely desirable with surprising price tags: the blue door from the film *Notting Hill* and the blue pinafore dress worn by Judy Garland in *The Wizard of Oz* went for a record £5,750 and £199,500, respectively. (⇨ *Map E*) ✉ *85 Old Brompton Rd., South Kensington, SW7* ☎ *020/7930–6074* Ⓤ *South Kensington.*

★ **Lots Road Auctions.** Established in the 1970s by two former Christie's employees and a King's Road dealer, these weekly auctions, held at 1 PM and 4 PM every Sunday, offer a grab bag of fine antiques, good-quality used furniture, and out and out tat. Popular with decorators and locals on Sunday outings, these auction rooms, off the King's Road, are not in the least intimidating and a great place for beginners to get a taste for the sport. (⇨ *Map F*) ✉ *71–73 Lots Rd., Chelsea, SW10* ☎ *020/7376–6800* Ⓤ *Fulham Broadway or Earl's Court.*

Sotheby's. There's a well-publicized calendar of regular auctions for the well-heeled, but you can also just look, ponder possible purchases, or break for lunch in the superb café. (⇨ *Map A*) ✉ *34–35 New Bond St., Mayfair, W1* ☎ *020/7293–5000* Ⓤ *Bond St.*

BOOKS

Charing Cross Road has long been a center of London bookselling. There's still quite a concentration of bookstores along its length, with specialist, antiquarian, and used bookstores tucked away in Cecil Court, a pedestrian alley linking it with St. Martin's Lane. (See ⊕ www. cecilcourt.co.uk for a full list of the shops in this unique enclave.) But books are big business in London and the trade spreads into many corners of the city. Look, in particular, for the finest rare books around Mayfair. Bloomsbury, around London University and the British Museum, is good territory for used books and eccentric specialists. Every decent London High Street has its Waterstones, Ottakers, Borders, or local independent complete with coffee shops and, in some cases, even cocktail bars.

19

GENERAL **Daunt Books.** The most striking feature of this original Edwardian bookshop is the airy, oak-galleried travel section at the back, illuminated by a lofty conservatory roof and stained-glass window, where guidebooks, poetry, and other literature are organized by country. There's an excellent children's section and, at the front, biography and fiction are piled on tables for eclectic browsing. There are also branches in Belsize Park, Hampstead, and Holland Park. (⇨ *Map B*) ✉ *83–84 Marylebone High St., Marylebone, W1* ☎ *020/7224–2295* Ⓜ *Baker St.*

Fodor's Choice **Foyles.** A quirky, labyrinthine, family-run business, this store was
★ founded by the Foyle brothers, who sold their own secondhand textbooks from the kitchen table after they failed the Civil Service exam. The Civil Service's loss was London book lovers' gain. Today Foyles' five floors carry almost every title imaginable. One of London's best sources for textbooks, the store stocks everything from popular fiction to military history, sheet music, opera scores, and fine arts. Christina Foyle instituted a literary luncheon, which since 1930 has attracted

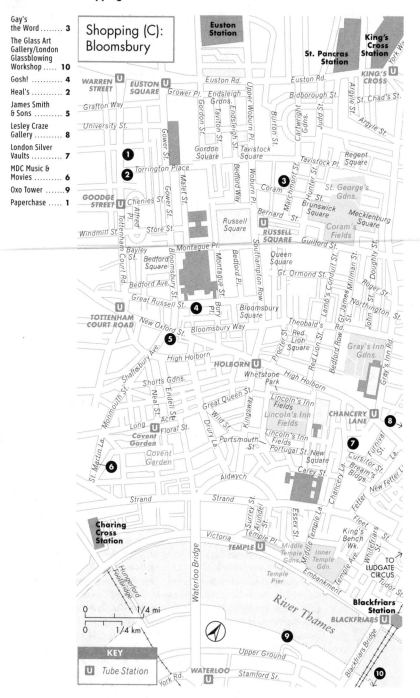

Shopping (C):
Bloomsbury

more than 700 top authors to speak at the ballroom in Grosvenor House. In 1999, following Christina's death, the family undertook a massive modernization program—installing elevators and air-conditioning. Store within a store Ray's Jazz has a cool café. In 2005, a new branch opened in the South Bank, followed by a concession within Selfridges department store in 2006. (➪ *Map D)* ⊠ *113–119 Charing Cross Rd., Soho, WC2* ☎ *020/7437–5660* Ⓤ *Tottenham Court Rd.* ⊠ *Royal Festival Hall, South Bank, SE1* ☎ *020/7437–5660* Ⓤ *Waterloo.*

Fodor'sChoice ★
Hatchards. This is one of London's well-established bookshops, beloved by writers themselves thanks to its cozy, independent character. Independence, however, is a matter of appearance only—Hatchards is owned by the same corporate giant as the omnipresent Waterstones chain. Nevertheless, you can revel in its old-fashioned charm while perusing the well-stocked shelves lining the winding stairs. The staff has retained old-fashioned helpfulness, too. (➪ *Map A)* ⊠ *187 Piccadilly, St. James's, W1* ☎ *020/7439–9921* Ⓤ *Piccadilly Circus.*

John Sandoe Books, Ltd. Enter this tiny shop off the King's Road in Chelsea and you may feel as if you've stepped through a time portal to an earlier century. More than 25,000 books fill the three, dollhouse-size floors of an 18th-century house. Organization? Forget it! Only the staff know where anything is. But they are knowledgeable, friendly, and full of great recommendations. You may be tempted to buy more than you can carry, but don't worry—they will pack and send your books anywhere in the world. Local writers, including William Boyd and Arabella Boxer, among others, are regulars and contribute to the shop's annual short publications. This is bookselling the way it used to be. (➪ *Map F)* ⊠ *10 Blacklands Terr., Chelsea, SW3* ☎ *020/7589–9473* Ⓤ *Sloane Square.*

Pan Bookshop. This crowded, independent Chelsea bookshop is full of charm. The staff are dedicated booksellers who know about books, care about book lovers, and take good care of local authors—the shop is known for its good selection of signed copies. (➪ *Map F)* ⊠ *158 Fulham Rd., Chelsea, SW10* ☎ *020/7373–4997* Ⓤ *South Kensington.*

Waterstone's. For book buying as a hedonistic leisure activity, the monster-size store by Piccadilly Circus caters to all tastes. The top floor boasts the 5th View Bar & Food, where until 10 PM you can sip a gin-and-tonic or get a bite while browsing through a book and admiring the view. Waterstone's is the country's leading book chain, and they've pulled out all the stops to make this, their flagship, as comfortable and relaxed as a bookstore can be. (➪ *Map A)* ⊠ *203–206 Piccadilly, St. James's, W1* ☎ *020/7851–2400* Ⓤ *Piccadilly Circus.*

SPECIALTY
Books for Cooks. It may seem odd to describe a bookshop as delicious smelling, but between the products of its test kitchen and its regularly scheduled cookery demonstrations, Books for Cooks is hard to resist. Just about every world cuisine is represented on its shelves, along with the complete lineup of celebrity-chef editions. You can spend hours perusing the volumes and sample lunch dishes, cakes, and coffee at one of a handful of tables in the back. ■ TIP➡ Before you come to London, visit the shop's Web site, ⊕ **www.booksforcooks.com,** to sign up for a

19

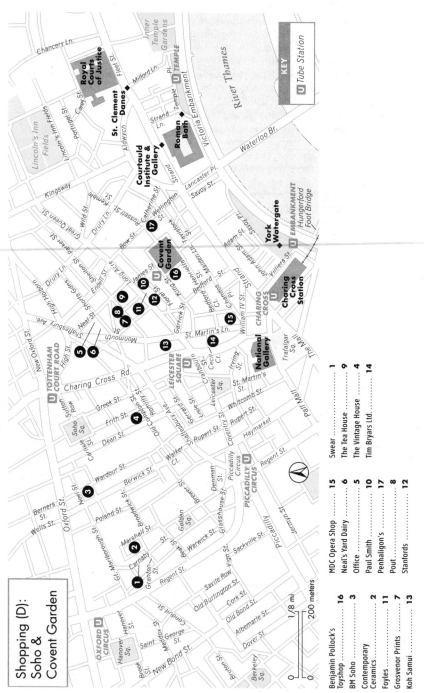

Shopping (D):
Soho &
Covent Garden

KEY

U Tube Station

Benjamin Pollock's
Toyshop **16**
BM Soho **3**
Contemporary
Ceramics **2**
Foyles **11**
Grosvenor Prints **7**
Koh Samui **13**

MDC Opera Shop **15**
Neal's Yard Dairy **6**
Office **5**
Paul Smith **10**
Penhaligon's **17**
Pout **8**
Stanfords **12**

Swear **1**
The Tea House **9**
The Vintage House **4**
Tim Bryars Ltd. **14**

1/8 mi

200 meters

cookery class. (⇨ *Map G*) ⊠ *4 Blenheim Crescent, Notting Hill, W11* ☎*020/7221–1992* Ⓤ *Notting Hill Gate.*

Children's Book Centre. Children are well catered to in London bookshops generally. This one, in addition to CDs, and the electronic paraphernalia kids demand, has the added treat of a basement full of toys. It's a very handy pacifier after you've done a bit of fashion shopping on Ken High Street. (⇨ *Map E*) ⊠ *237 Kensington High St., Kensington, W8* ☎*020/7937–7497* Ⓤ *High St. Kensington.*

Gay's the Word. Bloomsbury is where academia, eccentricity, and independence of spirit come together. It's also where London's largest and oldest gay and lesbian bookshop is located. You'll find thousands of titles, from literature and thoughtful nonfiction to erotica, multimedia, even comics. Opened in 1979, the shop has only recently had to compete with the gay and lesbian sections of some of London's mainstream bookstores—but it continues to lead the pack. (⇨ *Map C*) ⊠ *66 Marchmont St., Bloomsbury, WC1* ☎*020/7278–7654* Ⓤ *Russell Sq.*

Gosh! "Holy inky fingers, Batman! Is there a better comic book store in London?!" Probably not. Between the classic comics, graphic novels, manga, and independent minicomics this shop has got the genre covered. (⇨ *Map C*) ⊠ *39 Great Russell St., Bloomsbury, WC1* ☎*020/7636–1011* Ⓤ *Tottenham Court Rd.*

Stanfords. When it comes to encyclopedic coverage, there simply cannot be a better travel book and map shop on the planet. Stanfords is packed with a comprehensive selection of map and travel-book series. Their mail-order department is exemplary as well. Whether you're planning a junket to Surrey or a trip to the South Pole, this should be your first stop. (⇨ *Map D*) ⊠ *12–14 Long Acre, Covent Garden, WC2* ☎*020/7836–1321* Ⓤ *Covent Garden.*

Travel Bookshop. Across the street from Books for Cooks, this store covers the world on its shelves. It's great for globetrotters and armchair travelers alike, and is the kind of crowded and dusty bookshop that makes a great movie backdrop. Which is probably why it was Hugh Grant's bookstore in the movie *Notting Hill*. (⇨ *Map G*) ⊠ *13–15 Blenheim Crescent, Notting Hill, W11* ☎*020/7229–5260* Ⓤ *Notting Hill Gate.*

RARE & ANTIQUARIAN The English gentleman's library, with its glass-fronted cabinets full of rare leather-bound books, may be a film and literary cliché, but there's no denying that London is one of the world's great centers for rare book collectors. Browsers will find several shops along Cecil Court, off Charing Cross Road. For the most exquisite books, especially travel and natural history volumes with beautiful color plates, visit Mayfair around Maddox and Conduit streets.

Bernard J. Shapero Rare Books. Color plates are seen to best advantage in this bright, airy shop that vies with Maggs as one of the best antiquarian dealers in London. In addition to English and continental books that range from travel to medicine, there's also a gallery of maps and fine prints. (⇨ *Map A*) ⊠ *32 St. George St., Mayfair, W1* ☎*020/7493–0876* Ⓤ *Oxford Circus.*

Maggs Brothers Ltd. How could any book lover resist a shop with such a deliciously Dickensian name? In a Georgian town house in one of Mayfair's elegant squares, Maggs was established in 1853, and is one of the world's oldest and largest rare-book dealers. Shop staff act as advisors to important collectors but they are, nonetheless, friendly and helpful to all interested visitors. (⇨ Map A) ⊠ 50 Berkeley Sq., Mayfair, W1 ☎ 020/7493–7160 Ⓤ Green Park.

Simon Finch Rare Books Ltd. This unsnobbish dealer spans all periods, from Babylonian tablets to modern first editions. English history and literature, medical texts, and photography are among the eclectic specialties. The remarkably narrow, two-floor space is in the heart of Mayfair's rare-book territory, so it's convenient for a good afternoon's browse. (⇨ Map A) ⊠ 53 Maddox St., Mayfair, W1 ☎ 020/7499–0974 Ⓤ Oxford Circus.

Tim Bryars Ltd. Antiquarian books and maps, classical texts, illustrated travel books, and topographical and natural-history prints are among the specialties here. If you love first-person accounts by intrepid travelers from the 18th and 19th centuries, this is the place to look. (⇨ Map D) ⊠ 8 Cecil Ct., Charing Cross Rd., Covent Garden, WC2 ☎ 020/7836–1901 Ⓤ Leicester Sq.

CDS & RECORDS

The great megastores such as HMV and Virgin (which began as mail-order in the back pages of the music papers) that have taken over the globe started out in London. There are also specialty stores galore for cutting-edge music mixed by club DJs, and for stocking up your own collection of good old-fashioned vinyl. ■ TIP→**Before you get carried away, though, consider that CDs cost anywhere from 10% to as much as 50% more in the U.K. than they do in North America and continental Europe. So look for the kind of music you really can't find at home.** Several independent shops are clustered on Berwick Street in Soho, W1, including discount outlet Mr. CD (No. 80), the wide-ranging Sister Ray (Nos. 34–35), and Reckless Records (Nos. 26 and 30) for second-hand vinyl and CDs. Growing chain Fopp has a new flagship at 220–224 Tottenham Court Road, W1, offering good-value CDs, DVDs, records, and books, and a café-bar.

BM Soho. House, drum 'n' bass, electro, dubstep—this shop (formerly Blackmarket Records) stocks the hottest club music around. They carry some CDs, but this is really a shop for vinyl lovers. (⇨ Map D) ⊠ 25 D'Arblay St., Soho, W1 ☎ 020/7437–0478 Ⓤ Oxford Circus.

MDC Music & Movies. Relocated to the new retail development beneath the Royal Festival Hall, classical specialist MDC has expanded its stock and branched out into jazz and world music. Staff here, and at sister shop MDC Opera next to the ENO Coliseum, are knowledgeable and helpful. (⇨ Map C) ⊠ Festival Riverside, Royal Festival Hall, South Bank, SE1 ☎ 020/7620–0198 Ⓤ Waterloo.

Music & Video Exchange. This store—actually a conglomeration of several shops on Notting Hill Gate—is a convenient destination for seekers of unusual and mainstream chart music as well as classical and pop. Rare records and CDs are upstairs, the soul and dance branch is at No. 42,

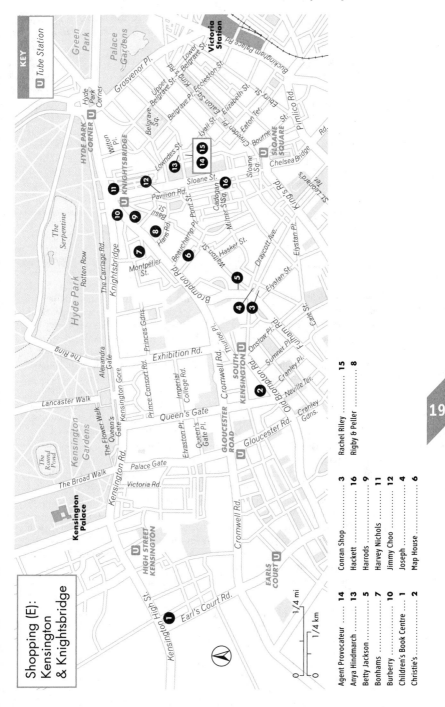

Shopping (E):
Kensington
& Knightsbridge

KEY
U Tube Station

1/4 mi

1/4 km

Agent Provocateur **14**
Anya Hindmarch **13**
Betty Jackson **5**
Bonhams **7**
Burberry **10**
Children's Book Centre **1**
Christie's **2**

Conran Shop **3**
Hackett **16**
Harrods **9**
Harvey Nichols **11**
Jimmy Choo **12**
Joseph **4**
Map House **6**

Rachel Riley **15**
Rigby & Peller **8**

19

and the classical branch is at No. 36. There are also branches in Soho and Camden. (⇨ *Map G)* ⊠*38 Notting Hill Gate, Notting Hill, W11* ☎*020/7243–8573* Ⓤ *Notting Hill Gate.*

CHINA & GLASS

English bone china is legendary, and the famous brands—Royal Doulton, Spode, Wedgwood, Minton, and the like—are still made in England, most in the Staffordshire towns around Stoke-on-Trent known as "The Potteries." The top brands are all over London, with the best selections in Harrods, Selfridges, and John Lewis. Look for unusual or hard-to-find pieces, but don't expect many bargains, and remember that sale markdowns are likely to be seconds. Regent Street's china shops sell conventional tourist favorites at tourist prices. Look for smart modern designs and unusual European tableware in the shops listed below, as well as at some of the design and houseware shops listed later in this chapter.

Emma Bridgewater. Look here for fun and funky casual plates, mugs, jugs, and breakfast tableware embellished with polka dots, hens, hearts and flowers, amusing mottoes, or matter-of-fact labels ("sugar" or "coffee"). (⇨ *Map B)* ⊠*81A Marylebone High St., Marylebone, W1* ☎*020/7486–6897* Ⓤ *Baker St. or Regents Park.*

★ **David Mellor.** Designer David Mellor has been creating modern cutlery in Sheffield stainless and silver plate since the 1950s. His cool and peaceful shop, tucked into a corner of Sloane Square, surrounds Mellor's own products with beautifully made, modern British tableware. (⇨ *Map F)* ⊠*4 Sloane Sq., Chelsea, SW1* ☎*020/7730–4259* Ⓤ *Sloane Square.*

★ **Divertimenti.** The store sells beautiful kitchenware, unusual culinary gifts—such as spoons made from polished horn—and lovely French pottery from Provence, and there is a pleasant café in the Marylebone branch. (⇨ *Maps B and F)* ⊠*33–34 Marylebone High St., Marylebone, W1* ☎*020/7935–0689* Ⓤ *Baker St. or Regents Park* ⊠*227–229 Brompton Rd., Knightsbridge, SW7* ☎*020/7581–8065* Ⓤ *Knightsbridge.*

Thomas Goode. This gigantic luxury homeware shop in the middle of Mayfair has been in business at the same location since 1827. The china, silver, crystal, and linens are either of the store's own design and manufacture or are simply the best that money can buy. Originally, customers here were mainly international royals and heads of state. The store still holds three royal warrants, but today anyone who can afford it can have their own bespoke set of china. ■TIP➜**If such luxury is beyond you, visit anyway for the shop's museum. Displays in the store include a 7-foot-tall china elephant and a sample of the plates Prince Charles designed for his own household.** (⇨ *Map A)* ⊠*19 S. Audley St., Mayfair, W1* ☎*020/7499–2823* Ⓤ *Green Park.*

CLOTHING

London is one of the world's fashion capitals, and every designer you've ever heard of is available. But it's the city's eccentric street style that gives fashion here its edge. London women may not look as soignée as French or Italian women, but many are daring and colorful fashion risk-takers. This is where the trends that show up on the European catwalks really begin.

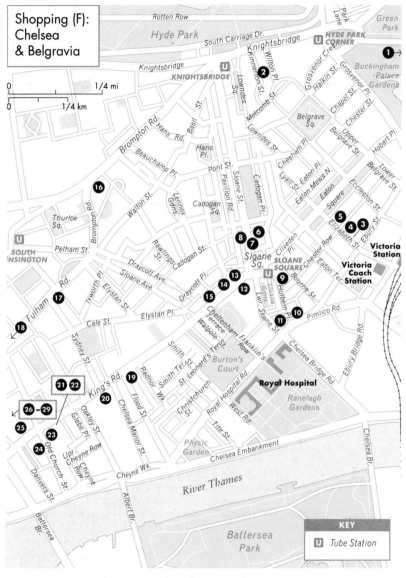

Shopping (F):
Chelsea
& Belgravia

What makes London clothes shopping so much fun—for both men and women—is that you can buy high-quality traditional British clothing, bespoke tailoring, today's best fashion labels, delicious vintage clothing, and outrageous directional street style without traveling farther than a couple of Tube stops.

ACCESSORIES   **Anya Hindmarch.** Exquisite leather bags and witty, printed canvas totes
★ are what made Hindmarch famous. Her designs are sold at Harrods and Harvey Nichols, but the real pleasure lies in her store, where you can see her complete collection of bags and shoes, and have your own photograph immortalized on a bag from a choice of sizes and styles. (⇨ *Map E*) ⊠ *15–17 Pont St., Knightsbridge, SW1* ☎ *020/7838–9177* Ⓤ *Sloane Square, Knightsbridge.*

★ **Bernstock Speirs.** Makers of colorful modern, street-smart pull-on and trilby hats, Paul Bernstock and Thelma Speirs have collected Madonna, Alicia Keys, and James Brown into their cult following. (⇨ *Map H*) ⊠ *234 Brick La., Spitalfields/East End, E2* ☎ *020/7739–7385* Ⓤ *Old St., Bethnal Green.*

Connolly. Connolly used to produce the leather for Ferraris and Aston Martins, and that heritage lives on in its deluxe motoring accessories, from sleek luggage to an espresso machine you plug into the dashboard lighter. You can also pick up less expensive, more practical items such as driving gloves or a leather-bound *London A to Z* (£65). Now owned by designer Joseph Ettedgui, the shop has broadened its range of luxurious clothing for men and women, including butter-soft leather and suede jackets. (⇨ *Map A*) ⊠ *41 Conduit St., Mayfair, W1* ☎ *020/7439–2510* Ⓤ *Oxford Circus, Bond St.*

James Lock & Co. Ltd. Need a silk opera hat, with a fitted leather box to match? A custom-made trilby or a traditional tweed flat cap? James Lock of St. James's has been making hats from its cozy little shop since 1676, and they have dressed the heads of Admiral Lord Nelson, Beau Brummel, Oscar Wilde, General de Gaulle, Jackie Onassis, Salvador Dalí, and Frank Sinatra. For bespoke hats, customers' measurements are taken on a circa 1850s contraption called a *conformateur* and kept on file forever. (⇨ *Map A*) ⊠ *6 St. James's St., St. James's, SW1* ☎ *020/7930–5849* Ⓤ *Green Park, Piccadilly Circus.*

James Smith & Sons Ltd. This has to be the world's ultimate umbrella shop, and a must for anyone interested in real Victorian London. Even if walking sticks and umbrellas are not on your shopping list, it's hard to resist a family-owned business that has traded since 1857 at the same New Oxford Street corner. This is a genuine landmark: most of the shop fittings—made by a full-time shop fitter employed by Mr. Smith—have not changed since the 19th century. (⇨ *Map C*) ⊠ *Hazelwood House, 53 New Oxford St., Bloomsbury, WC1* ☎ *020/7836–4731* Ⓤ *Tottenham Court Road, Holborn.*

★ **Lulu Guinness.** Famous for her flamboyant themed bags (memorable designs include a satin "bucket" topped with roses and an elaborately beaded red snakeskin "lips" clutch), Guinness also showcases a range of vintage-inspired vanity cases, change purses, shoes, and beauty products in this neat little shop. (⇨ *Map F*) ⊠ *3 Ellis St., Chelsea, SW1* ☎ *020/7823–4828* Ⓤ *Sloane Square.*

Shopping (G):
Notting Hill

KEY

U Tube Station

Mulberry. This is Britain's entry in the luxury and fashion leathergoods market. Mulberry's top-quality, slightly rustic handbags have been hot fashion property for several years now, but the company also makes belts, wallets, and luggage, as well as a collection of updated classic clothing for men and women. The boutique-size store at St. Christopher's Place stocks accessories only. (⇨ Map A) ⊠11–12 Gees Ct., St. Christopher's Pl., Mayfair, W1 ☎020/7493–2546 U Bond St. ⊠41–42 New Bond St., Mayfair, W1 ☎020/7491–3900 U Bond St. ⊠171–175 Brompton Rd., Knightsbridge, SW3 ☎020/7838–1411 U Knightsbridge ⊠199 Westbourne Grove, Notting Hill, W11 ☎020/7229–1635 U Notting Hill Gate.

Philip Treacy. Treacy's magnificent hats are annual showstoppers on Ladies Day at the Royal Ascot races and regularly grace the pages of *Harper's Bazaar.* Part Mad Hatter, part Cecil Beaton, Treacy's creations always guarantee a grand entrance. In addition to the extravagant confections custom-made in the atelier, ready-to-wear hats and bags are for sale in the shop. (⇨ Map F) ⊠69 Elizabeth St., Pimlico and Victoria, SW1 ☎020/7730–3992 U Victoria.

★ **Swaine Adeney Brigg.** This shop has been selling practical supplies for country pursuits since 1750. Not just for the horsey set, the store has golf umbrellas, walking sticks, and hip flasks—all beautifully crafted and ingenious. On a frosty morning, you shouldn't be without the

19

Bespoke London

Having anything made to order used to be an upper-class distinction in London. One had one's tailor, one's milliner, one's dressmaker, and so forth. Things are more democratic these days, but you can still have a remarkable number of things, besides Savile Row suits and shirts, custom-made.

Dress bespoke top to toe and inside out with undies from the Queen's corsetiere, **Rigby & Peller**; hats from **Philip Treacy** and **James Lock**; suits and shirts—for both men and women—from **Gieves and Hawkes,** **Ozwald Boateng, Kilgour,** or **Turnbull & Asser.** Finish the look with bespoke or handmade shoes from **Caroline Groves** or **John Lobb**; an umbrella or walking stick from **James Smith & Sons**; and a bespoke briefcase from **Swaine Adeney Brigg.** The ultimate bespoke service may be the one at **Thomas Goode,** where they'll help you design your own china pattern and produce a fine bone china service to your specifications. If all this is a bit traditional for your taste, have an old suit transformed into a cutting-edge garment of your choice at **Junky Styling.**

umbrella with a slim tipple-holder flask secreted inside the stick. Herbert Johnson, hatter, is housed downstairs. (⇨ *Map A)* ⊠ *54 St. James's St., St. James's, SW1* ☎ *020/7409–7277* Ⓤ *Piccadilly Circus.*

CHILDREN'S
WEAR

British children's wear has never been a bargain, and nothing has changed there. But since Britain has become more integrated with Europe, kids' gear is more fashionable. Gone are the days when young London mums asked their friends to bring home French, Italian, or American clothes from their vacations abroad. Several of the lower-price adult chains, including H&M, Next, Monsoon, and Zara, have cheap and cheerful children's lines. In select Jigsaw branches, Jigsaw Junior offers classics with a twist for girls. London parents love John Lewis for fair prices and quality goods. But if you're looking for something more than run of the mill, expect to pay for it.

Daisy & Tom. Cool kids love this magical King's Road emporium. While they're riding the carousel, cuddling soft toys, or having a haircut, parents can be checking out high-fashion children's togs from Kenzo, Polo, and the shop's own good-quality, reasonably priced label. Shoe shopping, for newborns to 10-year-olds, can actually be fun, and the colorful, packed bookshop has got to make a reader out of the most reluctant child. (⇨ *Map F)* ⊠ *181–183 King's Rd., Chelsea, SW3* ☎ *020/7352–5000* Ⓤ *Sloane Square.*

Rachel Riley. Looking for traditional English style on a small scale? Riley gives classics such as duffel coats, smocked dresses, Mary Jane shoes, and flannel pajamas a fresh modern spin. The children's clothes are complemented by a collection for mothers with a similarly nostalgic edge. Prices are high, but not prohibitive. (⇨ *Map E)* ⊠ *14 Pont St., Knightsbridge, SW1* ☎ *020/7259–5969* Ⓤ *Knightsbridge* ⊠ *82 Marylebone High St., Marylebone, W1* ☎ *020/7935–7007* Ⓤ *Baker St.*

Shopping (H):
Spitalfields &
the East End

Trotters. Trotters has the latest lines for parents who want to dress their darlings in traditional styles. The shop stocks trendy kids' labels and caters from top to toe (there's a hairdressing service, plus shoes). There are also videos, toys, and books to keep tempers cool. It's at the Sloane Square end of King's Road near the big Peter Jones branch of the John Lewis Department Store group. (⇨ Map F) ⊠34 King's Rd., Chelsea, SW3 ☎020/7259–9620 Ⓤ Sloane Square.

GENERAL **Aquascutum.** Known for its trenchcoats (worn by Churchill, no less), Aquascutum also offers clothing for men and women influenced by traditional British style, including a catwalk collection launched in 2005 playing on classic shapes. Now that this has been embraced by the fashion world, the house designers have turned their attention to revitalizing the less expensive (but certainly not cheap!) main line. The brand is also available at Harrods, Selfridges, and other big department stores around town. (⇨ Map A) ⊠100 Regent St., Soho, W1 ☎020/7675–8200 Ⓤ Piccadilly Circus.

b Store. On the end of Savile Row, b Store couldn't be farther away in terms of style from the traditional tailors down the street. Head here for cutting-edge pieces from avant-garde London designers such as Peter Jensen and Camilla Staerk, plus the store's quirky Buddhahood shoes.

19

(⇨ Map A) ⊠ 24A Savile Row, Mayfair, W1 ☎ 020/7734–6846 Ⓤ Bond St., Oxford Circus.

Burberry. The store tries to evoke an English heritage environment, with mahogany closets and stacks of neatly folded merchandise adorned with the trademark "Burberry Check" tartan. In addition to being seen on those famous raincoat linings, the tartan graces scarves, umbrellas, and hats. If you're up for a trek, there's a huge factory outlet in Hackney with clothing for men, women, and children, as well as accessories, at half price and less. *(⇨ Maps A and E) ⊠ 2 Brompton Rd., Knightsbridge, SW1 ☎ 020/7968–0000 Ⓤ Knightsbridge ⊠ 21–23 New Bond St., Mayfair, W1 ☎ 020/7968–0000 Ⓤ Piccadilly Circus ⊠ Burberry Factory Shop, 29–53 Chatham Pl., East End, E9 ☎ 020/8328–4287 Ⓤ Commuter rail: Hackney Central.*

Brora. The taste temperature is cool and conservative in this cashmere emporium for men, women, and kids. There are dressed-up camisoles, sweaters and cardigans, adorable baby ensembles, plus noncashmere items such as picnic blankets and scarves. Prices are surprisingly reasonable for the quality of the material. There are branches in Notting Hill and Marylebone. *(⇨ Map F) ⊠ 344 King's Rd., Chelsea, SW3 ☎ 020/7352–3697 Ⓤ Sloane Square.*

★ **Dover Street Market.** Visiting this six-floor emporium isn't just about buying; with its theatrical displays and eccentric mix of merchandise, it is as fascinating as any gallery. The creation of Comme des Garçons' Rei Kawakubo, it showcases all of the label's collections for men and women alongside other lofty designers such as Lanvin, Alaïa, and exclusive Japanese lines, plus curiosities including antique taxidermy, iconic 20th-century furniture, avant-garde art books, and vintage couture. You never know what you will find, which is half the fun. ■ TIP→**An outpost of the Rose Bakery on the top floor makes a handy pit stop.** *(⇨ Map A) ⊠ 17–18 Dover St., Mayfair, W1 ☎ 020/7518–0680 Ⓤ Green Park.*

Egg. Almost hidden in a residential mews a short walk from Harvey Nichols, this shop is the brainchild of Maureen Doherty, once Issey Miyake's right-hand person. She has described her customer as someone who likes clothes but is bored with fashion. Minimalist, unstructured styles for men and women in natural fabrics, such as silk, cashmere, and antique cotton, have an artisanal quality. The shop is a former Victorian dairy, and garments are casually hung on hooks or strewn over simple chairs in the simple, white, two-floor space. Unusual ceramics and jewelry are also on display. *(⇨ Map F) ⊠ 36 Kinnerton St., Knightsbridge, SW1 ☎ 020/7235–9315 Ⓤ Knightsbridge.*

Jaeger. A real London classic, Jaeger has been making conservative but stylish clothing for men and women since the mid-19th century. It's particularly good for coats, suits, and separates. Founded around a Victorian "scientific" theory about the healthy properties of animal fibers (wool, camel's hair, silk, vicuña), the label has long since embraced a more modern approach. But its woolens and silks remain very collectible. There are several London branches. The King's Road store carries both the men's and women's lines. *(⇨ Map F) ⊠ 145 King's Rd., Chelsea, SW3 ☎ 020/7352–1122 Ⓤ Sloane Square.*

★ **Junky Styling.** Gwen Stefani is a fan of outrageous designers Annika Sanders and Kerry Seager, who create "deconstructed," limited-edition clothing. They started by recycling traditional suits and shirts into wild clubbing outfits for themselves, and the business grew from there. The highly original (and eco-friendly) garments, for both men and women, are funky but retain the sophistication of their tailored origins. Their one-off Wardrobe Surgery service will recycle your old threads into something utterly original. (⇨ *Map H)* ⊠ *12 Dray Walk, Old Truman Brewery, 91–95 Brick La., Spitalfields/East End, E1* ☎ *020/7247– 1883* Ⓤ *Old St., Bethnal Green.*

★ **The Laden Showroom.** Victoria Beckham and Noel Gallagher are among the celebs who regularly check out new talent at this East End show-room for young designers. The store retails the work of more than 45 new designers, some selling no more than 12 items—so the look you find is likely to be exclusive. Prices are relatively reasonable: nothing is over £100. (⇨ *Map H)* ⊠ *103 Brick La., Spitalfields/East End, E1* ☎ *020/7247–2431* Ⓤ *Aldgate East.*

Margaret Howell. These quintessentially English clothes have a nostal-gic feel while managing to look utterly contemporary. Howell mixes impeccable British tailoring and traditional fabrics (Iinen, cashmere, tweed) with relaxed modern cuts. The designer also has a workwear-inspired line produced in collaboration with Japanese denim brand Edwin, and recent ventures with Anglepoise, Erco, and several other manufacturers have brought the Margaret Howell look to contem-porary housewares as well. (⇨ *Map B)* ⊠ *34 Wigmore St., Soho, W1* ☎ *020/7009–9009* Ⓤ *Oxford Circus* ⊠ *111 Fulham Rd., Chelsea, SW3* ☎ *020/7591–2255* Ⓤ *South Kensington.*

★ **Paul Smith.** British classics with colorful and irreverent twists define Paul Smith's collections for both women and men. Beautifully tailored men's suits in exceptional fabrics might sport flamboyant linings or unusual detailing. Women's lines tend to take familiar and traditional British ideas and turn them on their heads with humor and color. Accessories, including wallets, scarves, diaries—and even a soccer ball—in his sig-nature rainbow stripes make great gifts. There are several branches, including a Notting Hill mansion at 120–122 Kensington Park Road, W11; a small, funky outpost at 13 Park Street, SE1, near Borough Mar-ket; and a vintage furniture shop in Mayfair. (⇨ *Map D)* ⊠ *40–44 Floral St., Covent Garden, WC2* ☎ *020/7379–7133* Ⓤ *Covent Garden.*

★ **Topshop.** This London standby has successfully made the transition from what the British call "cheap and cheerful" to a genuine fashion hotspot at affordable prices. Clothing is geared to the younger end of the market (although women who are young at heart will find plenty of wearable clothing here) and the aim is to copy catwalk trends as fast as possible. Every season, a changing selection of front-of-the-pack young designers do small collections, and buyers cruise the end-of-term design shows at Central St. Martins College of Art and Design for the next big thing. Innovations, such as personal style advisors and an on-site "blow-dry bar," are constantly being introduced. Topman brings the same fashion approach to clothing for younger men. (⇨ *Map B)* ⊠ *214 Oxford St., Soho, W1* ☎ *020/7636–7700* Ⓤ *Oxford Circus.*

19

MENSWEAR   Except for Jigsaw, all the stores listed in General Clothing have good selections of menswear, especially the sublime Paul Smith. The department stores listed in this chapter have good menswear departments, but Selfridges and Liberty deserve special mentions for interesting designer offerings. London's Savile Row tailors are still the spot where a man orders a bespoke suit once he has really "arrived." But with European designers like Armani and the moderately priced Emporio Armani making inroads, styles, even in this bastion of British traditionalism, are noticeably loosening up. Ozwald Boateng, with his sharp designs, and colorful suitings and linings, is typical of the new wave of bespoke tailors. Those with more flash than cash should hotfoot to the trendsetting fashion chains: Topman, Reiss, and Zara.

★ **Bamford & Sons.** The men's and boys' wear at Bamford & Sons combines the British heritage of tailoring and fabrics with a suave modernity. Dashing city wear, romantically nonchalant country clothes, plus fine leather and cashmere accessories are all available. There is also a small women's collection. The Sloane Square store houses the Daylesford organic café in the basement. (⇨ *Map G)* ⊠ *The Old Workshop, 79–81 Ledbury Rd., Notting Hill, W11* ☎ *020/7792–9350* Ⓤ *Notting Hill Gate* ⊠ *31 Sloane Sq., Chelsea, SW1* ☎ *020/7881–8010* Ⓤ *Sloane Square.*

A Butcher of Distinction. This laid-back store is for men who are in tune with fashion but don't want to look like they're trying too hard. A Butcher stocks new British labels, such as Rushmoor and Clerk & Teller, alongside classics like Polo and Tricker's traditional shoes. Old tiles and meat hooks keep with the theme. (⇨ *Map H)* ⊠ *11 Dray Walk, Old Truman Brewery, East End, E1* ☎ *020/7770–6111* Ⓤ *Liverpool St.*

Gieves and Hawkes. One of the grandest of grand old names for London bespoke tailoring, this company made its name outfitting Britain's Royal Military officers and still supplies bespoke military uniforms. An alternative that costs almost a quarter of the price, personal tailoring is a six- to eight-week, made-to-measure service. Before you rush out for a bargain, consider that prices for a two-piece suit start from £795. The ready-to-wear Gieves line is a more affordable option. (⇨ *Map A)* ⊠ *1 Savile Row, Mayfair, W1* ☎ *020/7434–2001* Ⓤ *Piccadilly Circus.*

Hackett. Started as a posh thrift shop, Hackett once recycled cricket flannels, hunting pinks, Oxford brogues, and similar British wear. Now it makes its own attire, and it has become a genuine—and very good—gentlemen's outfitter. (⇨ *Map E)* ⊠ *Main store: 137–138 Sloane St., Knightsbridge, SW1* ☎ *020/7730–3331* Ⓤ *Sloane Square.*

Kilgour. Classic Savile Row tailoring has been updated with a luxury, ready-to-wear brand launched in 1998. The shop defines the essence of "Savile Row chic" as "lean shoulders, clean chest definition, and waisted silhouette" and does its best to provide it. Bespoke services include equestrian clothes and shirts as well as suits, and an "entry level bespoke" to ease customers into the concept. (⇨ *Map A)* ⊠ *8 Savile Row, Mayfair, W1* ☎ *020/7734–6905* Ⓤ *Piccadilly Circus.*

★ **Ozwald Boateng.** Ozwald Boateng's made-to-measure suits with their bright colors (even the more conservative suits sport bright silk linings), luxurious fabrics, and leading-edge styling used to be worn by rock and clubland luminaries. But the London scene has loosened up considerably since he opened his Savile Row atelier, and now any chap with enough alpha male confidence to cut a dash covets a Boateng (pronouned Bwa-teng) suit. If your wallet doesn't reach as far as bespoke, check out the ready-to-wear collection, along with accessories and scent, on Vigo Street. *(⇨ Map A)* ✉ *12A Savile Row, Mayfair, W1* ☏ *0870/777–1377* Ⓤ *Piccadilly Circus* ✉ *9 Vigo St., Mayfair, W1* ☏ *0870/777–1377* Ⓤ *Piccadilly Circus.*

Thomas Pink. The firm still makes some of the best dress shirts around, for both men and women. Bespoke shirts for men are available at the Jermyn Street branch. *(⇨ Map A)* ✉ *85 Jermyn St., St. James's, SW1* ☏ *020/7930–6364* Ⓤ *Green Park, Piccadilly Circus.*

★ **Turnbull & Asser.** This is *the* custom shirtmaker, dripping exclusivity from every fiber. Eighteen separate measurements are taken and the cloth, woven to their specifications, comes in 1,000 different patterns—the cottons feel as good as silk. The first order must be for a minimum of six shirts, from £150 each. There are less expensive, though still exquisite, ready-to-wear shirts available as well as jackets, cashmeres, suits, ties, and accessories. *(⇨ Map A)* ✉ *71–72 Jermyn St., St. James's, W1* ☏ *020/7808–3000* Ⓤ *Piccadilly Circus.*

WOMEN'S WEAR
As one of the world's great fashion capitals, London has shops to dress you in style—whether your style is rummage or royal, trendy or traditional. High-street chains like Miss Selfridges, Topshop, New Look, and All Saints take aim at the young, wild, and slim; Hobbs, Whistles, and Jaeger provide updated classics for the more sophisticated; and fashion-oriented department stores—Harvey Nichols, Harrods, Selfridges, Liberty, Fenwick—cater to women of all ages and tastes. The hottest names on the London catwalks have their headquarters here—Alexander McQueen's flagship store is at 4–5 Old Bond Street, Mayfair, W1, and, nearby, Stella McCartney's collections are showcased in a town house at 30 Bruton Street.

★ **Agent Provocateur.** Created by Vivienne Westwood's son, these shops purvey sexy, naughty-but-nice lingerie in gorgeous fabrics and lace. Locations say a lot, and this retailer has branches in the almost-red-light area of Soho, around the corner from the Bank of England, and in stylish familyland Notting Hill. Selections are available in Selfridges and at Heathrow's Terminal 4 as well. *(⇨ Map E)* ✉ *16 Pont St., Knightsbridge, SW1* ☏ *020/7235–0229* Ⓤ *Knightsbridge, Sloane Square.*

★ **Betty Jackson.** A low-key fixture on the London fashion scene since the early 1980s, Betty Jackson uses beautiful fabrics and judicious layering and shaping to create modern yet timeless clothes that manage to look wonderful on women of any age. Her knitwear and jackets have a subtle Britishness. *(⇨ Map E)* ✉ *311 Brompton Rd., Brompton Cross, SW3* ☏ *020/7589–7884* Ⓤ *South Kensington.*

★ **Browns.** This shop—actually a series of small shops on South Molton Street—was a pioneer designer boutique in the 1970s and continues to talent spot the newest and best around. You may find the windows showcasing the work of top graduates from this year's student shows or displaying well-established designers such as Marni, Chloé,

19

Juyna Watanabe, Yves Saint Laurent, Dries Van Noten, or Anne Demeulemeester. The men's store at No. 23 has a similar selection, while Browns Focus, across the street at Nos. 38–39, showcases young, hip designs and denim. Browns also has its own label, a bargain outlet at No. 50, and a designer bridal boutique at 59 Brook Street. *(⇨ Map A)* ⊠ *23–27 S. Molton St., Mayfair, W1* ☎ *020/7514–0000* Ⓤ *Bond St.*

The Cross. This ultrachic boutique has something for everyone. Downstairs is a jumble of

laid-back daywear, glamorous evening dresses, and accessories by an eclectic mix of British and international designers, including Temperley, Gharani Strok, Missoni, and Jenny Dyer. At ground level are pretty toiletries, embroidered Indian slippers, and the kinds of toys and kiddie clothes that Gwyneth's little Apple might be playing with and wearing. Cross The Road at No. 139 sells homewares and inexpensive gifts such as decorative tea lights and print shower caps. *(⇨ Map G)* ⊠ *141 Portland Rd., Notting Hill, W11* ☎ *020/7727–6760* Ⓤ *Notting Hill Gate.*

★ **Jigsaw.** Popular with women in their twenties through forties, Jigsaw sells separates that don't sacrifice quality to fashion. There's an accessories shop nearby at 49 South Molton Street, and other branches are around town. Kids get in on the act, too, with their own line, Jigsaw Junior. *(⇨ Map A)* ⊠ *126–127 New Bond St., Mayfair, W1* ☎ *020/7491–4484* Ⓤ *Bond St.*

Joseph. Movie stars, models, and well-heeled women have frequented Joseph's many Knightsbridge and Chelsea shops for years. Known for a kind of luxe minimalism, the designs are simple, chic, and executed in beautiful fabrics. In particular, there are stylish women who swear by Joseph's bottom-flattering trousers. This, the flagship store, also sells catwalk labels, such as Prada and Chloé, and features a fabulous designer shoe salon in the basement. There's a menswear shop around the corner at 74 Sloane Avenue and a sale shop at 53 King's Road (though much of the stock there is several seasons old). *(⇨ Map E)* ⊠ *77 Fulham Rd., Brompton Cross, SW3* ☎ *020/7823–9500* Ⓤ *South Kensington.*

★ **Koh Samui.** Named for an exclusive Thai resort, this shop stocks designer clothes for the kind of young, elegant woman that thinks nothing of flying there for a week's detox at the drop of a hat. On the rails are the likes of Marc Jacobs, Dries Van Noten, and Balenciaga, plus hot young design talent and select vintage pieces. *(⇨ Map D)* ⊠ *65–67 Monmouth St., Covent Garden, WC2* ☎ *020/7240–4280* Ⓤ *Covent Garden.*

Nicole Farhi. Busy women willing to invest in quality value Nicole Farhi's softly tailored, functional dresses and separates. The style manages to be contemporary yet timeless, making these standbys in many a working-woman's wardrobe. The store has numerous locations around the

CLOSE UP

Vintage London

The trend for vintage clothing on both sides of the Atlantic shows no sign of letting up, and the British, with their love of theatrical style, have embraced it with particular gusto. As well as a boom in specialist shops all over town, many boutiques have integrated vintage items into their stock. Liberty, Selfridges, and Topshop all have vintage sections. You can find throwaway retro from the recent past at Camden Market or on the fringes of Portobello Road and Brick Lane/Spitalfields. Here are some of the best:

Absolute Vintage is a warehouse of handpicked items from the 1930s through the 1980s, including more than 1,000 pairs of shoes, arranged on a rainbow wall of color. R&B star Kelis is reportedly a fan. Blondie, around the corner at 114–118 Commercial Street, is the "boutique" branch, selling an edited selection of items. ⊠ *15 Hanbury St., Spitalfields/East End, E1* ☎ *020/7247–3883* Ⓤ *Whitechapel, Liverpool St.*

Beyond Retro stocks 10,000 vintage and retro items for men and women. From cowboy boots to bowling shirts to prom dresses, they've got the largest collection of American Retro in the United Kingdom. Kiera Knightley and Kylie Minogue have been spotted here. ⊠ *110–112 Cheshire St., Spitalfields/East End, E2* ☎ *020/7613–3636* Ⓤ *Old St., Bethnal Green.*

Mary Moore Vintage is owned by sculptor Henry Moore's daughter, who turned a lifetime's passion for collecting into this little shop full of, basically, her own wardrobe. The dresses, in particular, are fabulous (most are around £300–£600). ⊠ *5 Clarendon Cross, Holland Park/Notting Hill, W11* ☎ *020/7229–5678* Ⓤ *Holland Park.*

One takes the concept of individual style a step farther, combining elements of two or more vintage garments to create an utterly unique piece. There is also a selection of unaltered, immaculate designer pieces by the likes of Chanel and Valentino. ⊠ *30 Ledbury Rd., Notting Hill, W11* ☎ *020/7221–5300* Ⓤ *Notting Hill Gate.*

Orsini is a tiny but choice Kensington boutique. Eveningwear with Hollywood-style glamour is the trademark here, with clothes from the 1920s to the 1970s. ⊠ *76 Earls Court Rd., Kensington, W8* ☎ *020/7937–2903* Ⓤ *Earls Court or High St. Kensington.*

Rokit consists of two shops along Brick Lane that stock everything from handbags and ball gowns to jeans, military, and Western wear. Magazine and rock stylists love it. There are also branches in Camden and Covent Garden. ⊠ *101–107 Brick La., Spitalfields/East End, E1* ☎ *020/7375–3864* Ⓤ *Aldgate East.*

Steinberg & Tolkien is a King's Road institution with two packed floors of genuine vintage haute couture. There's very good—and pricey—designer costume jewelry and the boxy plastic handbags that were ultrachic in the 1950s. ⊠ *193 King's Rd., Chelsea, SW3* ☎ *020/7376–3660* Ⓤ *Sloane Sq.*

Virginia, Virginia Baker's collection of antique and vintage clothing, may be the best in London. Dresses, hats, and accessories from early Victorian (circa 1850) to the early 1930s are available. These are wearable collectors' items and priced accordingly. The shop is kept dark to protect the fabrics—ring the bell to enter. ⊠ *98 Portland Rd., Clarendon Cross, Holland Park/Notting Hill, W11* ☎ *020/7727–9908* Ⓤ *Holland Park.*

19

city; the New Bond Street store sells clothes for both men and women, but the full men's collection is available at the Floral Street branch. *(⇨Map A) ⊠158 New Bond St., Mayfair, W1 ☎020/7499–8368* Ⓤ *Bond St. ☞Men's Collection: ⊠11 Floral St., Covent Garden, WC2 ☎020/7497–8713* Ⓤ *Covent Garden.*

Rigby & Peller. Those who love luxury lingerie shop here for brands like Prima Donna and Aubade, as well as R & P's own line. If the right fit eludes you, and you fancy being fitted by the Queen's corsetiere, have a bra made-to-measure (from £250). Most of the young royal and aristo women buy here, not just because the store holds the royal appointment, but because the quality and service are excellent and much friendlier than you might expect. *(⇨Map E) ⊠2 Hans Rd., Knightsbridge, SW3 ☎020/7589–9293* Ⓤ *Knightsbridge ⊠22A Conduit St., Mayfair, W1 ☎020/7491–2200* Ⓤ *Oxford St.*

Vivienne Westwood. This is where it all started: the Pompadour-punk ball gowns, Lady Hamilton vest coats, and foppish landmark getups are the core of Westwood's first boutique in Chelsea, where you can still buy ready-to-wear (mainly the more casual Anglomania diffusion line) under the sign of the spinning clock. The designer still represents the apex of high-style British couture. Head for the Conduit Street flagship for all the collections. The small Davies Street boutique sells only the Gold Label and made-to-measure couture. *(⇨Map A) ⊠6 Davies St., Mayfair, W1 ☎020/7629–3757* Ⓤ *Bond St. ☞Original boutique: ⊠430 King's Rd., Chelsea, SW3 ☎020/7352–6551* Ⓤ *Sloane Square or Earl's Court ⊠44 Conduit St., Mayfair, W1 ☎020/7439–1109* Ⓤ *Bond St.*

DESIGN

Britain has always encouraged design and applied arts. London, with its many design colleges, is a magnet for artisans and craftspeople in glass, textiles, jewelry making, ceramics, metal, leather, and woodwork. Open-studio weekends (usually late May/early June and late November/early December) allow you to buy direct from makers. Two of the most central are Clerkenwell Green (⊕www.cga.org.uk) and Cockpit Arts (⊕www.cockpitarts.com).

Contemporary Applied Arts. Expect to see quite a range of work by designers and craftspeople. Regular shows and exhibitions display everything from glassware and jewelry to furniture and lighting. *(⇨Map B) ⊠2 Percy St., Bloomsbury, W1 ☎020/7436–2344* Ⓤ *Tottenham Court Rd.*

★ **Contemporary Ceramics.** The gallery of the Craft Potters Association displays the work of Britain's best ceramic artists. Here you'll find a wide spectrum of pottery, from beautifully tactile and practical housewares to avant-garde sculpture. A good selection of books on the subject is also available. *(⇨Map D) ⊠7 Marshall St., Soho, W1 ☎020/7437–7605* Ⓤ *Oxford Circus.*

Designers Guild. Tricia Guild's colorful modern fabrics, wallpapers, paints, furniture, and bed linens have inspired several decades worth of home owners and apartment dwellers, and her soft-furnishings book has taught many a budget-conscious do-it-yourselfer how to reupholster a sofa or make lined draperies. The shop also stocks contemporary furniture, wallpapers, and home accessories by other designers. (⇨ *Map F)* ✉ *267–271 and 275–277 King's Rd., Chelsea, SW3* ☎ *020/7351– 5775* Ⓤ *Sloane Square.*

The Glass Art Gallery/London Glassblowing Workshop. Visitors to Peter Layton's workshop can feel the heat of molten glass as they watch creative glassblowers and designers at work. In addition to Layton, a team of glassblowers produce their own work for sale or commission at the studio. For £250 you can sign up for a full-day lesson in glass-blowing. In addition to domestic pieces, Layton's glasswork includes monumental sculpture and architectural commissions. ■ **TIP→Other craftspeople, printmakers, designers, and artists work in the industrial area known as Leathermarket, south of London Bridge, so it's worth having a nose around to see what you can find.** (⇨ *Map C)* ✉ *7 The Leathermarket, Weston St., South Bank, SE1* ☎ *020/7403–2800* Ⓤ *London Bridge.*

★ **Lesley Craze Gallery.** This serene gallery displays jewelry by some 100 young designers from around the world, with a strong British bias (fashion editors source upcoming talent here for their glossy spreads). In the textiles room, you'll find unusual and colorful handmade scarves, bags, and ties. Prices are remarkably reasonable. (⇨ *Map C)* ✉ *33–35A Clerkenwell Green, East End, EC1* ☎ *020/7608–0393* Ⓤ *Farringdon.*

Linley. Is Viscount David Linley really, as some say, one of today's finest furniture designers? Or is it simply that he's the Queen's only nephew? It doesn't really matter. What does is that his work in wood is beautiful, covetable, and definitely the heirlooms of the future. His desks, chairs, and chests of drawers have one foot in the 18th century, another in the 21st. His sculptural furniture is often decorated with marquetry or parquetry—patterns or pictures worked in fine veneers. The large pieces are suitably expensive, but small desk accessories and objets d'art are also available. (⇨ *Map F)* ✉ *60 Pimlico Rd., Pimlico and Victoria, SW1* ☎ *020/7730–7300* Ⓤ *Sloane Sq.* ✉ *46 Albemarle St., Mayfair, W1* ☎ *020/7290–1410* Ⓤ *Green Park.*

Oxo Tower. Many varied artisans have to pass rigorous selection procedures to set up in the prime riverside workshops where they make, display, and sell their work. The workshops are glass-walled, and you're welcome to explore, even if you're just browsing. You can commission pieces, too—anything from a cushion cover to custom-made jewelry, furniture, and sculpture. There are around 30 studios, spread over two floors, as well as exhibitions at Bargehouse and at *the.gallery@oxo.* The Oxo Tower Brasserie & Restaurant on the top floor is noisy and overpriced, but with its fantastic view across the river, it's worth popping up for a drink. There's also a public terrace where you can take in the view. (⇨ *Map C)* ✉ *Bargehouse St., South Bank, SE1* ☎ *020/7401– 2255* Ⓤ *Southwark.*

Themes & Variations. The name encapsulates the selection of styles and items found here, ranging from postwar to new-wave furniture, lighting, and decorative arts. Operated as a gallery, with changing exhibitions, you may find '50s and '70s furniture by named and unknown designers, surreal stools and ceramics by Fornasetti, contemporary British pieces by Tom Dixon or Mark Brazier-Jones, or a selection of Georg Jensen

19

silver jewelry. If you have a modernist space to fill, visit this gallery to wallow in the genre. *(⇨ Map G)* ⊠*231 Westbourne Grove, Notting Hill, W11* ☎*020/7727–5531* Ⓤ *Notting Hill Gate.*

FOOD HALLS & STORES

London excels at posh nosh, and the selection has gotten even bigger with European integration. The Food Halls at Harrods are internationally famous, almost as much for the beautiful displays and ceramic-tile ceilings as for the packaged teas, chocolates, biscuits, fresh foods, and game. Don't miss the legendary fish displays. Selfridges is less daunting but more international in its selection. There are ingredients from around the world and a good kosher department—their man-size salt-beef sandwiches are a must. Marks & Spencer has made such a name for its food in recent years that it has opened a chain of M&S Simply Food stores. Look for them everywhere. Their packaged shortbreads, chocolates, and bottled sauces are great take-home gifts.

Berry Bros. & Rudd. Londoners are relatively well-informed about wine. There are wine shops in every shopping district, and all the supermarkets sell high-quality selections. So a wine shop has to be really special to rise above the rest. This one is and it does. A family-run wine business since 1698, "BBR" stores its vintage bottles and casks in vaulted cellars that are more than 300 years old. The staff is extremely knowledgeable and the level of service simply unsurpassed. *(⇨ Map A)* ⊠*3 St. James's St., St. James's, SW1* ☎*020/7396–9600* ⊕*www.bbr.com* Ⓤ *Green Park.*

Charbonnel et Walker. Britain's master chocolatier since 1875, this Mayfair shop specializes in traditional sweets (violet and rose petal creams, for example) and was serving up beautifully packaged, high-quality chocolates long before most of the fashionable new brands appeared. ■**TIP→Some of their "drawing room" boxes are real works of art, and their drinking chocolate—coarsely grated fine chocolate in a tin—is worth carrying home in a suitcase.** *(⇨ Map A)* ⊠*1 the Royal Arcade, 28 Old Bond St., Mayfair, W1* ☎*020/7491–0939* Ⓤ *Green Park.*

The Chocolate Society. You can taste as well as buy at the Chocolate Society's shop—and you don't even have to be a member. Hot chocolate served in their small café contains 40 grams of pure chocolate. In addition to a selection of bonbons, truffles, and bars, the shop sells the Society's brownies, ice cream, and milk shakes. Yum. *(⇨ Map F)* ⊠*36 Elizabeth St., Pimlico and Victoria, SW1* ☎*020/7259–9222* Ⓤ *Victoria, Sloane Square.*

FodorśChoice
★
Fortnum & Mason. Although it's the Queen's grocer, this store is, paradoxically, the most egalitarian of gift shops; it has plenty of irresistibly packaged luxury foods, stamped with the gold BY APPOINTMENT crest, for less than £5. Try the teas, preserves, blocks of chocolate, tins of pâté, or a box of Duchy Originals oatcakes—like Paul Newman, the Prince of Wales has gone into the retail food business. Fortnum's celebrated its tercentenary in 2007 with a major refurbishment—although the impeccably mannered staff still sport traditional tailcoats. The ground floor food hall has expanded into the basement, which also houses a sleek wine bar. The rest of the store is devoted

to upscale gifts, toiletries, and housewares, and there are three more restaurants to choose from. (⇨ *Map A)* ⊠ *181 Piccadilly, St. James's, W1* ☎ *020/7734–8040* Ⓤ *Piccadilly Circus.*

L'Artisan du Chocolat. Praised by top chefs Gordon Ramsay and Heston Blumenthal and pronounced the best chocolate shop in the United Kingdom by *The Guardian*, L'Artisan raises chocolate to an art form with its abstract "Couture" chocolates, infused with fruits, nuts, and spices (including such exotic flavorings as szechuan pepper and tobacco). Leave the kiddies at home; this shop is total wish fulfillment for grown-up chocolate lovers. (⇨ *Map F)* ⊠ *89 Lower Sloane St., Chelsea, SW1* ☎ *020/7824–8365* Ⓤ *Sloane Square.*

Neal's Yard Dairy. NYD favors a traditional approach to small independent British cheese makers. Just outside a cobbled "yard" containing funky cafés and organic shops, the small premises are packed with cheeses whose names evoke the countryside, such as Shropshire Blue, Lincolnshire Poacher, and Sussex Golden Cross. (⇨ *Map D)* ⊠ *17 Shorts Gardens, Covent Garden, WC2* ☎ *020/7240–5700* Ⓤ *Covent Garden.*

★ **Paxton & Whitfield.** This is the most venerable of London's cheese shops, in business for more than 200 years. The fabulous aromas come from some of the world's greatest cheeses stacked on the shelves—in rounds, in boxes, and on straw, but always ready to be tasted. Whichever cheese is in season and ripe for eating is on display for sampling, and the staff is ready to help you pick the best wine to serve with it. (⇨ *Map A)* ⊠ *93 Jermyn St., St. James's, SW1* ☎ *020/7930–0259* Ⓤ *Piccadilly Circus.*

★ **Rococo.** Chantal Coady writes, eats, and lives for chocolate. Vegetable fats are forbidden words in this cocoa fantasyland, and there are interesting and offbeat additions to the main chocolate recipe, such as essence of Earl Grey, thyme, pepper, and chili (remarkably tasty). There's also a branch in Marylebone. (⇨ *Map F)* ⊠ *321 King's Rd., Chelsea, SW3* ☎ *020/7352–5857* Ⓤ *Sloane Square.* ⊠ *45 Marylebone High St., Marylebone, W1* ☎ *020/7935–7780* Ⓤ *Baker St.*

★ **The Spice Shop.** Birgit Erath set up a spice stall on Portobello Road as a weekend sideline while studying for a business degree in London. By the time she graduated, she had such a good business she opened her shop nearby. That was in the 1990s, and she hasn't looked back. Sourcing spices from all over the world, Birgit also creates her own blends and spice mixes. You can find any spice you can name among her usual stock of 2,500 products. (⇨ *Map G)* ⊠ *1 Blenheim Crescent, Notting Hill, W11* ☎ *020/7221–4448* Ⓤ *Notting Hill Gate.*

The Vintage House. If whiskey is more to your taste than wine, you may want to visit the Vintage House, which has the country's largest selection of single malts (more than 1,400), many notable for their age. The shop is open late—to 11 PM most nights. (⇨ *Map D)* ⊠ *42 Old Compton St., Soho, WC2* ☎ *020/7437–2592* Ⓤ *Piccadilly Circus, Leicester Square.*

19

GIFTS

These selections are ideal for browsing and inspired gift-giving. They offer plenty of choice, a good range of prices, and the opportunity to find something different and special. If you're hoping to find something particularly British, don't overlook London's museum shops. At the British Museum you might find reproductions of ancient Egyptian jewelry, or a dishcloth printed with the Rosetta Stone; at the Victoria & Albert look for Charles Rennie Mackintosh reproductions. The London Transport Museum sells transport models; the Natural History Museum has the largest selection of toy dinosaurs and real gemstones; the Science Museum carries models and items for would-be inventors; and the huge gift shop at the Tate Modern is chock-a-block with books, posters, novelties, and art materials for BritArt lovers.

GENERAL   **BBC Shop.** Whatever your favorite TV or radio show from the British Broadcasting Corporation, it's probably here in some form, from DVDs and computer games to books and toys. If you have a *Dr. Who* fan at home, this is the place to pick up a Tardis or an evil Dalek. Classic comedy by the Monty Python team shares shelf space with the latest giggles from *Little Britain.* (⇨ *Map B)* ⊠ *50 Margaret St., Marylebone, W1* ☎ *020/7631–4523* Ⓤ *Oxford Circus.*

General Trading Co. Known by its fans as the GTC, this sleek shop is where aristocrats and royals place their wedding lists—not because the goods are expensive (though sometimes they can be) but because the gifts, furniture, and homewares are interesting, tempting, and sometimes one or two of a kind. ■ TIP➜**Once you've explored the two spacious floors, you can rest your feet in the chic café.** (⇨ *Map F)* ⊠ *2 Symons St., Sloane Sq., Chelsea, SW3* ☎ *020/7730–0411* Ⓤ *Sloane Square.*

★   **National Trust Gift Shop.** If you can't make it out to one of the country houses owned by the Trust, then this shop–information center in the old Blewcoat School is the next best thing. This "poor" school was built in the Georgian period for children by a local brewer. The infinitely original and covetable gifts include neat pots of conserves, chocolate, china, books, body-care products, and more, whose origins and design are based upon the Trust houses and estates around the nation. (⇨ *Map F)* ⊠ *23 Caxton St., Westminster, SW1* ☎ *020/7222–2877* Ⓤ *St. James's Park.*

The Tea House. Alongside the varieties of tea (including traditional, green, and fruity blends) and a small selection of London cliché pots and caddies (London taxi, bus, phone booth), there are beautiful, handcrafted or hand-painted teapots, Japanese ceramic tea sets, and sweet, "tea-for-one" pots that nest inside generous matching cups. All the teapots, accessories, and gadgets are sourced from the countries where tea is grown. (⇨ *Map D)* ⊠ *15A Neal St., Covent Garden, WC2* ☎ *020/7240–7539* Ⓤ *Covent Garden.*

PERFUMES &   Both of London's most venerable perfumeries began life as barber
COSMETICS   shops. Mr. Floris brought his Mediterranean nose and perfumer's skill to London from Menorca, via Montpelier, in 1730. Mr. Penhaligon opened his original shop around 1870. Despite the advent of stylish new perfume and cosmetics shops, these grand old shops hold their own, and at least one, if not both, should be on the first time visitor's *must*

see list. Nicky Kinnaird dominates the cosmetics scene with her chain of Space NK stores, selling cult skincare, hair products, and make-up sourced from Europe and America as well as the UK. London's organic pioneer, Neal's Yard Remedies, has recently had a modern image make-over and added new shops to its empire on Marylebone High Street and Foubert's Place, Soho W1; the essential oils and unguents are effective without chemical nasties.

Fodor'sChoice **Floris.** One of the most beautiful shops in London, Floris boasts gleaming
★ glass and Spanish mahogany showcases (acquired from the Great Exhibition of 1851). As well as beautifully packaged soaps, bath essences, perfumes, and its famous rose-scented mouthwash, gift possibilities include goose-down powder puffs and cut-glass atomizers. Queen Victoria used to dab her favorite Floris fragrance on her lace handkerchief. True to its origins as a barbershop, Floris makes scent for both men and women as well as shaving products. *(⇨ Map A)* ⊠ *89 Jermyn St., St. James's, W1* ☎ *020/7930–2885* Ⓤ *Piccadilly Circus.*

Jo Malone. London's own passionate perfumer and cosmetician began blending scents and creams in the 1990s, and now has shops around the world. In addition to selling gorgeous products in discreet, modern packaging, the shops offer facials, and Fragrance Combining consultations. There are similar services at the 23 Brook Street Shop in Mayfair W1. *(⇨ Map F)* ⊠ *150 Sloane St., Chelsea, SW1* ☎ *020/7730–2100* Ⓤ *Sloane Square.*

Les Senteurs. An intimate, unglossy family-run perfumery, Les Senteurs sells some of the lesser-known, yet wonderfully timeless brands in town, such as Creed, Caron, and Frederic Malle's Editions de Parfums. *(⇨ Map F)* ⊠ *71 Elizabeth St., Pimlico and Victoria, SW1* ☎ *020/7730– 2322* Ⓤ *Sloane Square.*

★ **Penhaligon's.** William Penhaligon, court barber at the end of Queen Victoria's lengthy reign, established this shop. He blended perfumes and toilet waters and often created private concoctions for such customers as Lord Rothschild and Winston Churchill, using essential oils and natural, sometimes exotic ingredients. You can buy the very same formulations today, along with soaps, talcs, bath oils, and accessories. You'll find the strong whiff of Victoriana both inside and outside the flower-bedecked bottles and boxes. The shop is sumptuously outfitted with 19th-century perfumer furnishings. *(⇨ Maps A and D)* ⊠ *41 Wellington St., Covent Garden, WC2* ☎ *020/7836–2150* Ⓤ *Covent Garden* ⊠ *16 Burlington Arcade, Mayfair, W1* ☎ *020/7629–1416* Ⓤ *Piccadilly Circus.*

Pout. The creators of Pout know that makeup is really all about fun and serve up lippy (lipstick, Brit style) with a cheeky sense of humor. Product names include "Date Bait" lipstick, "Bite My Cherry" gloss, and "Rampant Rose" blush. You can try before you buy, in a fun, girlie boudoir setup, complete with pink walls and love-heart seating. It's irresistible. *(⇨ Map D)* ⊠ *32 Shelton St., Covent Garden, WC2* ☎ *020/7379–0379* Ⓤ *Covent Garden.*

STATIONERY & **Green & Stone.** This fabulous cave of artist materials, papers, art books,
GRAPHIC ARTS easels, and mannequins is one of the longest-running shops on the

19

King's Road, with a distinguished arts pedigree. It began life in 1927 as part of the Chenil Gallery, under the directorship of Augustus John and George Bernard Shaw. At the current location since 1934, it's always crowded and popular. It also has a framing service and a selection of antique paintboxes and artists' tools. *(⇨ Map F) ⊠259 King's Rd., Chelsea, SW3 ☎020/7352–0837 Ⓤ Sloane Square.*

Paperchase. The stationery superstore of London, it sells writing paper in every conceivable shade and in a dozen mediums. There are lovely cards, artists' materials, notebooks, and paperware. The three-floor store has a café. There are several branches in London, including 289 King's Road SW3 and the Piazza, Covent Garden WC2. *(⇨ Map C) ⊠213–215 Tottenham Court Rd., Bloomsbury, W1 ☎020/7467–6200 Ⓤ Goodge St.*

★ **Smythson of Bond Street.** This is, hands down, the classiest stationer in Britain. No hostess of any standing would consider having a leather-bound guest book made by anyone else, and the shop's distinctive pale blue–page diaries and social stationery are British through and through. Bespoke stationery sets come with a form and a sample so that recipients can personalize their gift. There are branches on Sloane Street, in Harvey Nicks, and at Selfridges. *(⇨ Map A) ⊠40 New Bond St., Mayfair, W1 ☎020/7629–8558 Ⓤ Bond St.*

TOYS &   **Armoury of St. James's.** The fine toy soldiers and military models in
MODELS   stock here are collectors' items. Painted and mounted knights only 6 inches high can cost more than £1,000 (though they start at a mere £4). Besides lead and tin soldiers, the shop has a full selection of regimental brooches, porcelain figures, military memorabilia, and antiques. *(⇨ Map A) ⊠17 Piccadilly Arcade, St. James's, SW1 ☎020/7493–5082 Ⓤ Piccadilly Circus.*

Benjamin Pollock's Toyshop. This Covent Garden shop carries on in the tradition of its founder and namesake who sold "theatrical sheets" for toy theaters from the mid-19th century to his death in 1937. Robert Louis Stevenson was a fan who wrote, "If you love art, folly, or the bright eyes of children, speed to Pollock's." Old-fashioned and magical toy theaters are the main stock in trade, but a selection of nostalgic puppets, mechanical toys, and zoetropes are also available. *(⇨ Map D) ⊠44 The Market, Covent Garden Piazza, WC2 ☎020/7379–7866 Ⓤ Covent Garden.*

Early Learning Centre. This is the ultimate stop for toys and educational games for babies and preschool children. The products are all clearly marked to explain what is appropriate for different age groups, and the staff is patient and helpful. If you bring your kids, you can still shop in relative peace while your youngsters play on some of the equipment. There are organized play sessions every Tuesday from 9:30 to 11:30 AM (except in the Christmas shopping season) for parent and child. *(⇨ Map F) ⊠36 King's Rd., Chelsea, SW3 ☎020/7581–5764 Ⓤ Sloane Square.*

Fodor's Choice   **Hamleys.** Every London child puts a trip to Hamleys at the top of his or
★   her wish list. A Regent Street institution, the shop has demonstrations, a play area, a café, and every cool toy on the planet—as soon as it's launched. The huge stock, including six floors of toys and games for chil-

dren and adults, ranges from traditional teddy bears to computer games and all the latest technological gimmickry. It's a mad rush at Christmastime, but Santa's grotto is one of the best in town. (⇨ *Map A)* ⊠ *188–196 Regent St., Soho, W1* ☎ *0870/333–2455* Ⓤ *Oxford Circus.*

HOUSEWARES

London's main department stores, such as John Lewis, Harrods, and Selfridges, have just about everything you might need. Terence Conran no longer owns Habitat, but his good design on a budget philosophy is still apparent. For something more unusual still, head to Cheshire Street in the East End. Independent home-design shops have sprouted up here over the past few years, including the wonderfully British Labour & Wait (No. 18), which sells stylish yet practical goods from traditional clothespegs to Welsh blankets. Most are only open on weekends, when the Brick Lane and Spitalfields markets bring customers to the area.

Cath Kidston. The stock in trade here is a collection of bright, girly prints—ginghams, polka dots, and miles and miles of roses—pasted over everything in sight, from ceramics and bedlinens to fine china, stationery, and dog beds. There are a few clothing and nightwear lines for women and children, along with handbags, beach bags, and diaper bags of different sizes, but everything in this shop is basically a canvas for Kidston's sugary prints. You'll either love them or loathe them. (⇨ *Map G)* ⊠ *8 Clarendon Cross, Notting Hill, W11* ☎ *020/7221–4000* Ⓤ *Notting Hill Gate.*

★ **Conran Shop.** This is the domain of Sir Terence Conran, who has been informing British taste since he opened Habitat in the '60s. Home enhancers from furniture to stemware—both handmade and mass-produced, by famous names and young designers—are displayed in a suitably gorgeous building that is a modernist design landmark in its own right. The household articles are almost objets d'art. The Conran Shop on Marylebone High Street, Marylebone W1, has similarly beautiful wares. (⇨ *Map E)* ⊠ *Michelin House, 81 Fulham Rd., South Kensington, SW3* ☎ *020/7589–7401* Ⓤ *South Kensington.*

Graham & Green. A Notting Hill stalwart before the area reached cult status, this lifestyle shop has something for everyone's home. Whether you prefer folksy, ethnic, European, or colonial, you can likely find cushions, throws, lanterns, mirrors, and more mundane housewares. A wide range of inexpensive novelties, traditional kids' toys, delicate nightwear and kimonos, jewelry, and decorative handbags make it a handy repository of affordable gifts. (⇨ *Map G)* ⊠ *4 and 10 Elgin Crescent, Notting Hill, W11* ☎ *020/7243–8908* Ⓤ *Ladbroke Grove.*

Heal's. The king of the furniture shops lining Tottenham Court Road, Heal's has designs that combine modern style with classicism, particularly beds and seating. The prices are high, but the store makes for delightful browsing, and the kitchenware and decorative pieces are more affordable. At Christmastime, Heal's decorative baubles are gorgeous. There's another, smaller store at 234 King's Road, Chelsea SW3. (⇨ *Map C)* ⊠ *196 Tottenham Court Rd., Bloomsbury, W1* ☎ *020/7636–1666* Ⓤ *Goodge St.*

19

Muji. If you're into minimalism, you'll love this Japanese chain. The merchandise, encompassing everything from tableware and bed linen to stationery and stackable Perspex storage in all sizes, is all geared towards practical yet stylish urban living. Skin-care products come in natural fragrances and white recyclable containers—including handy travel sizes—and there are great gadgets, such as a pair of portable cardboard speakers. The understated clothes—simple T-shirts (look out for the line sold in a shrink-wrapped "cube"), pants, and knits in neutral linens and cottons—round out the selection. Prices are very reasonable. There are branches everywhere: 187 Oxford Street, Soho W1; 135 Long Acre, Covent Garden WC2; 157 Kensington High Street, Kensington W8; 118 King's Road, Chelsea SW3. (⇨ *Map B)* ✉ *Unit 5, 6–17 Tottenham Court Rd., Bloomsbury, W1* ☎ *020/7436–1779* Ⓤ *Tottenham Court Rd.*

Paul Smith. The highly regarded British fashion designer, with successful, international collections for both men and women, opened his first exclusively home furnishings shop in Mayfair in 2005. Original, one-of-a-kind furniture pieces share space with what Smith terms "curiosities" in an ever-changing selection, sourced from all over the world. (⇨ *Map A)* ✉ *9 Albemarle St., Mayfair, W1* ☎ *020/7493–4565* Ⓤ *Bond St.*

JEWELRY

If you are suddenly overcome with the need to invest in serious rocks, London won't let you down. All the major international players are here: Cartier, Tiffany, Bulgari, Fred, Boucheron, De Beers, Van Cleef and Arpels, Graff, Kutchinsky, David Morris, and Britain's own Mappin & Webb among them. Bond Street, in particular, is good hunting grounds for megawatt stocking fillers. ∎ TIP→ **Bargain hunters who know their gems head for Hatton Garden, London's traditional diamond center. It's lined with small, independent dealers.** For a selection of unusual designer jewelry under one roof try Liberty or Fenwick. Widespread chain Links of London is a good bet for unfussy sterling silver and gold pieces, especially charm bracelets and cufflinks, and Lesley Craze Gallery is strong on hand-crafted jewelry.

★ **Asprey.** Exquisite jewelry and gifts are displayed in a discreet and very British environment at the "global flagship" store—opened in 2004, designed by Lord Foster and British interior designer David Mlinaric. The setting reeks money, good taste, and comfort. If you're in the market for an immaculate 1930s cigarette case, a crystal vase, a lizard-bound diary, or a pair of pavé diamond and sapphire earrings, you won't be disappointed. Bespoke jewelry is available as well. (⇨ *Map A)* ✉ *167 New Bond St., Mayfair, W1* ☎ *020/7493–6767* Ⓤ *Bond St.*

Fodor'sChoice **Butler & Wilson.** Long before anybody ever heard the word "bling," this
★ shop was marketing the look—in diamanté, colored rhinestones, and crystal—to movie stars and secretaries alike. Specialists in handmade, designer jewelry, they've added semi-precious stones and amber to the collections. The vintage-influenced clothes, once used only to display the jewelry, produced so many requests that they now sell filmy beaded dresses, handbags, and smashing capes as well. The crowded Chelsea Shop is like being inside a giant's jewel box; head upstairs for a

fine collection of genuine vintage items. There's also a smaller shop at 20 South Molton Street. *(⇨ Map F)* ✉*189 Fulham Rd., Chelsea, SW3* ☎*020/7352–3045* Ⓤ *South Kensington.*

Dinny Hall. Here you'll find a very simple collection of designs in mainly gold and silver. Pared-down necklaces with a single gemstone, slender drop or hoop earrings, and simple, sculptural silver pendants are indicative of the styles sold here. There's another branch at 292 Upper Street, Islington N1, and a selection is stocked at Liberty and Selfridges. *(⇨ Map G)* ✉*200 Westbourne Grove, Notting Hill, W11* ☎*020/7792–3913* Ⓤ *Notting Hill Gate.*

Garrard. Formally known as "Garrard, the Crown Jeweler," this is the company that, since Queen Victoria's day, has set the Kohinoor diamond into more than one royal crown. The focus is diamonds and precious gems in simple, classic settings. While recent collections such as the Wings pavé designs and the Regal line (featuring crown motifs, diamonds, rubies, and sapphires) are definitely bling, tradition rules and you can still drop in to pick up a jeweled tiara. *(⇨ Map A)* ✉*24 Albemarle St., Mayfair, W1* ☎*020/7758–8520* Ⓤ *Bond St.*

★ **Kabiri.** A dazzling array of exciting contemporary jewelry by emerging and established designers from around the world is packed into this small shop. There is something to suit most budgets and tastes, from flamboyant statement pieces to subtle, delicate adornment. Look out for British talent Sophie Towill, Scott Stephen, and Pippa Small, among many others. *(⇨ Map B)* ✉*37 Marylebone High St., Marylebone, W1* ☎*020/7224–1808* Ⓤ *Baker St., Bond St.*

Wright & Teague. Designers of superb pared-down jewelry made of gold, silver, and understated gems, this husband-and-wife team has crafted an exquisite collection that is more affordable than the upscale international jewelers on the adjacent Bond Street block. They describe their design philosophy as "glamour with gravitas." *(⇨ Map A)* ✉*1A Grafton St., Mayfair, W1* ☎*020/7629–2777* Ⓤ *Green Park.*

19

PRINTS

London prints, old and new, make great gifts. Below are some West End stores, but also try London's markets—in particular Camden Passage in Islington for fine antique prints, Antiquarius on the King's Road, and the shops lining Portobello Road. The antiquarian book sellers of Cecil Court, off Charing Cross Road, are sources of old prints, maps, and theater ephemera. Most of London's major galleries and museums have excellent art posters in their shops; check out the Tate Modern and Bankside Gallery (on the South Bank), Tate Britain, the National Gallery, and the Courtauld Institute—an often overlooked gem. In the bargain range, it's well worth making a date for one of the many art fairs during the year, such as the **Affordable Art Fair** (☎*020/8246–4848* ⊕*www.affordableartfair.co.uk*) around March and October at Battersea Park, where you can bag original work for under £3,000.

Classic Prints. The dusty windows of this little shop always have something worth looking at. A few doors away from Green & Stone *(see Stationery and Graphic Arts, above)*, it's worth browsing here if you're already on this choice stretch of the King's Road. *(⇨ Map F) ⊠ 265 King's Rd., Chelsea, SW3 ☎ 020/7376–5056 Ⓤ Sloane Squarre.*

★ **Grosvenor Prints.** London's largest collection of 17th- to early-20th-century prints includes a good selection of rare, early Americana. The main emphasis is London views and architecture as well as sporting and decorative prints. It's an eccentric collection, with prices ranging from £5 into the thousands. *(⇨ Map D) ⊠ 19 Shelton St., Covent Garden, WC2 ☎ 020/7836–1979 Ⓤ Covent Garden.*

Map House. Though a few items here are relatively inexpensive, this is mainly a shop for serious collectors of antique maps and globes—the sort of place that supplies prices on request. Much of its stock dates from the 16th century, and you can admire a very rare, Ptolemaic worldview that dates from 1493 (not for sale). A gallery of fine botanical, animal, and cityscape prints are also antique collectibles. *(⇨ Map E) ⊠ 54 Beauchamp Pl., Knightsbridge, SW3 ☎ 020/7589–4325 Ⓤ Knightsbridge.*

SHOES

It's no accident that Manolo Blahnik, the star footwear designer, made his name in London and still chooses to live here. The man who has shod fashionable women from Audrey Hepburn to Kate Moss and the "Sex and the City" girls still trades from his original shop in Chelsea, off the King's Road. Jimmy Choo is another "native son" who began his career quietly in London's East End. The British capital is still a hotbed of shoemaking talent: Georgina Goodman and Rupert Sanderson are two of the most exciting names of the moment. Besides some very good British leather and shoe merchants, London is a magnet for the best in Italian, Spanish, and French "pedi-couture." Stop in at one of the King's Road branches of Hobbs, Pied-A-Terre, or L.K. Bennett for British-designed shoes at more affordable prices.

★ **Caroline Groves.** Made to measure, stunning women's shoes echo classics of the 1920s, '30s, '40s, and '50s. Caroline Groves considers herself more of a craftsperson than a designer. If you loved raiding your grandmother's attic for her favorite footwear, this is the place to visit. *(⇨ Map B) ⊠ 37 Chiltern St., Marylebone, W1 ☎ 020/7935–2329 Ⓤ Baker St.*

★ **Georgina Goodman.** Former fashion stylist Georgina Goodman's original, colorful designs for women have been praised by the great Manolo himself. Featuring such signature flourishes as hand-painted leather and unusual heel shapes, her footwear is influenced by, but not enslaved to, current fashion. The pretty flat "slippers" in seasonally changing materials are affordable bestsellers, and you can also have couture shoes made to measure in the basement workshop. *(⇨ Map A) ⊠ 12–14 Shepherd St., Mayfair, W1 ☎ 020/7499–8599 Ⓤ Green Park.*

Jimmy Choo. It's the name on every supermodel's and fashion editor's feet. The exquisite, elegant designs combine luxurious materials and details with shapes (pointy toes and slim high heels are signatures) that are classic enough to have fashion staying power—essential given the prices. The handbags are also a hit with fans. *(⇨ Map E) ⊠ 32 Sloane St., Knightsbridge, SW1 ☎ 020/7823–1051 Ⓤ Knightsbridge.*

John Lobb. If you're planning to visit for your first pair of handmade shoes (after which your wooden "last," or foot mold, is kept), take note: this shop has a waiting list of six months plus. As well as plenty of time, you'll need plenty of money: around £2,000. But this buys a world of choice—from finest calf to exotic elk—and it will be your finest pair of shoes ever. *(⇨Map A) ⊠9 St. James's St., St. James's, SW1* 🕾 *020/7930–3664* Ⓤ *Piccadilly Circus.*

★ **Manolo Blahnik.** Blink and you'll miss the discreet sign of this little shoe shop. Here, in the heart of Chelsea, the man who single-handedly managed to revive the sexy stiletto and make it classier than ever has been trading since 1973. It's a must for shoe lovers with a healthy credit balance. If you're wearing your Manolos, hop on a bus or into a cab—the nearest Tube is about a mile and a half away. *(⇨Map F) ⊠49–51 Old Church St., Chelsea, SW3* 🕾 *020/7352–3863* Ⓤ *Sloane Square.*

Office. Inexpensive but imaginative takes on catwalk looks, with plenty of street cred, are the stock in trade at this popular chain. Styles for men and women feature trend-conscious shapes and funky patterns and finishes. Upscale sibling stores Poste (10 South Molton Street, W1) and Poste Mistress (61–63 Monmouth Street, Covent Garden, WC2) stock cutting-edge designer shoes for men and women, respectively. *(⇨Map D) ⊠57 Neal St., Covent Garden, WC2* 🕾 *020/7379–1896* Ⓤ *Covent Garden.*

Oliver Sweeney. Sweeney's "anatomical last," which supports the arch of the foot, ensures his updated classics for men feel as good as they look. Styles run the gamut from solid brogues and sleek loafers to sporty styles based on soccer shoes, in materials from calf and suede to "antique" leather and stingray. *(⇨Map F) ⊠29 King's Rd., Chelsea, SW3* 🕾 *020/7730–3666* Ⓤ *Sloane Square.*

★ **Rupert Sanderson.** Designed in London and made in Italy, Sanderson's elegant shoes have been a huge hit in fashion circles. Ladylike styles, bright colors, intricate effects, and a penchant for peep toes are signature elements. Prices reflect the impeccable craftsmanship. *(⇨Map A) ⊠33 Bruton Pl., Mayfair, W1* 🕾 *0870/750–9181* Ⓤ *Bond St.*

Swear. Wild and funky shoes iconoclasts, rubber fetishists, and rockers swear by. Styles tend to resemble sneakers and variations on traditional shoes such as lace-ups and pumps in bright, two-tone colors and metallics. The Carnaby Street shop now sells cutting-edge clothing labels, too. *(⇨Map D) ⊠22 Carnaby St., Soho, W1* 🕾 *020/7734–1690* Ⓤ *Oxford Circus.*

19

STREET MARKETS

For London's most famous markets, and the one's worth making a special trip to visit, see "To Market, To Market" feature. The markets listed below are also worth visiting if you happen to be nearby or, in the case of Camden Passage, if you're a serious and knowledgeable antiques buyer.

Berwick Street. Soho's fruit, vegetable, and dairy market is not very different from many small neighborhood markets—except that the neighborhood is Soho. Shops lining the edges include some good Italian grocers, butchers, and fishmongers alongside shops selling CDs and theatrical fabrics as well as those specializing in maribou-trimmed ladies undies and leather and rubber bondage gear! ⊠ *Soho, W1* ⊗ *Mon.–Sat. 9–5* Ⓤ *Oxford Circus, Piccadilly Circus.*

Camden Passage. Relatively new, as London markets go, this one set up in its 18th-century lanes in the early 1960s. Although Camden Passage was once lined with small antiques shops, these are gradually being taken over by boutiques, and one of the main arcades has been appropriated by a major clothing retailer. However, most of the new shops (selling everything from handmade chocolates and jewelry to designer home accessories and eco-friendly clothing) are tasteful, and many idiosyncratic dealers remain in the atmospheric Pierrepont Arcade and the clusters of stalls that open for business on Saturdays and Wednesdays. A few of the antiques shops will open midweek by appointment. In its historic setting, this is an expensive hunting ground with most of the shops run by specialist dealers who will only haggle with specialist buyers and those in the trade. Note that, despite the name, it's not in Camden but a couple of miles away in Islington. ⊠ *Islington, N1* ⊗ *Wed. 10 AM–2 PM, Sat. 10 AM–5 PM* Ⓤ *Angel.*

Covent Garden. Crafts stalls, jewelry designers, clothes makers—particularly of knitwear—potters, and many more artisans congregate in the undercover central area known as the Apple Market. Stall holders change depending on the day of the week, so if you see something you like, don't wait—buy it. Prices are high, but some of the merchandise, especially jewelry, can be clever and original. The Jubilee Market, toward Southampton Street, is less classy, with printed T-shirts and the like, but on Monday has a worthwhile selection of vintage collectibles. This area is, frankly, more of a tourist magnet than others, and you won't find many locals shopping the stalls. Keep that in mind when judging what you spend in this popular place. ⊠ *The Piazza, Covent Garden, WC2* ⊗ *Daily 9–5* Ⓤ *Covent Garden.*

TO MARKET, TO MARKET

Londoners love a good market. With their cluttered stalls and crowds of people, they are a visible reminder that, in this world of global chain stores and supermarkets, London is still, in many respects, an Old World European city.

Every neighborhood has its cluster of fruit, vegetable, and flower stalls, or its weekend car-boot sales—gigantic garage sales where ordinary people pay a fiver for the privilege of selling their castoffs. Some, like the North End Road Market in Fulham, run for miles. Others, like Brixton Market, Europe's biggest Caribbean-food market, specialize in ethnic ingredients and products. Still others crop up in the most unexpected places: on Berwick Street in the heart of Soho, for example, media moguls, designers, ad execs, actors, dancers, and ladies of the night mingle over the punnets of strawberries, wedges of cheddar, and slabs of wet fish.

The big specialty markets, open on weekends, are not only great for the occasional bargain but also for people-watching, photo ops, and all around great days out. And though the markets are popular with visitors, they aren't tourist traps. In fact, browsing the London markets is one of the few activities in London where natives and tourists mix and enjoy themselves as equals.

PORTOBELLO ROAD MARKET

🕐 **Sat. 6 AM–4:30 PM**

✉ Portobello Rd., Notting Hill

Ⓤ Ladbroke Grove (Hammersmith & City Line), Notting Hill (District, Circle, or Central Line), or Bus 52

☞ Antiques, fruits and vegetables, vintage clothing, household goods

A PORTOBELLO DAY

In good weather the market gets very crowded by midday. For a Londoner's day at Portobello, come as early as you can (7 AM) and enjoy the market when the traders have time for a chat and you can actually get near the stalls. By 10:30 you'll have seen plenty of the market and can stop for a late breakfast or brunch at the **Electric Brasserie** (✉ 191 Portobello Rd. ☎ 020/7908–9696), next to the area's famous Electric Cinema. If you still have the will to shop, move on to the less crowded boutiques along Westbourne Grove, Blenheim Crescent, or Ledbury Road.

London's most famous market still wins the prize for the all-around best. It sits in a lively multicultural part of town; the 1,500-odd antiques dealers don't rip you off (although you should haggle where you can); and it stretches over a mile, changing character completely as it goes.

The southern end is lined with antiques shops and arcades; the middle, above Elgin Crescent, is where locals buy fruits and vegetables. This middle area was the setting for the lovely sequence in the movie *Notting Hill* where Hugh Grant walks along the market and through the changing seasons. The section near the elevated highway (called the Westway) has the best flea market in town, with vintage-clothing stores along the edges. Here, young designers sell their wares in and around the Portobello Green arcade. After that, the market trails off into a giant rummage sale of the kinds of cheap household goods the British call tat.

Some say Portobello Road has become a bit of a tourist trap, but if you acknowledge that it's a circus and get into the spirit, it's a lot of fun. Perhaps you won't find many bargains, but this is such a cool part of town that just hanging out is a good enough excuse to come. There are some food and flower stalls throughout the week, but to see the market in full swing, Saturday is the only day to come.

BOROUGH MARKET

🕐 **Fri. noon–6, Sat. 9–4**

✉ Borough High St.,
South Bank

Ⓤ London Bridge (Jubilee or
Northern Line),
Borough (Nothern Line)

☞ Cheese, olives, coffee,
baked goods, meats, fish,
fruits, vegetables

There's been a market in Borough since Roman times. This one, spread under the arches and railway tracks leading to London Bridge Station, is the successor to a medieval market once held on London Bridge. Post-millennium, it has been transformed from a noisy collection of local stalls to a trendy foodie center. Named the best market in London by a local magazine and the best market in Britain by a national newspaper, the Farmers Market held on Fridays and Saturdays has attracted some of London's best merchants of comestibles. Fresh coffees, gorgeous cheeses, olives, and baked goods complement the organically farmed meats, fresh fish, fruit, and veggies.

Don't make any other lunch plans for the day; celebrity chef Jamie Oliver's scallop man cooks them up fresh at Shell Seekers; wild boar sausages sizzle on a grill, and there is much more that's tempting to gobble on the spot. There are chocolates, preserves, and Mrs. Bassa's handmade Indian condiments to take home, but the best souvenirs are the memories.

A BARGAIN DAY ON THE SOUTH BANK

Combine a visit to the Tate Modern (free) and a walk across the Millennium Bridge from the Tate to St. Paul's with a Thames-side picnic of goodies foraged at Borough Market. There are gourmet breads and farmhouse cheeses from France and Italy.

Or how about a wedge of Stinking Bishop cheese (Wallace and Gromit's favorite) from Neal's Yard Dairy? Fishmonger Applebee's serves up freshly sautéed garlic prawns in a wrap with chili and crème fraîche.

A PUB RIGHT OUT OF DICKENS

On the way back to Borough Tube station, stop for a pint at the **George Inn** (✉ 77 Borough High St., Southwark SE1 ☎ 020/7407–2056 Ⓤ London Bridge, Borough), mentioned by Dickens in *Little Dorrit*. This 17th-century coaching inn was a famous terminus in its day, and is the last galleried inn in London. Now owned by the National Trust, it is leased to a private company and still operates as a pub.

TO MARKET, TO MARKET

19

THE EAST END MARKETS

Brick Lane. The noisy center of the Bengali community is a hubbub of buying and selling. Sunday stalls have food, hardware, household goods, electrical goods, books, bikes, shoes, clothes, spices, and saris. The CDs and DVDs are as likely as not to be counterfeit, and the bargain iron may not have a plug—so be careful. But people come more to enjoy the ethnic buzz, eat curries and Bengali sweets, or indulge in salt beef on a bagel at Beigel Bake, London's 24-hour bagel bakery, a survivor of the neighborhood's Jewish past. Brick Lane's activity spills over into nearby Petticoat Lane Market with similar goods but less atmosphere.

From Brick Lane it's a stone's throw to the **Columbia Road Flower Market**. It's only 52 stalls, but markets don't get much more photogenic than this. Flowers, shrubs, bulbs, trees, garden tools, and accessories are sold wholesale. The local cafés are superb.

Stop to smell the roses and have Sunday brunch on Columbia Road before plunging into **Spitalfields**. The covered market (once London's wholesale meat market) is at the center of this area's boho revival. A modern shopping complex that respects the character of the original Victorian building has been developed around it, with a covered area housing additional stalls. At this writing, the original market hall interior was also being restored. Wares include crafts, retro clothing, handmade rugs, soap, and cakes. And, from Spanish tapas to Thai satays, it's possible to eat your way around the world.

BRICK LANE

🕙 **Sun. daybreak–noon**

✉ Brick La., East End

Ⓤ Aldgate East (Hammersmith & City or District Line), Shoreditch (East London Line)

☞ Food, hardware, household goods, electric goods, books, bikes, shoes, clothes, spices, saris

COLUMBIA ROAD FLOWER MARKET

🕙 **Sun. 8–2**

✉ Columbia Rd., East End

Ⓤ Old Street (Northern Line)

☞ Flowers, shrubs, bulbs, trees, garden tools, accessories

SPITALFIELDS

🕙 **Stalls weekdays 10–4, Sun. 9–5. Restaurants weekdays 11 AM–11 PM, Sun. 9–5. Retail shops daily 11 AM–7 PM.**

✉ Brushfield St., East End

Ⓤ Liverpool St. or Aldgate (Hammersmith & City, Circle, or Bakerloo Line), Aldgate East (Hammersmith & City or District Line)

☞ Crafts, foods, vintage clothing, rugs, soap, cakes

BERMONDSEY

Come before dawn and bring a flashlight to bag a bargain antique at this famous market. Dealers arrive as early as 4 AM to snap up the best bric-a-brac and silverware, paintings, objets d'art, fine arts, and furniture. The early start grew out of a wrinkle in the law under which thieves could sell stolen goods with impunity in the hours of darkness when provenance could not be ascertained. That law was changed, and the market has been shrinking ever since.

Once surrounded by an indoor market and furniture warehouses, Bermondsey is now confined to outdoor stalls, though they retain their character and some interesting wares. Bermondsey Square is being redeveloped, with a hotel, art-house cinema, shops, and restaurants in the works—it's due to be completed at the end of 2008. The local government has pledged to preserve the original modest flavor of the market, despite the upcoming luxuries.

- ⊙ **Fri. 4 AM–about noon**
- ✉ Long La. and Bermondsey Sq., South Bank
- Ⓤ London Bridge (Jubilee or Northern Line), Borough (Nothern Line)
- ☞ Antiques (silverware, paintings, furniture)

THE CAMDEN MARKETS

Now that more stalls and a faux warehouse have been inserted into the surrounding brick railway buildings, some of the haphazard charm of this area—actually several markets gathered around a pair of locks in the Regent's Canal—is lost. Still, the variety of merchandise is mind-blowing: vintage and new clothes, antiques and junk, jewelry and scarves, candlesticks, ceramics, mirrors, and toys.

The markets on Camden High Streem (both outdoors and within the Electric Ballroom) mainly sell cheap T-shirts, secondhand clothes, and tacky pop-culture paraphernalia; it's best to head to Camden Lock and Stable Markets. Though much of the merchandise is youth oriented, the markets have a lively appeal to aging hippies, fashion designers, and anyone with a taste for the bohemian who doesn't mind crowds and a bit of a madhouse scene. Don't miss the Horse Hospital for quirky antiques dealers.

CAMDEN MARKET
- ⊙ **Thurs.–Sun. 9–5:30**

CAMDEN LOCK MARKET, STABLES MARKET, AND CANAL MARKET
- ⊙ **Weekends 10–6**

ELECTRIC MARKET
- ⊙ **Sun. 9–5:30**
- ✉ Camden Town
- Ⓤ Camden Town (Northern Line)
- ☞ Vintage clothing, antiques, jewelry, candlesticks, ceramics, mirrors, toys

TO MARKET, TO MARKET

19

THE GREENWICH MARKET

🕑 **Thurs.–Sun. 9:30–5:30**

✉ **Greenwich High Rd., Greenwich**

Ⓤ **DLR: Cutty Sark for Maritime Greenwich**

☞ **Antiques, arts, crafts, books, toys, paraphernalia**

On weekends, the focus is on crafts, while on Thursdays and Fridays it's on antques: china, old books, cameras, vintage clothing, marine memorabilia, and other curiosities. On weekends, the Village Market down the road offers yet more flea-market miscellany and cheap goods. Less crowded than Camden, less touristy than Covent Garden, this part-indoor, part-outdoor market is surrounded by interesting shops and close to historic sites. If you make a day of it, you can see the Greenwich Observatory and stand on Longitude 0 (marked in brass and stone in front of the observatory), visit the tall ship *Cutty Sark*, and shop till you drop.

Know-How

■ **TWO MARKET TIPS TO REMEMBER→** In the end, if you like something and you can afford it, it's worth buying; you're the best judge of that. But it's annoying to buy an "English antique" only to find the Made in China label when you get home. To avoid disappointment:

Look for hallmarks. A lot of what passes for English silver is plate or outright fake. English gold and silver must, by law, be marked with hallmarks that indicate their material and the year in which they were made. Books of hallmarks are inexpensive to buy in London bookshops.

Buy crafts items directly from the makers. Ceramicists, jewelers, needleworkers and other artisans often sell their own work at markets. Besides buying the item, you may have a conversation worth remembering.

■ **MARKET ETIQUETTE →** You've probably heard that you're expected to bargain with the market traders to get the best price. That's true to a degree, but London markets are not Middle Eastern souks, and most bargaining is modest. Unless you are an expert in the item you want to buy and really know how low you can go, don't offer a ridiculously low price. Instead ask the dealer, "Is that the best you can do?" If the dealer is willing to bargain, he or she will suggest a slightly lower price, maybe 10% less. You might try to get another 10% off and end up meeting in the middle.

Side Trips from London

WORD OF MOUTH

"You can do many day trips. Places like Windsor, Hampton Court, Greenwich, Warwick Castle, Canterbury, Cambridge, Bath, and Salisbury (and the list goes on) are very easy to get to via train from London."

—Lori

SIDE TRIPS FROM LONDON PLANNER

Getting Around

Normally the towns covered in this chapter are best reached by train. Bus travel costs less, but can take twice as long. However, train routes throughout Britain are often subject to delays. Wherever you're going, plan ahead: check the latest timetables before you set off, and try to get an early start.

STATION TIPS

You can reach any of London's main line train stations by Tube. London's bus stations can be confusing for the uninitiated. Here's a quick breakdown:

Victoria Coach Station is on Buckingham Palace Road: it's a 5-minute walk from Victoria Tube station. This is where to go for coach departures; arrivals are at a different location, a short walk from here.

Victoria Bus Station is where many of the local London bus services arrive and depart, and is directly outside the main exits of the train and Tube stations.

Green Line Coach Station is on Bulleid Way (in front of the Colonnades Shopping Centre on Buckingham Palace Road) and is the departure point for most Green Line and Megabus services.

⇨ For more details and contact information for rail and bus lines, see London Essentials.

Visitor Information

Bath (☎0906/711–2000 50p per minute⊕www.visitbath.co.uk). **Brighton** (☎0906/711–2255 50p per minute⊕www.visitbrighton.com). **Cambridge** (☎0871/226–8006, 01223/464–732 from outside U.K.⊕www.visitcambridge.org). **Canterbury** (☎01227/378–100⊕www.canterbury.co.uk). **Oxford** (☎01865/726–871⊕www.oxford.gov.uk/tourism). **Stratford-upon-Avon**(☎0870/160–7930⊕www.shakespeare-country.co.uk).**Windsor** (☎01753/743–900⊕www.windsor.gov.uk).

TO GET TO...	TAKE THE TRAIN FROM...	TAKE THE BUS FROM...
Bath	Paddington (90 minutes; half-hourly departures)	Victoria Coach Station (3 hours, 50 minutes; hourly departures)
Brighton	Victoria (1–1½ hours; half-hourly) or London Bridge (95 minutes; departures every 15 minutes)	Victoria Coach (2 hours; hourly)
Cambridge	King's Cross (1 hour; hourly)	Victoria Coach (about 2 hours; hourly)
Canterbury	Victoria (85 minutes; hourly)	Victoria Coach (1 hour, 50 minutes; hourly)
Oxford	Paddington (55 minutes; half-hourly)	Victoria Coach (1 hour, 40 minutes; half-hourly)
Stratford-upon-Avon	Paddington (2 hours, 20 minutes); Marylebone (2½ hours); or Euston (2½ hours)	Victoria Coach (3 hours; about three times daily)
Windsor	Paddington (40 minutes; hourly) or Waterloo (1 hour; hourly)	Green Line Coach Station (1½ hours)

Updated by Robert Andrews, Christi Daugherty, and Julius Honnor

London is exciting and entertaining, but it's not all Britain has to offer. If you have even one day to spare, head out of the city. A train ride past hills dotted with sheep, a stroll through a medieval town, or a visit to one of England's great castles could make you feel as though you've added another week to your vacation.

Londoners are undeniably lucky. Few urban populations enjoy such glorious—and easily accessible—options for day-tripping. England is extremely compact, and the train and bus networks, although somewhat inefficient and expensive compared to their European counterparts, are extensive and user-friendly.

Although you could tackle any one of the towns in this chapter on a frenzied day trip—heavy summer crowds make it difficult to cover the sights in a relaxed manner—consider staying for a day or two. You'd then have time to explore a very different England—one blessed with quiet country pubs, fluffy sheep, and neatly trimmed farms. No matter where you go, lodging reservations are a good idea from June through September, when foreign visitors saturate the English countryside.

20

BATH

115 mi west of London.

"I really believe I shall always be talking of Bath … I do like it so very much. Oh! Who can ever be tired of Bath?" wrote Jane Austen in *Northanger Abbey*. Today thousands of visitors heartily concur. A remarkably unsullied Georgian city with remnants of its Roman occupation, Bath looks as if John Wood (circa 1705–54), its chief architect; "Beau" Nash (1674–1762), its principal dandy; and Jane Austen (1775–1817) might still be seen strolling on the promenade. Stepping out of the train station puts you right in the center, and Bath is compact enough to explore on foot. A single day is sufficient for you to take in the glorious yellow-stone buildings, tour the Roman baths, and stop

·for tea, though it will give you only a brief hint of the cultural life that thrives in this vibrant town.

EXPLORING BATH

Fodor'sChoice   The **Pump Room and Roman Baths** are among the most popular sights
★   outside London. The Romans set about building the baths here around the healing spring of the English goddess Aquae Sulis in AD 60, after wars with the Brits had laid the city to waste. The site became famous as a temple to Minerva, the Roman goddess of wisdom. Legend has it the first taker of these sacred waters was King Lear's leprous father, Prince Bladud, in the 9th century BC. (Yes, it's claimed he was cured.) The British added the Pump Room—oft-described in Austen's works, and now beautifully restored—in the 18th century. You can drink the spa waters here, or have a more agreeable cup of tea. Below the Pump Room is a museum of quirky objects found during excavations. Allow at least 90 minutes for the museum. ⊠*Abbey Churchyard* 🕾*01225/477–784* ⊕*www.romanbaths.co.uk* 🖃*£10.25, July and Aug. £11.25, combined ticket with Assembly Rooms £13.50* ⊘*Mar.–June, Sept., and Oct., daily 9–6; July and Aug., daily 9 AM–9 PM; Nov.–Feb., daily 9:30–5:30; last admission 1 hr before closing.*

Bath Abbey was commissioned by God. Really. The design came to Bishop Oliver King in a dream, and was built during the 15th century. Look up at the fan-vaulted ceiling in the nave and the carved angels on the restored West Front. In the **Heritage Vaults** is a museum of archaeological finds, with a scale model of 13th-century Bath. ⊠*Abbey Churchyard* 🕾*01225/422–462* ⊕*www.bathabbey.org* 🖃*Abbey free, suggested donation £2.50, Heritage Vaults free* ⊘*Abbey Apr.–Oct., Mon.–Sat. 9–6, Sun. 1–2:30 and 4:30–5:30; Nov.–Mar., Mon.–Sat. 9–4:30, Sun. 1–2:30. Heritage Vaults Mon.–Sat. 10–4.*

NEED A BREAK?
Sally Lunn's Refreshment House & Museum (⊠ **4 N. Parade Passage** 🕾**01225/461–634**) **claims to be Bath's oldest house (1482). The cellars hold a museum where you can view the old foundation of the house, plus the original kitchen. It's open 10 to 10 Monday through Saturday and 11 to 10 on Sunday.**

One of the most famous landmarks of the city, **Pulteney Bridge** (⊠*Off Bridge St. at Grand Parade*), was the great Georgian architect Robert Adam's sole contribution to Bath. In its way, the bridge is as fine as the only other bridge in the world with shops lining either side: the Ponte Vecchio in Florence.

★   Among Bath's remarkable architectural achievements is **The Circus** (⊠*Intersection of Brock, Gay, and Bennett Sts.*), a perfectly circular ring of three-story stone houses designed by John Wood. The painter Thomas Gainsborough (1727–88) lived at No. 17 from 1760 to 1774.

On the east side of Bath's Circus are thrills for Austen readers: her much-mentioned **Assembly Rooms**, where the upper class would gather for concerts and dances. Within the rooms is the **Museum of Costume**, which displays fashions from the 17th through 20th centuries. Allow at least

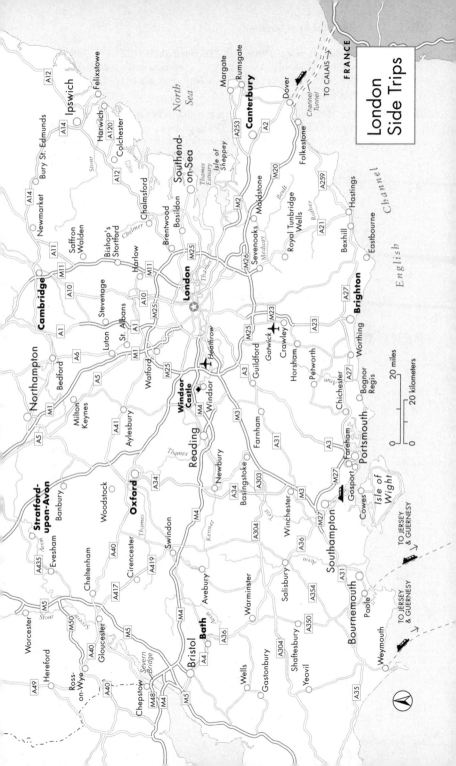

London Side Trips

an hour to tour the museum. ⊠ *Bennett St.* ☏ *01225/477–789* ⊕ *www. museumofcostume.co.uk* 🖃 *£6.75, combined ticket with Roman Baths £13.50* ⊙ *Mar.–Oct., daily 11–6; Nov.–Feb., daily 11–5; last admission 1 hr before closing.*

Fodor'sChoice
★
★

The 18th-century **Royal Crescent** is the most famous site in Bath, and you can't help but see why. Designed by John Wood the Younger, it's perfectly proportioned and beautifully sited, with sweeping views over parkland. A marvelous museum at **Number 1 Royal Crescent** shows life as Beau Nash would have lived it circa 1765. ⊠ *1 Royal Crescent* ☏ *01225/428–126* ⊕ *www.bath-preservation-trust.org.uk* 🖃 *£5* ⊙ *Feb.– Oct., Tues.–Sun. 10:30–5; Nov., Tues.–Sun. 10:30–4; last admission 30 min before closing.*

WHERE TO EAT

££–£££   **Number Five.** Just over the Pulteney Bridge from the center of town, this airy bistro, with its plants, framed posters, and cane-back chairs, is an ideal spot for a light lunch. The regularly changing continental menu includes tasty homemade soups, crostini of goat's cheese and cherry tomatoes, and grilled rib of beef with a red wine sauce. ⊠ *5 Argyle St.* ☏ *01225/444–499* 🖃 *AE, DC, MC, V.*

BRIGHTON

52 mi south of London.

Ever since the Prince Regent first visited in 1783, Brighton has been England's most exciting seaside city, and today it's as eccentric and cosmopolitan as ever. With its rich cultural mix—Regency architecture, an amusement pier, specialist shops, pavement cafés, lively arts, and, of course, the odd and exotic Royal Pavilion—Brighton is a truly extraordinary city by the sea. For most of the 20th century the city was known for its tarnished allure and faded glamour. Happily, a young, bustling spirit has given a face-lift to this ever-popular resort, which shares its city status with neighboring Hove, as genteel a retreat as Brighton is abuzz.

EXPLORING BRIGHTON

In the 1850s, the county of Sussex featured the first examples of that peculiarly British institution, the amusement pier.

★   **Brighton Pier,** which opened in 1899, followed in the great tradition, with a crowded maze of arcade games, amusement-park rides, and chip shops. The decaying ghost of a Victorian structure down the beach from Brighton Pier is **West Pier** (☏ *01273/321–499* ⊕ *www.westpier.co.uk*). Built in 1866, it was the more upscale of Brighton's piers and was for many years the most recognizable landmark of the city. Sadly, storms and fires have ravaged the structure over the last 30 years, leaving only a charred skeleton cut off from land. Now plans have been approved for construction of a £20 million Spaceneedle-style observation tower where the graceful pier once touched the shore. Called i360, the tower will carry passengers up 400 feet in a glass pod. It's scheduled to open in summer 2008. Local groups plan to use the success of the i360 to raise funds for rebuilding the West Pier. ✉ *Waterfront along Madeira Dr.* ☎ *01273/609–361* ⊕ *www. brightonpier.co.uk* ✉ *Free, costs of rides vary* ⊙ *June–Aug., daily 9* AM*–2* AM*; Sept.–May, daily 10* AM*–midnight.*

The heart of Brighton is the **Steine** (pronounced *steen*), a long, narrow park close to the seafront. This was a river mouth until the Prince of Wales (later the Prince Regent) had it drained in 1793.

Fodor's Choice ★ The most remarkable building on the Steine, perhaps in all Britain, is unquestionably the extravagant, fairy-tale **Royal Pavilion.** Built by architect Henry Holland in 1787 as a simple seaside villa, the Pavilion was transformed by John Nash between 1815 and 1823 for the Prince Regent (later George IV), who favored an exotic, Eastern design with opulent Chinese interiors. When Queen Victoria came to the throne in 1837, she disapproved of the palace and planned to demolish it. Fortunately, the local council bought it from her, and after a lengthy process of restoration the Pavilion looks much as it did in its Regency heyday. Take particular note of the spectacular **Music Room,** styled as a Chinese pavilion, and the **Banqueting Room,** with its enormous flying-dragon gasolier, or gaslight chandelier, a revolutionary invention in the early 19th century. The gardens, too, have been restored to Regency splendor, following John Nash's naturalistic design of 1826. ✉ *Old Steine* ☎ *01273/290–900* ⊕ *www.royalpavilion.org.uk* ✉ *£7.50* ⊙ *Oct.–Mar., daily 10–5:15; Apr.–Sept., daily 9:30–5:45; last admission 45 min before closing.*

The grounds of the Royal Pavilion contain the **Brighton Museum and Art Gallery,** whose buildings were designed as a stable block for the Prince Regent's horses. The museum, which recently underwent a £10 million facelift, has particularly interesting art nouveau and art deco collections. Look out for Salvador Dalí's famous sofa in the shape of Mae West's lips, and pause at the Balcony Café for its bird's-eye view over the 20th-century Art and Design collection. ✉ *Church St.* ☎ *01273/290–900* ⊕ *www.brighton.virtualmuseum.info* ✉ *Free* ⊙ *Tues. 10–7, Wed.–Sat. 10–5, Sun. 2–5; closed Mon. except public holidays.*

The Lanes (✉ *Bordered by West, North, East, and Prince Albert Sts.*), a maze of alleys and passageways, once held the homes of fishermen and their families. Closed to vehicular traffic, those cobbled streets are now the city's shopping hotspot, filled with interesting restaurants, boutiques, and antiques shops. Fish and seafood restaurants line the heart of the Lanes, at Market Street and Market Square.

☺ **Volk's Electric Railway,** built by inventor Magnus Volk in 1883, was the first public electric railroad in Britain. In summer you can take the 1¼-mi trip along Marine Parade. ✉ *Marine Parade* ☎ *01273/292–*

20

718 ⬚£1.50 one-way, £2.50 round-trip ⊙ Late Mar.–Sept., weekdays 10:30–5, weekends 10:30–6.

WHERE TO EAT

££–£££ **Due South.** Arguably the first quality dining option on Brighton's seafront, Due South is really making waves on Brighton's food scene. The menu features clever, classic seafood dishes, with locally sourced organic fruit and vegetables. ⊠ *139 Kings Road Arches* ☎ *01273/821–218* ▭ *AE, MC, V.*

££–£££ **English's of Brighton.** One of the few old-fashioned seafood havens left in England is buried in the Lanes in three fisherfolk's cottages. It's been a restaurant for more than 150 years and a family business for more than 50. You can eat succulent oysters and other seafood dishes at the counter or take a table in the smart restaurant section. The restaurant's popularity means it's usually busy, and service can sometimes be slow. ⊠ *29–31 East St.* ☎ *01273/327–980* ▭ *AE, DC, MC, V.*

££–£££ **Havana.** The mock Cuban building, high ceilings, rattan chairs, tan leather furnishings, and sophisticated food at Havana might make you think you're in London. Don't let that deter you, however—this place is a pleasure. Expect modern twists on British classics: the sautéed sea bream, for example, comes on a bed of braised fennel. The chic bar area is a perfect place to rest your feet at the end of the day. ⊠ *32 Duke St.* ☎ *01273/773–388* ▭ *AE, MC, V.*

★ ££ **Terre à Terre.** This inspiring vegetarian restaurant is popular, so come early for a light lunch, or book a table for an evening meal. The Jerusalem artichoke soufflé, tangy olive-cranberry couscous, and an eclectic choice of salads should satisfy most palates, and dishes have names to match their culinary inventiveness, such as Blackbean Cellophane Frisbee and Jabba Jabba Beefy Tea. ⊠ *71 East St.* ☎ *01273/729–051* ⌖ *Reservations essential* ▭ *AE, DC, MC, V* ⊙ *No lunch Mon.; in winter, closed Mon., no lunch Tues. and Wed.*

£–££ **Nia Café.** In the interesting North Laine area, Nia has views down Trafalgar Street from its pavement tables. In addition to good coffees and leaf teas, excellent café food is available all day, from simple (but freshly made) sandwiches to fillets of cod stuffed with wild mushrooms. The dining room is simple, but large windows and fresh flowers add a friendly feel. It's also near the station, which is handy if you have time to kill before a train or you need to reenergize before a busy day's sightseeing. ⊠ *87–88 Trafalgar St.* ☎ *01273/671–371.*

CAMBRIDGE

60 mi north-northeast of London.

With the spires of its university buildings framed by towering trees and expansive meadows, its medieval streets and passages enhanced by gardens and riverbanks, the city of Cambridge is among the loveliest in England. The city predates the Roman occupation of Britain but the university was not founded until the 13th century. There's disagreement about the birth of the university: one story attributes its founding to impoverished students from Oxford, who came in search of eels—a cheap source of nourishment. Today a healthy rivalry persists between the two schools.

This university town may be beautiful, but it's no museum. Even when the students are on vacation there's a cultural and intellectual buzz here. It's a preserved medieval city of some 109,000 souls and growing, dominated culturally and architecturally by its famous university (whose students make up around one-fifth of the inhabitants), and beautified by parks, gardens, and the quietly flowing River Cam. Punting on the Cam (one occupant propels the narrow, square-end, flat-bottom boat with a long pole) is a quintessential Cambridge pursuit, followed by a stroll along the Backs, the left bank of the river fringed by St. John's, Trinity, Clare, King's, and Queens' colleges, and Trinity Hall.

VISITING THE COLLEGES College visits are certainly a highlight of a Cambridge tour, but remember that the colleges are private homes and workplaces, even when school isn't in session. Each is an independent entity within the university; some are closed to the public, but at others you can see the chapels, dining rooms (called halls), and sometimes the libraries, too. Some colleges charge a small fee for the privilege of nosing around. All are closed during exams, usually from mid-April to late June, and the opening hours often vary. For details about visiting specific colleges not listed here, contact **Cambridge University** (☎*01223/337–733* ⊕*www. cam.ac.uk*).

By far the best way to gain access without annoying anyone is to join a walking tour led by an official Blue Badge guide—in fact, many areas are off-limits unless you do. The two-hour tours (£8–£9) leave daily from the **Tourist Information Centre** (⊠*The Old Library, Wheeler St.* ☎*0871/226–8006, 0044/1223–464732 from abroad* ⊕*www.visitcambridge.org* ☉*Easter–Sept., weekdays 10–5:30, Sat. 10–5, Sun. 11–4; Oct.–Easter, weekdays 10–5:30, Sat. 10–5*).

EXPLORING CAMBRIDGE

Emmanuel College (1584) is the alma mater of one John Harvard, who gave his books and his name to the American university. A number of the Pilgrims were Emmanuel alumni; they named Cambridge, Massachusetts, after their one-time home. ⊠*Emmanuel and St. Andrew's Sts.* ☎*01223/334–200* ⊕*www.emma.cam.ac.uk* ☎*Free* ☉*Daily 9–6*.

Fodor'sChoice One of England's finest art galleries, the **Fitzwilliam Museum** houses an
★ outstanding collection of art, as well as striking antiquities from ancient Egypt, Greece, and Rome. Highlights include two large Titians, an extensive collection of French Impressionist painting, and many paintings by Matisse and Picasso. The gallery holds occasional free classical music concerts. ⊠*Trumpington St.* ☎*01223/332–900* ⊕*www.fitzmuseum.cam.ac.uk* ☎*Free* ☉*Tues.–Sat. 10–5, Sun. noon–5*.

Fodor'sChoice **King's College** (1441) is notable as the site of the world-famous Gothic-
★ style **King's College Chapel** (built 1446–1547). Some deem its great fan-vaulted roof, supported by a delicate tracery of columns, the most glorious example of Perpendicular Gothic in Britain. It's the home of the famous choristers, and, to cap it all, Rubens's *Adoration of the Magi*

20

is secreted behind the altar. The college's Back Lawn leads down to the river, from where the panorama of college and chapel is one of the university's most photographed views. ⊠*King's Parade* ☎*01223/331–100 college, 01223/331155 chapel* ⊕*www.kings.cam.ac.uk* ✉*£4.50* ⊙*Oct.– June, weekdays 9:30–3:30, Sat. 9:30–3:15, Sun. 1:15–2:15; July–Sept., Mon.–Sat. 9:30–4:30, Sun. 1:15–2:15 and 5–5:30; hrs vary with services, so call to confirm before visiting.*

Pembroke College (1347) has delightful gardens and bowling greens. Its chapel, completed in 1665, was the architect Christopher Wren's first commission. ⊠*Trumpington St.* ☎*01223/338–100* ⊕*www.pem.cam. ac.uk* ✉*Free* ⊙*Daily 9–dusk.*

In 1284 the Bishop of Ely founded **Peterhouse College,** Cambridge's smallest and oldest college. Take a tranquil walk through its former deer park, by the river side of its ivy-clad buildings. ⊠*Trumpington St.* ☎*01223/338–200* ⊕*www.pet.cam.ac.uk* ✉*Free* ⊙*Daily 9–5.*

★ **Queens' College**—built around 1448, and named after Margaret, queen of Henry VI, and Elizabeth, queen of Edward IV—enjoys a reputation as one of Cambridge's most eye-catching colleges. Enter over the **Mathematical Bridge,** the original version of which is said to have been built by Isaac Newton without any binding save gravity, then dismantled by curious scholars anxious to learn Sir Isaac's secret. The college maintains, however, that the bridge wasn't actually put together until 1749, 22 years after Newton's death, thus debunking the popular myth. ⊠*Queens' La.* ☎*01223/335–511* ⊕*www.quns.cam.ac.uk* ✉*£1.50, free Nov.–mid-Mar.* ⊙*Mid-Mar.–Oct., daily hrs vary; Nov.–mid-Mar., daily 1:45–4:30.*

Along King's Parade is **Corpus Christi College.** If you visit only one quadrangle, make it the beautiful, serene, 14th-century Old Court here; it's the oldest continuously inhabited college quadrangle in Cambridge. ⊠*King's Parade* ☎*01223/338–000* ⊕*www.corpus.cam. ac.uk* ✉*Free* ⊙*Daily dawn–dusk.*

St. John's College (1511), the university's second largest, has noted alumni (Wordsworth studied here), a series of beautiful courtyards, and two of the finest sights in town: the **School of Pythagoras,** the oldest house in Cambridge; and the 1831 **Bridge of Sighs,** whose only resemblance to its Venetian counterpart is its covering. The windowed, covered stone bridge reaches across the Cam to the mock-Gothic New Court (1825–31). The New Court's cupola's white crenellations have earned it the nickname "the wedding cake." ⊠*St. John's St.* ☎*01223/338– 600* ⊕*www.joh.cam.ac.uk* ✉*£2.50* ⊙*Mar.–Oct., daily 10–5.30; Nov.– Feb. hrs vary.*

Fodor'sChoice **Trinity College** was founded by Henry VIII in 1546, and has the largest
★ student population of all the colleges. It's also famous for having been attended by Byron, Thackeray, Tennyson, Bertrand Russell, Nabokov, Nehru, and 31 Nobel prize winners. Many of Trinity's features reflect its status as Cambridge's largest college, not least its 17th-century "great court" and the massive gatehouse that contains Great Tom, a giant

clock that strikes each hour with high and low notes. Don't miss the wonderful library by Christopher Wren, where you can see a letter written by alumnus Isaac Newton with early notes on gravity, and A. A. Milne's handwritten manuscript of *The House at Pooh Corner.* ⊠*St. John's St.* ☎*01223/338–400* ⊕*www.trin.cam.ac.uk* ✑*£2.20 Mar.–Oct.* ☉*College daily 10–5; library weekdays 10–2, Sat. 10:30–noon; hall and chapel open to visitors but hrs vary.*

WHERE TO EAT

★**££–£££** **Midsummer House.** In fine weather the gray-brick Midsummer House's conservatory, beside the River Cam, makes for a memorable lunchtime jaunt. Choose from a selection of innovative French and Mediterranean dishes. You might get tender local lamb, a smoked eel salad, or grilled pigeon adorned with inventively presented vegetables. ⊠*Midsummer Common* ☎*01223/369–299* ⚱*Reservations essential* ▤*AE, MC, V* ☉*Closed Mon. No lunch Sun.–Thurs., no dinner Sun.*

£–££ **Vaults.** Ochre and deep-red walls and metal chairs on slate floors lend a sleek, contemporary twist to the underground vaults. The zinc-topped bar with red sofas is the perfect place for lounging with a cocktail, and there's live music four nights a week. The evening menu is tapas style: lots of small portions of an eclectic mix of international cuisine. Lunchtime menus are more traditional. ⊠*14A Trinity St.* ☎*01223/506–090* ▤*AE, MC, V.*

CANTERBURY

60 mi north of London.

A bustling medieval Cathedral town, charming Canterbury has good shopping, plenty of history, and just enough to see in a day—making it an ideal day trip from London.

As you might remember from high school English classes spent studying Chaucer's *Canterbury Tales,* the height of Canterbury's popularity came in the 12th century, when thousands of pilgrims flocked here to see the shrine of Archbishop St. Thomas à Becket, murdered when two knights misunderstood King Henry II's complaints about the "troublesome priest." The humble ancient buildings that served as pilgrims' inns still dominate the streets of Canterbury's pedestrian center.

Dig a little deeper and there's evidence of prosperous society in the Canterbury area as early as the Bronze Age (around 1000 BC). Canterbury was an important Roman city, as well as an Anglo-Saxon center in the Kingdom of Kent; it's currently headquarters of the Anglican Church. The town remains a lively place, a fact that has impressed visitors since 1388, when Chaucer wrote his stories.

20

EXPLORING CANTERBURY

You can easily cover Canterbury in a day. The 90-minute journey south from London's Victoria Station leaves plenty of time for a tour of the cathedral, a museum visit or two, and (if the weather's right) a walk around the perimeter of the old walled town. Canterbury is bisected by a road running northwest, along which the major tourist sites cluster.

This road begins as St. George's Street, then becomes High Street, and finally turns into St. Peter's Street.

If you're seeing several sights while in town, consider purchasing an "Attractions Passport" from the visitor center. It costs £15, and gives you admission to the Canterbury Cathedral, the Canterbury Tales, St. Augustine's Abbey, and another museum of your choice.

On St. George's Street a lone church tower marks the site of **St. George's Church**—the rest of the building was destroyed in World War II—where playwright Christopher Marlowe was baptized in 1564.

★ The **Canterbury Roman Museum** is below ground level, in the ruins of the original Roman town. There's a colorful restored Roman mosaic pavement and a hypocaust (the Roman version of central heating), as well as a display of excavated objects. Get a feel for what it once looked like via the computer-generated reconstructions of Roman buildings. ⊠ *Butchery La.* ☎ *01227/785–575* ⊕ *www.canterbury-museums. co.uk* ✉ *£3* ♡ *June–Oct., Mon.–Sat. 10–5, Sun. 1:30–5; Nov.–May, Mon.–Sat. 10–5; last entry at 4. Closed last wk in Dec.*

Mercery Lane, with its medieval-style cottages and massive, overhanging timber roofs, runs right off High Street and ends in the tiny **Buttermarket,** a market square that was known in the 15th century as the Bullstake: animals were tied here for baiting before slaughter. Today it's a small market where you can buy books or homemade jam.

The immense **Christchurch Gate**, built in 1517, leads into the cathedral close. As you pass through, look up at the sculpted heads of two young figures: Prince Arthur, elder brother of Henry VIII, and the young Catherine of Aragon, to whom he was betrothed. After Arthur's death, Catherine married Henry. Her inability to produce a male heir after 25 years of marriage led to Henry's decision to divorce her, creating an irrevocable breach with the Roman Catholic Church and altering the course of English history.

Fodor'sChoice The massive heart of the town, towering **Canterbury Cathedral** was the
★ first of England's great Norman cathedrals. The nucleus of worldwide Anglicanism, the Cathedral Church of Christ Canterbury (its formal name) is a living textbook of medieval architecture.

The cathedral was only a century old, and still relatively small in size, when Thomas à Becket, the Archbishop of Canterbury, was murdered here in 1170. An uncompromising defender of ecclesiastical interests, Becket had angered his friend Henry II, who supposedly exclaimed, "Who will rid me of this troublesome priest?" Thinking they were carrying out the king's wishes, four knights burst in on Becket in one of the church's side chapels, chased him through the halls, and stabbed him to death. Two years later Becket was canonized, and Henry II's subsequent penitence helped establish the cathedral as the undisputed center of English Christianity.

Becket's tomb, destroyed by Henry VIII in 1538 as part of his campaign to reduce the power of the Church and confiscate its treasures, was one of the most extravagant shrines in Christendom. In **Trinity Chapel,** which held the shrine, you can still see a series of 13th-century stained-glass windows illustrating Becket's miracles. The actual site of Becket's murder is down a flight of steps just to the left of the nave, and marked with a simple sign that says only "Becket." If time permits, be sure to explore the **Cloisters** and other small monastic buildings north of the cathedral. ✉ *Cathedral Precincts* ☎ *01227/762–862* 🌐 *www.canterbury-cathedral.org* 🎫 *£6; free for services and for ½ hr before closing* ⏲ *Easter–Sept., Mon.–Sat. 9–6, Sun. 12:30–2:30 and 4:30–5:30; Oct.–Easter, Mon.–Sat. 9–4:30, Sun. 12:30–2:30 and 4:30–5:30. Restricted access during services.*

To vivify some of Canterbury's history, spend some time at an exhibition called **The Canterbury Tales,** an audiovisual (and occasionally olfactory) dramatization of 14th-century English life. You'll "meet" Chaucer's pilgrims at the Tabard Inn near London and view tableaux illustrating five tales. Actors clad in period costumes play out the town's history. ✉ *St. Margaret's St.* ☎ *01227/479–227* 🌐 *www.canterburytales.org.uk* 🎫 *£7.25* ⏲ *Nov.–Feb., daily 10–4:30; Mar.–June, Sept., and Oct., daily 10–5; July and Aug., daily 9:30–5.*

★ The medieval Poor Priests' Hospital is now the site of the **Museum of Canterbury** (previously the Canterbury Heritage Museum). The exhibits provide an excellent overview of the city's history and architecture from Roman times to World War II, although the displays are a strange mix of the serious (the Blitz) and the silly (cartoon characters Bagpuss and Rupert Bear). It even touches on the mysterious death of the 16th-century poet and playwright Christopher Marlowe. You can look at "medieval poo" under a microscope. Visit early in the day to avoid the crowds. ✉ *20 Stour St.* ☎ *01227/475–202* 🌐 *www.canterbury-museums.co.uk* 🎫 *£3.30* ⏲ *Jan.–May and Oct.–Dec., Mon.–Sat. 10:30–5; June–Sept., Mon.–Sat. 10:30–5, Sun. 1:30–5; last admission at 4.*

Only one of the city's seven medieval gatehouses survives, complete with twin castellated towers; it now contains the **West Gate Museum.** Inside are medieval bric-a-brac and armaments used by the city guard, as well as more contemporary weaponry. The building became a jail in the 14th century, and you can view the prison cells. Climb to the roof for a panoramic view of the city spires. Because it's accessed by spiral stone stairs, this museum is only for those without mobility problems. ☎ *01227/789–576* 🌐 *www.canterbury-museums.co.uk* 🎫 *£1.20* ⏲ *Mon.–Sat. 11–12:30 and 1:30–3:30; last admission 1 hr before closing. Closed Christmas wk and Good Friday.*

Perhaps the best view of Canterbury's medieval past comes from following its 13th- and 14th-century **medieval city walls,** which were themselves built on the line of the original Roman walls. Those to the east have survived intact, towering some 20 feet high and offering a sweeping view of the town. You can access these from a number of places, including Castle and Broad streets.

Augustine, England's first Christian missionary, was buried in 597 at **St. Augustine's Abbey,** one of the oldest monastic sites in the country. When

Henry VIII seized the abbey in the 16th century, he destroyed some of the buildings and converted others into a royal manor for his fourth wife, Anne of Cleves. A free interactive audio tour vividly puts events into context. The abbey is the base for Canterbury's biennial Sculpture Festival (held on odd-number years). Contemporary sculpture is placed on the grounds, and in other locations in the city, May through August. ⊠*Longport* ☎*01227/767–345* ⊕*www.english-heritage.org. uk* ☎*£3.90* ⊗*Apr.–Sept., daily 10–6; Oct.–Mar., Wed.–Sat. 10–4.*

☾ There's not much left of the aptly named **Dane John Mound**, just opposite the Canterbury East train station, but it was originally a fortress and part of the city defenses. But among what does remain is a fantastic medieval maze.

WHERE TO EAT

£££–££££ **Michael Caines Restaurant.** One of the very few fine dining restaurants in Canterbury, the new Michael Caines Restaurant in the ABode hotel has been earning rave reviews since it opened in 2006. It takes a European approach to British cuisine—wrapping monkfish in Parma ham, serving local lamb with a kidney brochette. This is where to go if you feel like a splurge. ⊠*ABode Canterbury Hotel, High St.* ☎*01227/826–684* ⊟*AE, MC, V.*

★**££–£££** **Lloyds.** The magnificent beamed barn roof of this older building remains, but the interior—stripped wooden floors, and white walls enlivened by modern art—and the contemporary cooking are definitely up-to-the-minute. A crew of young chefs creates such dishes as roasted-pumpkin-and-amaretto ravioli with Parmesan, and pheasant with kumquats and juniper berries. The ice creams are homemade. ⊠*89–90 St. Dunstan's St.* ☎*01227/768–222* ⊟*AE, MC, V.*

£–££ **Duck Inn.** About 5 mi outside of Canterbury, this lovely, low-roof traditional pub is a great favorite among regular visitors to the city. Its pleasant rural location yields a bit of country charm, while dishes such as game pies are delightfully traditional. The name is said to come from the fact that the beams above the entrance are so low that you must duck as you enter or risk bashing your head. ⊠*Pett Bottom, near bridge* ☎*01227/830–354* ⊟*No credit cards.*

★**£–££** **Weavers.** In one of the Weavers' Houses (the Weavers were Huguenots and Walloons who fled persecution in continental Europe in the 16th and 17th centuries) on the River Stour, this popular restaurant in the center of town is an ideal place to revel in the Tudor surroundings and feast on generous portions of British comfort food. Traditional pies, seafood, and pasta dishes are served along with a good selection of wines. Ask for a table in the more sedate ground-floor dining area. ⊠*1 St. Peter's St.* ☎*01227/464–660* ⊟*AE, MC, V.*

£ **City Fish Bar.** Long lines and lots of satisfied finger-licking attest to the deserved popularity of this excellent fish-and-chips outlet in the center of town. Everything is freshly fried, the batter is crisp, and the fish is tasty; the fried mushrooms are also surprisingly good. It closes at 7. ⊠*30 St. Margarets St.* ☎*01227/760–873* ⊟*No credit cards.*

OXFORD

62 mi north of London.

The university system that educated Prime Minister Tony Blair, former President Bill Clinton, and writers J. R. R. Tolkien, Percy Bysshe Shelley, Oscar Wilde, W. H. Auden, and C. S. Lewis is the heart and soul of the town. Its fabled "dreaming spires" can be seen for miles around, and it's not at all unusual to see robed students rushing to exams, or harried dons clutching their mortar boards as they race to class on bicycles.

Dating from the 12th century, Oxford University is older than Cambridge, and the city is bigger and more cosmopolitan than its competitor to the east. It's satisfyingly filled with hushed quadrangles, chapels, canals, rivers, and vivid gardens. Bikes are inevitably propped against picturesque wrought-iron railings, and students propel flat-bottom boats down the little River Cherwell with long poles. (It's harder than it looks, but you can rent a punt yourself at the foot of Magdalen Bridge.)

In the end, though, central Oxford is also a bit of an illusion. Outside of the eminently photographable university area, it's a major industrial center, with sprawling modern suburbs and large car and steel plants around its fringes.

VISITING THE COLLEGES
The same concerns for people's work and privacy hold here as in Cambridge. Note that many of the colleges and university buildings are closed around Christmas (sometimes Easter, too) and on certain days from April to June for exams and degree ceremonies.

If you have limited time, get a detailed map from the tourist office and focus on selected sights. The Oxford University Web site (⊕ *www.ox.ac. uk*) is a great source of information if you're planning to go it alone.

Guided city walking tours leave the **Oxford Information Centre** twice a day. ⊠ *15–16 Broad St.* ☎ *01865/726–871* ⊕ *www.oxford.gov.uk/tourism* 🖼 *£6.50 Sun.–Fri., £7.50 Sat.* ⊙ *Tours daily at 11 and 4.*

20

EXPLORING OXFORD

Any Oxford visit should begin at its very center—a pleasant walk of 10 minutes or so east from the train station—with the splendid **University Church of St. Mary the Virgin** (1280). Climb 127 steps to the top of its 14th-century tower for a panoramic view of the city. ⊠ *High St.* ☎ *01865/279–111* ⊕ *www.university-church.ox.ac.uk* 🖼 *Church free, tower £2* ⊙ *Sept.–June, Mon.–Sat. 9–5, Sun. noon–5; July and Aug., Mon.–Sat. 9–6, Sun. noon–6; last admission to tower 30 min before closing.*

Fodor'sChoice
★
Among Oxford's most famous sights, the gorgeous, round **Radcliffe Camera** (1737–49) is the most beautiful of the buildings housing the extensive contents of the august **Bodleian Library**. The baroque domed rotunda with an octagonal base sits in a lovely square where your photographic instincts can run riot. Not many of the 6-million-plus volumes are on view to those who aren't dons, but you can see part of the collection

on a tour. Call ahead to prebook a tour. Note that children under 14 are not admitted. ✉ *Broad St.* ☎ *01865/277–224* ⊕ *www.bodley.ox.ac.uk* 🖼 *£4, extended tour £7* ⊘ *Bodleian tours Mar.–Oct., weekdays at 10:30, 11:30, 2, and 3, and Sat. at 10:30 and 11:30; Nov.–Feb., weekdays at 2 and 3, and Sat. at 10:30 and 11:30. Divinity School weekdays 9–4:45, Sat. 9–12:30.*

★ The **Sheldonian Theatre,** built between 1664 and 1668, was Sir Christopher Wren's first major work (the chapel at Pembroke College was his first commission). The theater, which he modeled on a Roman amphitheater, made his reputation. It was built as a venue for the university's public ceremonies, and graduations are still held here—entirely in Latin, as befits the building's spirit. Outside is one of Oxford's most striking sights—a metal fence topped with stone busts of 18 Roman emperors (modern reproductions of the originals, which were eaten away by pollution). ✉ *Broad St.* ☎ *01865/277–299* ⊕ *www.sheldon.ox.ac.uk* 🖼 *£2* ⊘ *Mar.–mid-Nov., Mon.–Sat. 10–12:30 and 2–4:30; mid-Nov.–Feb., Mon.–Sat. 10–12:30 and 2–3:30. Closed for 10 days at Christmas and Easter and for degree ceremonies and events.*

☾ Brush up on local history at the **Oxford Story.** Take your place at a medieval student's desk as it trundles, Disney-style, through 800 years of Oxford history. In 20 minutes you can see Edmund Halley discover his comet, and watch the Scholastica's Day Riot of 1355. This one's mostly geared toward kids. ✉ *6 Broad St.* ☎ *01865/728–822* ⊕ *www.oxfordstory.co.uk* 🖼 *£7.25* ⊘ *July and Aug., daily 9:30–5; Sept.–June, Mon.–Sat. 10–4:30, Sun. 11–4:30.*

Outside the "new" (they're actually Victorian) college gates of prestigious **Balliol College** (1263), a cobblestone cross in the sidewalk marks the spot where Archbishop Cranmer and Bishops Latimer and Ridley were burned in 1555 for their Protestant beliefs. The original college gates (rumored to have existed at the time of the scorching) hang in the library passage, between the inner and outer quadrangles. ✉ *St. Giles St.* ☎ *01865/277–777* ⊕ *www.balliol.ox.ac.uk* 🖼 *£1* ⊘ *Daily 2–5, or dusk if earlier.*

★ The **chapel of Trinity College** (1555) is an architectural gem—a tiny place with a delicately painted ceiling, gorgeously tiled floor, and elaborate wood carvings on the pews, pulpit, and walls. Some of the superb wood carvings were done by Grinling Gibbons, a 17th-century master carver whose work can also be seen in Hampton Court Palace and St. Paul's Cathedral, and who inspired the 18th-century cabinetmaker Thomas Chippendale. ✉ *Broad St.* ☎ *01865/279–900* ⊕ *www.trinity.ox.ac.uk* 🖼 *£2* ⊘ *Daily 10–noon and 2–4, or dusk if earlier.*

Fodor's Choice
★ The **Ashmolean Museum,** founded in 1683, is Britain's oldest public museum. Some of the world's most precious art objects are stashed here—drawings by Michelangelo and Raphael, European silverware and ceramics, a world-class numismatic collection, and Egyptian, Greek, and Roman artifacts. The museum is currently being renovated one section at a time, so some galleries may be closed when you visit. Check the Web site in advance if you had a particular display in mind. ⊠ *Beaumont St.* ☎ *01865/278–000* ⊕ *www.ashmolean.org* ⊡ *Free* ⊙ *Tues.–Sat. 10–5, Sun. noon–5.*

St. John's College (1555), Prime Minister Tony Blair's alma mater, is worth a stop for its historic courtyards, neatly arrayed symmetrical gardens, and its library, where you can view some of Jane Austen's letters and an illustrated 1482 edition of *The Canterbury Tales* by the English printer William Caxton. ⊠ *St. Giles St.* ☎ *01865/277–300* ⊕ *www.sjc. ox.ac.uk* ⊡ *Free* ⊙ *Daily 1–dusk.*

Tom Tower, designed by Christopher Wren, marks the entrance to the largest college of the southern half of Oxford:

★ **Christ Church College.** Traditionally called "the House" by its students,
☪ Christ Church has the largest quadrangle in town. This is where Charles Dodgson, better known as Lewis Carroll, was a math don; a shop across from the parkland (known as "the meadows") on St. Aldate's was the inspiration for the shop in *Through the Looking Glass.* Don't miss the 800-year-old chapel, or the medieval dining hall, with its portraits of former students—John Wesley, William Penn, and 14 prime ministers. ⊠ *St. Aldate's* ☎ *01865/276–150* ⊕ *www.chch.ox.ac. uk* ⊡ *£4.70* ⊙ *Mon.–Sat. 9–5:30, Sun. 1–5:30.*

WHERE TO EAT

★ ££–£££ **Le Petit Blanc.** Raymond Blanc's Conran-designed brasserie is sophisticated even by London standards. The top British chef populates his menu with modern European and regional French dishes: you might see herb pancakes with Gruyère and ham, or a hake fillet panfried in hazelnut butter. At £12 for two courses or £14.50 for three, the prix-fixe lunch is an incredible value, and well worth the short walk north of the town center. ⊠ *71–72 Walton St.* ☎ *01865/510–999* ⚑ *Reservations essential* ⊟ *AE, DC, MC, V.*

£ **Grand Café.** In a lovely 1920s building, this inexpensive café looks as if it should cost the world. Golden tiles, carved columns, and antique marble tables fill the place with charm, while the menu of tasty sandwiches, salads, and tarts, as well as perfect coffee drinks and desserts, make it a great place for lunch or an afternoon break. ⊠ *84 High St.* ☎ *01865/204–463* ⊟ *AE, DC, MC, V.*

£ **Pizza Express.** Many people are surprised to discover that this unique restaurant in the former sitting room of the 15th-century Golden Cross—Shakespeare's stopover lodging on his frequent trips from Stratford to London—is part of a nationwide chain. Creativity is encouraged here, so vegetarians, vegans, and meat eaters alike can enjoy inventing their own dream pizzas. A terrace is open in summer, but be sure to check out the medieval paintings and friezes inside the restaurant before heading

20

out. ⊠*8 The Golden Cross, Cornmarket St.* ☎*01865/790–442* ▭*AE, DC, MC, V.*

STRATFORD-UPON-AVON

104 mi north of London.

Stratford-upon-Avon has become adept at accommodating the hordes of people who come for a glimpse of William Shakespeare's world. Filled with all the distinctive, Tudor half-timber buildings your heart could desire, this is certainly a handsome town. But it can feel, at times, like a literary amusement park, so if you're not a fan of the Bard, you'd probably do better to explore some other quaint English village.

That said, how best to maximize your immersion in Shakespeare's works?

It's difficult to avoid feeling like a herd animal as you board the Shakespeare bus, but tours like **Stratford and the Shakespeare Story** (⊠*14 Rother St.* ☎*01789/294–466* ⊕*www.city-sightseeing.com* ▭*£9*), with a hop-on, hop-off route around the five Shakespeare Birthplace Trust properties (two of which are out of town), can make a visit infinitely easier if you don't have a car.

If you've never been here before, and you want to see everything, it's worth purchasing a combined ticket to the **Shakespeare's Birthplace Trust properties,** which include Shakespeare's Birthplace Museum, Nash's House, Hall's Croft, Anne Hathaway's Cottage, and the Shakespeare Countryside Museum. The ticket, which is valid for one year and is available at any of the properties, costs £14 for all the sites, or £11 for the three in-town properties (not including Anne Hathaway's Cottage and Mary Arden's House). ☎*01789/204–016* ⊕*www.shakespeare.org.uk.*

EXPLORING STRATFORD-UPON-AVON

Most visitors to Stratford start at **Shakespeare's Birthplace Museum.** The half-timber building in which Shakespeare was born in 1564 is a national treasure. It was owned by his descendants until the 19th century, and it became a national memorial in 1847. It's been furnished and decorated in bright colors that were popular in Shakespeare's time. All the fabrics have been hand-dyed using period methods. The visitor center tells the story of Shakespeare's life in great detail, which makes a good starting point for any tour of Stratford. ⊠*Henley St.* ☎*01789/204–016* ⊕*www. shakespeare.org.uk* ▭*£7* ⊙*Late Mar.–late Oct., Mon.–Sat. 9–5, Sun. 9:30–5; late Oct.–late Mar., Mon.–Sat. 9:30–4, Sun. 10–4.*

Nash's House contains an exhibit charting the history of Stratford, against a backdrop of period furniture and tapestries. The main attraction is really the vainglorious gardens around the adjacent remains of **New Place,** the home where Shakespeare spent his last years, and where he died in 1616.

> ## FAMILY TREES
>
> Nash's House belonged to Thomas Nash, first husband of Shakespeare's granddaughter Elizabeth Hall: you can see how tenuous the Shakespearean links can get around here.

A gorgeous Elizabethan knot garden, based on drawings of gardens from Shakespeare's time, grows around the remaining foundation of the house, which was destroyed in 1759 by its last owner, Reverend Francis Gastrell, in an attempt to stop the tide of visitors. ⊠ *Chapel St.* ☎ *01789/204–016* ⊕ *www.shakespeare.org.uk* 🖼 *£3.75* ⊘ *Nov.–Mar., daily 11–4; Apr., May, Sept., and Oct., daily 11–5; June–Aug., Mon.–Sat. 9:30–5, Sun. 10–5; last entry 30 min before closing.*

★ **Hall's Croft** is Stratford's most beautiful Tudor town house. This was—almost definitely—the home of Shakespeare's daughter Susanna and her husband, Dr. John Hall. It's outfitted with furniture of the period and the doctor's dispensary. The walled garden is delightful. ⊠ *Old Town St.* ☎ *01789/204–016* ⊕ *www.shakespeare.org.uk* 🖼 *£3.75* ⊘ *Nov.–Mar., daily 11–4; Apr., May, Sept., and Oct., daily 11–5; June–Aug., Mon.–Sat. 9:30–5, Sun. 10–5; last entry 30 min before closing.*

"Shakespeare's church," the 13th-century **Holy Trinity,** is fronted by a beautiful avenue of lime trees. Shakespeare is buried here, in the chancel. The bust of the Bard is thought to be an authentic likeness, executed a few years after his death. ⊠ *Trinity St.* ☎ *01789/266–316* 🖼 *Church free, chancel £1* ⊘ *Mar., Mon.–Sat. 9–5, Sun. 12:30–5; Apr.–Oct., Mon.–Sat. 8:30–6, Sun. 12:30–5; Nov.–Feb., Mon.–Sat. 9–4, Sun. 12:30–5; last admission 20 min before closing.*

Fodor'sChoice
★ The **Royal Shakespeare Theatre** on the bank of the Avon is the home of the Royal Shakespeare Company in Stratford, but since a massive renovation project began in 2007, it's been closed to the loyal fans who usually fill its seats for several productions a year. Similarly, the smaller **Swan Theatre,** in the same building, is closed for now as well. Both are slated to reopen in 2010. But never fear: you can still see the latest Royal Shakespeare Company productions at the two alternate theaters, the Other Place and the Courtyard. Check the Web site to see what's going to be on during your visit. It's always best to book in advance, but day-of-performance tickets are usually available. ⊠ *Waterside* ☎ *0870/609–1110 ticket hotline, 01789/296–655 information, 01789/403–405 tours* ⊕ *www.rsc.org.uk.*

20

STRATFORD ENVIRONS
The two remaining stops on the Shakespeare trail are just outside Stratford.

★ **Anne Hathaway's Cottage,** the early home of the playwright's wife, is a picturesque thatched cottage restored to reflect the comfortable middle-class Hathaway life. You can walk here from town—it's just over a mile from central Stratford. ⊠ *Cottage La., Shottery* ☎ *01789/204–016* ⊕ *www.shakespeare.org.uk* ⊡ *£5.50* ⊙ *Apr., May, Sept., and Oct., Mon.–Sat. 9:30–5, Sun. 10–5; June–Aug., Mon.–Sat. 9–5, Sun. 9:30–5; Nov.–Mar., Mon.–Sat. 10–4, Sun. 10:30–4; last entry 30 min before closing.*

☉ The **Shakespeare Countryside Museum,** with displays that illustrate life in the English countryside from Shakespeare's time to the present day, is the main attraction at **Palmer's Farm,** the site of a recent and radical Shakespearean revelation. In late 2000, research findings based on newly discovered real estate records revealed that the property, which had been referred to since the 18th century as Mary Arden's House, was not in fact the house in which Shakespeare's mother grew up. The real **Mary Arden's House,** hitherto known as Glebe Farm, was actually nearby and (thankfully) already owned by the Shakespeare Birthplace Trust. ⊠ *Wilmcote* ☎ *01789/204–016, 01789/293–455 for information on special events* ⊕ *www.shakespeare.org.uk* ⊡ *£6* ⊙ *Nov.–Mar., Mon.–Sat. 10–4, Sun. 10:30–4; Sept., Oct., Apr., and May, Mon.–Sat. 10–5, Sun. 10:30–5; June–Aug., Mon.–Sat. 9:30–5, Sun. 10–5; last entry 30 min before closing.*

☉ Some 8 mi north of Stratford in the medieval town of Warwick, **War-**
★ **wick Castle** fulfills the most clichéd Camelot daydreams. This medieval, fortified, much-restored, castellated, moated, landscaped (by Capability Brown) castle, now managed by the experts at Madame Tussauds, is a true period museum—complete with dungeons and a torture chamber, state rooms, and the occasional battle reenactment. ⊠ *Castle La. off Mill St., Warwick* ☎ *01926/495–421, 08704/422–000 24-hr information line* ⊕ *www.warwick-castle.co.uk* ⊡ *Nov.–Feb. £13.95, Mar.–mid-July £15.95, mid-July–Oct. £17.95* ⊙ *Apr.–July and Sept., daily 10–6; Aug., weekdays 10–6, weekends 10–7; Oct.–Mar., daily 10–5.*

WHERE TO EAT

££–£££ **Callands.** This brightly painted restaurant wins high marks for outstanding contemporary cuisine, as well as for good-value fixed-price menus (£20 for a pretheater dinner, for example). Start with tomato and paprika soup or Thai fish cakes with sweet dipping sauce, and move on to crab risotto, Moroccan-spice chicken, or grilled lemon sole. ⊠ *13–14 Meer St.* ☎ *01789/269–304.*

££ **Lambs of Sheep Street.** This friendly place is making a name for itself as one of the best restaurants in the region. You can try everything from fresh local sausages and mashed potatoes to creamy Thai green-curry chicken. Hardwood floors and oak beams make for a cozier ambience downstairs. The two- and three-course set menus (£11.50 and £14, respectively) are particularly good deals. ⊠ *12 Sheep St.* ☎ *01789/292–554* ⌂ *Reservations essential* ⊟ *AE, MC, V.*

£–££ **Black Swan.** Known locally as the Dirty Duck, this is one of Stratford's most celebrated pubs—it has attracted actors since the 18th-century thespian David Garrick's days. A little veranda overlooks the theaters and the river here. Along with a pint of bitter, it's a fine place to enjoy English grill specialties, as well as braised oxtail and honey-roasted duck. You can also choose from an assortment of bar meals. ⊠ *Water-side* ☎ *01789/297–312* ⊟ *AE, MC, V* ☺ *No dinner Sun.*

WINDSOR CASTLE

24 mi west of London.

The tall turrets of Windsor Castle, the largest inhabited castle in the world, can be seen for miles around. The grand stone castle is the star attraction in this quiet medieval town—though Eton College, England's most famous public school, is also just a lovely walk away across the Thames. The castle is the only royal residence to have been in continuous royal use since the days of William the Conqueror, who chose this site to build a timber stockade soon after his conquest of Britain in 1066. It was Edward III in the 1300s who really founded the castle: he built the Norman gateway, the great Round Tower, and the State Apartments. Charles II restored the State Apartments during the 1600s, and, during the 1820s George IV—with his mania for building—converted what was still essentially a medieval castle into the palace you see today.

EXPLORING WINDSOR CASTLE

The massive citadel of **Windsor Castle** occupies 13 acres, but the first part you notice on entering is the **Round Tower,** on top of which the Standard is flown and at the base of which is the 11th-century Moat Garden. Passing under the portcullis at the Norman Gate, you reach the **Upper Ward,** the quadrangle containing the State Apartments—which you may tour when the queen is out—and the sovereign's Private Apartments. Processions for foreign heads of state and other ceremonies take place here, as does the Changing of the Guard when the queen is in. A short walk takes you to the Lower Ward, where the high point is the magnificent **St. George's Chapel,** symbolic and actual guardian of the Order of the Garter, the highest chivalric order in the land, founded in 1348 by Edward III. Ten sovereigns are buried in the chapel—a fantastic Perpendicular Gothic vision 230 feet long, complete with gargoyles, buttresses, banners, swords, and choir stalls. This is also where royal weddings usually take place.

The **State Apartments** are grander than Buckingham Palace's and have the added attraction of a few gems from the queen's vast art collection: choice canvases by Rubens, Rembrandt, Van Dyck, Gainsborough, Canaletto, and Holbein; da Vinci drawings; Gobelin tapestries; and lime-wood carvings by Grinling Gibbons. The entrance is through a grand hall holding cases crammed with precious china—some still used for royal banquets. Don't miss the outsize suit of armor, made for

20

> **DID YOU KNOW?**
>
> The queen uses Windsor often—it's said she likes it much more than Buckingham Palace—spending most weekends here, often joined by family and friends. You know she's in when the Royal Standard is flown above the Round Tower but not when you see the Union Jack.

Henry VIII, in the armory. Make sure you take in the magnificent views across to Windsor Great Park, which are the remains of a former royal hunting forest.

☾ One unmissable treat is **Queen Mary's Dolls' House,** a 12:1 scale, seven-story palace with electricity, running water, and working elevators, designed in 1924 by Sir Edwin Lutyens. The detail is incredible—even the diminutive wine bottles hold the real thing.

⊠ *Windsor Castle* ☎ *020/7766–7304 tickets* ⊕ *www.royalresidences. com* ✉ *£13.50 for Precincts, State Apartments, Gallery, St. George's Chapel, Albert Memorial Chapel, and Queen Mary's Dolls' House; £7 when State Apartments are closed* ☉ *Mar.–Oct., daily 9:45–5:15, last admission at 4; Nov.–Feb., daily 9:45–4:15, last admission at 3; St. George's Chapel closed Sun. except to worshippers.*

★ The splendid redbrick Tudor-style buildings of **Eton College,** founded in 1440 by King Henry VI, border the north end of High Street. During the college semesters, schoolboys dress in their distinctive striped trousers, swallow-tailed coats, and stiff collars to walk to class—it's all terrifically photogenic. The Gothic **Chapel** rivals St. George's at Windsor in size and magnificence, and is both austere and intimate. The **Museum of Eton Life** has displays on the school's history. ⊠ *Main entrance Brewhouse Yard* ☎ *01753/671–177* ⊕ *www.etoncollege.com* ✉ *£4, £5 with one-hour tour of school and chapel* ☉ *Mar.–mid-Apr., July, and Aug., daily 10:30–4:30; mid-Apr.–June and Sept., daily 2–4:30; guided tours mid-Mar.–Sept., daily at 2:15 and 3:15.*

WHERE TO EAT

£ **Two Brewers.** Two small, low-ceiling rooms make up this 17th-century pub where locals congregate. Children are not welcome, but adults will find a suitable collection of wine, espresso, and local beer, plus an excellent little menu. Reservations are essential on Sunday, when the pub serves a traditional roast. ⊠ *34 Park St.* ☎ *01753/855–426* ▭ *AE, MC, V* ☉ *No dinner Fri. or Sat.*

UNDERSTANDING LONDON

LONDON AT-A-GLANCE

FAST FACTS

Type of government: Representative democracy. In 1999 the Greater London Authority Act reestablished a single local governing body for the Greater London area, consisting of an elected mayor and the 25-member London Assembly. Elections, first held in 2000, take place every 4 years.

Population: City 7.4 million, metro area 11.2 million

Population density: 11,841 people per square mi

Median age: 38.4

Infant mortality rate: 5.7 per 1,000 births

Language: English. More than 300 languages are spoken in London. All city government documents are translated into Arabic, Bengali, Chinese, Greek, Gujurati, Hindi, Punjabi, Turkish, Urdu, and Vietnamese.

Ethnic and racial groups: White 71%, Indian 6%, other 6%, black African 5%, black Caribbean 5%, Bangladeshi 2%, other Asian 2%, Pakistani 2%, Chinese 1%

Religion: Christian 58%, non-affiliated 24%, Muslim 8%, Hindu 4%, Jewish 2%, Sikh 1%, other religion 1%, Buddhist 0.8%

When a man is tired of London, he is tired of life; for there is in London all that life can afford.

—Samuel Johnson

GEOGRAPHY & ENVIRONMENT

Latitude: 51° N (same as Calgary, Canada; Kiev, Russia; Prague, Czech Republic)

Longitude: 0° (same as Accra, Ghana). A brass line in the ground in Greenwich marks the prime meridian (0° longitude).

Elevation: 49 feet

Land area: City, 67 square mi; metro area, 625 square mi

Terrain: River plain, rolling hills, and parkland

Natural hazards: Drought in warmer summers, flooding of the Thames due to surge tides from the North Atlantic

Environmental issues: Up to 1,600 people die each year from health problems related to London's polluted air. The city has been improving its air quality but is unlikely to meet goals it set for 2005. Only half of London's rivers and canals received passing grades for water quality from 1999 through 2001. Over £12 million ($22 million) is spent annually to ensure the city's food safety.

I'm leaving because the weather is too good. I hate London when it's not raining.

—Groucho Marx

ECONOMY

Work force: 5.3 million; financial/real estate 28%, health care 10%, manufacturing 8%, education 7%, construction 5%, public administration 5%

Unemployment: 6.9%

Major industries: The arts, banking, government, insurance, tourism

London: a nation, not a city.

—Benjamin Disraeli, Lothair

ENGLISH VOCABULARY

You and a Londoner may speak the same language, but some phrases definitely get lost in translation once they cross the Atlantic. Here's a handy guide to help you avoid confusion.

BRITISH ENGLISH	AMERICAN ENGLISH
BASIC TERMS AND EVERYDAY ITEMS	
bill	check
flat	apartment
lift	elevator
nappie	diaper
holiday	vacation
note	bill (currency)
plaster	Band-Aid
queue	line
row	argument
rubbish	trash
tin	can
toilet/ loo/ WC	bathroom
CLOTHING	
braces	suspenders
bum bag	fanny pack
dressing	gown robe
handbag	purse
jumper	sweater
pants/ undies	underpants/ briefs
rucksack	backpack
suspender	garter
tights	pantyhose
trainers	sneakers
trousers	pants
vest	undershirt
waistcoat	vest
TRANSPORTATION	
bonnet	hood
boot	trunk
coach	long-distance bus
pavement	sidewalk

petrol	gas
pram	baby carriage
puncture	flat
windscreen	windshield

FOOD

afters	dessert
aubergine	eggplant
banger	sausage
biscuit	cookie
chips	fries
courgette	zucchini
crisps	potato chips
greasy spoon	café serving traditional English breakfasts, all day
jam	jelly
jelly	Jello
pips	seeds
rocket	arugula
spud	potato
starter	appetizer
sweet	candy
tea	early dinner

SLANG

all right	hi there
bird	woman
bloke, chap	guy
cheers	thank you
chuffed	pleased
geezer	dude
guv'nor, gaffer	boss
hard	tough
mate	buddy
randy	horny
sound	good
ta	thank you
wicked	cool

London has been the focus of countless books and essays. For sonorous eloquence, you still must reach back more than half a century to Henry James's *English Hours* and Virginia Woolf's *The London Scene*. Today most suggested reading lists begin with V. S. Pritchett's *London Perceived* and H. V. Morton's *In Search of London,* both decades old. Three more up-to-date books with a general compass are: Peter Ackroyd's anecdotal *London: The Biography,* which traces the city's growth from the Druids to the 21st century, John Russell's *London,* a sumptuously illustrated art book, and Christopher Hibbert's *In London: The Biography of a City.* Stephen Inwood's *A History of London* explores the city from its Roman roots to its swinging '60s heyday. Piet Schreuders's *The Beatles' London* follows the footsteps of the Fab Four.

That noted, there are books galore on the various facets of the city. *The Art and Architecture of London* by Ann Saunders is fairly comprehensive. *Inside London: Discovering the Classic Interiors of London,* by Joe Friedman and Peter Aprahamian, has magnificent color photographs of hidden and overlooked shops, clubs, and town houses. For a wonderful take on the golden age of the city's regal mansions, see Christopher Simon Sykes's *Private Palaces: Life in the Great London Houses.* For various other aspects of the city, consult Mervyn Blatch's helpful *A Guide to London's Churches,* Andrew Crowe's *The Parks and Woodlands of London,* Sheila Fairfield's *The Streets of London,* Ann Saunders's *Regent's Park,* Ian Norrie's *Hampstead, Highgate Village, and Kenwood,* and Suzanne Ebel's *A Guide to London's Riverside: Hampton Court to Greenwich.* For keen walkers, there are two books by Andrew Duncan: *Secret London* and *Walking Village London.* *City Secrets: London,* edited by Robert Kahn, is a handsome little red-linen book of anecdotes from London writers,

artists, and historians about their favorite places in the city. For the last word on just about every subject, see *The London Encyclopaedia,* edited by Ben Weinreb and Christopher Hibbert. HarperCollins's *London Photographic Atlas* has a plethora of bird's-eye images of the capital. For an alternative view of the city, it would be hard to better Ian Sinclair's witty and intelligent *London Orbital: A Walk Around the M25* in which he scrutinizes the history, mythology, and politics of London from the viewpoint of its ugly ringroad.

Of course, the history and spirit of the city are also to be found in celebrations of great authors, British heroes, and architects. Peter Ackroyd's massive *Dickens* elucidates how the great author shaped today's view of the city; Martin Gilbert's magisterial, multivolume *Churchill* traces the city through some of its greatest trials; J. Mansbridge's *John Nash* details the London buildings of this great architect. Liza Picard evokes mid-18th-century London in *Dr. Johnson's London.* For musical theater buffs, Mike Leigh's *Gilbert and Sullivan's London* takes a romantic look at the two artists' lives and times in the capital's grand theaters and wild nightspots. *Rodinsky's Room* by Rachel Lichtenstein and Iain Sinclair is a fascinating exploration of East End Jewish London and the mysterious disappearance of one of its occupants.

Nineteenth-century London—the city of Queen Victoria, Tennyson, and Dickens—comes alive through *Mayhew's London,* a massive study of the London poor, and Gustave Doré's *London,* an unforgettable series of engravings of the city (often reprinted in modern editions) that detail its horrifying slums and grand avenues. Maureen Waller's *1700: Scenes from London Life* is a fascinating look at the daily life of Londoners in the 18th century. When it comes to fiction, of course, Dickens's immortal works top the list. Stay-at-home detectives have long walked the streets of London, thanks to great mysteries by Sir Arthur Conan Doyle, Dorothy L. Sayers, Agatha Christie, Ngaio Marsh, and Antonia Fraser. Cops and bad guys wind their way around 1960s London in Jake Arnott's pulp fiction books, *The Long Firm* and *He Kills Coppers*. Martin Amis's *London Fields* tracks a murder mystery through West London. For so-called "tart noir," pick up any Stella Duffy book. Marie Belloc-Lowndes's *The Lodger* is a fictional account of London's most deadly villain, Jack the Ripper. Victorian London was never so salacious as in Sarah Waters' story of a young girl who travels the theaters as a singer, the Soho squares as a male prostitute, and the East End as a communist in *Tipping the Velvet*. Late-20th-century London, with its diverse ethnic makeup, is the star of Zadie Smith's famed novel *White Teeth*. The vibrancy and cultural diversity of London's East End come to life in Monica Ali's *Brick Lane*.

There are any number of films—from *Waterloo Bridge* and *Georgy Girl* to *Secrets and Lies* and *Notting Hill*—that have used London as their setting. But always near the top of anyone's list are four films that rank among the greatest musicals of all time: Walt Disney's *Mary Poppins* (complete with Dick Van Dyke's laughable Cockney accent), George Cukor's *My Fair Lady*, Sir Carol Reed's *Oliver!*, and The Beatles' *A Hard Day's Night*.

Children of all ages enjoy Stephen Herek's *101 Dalmatians*, with Glenn Close as fashion-savvy Cruella de Vil. King's Cross Station in London was shot to cinematic fame by the movie version of J.K. Rowling's *Harry Potter and the Philosopher's Stone*. Look for cameos by the city in all other *Harry Potter* films.

The swinging '60s are loosely portrayed in M. Jay Roach's *Austin Powers: International Man of Mystery*, full of references to British slang and some great opening scenes in London. For a truer picture of the '60s in London, Michaelangelo Antonioni weaves a mystery plot around the world of London fashion photographer in *Blow-Up*. British gangster films came into their own with Guy Ritchie's amusing tales of London thieves in *Lock, Stock, and Two Smoking Barrels*, filmed almost entirely in London, and the follow-up *Snatch*, with a comedic turn by Brad Pitt. Of course, the original tough guy is 007, and his best exploits in London are featured in the introductory chase scene in *The World Is Not Enough*.

Sir Arthur Conan Doyle knew the potential of London as a chilling setting, and John Landis's *An American Werewolf in London* and Hitchcock's *39 Steps* exploit the Gothic and sinister qualities of the city. St. Ermine's Hotel stands in for the 19th-century Savoy dining room in Oliver Parker's *The Importance of Being Earnest*. For a fascinating look at Renaissance London, watch John Madden's *Shakespeare in Love*.

Some modern-day romantic comedies that use London as a backdrop are Peter Howitt's *Sliding Doors* with Gwyneth Paltrow; Nick Hamm's sweet, romantic comedy about an American backpacker, *Martha Meet Frank, Daniel and Laurence (aka The Very Thought of You)*; the screen adaptations of Helen Fielding's *Bridget Jones's Diary* (and its sequel), starring Renée Zellweger, Hugh Grant, and Colin Firth; and Richard Curtis's holiday feel-good flick *Love Actually*, which included as many threaded-together romantic misadventures as it did A-list British actors. For a slice of Indian London, you can't do better than Gurinder Chadha's tale of a girl who wants to play soccer in *Bend It Like Beckham*.

London Essentials

There are planners and there are those who, excuse the pun, fly by the seat of their pants. We happily place ourselves among the planners. Our writers and editors try to anticipate all the issues you may face before and during any journey, and then they do their research. This section is the product of their efforts. Use it to get excited about your trip to London, to inform your travel planning, or to guide you on the road should the seat of your pants start to feel threadbare.

GETTING STARTED

We're really proud of our Web site: Fodors.com is a great place to begin any journey. Scan Travel Wire for suggested itineraries, travel deals, restaurant and hotel openings, and other up-to-the-minute info. Check out Booking to research prices and book plane tickets, hotel rooms, rental cars, and vacation packages. Head to Talk for on-the-ground pointers from travelers who frequent our message boards. You can also link to loads of other travel-related resources.

■ RESOURCES

ONLINE TRAVEL TOOLS

For more information specifically on London, visit one of the following:

The official London Web site is ⊕*www.visitlondon.com*, which supplies event information and has accommodations booking with guaranteed lowest rates: if you book through its site and then find a lower price at the same hotel within 24 hours, they'll refund the difference.

Other sites of interest include ⊕*www.londontown.com*, the *Evening Standard*'s online ⊕*www.thisislondon.com*, Transport for London (⊕*www.tfl.gov.uk*), No. 10 Downing Street (⊕*www.number-10.gov.uk*), and the BBC (⊕*www.bbc.co.uk*).

For London events and news months in advance, visit the following culture and entertainment Web sites: ⊕*www.timeout.co.uk*, ⊕*www.officiallondontheatre.co.uk*, and ⊕*www.kidslovelondon.com*. At ⊕*www.londonfreelist.com* you can find great listings of free and nearly free events and attractions.

Currency Conversion Google (⊕www.google.com) does currency conversion. Just type in the amount you want to convert and an explanation of how you want it converted (e.g., "14 Swiss francs in dollars"), and then voilà. **Oanda.com** (⊕www.oanda.com) also allows you to print out a handy table with the current day's conversion rates. **XE.com** (⊕www.xe.com) is a good currency conversion Web site.

Safety Transportation Security Administration ([TSA;] ⊕www.tsa.gov)

Time Zones Timeanddate.com (⊕www.timeanddate.com/worldclock) can help you figure out the correct time anywhere in the world.

Weather Accuweather.com (⊕www.accuweather.com) is an independent weather-forecasting service with especially good coverage of hurricanes. **Weather.com** (⊕www.weather.com) is the Web site for the Weather Channel.

Other Resources CIA World Factbook (⊕www.odci.gov/cia/publications/factbook/index.html) has profiles of every country in the world. It's a good source if you need some quick facts and figures.

VISITOR INFORMATION

When you arrive in London, you can get good information at the London Visitor Centre near the Eurostar arrivals area at Waterloo train station. There's also an information office at Victoria Station. These are helpful if you're looking for brochures for London sights, or if something's gone horribly wrong with your hotel reservation—if, for example, you don't have one—as they have a useful reservations service. All visitor stations are open from 9 AM until after 10 PM, later in the summer. The Britain and London Visitor Centre is a worthwhile stop for travel, hotel, and entertainment information. It's open June–October, weekdays 9:30–6:30, Saturday 9–5, Sunday 10–4; and November–May, weekdays 9:30–6:30, weekends

10–4. The London Tourist Information Centre has branches in Greenwich and in Southwark. If you want basic information and none of these centers are handy, call the Londonline for tips on sightseeing. (Note that the Londonline is a premium rate phone number, so you'll be charged more for calling it than you would for a local number.)

The official Web site of VisitBritain, the British Tourist Authority is ⊕*www.visitbritain.com*. Its "gateway" Web site, ⊕*www.visitbritain.com/usa*, provides information most helpful to Britain-bound U.S. travelers.

Contacts **VisitBritain** (☎212/986–2200 or 800/462–2748 ⊕www.visitbritain.com/usa).

In London **Britain and London Visitor Centre** (✉1 Regent St., Piccadilly Circus, SW1Y 4NX). **London Tourist Information Centre** (✉Pepys House, 2 Cutty Sark Gardens, Greenwich, SE10 9LW ☎0870/608–2000 ⊕www. visitlondon.com ✉Vinopolis, 1 Bank End, Southwark, SE1 9BU ☎020/7357–9168). **Londonline** (☎090/6866–3344 ⊕www.london-line.co.uk).

❚ THINGS TO CONSIDER

GOVERNMENT ADVISORIES
As different countries have different world views, look at travel advisories from a range of governments to get more of a sense of what's going on out there. And be sure to parse the language carefully. For example, a warning to "avoid all travel" carries more weight than one urging you to "avoid nonessential travel," and both are much stronger than a plea to "exercise caution." A U.S. government travel warning is more permanent (though not necessarily more serious) than a so-called public announcement, which carries an expiration date.

The U.S. Department of State's Web site has more than just travel warnings and advisories. The consular information sheets issued for every country have general safety tips, entry requirements (though

be sure to verify these with the country's embassy), and other useful details.

❚TIP➡**If you're a U.S. citizen traveling abroad, consider registering online with the State Department (https://travelregistration.state.gov/ibrs/), so the government will know to look for you should a crisis occur in the country you're visiting. If you travel frequently, look into the TSA's Registered Traveler program. The program, which is still being tested in several U.S. airports, is designed to cut down on gridlock at security checkpoints by allowing prescreened travelers to pass quickly through kiosks that scan an iris and/or a fingerprint. How sci-fi is that?**

General Information & Warnings **Australian Department of Foreign Affairs & Trade** (⊕www.smartraveller.gov.au). **Consular Affairs Bureau of Canada** (⊕www.voyage. gc.ca). **U.K. Foreign & Commonwealth Office** (⊕www.fco.gov.uk/travel). **U.S. Department of State** (⊕www.travel.state.gov).

GEAR
London's weather is unpredictable. It can be cool, damp, and overcast, even in summer, but recent summers have been real scorchers—with days when temperatures neared 100°F for weeks at a time, which can be miserable as not very many hotels, restaurants, and bars are air-conditioned. In general, you'll need a heavy coat for winter and short-sleeved, light clothes for summer, along with a lightweight coat or jacket. Always pack a small umbrella that you can easily carry around with you. Pack as you would for any American city: jackets and ties for expensive restaurants and nightspots, casual clothes elsewhere. Jeans are popular in London and are perfectly acceptable for sightseeing and informal dining. Blazers and sports jackets are popular with men. In five-star hotels men can expect to be asked to wear a jacket and tie in the restaurant and bar, while women might feel out of place unless they're in smart clothes. Otherwise, for women, ordinary dress is acceptable just about everywhere.

SHIPPING LUGGAGE AHEAD

Imagine globetrotting with only a carry-on in tow. Shipping your luggage in advance via an air-freight service is a great way to cut down on backaches, hassles, and stress—especially if your packing list includes strollers, car-seats, etc. There are some things to be aware of, though. First, research carry-on restrictions; if you absolutely need something that's isn't practical to ship and isn't allowed in carry-ons, this strategy isn't for you. Second, plan to send your bags several days in advance to U.S. destinations and as much as two weeks in advance to some international destinations. Third, plan to spend some money: it will cost least $100 to send a small piece of luggage, a golf bag, or a pair of skis to a domestic destination, much more to places overseas. Some people use Federal Express to ship their bags, but this can cost even more than air-freight services. All these services insure your bag (for most, the limit is $1,000, but you should verify that amount); you can, however, purchase additional insurance for about $1 per $100 of value.

Contacts Luggage Concierge (☎ 800/288–9818 ⊕ www.luggageconcierge.com). **Luggage Express** (☎ 866/744–7224 ⊕ www.usxpluggageexpress.com). **Luggage Free** (☎ 800/361–6871 ⊕ www.luggagefree.com). **Sports Express** (☎ 800/357–4174 ⊕ www.sportsexpress.com) specializes in shipping golf clubs and other sports equipment. **Virtual Bellhop** (☎ 877/235–5467 ⊕ www.virtualbellhop.com).

PASSPORTS & VISAS

U.S. citizens need only a valid passport to enter Great Britain for stays of up to six months. If you're within six months of your passport's expiration date, renew it before you leave—nearly extinct passports are not strictly banned, but they make immigration officials very anxious, and may cause you problems.

PASSPORTS

We're always surprised at how few Americans have passports—only 25% at this writing. This number is expected to grow in coming years, when it becomes impossible to re-enter the United States from trips to neighboring Canada or Mexico without one. Remember this: A passport verifies both your identity and nationality—a great reason to have one.

U.S. passports are valid for 10 years. You must apply in person if you're getting a passport for the first time; if your previous passport was lost, stolen, or damaged; or if your previous passport has expired and was issued more than 15 years ago or when you were under 16. All children under 18 must appear in person to apply for or renew a passport. Both parents must accompany any child under 14 (or send a notarized statement with their permission) and provide proof of their relationship to the child.

There are 13 regional passport offices, as well as 7,000 passport acceptance facilities in post offices, public libraries, and other governmental offices. If you're renewing a passport, you can do so by mail. Forms are available at passport acceptance facilities and online.

The cost to apply for a new passport is $97 for adults, $82 for children under 16; renewals are $67. Allow six weeks for processing, both for first-time passports and renewals. For an expediting fee of $60 you can reduce this time to about two weeks. If your trip is less than two weeks away, you can get a passport even more rapidly by going to a passport office with the necessary documentation. Private expediters can get things done in as little as 48 hours, but charge hefty fees for their services.

■TIP➔Before your trip, make two copies of your passport's data page (one for someone at home and another for you to carry separately). Or scan the page and e-mail it to someone at home and/or yourself.

PACKING 101

Why do some people travel with a convoy of huge suitcases yet never have a thing to wear? How do others pack a duffle with a week's worth of outfits *and* supplies for every contingency? We realize that packing is a matter of style, but there's a lot to be said for traveling light. These tips help fight the battle of the bulging bag.

Make a list. In a recent Fodor's survey, 29% of respondents said they make lists (and often pack) a week before a trip. You can use your list to pack and to repack at the end of your trip. It can also serve as record of the contents of your suitcase—in case it disappears in transit.

Think it through. What's the weather like? Is this a business trip? A cruise? Going abroad? In some places dress may be more or less conservative than you're used to. As you create your itinerary, note outfits next to each activity (don't forget accessories).

Edit your wardrobe. Plan to wear everything twice (better yet, thrice) and to do laundry along the way. Stick to one basic look—urban chic, sporty casual, etc. Build around one or two neutrals and an accent (e.g., black, white, and olive green). Women can freshen looks by changing scarves or jewelry. For a week's trip, you can look smashing with three bottoms, four or five tops, a sweater, and a jacket.

Be practical. Put comfortable shoes atop your list. (Did we need to say this?) Pack lightweight, wrinkle-resistent, compact, washable items. (Or this?) Stack and roll clothes, so they'll wrinkle less. Unless you're on a guided tour or a cruise, select luggage you can readily carry. Porters, like good butlers, are hard to find these days.

Check weight & size limitations. In the U.S. you may be charged extra for checked bags weighing more than 50 pounds. Some airlines don't allow you to check bags over 60 to 70 pounds, or they charge outrageous fees for every excess pound—or bag. Carry-on size limitations can be stringent, too.

Check carry-on restrictions. Research restrictions with the TSA. Rules vary abroad, so check them with your airline if you're traveling overseas on a foreign carrier. Consider packing all but essentials (travel documents, prescription meds, wallet) in checked luggage. This leads to a "pack only what you can afford to lose" approach that might help you streamline.

Rethink valuables. On U.S. flights, airlines are liable for only about $2,800 per person for bags. On international flights, the liability limit is around $635 per bag. But items like computers, cameras, and jewelry aren't covered, and as gadgetry can go on and of the list of carry-on no-no's, you can't count on keeping things safe by keeping them close. Although comprehensive travel policies may cover luggage, the liability limit is often a pittance. Your homeowner's policy may cover you sufficiently when you travel—or not.

Lock it up. If you must pack valuables, use TSA-approved locks (about $10) that can be unlocked by all U.S. security personnel.

Tag it. Always tag your luggage; use your business address if you don't want people to know your home address. Put the same information (and a copy of your itinerary) inside your luggage, too.

Report problems immediately. If your bags—or things inside them—are damaged or go astray, file a written claim with your airline *before leaving the airport.* If the airline is at fault, it may give you money for essentials until your luggage arrives. Most lost bags are found within 48 hours, so alert the airline to your whereabouts for two or three days. If your bag was opened for security reasons in the United States and something is missing, file a claim with the TSA.

VISAS

A visa is essentially formal permission to enter a country. Visas allow countries to keep track of you and other visitors—and generate revenue (from application fees). You *always* need a visa to enter a foreign country; however, many countries routinely issue tourist visas on arrival, particularly to U.S. citizens. When your passport is stamped or scanned in the immigration line, you're actually being issued a visa. Sometimes you have to stand in a separate line and pay a small fee to get your stamp before going through immigration, but you can still do this at the airport on arrival. Getting a visa isn't always that easy. Some countries require that you arrange for one in advance of your trip. There's usually—but not always—a fee involved, and said fee may be nominal ($10 or less) or substantial ($100 or more).

If you must apply for a visa in advance, you can usually do it in person or by mail. When you apply by mail, you send your passport to a designated consulate, where your passport will be examined and the visa issued. Expediters—usually the same ones who handle expedited passport applications—can do all the work of obtaining your visa for you; however, there's always an additional cost (often more than $50 per visa).

Most visas limit you to a single trip—basically during the actual dates of your planned vacation. Other visas allow you to visit as many times as you wish for a specific period of time. Remember that requirements change, sometimes at the drop of a hat, and the burden is on you to make sure that you have the appropriate visas. Otherwise, you'll be turned away at the airport or, worse, deported after you arrive in the country. No company or travel insurer gives refunds if your travel plans are disrupted because you didn't have the correct visa.

U.S. Passport Information U.S. Department of State (☎877/487-2778 ⊕http://travel. state.gov/passport).

U.S. Passport & Visa Expediters A. Briggs Passport & Visa Expeditors (☎800/806-0581 or 202/464-3000 ⊕www. abriggs.com). **American Passport Express** (☎800/455-5166 or 603/559-9888 ⊕www. americanpassport.com). **Passport Express** (☎800/362-8196 or 401/272-4612 ⊕www. passportexpress.com). **Travel Document Systems** (☎800/874-5100 or 202/638-3800 ⊕www.traveldocs.com). **Travel the World Visas** (☎866/886-8472 or 301/495-7700 ⊕www.world-visa.com).

SHOTS & MEDICATIONS

For more information see ⇨Health under On the Ground in London, below.

■ TIP→**If you travel a lot internationally—particularly to developing nations—refer to the CDC's** *Health Information for International Travel* **(aka Traveler's Health Yellow Book). Info from it is posted on the CDC Web site (** ⊕www.cdc.gov/travel/yb**), or you can buy a copy from your local bookstore for $24.95.**

Health Warnings National Centers for Disease Control & Prevention ([CDC] ☎877/394-8747 international travelers' health line ⊕www.cdc.gov/travel). **World Health Organization** ([WHO] ⊕www.who.int).

TRIP INSURANCE

What kind of coverage do you honestly need? Do you even need trip insurance at all? Take a deep breath and read on.

We believe that comprehensive trip insurance is especially valuable if you're booking a very expensive or complicated trip (particularly to an isolated region) or if you're booking far in advance. Who knows what could happen six months down the road? But whether or not you get insurance has more to do with how comfortable you are assuming all that risk yourself.

Comprehensive travel policies typically cover trip-cancellation and interruption, letting you cancel or cut your trip short because of a personal emergency, illness, or, in some cases, acts of terrorism in

Trip Insurance Resources

INSURANCE COMPARISON SITES		
Insure My Trip.com	800/487-4722	www.insuremytrip.com
Square Mouth.com	800/240-0369	www.quotetravelinsurance.com
COMPREHENSIVE TRAVEL INSURERS		
Access America	866/807-3982	www.accessamerica.com
CSA Travel Protection	800/873-9855	www.csatravelprotection.com
HTH Worldwide	610/254-8700 or 888/243-2358	www.hthworldwide.com
Travelex Insurance	888/457-4602	www.travelex-insurance.com
Travel Guard International	715/345-0505 or 800/826-4919	www.travelguard.com
Travel Insured International	800/243-3174	www.travelinsured.com
MEDICAL-ONLY INSURERS		
International Medical Group	800/628-4664	www.imglobal.com
International SOS	215/942-8000 or 713/521-7611	www.internationalsos.com
Wallach & Company	800/237-6615 or 504/687-3166	www.wallach.com

your destination. Such policies also cover evacuation and medical care. Some also cover you for trip delays because of bad weather or mechanical problems as well as for lost or delayed baggage. Another type of coverage to look for is financial default—that is, when your trip is disrupted because a tour operator, airline, or cruise line goes out of business. Generally you must buy this when you book your trip or shortly thereafter, and it's only available to you if your operator isn't on a list of excluded companies.

If you're going abroad, consider buying medical-only coverage at the very least. Neither Medicare nor some private insurers cover medical expenses anywhere outside of the United States besides Mexico and Canada (including time aboard a cruise ship, even if it leaves from a U.S. port). Medical-only policies typically reimburse you for medical care (excluding that related to pre-existing conditions) and hospitalization abroad, and provide for evacuation. You still have to pay the bills and await reimbursement from the insurer, though.

Although England has a subsidized National Health Service, free at the point of service for British residents, foreign visitors are required to pay for any health treatment they receive. So be sure you have adequate health insurance before you travel. Expect comprehensive travel insurance policies to cost about 4% to 7% of the total price of your trip (it's more like 12% if you're over age 70). A medical-only policy may or may not be cheaper than a comprehensive policy. Always read the fine print of your policy to make sure that you are covered for the risks that are of most concern to you. Compare several policies to make sure you're getting the best price and range of coverage available.

BOOKING YOUR TRIP

Unless your cousin is a travel agent, you're probably among the millions of people who make most of their travel arrangements online. But have you ever wondered just what the differences are between an online travel agent (a Web site through which you make reservations instead of going directly to the airline, hotel, or car-rental company), a discounter (a firm that does a high volume of business with a hotel chain or airline and accordingly gets good prices), a wholesaler (one that makes cheap reservations in bulk and then re-sells them to people like you), and an aggregator (one that compares all the offerings so you don't have to)? Is it truly better to book directly on an airline or hotel Web site? And when does a real live travel agent come in handy?

ONLINE

You really have to shop around. A travel wholesaler such as Hotels.com or Hotel-Club.net can be a source of good rates, as can discounters such as Hotwire or Priceline, particularly if you can bid for your hotel room or airfare. Indeed, such sites sometimes have deals that are unavailable elsewhere. They do, however, tend to work only with hotel chains (which makes them just plain useless for getting hotel reservations outside of major cities) or big airlines (so that often leaves out upstarts like jetBlue and some foreign carriers like Air India). Also, with discounters and wholesalers you must generally prepay, and everything is nonrefundable. And before you fork over the dough, be sure to check the terms and conditions, so you know what a given company will do for you if there's a problem and what you'll have to deal with on your own.

■TIP→**To be absolutely sure everything was processed correctly, confirm reservations made through online travel agents, discounters, and wholesalers directly with your hotel before leaving home.**

Booking engines like Expedia, Travelocity, and Orbitz are actually travel agents, albeit high-volume, online ones. And airline travel packagers like American Airlines Vacations and Virgin Vacations—well, they're travel agents, too. But they may still not work with all the world's hotels.

An aggregator site will search many sites and pull the best prices for airfares, hotels, and rental cars from them. Most aggregators compare the major travel-booking sites such as Expedia, Travelocity, and Orbitz; some also look at airline Web sites, though rarely the sites of smaller budget airlines. Some aggregators also compare other travel products, including complex packages—a good thing, as you can sometimes get the best overall deal by booking an air-and-hotel package.

WITH A TRAVEL AGENT

If you use an agent—brick-and-mortar or virtual—you'll pay a fee for the service. And know that the service you get from some online agents isn't comprehensive. For example Expedia and Travelocity don't search for prices on budget airlines like jetBlue, Southwest, or small foreign carriers. That said, some agents (online or not) *do* have access to fares that are difficult to find otherwise, and the savings can more than make up for any surcharge.

A knowledgeable brick-and-mortar travel agent can be a godsend if you're booking a cruise, a package trip that's not available to you directly, an air pass, or a complicated itinerary including several overseas flights. What's more, travel agents that specialize in a destination may have exclusive access to certain deals and insider information on things such as charter flights. Agents who specialize in types of travelers (senior citizens, gays and lesbians, naturists) or types of trips (cruises, luxury travel, safaris) can also be invaluable.

A top-notch agent planning your trip to Russia will make sure you get the correct visa application and complete it on time; the one booking your cruise may get you a cabin upgrade or arrange to have bottle of champagne chilling in your cabin when you embark. And complain about the surcharges all you like, but when things don't work out the way you'd hoped, it's nice to have an agent to put things right.

■ TIP → Remember that Expedia, Travelocity, and Orbitz are travel agents, not just booking engines. To resolve any problems with a reservation made through these companies, contact them first.

Travel novices might feel more comfortable booking their trip to the U.K. through an established travel agent, as they can give recommendations about the best neighborhoods for you to stay in to fit your interests, and steer you away from easy travel mistakes. More experienced travelers often book online to get the best deals, and prefer to handle their own scheduling and and reservations.

Agent Resources **American Society of Travel Agents** (☎ 703/739–2782 ⊕ www.travelsense.org).

London Travel Agents **Preference Travel Limited** (☎ 0207/373–9322 ⊕ www.preferencetravel.co.uk) is a reliable option in Chelsea, good for exotic holidays or simpler journeys. **STA Travel** (☎ 0871/230–0040 ⊕ www.statravel.co.uk) has offices all over town that specialize in budget travel for the young, and the young at heart.

▌ **AIRLINE TICKETS**

Most domestic airline tickets are electronic; international tickets may be either electronic or paper. With an e-ticket the only thing you receive is an e-mailed receipt citing your itinerary and reservation and ticket numbers. The greatest advantage of an e-ticket is that if you lose your receipt, you can simply print out another copy or ask the airline to do it for you at check-in. You usually pay a sur-

10 WAYS TO SAVE

1. Nonrefundable is best. If saving money is more important than flexibility, then nonrefundable tickets work. Just remember that you'll pay dearly (as much as $100) if you change your plans.

2. Comparison shop. Web sites and travel agents can have different arrangements with the airlines and offer different prices for exactly the same flights.

3. Beware those prices. Many airline Web sites—and most ads—show prices *without* taxes and surcharges. Don't buy until you know the full price.

4. Stay loyal. Stick with one or two frequent-flier programs. You'll rack up free trips faster and you'll accumulate more quickly the perks that make trips easier. On some airlines these include a special reservations number, early boarding, and access to upgrades.

5. Watch those ticketing fees. Surcharges are usually added when you buy your ticket anywhere but on an airline Web site. (That includes by phone—even if you call the airline directly—and paper tickets regardless of how you book).

6. Check early and often. Start looking for cheap fares up to a year in advance, and keep looking until you see something you can live with.

7. Don't work alone. Some Web sites have tracking features that will e-mail you immediately when good deals are posted.

8. Fly mid-week. Look for departures on Tuesday, Wednesday, and Thursday, typically the cheapest days to travel.

9. Be flexible. Check on prices for departures at different times and to and from alternative airports.

10. Weigh your options. What you get can be as important as what you save. A cheaper flight might have a long layover, or it might land at a secondary airport, where your ground transportation costs might be higher.

Online Booking Resources

AGGREGATORS

Kayak	www.kayak.com	also looks at cruises and vacation packages.
Mobissimo	www.mobissimo.com	also looks at car rental rates and activities.
Qixo	www.qixo.com	also compares cruises, vacation packages, and even travel insurance.
Sidestep	www.sidestep.com	also compares vacation packages and lists travel deals.
Travelgrove	www.travelgrove.com	also compares cruises and packages.

BOOKING ENGINES

Cheap Tickets	www.cheaptickets.com	a discounter.
Expedia	www.expedia.com	a large online agency that charges a booking fee for airline tickets.
Hotwire	www.hotwire.com	a discounter.
lastminute.com	www.lastminute.com	specializes in last-minute travel the main site is for the U.K., but it has a link to a U.S. site.
Luxury Link	www.luxurylink.com	has auctions (surprisingly good deals) as well as offers on the high-end side of travel.
Onetravel.com	www.onetravel.com	a discounter for hotels, car rentals, airfares, and packages.
Orbitz	www.orbitz.com	charges a booking fee for airline tickets, but gives a clear breakdown of fees and taxes before you book.
Priceline.com	www.priceline.com	a discounter that also allows bidding.
Travel.com	www.travel.com	allows you to compare its rates with those of other booking engines.
Travelocity	www.travelocity.com	charges a booking fee for airline tickets, but promises good problem resolution.

ONLINE ACCOMMODATIONS

Hotelbook.com	www.hotelbook.com	focuses on independent hotels worldwide.
Hotel Club	www.hotelclub.net	good for major cities worldwide.
Hotels.com	www.hotels.com	a big Expedia-owned wholesaler that offers rooms in hotels all over the world.
Quikbook	www.quikbook.com	offers "pay when you stay" reservations that let you settle your bill at check out, not when you book.

OTHER RESOURCES

Bidding For Travel	www.biddingfortravel.com	a good place to figure out what you can get and for how much before you start bidding on, say, Priceline.

charge (up to $50) to get a paper ticket, if you can get one at all. The sole advantage of a paper ticket is that it may be easier to endorse over to another airline if your flight is canceled and the airline with which you booked can't accommodate you on another flight.

■TIP➡Discount air passes that let you travel economically in a country or region must often be purchased before you leave home. In some cases you can only get them through a travel agent.

▌ RENTAL CARS

When you reserve a car, ask about cancellation penalties, taxes, drop-off charges (if you're planning to pick up the car in one city and leave it in another), and surcharges (for being under or over a certain age, for additional drivers, or for driving across state or country borders or beyond a specific distance from your point of rental). All these things can add substantially to your costs. Request car seats and extras such as GPS when you book.

Rates are sometimes—but not always—better if you book in advance or reserve through a rental agency's Web site. There are other reasons to book ahead, though: for popular destinations, during busy times of the year, or to ensure that you get certain types of cars (vans, SUVs, exotic sports cars).

■TIP➡Make sure that a confirmed reservation guarantees you a car. Agencies sometimes overbook, particularly for busy weekends and holiday periods.

If you are staying just in London on this trip, there's virtually no reason to rent a car since the city and its suburbs are widely covered by public transportation. However, you might want a car for day trips to castles or stately homes out in the countryside. Rental rates are generally reasonable, and insurance costs are lower than in comparable U.S. cities.

Driving in London's traffic congestion is hellish, however; so if you only want the car for country trips, consider renting your car in a medium-size town in the area where you'll be traveling, and then journeying there by train and picking up the car once you arrive. Moreover, rental rates are slightly cheaper out in the country, and it will save you from having to traverse London's notoriously complex road system.

Rental rates in London vary widely. Rates generally begin at £35 a day and £160 a week for a small economy car (such as a subcompact General Motors Vauxhall, Corsa, or Renault Clio), usually with manual transmission. Air-conditioning and unlimited mileage generally come with the larger-size automatic cars. Rates are generally cheapest at European rental agencies such as Europcar (⇨Local Agencies).

Age restrictions vary by rental car agency, but most will not rent to drivers under 25 or over 70.

Some rental agencies will offer a car seat for babies for a small extra fee. Most agencies do not charge extra for additional drivers.

CAR-RENTAL INSURANCE

Everyone who rents a car wonders whether the insurance that the rental companies offer is worth the expense. No one—including us—has a simple answer. It all depends on how much regular insurance you have, how comfortable you are with risk, and whether or not money is an issue.

If you own a car, your personal auto insurance may cover a rental to some degree, though not all policies protect you abroad; always read your policy's fine print. If you don't have auto insurance, then seriously consider buying the collision- or loss-damage waiver (CDW or LDW) from the car-rental company, which eliminates your liability for damage to the car. Some credit cards offer CDW coverage, but it's usually supplemental to your own insurance and rarely covers SUVs, minivans, luxury models, and the like. If your coverage is secondary, you may still be liable for loss-of-use costs from the car-rental company. But no credit-card insurance is valid unless you use that card for *all* transactions, from reserving to paying the final bill. All companies exclude car rental in some countries, so be sure to find out about the destination to which you are traveling.

■TIP➡Diners Club offers primary CDW coverage on all rentals reserved and paid for with the card. This means that Diners Club's company—not your own car insurance—pays in case of an accident. It *doesn't* mean your car-insurance company won't raise your rates once it discovers you had an accident.

In Britain, basic car rental insurance is generally included in the daily price of the rental vehicle; however, the deductible is usually very high—as much as £500 is not unusual. For a daily fee—which can be as low as £10—you can lower the deductible to £0. However, your own insurance or credit cards may cover the deductible, so inquire with your insurance or card company before you rent.

■TIP➡You can decline the insurance from the rental company and purchase it through a third-party provider such as Travel Guard (www.travelguard.com)—$9 per day for $35,000 of coverage. That's sometimes just under half the price of the CDW offered by some car-rental companies.

TRAIN TICKETS

Train tickets in Britain are much cheaper if purchased in advance. Prices for the same journey can vary by hundreds of pounds depending upon when you buy the ticket. A journey from, say, London to Cardiff, will cost around £38 if purchased more than two weeks in advance, but if purchased on the day you travel it can cost more than £150. However, journeys within commuting distance of city centers are sold at unvarying set prices, and those

can be purchased on the day you expect to make your journey without any financial penalty. Note that, in busy city centers such as London, all travel costs more during morning rush hour. *For more information about how to purchase your tickets in advance, see ➪the Transportation By Train section.*

▮ VACATION PACKAGES

Packages *are not* guided excursions. Packages combine airfare, accommodations, and perhaps a rental car or other extras (theater tickets, guided excursions, boat trips, reserved entry to popular museums, transit passes), but they let you do your own thing. During busy periods packages may be your only option, as flights and rooms may be sold out otherwise. Packages will definitely save you time. They can also save you money, particularly in peak seasons, but—and this is a really big "but"—you should price each part of the package separately to be sure. And be aware that prices advertised on Web sites and in newspapers rarely include service charges or taxes, which can up your costs by hundreds of dollars.

■TIP➡Some packages are sold only through travel agents. Don't always assume that you can get the best deal by booking everything yourself.

Each year consumers are stranded or lose their money when packagers—even large ones with excellent reputations—go out of business. How can you protect yourself? First, always pay with a credit card; if you have a problem, your credit-card company may help you resolve it. Second, buy trip insurance that covers default. Third, choose a company that belongs to the United States Tour Operators Association, whose members must set aside funds to cover defaults. Finally, choose a company that also participates in the Tour Operator Program of the American Society of Travel Agents (ASTA), which will act as mediator in any disputes. You can also check on the tour operator's reputation among travelers by posting an inquiry on one of the Fodors.com forums.

Because of its extensive public transport and a wide network of taxicabs, visiting London on a fully escorted tour can feel a bit unnecessary. There are ample tour companies offering day tours to the city's sights highlights, and getting around is usually quite easy. However, there can be cost advantages to booking all-inclusive trips, and novice travelers might find the extra guidance comforting.

If you're planning to see the countryside outside the city, though, packaged tours can be very useful, particularly for those who don't want to rent a car and strike out on their own. If, for example, you feel you'll find it hard to drive on the left side of the road, or if you're traveling alone and will not have anybody to help you navigate the unfamiliar and narrow byways, joining a tour group and seeing it all from the comfort of a modern bus is a valid option.

There are a few downsides: rooms in castles and medieval houses tend to be small and can feel overrun when tour groups roll in. You will also be quite limited in terms of experiencing local life and meeting local residents.

Organizations American Society of Travel Agents ([ASTA] ☎703/739–2782 or 800/965–2782 ⊕ www.astanet.com). **United States Tour Operators Association** ([USTOA] ☎212/599–6599 ⊕ www.ustoa.com).

■ TIP→ **Local tourism boards can provide information about lesser-known and small-niche operators.**

▮ GUIDED TOURS

Guided tours are a good option when you don't want to do it all yourself. You travel along with a group (sometimes large, sometimes small), stay in prebooked hotels, eat with your fellow travelers (the cost of meals sometimes included in the

10 WAYS TO SAVE

1. Join "frequent guest" programs. You may get preferential treatment in room choice and/or upgrades.

2. Call direct. You can sometimes get a better price if you call a hotel's local toll-free number (if available) rather than a central reservations number.

3. Check online. Check hotel Web sites, as not all chains are represented on all travel sites.

4. Look for specials. Always inquire about packages and corporate rates.

5. Look for price guarantees. For overseas trips, look for guaranteed rates. With your rate locked in you won't pay more, even if the price goes up in the local currency.

6. Look for weekend deals at business hotels. High-end chains catering to business travelers are often busy only on weekdays; to fill rooms they often drop rates dramatically on weekends.

7. Ask about taxes. Verify whether local hotel taxes are included in quoted rates. In some places taxes can add 20% or more to your bill.

8. Read the fine print. Watch for add-ons, including resort fees, energy surcharges, and "convenience" fees for such things as unlimited local phone service you won't use or a free newspaper in a language you can't read.

9. Know when to go. If high season is December through April and you're trying to book, say, in late April, you might save money by changing your dates by a week or two. Ask when rates go down, though: if your dates straddle peak and nonpeak seasons, a property may still charge peak-season rates for the entire stay.

10. Weigh your options (we can't say this enough). Weigh transportation times and costs against the savings of staying in a hotel that's cheaper because it's out of the way.

price of your tour, sometimes not), and follow a schedule. But not all guided tours are an if-it's-Tuesday-this-must-be-Belgium experience. A knowledgeable guide can take you places that you might never discover on your own, and you may be pushed to see more than you would have otherwise. Tours aren't for everyone, but they can be just the thing for trips to places where making travel arrangements is difficult or time-consuming (particularly when you don't speak the language). Whenever you book a guided tour, find out what's included and what isn't. A "land-only" tour includes all your travel (by bus, in most cases) in the destination, but not necessarily your flights to and from or even within it. Also, in most cases prices in tour brochures don't include fees and taxes. And remember that you'll be expected to tip your guide (in cash) at the end of the tour.

Dozens of companies offer fully guided tours of London and the region around it. Most of these are full packages including hotels, food, and transportation costs in one flat fee. Because each tour company has different specialties, do a bit of research—either on your own or through a travel agent—before booking. You'll want to know about the hotels you'll be staying in along the way, how big your group is, precisely how your days will be structured (how much rest time you'll have, for example), and who your travel companions are likely to be. Knowing the answers to these questions will help you make the right choices in picking the best tour for you.

Among the most reliable tour companies, two U.S.-based companies—Trafalgar Tours and Globus & Cosmos Tours—specialize in moderately priced trips that feature plenty of sights, but not much in the way of five-star hotels. Both offer fairly comprehensive, two-week tours within Britain, as well as shorter trip options.

At the opposite end of the price scale is Abercrombie & Kent, which is known for its luxurious tours that feature everything from castle hotels to journeys on vintage railways. In between the two is Wallace Arnold Holidays, a favorite of British travelers exploring their own country. Its rather heartwarming motto is, "We take care of everything."

Recommended Companies **Trafalgar Tours** (☎800/854–0103 ⊕www.trafalgartours.com). **Globus & Cosmos Tours** (☎800/338–7092 ⊕www.globusandcosmos.com). **Wallace Arnold Holidays** (☎0208/686–2378 ⊕www.wallacearnold.com). **Abercrombie & Kent** (☎800/323–7308 ⊕www.abercrombiekent.com).

TRANSPORTATION

Central London and its surrounding districts are divided into 32 boroughs—33, counting the City of London. More useful for finding your way around, however, are the subdivisions of London into postal districts. Throughout the guide we've given the full postal code for most listings. The first one or two letters give the location: N means north, NW means northwest, and so on. Don't expect the numbering to be logical, however. You won't, for example, find W2 next to W3. The general rule is that the lower numbers, such as W1 or SW1, are closest to the city center, but that rule is not followed with any consistency—SE21 is closer to the city center than E8, for example.

▍ BY AIR

Flying time to London is about 6½ hours from New York, 7½ hours from Chicago, 11 hours from San Francisco, and 21½ hours from Sydney.

For flights out of London, the general rule is that you arrive one hour before your scheduled departure time for domestic flights and two hours before international flights for off-peak travel.

Airlines & Airports Airline and Airport Links.com (⊕www.airlineandairportlinks.com) has links to many of the world's airlines and airports.

Airline Security Issues Transportation Security Administration (⊕www.tsa.gov)has answers for almost every question that might come up.

AIRPORTS

International flights to London arrive at either Heathrow Airport (LHR), 15 mi west of London, or at Gatwick Airport (LGW), 27 mi south of the capital. Most flights from the United States go to Heathrow, which is the busiest and is divided into four terminals, with Terminals 3 and 4 handling transatlantic flights (British

NAVIGATING LONDON

London is a confusing city to navigate, even for people who've visited it a few times. Its streets are arranged in medieval patterns that no longer make much sense, meaning that you can't always use logic to find your way around. A good map is essential, and public transportation can be a lifesaver: buses will take you magically from point A to point B, while the Tube is often the quickest way to reach your destination. Here are some basic tips to help you find your way around:

■ While free tourist maps can be handy, they're usually quite basic and only include major streets. If you're going to be doing lots of wandering around, buy the pocket-size map book "London A–Z" sold in book stores and Tube and train stations throughout the city. Its detailed maps are lifesavers.

■ To find your way, look for tall landmarks near where you were headed: the towering statue of Admiral Nelson in Trafalgar Square, for example, or the cross atop St. Paul's Cathedral—or the most obvious of all, Big Ben.

■ If you get properly lost, the best people to ask are the Londoners hustling buy you, who know the area like nobody else. The worst people to ask are the people working in souvenir kiosks and street vendors selling the local *Evening Standard* newspaper; they're famously rude and unhelpful to lost tourists.

■ The tourist hubs of Soho, Covent Garden, Leicester Square, and Trafalgar Square are separated from one another by only a few blocks. Taking the Tube from one to another actually takes longer than walking.

■ On the other hand, when you're lost, the Tube is often the shortest distance between two points. Don't hesitate to use it.

London
Postal Districts

FLYING 101

Flying may not be as carefree as it once was, but there are some things you can do to make your trip smoother.

Minimize the time spent standing in line. Buy an e-ticket, check in at an electronic kiosk, or—even better—check in on your airline's Web site before leaving home. Pack light and limit carry-on items to only the essentials.

Arrive when you need to. Research your airline's policy. It's usually at least an hour before domestic flights and two to three hours before international flights. But airlines at some busy airports have more stringent requirements. Check the TSA Web site for estimated security waiting times at major airports.

Get to the gate. If you aren't at the gate at least 10 minutes before your flight is scheduled to take off (sometimes earlier), you won't be allowed to board.

Double-check your flight times. Do this especially if you reserved far in advance. Schedules change, and alerts may not reach you.

Don't go hungry. Ask whether your airline offers anything to eat; even when it does, be prepared to pay.

Get the seat you want. Often you can pick a seat when you buy your ticket on an airline Web site. But it's not guaranteed; the airline could change the plane after you book, so double-check. You can also select a seat if you check in electronically. Avoid seats on the aisle directly across from the lavatories. Frequent fliers say those are even worse than back-row seats that don't recline.

Got kids? Get info. Ask the airline about its children's menus, activities, and fares. Sometimes infants and toddlers fly free if they sit on a parent's lap, and older children fly for half price in their own seats. Also inquire about policies involving car seats; having one may limit seating options. Also ask about seat-belt extenders for car seats. And note that you can't count on a flight attendant to produce an extender; you may have to ask for one when you board.

Check your scheduling. Don't buy a ticket if there's less than an hour between connecting flights. Although schedules are padded, if anything goes wrong you might miss your connection. If you're traveling to an important function, consider departing a day early.

Bring paper. Even when using an e-ticket, always carry a hard copy of your receipt; you may need it to get your boarding pass, which most airports require to get past security.

Complain at the airport. If your baggage goes astray or your flight goes awry, complain before leaving the airport. Most carriers require that you file a claim immediately.

Beware of overbooked flights. If a flight is oversold, the gate agent will usually ask for volunteers and offer some sort of compensation for taking a different flight. If you're bumped from a flight *involuntarily,* the airline must give you some kind of compensation if an alternate flight can't be found within one hour.

Know your rights. If your flight is delayed because of something within the airline's control (bad weather doesn't count), the airline must get you to your destination on the same day, even if they have to book you on another airline and in an upgraded class. Read the Contract of Carriage, which is usually buried on the airline's Web site.

Be prepared. The Boy Scout motto is especially important if you're traveling during a stormy season. To quickly adjust your plans, program a few numbers into your cell: your airline, an airport hotel or two, your destination hotel, your car service, and/or your travel agent.

Airways uses Terminal 4). A fifth terminal is currently under construction. Gatwick is London's second gateway. It has grown from a European airport into an airport that serves dozens of U.S. destinations. A smaller third airport, Stansted (STN), is 35 mi east of the city. It handles mainly European and domestic traffic, although there's also scheduled service from New York. A fourth airport, Luton (LTN), 30 mi north of town, is also small and mainly handles flights to Europe.

Airport Information **Gatwick Airport** (☎0870/000–2468 ⊕www.gatwickairport. com). **Heathrow Airport** (☎0870/000– 0123 ⊕www.heathrowairport.com). **Luton Airport** (☎01582/405–100 ⊕www.london- luton.co.uk). **Stansted Airport** (☎0870/000– 0303 ⊕www.stanstedairport.com).

GROUND TRANSPORTATION

London has excellent bus and train connections between its airports and downtown. If you're arriving at Heathrow, you can pick up a map and fare schedule at a Transport for London (TfL) Information Centre (in Terminals 1 and 2). Train service can be quick, but the downside (for trains from all airports) is that you must get yourself and your luggage to the train via a series of escalators and connecting trams. Airport link buses (generally National Express Airport buses) may ease the luggage factor and drop you closer to central hotels, but they're subject to London traffic, which can be horrendous. Taxis can be more convenient than buses, but beware that prices can go through the roof. Airport Travel Line has additional transfer information and takes advance booking for transfers between airports and into London.

Heathrow by Bus: National Express takes 1½ hours and costs £8 one-way and £15 round-trip. It leaves for King's Cross, with stops at Notting Hill Gate, Bayswater, Marble Arch, Marylebone Road, Euston, and Russell Square, every 30 minutes 5:30 AM–9:45 PM, but there are around 14 stops along the route, so it can be tedious. The

N9 night bus runs every half hour from midnight to 4:30 AM to Trafalgar Square; it takes an hour and costs £1. For the same price and a journey closer to an hour, National Express buses leave every hour for Victoria Coach Station from 5:40 AM to 9:30 PM.

Heathrow by Train: The cheap, direct route into London is via the Piccadilly line of the Underground (London's extensive subway system, or "Tube"). Trains normally run every four to eight minutes from all terminals from early morning until just before midnight. The 50-minute trip into central London costs £4.80 one-way and connects with other central Tube lines. The Heathrow Express train is comfortable and very convenient, speeding into London's Paddington Station in 15 minutes, but is more expensive than the Tube. Standard one-way tickets cost £15 (£27 round-trip) and £27 for first class. There's daily service from 5:10 AM (5:50 AM on Sunday) to 11:40 PM (10:50 PM on Sunday), with departures every 15 minutes. At Paddington you can board the Hotel Express bus to get to a number of central London hotels for £2.50. There are also local trains that make multiple stops; these are cheaper, but slower, than the Heathrow Express.

Gatwick by Bus: Hourly bus service runs from Gatwick's south terminal to Victoria Station with stops at Hooley, Coulsdon, Mitcham, Streatham, Stockwell, and Pimlico. The journey takes 90 minutes and costs £11 one-way. Make sure you get on a direct bus that does not require you to change—otherwise the journey could take hours.

Gatwick by Train: The fast, nonstop Gatwick Express leaves for Victoria Station every 15 minutes 5:15 AM–midnight. The 30-minute trip costs £13.50 one-way, £25.30 round-trip. The Thameslink train runs regularly throughout the day until 11:30 PM to King's Cross, London Bridge, and Blackfriars stations; departures are every 15 to 30 minutes, and the journey takes almost one hour. Tickets are about £11 one-way.

Stansted by Bus: Hourly service on National Express Airport bus A6 (24 hours a day) to Victoria Coach Station costs £10 one-way, £15 round-trip, and takes about 1 hour and 40 minutes. Stops include Golders Green, Finchley Road, St. John's Wood, Baker Street, Marble Arch, and Hyde Park Corner.

Stansted by Train: The 45-minute journey on Stansted Express to Liverpool Street Station (with a stop at Tottenham Hale) runs every 15 minutes 8 AM–5 PM weekdays, and every 30 minutes 5 PM–midnight and 6 AM–8 AM weekdays, and all day on weekends. The trip costs £14.50 one-way, £24 round-trip.

Luton by Bus and Train: A free airport shuttle runs from Luton Airport to the nearby Luton Airport Parkway Station, from which you can take a train or bus into London. From there, the Thameslink train service runs to several London stations, terminating at King's Cross. The journey takes about 35 minutes. Trains leave every 10 minutes or so 24 hours a day and cost £10.70 one-way, £19 round-trip. For a cheaper journey, take the Green Line 757 bus service from Luton to Victoria Station. It runs three times an hour, takes about 90 minutes, and costs £7.50.

Heathrow, Gatwick, Stansted, and Luton by Taxi: Taxis can get caught in traffic; the trip from Heathrow, for example, can take more than an hour and cost anywhere from £35 to more than £50. From Gatwick, the taxi fare is at least £70, with a journey time of about an hour and a half. From Stansted, the £75 journey takes a little more than an hour. From Luton, the approximately one-hour journey should cost around £65. Your hotel may be able to recommend a car service for airport transfers. Charges are usually about £35 to any airport. Add a tip of 10% to 15% to the basic fare.

TRANSFERS BETWEEN AIRPORTS

Allow at least 2–3 hours for an interairport transfer. The cheapest option is public transport: from Gatwick to Stansted, for instance, you can catch the nonexpress commuter train from Gatwick to Victoria Station, take the Tube to Liverpool Street station, then catch the train to Stansted from there. To get from Heathrow to Gatwick by public transport, take the Tube to King's Cross, then change to the Victoria Line, get to Victoria Station, and then take the commuter train to Gatwick. Both of these trips would take about two hours.

The National Express Airport bus is the most direct option between Gatwick and Heathrow. Buses pick up passengers every 15 minutes from 5 AM to 10 PM from both airports. The trip takes 1½–2 hours, and the fare is £17.50 one-way, £35 round-trip. It's advisable to book tickets in advance via National Express, especially during peak travel seasons, but you can also buy tickets in the terminals. National Express also runs shuttles between all the other airports, except between Luton and Stansted. Finally, some airlines may offer shuttle services as well—check with your travel agent in advance of your journey.

Contacts Gatwick Express (☎0870/530–1530 ⊕www.gatwickexpress.com). **Green Line** (☎0870/608–7261 ⊕www.greenline.co.uk). **Heathrow Express** (☎0845/600–1515 ⊕www.heathrowexpress.com). **National Express** (☎0870/580–8080 ⊕www.nationalexpress.com). **Stansted Express and Thameslink** (☎0845/748–4950 ⊕www.stanstedexpress.com). **Taxi at Gatwick Airport** (☎0800/747–737). **Taxi at Heathrow** (☎020/8745–7487). **Taxi at Luton** (☎01582/595–555 or 01582/736–666). **Taxi at Stansted Airport** (☎01279/662–444).

Transfer Information Airport Travel Line (☎0870/574–7777).

FLIGHTS

British Airways is the national flagship carrier and offers mostly nonstop flights from 18 U.S. cities to Heathrow and Gatwick airports, along with flights to Manchester, Birmingham, and Glasgow. As the leading British airline, it has a vast program of discount airfare-hotel packages.

Airline Contacts **American Airlines** (☎800/433–7300, 020/7365–0777 in London ⊕www.aa.com). **British Airways** (☎800/247–9297, 0870/850–9850 in London ⊕www.ba.com)to Heathrow, Gatwick. **Continental Airlines** (☎800/523–3273 for U.S. and Mexico reservations, 800/231–0856 for international reservations, 01293/776464, 0845/607–6760 in London ⊕www.continental. com). **Delta Airlines** (☎800/221–1212 for U.S. reservations, 800/241–4141 for international reservations, 0800/414–767 in London ⊕www. delta.com). **Northwest Airlines** (☎800/225–2525, 0870/507–4074 in London ⊕www.nwa. com). **United Airlines** (☎800/864–8331 for U.S. reservations, 800/538–2929 for international reservations, 0845/844–4777 in London ⊕www.united.com). **USAirways** (☎800/428–4322 for U.S. and Canada reservations, 800/622–1015 for international reservations, 0845/600–3300 in London ⊕www. usairways.com). **Virgin Atlantic** (☎800/862–8621, 01293/450150 in London ⊕www.virgin-atlantic.com)to Heathrow, Gatwick.

▮ BY BUS

ARRIVING & DEPARTING

National Express is the biggest British coach operator and the nearest equivalent to Greyhound. It's fast (particularly its Rapide services, which do not detour to make pickups and have steward service for refreshments) and comfortable (with washroom facilities on board). Services depart mainly from Victoria Coach Station, a well-signposted short walk behind the Victoria mainline rail station. The departures point is on the corner of Buckingham Palace Road; this is also the main information point. The arrivals point is opposite at Elizabeth Bridge. National Express buses travel to all large and midsize cities in southern England and the midlands. Scotland and the north are not as well served. The station is extremely busy around holidays

and weekends. It's wise to arrive at least 30 minutes before departure so you can find the correct exit gate. Smoking is not permitted on board.

A newcomer on the bus travel scene, Megabus, has been packing in the budget travelers, since it offers cross-country fares for as little as £1 per person. The company's double-decker buses serve an extensive array of cities across Great Britain. Though it's relatively new, it has been giving National Express a run for its money, taking it on with rock-bottom fares, new buses, and a cheerful budget attitude. In London, buses for all destinations depart from the Green Line bus stand at Victoria Station.

Megabus does not accommodate wheelchairs, and the company strictly limits luggage to one piece per person checked, and one piece of hand luggage.

Green Line serves the counties surrounding London, as well as airports. Bus stops (there's no central bus station) are on Buckingham Palace Road, between the Victoria mainline station and Victoria Coach Station.

Tickets on some long-distance routes are cheaper if purchased in advance, and traveling midweek is cheaper than over weekends and at holiday periods. Tourist Trail Passes, sold by British Travel International, offer great savings if you plan to tour Britain, and they can be bought in advance. Prices run from about £49 for two days of unlimited travel within three days to more than £200 for 15 days of unlimited travel within two months. The Discount Coachcard for students costs £11 and qualifies you for 20% to 30% off many standard fares over a one-year period.

Tickets for National Express can be bought from the Victoria, Heathrow, or Gatwick coach stations by phone with a credit card, via the National Express Web site, or from travel agencies. Tickets for Megabus must be purchased online in advance, or by phone. Tickets bought online in advance rarely rise above £5.

GETTING AROUND LONDON

Red Transport for London (TfL) buses travel all over town, whereas buses in other colors cover the suburbs. Although London is famous for its double-decker buses, change is underway. The city has embraced long articulated buses (locally known as "bendy buses"), which have fully replaced the oldest buses—the beloved rattletrap "routemasters," which had the jump-on/off back platforms. Two routemaster "heritage" routes keep the old familiar routemaster buses working, however: the No. 9 travels through Piccadilly, Trafalgar Square, and Knightsbridge, and the No. 15 clatters its way through Trafalgar Square down Fleet Street and on to St. Paul's Cathedral.

Bus stops are clearly indicated; signs at bus stops feature a red TfL symbol on a plain white background. When the word REQUEST is written across the sign, you must flag the bus down. When the sign simply says "bus stop," the bus must stop whether or not it's flagged. Each numbered route is listed on the main stop, and buses have a large number on the front with their end destination (other major destinations will be listed on a lighted sign the left side of the bus). Not all buses run the full route at all times; check with the driver to be sure. If you want to decipher the numbers, pick up a free bus guide at a TfL Travel Information Centre (at Euston, Liverpool Street, Piccadilly Circus, and Victoria Tube stations; at West Croydon bus station; and at Heathrow Airport).

Buses are a good way of seeing the town, particularly if you plan to hop on and off to cover many sights, but don't take a bus if you're in a hurry as traffic can really slow them down. To get off, pull the cord running above the windows on old buses, or, on more modern buses, press the red exit buttons mounted on poles near the doors. Expect to get very squashed during rush hour, from 8 AM to 9:30 AM and 4:30 PM to 6:30 PM.

Night buses, denoted by an N before their route numbers, run from midnight to 5 AM on a more restricted route than day buses. All night buses run by request stop, so flag them down if you're waiting or push the button or pull the cord if you want to alight.

All journeys cost £1.50. If you plan to make a number of journeys in one day, consider buying a bus pass (£3) or a Travelcard (⇨ *Underground Tube Travel*), good for both Tube and bus travel. Traveling without a valid ticket makes you liable for a fine (£10–£20). Buses are supposed to swing by most stops every five or six minutes, but, in reality, you can often expect to wait a bit longer, although those in the center of town are quite reliable.

In central London you must pay before you board the bus. Automated ticket kiosks are set up at these bus stops, which are clearly marked with a yellow sign BUY TICKETS BEFORE BOARDING. Otherwise, you can buy tickets at most central London Tube stations as well as at newsagents, and shops that display the sign BUY YOUR TRAVELCARDS & BUS PASSES HERE. Outside the central zone, payment may be made to the driver as you enter (exact change is best so as to avoid incurring the driver's wrath). On some of the old buses, a conductor issues you a ticket.

Bus Information **British Travel International** (☎800/327–6097 within the U.S.). **Green Line** (☎0870/608–7261 ⊕www. greenline.co.uk). **Megabus** (☎0900/160–0900 ⊕www.megabus.com). **National Express** (☎0870/580–8080 ⊕www.nationalexpress. com). **Transport for London** (☎020/7222–1234 ⊕www.tfl.gov.uk). **Victoria Coach Station** (☎020/7730–3499).

▌BY CAR

In London your U.S. driver's license is acceptable (as long as you are over 23 years old, with no endorsements or driving convictions). If you have a driver's license from a country other than the United States, it may not be recognized in the United Kingdom. An International Driver's Permit is a good idea no matter what; it's available from the American (AAA) or Canadian Automobile Association and, in the United Kingdom, from the Automobile Association (AA) or Royal Automobile Club (RAC). International permits are universally recognized, and having one may save you a problem with the local authorities.

The best advice on driving in London is: don't. London's streets are a winding mass of chaos, made worse by one-way roads. Parking is also restrictive and expensive, and traffic is tediously slow at most times of the day; during rush hours—from 8 AM to 9:30 AM and 4:30 PM to 6:30 PM—it often grinds to a standstill, particularly on Friday, when everyone wants to leave town. Avoid city-center shopping areas, including the roads feeding Oxford Street, Kensington, and Knightsbridge. Other main roads into the city center are also busy, such as King's Cross and Euston in the north. Watch out also for cyclists and motorcycle couriers who weave between cars and pedestrians and seem to come out of nowhere.

Remember that Britain drives on the left, and the rest of Europe on the right. Therefore, you may want to leave your rented car in Britain and pick up a left-side drive if you cross the Channel (⇨ *The Channel Tunnel*).

CONGESTION CHARGE

Designed to reduce traffic through central London, a congestion charge has been instituted. Vehicles (with some exemptions) entering central London on weekdays from 7 AM to 6:30 PM (excluding public holidays) have to pay a £8 per day fee; it can be paid up to 90 days in advance, or on the day you need it. Day-, week-, month-, and year-long passes are available on the Congestion Charge Customer Service Web site, at gas stations, parking lots (car parks), by mail, by phone, by SMS text message, and at BT Internet kiosks. Traffic signs designate the entrance to congestion areas, and cameras read car license plates and send the information to a database. Drivers who don't pay the congestion charge by midnight after the day of driving are penalized £80, which is reduced to £40 if paid within 14 days.

Information **Congestion Charge Customer Service** (✉ Box 2985, Coventry CV7 8ZR ☎ 0845/900–1234 ⊕ www.cclondon.com).

GASOLINE

Gasoline (petrol) is sold in liters and is expensive (about 91p per liter—nearly $8 per gallon—at this writing). Unleaded petrol, denoted by green pump lines, is predominant. Premium and Super Premium are the two varieties, and most cars run on regular Premium. Supermarket pumps usually offer the best value, although they are often on the edge of town. You won't find many service stations in the center of town; these are generally on main, multilane trunk roads out of the center. Service is self-serve, except in small villages, where gas stations are likely to be closed on Sunday and late evening. Most stations accept major credit cards.

PARKING

During the day—and probably at all times—it's safest to believe that you can park nowhere except at a meter, in a garage, or where you are sure there are no lines or signs; otherwise, you run the risk of a towing cost of about £100 or a wheel clamp, which costs about the same, since you pay to have the clamp removed plus the cost of the one or two tickets you'll have earned first. Restrictions are indicated by the NO WAITING parking signpost on the sidewalk (these restrictions vary from street to street), and restricted areas include single yellow lines or double yellow lines. Parking at a bus stop or in a red-line bus lane is also restricted. It's illegal to park on the sidewalk, across entrances, or on white zigzag lines approaching a pedestrian crossing.

Meters have an insatiable hunger in the inner city—a 20p piece buys just six minutes—and some will only permit a two-hour stay. Meters take 10p, 20p, 50p, and £1 coins. In the evening, after restrictions end, meter bays are free. In the daytime, take advantage of the many N.C.P. parking lots in the center of town, which are often a better value (about £2.50–£3 per hour, up to eight hours). A London street map should have the parking lots marked.

ROADSIDE EMERGENCIES

If your car is stolen, you're in a car accident, or your car breaks down and there's nobody around to help you, contact the police by dialing ☎999.

The general procedure for a breakdown is the following: position the red hazard triangle (which should be in the trunk of the car) a few paces away from the rear of the car. Leave the hazard warning lights on. Along highways (motorways), emergency roadside telephone booths are positioned at intervals within walking distance. Contact the car-rental company or an auto club. The main auto clubs in the United Kingdom are the Automobile Association (AA) and the Royal Automobile Club (RAC). If you're a member of the American Automobile Association (AAA), check your membership details before you depart for Britain as, under a reciprocal agreement, roadside assistance in the United Kingdom should cost you nothing. You can join and receive roadside assistance from the AA on the spot, but the charge is higher—around £75—than a simple membership fee.

Emergency Services **American Automobile Association** (☎800/564–6222). **Automobile Association** (☎0870/550–0600, 0800/887–766 for emergency roadside assistance). **Royal Automobile Club** (☎0870/572–2722).

RULES OF THE ROAD

London is a morass of narrow, one-way roads, and narrow, two-way streets that are no bigger than the one-way roads. If you must risk life and limb and drive in London, note that the speed limit is 30 mph in the royal parks, as well as in all streets (20 mph on the narrowest streets)—unless you see the large 40 mph signs found only in the suburbs. Speed bumps are sprinkled about with abandon in case you forget. Speed is strictly controlled by cameras mounted absolutely everywhere, which ruthlessly photograph speeders for future ticketing.

Medium-size intersections are often designed as "roundabouts" (marked by signs in which three arrows curve into a circle). On these, cars travel in a circle and incoming cars must yield to those already on their way around.

Jaywalking is not illegal in London, and everybody does it, despite the fact that striped crossings with blinking yellow lights mounted on poles at either end—called "zebra crossings"—give pedestrians the right of way to cross. Cars should treat zebra crossings like stop signs if a pedestrian is waiting to cross or already starting to cross. It's illegal to pass another vehicle at a zebra crossing. At other crossings pedestrians must yield to traffic, but they do have the right-of-way over traffic turning left at controlled crossings—if they have the nerve.

Traffic lights sometimes have arrows directing left or right turns; try to catch a glimpse of the road markings in time, and don't get into the turn lane if you mean to go straight ahead. A right turn is not permitted on a red light. Signs at the beginning and end of designated bus lanes give the time restrictions for use (usually during peak hours); if you're caught driving on bus lanes during restricted hours, you could be fined. The use of horns is prohibited between 11:30 PM and 7 AM. By law, seat belts must be worn in the front and back seats. Drunk-driving laws are strictly enforced, and it's safest to avoid alcohol altogether if you'll be driving. The legal limit is 80 milligrams of alcohol, which roughly translated means two units of alcohol—two glasses of wine, one pint of beer, or one glass of whiskey.

∎ BY UNDERGROUND TUBE

London's extensive Underground train (Tube) system has color-coded routes, clear signage, and many connections. Trains run out into the suburbs, and all stations are marked with the London Underground circular symbol. (Do not be confused by similar looking signs reading "subway"—in Britain, the word "subway" means "pedestrian underpass.") Trains are all one class; smoking is *not* allowed on board or in the stations.

Some lines have multiple branches (Central, District, Northern, Metropolitan, and Piccadilly), so be sure to note which branch is needed for your particular destination. Do this by noting the end destination on the lighted sign on the platform, which also tells you how long you'll have to wait until the train arrives. Compare that with the end destination of the branch you want. When the two match, that's your train. ∎TIP→**Service on many Tube lines will be disrupted in 2008 as a widespread improvements program is underway. Some major stations will be closed for short periods of time. Look for information signs near Tube entrances for closures happening while you're in town.**

London is divided into six concentric zones (ask at Underground ticket booths for a map and booklet, which give details of the ticket options), so be sure to buy a ticket for the correct zone or you may be liable for an on-the-spot fine of £20. Don't panic if you do forget to buy a ticket for the right zone: just tell a station attendant that you need to buy an "extension" to your ticket. Although you're meant to do that in advance, generally if you're an out-of-towner, they don't give you a hard time.

You can buy a single or return ticket, the equivalent of a one-way and a round-trip, for travel anytime on the day of issue. For single fares, a flat £4 price per journey now applies across all six zones, whether you're traveling one stop or 12 stops. If you're planning several trips in one day, then consider a travelcard, which is good for unrestricted travel on the Tube, buses, and some overground railways. Bear in mind that travelcards cost much more if purchased before the 9:30 AM rush hour threshold. A one-day travelcard for zones 1–2 costs £6.60 if purchased before 9:30 AM, and £5.10 if bought after 9:30 AM. The more zones included in your travel (if, for example, you'll be traveling to Kew or Wimbledon), the more the travelcard will cost. If you're going to be in town for several days, buy a three-day travelcard. There are a variety of travelcard options: a seven-day travelcard (£21 for zones 1–2) can offer significant savings, but only if you'll be traveling by public transport every day. Children under 11 travel free on the Tube and buses after 9:30 AM, while children ages 11–15 travel free on buses as long as they order an Oyster card *(see below)* at least four weeks before they travel.

The cheapest way to travel is by purchasing an Oyster card, which can be charged with a cash value and then used for travel throughout the city. Each time you take the Tube or bus, you swipe the blue card across the yellow readers at the entrance and the amount of your fare is deducted. The London mayor is so eager to promote the cards that he set up a system in which those using Oyster cards pay discounted rates, making them the cheapest way to get around London. You can purchase an Oyster card for £3 at any London Underground station, and then prepay any amount you wish for your expected travel while in the city. (Alternatively, you can download an application form for an Oyster card online, fill it out and mail it to Transport for London, and it will be posted to your house in the U.S. before you leave for the U.K. This, however, takes considerably longer and is somewhat unnecessary.) Using an Oyster card, bus fares are £1 instead of £2, and underground singles within Zone 1 cost £1.50 instead of £4. If you make numerous journeys in a single day, your Oyster card deductions will always be capped at the standard price of a one-day travelcard.

Trains begin running just after 5 AM Monday–Saturday; the last services leave central London between midnight and 12:30 AM. On Sunday, trains start two hours later and finish about an hour earlier. The frequency of trains depends on the route and the time of day, but normally you should not have to wait more than 10 minutes in central areas.

There are TfL Travel Information Centres at the following Tube stations: Euston, Liverpool Street, Piccadilly Circus, and Victoria, open 7:15 AM–10 PM; and at Heathrow Airport (in terminals 1, 2, and 4), open 6 AM–3 PM.

Underground and Bus Information Trans-port for London (☎020/7222–1234 ⊕www.tfl.gov.uk).

▌ BY TAXI

Universally known as "black cabs," the traditional big black London taxicabs are as much a part of the city's streetscape as red double-decker buses, and for good reason: the unique, spacious taxis easily hold five people, plus luggage. In order to earn a taxi license, drivers must undergo intensive training on the history and geography of London. The course, and all that the drivers have learned in it, is known simply as "the Knowledge." There's almost nothing your taxi driver won't know about the city.

Hotels and main tourist areas have cab stands (just take the first in line), but you can also flag one down from the roadside. If the yellow FOR HIRE sign on the top is lit, the taxi is available. Cab drivers often cruise at night with their signs unlit so that they can choose their passengers and avoid those they think might cause trouble. If you see an unlit, passengerless cab, hail it: you might be lucky.

Fares start at £2 and increase by about £1.80 for every mile or 30p per minute. Taxis cost about double after 10 PM, when they charge by the minute rather than by the mile. (This system was designed to convince more taxi drivers to work at night, but it has resulted in extortionate fares.) Surcharges are a tricky extra, ranging from 40p for additional passengers or bulky luggage to £2 for ordering by phone. At Christmas and New Year, the surcharge is £3. Fares are occasionally raised from year to year. Tip taxi drivers 10%–15% of the tab.

Minicabs, which operate out of small, curb-side offices throughout the city, are generally cheaper than black cabs, but are less reliable and trusted. These are usually unmarked passenger cars, and their drivers are often not native Londoners, and do not have to take or pass "the Knowledge" test. Still, Londoners use them in droves because they are plentiful and cheap. If you choose to use them, do not ever take an unlicensed cab: anyone who curb-crawls looking for customers is likely to be unlicensed. Unlicensed cabs have been associated with many crimes and can be dangerous. All cab companies with proper dispatch offices are likely to be licensed. Look out for a yellow license disk on the front or rear window of the cab to be sure.

There are plenty of trustworthy and licensed minicab firms. For Londonwide service try Lady Cabs, which employs only women drivers, or Addison Lee, which uses comfortable minivans but requires that you know the postcode for both your pickup location and your destination. When using a minicab, always ask the price in advance when you phone for the car, then verify with the driver before the journey begins.

Black Cabs **Dial-a-Cab** (☎0207/253–5000). **Radio Taxis** (☎0207/272–0272).

Minicabs **Addison Lee** (☎0207/387–8888). **Lady Cabs** (☎0207/272–3300)

▌BY TRAIN

London has eight major train stations that serve as arteries to the rest of the country (and to Europe). All are served by the Underground. As a general rule of thumb, the stations' location in the city matches the part of the country they serve.

■ Charing Cross serves southeast England, including Canterbury and Dover/Folkestone for Europe.

■ Euston serves the Midlands, north Wales, northwest England, and western Scotland.

■ King's Cross marks the end of the Great Northern Line, serving northeast England and Scotland.

■ Liverpool Street serves East Anglia, including Cambridge and Norwich.

■ Paddington mainly serves south Wales and the West Country, as well as Reading, Oxford, and Bristol.

■ St. Pancras serves Leicester, Nottingham, and Sheffield in south Yorkshire.

■ Victoria serves southern England, including Brighton, Dover/Folkestone, and the south coast.

■ Waterloo serves southeastern destinations, including Portsmouth and Southampton. The Eurostar service to France and Belgium departs from Waterloo International, within Waterloo Station.

For the best rates, buy your tickets well in advance. Tickets bought two to three weeks in advance can cost a quarter of the price of tickets bought on the day of travel. You can purchase tickets online, by phone, or at any rail station in the United Kingdom. The best way to find out which train to catch, and where to catch it, is to call National Rail Enquiries. Operators there can put you in touch with the right train company, and give you a breakdown of available ticket prices. You cannot buy tickets from National Rail, but they'll put you in touch with the individual train company ticket offices.

Regardless of which train company is involved, many discount passes are available, such as the Young Person's Railcard (for which you must be under 26 and provide a passport-size photo) and the Family Travelcard, which can be bought from most mainline stations. But if you intend to make several long-distance rail journeys, it's can be a good idea to invest in a BritRail Pass (which you must buy in the United States).

BritRail passes come in two basic varieties. The Classic pass allows travel on consecutive days, and the FlexiPass allows a number of travel days within a set period of time. The cost (in U.S. dollars) of a BritRail Consecutive Pass adult ticket for 8 days is $269 standard and $405 first-class; for 15 days, $405 and $609; for 22 days, $515 and $769; and for a month, $609 and $915. The cost of a BritRail FlexiPass adult ticket for 4 days' travel in two months is $235 standard and $355 first-class; for 8 days' travel in two months, $349 and $519; and for 15 days' travel in two months, $525 and $779. Prices drop by about 25% for off-peak travel passes between October and March. Passes for students, seniors, and ages 16–25 are discounted, too.

Some trains have refreshment carriages, called buffet cars. Most trains these days have "quiet cars" where use of cell phones and music devices is banned, but these rules are not enforced with any enthusiasm. Smoking is forbidden in all rail carriages.

Generally speaking, rail travel in the U.K. is expensive: for instance, a round-trip ticket to Bath from London can cost around £60 per person at peak times. The fee drops to around £35 at other times, so it's best to travel before or after the frantic business commuter rush (before 4:30 PM and after 9:30 AM). Credit cards are accepted for train fares paid both in person and by phone.

Delays are not uncommon, but they're rarely long. Unfortunately, you almost always have to go to the station to find out if there's going to be one (because delays tend to happen at the last minute). Luckily, most stations have coffee shops, restaurants, and pubs where you can cool your heels while you wait for the train to get rolling. National Rail Enquiries provides an up-to-date state-of-the-railways schedule.

Most of the time, first-class train travel in England isn't particularly first-class. Some train companies don't offer at-seat service, so you still have to get up and go to the buffet car for food or drinks. First class is generally booked by business travelers on expense accounts because crying babies and noisy families are quite rare in first class, and quite common in standard class.

Information **BritRail Travel** (☎877/677–1066 in U.S.). **Eurostar** (☎0870/518–6186, in the U.K. ⊕www.eurostar.co.uk). **National Rail Enquiries** (☎0845/748–4950, 0161/236–3522 outside U.K.).

Channel Tunnel Car Transport **Eurotunnel** (☎0870/535–3535 in the U.K., 070/223–210 in Belgium, 03–21–00–61–00 in France ⊕www.eurotunnel.com). **Rail Europe** (☎888/382–7245 in the U.S., 0870/584–8848 in the U.K. inquiries and credit-card bookings ⊕www.raileurope.com).

ON THE GROUND

■ BUSINESS SERVICES & FACILITIES

There are several Kinko's and Mail Boxes Etc. locations in London to handle your photocopying, next-day mail, and packaging needs. Check their Web sites for more locations.

Contacts **Kinko's** (⊠1 Curzon St., Soho, London W1Y 7FN ☎020/7717–4900 ⊕www.kinkos.co.uk). **Mail Boxes Etc.** (⊠4 Montpelier St., Knightsbridge, London SW7 1EE ☎020/7225–2828 ⊕www.mbe.co.uk).

■ COMMUNICATIONS

INTERNET

If you're traveling with a laptop, carry a spare battery and adapter: new batteries and replacement adapters are expensive; if you do need to replace them, head to Tottenham Court Road (W1), which is lined with computer specialists. John Lewis department store and Selfridges, on Oxford Street (W1), also carry a limited range. Never plug your computer into any socket before asking about surge protection. Some hotels do not have built-in current stabilizers, and extreme electrical fluctuations and surges, while very rare, can short your adapter or even destroy your computer. IBM sells an invaluable pen-size modem tester that plugs into a telephone jack to check if the line is safe to use.

The U.K. is finally catching up to the U.S. in terms of the spread of broadband and Wi-Fi. In London, Wi-Fi is increasingly available in hotels, and broadband coverage is widespread; generally speaking, the pricier the hotel, the more likely you are to find Wi-Fi there. Wireless access is still rare in cafés and coffeeshops, but Starbucks is spreading the word, and competition being what it is, its popularity is likely to increase elsewhere quickly.

Contacts **Cybercafes** (⊕www.cybercafes.com)lists over 4,000 Internet cafés worldwide.

PHONES

The good news is that you can now make a direct-dial telephone call from virtually any point on earth. The bad news? You can't always do so cheaply. Calling from a hotel is almost always the most expensive option; hotels usually add huge surcharges to all calls, particularly international ones. In some countries you can phone from call centers or even the post office. Calling cards usually keep costs to a minimum, but only if you purchase them locally. And then there are mobile phones *(⇨below)*, which are sometimes more prevalent—particularly in the developing world—than land lines; as expensive as mobile phone calls can be, they are still usually a much cheaper option than calling from your hotel.

All calls made within the United Kingdom are charged according to the time of day. The standard rate applies weekdays 8 AM–6 PM; a cheaper rate is in effect weekdays 6 PM–8 AM and all day on weekends, when it's even cheaper. A local call before 6 PM costs 15p for three minutes; this doubles to 30p for the same from a pay phone. A daytime call to the United States will cost 24p a minute on a regular phone (weekends are cheaper), 80p on a pay phone.

The country code for Great Britain is 44. When dialing from abroad, drop the initial "0" from the local area code. The code for London is 020, followed by a 7 for numbers in central London, or an 8 for numbers in the Greater London area. Freephone (toll-free) numbers start with 0800 or 0808; national information numbers start with 0845.

A word of warning: 0870 numbers are *not* toll-free numbers; in fact, numbers beginning with this, 0871 or the 0900 prefix are "premium rate" numbers, and it costs extra to call them. The amount varies and is usually relatively small when dialed from within the country but can be excessive when dialed from outside the U.K.

CALLING WITHIN BRITAIN

There are three types of phones: those that accept (1) only coins, (2) only British Telecom (BT) phone cards, or (3) BT phone cards and credit cards.

The coin-operated phones are of the push-button variety; the workings of coin-operated telephones vary, but there are usually instructions on each unit. Most take 10p, 20p, 50p, and £1 coins. Insert the coins *before* dialing (the minimum charge is 10p). If you hear a repeated single tone after dialing, the line is busy; a continual tone means the number is unobtainable (or that you have dialed the wrong—or no—prefix). The indicator panel shows you how much money is left; add more whenever you like. If there is no answer, replace the receiver and your money will be returned.

There are several different directory-assistance providers. For information anywhere in Britain, try dialing 118–888 or 118–118; you'll need to know the town and the street (or at least the neighborhood) of the person or organization for which you're requesting information. For the operator, dial 100.

You don't have to dial London's central area code (020) if you are calling inside London itself—just the eight-digit telephone number.

For long-distance calls within Britain, dial the area code (which begins with 01), followed by the number. The area-code prefix is used only when you are dialing from outside the city. In provincial areas, the dialing codes for nearby towns are often posted in the booth.

CALLING OUTSIDE BRITAIN

For assistance with international calls, dial 155.

To make an international call from London, dial 00, followed by the country code and the local number.

When calling from overseas to access a London telephone number, drop the first 0 from the prefix and dial only 20 (or any other British area code) and then the eight-digit phone number.

You can also pick up one of the many instant international phone cards from newsstands, which can be used from residential, hotel, and public pay phones. With these, you can call the United States for as little as 5p per minute.

The country code for the United States is 1.

Access Codes AT&T Direct (☎0500/890–011). MCI WorldPhone (☎0800/279–5088 in U.K., 800/444–4141 for U.S. and other areas). Sprint International Access (☎0800/890–877).

CALLING CARDS

Public card phones operate with either cash or with special cards that you can buy from post offices or newsstands. Ideal for longer calls, they are composed of units of 10p, and come in values of £3, £5, £10, and more. To use a card phone, lift the receiver, insert your card, and dial the number. An indicator panel shows the number of units used. At the end of your call, the card will be returned. Where credit cards are taken, slide the card through, as indicated.

MOBILE PHONES

If you have a multiband phone (some countries use different frequencies from what's used in the United States) and your service provider uses the world-standard GSM network (as do T-Mobile, Cingular, and Verizon), you can probably use your phone abroad. Roaming fees can be steep, however: 99¢ a minute is considered reasonable. And overseas you normally pay the toll charges for incoming calls. It's almost always cheaper to send a text message than to make a call, since text messages have a very low set fee (often less than 5¢).

If you just want to make local calls, consider buying a new SIM card (note that your provider may have to unlock your phone for you to use a different SIM card) and a prepaid service plan in the destination. You'll then have a local number and can make local calls at local rates. If your trip is extensive, you could also simply buy a new cell phone in your destination, as the initial cost will be offset over time.

■TIP➜If you travel internationally frequently, save one of your old mobile phones or buy a cheap one on the Internet; ask your cell phone company to unlock it for you, and take it with you as a travel phone, buying a new SIM card with pay-as-you-go service in each destination.

Any cell phone can be used in Europe if it's tri-band/GSM. Travelers should ask their cell phone company if their phone is tri-band, and make sure it is activated for international calling before leaving their home country.

You can rent a cell phone from most car rental agencies in London. Some upscale hotels now provide loaner cell phones to their guests. Beware, however, of the per-minute rates charged, as these can be shockingly high. You can also rent a mobile phone through www.rent-mobile-phone.com (☎0870/750–0770) for £1 per day plus usage.

Contacts **Cellular Abroad** (☎800/287–5072 ⊕www.cellularabroad.com)rents and sells GMS phones and sells SIM cards that work in many countries. **Mobal** (☎888/888–9162 ⊕www.mobalrental.com)rents mobiles and sells GSM phones (starting at $49) that will operate in 140 countries. Per-call rates vary throughout the world. **Planet Fone** (☎888/988–4777 ⊕www.planetfone.com) rents cell phones, but the per-minute rates are expensive.

▌ CUSTOMS & DUTIES

You're always allowed to bring goods of a certain value back home without having to pay any duty or import tax. But there's a limit on the amount of tobacco and liquor you can bring back duty-free, and some countries have separate limits for perfumes; for exact figures, check with your customs department. The values of so-called "duty-free" goods are included in these amounts. When you shop abroad, save all your receipts, as customs inspectors may ask to see them as well as the items you purchased. If the total value of your goods is more than the duty-free limit, you'll have to pay a tax (most often a flat percentage) on the value of everything beyond that limit.

There are two levels of duty-free allowance for entering Britain: one for goods bought outside the European Union (EU) and the other for goods bought within the EU.

Of goods bought outside the EU you may import duty-free: 200 cigarettes or 100 cigarillos or 50 cigars or 250 grams of tobacco; two liters of table wine and, in addition, (a) one liter of alcohol over 22% by volume (most spirits), (b) two liters of alcohol under 22% by volume (fortified or sparkling wine or liqueurs), or (c) two more liters of table wine; 60 ml of perfume; ¼ liter (250 ml) of toilet water; and other goods up to a value of £145, but not more than 50 liters of beer or 25 cigarette lighters.

Of goods bought within the EU, you should not exceed (unless you can prove they are for personal use): 3,200 cigarettes, 400 cigarillos, 200 cigars, or 1 kilogram of tobacco, plus 10 liters of spirits, 20 liters of fortified wine, 90 liters of wine, or 110 liters of beer.

Pets (dogs and cats) can be brought into the United Kingdom from the United States without six months' quarantine, provided that the animal meets all the PETS (Pet Travel Scheme) requirements. The process takes about six months to complete and involves detailed steps. Other pets have to undergo a lengthy quarantine, and penalties for breaking this law are severe and strictly enforced.

Fresh meats, plants and vegetables, unpasteurized milk, controlled drugs, and firearms and ammunition may not be brought into the United Kingdom.

Information in London HM Customs and Excise (✉ Portcullis House, 21 Cowbridge Rd. E, Cardiff CF11 9SS ☎0845/010–9000, 0208/929–0152 advice service, 0208/929–6731, 0208/910–3602 complaints ⊕www. hmce.gov.uk).

U.S. Information U.S. Customs and Border Protection (⊕www.cbp.gov).

▌ DAY TOURS & GUIDES

BIKE TOURS
Tour Operator Humdinger Bike Tours (☎01689/827–371). London Bicycle Tour (☎020/7928-6838 ⊕www.londonbicycle.com).

BOAT TOURS
All year-round, but more frequently from April to October, boats cruise the Thames, offering a different view of the London skyline. Most leave from Westminster Pier, Charing Cross Pier, and Tower Pier. Downstream routes go to the Tower of London, Greenwich, and the Thames Barrier via Canary Wharf. Upstream destinations include Kew, Richmond, and Hampton Court (mainly in summer). Most of the launches seat between 100 and 250 passengers, have a public-address system, and provide a running commentary on passing points of interest. Depending upon the destination, river trips may last from one to four hours.

A Sail and Rail ticket combines the modern wonders of Canary Wharf by Docklands Light Railway with a trip on the river. Tickets are available year-round from Westminster Pier or DLR stations; ticket holders also get discounted tickets to the London Aquarium in Westminster

and the National Maritime Museum in Greenwich.

Details on all other river-cruise operators are available from London River Services.

River Cruise Operators Catamaran Cruisers (☎020/7987–1185). London Duck Tours (☎020/7928–3132). London River Services (☎020/7941–2400). Sail and Rail (☎020/7363–9700). Thames Cruises (☎020/7930–4097). Westminster Passenger Boat Services (☎020/7930–4097).

BUS TOURS
Guided sightseeing tours from the top of double-decker buses, which are open-top in summer, are a good introduction to the city, as they cover all the main central sights. Numerous companies run daily bus tours that depart (usually between 8:30 and 9 AM) from central points. You may board or alight at any of the numerous stops to view the sights, and reboard on the next bus. Tickets can be bought from the driver and are good all day. Prices vary according to the type of tour, although £15 is the benchmark.

Tour Operators Big Bus Company (☎020/7233-9533 ⊕www.bigbus.co.uk). Big Value Tours (☎020/7233-7797). Black Taxi Tour of London (☎020/7289-4371 ⊕www.blacktaxitours.co.uk). Golden Tours (☎020/7233-7030). London Pride (☎020/7520-2050). London Spy Tours (☎0870/060-0100). Original London Sightseeing Tour (☎020/8877-1722 ⊕www. theoriginaltour.com). Premium Tours (☎020/7278-5300).

CANAL TOURS
The tranquil side of London can be found on narrow boats that cruise the city's two canals, the Grand Union and Regent's Canal; most vessels operate on the latter, which runs between Little Venice in the west (nearest Tube: Warwick Avenue on the Bakerloo Line) and Camden Lock (about 200 yards north of Camden Town Tube station). Fares are about £5 for 1½-hour cruises.

LOCAL DO'S & TABOOS

CUSTOMS OF THE COUNTRY

In general, British and American rules of etiquette are much the same. Differences are subtle. British people find American and Canadian bluntness somewhat startling from time to time, but are charmed by their friendliness. British people tend to take politeness extremely seriously. They say "thank you" at every stage of a financial transaction, but are less likely to offer a "God bless you" should a stranger sneeze.

The famous British stiff upper lip is more relaxed these days, but on social occasions the best option is to observe what the others do, and then go with the flow. If you're visiting a family home, a gift of flowers is welcome, as is a bottle of wine, or maybe some candy for the children—but not all three.

GREETINGS

British people will shake hands on greeting old friends or acquaintances; female friends may greet each other with a kiss on the cheek. In Britain, you can never say please, thank you, or sorry too often; to thank your host, a phone call or thank-you card does nicely.

SIGHTSEEING

As in the U.S., in public places it is considered polite to give up your seat to an elderly person, to a pregnant woman, or a burdened parent struggling with young children and bags. Sometimes if only a woman is standing, men will offer her their seats.

Jaywalking is not illegal in England and everybody does it.

British people take waiting in line (called "queuing") incredibly seriously. They highly value patience, and will turn on "queue jumpers" who try to cut in line with some ferocity. Complaining while waiting in line is considered wimpy. Enduring the wait with good humor is considered a sign of strong moral character.

OUT ON THE TOWN

Etiquette in restaurants is much the same in London as in any major U.S. city. In restaurants you hail a waiter by saying "Excuse me … " as one passes by, or by trying to catch their eye by politely signaling with subtle hand signals. Friends and co-workers frequently gather in pubs, but you don't have to drink alcohol—many people in the pub drink juice or sodas. Drunkenness is very common after about 9 PM—London has a serious binge-drinking culture—and many people avoid taking the Tube or bus late in the evening in order to avoid drunk travelers.

You're generally expected to dress "casually smart" for the theater (suits or nice jackets for men, skirts or nice slacks for women), and those going to nightclubs will dress just the same here as they would in New York or Chicago—the flashier the better. Pubs are very casual places, however, and jeans and tennis shoes are perfectly acceptable there.

The single thing you can do that will most mark you as a tourist—and an impolite one—is failing to observe the written and spoken rule that, on virtually all escalators but especially those in Tube stations, you stand on the right side of the escalator and leave room for people to walk past you on the left. Commuters are far too impatient to wait for the escalator to make its way to the top or the bottom, and they need to be able to rush by you. If you're in their way, they'll never forgive you.

As of 2007, there is a ban on smoking in public places, including in bars and restaurants.

DOING BUSINESS

In business, punctuality is of prime importance; if you anticipate a late arrival, call ahead. For business dinners, it's not assumed that spouses will attend unless prearranged, and if you proffered the invitation it's usually assumed that you will pick up the tab. If you're the visitor, however, it's good form for the host to pay the bill. Alternatively, play it safe and offer to split the check.

Cruise Operators Canal Cruises (☎020/8440–8962). **Jason's Trip** (☎020/7286–3428). **London Waterbus Company** (☎020/7482–2660).

EXCURSIONS

Evan Evans, Green Line, and National Express all offer day excursions by bus to places within easy reach of London, such as Hampton Court, Oxford, Stratford, and Bath.

Tour Operators Evan Evans (☎020/7950–1777). **Green Line** (☎0870/608–7261 ⊕www.greenline.co.uk). **National Express** (☎0870/580–8080 ⊕www.nationalexpress.com).

WALKING TOURS

One of the best ways to get to know London is on foot, and there are many guided and themed walking tours from which to choose. The city's Jack the Ripper Mystery Walks are famous worldwide for their chilling comprehensiveness in following in the footsteps of the titular killer. The Original London Walks Company is one of the city's most reliably good walking tour companies, with a variety of tour themes that change with the time of year and the time of day. Offerings can vary in a day from the "Soho in the Morning" walk early in the day to the "Inns of Court" walk in the afternoon, and the "Haunted London" tour at night. For more options, pick up a copy of *Time Out* magazine and check the weekly listings for upcoming special tours.

Tour Operators Blood and Tears Walk (☎020/8348–9022). **Blue Badge** (☎020/7495–5504). **Citisights** (☎020/8806–4325). **Great London Treasure Hunt** (☎020/7928–2627). **Historical Walks** (☎020/8668–4019). **Jack the Ripper Mystery Walks** (☎020/8558–9446 ⊕www.jack-the-ripper-walk.co.uk). **Original London Walks** (☎020/7624–3978 ⊕www.walks.com). **Shakespeare City Walk** (☎020/7625–5155 ⊕www.shakespeareguide.com).

ELECTRICITY

The electrical current in London is 220–240 volts (coming into line with the rest of Europe at 230 volts), 50 cycles alternating current (AC); wall outlets take three-pin plugs, and shaver sockets take two round, oversize prongs. For converters, adapters, and advice, stop in one of the many STA Travel shops around London or at Nomad Travel.

Consider making a small investment in a universal adapter, which has several types of plugs in one lightweight, compact unit. Most laptops and mobile phone chargers are dual voltage (i.e., they operate equally well on 110 and 220 volts), and thus require only an adapter. These days the same is true of small appliances such as hair dryers. Always check labels and manufacturer instructions to be sure. Don't use 110-volt outlets marked FOR SHAVERS ONLY for high-wattage appliances such as hair-dryers.

Contacts Nomad Travel (✉40 Bernard St., Bloomsbury, WC1N 1LJ ☎020/7833–4114 ✉52 Grosvenor Gardens, Victoria, SW1W 0AG ☎020/7823–5823). **STA Travel** (⊕www.statravel.co.uk). **Steve Kropla's Help for World Traveler's** (⊕www.kropla.com)has information on electrical and telephone plugs around the world. **Walkabout Travel Gear** (⊕www.walkabouttravelgear.com)has a good coverage of electricity under "adapters."

EMERGENCIES

London is a relatively safe city, though crime does happen. If you need to report a theft or an attack, head to the nearest police station (listed in the Yellow Pages or the local directory) or dial 999 for police, fire, or ambulance (be prepared to give the telephone number you're calling from). National Health Service hospitals, several of which are listed below, give free, round-the-clock treatment in Accident and Emergency sections, where delays can be an hour or more. Prescriptions are valid only if made out by doctors registered in the United Kingdom.

Doctors & Dentists **Dental Emergency Care Service** (☎020/7955–2186). **Doctor's Call** (☎020/8900–1000). **Eastman Dental Hospital** (✉256 Gray's Inn Rd., WC1 ☎020/7915–1000). **Medical Express** (✉117A Harley St., W1 ☎020/7499–1991).

Foreign Embassies **U.S. Embassy** (✉24 Grosvenor Sq., Mayfair, W1 ☎020/7499–9000, 020/7894–0563 for Passport Unit ⊕www.usembassy.org.uk).

General Emergency Contacts **Ambulance, fire, police** (☎999).

Hospitals & Clinics **Charing Cross Hospital** (✉Fulham Palace Rd., Fulham, W6 ☎020/8846–1234). **Royal Free Hospital** (✉Pond St., Hampstead, NW3 ☎020/7794–0500). **St. Thomas's Hospital** (✉Lambeth Palace Rd., Battersea, SE1 ☎020/7928–9292). **University College Hospital** (✉Grafton Way, Bloomsbury, WC1 ☎020/7387–9300).

Hotlines **Samaritans** (☎020/7734–2800) for counseling. **Victim Support** (☎020/7735–9166, 020/7582–5712 after office hours).

Pharmacies **Bliss the Chemist** (✉5 Marble Arch, Marble Arch, W1 ☎020/7723–6116).

▌ HEALTH

SPECIFIC ISSUES IN LONDON

In the past, Great Britain had been plagued by concerns about bovine spongiform encephalopathy (BSE), or mad cow disease, but the scare is over. New rules regulate British meat, which is considered perfectly safe to eat. For the latest information, contact the National Centers for Disease Control and Prevention.

OVER-THE-COUNTER REMEDIES

Over-the-counter medications in Britain are similar to those in the U.S., with a few significant differences. For one thing, medications are sold in boxes rather than bottles, and are sold in very small amounts—usually no more than 12 pills per package. There are also fewer brands than you're likely to be used to—you can, for example, find aspirin, but usually only one kind in a store, unbuffered, often in a plain white box. All headache medicine is usually filed under the heading of "pain-killers." You can buy generic ibuprofen or a popular European brand of ibuprofen, Nurofen, which is sold everywhere. Tylenol is not sold in the U.K., but its main ingredient, acetaminophen, is—although, confusingly, it's called paracetomol.

Among sinus and allergy medicines, Claritin is the main option here; it's the same brand sold in the U.S. Some medicines are pretty much the same as brands sold in the U.S.—instead of Nyquil cold medicine, there's "Night Nurse," and instead of Dayquil, there's "Day Nurse." The most popular over-the-counter cough medicine is Benylin.

Drugstores are generally called pharmacies, but sometimes referred to as chemists' shops. The biggest drug store chain in the country is Boots—there are outlets everywhere, save for the smallest towns. If you're in a rural area look out for shops marked with a sign of a green cross; almost all small drug stores have one of these.

Supermarkets and news agents all usually have a small supply of cold and headache medicines, often behind the cash register. As in the U.S., large supermarkets will have a bigger supply on offer.

British people have more faith in herbal cures than Americans, and in some drugstores—including some Boots—you'll find more herbal and vitamin offerings than actual medicine. If you can't find what you're looking for, just ask at the counter; many over-the-counter medicines are kept behind the cash register. Pharmacy workers are trained to ensure you know basic safety issues with all drugs, so don't be surprised if you're asked a few questions about what else you're taking and how you're planning to use the medicine.

▌ HOLIDAYS

Standard holidays include: New Year's Day, Good Friday, Easter Monday, May Day (1st Mon. in May), spring and summer bank holidays (last Mon. in May and Aug., respectively), Christmas, and Boxing Day (Dec. 26). On Christmas Eve and New Year's Eve, some shops, restaurants, and businesses close early. Some museums and tourist attractions are also closed then.

▌ MAIL

Stamps can be bought from post offices (generally open weekdays 9–5:30, Saturday 9–noon), from stamp machines outside post offices, and from newsagents' stores and newsstands. Mailboxes are known as post or letter boxes and are painted bright red; large tubular ones are set on the edge of sidewalks, whereas smaller boxes are set into post-office walls. Allow seven days for a letter to reach the United States. To contact the post office by phone, call the main office at ☎08457/740740. Check the Yellow Pages for a complete list of branches, though you cannot reach individual offices by phone.

Airmail letters up to 10 grams (0.35 ounce) to North America, Australia, and New Zealand cost 70p, postcards cost 50p. Letters within Britain are 39p for first class, 28p for second class (these rates are subject to change).

If you're uncertain where you'll be staying, you can have mail sent to you at the London Main Post Office, c/o poste restante. The post office will hold international mail for one month.

Main Branches **London Main Post Office** (✉24–28 William IV St., Covent Garden, WC2N 4DL ☎08457/740740 ⊕www.royalmail.com). (✉17 Euston Rd., NW1 ✉125–131 Westminster Bridge Rd., Westminster, SW1 ✉110 Victoria St., Victoria, SW1 ✉15 Broadwick St., Soho, W1 ✉54 Great Portland St., Soho, W1 ✉43 Seymour St., Marble Arch, W1 ✉The Science Museum, South Kensington, SW7 ✉24 William IV St., Trafalgar Sq., WC2).

SHIPPING PACKAGES

Most department stores and retail outlets can ship your goods home. You should check your insurance for coverage of possible damage. Private delivery companies such as DHL, FedEx, and Parcelforce offer two-day delivery service to the U.S., but you'll pay a considerable amount for the privilege.

Express Services **DHL** (☎0845/710–0300 ⊕www.dhl.com). **FedEx** (☎0800/123–800 ⊕www.fedex.com). **Parcelforce** (☎0800/224–466 ⊕www.parcelforce.com).

▌ MONEY

No doubt about it, London is one of the most expensive cities in the world: getting around is expensive, eating can be expensive, theaters are pricey, and hotels aren't cheap. However, for every yin there's a yang, and travelers do get a break in other places: most museums are free, for example, and Oyster cards help cut the price of travel.

ATMS & BANKS

Your own bank will probably charge a fee for using ATMs abroad; the foreign bank you use may also charge a fee. Nevertheless, you'll usually get a better rate of exchange at an ATM than you will at a currency-exchange office or even when changing money in a bank. And extracting funds as you need them is a safer option than carrying around a large amount of cash.

■TIP➔ PIN numbers with more than four digits are not recognized at ATMs in many countries. If yours has five or more, remember to change it before you leave.

Credit cards or debit cards (also known as check cards) will get you cash advances at ATMs, which are widely available in London. To make sure that your Cirrus or Plus card (to cite just two of the leading names) works in European ATMs, have your bank reset it to use a four-digit PIN number before your departure.

CREDIT CARDS

Throughout this guide, the following abbreviations are used: **AE**, American Express; **DC**, Diners Club; **MC**, Master-Card; and **V**, Visa.

If you plan to use your credit card for cash advances, you'll need to apply for a PIN at least two weeks before your trip. Although it's usually cheaper (and safer) to use a credit card abroad for large purchases (so you can cancel payments or be reimbursed if there's a problem), note that some credit-card companies *and* the banks that issue them add substantial percentages to all foreign transactions, whether they're in a foreign currency or not. Check on these fees before leaving home, so there won't be any surprises when you get the bill.

■TIP→Before you charge something, ask the merchant whether or not he or she plans to do a dynamic currency conversion (DCC). In such a transaction the credit-card *processor* (shop, restaurant, or hotel, not Visa or MasterCard) converts the currency and charges you in dollars. In most cases you'll pay the merchant a 3% fee for this service in addition to any credit-card company and issuing-bank foreign-transaction surcharges.

Dynamic currency conversion programs are becoming increasingly widespread. Merchants who participate in them are supposed to ask whether you want to be charged in dollars or the local currency, but they don't always do so. And even if they do offer you a choice, they may well avoid mentioning the additional surcharges. The good news is that you *do* have a choice. And if this practice really gets your goat, you can avoid it entirely thanks to American Express; with its cards, DCC simply isn't an option.

Credit cards are accepted virtually everywhere in London.

Reporting Lost Cards American Express (☎800/992–3404 in the U.S. or 01273/696–933 in the U.K. ⊕www.americanexpress.com) . **Diners Club** (☎800/234–6377 in the U.S. or 0800/460–800 in the U.K. ⊕www.dinersclub.com). **MasterCard** (☎800/622–7747 in the U.S. or 0800/964–767 in the U.K. ⊕www.mastercard.com). **Visa** (☎800/847–2911 in the U.S. or 0800/891–725 in the U.K. ⊕www.visa.com).

CURRENCY & EXCHANGE

The units of currency in Great Britain are the pound sterling (£) and pence (p): £50, £20, £10, and £5 bills (called notes); £2, £1 (100p), 50p, 20p, 10p, 5p, 2p, and 1p coins. At this writing, the exchange rate was about Australian $2.42, Canadian $2.31, New Zealand $2.59, U.S. $1.92, and €1.44 to the pound (also known as quid).

Even if a currency-exchange booth has a sign promising no commission, rest assured that there's some kind of huge, hidden fee. (Oh … that's right. The sign didn't say no fee.) And as for rates, you're almost always better off getting foreign currency at an ATM or exchanging money at a bank.

■TIP→Banks never have every foreign currency on hand, and it may take as long as a week to order. If you're planning to exchange funds before leaving home, don't wait until the last minute.

TRAVELER'S CHECKS & CARDS

Some consider this the currency of the cave man, and it's true that fewer establishments accept traveler's checks these days. Nevertheless, they're a cheap and secure way to carry extra money, particularly on trips to urban areas. Both Citibank (under the Visa brand) and American Express issue traveler's checks in the United States, but Amex is better known and more widely accepted; you can also avoid hefty surcharges by cashing Amex checks at Amex offices. Whatever you do, keep track of all the serial numbers in case the checks are lost or stolen.

Contacts **American Express** (☎888/412–6945 in the U.S., 801/945–9450 collect outside of the U.S. to add value or speak to customer service ⊕ www.americanexpress.com).

▌ RESTROOMS

Restrooms in London are very similar to those in the U.S., except they're not called restrooms or bathrooms, they're called any of the following: toilets, loos, ladies, or gents. Pay toilets are very rare. You'll see them largely in train stations, where you can expect to pay 20 pence to get in. Toilet attendants are extremely rare, and tip plates for them are even rarer. If you're desperate for a loo and there's no public toilet around, you can often pop into a nearby pub and slip into the restroom unnoticed. If the place is empty, though, you might need to buy a soft drink as an act of politeness.

Find a Loo **The Bathroom Diaries** (⊕ www.thebathroomdiaries.com)is flush with unsanitized info on restrooms the world over—each one located, reviewed, and rated.

▌ SAFETY

The rules for safety in London are the same as in New York or any big city. If you're carrying a considerable amount of cash and do not have a safe in your hotel room, it's a good idea to keep it in something like a money belt or a neck pouch, but don't get cash out of it in public. Keep a small amount of cash for immediate purchases in your pocket or handbag.

Beyond that, use common sense. In central London, nobody will raise an eyebrow at tourists studying maps on street corners, and don't hesitate to ask directions. However, outside of the center, exercise general caution about the neighborhoods you walk in: if they don't look safe, take a cab. After midnight, outside of the center, take cabs rather than waiting for a night bus. Although London has plenty of so-called "mini-cabs"—normal cars driven by self-employed drivers in a cab service—don't ever get into an unmarked car that pulls up offering you "cab service." Only take a licensed minicab from a cab office, or, preferably, a normal London "black cab," which you flag down on the street. Unlicensed mini-cab drivers have been associated with a slate of violent crimes in recent years.

If you carry a purse, choose one with a zipper and a thick strap that you can drape across your body; adjust the length so that the purse sits in front of you at or above hip level. Store only enough money in the purse to cover casual spending. Distribute the rest of your cash and any valuables among deep front pockets, inside jacket or vest pockets, and a concealed money pouch. Many pubs, restaurants, and bars have "Chelsea clips" under the tables where you can hang your handbag at your knee. These keep your bag safe, and make it hard for anybody to grab it. Never leave your bag beside your chair or hanging from the back of your chair. Be careful with backpacks, as pickpockets can unzip them on the Tube, or even as you're traveling up an escalator.

▌TIP→Distribute your cash, credit cards, IDs, and other valuables between a deep front pocket, an inside jacket or vest pocket, and a hidden money pouch. Don't reach for the money pouch once you're in public.

▌ TAXES

An airport departure tax of £20 (£10 for flights within the United Kingdom and other EU countries) per person is included in the price of your ticket. The fee is subject to government tax increases.

The British sales tax (V.A.T., value-added tax) is 17½%. The tax is almost always included in quoted prices in shops, hotels, and restaurants.

Most travelers can get a V.A.T. refund by either the Retail Export or the more cumbersome Direct Export method. Many, but not all, large stores provide these services, but only if you request them; they will handle the paperwork. For the Retail Export method, you must ask the store for Form VAT 407 when making a purchase (you must have identification—passports are best). Have the form stamped like any customs form by customs officials when you leave the country or, if you're visiting several European Union countries, when you leave the EU. After you're through passport control, take the form to a refund-service counter for an on-the-spot refund (which is usually the quickest and easiest option), or mail it to the address on the form (or the envelope with it) after you arrive home. You receive the total refund stated on the form, but the processing time can be long, especially if you request a credit-card adjustment.

With the Direct Export method, the goods are shipped directly to your home. You must have a Form VAT 407 certified by customs, the police, or a notary public when you get home and then send it back to the store, which will refund your money. For inquiries, contact Her Majesty's Customs & Excise office.

V.A.T. Refunds Global Refund (☎800/566–9828 ⊕www.globalrefund.com). **Her Majesty's Customs & Excise office** (☎0845/010–9000 within U.K., 208/929–0152 from outside U.K. ⊕http://customs.hmrc.gov.uk).

▮ TIME

London is five hours ahead of New York City. In other words, when it's 3 PM in New York (or noon in Los Angeles) it's 8 PM in London. Note that Great Britain and most European countries also move their clocks ahead for the one-hour differential when daylight saving time goes into effect (although they make the changeover several days after the United States).

▮ TIPPING

Tipping is done in Britain just as in the U.S., but at a lower level. So, while it might make you uncomfortable, tipping less than you would back home in restaurants—and not tipping at all in pubs—is not only accepted, but standard. Tipping more can look like you're showing off. Do not tip movie or theater ushers, elevator operators, or bar staff in pubs—although you can always offer to buy them a drink.

Tipping Guidelines for London	
Bartender	In cocktail bars, on the other hand, if you see a tip plate it's fine to leave £1 or £2. For table service, tip 10% of the cost of the bill. However, the gratuity is often included in the check at more expensive bars.
Bellhop	£1–£2 for carrying bags
Hotel Concierge	It is not necessary to tip your concierge and could be perceived as insulting.
Hotel Doorman	£1 for hailing taxis or for carrying bags to check-in desk
Hotel Maid	It's extremely rare for hotel maids to be tipped; £1 or £2 would be generous.
Porter at Airport or Train Station	£1 per bag
Skycap at Airport	£1–£3 per bag
Taxi Driver	10%–15%, perhaps a little more for a short ride
Tour Guide	Tipping optional; £1 or £2 would be generous.
Waiter	10%–15%, with 15% being the norm at high-end restaurants; nothing additional if a service charge is added to the bill.
Other	Restroom attendants in more expensive restaurants expect some small change (20p or so).

INDEX

ABOUT OUR WRITERS

Longtime contributor Robert Andrews loves warm beer and soggy moors, both of which he found in abundance while updating Bath for the Side Trips chapter.

Former Fodor's editor Nuha Ansari has since childhood been an explorer of London's urban spaces, architecture, and monuments. She currently divides her time between London and Geneva, Switzerland, where she works for the Aga Khan Award for Architecture. For this edition, Nuha updated the neighborhoods chapters.

Puja Chugani is a freelance travel writer who is willing to search high and low for the world's best restaurants. She shared her hidden finds and insider tips about London's dining scene for the "Bloombury & Fitzrovia" and "Notting Hill & Bayswater" spotlights in the Where to Eat chapter.

Texan by birth, New Orleanian by nature, and Anglophile at heart, Christi Daugherty now lives miles from home in London, where she works as a freelance writer and editor. She updated London Essentials, the Where to Stay chapter, and the Stratford side trip. Her mother wants her to move home.

Julius Honnor has traveled widely but now lives in London. He has written or updated several guidebooks and is a contributor to *Fodor's Great Britain*. For this book he updated the Pubs & Nightlife and Arts & Entertainment chapters, as well as the Cambridge side trip.

An Essex boy by birth, James Knight has never quite managed to lose a wide-eyed sense of awe at London that comes only from being brought up just outside it James has written for Reuters, the BBC, the *Sunday Times,* the *Economist,* the *New Statesman,* and other publications.

Helen Lewis wrote the "City, South Bank & Clerkenwell" and "Soho & Covent Garden" spotlights in the Where to Eat chapter.

Life-long London resident Katrina Manson has sailed the Thames in a wooden bathtub, danced on the stage of the London Palladium, and sold cheese at one of its smartest delis. She has written for Reuters, the BBC, the *Times,* the *Independent,* the *Guardian,* and several magazines

James Knight and Katrina Manson co-wrote the Experience London, Westminster & Royal London, the City, Greenwich, and the Thames Upstream chapters, including the Tour of the Thames and Tower of London features.

Christina Valhouli is a globe-trotting travel writer who contributes to the New York Times and Town & Country among others. She wrote the "Chelsea, Kensington & and Knightsbridge" and "Mayfair, St. James's & Marylebone" spotlights in the Where to Eat chapter.

By day, Londoner Alex Wijeratna works as an activist for ActionAid International; by night, he truffles out the best eateries in town for the Where to Eat chapter. With his mixed roots, Alex is well aware that London's restaurant boom is built on its ethnic diversity—and on a wall of money from the City's global finance center. He has written for the *Daily Mail* and the *London Times*. For this edition, Alex updated the Where to Eat chapter.